Beyond Television

Andreas Halskov

Beyond Television
TV Production in the Multiplatform Era

Beyond Television:
TV Production in the Multiplatform Era

University of Southern Denmark Studies in Art History, vol. 13

© 2021 Andreas Halskov, Thomas Schwartz Larsen
and University Press of Southern Denmark.

ISBN: 978-87-408-3350-8

Cover design by Thomas Thorhauge.
Book design and frame enlargements by Thomas Schwartz Larsen.

The book is set in Barlow.
Printed by: Specialtrykkeriet Arco A/S.

Printed in Denmark 2021. First edition.

University Press of Southern Denmark
Campusvej 55
DK-5230 Odense M
press@forlag.sdu.dk
www.universitypress.dk

Distribution in the United States and Canada:
Independent Publishers Group
www.ipgbook.com

Distribution in the United Kingdom and Ireland:
Gazelle Book Services
www.gazellebookservices.co.uk

All rights reserved. No part of this publication may be reproduced, distributed, or transmitted in any form or by any means, including photocopying, recording, or other electronic or mechanical methods, without the prior written permission of the publisher, except in the case of brief quotations embodied in critical reviews and certain other non-commercial uses permitted by copyright law.

Contents

Foreword (*by writer-producer Harley Peyton*) 6
Preface & Acknowledgements 7

Part I: Beyond the TV Landscape: Industry & Infrastructure 9

Chapter 1: "It's Not TV. It's HBO": Prestige Television and Not-TV Branding in the Cable Era 15
Feature Interview #1: The Cable Vanguard: Interview with Tom Fontana (*Oz*), David Chase (*The Sopranos*) and David Simon (*The Wire*) 40

Chapter 2: TV in the Age of Plenty: Streaming, Bingeing and Redefining Television 53
Feature Interview #2: The Pioneers of Streaming: Interview with Anne Bjørnstad & Eilif Skodvin (*Lilyhammer*) and Beau Willimon (*House of Cards*) 82

Chapter 3: Beyond Borders: Transnational Television and Glocal Perspectives 93
Feature Interview #3: Local is Global: Interview with Kelly Luegenbiehl (Vice President of Local-Language Originals, Netflix) 124

Part II: Beyond Traditional Television: New Approaches to Storytelling, Style and Genre 131

Chapter 4: A Complex Affair: Transmedia Storytelling and Complex TV 135
Feature Interview #4: Building Worlds & Crafting Stories: Interview with Angela Kang (*The Walking Dead*) and Mark Frost (*Twin Peaks*) 169

Chapter 5: The Art of Television: Stylistic Experimentation and TV Auteurism 176
Feature Interview #5: Artists and Tele-visionaries: Interview with Sabrina Sutherland (*Twin Peaks: The Return*), Peter Gould (*Breaking Bad, Better Call Saul*), Mary Harron (*Alias Grace*) and Derek Cianfrance (*I Know This Much Is True*) 246

Chapter 6: Unboxing Television: Hybridity and New Approaches to Genre .263
Feature Interview #6: Beyond the Generic: Interview with Nic Pizzolatto (*True Detective*), Sam Levinson (*Euphoria*) and Jay Duplass (*Togetherness, Transparent*) 337

Epilogue: Television in the *Multiplatform Era* 350
Bibliography 356
Notes 373

Foreword

Television found me, changed me, and made me. From my first viewing to the present day, a modest landscape once defined and tightly controlled by three networks that became a vast inexplicable continent.

At the start, the trick was to find and hold the stories that you loved, precious metal amid the dross. So you watch *The Twilight Zone*, and it teaches you another way to tell stories. So you watch *Saturday Night Live*, and it teaches you another way to laugh. So you watch *Miami Vice*, and it teaches you another way to crime.

So you work on *Twin Peaks*, and it changes your life.

There was a day when finding the shows you loved involved nothing more than the desire to make time for them, modest curation in a context easily held in one's hands (or mind). But that was then and this is –

The Wire and *Lost* and *Life On Mars* and *Stranger Things* and *Utopia* and *Breaking Bad* and *Borgen* and *Sex Education* and *Forbrydelsen* and *Spiral* and *Watchmen*; the world of television is now truly a *world*. Vast, daunting, and requiring determined exploration rather than the modest curation.
But the experience of it, the loving of it, remains the same. Shows that teach us another way to tell stories, that teach us another way to laugh, that teach us another way to crime. Everything has changed but nothing has changed too. Television will find you, change you, and if you're lucky it will make you too.

Andreas not only understands this, he's written a book about it. Interviews with the men and women who created the television that found us. Further investigation into industrial and systemic alteration in the business that changed us. Valuable insights into the television shows that made us too. More simply and more accurately: Andreas loves television every bit as much as I (and likely you) do.

Let's read his book together.

- Harley Peyton, writer-producer

Preface & Acknowledgements

> [A] major industrial shift is occurring in the nature of viewing devices, modes of production, and distribution systems. [...] Television is no longer associated with authorized and regulated production systems, a universal and familiar device, or any device at all. Television is not a discrete object or a privileged device. It is a visual content that emanates from a wide variety of production systems, embodies all genres and narrative forms, and flows across multiple types of screens and into all manner of electronic gadgets.
> - Michael Strangelove, TV scholar[1]

Standing in the middle of a changing landscape and trying to map that landscape, accounting for the structural changes and their complex impact on production, style and storytelling, is a difficult and daunting task. But also an interesting and hopefully fruitful one. Many scholars argue that the TV landscape is changing, and most practitioners claim that those changes are influencing the way that they produce and tell their stories.[2] Changes in the industry and infrastructure influence the way that TV series are created and the shape that they take. This narrative is already well-known - eagerly circulated among TV creators, executives, critics and journalists - but behind the popular narrative there is a complex story that involves multiple factors and a long history of experimentation and transformation.

In this book, I explore and try to chart the current TV landscape, focusing primarily on the American TV industry and American TV series from the new millennium (what Trisha Dunleavy calls *the multiplatform era*).[3] Though focusing on American television and the American TV industry, I argue that the current TV landscape is a complex and fluid one where TV productions often transgress or connect different territories, industries and distribution technologies.

Beyond Television is a labor of love, but it is also the result of a profound curiosity, a long research phase and a deep exploration. In 2009, I co-wrote two articles on the American TV landscape for the Danish journal *16:9*, and in 2011 I co-edited and -wrote the first Danish anthology on American television in the so-called *cable era* (*Fjernsyn for viderekomne*). That book was soon followed by other monographs, anthologies and articles, exploring specific aspects of the American and global TV landscape. From television comedy to adaptations, remakes and reboots. In 2015, then, I wrote my first English book, *TV Peaks: Twin Peaks and Modern Television Drama*, which used *Twin Peaks* (ABC, 1990-1991) as a concrete example through which to describe the changes in the TV landscape from 1990 to 2015. As part of that book, I interviewed the cast and crew from *Twin Peaks*, and in the last five years I have interviewed more than 100 people from the TV industry, hoping to gain a wider and more profound understanding of TV production and how the practitioners themselves describe the changes in their trade and the TV landscape.

Working with Kim Sørensen, Lasse Lorenzen, Jan Oxholm and HBO Nordic, I have travelled the American TV landscape, visiting popular sets and locations and meeting different practitioners in their homes or at their respective studios. I am greatly indebted to all these creators and craftsmen, and there are far too many for me to mention them all individually. I especially wish to thank the producers and directors behind the major cases in this book – people like Tom Fontana, David Chase, David Simon, Anne Bjørnstad, Eilif Skodvin, Beau Willimon, Kelly Luegenbiehl, Mark Frost, Angela Kang, Jesse Armstrong, Sabrina Sutherland, Tom Perrotta, Mary Harron, Derek Cianfrance, Nic Pizzolatto, Sam Levinson, Tricia Brock, Michael Lannan, Jay Duplass, Susanne Bier, Joel Fields and Peter Gould – and I want to convey my deepest gratitude to Harley Peyton who has helped me while working on this book. In this context, I also wish to thank my former colleagues at the universities of Copenhagen and Aarhus and my current colleagues at the Danish film and TV journal *16:9*, the radio program *Stream and Chill* and *Aarhus Series Festival*. Furthermore, I wish to thank the illustrious TV scholar Kim Akass, who urged me to write for CSTOnline on a regular basis and who has given me a lot of valuable encouragement and feedback while working on this book. The same thing could be said of people like Keld Reinicke, Mikkel Hollænder Jensen, Kim Bøg Brandt, Per Martin Halskov, Esben Bue Halskov and Ingrid Stage, who have willingly shared their time and knowledge. Finally, I want to thank my peer reviewer, my editor (Michael Dam Petersen) and my proofreader (Karen Bek-Pedersen), not to mention the two wonderful artists, Thomas Thorhauge and Thomas Schwartz Larsen, who have designed the cover and the general look of this book. Like a TV series, this book is a collective effort that could not have been achieved without the help and contribution of many different people and institutions.

    The TV landscape might be changing rapidly, but I hope my findings will be relevant for many years to come.

Part I

Beyond the TV Landscape

Industry & Infrastructure

As artists, we have been given this gigantic tool box which is new media. And if we remember the fundamental thing that goes back to the beginning of time, around the campfire, which is trying to tell a good story well, what we now have is the possibility to not just have it happen around one campfire or in one country. We've got the world at our fingertips.
- Maggie Monteith (producer)[4]

There are now so many venues - Netflix alone is just like a behemoth - so I think the landscape is changing, pushing people to be more original, more outrageous and show us something that we haven't seen before.
- Tricia Brock (writer-director)[5]

The hardest thing about creating television now is that there is so much content, on so many different venues, that we writers are told to be outrageous just for the sake of making noise.
- Tom Fontana (writer-producer)[6]

How have streaming channels changed the TV landscape? In some ways fundamentally and in some ways not at all.
- Beau Willimon (writer-producer)[7]

Introduction: From a Ripple to a Stream

We are living in the midst of a transition or even a potential disruption. New forms of production and distribution have been introduced within the last few decades, resulting in a plethora of new platforms and productions. Some of the most significant changes are implied in the comments above, suggesting that the television landscape has become globalized, opening up to new forms of content from various venues and cultures and reconfiguring traditional formats, genres and modes of production, if not, in fact, redefining television altogether.

These points are hardly revolutionary, and they come from four people who have themselves introduced a series of 'firsts' within television. In 1997, the seasoned writer-producer Tom Fontana, who worked on two of the most influential shows from the 1980s and 1990s, *St. Elsewhere* (NBC, 1982-1988) and *Homicide: Life on the Street* (NBC, 1993-1999), created the first *premium cable* series, *Oz* (HBO, 1997-2003), initiating a small revolution or 'Golden Age' within American television.[8] Sixteen years later, Beau Willimon created *House of Cards* (2013-2018), the first original TV series produced for Netflix and the first series that was made available to a global audience simultaneously, all episodes from the first season launched at once. Following that, Tricia Brock directed all the episodes of *Margot vs. Lily* (2016), an early example of *branded content* or *long-form commercial* produced by Nike and distributed as an eight-episode comedy series for YouTube, and *Dummy* (2020), which was one of the first series to be launched by the short-lived mobile video platform Quibi. Finally, Maggie Monteith, in light of COVID-19, created a pilot episode for what might become the first truly global TV series, *The Agoraphobics De-*

tective Society, which is shot by the different performers in their respective homes, using their mobile devices and the virtual communication software called Zoom, and launched on the Pinpoint Presents website. In that sense, *Agoraphobics Detective Society*, though potentially nothing more than a digital curiosity, represents a new mediascape where productions can be shot remotely across many different countries and distributed, simultaneously, to a global audience.

The Structure of This Book

Indeed, the TV landscape has changed in various ways in the last 20 years, and this book explores some of those changes and how they have affected the style, storytelling and genericity of modern TV series. The book examines industrial changes and infrastructural aspects of the modern TV landscape - what Trisha Dunleavy describes as *the multiplatform era* - focusing particularly on the American TV industry, but also including examples from other countries and global trends and perspectives. Building on academic studies by scholars such as Dunleavy, Amanda D. Lotz, Ramon Lobato and Jakob Isak Nielsen, the book argues that television has been reconfigured with the advent of cable and streaming, but there is no evidence to support the popular assumptions about the death of *linear TV* or television drama as such.

The introductory chapters explore the modern TV landscape from an infrastructural perspective and try to arrive at a more nuanced understanding of the concept 'TV series' and the potential effects of streaming on the modern TV landscape. The first chapter deals with what might be described as the preliminary phase of the *multiplatform era*, i.e. the cable revolution of the late 1990s and early 2000s. This phase is seen as an important prelude to the modern TV landscape due to the introduction of cable and DVD, but *Beyond Television* focuses primarily on the second phase of the *multiplatform era* where Netflix and other streamers entered the TV landscape and challenged our understandings further about what television is or could be. *The multiplatform era* is a phase in modern television, which is characterized by TV series that are distributed through various media and platforms (e.g. broadcast networks, cable and satellite television, DVD, Blu-ray and streaming). During this era, audiences engage with TV series in new ways, and TV series are often tailored to new media and forms of consumption, if not, in fact, using multiple platforms as part of their storytelling and engagement structure.

The second chapter deals with the advent of streaming, whereas the third chapter explores *the global turn* in modern television where TV is becoming a less insular or "siloized" phenomenon.[9] Through international collaborations and co-productions, *transnational remakes* and *local-language originals* by global streamers like Netflix, the TV landscape is changing and opening up to mutual inspiration and "circular influences" (as Nic Pizzolatto puts it).[10] These elements and the migration of talents and TV formats have created a TV landscape where American TV series are affected by global tendencies and non-American productions (through adaptations, remakes, co-financing, co-productions or a more general inspiration).

The first part of the book (chapters 1-3) explores the changes in the modern TV landscape, and the second part of the book examines different aspects of modern TV series: from new modes of storytelling and new approaches to genre to *TV auteurism* and stylistic innovation. In exploring those aspects, the book draws on various scholars, from Jason Mittell and Henry Jenkins to Kristin Thompson and Luca Barra, yet it does not rely solely on such scholarly accounts. Rather, it seeks to gain a more complex and valid understanding of TV production in the *multiplatform era* by combining interviews with more than 100 people from the television industry with different theoretical understandings and analyses of selected TV series that display a groundbreaking or innovative approach to one or more of the aforementioned aspects.

Stories We Tell: Trade Stories and Production Analysis

Production analysis may entail many different forms of investigation and data collection, from interviews with practitioners to observational studies (what Clifford Geertz would call "interpretive anthropology").[11] A typical challenge concerning production studies is that they are often based on a limited set of interviewees from *above-the-line creative sectors* (writers, directors and producers), underemphasizing or totally ignoring what John T. Caldwell describes as *below-the-line technical crafts* (e.g. cinematographers, re-recording mixers and editors).[12]

Hoping to get a deeper and more valid insight into the production process, this book includes a wide variety of practitioners and sectors - something that seems particularly relevant when dealing with not just *above-the-line* creative visions, but also specific stylistic choices and technical aspects.

Thus, apart from textual analyses, various statistics and secondary sources, this book is based on interviews with an extensive group of people from different sectors in the industry. This includes creators, writers and showrunners (e.g. David Chase, David Simon, Julie Andem, Jay Duplass, Angela Kang and Nic Pizzolatto), directors (e.g. Mary Harron, Tricia Brock and Sam Miller) and producers (e.g. Sabrina Sutherland and Kelly Luegenbiehl), but also cinematographers (e.g. Patrick Capone and Migue Amoedo), editors (e.g. Duwayne Dunham and Sidney Wolinsky), sound designers (e.g. Paula Fairfield and Craig Henighan), composers (e.g. Angelo Badalamenti and Dave Porter) and title sequence designers (e.g. Michelle Dougherty and Patrick Clair).

Different types of practitioners can give insights into different parts of the production process, and they might also have different stories to tell about the process itself and television production in general. In that sense, *Beyond Television* hopes to go beyond television production in the *multiplatform era* by drawing on numerous interviews and by exploring the different narratives that we find within the industry. As Caldwell writes, knowledge about the industry tends to be "highly coded, managed and inflected", and the higher up you get in the food chain, the more managed and controlled these narratives tend to get (Caldwell describes this as "the inverse credibility law").[13] In that sense, this book is based on a wide range of interviews, not just to give validity to the different statements about industrial and productional issues, but to cross-reference those stories and reveal some more general *trade narratives* about modern television and the current TV landscape. Film and TV studies "matured in part by embracing narrative theory as one of its defining methods," as Caldwell poignantly puts it. "Yet little or no attention has been paid to the trade stories that practitioners tell among themselves."[14]

Beyond Television takes the reader behind the scenes of TV production in the *multiplatform era*, yet it also goes beyond the selected TV series and explores how they, in different ways, challenge the boundaries and conventions of television. Finally, it tries to reveal the metanarratives about modern television that exist *within* the industry. Hence, the interviews are used in different ways. Part of the interviews are used as quotes throughout the book - alongside statistics and various academic sources - to illustrate different views on the current TV landscape. Elsewhere, the interviewees are used as *exclusive informants* who provide exclusive insight into or expert knowledge about a given TV production (e.g. the use of filters, lenses or musical motifs).[15] In the first case, the interviewees function as relevant voices, whose opinions are of interest due to their position within and experience from the industry. In the second case, the interviewees function as experts due to their privileged insight into a given field and a concrete production.

Finally, the book includes a feature interview at the end of each chapter, either in the form of a solo interview or a small cluster of related interviews with TV executives and creators. These interviews could be seen as vertical breakers that punctuate the horizontal narrative of the book, yet they resonate with the neighboring chapters and reflect how the industry people, themselves, see the changes in the TV landscape. In that sense, *Beyond Television* could be described almost as a TV series. It can be read in a linear fashion, although it has breaks at the end of each chapter, but it can also be read in a non-linear way, each chapter exploring a new aspect of the current TV landscape and resonating in complex ways with the other chapters and interludes.

The book is based on extensive research and an interview period spanning six years (from 2014 to 2020), yet the book does not claim to give a definitive, let alone an exhaustive, account of TV production in the *multiplatform era*. It focuses mainly on modern American television, exploring new approaches to storytelling, style and genre, but it also includes global perspectives and non-American cases, inasmuch as modern TV series often transcend national borders and find global distribution and audiences. Throughout the book, various TV series are used to illustrate and exemplify the different points, but the most central cases are *Breaking Bad* (AMC, 2008-2013), *House of Cards* (Netflix, 2013-2018), *True Detective* (HBO, 2014-2019), *American Crime* (ABC, 2015-2017), *Better Call Saul* (AMC, 2015-), *Stranger Things* (Netflix, 2016-), *Twin Peaks: The Return* (Showtime, 2017) and *Euphoria* (HBO, 2019-).

There are many insightful studies of modern TV series and the current TV landscape. Some of these focus on industrial and infrastructural perspectives (cf. Catherine Johnson's *Online TV* and Amanda D. Lotz's *We Now Disrupt This Broadcast*), while others explore productional and technical aspects (cf. Neil Landau's *TV Outside the Box*) or textual and authorial qualities in specific series (cf. Martha Nochimson's *Television Rewired*). This book is not interested in these aspects as isolated phenomena, but in the intersection between them and how infrastructural and industrial changes influence or reflect changes in terms of production, style and storytelling.

It is a central argument in the book that modern TV series often challenge traditional understandings of television, moving beyond traditional stylistic choices, traditional modes of storytelling and conventional genres and formats, yet they still have a serialized structure and, in different ways, adhere to televisual conventions. In terms of distribution, many series might have moved "beyond television", and modern TV series challenge our understandings of television in various ways. *The multiplatform era*, however, is characterized by both change and continuity, and this study seeks to illustrate how modern and innovative TV series embody those opposites, challenging some conventions while respecting and drawing on others. The study focuses on productional, narrative and aesthetic aspects, and although it gives a preliminary account of the modern TV landscape (from the advent of cable to the current streaming age), it is not a technical study of interfaces, distribution and *media infrastructures*.[16] Though including infrastructural perspectives, through reference to various statistics and scholars like Ramon Lobato, Lisa Parks, Shanti Kumar and Amanda D. Lotz, a fully-fledged technical account of modern types of digital distribution is well beyond the scope of this book. What this book promises is not an exhaustive technical account of the modern TV landscape, but an extensive study of new forms of production and new approaches to style, storytelling and genre in modern TV series, executed through a combination of case analyses and qualitative interviews.

Chapter 1

"It's Not TV. It's HBO": Prestige Television and Not-TV Branding in the Cable Era

> There is a feeling about HBO that when the name goes on a program, you at least know that it's going to be – whatever genre – the top of the line.
> - Ray Solley, Executive Director of the Tower Theatre Foundation (TFF)[17]

The 1990s was a period of change in American television, an era that saw the launching of new TV stations, new ways of transmitting, distributing and consuming television and new types of programming.

A linear descendant of DuMont Television, Fox was launched in 1986, and other networks, for example The WB and UPN, appeared in 1995. In 1996, then, the Federal Communications Committee (FCC) deregulated the American TV landscape, letting "anyone enter the communications business - to let any communications business compete in any market against any other."[18] Amending the *Communications Act* of 1934, the new act from 1996, signed by Bill Clinton, sought to deregulate the market and allow telephony services like AT&T to "participate in various other services such as Internet provision, broadcasting, and news publication."[19]

These were important changes that would pave the way for a fundamental reshaping of the American TV landscape, but two separate events from 1997 would alter the infrastructure of American (and global) television even further. A descendant of VHS (Video Home System), which was released in Japan and America in 1976 and 1977, the DVD (Digital Versatile Disc) now made its commercial debut and was recognized as the "fastest selling media format of all time."[20] Though initially meant for feature films, the DVD would soon become a new medium for serialized content, transforming "the flow of broadcasting into tangible texts," and a new way to approach and consume television programs.[21]

An even more game-changing debut, *Oz* (1997-2003) premiered on HBO, becoming the first example of their *original programming* strategy and the first *premium cable* series in the history of American television.

This chapter deals with the changes in American (and global) television from the 1990s through the early 2000s - what could be described as the first ripple of the *multiplatform era* - and it discusses the different periodizations of American TV history and their potential limitations.[22]

The Stories of TV History: Phases and Periodizations

TV history is a story about serialized narratives, but American television history, in itself, is a series of narratives often neatly divided into valleys and peaks, 'wastelands' and 'Golden Ages'.[23]

In his seminal book *Television's Second Golden Age* (1996), TV critic Robert J. Thompson, for example, claims that American TV history had its *First Golden Age* in the 1940s and 1950s, coinciding with influential anthology series such as *Kraft Television Theatre* (NBC, 1947-1955), *The Philco Televison Playhouse* (NBC, 1948-1955) and *Alfred Hitchcock Presents* (CBS/NBC, 1955-1962). Amid traditional TV genres, like soap operas and sitcoms with their 30-minute episode lengths and somewhat formulaic style and structure, *live television dramas* represented a type of television that was elevated into an art form through its conceptualizing creators and producers (e.g. Alfred Hitchcock) and its reference to critically acclaimed stage plays. At the same time, Thompson argues, the early anthology dramas became a breeding ground for new talents (e.g. Robert Altman, John Frankenheimer, Sidney Lumet and George Roy Hill) who would later migrate to the film industry and help define American cinema.[24]

According to Thompson, the *First Golden Age* was followed by an era of repetition and standardization within American television, but a small group of groundbreaking series (e.g. *Hill Street Blues*, *Miami Vice*, *L.A. Law*, *Homicide*, *Twin Peaks* and *ER*) formed a sort of *Second Golden Age* in the mid-1980s and early 1990s within an otherwise conservative TV landscape.[25]

In his hugely influential book, Thompson points out 11 characteristics of "Quality TV" - characteristics that are often mentioned when describing cable dramas of the early 2000s or modern streaming series.[26] Firstly, he argues, quality series are often best defined by what they are not ("regular" TV), inasmuch as they break many of the rules and conventions that we typically associate with television. Secondly, they often have a "quality pedigree" through their creators/producers (e.g. Michael Mann and David Lynch) who are known from other and more respected media, and they tend to attract audiences with "blue-chip demographics". Thirdly, quality series typically mix different genres, explore controversial topics in a self-conscious, metafictional way or in an unpackaged and realistic style that you rarely see in television. Finally, quality series tend to have large ensembles and cumulative plots that require a high degree of attention and memory on the part of the viewer and even a certain understanding of the medium itself (what David Bianculli calls *teleliteracy*).[27]

Golden Ages and Evolutionary Histories

Other critics and scholars have described American TV history in evolutionary terms, adopting Thompson's "Golden Age" rhetoric and distinguishing between traditional television (often seen as simple and formulaic) and modern

TV series (described as mature or complex). Expanding on Thompson, scholars such as Henrik Højer, Michael Mario Albrecht and Margaret Tally have written about a *Third Golden Age* in American television where the cable revolution of the late 1990s and early 2000s is seen as a new phase or "Golden Age" rather than a simple continuation of the development that took place in the late 1980s and mid-1990s.[28] Critics and reviewers have followed suit, making *The Third Golden Age* an almost ubiquitous term for today's TV landscape.[29] Even people from the industry talk about TV history in evolutionary terms, referring to different Golden Ages in American Television (as in the interview with Tom Fontana later in this book) and talking about American TV history as a story of 'maturation' (as in the interview with David Simon). Neither Fontana nor Simon, however, adhere to a simple understanding of American television, and Fontana rejects the general devaluation of television and the tendency to forget the long and complex history of experimentation within TV history. An often forgotten example of experimentation within early TV history was seen in the pilot episode for Orson Welles' anthology series *The Fountain of Youth* (NBC, 1958), which used voice-over narration, backprojection and blackouts in a fairly unique and radical way. *The Fountain of Youth*, as Welles said, was his "first film conceived for the box," but was ultimately rejected by Desilu Studios due to budgetary issues and Welles' unwillingness to compromise his vision.[30]

Albeit influential, Thompson's terminology has been rejected by many scholars, such as Elana Levine, inasmuch as it "neglects a long history of innovation in television and [...] tends to privilege shows that are valued by elite audiences over those more widely watched".[31] Apart from the normative tendency, Thompson's book and other "Golden Age" histories seem to underemphasize the global aspects and the many precursors that exist - and have always existed - outside America.

Undoubtedly, it was significant to American TV history when film directors like Michael Mann and David Lynch migrated to television and produced two of the most influential TV series of the 1980s and 1990s. Mann, who had worked as an episode director on different shows before receiving a Palme d'Or nomination for his expressive neo-noir thriller *Thief* (1981), turned to television and produced the notoriously flamboyant cop show *Miami Vice* (NBC, 1984-1990), known for its MTV-like use of montage editing, non-diegetic music, wide lenses and flashy colors.[32] In terms of sound, *Miami Vice* was also ahead of its time, using analogue Nagras and two-track recording in an innovative way.[33] "Between the music, the popular songs, the car chases and the explosions, I think Michael really carved new ground," as sound effects editor Scott Hecker puts it:

> Prior to *Miami Vice*, I had worked with Michael on his films *Thief* and *Manhunter*. If you go back and watch *Thief*, there are many shots of the front hood of the car where all of the cars that pass it are reflected in it in a Doppler way, and I think that motif carried on into *Miami Vice*. The way light reflected off the car, the close-ups of the wheels, the sounds. Those are his trademarks in a way.[34]

After directing the expressionistic midnight movie *Eraserhead* (1977), David Lynch had made a name for himself in the arthouse circuit, and he brought his trademark combination of moody surrealism, Americana and genre-bending art cinema with him to the small screen. Here, Lynch's unique sensibilities would be paired with the storytelling qualities of Mark Frost, a seasoned TV writer known for his work on *The Six Million Dollar Man* (ABC, 1973-1978) and *Hill Street Blues* (NBC, 1981-1987). Though clearly a shared vision, *Twin Peaks* was often branded as a David Lynch creation or described as a combination of Lynch's audiovisual artistry and Frost's understanding of serialized narratives and the TV medium.[35] "Those *are* probably our individual strengths," as Frost admits, "but there is something that happens when you put your heads together where the whole is more than the sum of the parts."[36]

Despite working on other projects, David Lynch was personally involved in many aspects of *Twin Peaks*, and even though he allowed the different episode directors a lot of creative freedom, he would comment on the editing, ask for revisions or even create new practical effects and Foley sounds during post-production.[37]

Unquestionably, this was news in America where the film and TV industries were often seen as two separate worlds at different ends of an industrial and cultural hierarchy. Coming from television and "break[ing] into movies", as David Chase says, was all but "impossible" in the 1980s, and the thought of migrating from film to television was surprising, if not unthinkable.[38]

This might well be the case in American television, yet in terms of global TV history, Mann and Lynch were not the first film directors with an arthouse pedigree to migrate between cinema and television. In Sweden, Ingmar Bergman had created the miniseries *Scener ur ett äktenskap* (SVT, 1973) and *Fanny och Alexander* (SVT, 1982), two critically lauded chamber plays that are mentioned as points of inspiration by numerous interviewees for this book, including David Chase (*The Sopranos*), Hagai Levi (*BeTipul*), Beau Willimon (*House of Cards*) and Tricia Brock (*Halt and Catch Fire*).[39] In the words of writer-director Derek Cianfrance:

> I had never seen *Fanny and Alexander*, but as I was writing *I Know This Much Is True*, the Film Forum in New York was playing *Fanny and Alexander* over the course of a couple of days, so I went and watched Bergman's TV show in the movie theater. It was a great inspiration for me to think that Bergman was doing his thing: It might have been for the small screen, but he was doing exactly what he wanted, and the thing that he made for the small screen still works on the big screen too.[40]

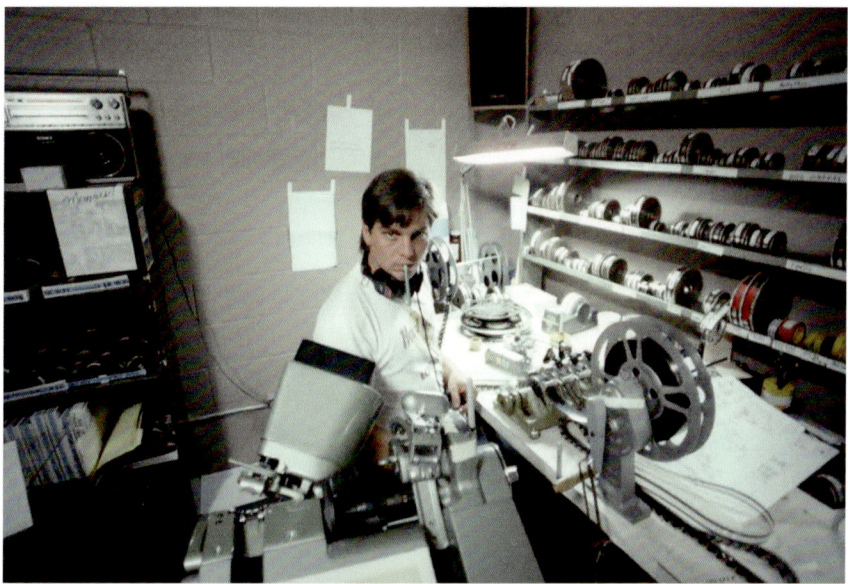

Fig. 1-2: *Miami Vice* (created by Anthony Yerkovich) and *Twin Peaks* broke new ground in the 1980s and 1990s, both experimenting with new approaches to sound. *Miami Vice* used two-track analogue recording, and *Twin Peaks* was born during the early stages of television surround sound. Above we see the sound effects editor Scott Hecker (*Miami Vice*). Below we see Lori Eschler Frystak, who remembers how David Lynch would create Foley sounds himself while overseeing other directors' episodes for *Twin Peaks*. Courtesy of Scott Hecker and Lori Eschler Frystak.

Other famous European filmmakers had done the same - from Rainer Werner Fassbinder in Germany (*Berlin Alexanderplatz*, Das Erste, 1980) to Krzysztof Kieślowski in Poland (*Dekalog*, TVP, 1989) - and directors such as Ken Loach in England and Erik Balling in Denmark commuted freely between the film and TV industries. In Denmark, in fact, there has been a natural crossover between the film and TV industries ever since the 1970s, long before Lars von Trier became famous for directing his *Twin Peaks*-inspired miniseries *Riget* (DR, 1994), which is currently being revived, and many decades before *crossover* became an actual dogma for DR (Danish Broadcasting Corporation).[41]

However significant and interesting, Thompson's periodization of American TV history includes a few potential oversights, neglecting the long history of experimentation and innovation in (American) TV history and almost ignoring the trends and influences from other countries and industries. Finally, one could argue that the "Golden Age" rhetoric, by pointing to the innovative or untraditional qualities of modern TV series, tends to overlook the conventional and *classically televisual* qualities of those same series. As we shall see elsewhere in this book, for example, the creators of *Six Feet Under* (HBO, 2001-2005), *House of Cards* (Netflix, 2013-2018) and *Arvingerne* (DR, 2014-2017) willingly describe their series as offshoots of the *serial melodrama* (soap opera) - a connection that is rarely emphasized by the critics.

Nevertheless, Thompson's seminal book does give an insightful description of the American TV landscape in the 1990s, and many scholars borrow from Thompson, even if they reject his "Golden Age" terminology.

Industrial Circumstances and Structural Histories

In less categorical manners, other TV histories focus solely on technological inventions and industrial shifts. This is the case with John Ellis who, in his book *Seeing Things: Television in the Age of Uncertainty*, distinguishes between three phases in TV history (TVI, TVII and TVIII) characterized by *scarcity*, *availability* and *plenty*.[42] The first era was defined by mass market consumerism, standardization and a scarcity in terms of channels and TV series.

In the 1980s, Channel 4 and other new networks began to emerge in Britain (Ellis focuses primarily on a British context), and many of those channels abandoned the tenets of scarcity and paved the way for a new phase in TV history. Around the turn of the century, British television had reached an era of *plenty* where audiences were being flooded with new channels, outlets and content. As Ellis, almost prophetically, puts it:

> The television industry enters the new millennium in a state of profound uncertainty. Changes are taking place on all fronts. New production technologies are altering the ways that programmes are made; new distribution technologies are altering the experience of television viewing itself.[43]

Ellis' industrial model, focusing on the gradual expansion of television services in Britain, has become greatly influential, and a similar framework has been used by Rogers, Epstein and Reeves to describe American TV history.[44]

In her book *Netflix and the Re-Invention of Television* (2018), Mareike Jenner also builds on Ellis' model, suggesting that the current phase in the TV landscape should be dubbed TVIV. "Looking at these phases as technological shifts," Jenner writes, "changes to content and marketing strategies that target increasingly smaller audience segments (from mass medium to niche medium) justify a categorization of contemporary shifts as TVIV."[45]

A similar model is introduced by Amanda D. Lotz who gives an industrial and infrastructural account of American TV history, dividing it into three distinct phases called *the network era*, *the multi-channel transition* and *the post-network era*. *The network era* is a lengthy phase in American television history, from the early days of the medium in the 1940s to the beginning of the 1980s. This was an era largely dominated by three major broadcast networks (NBC, CBS and ABC), relying on standardized genres (soap operas, sitcoms, sketch shows, talk shows etc.), tried-and-true formulas and mass consumption. According to Lotz, the first phase in American TV history was an era defined by a broadcast structure and a small monopoly of networks, not unlike the studio system in Hollywood, but it was a period of both standardization and innovation.

The 1980s and early 1990s, then, was a transitional phase. This era saw the birth of Fox, which spawned a number of different TV channels (not unlike the original broadcast networks, which were all subdivided into different channels).[46] The era also saw the launching of new cable channels, and even though cable channels did not begin to produce original TV series until the end of the 1990s, cable was already beginning to transform American television. It is worth noting in this context that the core of the cable industry was not originally the cable channels themselves; the primary function of the cable business was *distribution*, and cable was used to deliver both cable channels (e.g. CNN and MTV) and traditional broadcast networks which could also be received via the antenna. "The word *cable* is used a lot like *Hollywood* in American culture," as Lotz notices. "While it references something quite specific, it also stands in for much more and describes two separate entities."[47] The cable business has a long history, going back to the 1940s, but until the 1970s – HBO was launched in 1972 and AMC in 1984 – it was primarily used to transmit signals. "Cable first developed to solve a problem of geography - the inability of towns, typically in mountainous areas, to receive broadcast signals", writes Lotz, and the cable service providers (such as Charter and Cox) are often unrelated to the cable channels (e.g. HBO and Showtime) that provide premium cable series.[48]

After 1975, the VCR also became an increasingly visible part of the American TV landscape (the VCR penetration grew from 1% in 1980 to 68.6% in 1990 and 91.5% in 2003). At the same time, there was an increase in the number of American households with two or more television sets (from 1% in 1950 to 50.1% in 1980 and 84.4% in 2010), and VHS also entered the market and helped transform the way people watched and consumed television.[49]

The 1980s and early 1990s may be seen as a *Second Golden Age* in television, focusing on genre-bending and groundbreaking series like *The Singing Detective* (BBC One, 1986), *Moonlighting* (ABC, 1985-1989), *Twin Peaks* and *Riget* and featuring famous film directors who migrated to the TV industry. In this context, it would also be natural to mention series such as *St. Elsewhere* (NBC, 1982-1988), *ER* (NBC, 1994-2009), *Homicide: Life on the Street* (NBC, 1993-1999) and *NYPD Blue* (ABC, 1993-2005), which all but reinvented two of the most traditional TV genres: the medical show and the cop show. *Homicide*, *NYPD Blue* and *ER* became famous for their authentic qualities and use of handheld camera - something that would later inspire the Danish producer Sven Clausen who went on a "research trip" to the US and brought back notes that would influence Danish TV in the years to come (even if the Danish series *Een gang strømer* had introduced a similar style in 1987).[50] On *ER*, the goal of authenticity was achieved by means of unsteady handheld camera and a complex, realistic sound design. In the words of re-recording mixer Adam Sawelson:

> *ER* was quite a complicated show in terms of sound. First of all, we tried to create a lot of different layers for each location, specifically at the hospital. There were a lot of details that went into it. The other thing that we did was to orchestrate all of the different beeps of the machines, partly to give the audience a sense of authenticity – that those machines were actually there – and partly to build suspense. We actually had a few doctors on the show who were there to make sure that everything sounded right. The way the beeps were orchestrated as the drama was intensified was an important thing we did. We did a lot of those things, off-stage sirens and babies crying in the background. There was just an enormous level of detail that went into it. We had a license to be creative, but the showrunners were also very involved, and it was very important that it sounded authentic.[51]

Even more influential, *Homicide* was inspired by real events, and the production process was notably different from most other cop and crime shows of the time. According to executive producer Tom Fontana:

> Barry Levinson directed the pilot of *Homicide: Life on the Street*, and he decided that every episode would be filmed with a handheld camera, giving the series a quasi-documentary feel. The camera was as volatile as the stories we were telling, constantly moving, always searching for the most dramatic moment, rather than the prettiest shot. We never did a perfect master, so the actors never knew if the camera was on them. That meant they had to be in character at every moment, giving their all. In terms of the storytelling, we used every kernel in David's non-fiction book, which is, I think, the most honest and authentic crime book ever written. Our detectives were fallible, petulant, self-serving, irritating and

> yet determined to "speak for the dead." And, as I said, we didn't always solve the murders. For example, we, purposely, didn't "close" the Adena Watson case because the story was based on a real murder in *Homicide: A Year on the Killing Streets*, which is unsolved to this day. We felt coming up with a fictional solution would be disrespectful.[52]

Mary Harron, who worked as an episode director on *Homicide*, describes it in a similar manner - mentioning the impossibility of planning shots as a liberating factor - and she points to the use of directors from the independent film sector as another noteworthy and groundbreaking feature.[53] A similar point has been made about *Twin Peaks* where Mark Frost and David Lynch employed untried directors (like Duwayne Dunham) and film directors who had made their mark in foreign and independent cinema (e.g. Tim Hunter, Tina Rathborne, Uli Edel and James Foley).

Homicide could be described as a reinvention of the cop show and *Twin Peaks* as an unusual hybrid of detective series, soap opera and surrealism.[54] *St. Elsewhere* also challenged generic formulas, drawing on game-changing precursors from the 1970s. In the words of Fontana:

> *St. Elsewhere* was the opposite of the standard medical shows which had been on TV since the beginning, from *Dr. Kildare* to *Marcus Welby, M.D.* Like *Homicide*, our doctors and nurses were damaged souls, yet they cared about healing – themselves and their patients. But, to give credit where credit is due, we writers on *St. Elsewhere* were inspired by the comedy series *M*A*S*H*, which transcended the half-hour "sitcom" form and showed us how you can reinvent your show on a weekly basis.[55]

Whether or not we accept Fontana's description, the 1980s and 1990s were a transitional phase in TV history, and it could be described as a "Golden Age" with reference to groundbreaking American series such as *Hill Street Blues*, *St. Elsewhere*, *Twin Peaks* and *Homicide* and influential European series such as *The Singing Detective*, *Berlin Alexanderplatz* and *Riget*.[56] Without buying into the "Golden Age" rhetoric, we could also simply describe the period as a transitional phase in TV history due to the growth in TV ownership, the gradual restructuring of the TV landscape (with new channels, cable and satellite television, VCR and VHS) and how this affected TV programming and consumption. In that sense, the game-changing series of the 1980s and 1990s might be seen as a result of a new strategy from the broadcast networks that experienced "declining audience shares, decreasing revenues [and] competition from cable networks." It was within this context that some broadcast networks began taking risks and tried to reposition themselves in the marketplace. As NBC's Brandon Tartikoff poignantly put it: "Tried and true is dead and buried."[57]

The last phase mentioned in Lotz's TV history is called *The Post-Network Era*, in the sense that the American TV landscape is no longer dominated by a limited number of broadcast networks. In this context, however, I prefer Trisha Dunleavy's term *the multiplatform era*, a phrase that seeks to describe the complex and potentially confusing era in television history from 2000 and onwards.[58] What is particularly appealing about Dunleavy's terminology is that it does not focus exclusively on how modern series differ from traditional television. Rather, Dunleavy describes the *multiplatform era* as a period characterized by many different channels and platforms and a diverse TV landscape that is noticeably *dissimilar from* traditional television, but also, in complex ways, *related to* and *contingent on* traditional TV.

The HBO Playbook

In 1991 David Simon wrote a journalistic book entitled *Homicide: A Year on the Killing Streets*, depicting a police department in the crime-ridden area of Baltimore, and the subsequent TV adaptation of that book, *Homicide: Life on the Street* (NBC, 1993-1999), helped pave the way for the cable revolution at the end of the 1990s. The TV landscape did not change dramatically, though, until the advent of the major cable networks and their introduction of *original programming* at the turn of the century.

Two decades before they would come to change television, HBO went to court against FCC (Federal Communications Commission), arguing that *premium cable* channels like HBO could not be expected to follow the same guidelines as traditional broadcast networks. Historically, broadcast networks have imposed restrictions and censorship on themselves, trying not to scare off viewers or advertisers, and in the 1960s, NBC executive Paul L. Klein coined the phrase *least objectionable programming* to describe the broadcast ideal of getting people to tune in and stay on.[59] Knowing that viewers often turned on their television sets to watch television in a broad sense, not for any *one* program, broadcast networks tried to eschew graphic violence and nudity, transgressive behavior and "any obscene, indecent or profane language" (as mentioned in the *Communications Act of 1934*).[60]

In 1977, however, HBO won the case against FCC by pointing to the First Amendment and the freedom of expression. Given that they had a subscription model, *premium cable* networks could not be compared with broadcast networks that were available to everyone with an antenna. The court held that the regulations against HBO were in violation of the First Amendment because they did not serve "any important or substantial interest", and that decision would prove important for HBO twenty years later and potentially transformative for the TV landscape.[61]

HBO is often seen as a central game-changer in American TV history, promoting itself as something *more* than traditional television, and their prestigious drama series are often seen as something other, entirely, than conventional TV serials. There has even been talk of an *HBO Playbook* which the other cable networks and major broadcasters hoped to emulate: a set of stylistic and narrative principles that HBO had almost been able to claim as their own. These included:

- transgressive content and moral ambiguity
- narrative complexity and large ensembles
- social and institutional critique
- flawed characters and antiheroes
- niche-marketing and narrowcasting
- TV auteurism and signature styles
- High production values and limited seasons.[62]

This is a well-known story by now, and many books have been written on the *tradition of quality* or *cable revolution* in American television.[63] The importance of HBO in this context is also well documented, and the TV scholars Kim Akass and Janet McCabe summarize HBO's history and importance in the following way:

> Across its history HBO has repeatedly pushed the boundaries of the medium – in terms of delivery, form and content – motivated by its economically precarious and, at times, institutionally marginal position in the US audiovisual media ecology. HBO started as a small enterprise situated on the very fringes of the US TV industry. Without much media fanfare HBO launched on 8 November 1972, with the 1971 film *Sometimes a Great Notion* (dir. Paul Newman, 1970) starring Paul Newman and Henry Fonda, followed by a NHL hockey game between the New York Rangers and the Vancouver Canucks. Three hundred and sixty-five Service Electric subscribers in Wilkes-Barre, Pennsylvania were the first to receive HBO (DeFino 2014). As of December 2013, HBO had an established 43 million domestic subscribers and by 2015 that figure had risen to 49 million, which included users of its newly launched streaming service, HBO NOW (Statista). HBO has gone from a small, almost regional service in the northeastern and Mid-Atlantic area of the United States to become a truly global brand and an internationally networked owner-syndicator.[64]

Akass and McCabe point to HBO as a sort of 'first-mover', and they write about HBO's ability to brand their content as particularly worthy and "exclusive". On the following pages, I will illustrate some of the aspects of *The HBO Playbook* through reference to selected TV series that resonate in different ways with the first feature interview at the end of the chapter.

No Place Like Home: Transgression and Subversion in *Oz*

"It's No Place Like Home." Thus reads the tagline of the transgressive prison show *Oz*, which premiered on HBO in 1997. The title and the tagline of the show are naturally ironic, alluding to the famous *fairy tale*-musical *The Wizard of Oz* (1939) and hinting at the rough and transgressive sensibility of Tom Fontana's series, which is far removed from Victor Fleming and (techni)colorful fantasies from the classical Hollywood era.⁶⁵

When *Oz* came out, it constituted a shock to the American television system with its graphic portrayal of sex, violence and decay in the American prison system, and it is worth noting that Tom Fontana had tried pitching it to many of the established networks before opting for HBO as his platform.⁶⁶ Having struggled with the different networks on series like *St. Elsewhere* and *Homicide*, Fontana finally succeeded in selling *Oz* to Chris Albrecht who saw HBO (with its critically acclaimed prison documentaries) as the natural home for *Oz*, and assured Fontana that his characters did not have to be "likeable" as long as they were interesting.⁶⁷ Albrecht gave Fontana an unprecedented amount of creative freedom, and Fontana used this freedom to create a radical and subversive prison series, employing an overt visual style and exposing the "dehumanizing nature of the prison experience."⁶⁸

Apart from alluding to *The Wizard of Oz*, the tagline, "It's No Place Like Home", could also be a reference to HBO itself. Following the legal dispute with FCC in 1977, HBO ventured into *original programming* in the 1990s, and with a triad of shows, *Oz* (1997-2003), *Sex and the City* (1998-2004) and *The Sopranos* (1999-2007), they introduced a type of niche-oriented television drama which would not have been possible to present on network television. This kind of niche-oriented TV drama also included adult-oriented programming, which, in itself, was a trademark of arthouse cinema that, along with the well-known film directors, could help attract famous movie stars to the television medium.

This move from HBO into *original programming* would soon become a central factor in the ever-changing TV landscape, and the slogan of HBO (at the time) would come to indicate the channel's attempt to distance itself from traditional or stereotypical notions of television: "It's Not TV. It's HBO."⁶⁹ If the "not TV"-slogan of HBO seemed to echo the tagline of the drama series *Oz*, then the 1982-1983-slogan was even more similar to the aforementioned tagline, saying "There's No Place Like HBO."

According to Marc Leverette, HBO has been part of a "not TV industry," trying to lure urban, educated viewers by promoting itself as a producer of unconventional, *high-end* television drama.⁷⁰ As Amanda D. Lotz puts it: "HBO thrives by defying program standards that appeal to the mass audience, and succeeds by exploiting limited access as the means to acceptance as high (or at least higher) elite art."⁷¹

Apart from its graphic portrayal of violence, sex and perversity, *Oz* is mostly known for its use of an embedded on-screen narrator (Augustus Hill played by Harold Perrineau) - a black man seated in a wheelchair and talking directly to the audience. This stylistic signature functions as a sort of Brechtian or Godardian type of *defamiliarization*, and it lends a certain element of formalism to an otherwise realistic show.

In general, *Oz* would become known for its violent content and its depraved characters (in the maximum security wing called Emerald City), and stylistically it would employ extreme angles, wide lenses and expressive colors and lighting. The gritty realism of the content, in other words, was often juxtaposed by a heavily expressive and intensified style.

In the episode called "Animal Farm" (2:7, 1998), for example, we follow different characters and plot arcs. One storyline deals with Robert Sippel (David Lansbury), a religious inmate who was convicted after confessing that he had molested a 14-year-old boy named Frances Hansell, and that storyline echoes a classic theme in the works of Fontana and episode director Mary Harron: The fluid boundary between righteousness and sin, virtue and vice. Similarly, the story of Robert Sippel, priest turned pedophile, touches upon a general question of sexuality and transgression that is often explored in *Oz*, and the name of the molested boy seems to allude to the Grimm fairy tale about Hansel and Gretel (*Hänsel und Gretel*, 1812). In the original story, two children are lured into a house constructed of cake and confectionery by an old and treacherous witch, and in *Oz* the classic fairy tale is turned into a realistic, yet equally nightmarish, story about an adolescent boy who is molested by a seemingly trustworthy man. A man of God, no less.

Another storyline in "Animal Farm" focuses on Ryan O'Reily (Dean Winters), who is reunited with his brother Cyril after a period of forced separation. This plotline, blending elements of comedy, raw realism and melodrama, touches upon another central theme of the series: The deconstruction of the family and the redefinition of "home". The two O'Reilys are being separated, torn apart. But as they reunite – as Cyril comes "home" – their reunion spells a total redefinition of both family values and "home". Cyril and Ryan are reunited in prison after Cyril has killed Dr. Gloria Nathan's husband, and in that sense the *reunion* of the two O'Reilys is predicated on the *destruction* of another family: the Nathans.

A similar thing could be said of the Rob Rebadow arc. Rebadow's grandson is dying of leukemia, and hoping to grant him his final wish (to go to Disneyland), Rob Rebadow gets money from the other inmates. Using a subtle montage technique, Harron illustrates the interconnections of vice and virtue – money changing hands between different inmates in order to help a dying child and bridge the gap between him and his estranged grandfather – and she shows us how Rebadow is trying to mend the wounds of his biological family by acquiring help from his new family: the other prisoners.

The title of the episode, "Animal Farm", alludes to George Orwell and hints at the social critique in Fontana's series and its metafictional or even Brechtian tendencies. From its overt use of wide lenses, colors and direct address,

Fontana's series was nothing like a traditional prison drama, and had it not been for a cable network known for its raw and prestigious prison documentaries, it might never have found a home in American television.

Artistic Influences and Tonal Ambiguity in *The Sopranos*

Like Tom Fontana before him, David Chase had a difficult time pitching and selling *The Sopranos*, a series that was inspired by interviews, real events, biographical experiences and various cinematic influences.[72]

Chase took his idea to all of the major networks, but they all turned it down or asked for revisions or concessions that Chase did not want to make.[73] Inspired by Martin Scorsese's gangster films, Francis Ford Coppola's *Godfather* trilogy (1972, 1974 and 1990) and European art directors such as Ingmar Bergman and Jean-Luc Godard, Chase wanted to create a TV series that broke the traditional paradigms of television and challenged the generic conventions of the gangster genre. Eventually, HBO accepted his proposal and chose to air *The Sopranos* (HBO, 1999-2007), a clever combination of gangster series, family-melodrama and humor that would soon become a modern classic. With more than 22 million people watching the Season 3 premiere, *The Sopranos* was an unprecedented audience success for HBO, and it was soon lauded as one of the best TV series ever made.[74]

The qualities of *The Sopranos* are difficult to pinpoint within a few pages, but two of the most striking factors are: (1) The way in which it embraces ambiguity, often using Eisensteinian montage editing, counterpoint and extreme tonal shifts, and (2) its reconfiguration of the gangster genre, alluding to classic gangster movies, but avoiding the traditional rise-and-fall template.

Before migrating to television, Chase had gone to film school and worked as a production manager and writer on low-budget genre movies in the 1960s and 1970s (including John Hayes' *The Cut-Throats* and *Grave of the Vampire*). Unwillingly, Chase turned his attention to television, as he found it difficult to get an actual breakthrough in the film industry. In television, Chase worked as an episode director on the new version of *Alfred Hitchcock Presents* (NBC/USA Network, 1985-1989) and a staff writer on the *Twin Peaks*-inspired and critically acclaimed small town series *Northern Exposure* (CBS, 1990-1995). Still, Chase was critical of traditional television and the TV industry in general, claiming that television "trivializes everything"[75] and describing American TV as a "prisoner of dialogue":

> Television is really an outgrowth of radio. And radio is just all yak-yak-yak-yak. And that's what television is: yak-yak-yak-tak. It's a prisoner of dialogue, film of people talking.[76]

Hoping to avoid the anecdotal style of traditional television, Chase, who created and wrote *The Sopranos* and directed the pilot episode and the iconic finale, staged the dialogues differently, often using wide lenses and, at times, letting the camera drift away from the characters.

At the end of the pilot episode, for example, different people are assembled at the Soprano residence for a barbeque, but as the guests move out of the picture towards the house, the camera lingers and eventually turns in the other direction, ending in a wide shot of the empty pool. This camera movement, though potentially unnoticed by many viewers, is a good example of the alternative staging and *art TV*-qualities of *The Sopranos*.[77] Chase, himself, admits that it might seem like a surprising or counterintuitive camera movement, but to him it was the "obvious choice", perhaps because it metaphorically references Tony Soprano's beloved ducks that have now left the pool and, by extension, the sense of absence or emptiness that many of the characters feel.[78] Mirroring a shot in *Taxi Driver* (1976) where the camera drifts away from the main character and into an empty hallway, the final shot of Chase's pilot episode is a so-called "Antonioni Pirouette" (also known from the ending of Michelangelo Antonioni's *Professione: reporter*).[79] This type of camera movement is associated mainly with art cinema, and it is used by Scorsese and Antonioni to emphasize the existential sense of spleen or emptiness of their main characters.

This would only seem fitting to *The Sopranos*, a series that was originally conceived as a feature film about "a mobster in therapy having problems with his mother," created by a film aficionado who despised traditional television and veered toward the visual sophistication of arthouse cinema.[80] In the words of film and TV director Mary Harron:

> One thing that happened is that television became more visually sophisticated because it took on some of the style and the experimentation of independent film, and the audience became much more visually sophisticated. It started with *The Sopranos*, I would say - that was probably the big groundbreaker - and then *Deadwood*, *Breaking Bad* and a few other shows that were visually extraordinary. The first season of *Westworld* too. That was also extraordinary, and it had a huge budget.[81]

Tony Soprano (James Gandolfini) is not a typical film or TV mobster, and Chase has said on different occasions that he wanted to depict a gangster who experienced a rise and fall every day and a world so selfish and self-involved that even the gangsters went to therapy.[82] Inspired by directors like Ingmar Bergman and David Lynch, Chase included therapy sessions, elements of psychological realism and surreal dream sequences, and the depressed main character, Tony Soprano, came to represent a popular trope in cable television: the antihero.[83] As seen in the interview with Beau Willimon elsewhere in this book, the main characters in *House of Cards* (Netflix, 2013-2018) were inspired by Shakespearean tragedies, but also the kind of antihero that had not been seen in television, at least not extensively, before Tony Soprano.[84] Other series that were directly inspired by *The Sopranos*, in terms of its main character and the *apparently perverse allegiance* between him and the audience, included *The Shield* (FX, 2002-2008), *Dexter* (Showtime, 2006-2021), *Breaking Bad* (AMC, 2008-2013), *Hannibal* (NBC, 2013-2015) and *The Americans* (FX, 2013-2018). "We pitched *The Americans* around to a lot of places and got a lot of respectful nods, but deep down inside there was a lot of horror at the idea that you could take KGB spies and turn them into the heroes of a show," as the creator Joseph Weisberg said at the Split Screens Festival in 2018. "That was not really appealing to anyone except at FX who thought the idea was fantastic, because that was the network where doing things that were unconventional, different or weird was what appealed to them."[85]

Chase himself refuses to describe *The Sopranos* as a reinvention of the gangster genre, but admits that it might have "widened" or challenged the genre in various ways. This is evident from a sequence in the pilot episode where Tony's protégé, Christopher Moltisanti (Michael Imperioli), kills Emil Kolar (Bruce Smolanoff). As Emil bends down to test Christopher's drugs, Christopher shoots him in the back of his head several times, and for each shot we cut to a close-up of an image on the wall. In an almost Eisensteinian way, the cuts to the different images of Humphrey Bogart, Dean Martin and Edward G. Robinson (who are all associated with the mob or classic gangster films) seem to symbolize Christopher's attempt to imitate his heroes or act like a gangster.[86] Not unlike the scene in Godard's *À bout de souffle* (1960, *Breathless*) where Michel (Jean-Paul Belmondo) looks at a poster of Humphrey Bogart and tries to imitate his role model, the scene in *The Sopranos* seems to reference the gangster genre and simultaneously portray Christopher as a (tragic) would-be gangster. Though not intentionally referencing Godard, Chase says that it might well have been an unconscious source of inspiration, since Godard's movie played a vital role in the formation of Chase as a film and TV director.[87]

The characters in *The Sopranos* often quote gangster movies (from *The Godfather* to *Goodfellas*), and there is a high degree of ambiguity which is created through contrast editing, contrapuntal music and sudden tonal shifts. In another episode, for example, Christopher's friend Brendan Filone (Anthony DeSando) is executed by Mikey Palmice (Al Sapienza), and the execution is intercut with Meadow's recital, using the diegetic choir version of the lullaby "All Through the Night" as a musical counterpoint. These kinds of tonal shifts are seen throughout (e.g. when Tony plays a video game with his son, switching between a somewhat caring personality and an almost abusive one, and when Tony intentionally runs Mahaffey down in the pilot episode, breaking his leg, and then follows up with a snappy comment about HMOs).[88]

A famous example of these contrasts is seen in the episode "College" (1:5) where Tony takes his daughter college hunting in Maine. In a particularly suspenseful scene, Tony strangles a Mafia informant named Fabian Petrulio (Tony Ray Rossi), upon which we cut to an extreme high-angle shot of our main antihero who notices a flock of flying ducks in the air (a recurring symbol in the series). While characterizing Tony as both a caring father and a ruthless gangster, this sequence moreover utilizes a strong sonic contrast and dynamic range, going from "ominous silence" (as Alfred Hitchcock calls it) to sudden bursts of noise (coming from Tony and the flapping wings of the ducks).[89] In the words of re-recording mixer Adam Sawelson:

> We had a sort of general rule on *The Sopranos*: We tried to lead the audience to the edge of a cliff, and sometimes the use of silence can make something more intense and leave the audience at the edge of the cliff, before they suddenly fall down. If you never have quiet or silence, you won't get anything out of those loud or intense sounds. We wanted a sense of *vertical activity* on the track.
>
> If you do a big action scene or a car chase or something, it's very dense and effective, but it's actually very straight-forward and simpler to do, and the subtler soundtracks and sequences are, many times, far more difficult to do. I have worked in the industry for a long time, and one of the people who inspired and influenced me a lot was H.L. Bird. He mixed *2001 – a Space Odyssey* (1968), and he created that absolute silence in space, back in the analogue days. There was no sound whatsoever. I thought that was a pretty cool thing, and it just shows you how effective silence can be.
>
> David Chase would come in, and we would play back the final mix for him. He was very involved in every episode. Many of those ideas concerning the contrasts and uses of silence were his ideas, actually.[90]

From the very onset of his series, David Chase seems to indicate that this is not your average gangster show, infusing it with elements of humor and melodrama and re-situating the action to a bucolic setting. In a geographical sense, New Jersey may be in close proximity to Scorsese's New York, but culturally they seem to represent two different worlds, and already from the title sequence it is made clear that this is a different kind of gangster series in a different kind of environment.[91]

Though not as overtly experimental and stylistically flashy as some of the other series in this book, *The Sopranos* was visually and tonally innovative, and it also has a fairly radical ending, written and directed by Chase himself. In the final sequence, we crosscut between Tony's daughter Meadow (Jamie-Lynn Sigler) who is attempting to parallel park her car outside of their favorite diner, and the rest of the family who are inside the diner. As Tony enters the diner, there is an interesting series of cuts, as we cut from a *point glance* of Tony to a *point object* of Tony sitting at the booth (apparently seen from Tony's own point of view). This series of cuts seems to indicate that Tony is seeing himself, perhaps envisioning his own death, or that he is already dead.

Characters that enter their own points of view constitute a stylistic trait in art films like Wim Wenders' *Der Himmer über Berlin* (1987, *Wings of Desire*) and David Lynch's *Mulholland Dr.* (2001), but it is a rare feature in TV series.[92] And the finale of *The Sopranos* closes at an extremely ambiguous point, suddenly cutting to black at the sound of the line "Don't Stop" from Journey's "Don't Stop Believin'" (1981). In the words of editor Sidney Wolinsky:

> David figured out a way of ending it like nobody else would end it. And I kind of like it because whatever ending he could have thought of and written and carefully crafted, people would say: "That does not make sense. This should have happened, or that should have happened. He should have been punished, or he wasn't punished enough". Or it would have been a big shootout. And this way, it stops, and it's like there is no real ending, so I thought it was brilliant.[93]

"All about the Systemic": Institutional Critique in the Works of David Simon

We all know the story: An external force is threatening to eliminate the world and disturb the social order, as we know it. A strong man is put on the case and uses his will and agency to overcome the external threat and his inner conflict before restoring order as well as our collective faith in society and humankind. The typical Hollywood film follows a fairly well-known formula. It has a clear and well-defined plot, follows a *straight corridor* and takes few excursions on the way toward the happy ending. It has a strong protagonist at the center of the story – a character who is promptly introduced and who sets off the plot, which then unfolds as a neat series of causes and effects. This principle of *individualized causality* is seen in most Hollywood films, and many of these maxims are also apparent in the serialized fiction that we find in American television.[94]

These characteristics, however, are not typical of the fictional stories by TV creator and showrunner David Simon, who began his career as a journalist and became something of a flagship for HBO. Through lauded TV classics like *Homicide: Life on the Street* (NBC, 1993-1999), *The Corner* (HBO, 2000), *The Wire* (HBO, 2002-2008), *Generation Kill* (HBO, 2008), *Treme* (HBO, 2010-2013), *The Deuce* (HBO, 2017-2019) and *The Plot Against America* (HBO, 2020), Simon has come to define a pivotal shift in American television, largely by going against the grain of American politics and traditional formulas known from Hollywood and American television. If the classical Hollywood film deals with strong individuals who prevail and restore the social order, then Simon's fictions are often about structural issues and institutions that fail. And while a classical Hollywood film has one clear protagonist with a clearly defined goal, then Simon's stories are more anthropological and ambiguous in nature, without a clear center or an evident *telos*.

David Simon is a powerful voice in the political debate, a crucial figure for HBO and one of the most central and critically acclaimed *TV auteurs* in the modern mediascape.[95] As is evident from the feature interview at the end of this chapter, Simon often talks about his TV series as "pieces" or different parts of his personal exploration of American society and institutions. When advertising *The Deuce*, HBO played into this narrative, as Mikkel Jensen notices, and urged the viewers to see the new series as part of a larger whole by writing the following entry on their website: "What David Simon and George Pelecanos Want You to Know About Their Shows".[96]

HBO may contribute to the authorial reading of Simon's different series for understandable branding purposes, but that reading does seem natural given the way Simon frames his oeuvre. Whereas David Chase and David Lynch are reluctant to discuss the meaning of their work - avoiding interpretive questions, answering in vague or sparse manners or, in the case of Lynch, rejecting to make audio commentary for his productions - Simon speaks willingly about his work. In that sense, Jason Mittell may be right when he argues that:

> we read the politics of *The Wire* and *Treme* off each other and in the context of David Simon's copious writings and interviews, providing an interpretive frame based on an authorial identity that is more unified and consistent than are actual creative processes.[97]

Despite the poignancy of Mittell's comment, it does make sense to look at Simon's TV series as parts of a larger exploration of America, focusing on different institutions, cities and eras. *Generation Kill* focuses on the Marine Corps during the Invasion of Iraq in 2003; *The Wire* is set in Baltimore and focuses on the drug trade and the potential corruption of different institutions, including the police force and the school system; and *Treme* is about New Orleans in the wake of Hurricane Katrina. *Show Me a Hero* and *The Plot Against America*, in turn, deal with the political system in the 1940s and 1980s, respectively, and take place in Yonkers and Newark, while *The Deuce* depicts New York from the 1970s to the present day and develops into a systemic critique of the sex industry and American society in general. As the actor Michael Potts (*The Wire* and *Show Me a Hero*) eloquently puts it:

> David came in, and what you had was long-form storytelling. Characters that were nuanced, stories that were nuanced, that required your attention and required you to follow it. Nothing was wrapped up at the end of one episode or one hour. It continued. It was sort of like a novel. I think it's a visual novel – the way he looked at it.
>
> People look at television, and you see the lead character, and you think that's the protagonist. But I think, for David, the protagonist is actually America. American society is always the protagonist.[98]

Though hardly his most famous or recognized piece, *Treme* is a good example of Simon's sensibility. The first episode opens on a black screen. After 10 seconds, some muffled voices are heard on the soundtrack, and two captions enter the frame: "New Orleans, Louisiana", "Three Months After". The different voices grow louder and more distinct, and at the sound of a trombone we cut to an extreme close-up of a mouth chewing on a popsicle, gradually coming into focus. Slowly the sequence develops into a montage of close-ups, all shot with a curious handheld camera and an eager use of *rack focus*, as if the story were slowly coming into focus through the polyphony of different voices and impressions. The moving camera tilts upwards, revealing the words "New Orleans" on a liquor bottle and pans around to display a number of soldiers from the US Army and various musicians practicing their instruments. After one minute, there has been no central or audible line of dialogue, and no seeming protagonist has been introduced, but the environment and social issues are becoming clearer: This is a story, the opening seems to imply, about a city "steeped in culture" but affected by a natural disaster and its potential social repercussions.[99]

Though not a typical example of narrative complexity (a phenomenon that will be explored later in this book), *Treme* might be described as a *polyphonous* or *polycentric* text. Mikhail Bakhtin's concept of *polyphony* refers to a text with many different simultaneous voices, perspectives and points of view, and TV scholar Angela Ndalianis draws on Bakhtin's concept when trying to describe the kind of complexity that we see in modern serials.[100]

In a metaphorical sense, Simon's "pieces" might be described as *polyphonous*, but this description also makes sense in a literal and concrete way, inasmuch as Simon writes rich and intricate background dialogues for his TV series. Even the voices that are inaudible or barely intelligible are written into the script, and this makes for an almost Altmanesque cacophony on the soundtrack.[101] According to sound mixer Bruce Litecky, David Simon is influenced by Robert Altman's use of overlapping dialogue and different simultaneous on- and off-screen voices, but, in a way, his poetics is closer to David Fincher who often writes off-screen dialogue into his scripts.[102]

Simon began his career in journalism, and Litecky came from documentary. Those beginnings may well have colored their respective approaches to sound and authenticity, and Litecky argues that Simon's use of background voices has developed over the course of time, from a raw and realistic polyphony in *The Wire* to an almost musical mix between different voices, sounds and instruments in *Treme*.

The musical and sonic authenticity is evident in most episodes of *Treme* where the different characters perform at jazz clubs, practice and talk in the street (often interrupted or partially drowned out by music or background voices) or record conversations and live renditions of popular jazz and blues

Bruce Litecky (sound mixer) on David Simon's approach to sound

Sound and authenticity in *The Wire*: David Simon started off as a newspaper man, and I always got the sense that the reality or realism of the dialogue came from him being a good listener. The dialogue in *The Wire* was pretty close to the script actually, but the scripts were just so realistic. We did go out into the streets, though, to record some snippets of conversations to give it a level of authenticity. From a strictly legal standpoint you couldn't record and air so many conversations from people in the streets, so we recorded some different conversations, arguments and people talking together in the actual streets and we passed them on to a *loop group*. They would put it together using snippets of the different recordings to capture that sense of realism. There was a battle going on all the time between authenticity and intelligibility. It was always a sort of trade-off. What happened a lot was that we had radio microphones that we would use to record the dialogue. If you would look at the thing through a long lens, for example, you couldn't use a boom microphone, so we would use radio mics to give a certain perspective.

Sound and music in *Treme*: You have to have certain skills to be in your face, as you do in a documentary, and that also helped me when working on *The Wire*. In *The Wire* we had to build a world. It wasn't just a stage. When we were in The Projects, we were in the actual Projects. When we were in a dangerous street, we were actually *in* that street. In *The Wire*, the dialogue would sometimes be a little in the back, so to make it intelligible we would try to do our best to control the background noise. When we were down at the docks, for example, we spent a whole day just recording the trucks going by, just to give us an authentic sense of the environment. There's a responsibility of trying to remain honest to that environment. That was important when doing *The Wire*, but even more so in *Treme*. In *Treme*, we said that we treated the music as another character. We would follow and get involved in the music, just like we would follow and get involved in the other characters in the show. The recording of the music was even part of the production. They wanted it to be captured live, so we carried around our own speakers and mics.

We went from *The Wire* to *Treme*, David became far more involved in the sound, and the question of intelligibility vs. unintelligibility was something that we debated. David was really a stickler for the reality of the thing. As he went along, his involvement in the sound became much greater, and I was flabbergasted with how much he wanted to be involved in and talk about the sound. Normally a producer is not that involved with the sound – sound is usually second cousin to everything else in a film or television show – but David was very involved.[103]

tracks. At the opening of Ep. 1:2, for example, we see Davis McAlary (Steve Zahn) listening to a live performance by Coco Robicheaux, played by the blues musician himself. The music by Robicheaux is not only performed live within the diegesis of *Treme*, but is also *recorded* live by Litecky and the rest of the sound crew (as is the case with the street musicians later in the same episode). This strategy is reminiscent of Robert Altman's *Nashville* (1975) and Jean-Marie Straub and Danièle Huillet's *Chronik der Anna Magdalena Bach* (1968), and it contributes to the raw sense of realism and liveness in Simon's work.[104] In a thematic and narrative sense, there is no (one) center in *Treme*, only different people, stories and voices, and this polyphonous or polycentric approach is mirrored in the audiovisual style through *rack focus*, handheld camera, overlapping dialogue and ambient noises.

Anne Gjelsvik and Jørgen Bruhn have presented a similar Bakhtinian reading of *The Wire*, arguing that it differs from other quality series of its time by focusing on environment rather than plot, structures rather than strong individuals, and by changing the setting and the focal points with each season. In that sense, Gjelsvik and Bruhn argue, *The Wire* becomes an open and *dialogic* exploration of Baltimore, different American institutions and, by extension, American society on the whole.[105]

Given its dialogic qualities, *The Wire* has also been described as "made for DVD" (a medium that expanded rapidly in the early 2000s).[106] Amanda D. Lotz and J.P. Kelly have used the term *compressed consumption* to describe the act of 'bingeing' many episodes or even seasons in only a few sittings, without being interrupted by commercial breaks or having to follow the traditional flow of a television schedule.[107] "That particular way of watching or consuming television - where you can watch many episodes in a row, pausing and rewatching sequences that require further attention - seems particularly suited to complex or *polycentric* series such as *The Wire* and *Treme*.

Agreeing with Gjelsvik and Bruhn, the Norwegian TV scholar Erlend Lavik points to *The Wire* as the most paradigmatic example of *quality TV* and the most crucial work of the cable era.[108] An influential and culturally relevant series, *The Wire* has inspired numerous modern shows, as we shall see, from the financial crime thriller *Bedrag* (*Follow the Money*, DR, 2016-2019) to the gritty reflection of the international drug trade in *ZeroZeroZero* (SkyAtlantic/Canal+/Prime Video, 2020). *The Wire* is also mentioned by Alan Sepinwall and Matt Zoller Seitz as one of the greatest American TV series of all time, and they, fittingly, use a string of questions when trying to summarize the plot in all of its complexity:

> *The Wire* is about a clever cop who doesn't play by his bosses' rules.
> Or is it about how that cop pushes his bosses to create a task force to take down a dangerous inner-city drug crew?

> Maybe it's about the charismatic leaders of that drug crew?
> Could it be about dysfunction inside the police department?
> Wait... now it's about the stevedores' union?
> Only now the mayoral campaign is the most important thing?
> How is the show suddenly about four boys in middle school?
> And here at the end it's about the inner workings of the city's biggest newspaper?
> What on earth is the show supposed to be about, people? [109]

Treme and *The Wire* have many immediate similarities - similarities that might naturally be attributed to David Simon as an auteur - but they are tonally rather different. *The Wire* seems much bleaker and unforgiving compared to *Treme*, and you can feel it when watching the show, as well as recognize it in the descriptions presented by the people who were part of it. As Michael Potts (Brother Mouzone) eloquently puts it:

> Baltimore is the environment of destitution. Really, you would feel that. You would be standing in one part of Baltimore: completely dilapidated homes and buildings falling apart, overgrown, high-crime areas. Very, very poor areas. And you'd look up two blocks away, and there'd be Johns Hopkins University. So it would be this weird juxtaposition where one part of Baltimore is impoverished, and the other part is wealthy. That couldn't help but be a part of the story that David is telling: the wealth gap.
>   How is this allowed to happen? How are we living these two Americas, blocks away from each other.[110]

As the two series explore different areas and different contexts, they naturally have different tonalities and different textual qualities. A good explanation for this tonal contrast, according to TV scholar Mikkel Jensen, is that *The Wire* "seeks to explain how the war on drugs could be perpetuated across several decades", whereas *Treme* "tries to argue that New Orleans was worth saving in the wake of Hurricane Katrina." A similar argument is seen in a recent article by film and TV critic Bryan O'Donnell: "*The Wire* is not a happy show. A lot of characters end up with a raw deal – or wind up dead," as he writes. "The people are stuck in an endless cycle of corruption and crime that isn't getting better... The end of the final montage switches gears to flashing stills of real Baltimore residents – not actors in the show, but real people... The show had gone through five seasons of ups and downs and the people of Baltimore basically ended up where everything started."[111]

In any case, both *The Wire* and *Treme* can be seen as "an argument for the city," and that understanding of Simon's work might naturally be affected by Simon's ample comments on his own work and HBO's attempt to advertise his different series as parts of his oeuvre. Simon has been the object of much critical acclaim and scholarly scrutiny. At the point of writing this book, at least five monographs have been published about David Simon and his different series. Moreover, he is a central example in numerous books on showrunners and TV auteurism (aspects that will be explored later in this book).[112]

David Simon wrote the book behind *Homicide*, the series that many critics and scholars forget when writing about modern television, and it was while working on this show that he learned to write for television from the showrunner Tom Fontana.[113] In that sense, it would not be unfair to claim that Fontana, Chase and Simon were pioneers during the first phase of the *multiplatform era*, and in the following feature interview they discuss their work, the cable revolution and changes in the TV landscape.

Chase has described traditional television as a "prisoner of dialogue," and Simon has argued that television "is the optimum tool" for "quiet masturbation," comparing TV consumption to a shameful and potentially addictive habit.[114] By comparison, Fontana is less critical of traditional television, but all three showrunners describe TV history as a story of maturation where cable channels, such as HBO, in the early 2000s paved the way for a more ambiguous, transgressive and sophisticated type of programming. This story could be seen as the first phase of the *multiplatform era*, followed by a complex era in TV history where video platforms and streaming channels like YouTube, Netflix, Amazon and Disney+ are flooding the market with content and perhaps reintroducing a new form of *vertical integration*. In the following feature interview, Fontana, Chase and Simon focus on the first stage of this development, though also touching upon the current streaming age, and they discuss their own canonical series in light of this transitional phase. In the following chapters, then, we shall turn our attention to the second phase of the *multiplatform era*: Television in the global age of streaming.

Fig. 3: Editor Sidney Wolinsky talking about the iconic finale of *The Sopranos* (HBO, 1999-2007). In a roundtable discussion with Alan Sepinwall and Matt Zoller Seitz, David Chase, perhaps inadvertently, described the final scene as the "death scene", but Wolinsky stresses the open-endedness and ambiguity of the final sequence as one of its most profound qualities (cf. Seitz & Sepinwall 2019, pp. 314-414). © Jan Oxholm, Los Angeles, 2019.

Fig. 4: David Simon at the 63rd Annual Peabody Award with two actors from *The Wire:* Lawrence Gilliard, Jr. (left) and Dominic West (right). Photo: Anders Krusberg / Peabody Awards, 63rd Annual Peabody Awards Luncheon, Waldorf Astoria Hotel, May 17, 2004. Creative Commons.

Feature Interview #1

The Cable Vanguard: Interview with Tom Fontana (*Oz*), David Chase (*The Sopranos*) and David Simon (*The Wire*)

The TV landscape did not change over night. The so-called *cable revolution*, which began in the late 1990s, was a significant precursor to the current streaming age, paving the way for a whole new type of television, not just a new way of transmitting TV signals and receiving televisual content. This *cable revolution* could be seen as the first phase in a series of changes that have occurred since the beginning of the new millennium, and in this cluster of interviews three of the most significant representatives of this phase discuss their groundbreaking cable series and the changes that have occurred in the TV landscape since the advent of cable television.

Tom Fontana created the first premium cable series, *Oz* (1997-2003), and David Chase and David Simon later produced two of the most emblematic and critically acclaimed cable series: *The Sopranos* (1999-2007) and *The Wire* (2002-2008). Together, the three creators reflect upon the differences between network and cable television and discuss how - and to what degree - cable channels such as HBO have transformed television in terms of genre, style and storytelling.

"We're Not in Kansas Anymore": Tom Fontana

You created the first ever cable series. How did you conceive of this series, and how did you pitch it to HBO, which at that time was mainly known for showing uncensored films, documentaries and sports events?

Fontana: *Oz* came in my head, while I was in the middle of filming *Homicide: Life on the Street*. Though we didn't always catch the murderer on *HLOTS*, when we did, he was sent off to prison. That got me thinking: We never see that part of the story, we never see what happens to all those bad guys once they're crammed together in maximum security. Also, when I was a teenager, there was a riot at Attica, the prison not far from my hometown, Buffalo. The Governor ordered the National Guard to attack the compound and forty-three people — prisoners and correctional officers —were killed. That made me wonder: What had caused life inside Attica to reach this deadly climax. I pitched my idea of a prison series to the three broadcast networks.

The executives couldn't wait for me to get out of their offices. Meanwhile, HBO was looking for its first drama series and a friend of mine, Rob Kenneally, had a meeting with Chris Albrecht, during which Chris said that maybe they wanted a prison show. Rob left the meeting, called me in New York and said, "Get your ass out here." I flew to LA, met with Chris and Anne Thomopoulos, told them what was in my head, and they ordered a pilot script. After that, we made a fifteen minute presentation and, having watched that, Chris ordered eight episodes.

I have heard that some of your friends in the industry reacted in a somewhat surprising manner to you choosing to make *Oz* on HBO. Is it true that many people in the business thought that nobody would watch *Oz*?

Fontana: Some of my best friends, very knowledgeable about the business, said to me that no one would see *Oz*. I said, "I don't care, they're gonna let me do what I want." One dear friend read the pilot script and said the show would end my career.

Before going into original programming, HBO had a tradition for making documentaries. Was there a link between that tradition and the gritty authenticity of *Oz*?

Fontana: Chris Albrecht mentioned the network had a lot of success with their prison documentaries, so he thought his subscribers could handle a gritty drama series in the same arena. He said to me, "I don't care if the characters are likable, as long as they're interesting." After years in broadcast TV, fighting the networks to make the characters on *St. Elsewhere* and *Homicide* "more heroic," Chris' dictum was music to my ears.

How was it different creating a TV series for HBO as opposed to creating a traditional network series, and how did it affect the style, tone and story of your series?

Fontana: Without having to stop the narrative to cut to a commercial, I felt very free to abandon the traditional style of the TV shows airing at that time, you know, going from the A story to the B story to the C story, then back to the A story, etc. I wanted to write a series of short stories in each episode, featuring different characters who would then be secondary characters in the other stories in that same episode.

***Oz* was directed by a number of different episode directors, and many of**

those directors had an interesting pedigree, either coming from the independent film circuit, foreign films or other TV series with an art-like quality. Could you say a few words on the choice of directors for *Oz*?

Fontana: Once the groundwork was laid down for something freewheeling, the directors embraced the style. And, yes, the directors were a mix of seasoned TV veterans, indie filmmakers, foreign artists, film school grads and actors directing for the first time. Not being a director, I relied on our directors to fulfill the potential of cable television and be true to the spirit of *Oz*. I tried not to dictate a look for the series, encouraging people to surprise me, especially when it came to the August Hill monologues in the big glass box.

The tagline "It's no place like home", which like the title alluded to *The Wizard of Oz*, also seemed fitting to HBO and its popular slogan (at the time): "It's not TV. It's HBO". That slogan was clever in terms of branding, but do you think that we sometimes tend to forget or underemphasize the great series that preceded the cable revolution? And do you think that times have changed to the point where a TV series can proudly describe itself as television?

Fontana: I've now been a part of two "Golden Ages of Television" — and that doesn't count the "Golden Age" which took place in the 1950s. I think television viewers have very short memories and, like most people, are uninterested in history. The list of quality drama series, prior to the "cable revolution," is long and impressive — starting with *Naked City* and *The Defenders* to *Hill Street Blues* and *St. Elsewhere*. I am proud to work in *television*.

What are the most essential changes that have happened in the TV landscape since the premiere of *Oz*, and how would you describe the state of television today?

Fontana: A lot of television today is outstanding. Why? Perhaps because "reality" shows are so over-the-top, that comedies and dramas need to go even further over-the-top, in order to grab the audience's attention. My concern is that some quality shows focus on the quirkiness of their characters, but avoid commenting on the world in which we live. I don't mean that stories need to be polemics, but they should reflect society as a whole. We are supposed to enlighten and mirror. Maybe that'll happen more in a post-pandemic world. The hardest thing about creating television now is that there is so much content, on so many different venues, that we writers are told to be outrageous just for the sake of making noise. I'm not interested in simply making noise, I want to ask questions which will keep the viewers up at night...

Embracing Ambiguity: David Chase

The Sopranos has been lauded for its combination of different genres and tonalities. One could describe *Oz, Sex and the City* and *The Sopranos*, the triad of shows that launched HBO as a producer of original high-end TV series, as reinventions of traditional genres. *Oz* could be said to have reinvented the prison series, *Sex and the City* was a sort of *sexcom* that all but redefined the dramedy genre, and *The Sopranos* has been described as a subversion or reinvention of the gangster genre. How do you see it?

Chase: I don't think *The Sopranos* reinvented much. It widened the gangster genre, and it encompassed more.

But it certainly seems ambiguous, more so than many of the traditional gangster movies, and it uses contrast and counterpoint repeatedly.

Chase: There are many great films, novels, poems etc. that work with ambiguity. In fact, maybe all the really great ones do. But not American television. There was no ambiguity in American television, except in David Lynch's show. There were many great shows, but they were never ambiguous, and I missed that very much and wanted to see it. The other aspect of that - I have said this before - is that I still don't know whether *The Sopranos* was a drama or a comedy, but that mixture was extremely important. So people can say: "It's ambiguous. Is that supposed to be funny? He's so mean to his son. Is that supposed to be funny?" The ambiguity has to do with the tone.

There is an interesting scene that illustrates the ambiguous relationship between *The Sopranos* and traditional gangster films. I am thinking of the scene where Christopher kills Emil. In that scene, you use montage editing in an almost Eisensteinian fashion, cutting for each gun shot to a picture of a performer: Humphrey Bogart, Dean Martin and Edward G. Robinson. Those faces are naturally associated with the mafia and/or noir and gangster films from the classical Hollywood era, so the scene seems to reference the cinematic tradition that you are inspired by. But it also seems to indicate that Christopher is "playing" a gangster, somewhat like Michel in *À bout de souffle* who looks at posters of Bogart and tries to imitate him. What was the idea behind that sequence?

Chase: I remember that scene from Godard's film very well, when he's standing there looking at the poster, and he smokes cigarettes and is a bohemian, and I guess that did influence me without my knowledge. The more Godard went on, the harder it was to classify his films and to say what he was doing. *Breathless* was a very important movie to me at that time.

In general, there seems to be a relationship between *The Sopranos* and the kind of films that were made during the 1960s and 1970s. There is a certain New Wave sensibility and an element of psychological realism that you would see in many films from that decade, for example in France and Scandinavia.

Chase: I was going to film school at that time, wanting to be a filmmaker, and that was when Bergman hit the United States, and Godard, Truffaut, Fellini, you name it. All those people. The foreign films became really interesting to young people at the time. And the comment about psychological realism is interesting. We *were* trying to do that, and, yes, that has certainly been popular in Scandinavia, going back to Bergman.

The title sequence was also quite interesting, and it seemed to point to a different environment than what you often see in gangster films. What were you going for?

Chase: It did have a purpose. I wanted to show an audience that you are no longer in New York where almost all the mob films take place, and that was all that was in my mind. *The Godfather* films and, more importantly, all the Scorsese movies took place in New York. Here, you were going some place different, which was New Jersey, across the river, and a lot of people in the United States and the world wouldn't know that. Wouldn't know they're in a different place. And New Jersey is a little bit more bucolic.

You have argued that television was once a prisoner of dialogue. Has television changed markedly since you said that, or is television still mostly "yak-yak-yak-yak"?

Chase: I don't think television is a prisoner of dialogue quite as much today as it was earlier. It's really easy to explain why it has been a prisoner of dialogue. Dialogue is the cheapest thing to shoot. You set up a table - a person at one end, another person at the other and two cups of coffee - and they're now talking to each other. And, really, you can do it in a two-shot or you can go out on a limb and do a series of close-ups, but it's not very beautiful filmmaking.

I really did want to not do classic television coverage. I wanted it to be more cinematic, and I tried very hard, and I give a lot of credit to our DP, Alik Sakharov. We had a really great time making that series together. We used a lot of wide lenses.

As the series went on, we had different directors coming on board, and they brought the kind of things that they like, and I believe that a lot of that wide-lens stuff kind of fell by the wayside, which I kind of think was too bad because I loved it, but they were all very creative, and they all had different eyes, so I'm very satisfied with it.

It does not look like traditional television.

Chase: No, it does not.

Beau Willimon has argued that *binge-watching* is not, in itself, a new phenomenon, and he claims that the DVD box set of *The Sopranos* might, in a way, have been the first example of that type of viewer engagement. Does that make sense to you?

Chase: I don't want to sound too arrogant, but I agree with that. I don't know when we started doing those box sets. But every season, when we were doing the show, we would get requests from people in show business - Steven Soderbergh, Robert Evans and all these other people who had some clout - asking us for all the shows in advance on DVD. And more often than not, we would do it because they were working on location, but that had never happened to me before.

In the US, television and cinema were usually two very separate industries. There is more crossover these days. In many European countries, however, the television and film industries have not, historically, been as separate as in America, perhaps because America is bigger than any European country. Ingmar Bergman, for example, could easily make both films and television.

Chase: Exactly. He wasn't slumming when doing television...

People have no idea how difficult it was before, here in America. If you were a director or a writer in television, and you wanted to break into movies, it was impossible. You just weren't welcome. Some people did; there were a few, of course.

Some people might say that today it is more difficult to distinguish be-

tween film and television. Perhaps that distinction itself is arbitrary.

Chase: That's an interesting point. Now we have television series that are only eight episodes long or six episodes. Television was always about 22 episodes. That was a season, at least in American television.

There is a tendency these days to make films based on TV series and to give episodes from TV series a theatrical release. Next year, for example, you are releasing The Many Saints of Newark, **a cinematic prequel to** The Sopranos. **How did that come about, and where will it be released?**

Chase: The intention was to open it in theaters and have a theatrical run. When that was over, then it would go on HBO. Now, who knows? Maybe there won't be a theatrical release. Who knows if audiences want to go into a movie theater.
   But I have to tell you: I haven't been plagued by people to make more of The Sopranos. It has never happened. The studio head at New Line, Toby Emmerich, who is now the head of Warner Bros., always wanted to do more of The Sopranos, but I wasn't really approached by other people.

What is the most significant change we have seen in the TV landscape after the cable revolution?

Chase: That's a really challenging question, but one thing is that TV is becoming global, and I think that's wonderful. To be able to watch cinema or television - I guess they aren't the same, they still aren't the same - from other countries is a blessing to everyone.

Tales of the City: David Simon

The Wire **is easily one of the most widely debated and critically acclaimed TV series, exploring the problematic structures and failed institutions in the USA, instead of focusing on strong individuals and immediately exciting plots. It has been described as neo-realism, sociology, anthropology, a systemic critique of America and many other things. How do you see it?**

Simon: It's a critique of why we can't solve any of our problems nationally. There are problems that have to do with how we live together, and how we live together in the 21st century is inevitably an urban question. Urbanity is now the future of humankind, and the shape and structure and viability of the city is going to determine whether or not we survive as a species. In that sense, we're using the city allegorically to make arguments about what has gone wrong with our society that our institutions no longer perform or even attempt to perform as they once did, and how problems and even the attempts to solve problems become more and more elusive – and why the center of our society, which used to be some communal sense of responsibility, can no longer hold.

I have no interest in telling stories about characters. Characters are building blocks, and you have to write interesting characters, and you have to care about your characters as a writer, but characters are basically a tool in the tool box to tell a story about something larger. At least it is in our construct of what we're doing, and that's true not just for *The Wire*, but for all of our pieces. Every single one. They're all about structure. They're all about the systemic. And that has to prevail for us to care about it.

And one of the reasons we found that to be a plausible pursuit is that we're doing long-form. We're doing long-form television shows. We're doing miniseries and series, so there's time to lay out the structural critique. There's no time to do that in a two-hour movie. It's an improbable thing to do in a two-hour movie. Around a small structure, you can do something specific about a problem in a certain institution, maybe, in two hours, but you're not going to be able to critique the larger constructs of society in an hour and a half, two hours or even two and a half hours. For that, you are going to need six, twelve or twenty hours, depending on what you're talking about.

Many people have also pointed to the level of attention and patience that a show like *The Wire* requires. I guess we could say the same thing about *Treme* (a show about the effects of Hurricane Katrina as both a natural and social disaster), which had such an interesting opening, almost reminiscent of Italian Neo-Realism, and such a jazzy, slow-paced style.

Simon: I'm particularly proud of that one, actually, in that it avoids, it denies itself, all of the tropes and metrics by which American television usually measures itself. It only has enough violence to depict the actuality of violence in the city. It only has enough sexuality to accurately chronicle the lives of ordinary people. It's not trading on the things that make television shows go forward. It's a lot harder to get people to watch a show where you put a trombone in a guy's hand, than if you put a gun or a blonde, and we were determined to say something, again, about the American city. What in urbanity matters? What is resilient? What must endure? *Treme* is a show about culture. It's about the culture of a city that's steeped in culture, and it survives only because of culture. It was an attempt to make an argument for the city.

There were a lot of people who watched *The Wire* and said, "Man, why don't they leave?", which I thought was an astonishing reply to what *The Wire* was presenting. Nobody's going anywhere. Baltimore's going to be there tomorrow. The question is what it will be and whether or not we have the national stamina to address our problems. So I was a little bit distressed to find that people thought Baltimore was in any way aberrant or was enduring more than many other American cities like it. Baltimore is no different than St. Louis, Cleveland or New Orleans. In fact, there are only three cities in America that have any reprieve from these forces that are arrayed against them, and that's New York, Los Angeles and Washington. And the reasons are obvious. New York is the financial capital of the world, and so the run-up on Wall Street eventually trickles down and allows them to rebuild the city and an incredible revenue stream. Los Angeles, at least the west side of Los Angeles, is floated by the American entertainment industry, which is recession-proof. And Washington, being the federal city, which survives on the largesse of the government itself, is also recession-proof. Everything else in America has to fight. We have to fight the poverty of our politics and the poverty of our spirit, and we have to fight bombs of national contempt for the idea of the city, which is self-defeating.

I know that you still live in Baltimore, and I was wondering whether your projects would even be possible if you lived in LA – far removed, both geographically and conceptually, from the places that you explore and depict in your shows?

Simon: Listen, the last three projects I've done have been in the New York and New Jersey area, and I'm from Baltimore, so the trick is to do as much research as you can, spend as much time on the ground as you can, so your view is clarified, hire other writers, researchers and experts who know the material and know the geography – which we did in New Orleans and which we did, when it came to the Marine Corps in *Generation Kill*, and which we did in New York. Do the work. That's it. You're obliged to do the work. There's nothing to say that someone from LA can't write a good and precise piece about Baltimore, but they have to go there. They have to meet people, they have to do the research, and they have to deliver. If they're just going to sit where they are and guess from what they know in LA – or, even worse, West LA – then you can imagine how it's going to turn out.

Your series could be seen as a modernized version of Italian Neo-Realism – a movement which was recognized for its use of location shooting, open-ended and decentralized stories, and amateurs who speak in dialect

and the vernacular. The ideas behind the Neo-Realist movement were formulated by the writer Cesare Zavattini, who claimed that all good movies depict "the pressing issues of their time". Would you agree with Zavattini, or is it a far-fetched comparison?

Simon: I would not be so limiting. I would say that's what my work has to be because my training is in journalism, not in film and certainly not in the entertainment industry. So what I'm chasing has some rooted logic in journalism, and journalism is about the issues of our time. From my point of view, this is all I know how to do, but I can certainly conceive of great art that targets not simply the social issues of our time, but maybe just the human condition in general. Or maybe I'm speaking in such generalities that those are always issues of our time. Shakespeare works and the Greek plays work because man is man and his nature is his nature, and the forms by which power and dignity ground themselves, through humanity or through the human condition, don't really ever change. The scale of hope and risk for human beings is the same for Hamlet as it is for Oedipus. This stuff works because we can watch Medea and we can encounter her trauma through our own knowledge of domestic pain and gender. And it's not really of our time, it's of every time. I don't know, sometimes a good story is just a good story, right? I don't want to get in the way of a good story by saying it's all going to be rooted in contemporary politics, but I know there are things I can't do, and what I can do is rooted in where I came from, which is journalism.

The Deuce is also quite topical, dealing with issues concerning gender and sexual commodification. This theme of sexual exploitation is particularly interesting for a cable series, inasmuch as cable television often utilizes nudity and sex as a sort of attraction. How do you toe the line in a series like *The Deuce* between depicting sex and exploitation without becoming potentially exploitative yourself?

Simon: In the entertainment industry, I've seen the demeanor of people change, and largely for the better. Structurally, on set. Even on *The Deuce* we've improved the means by which we depict sexuality. We started to contemplate and emphasize certain structural changes in terms of how we shoot simulated sex, which is a big deal for performers. People have taken pause, and it's a good thing. And, I think, certainly you want the most egregious cases to be the paradigm examples of reform. I mean, Les Moonves, Bill Cosby and Harvey Weinstein are fundamental, and there's a reason they stand out. They should stand out.

To give one note of caution, which I think is fair to say: If we're going to replace The Court of Law and a determination of who is a sexual predator with judgment of employers and corporations as to whether or not someone can be employed or not employed, then that requires a certain amount of nuance, clarity and attention to detail. In the initial stages of #MeToo and #TimesUp, all of the targets did seem to be those who were operating at great extremity and those who were actually being sexual predators.

I had an experience on *The Deuce* where one of our actors, Mr. Franco, was critiqued. There was a piece in one of the newspapers about problems he had had making independent films and teaching film courses, and there came a moment where we had to look at it very seriously. Obviously, because of what the show is about, it was even more important for us. We looked at it with great care, case by case, detail by detail. And what we found was – while there certainly may have been mistakes made with people's level of comfort on a film set, and there may have been mistakes made with Mr. Franco himself being a little bit oblivious to his own power to convince people or to get people to do what they would later on regret in terms of nudity (I don't think he was aware of his own James Franconess, to be honest with you) – but what was missing from all those critiques, which was obvious to the Weinstein, Cosby, Moonves cohort, was that James Franco wasn't trying to sleep with anybody. He wasn't trying to trade his power. He never asked for sexual favors. Obviously things went wrong, and people were unhappy – I don't mean to dismiss that unhappiness; that's a cause for looking at it and a cause for reform – but I was faced with working with someone who genuinely had not tried to use his position to achieve any sexual favor with anyone. He hadn't asked anybody, and nobody was accusing him of that, so I got to the point – we were confronted with a lot of calls to exile James Franco from the production – where none of us at HBO could find the justification to do that. That would have been an inappropriate level of response. That's not to suggest that what was critiqued isn't deserving of critique or that James should not respond to that, but to have him in the same category as Weinstein or Moonves is an affront to the facts, and it actually diminishes the value and the purpose of #MeToo.

When you flatten all offense and all error and make everything the same thing, you're not helping the cause. You're, in fact, making what is a substantial critique of sexual predation less substantial. So, if you're asking about the movement, I support this thing, and I understand that it actually has the capacity to change things within the industry. But, on the other hand, its initial application has been rather a blunt weapon, and I don't know how we fix that. It's not like there's a Board of Review. It's a very informal thing that happens which is, basically, it hits the newspapers and we all contemplate it. But it's not like there's some governing body which you can appeal to and there's a ruling as to what is sexual predation and what is mere error.

We made errors. In the first season of filming *The Deuce*, we made errors in terms of contributing to people's discomfort at times, and we certainly weren't trying to do it because we knew what we were chasing and how hard it was to film it. But we got better as we went. So that would be my only critique: As we go on with this thing, I think everybody has to get smarter about what is x and what is y.

We thought about every frame of film on this show because we understand that if you create porn to critique porn, there's a latent hypocrisy that the piece can't overcome. So we were very conscious about every frame: How long the camera stays, what the camera sees, why the camera sees it. These discussions were had on every episode.

Three of your most recent series, *Show Me a Hero*, *The Deuce* and *The Plot Against America*, are all period dramas. Period dramas are in vogue these days, often presenting a nostalgic or romanticized version of the past. In your work, however, it seems as if you use the past to speak about the current political climate or situation. Is that the case?

Simon: Absolutely. There's no point in doing period drama, if you're not reflecting on the world that currently exists. The problems of a hyper-segregated society and inequality are even more profound today than they were at the time of *Show Me a Hero*. The same things are going on in every city about what to do with the poor, where to put the poor. At this moment, there'll be 67,000 people in the homeless shelters in New York City, which is an all-time record in one of the most affluent cities in the world. That is, in fact, the case. There's a dearth of affordable housing. The city is a playground for the rich and hell for the poor. So there is nothing being said about Yonkers in the 1980s in *Show Me a Hero* that can't be applied now to our current society.

Similarly, *The Deuce* is about misogyny, sexual commodification and labor and gender, and those topics are still relevant. The status of women in society is being questioned as aggressively today with #MeToo and #TimesUp as it ever has been. The same arguments are still unresolved. So, if you're not speaking of the present, you've got no business accessing the past.

All of your so-called 'pieces' have been produced by HBO. That begs the question: How did cable channels like HBO change the TV landscape?

Simon: American television was a juvenile form in fundamental ways, until there were some channels that could get rid of advertising and commercials as the revenue stream. When they were the revenue stream, you could not present a story that was particularly dark or disturbing or problematic or argumentative in a political sense because it disturbed the consumer class. It disturbed the dynamic between the advertiser and the consumer. It didn't put anyone in the mood to buy cars or blue jeans or iPods or anything. But once you got rid of the advertisers and made it a subscription model, now you started having grown-up stories.

Chapter 2

TV in the Age of Plenty: Streaming, Bingeing and Redefining Television

> The precise contours of television, film, or video production in a mature phase of internet-distributed services remain too preliminary and unclear to suggest distinguishable norms of streaming. A blending of change and continuity has allowed for experimentation.
> - Amanda D. Lotz, TV scholar[115]

> There's a whole world of possibilities in television and streaming.
> - Derek Cianfrance, writer-director[116]

As mentioned earlier, the 1990s was a period of change in American television. A lot has happened, though, since the premieres of *Oz*, *The Sopranos* and *The Wire*, and we could possibly talk of a new paradigm shift in the American and global mediascape during the last decade. Since the birth of YouTube in 2005 and the premiere of the first original Netflix series, *House of Cards* (2013-2018), television has moved "outside the box" (as Neil Landau puts it).[117] This development, too, goes back to the years of *Oz* and *The Wire* when the Internet expanded (from 16 million users in December 1995 to 1.018 billion users in December 2005) and when Netflix was founded in 1997 (initially renting out DVDs by mail).[118]

Many critics and scholars agree that television is being redefined these days, and some writers go even further, arguing that television has been completely "rewired" or that we have entered a new phase in media history where TV series have been replaced by a new type of seriality with few or no ties to television as a concept.[119] "When did 'watching television' become an outdated term?", as TV columnist Frazier Moore asked in an article from 2008, referencing the noticeable shift from the days of *All in the Family* to the modern mediascape. Or as TV scholar Lynn Spiegel writes:

> If TV refers to the technologies, industrial formations, government policies, and practices of looking that were associated with the medium in the classical public service and three-network era, it appears that we are now entering a new phase of television - the phase that comes after TV.[120]

The German TV historian Sven Stollfuß has suggested the term *AV series* as a more fitting description for series that are made in the digital age (whether made directly for streaming or made for both streaming and television), and popular media have published numerous articles announcing the death of television.[121] However common, such obituaries tend to simplify or reduce the complexity of today's mediascape, and while they emphasize the radical newness of the current TV landscape (using words like "revolution" or "disruption"), they often overlook or underemphasize the continuity between traditional and modern TV series.[122] As the media and communication lecturer Michael Strangelove poignantly puts it:

> Television still has a stranglehold on popular culture and cultural values, but its identity and future remain unresolved issues. There is confusion and uncertainty over what qualifies as television. [...] As television viewing becomes dissociated from a singular device, at the same time it becomes ubiquitous. In the post-television age television is everywhere. But this does not mean that it is simply more of the same old thing.[123]

The modern TV series is seen on many different platforms and in various contexts, and phenomena like Video on Demand (VOD), DVD and Blu-ray boxes, smartphones and tablets have all contributed to the ongoing changes. According to Kim Akass and Janet McCabe, "the TV viewer has been remade within these technologies and the new technologies have [...] allowed for new ways of consuming, watching and appreciating television."[124] In the modern streaming landscape, the competition between different outlets, platforms and producers is bigger, and companies and conglomerates such as Comcast, Apple, Disney and Netflix have moved the tent-poles and challenged the status of traditional broadcasters and cable networks like HBO.

This chapter explores the current streaming landscape, focusing on an American context, but also including examples and statistics from other countries and industries for comparison. Apart from giving a preliminary introduction to streaming as an idea and a distribution mechanism, it addresses some of the most pressing questions and issues concerning today's mediascape:

- If *non-linear TV* is on the rise, does that mean that *linear TV* is dying?
- If streaming services are booming, does that mean that television is waning?
- If a series is not being broadcast and shown on a TV screen, is it then a TV series?
- If the amount of platforms, distributors and content is growing, does that mean that we are seeing a de-monopolization of the media landscape?

Selective Television: From Ideal to Reality

In computer terms, streaming refers to the "display of media while they are still being received" (without having to download an entire video file before playing it).[125] Up until the 1990s, this form of digital video distribution was all but unthinkable due to the small bandwidth of copper telephone cables and the limited power of personal computers and networks.[126] However, with the invention of ADSL (Asymmetric Digital Subscriber Line), improvements in video compression and a new kind of distribution network, the idea of streaming audiovisual media became more viable, and in 1995 an audio coverage of a baseball game between Seattle Mariners and New York Yankees was the first-ever live event to be streamed over the Internet.[127]

As early as 1967, the computer scientist and Internet pioneer J.C.R. Licklider had envisioned a form of "selective television" where the Internet, unlike broadcast television, which offered "everyone the same thing" at the same time, could "give viewers a direct way of participating."[128] These thoughts were vague ideas and distant dreams in the 1960s, but with new technological inventions and a new distribution network, some of Licklider's ideas became feasible (whether the current mediascape mirrors the philosophy behind Licklider's ideas is, however, debatable). The new kind of distribution network, which "detects where a video request originates [...] and then directs that request to a server that is as close to the request as possible," can be likened to the Aesop parable of "The Tortoise and the Hare". In Aesop's fable, a slow-moving tortoise challenges a hare to a race, and the hare seems destined to win the race, but takes a rest while he is in front, only to discover that the tortoise, crawling slowly but steadily towards the finishing line, has arrived before him. In metaphorical terms, this might describe the idea behind the buffer, i.e. the amount of data that is sent to the receiver in advance, as s/he is streaming a file. Instead of sending the receiver a large amount of data at once, s/he receives a small portion of data in advance, in case s/he should experience a short hiccup or loss of Internet connection. But the steady flow of data usually makes it possible for the user to stream the program without experiencing quality reduction or sudden interruptions (when the program is "buffering").[129]

What was once an ideal or a vague dream became a feasibility in the 1990s and a fully-fledged reality in the 2010s, but the question is how and to what degree the new distribution technology affects TV production and programming. In the words of Amanda D. Lotz:

> Streaming - or internet-distributed video - first proved to be a new mechanism of distributing video somewhat akin to what cable and satellite meant to the pre-existing broadcast industry. [...] But over time, the peculiar features of internet-distributed services - such as their cultivation of libraries rather than schedules and their tendency towards subscription funding - have inspired changes in production norms; perhaps enough so as to distinguish them from their foundation in television and film.[130]

Rethinking Television

The introduction of internet-distributed television - something that was initially called "web TV" and used as a label for early experiments in online series - has reintroduced some of the most basic questions and conundrums in Media Studies and asked us, as audiences and critics, to rethink or redefine television as a concept. Film critics have often posed the question: "What is cinema?", whether as a means for creating a poetics (as in the case of André Bazin) or a more philosophically valid and consistent definition of film as a medium and phenomenon (as in the case of Noël Carroll).[131] Similarly, the current mediascape has prompted critics and scholars to reconsider the word "TV series" and its relevance in an era where many series are distributed online and where some series even have theatrical releases (both *Top of the Lake: China Girl* and *Twin Peaks: The Return* premiered at the Cannes Film Festival in 2017).

"In addition to contemplating the perennial question of 'what is the future of television?'," as Max Dawson writes, "some commentators asked whether or not television had a future at all in a world in which computers, game consoles, iPods, and cellular phones all could receive and display television programming."[132]

In this context, Amanda D. Lotz introduces a relevant distinction between *media* and *distribution technology* - a distinction that is inspired by Henry Jenkins and which is meant to illustrate that

> television is a medium, whereas broadcast signals, cable wires, and internet protocols are all delivery systems or distribution technologies. [...] [B]oth film and television are audiovisual messaging systems, but they are distinct media because of their discrepant industrial formations, government policies, and practices of looking.[133]

To some extent, a TV series may be informed by its distribution technology, but it is also shaped by cultural practices, historical traditions and storytelling conventions. To put it in almost McLuhanesque terms: *The medium forms the message; the distribution technology informs it.*[134]

As Mittell correctly notes, traditional American TV series during the *three-network era* were of course shaped by network television, which demanded commercial breaks, unobjectionable programming and possibilities for syndication. The commercial breaks could naturally have affected the structure of TV series and other television programs, prompting TV creators to think in *beats* and *intra-episodic cliffhangers* before each commercial break, and the television schedules likewise affected the typical length and format of a TV series. Moreover, the principle of syndication may have led to an almost 'episodic ideal'; episodic series with self-contained episodes were better suited for syndication, inasmuch as they might be shown out of order when being syndicated on a new channel.[135]

Those elements unsurprisingly informed TV series during the *three-network era* in the US, whereas Danish television programming during the same era was informed by a long-standing public service tradition. But many of these elements have to do with the revenue stream just as much as, or arguably more than, the distribution technology itself. Given that traditional broadcast networks are financed through advertisements, they have to adhere to other norms and standards than premium cable channels, and in that sense the difference between a cable series and a network series might well be bigger than the difference between a cable series and a Netflix series (both of which use a subscription model). Netflix uses a different distribution technology than traditional cable channels and enables "non-linear" viewing, but they have a similar revenue stream and are shaped by similar financial models and inherited storytelling traditions.[136]

In that sense, it seems premature to suggest that internet-distributed television (or *online TV*, as Catherine Johnson calls it) is so different from traditional TV series that it warrants a new and independent nametag. And it would seem just as natural to call *Stranger Things* (Netflix, 2016-) a TV series, despite it never having aired on a traditional TV network, as it is to describe straight-to-DVD movies like *Submerged* (2005) or Netflix productions like *Marriage Story* (2019) as films, despite them having had a limited or no theatrical run. Naturally, though, it is a vast and complex mediascape, and, as we shall see, there are important variations and crucial differences between streaming channels and mobile video platforms such as Netflix, Amazon and Quibi, on the one hand, and those connected to traditional TV networks and different *content businesses* on the other. As Lisa Parks and Nicole Starosielski put it:

> Today, broadcasting, cable, satellite, Internet, and mobile telephone systems are used simultaneously, and sometimes in coordinated ways, to route signal traffic to and from sites around the world. The content and form of contemporary media - whether television programs or online games - are shaped in relation to the properties and locations of these distribution systems. Simply put, our current mediascapes would not exist without our current media infrastructures.[137]

A Complex Landscape

The study of media infrastructures and industries is popular these days, and most of the scholarly accounts within this field focus on one particular industry, acknowledging the major structural differences between specific industries and national traditions. This type of "siloization" makes sense given the complexity of the current mediascape. But Daniel Herbert, Amanda D. Lotz and Marshall Lee make a convincing case for comparative industrial studies when it comes to dealing particularly with the current streaming landscape - a global landscape defined by new players and, hence, a potential for new industrial patterns and forms of organization, as well as a convergence between different nations and industries.[138]

As mentioned earlier, the concept of 'streaming' emerged in the 1990s, and it has been something of a fluffy concept, referring specifically to music or audiovisual content that is experienced in 'real time' (without having to download a file to a local drive), but it has also been used more broadly to describe "on-demand services regardless of the technical means of transmission."[139] Referencing Michele Hilmes, Lotz has described the attempt to make any specific claims of streaming as "nailing mercury; in which any pressure to fix the substance simply leads it to slide off in another direction."[140] And the strict focus on an American context and streaming channels with a subscription model may be an issue in Lotz's own - though otherwise convincing– description. By focusing on subscription funded streaming channels such as Netflix and Amazon Prime and practically ignoring other types of streaming channels (e.g. open-access services and streaming services provided by broadcasters in England, Denmark and other European countries, which are funded either by advertising or media licence), Lotz's model is somewhat reductive.[141]

TV Natives, Online Natives and Content Natives

An appealing framework, then, is presented in Catherine Johnson's book *Online TV* (2016) where she distinguishes between three different types of online TV providers. The first type is called *TV natives*. These are streaming services connected to already existing TV networks, whether broadcast networks, cable networks, satellite channels or public service channels. Consequently, the *TV natives* "need to consider the impact of their online TV service on their existing television business and to protect extant business models and revenue streams," and they sometimes offer extra channels to their existing catalogue or possibilities of viewer engagement and transmedia storytelling.[142]

As may be evident, this is a fairly heterogeneous group of services - some are funded through media licences (as in the case of DR's internet-distributed TV service DRTV), others by advertising or subscriptions (as in the case of Showtime Anytime or Sky Go, which is provided free of charge for Sky subscribers). In this context, Johnson also mentions telecom providers like TalkTalk that have "extended their media infrastructure business into the provision of TV services," offering "online versions of their subscription TV packages as well as the ability to buy/rent films and TV programmes online."[143]

Most of these *TV natives* are geoblocked, and they often include a vast catalogue of programs and options for both *linear* and *non-linear* viewing (where you either watch the programs online as they are being aired on TV or watch them at your leisure, until the given program is removed from the streaming service). In Denmark, for example, the channels DR3 and DR Ultra, both of which were aimed at the younger demographic, were discontinued as *flow TV* channels and transferred to streaming-only channels on DRTV, and the two culture-oriented channels DR2 and DRK were merged into one channel (DR2) on *flow TV*, while an online addendum (DR2+) was added to the streaming service.[144]

The second category in Johnson's model is called *online natives*, in the sense that these providers are not tied to an existing TV network, but an existing online business. This is the case with Amazon Prime, which is connected to one of the major online retailers in the world, and Netflix which originally rented out DVDs by mail and later began curating and streaming films, before eventually producing original TV series like *House of Cards* and *Stranger Things*. Netflix and Amazon dominate the OTT (over the top) market, together with Disney+, and Apple TV+, which is connected to one of the giants of home computing, is also a noteworthy example.

Another and slightly more radical example is the mobile video platform Quibi, which is known for its short fictional series with brief episode lengths of approximately 8-10 minutes ("**Qui**ck **bi**tes)" and the technical option called "turnstyle" where you can seamlessly switch between "landscape and portrait video orientation depending on how you hold your phone."[145] When Quibi was first promoted, it was advertised as an ideal video platform for commuters – something that was eclipsed by the unexpected COVID-19 pandemic, which coincided with the time when Quibi finally launched.[146] Often criticized, Quibi sold itself as a producer of short and 'snackable' series (e.g. comedies and dramedies like *Dummy* and anthology series like *50 States of Fright*) in a TV landscape dominated by long serials and hour-long episodes. In that sense, Quibi might have been trying to monetize the short format and the limited series – a field that is increasingly popular among TV creators and critics – yet the platform was described as "speculative," "uninvolving" or even "unnecessary". "Shortform sub-Netflix shows aren't long for this world," as Benjamin Lee of *The Guardian* wrote.[147] Or as TV creator Michael Lannan puts it:

> I think the Quibi disaster proves there are limits to how much you can try to reinvent certain human instincts in relation to storytelling. Especially if you're extremely cynical and primarily focused on monetizing your audience. But I still think there's so much exciting stuff to be discovered beyond what exists now.[148]

While Netflix and Amazon Prime have largely followed well-known TV genres and formats in their original productions, Quibi is less directly tied to television norms and traditions, and up until recently it was not even possible to watch a Quibi show on your television set using "streaming devices" such as Chromecast or Roku Streaming Stick+.[149] The ultra-short episode lenghts make for a format that differs markedly from traditional TV formats, and the production process on a Quibi show also differs from traditional TV production, inasmuch as Quibi shows are *cross-boarded* and shot like a film - all of it typically directed by one person - before dividing it into short chapters.[150] Still, the 1.75 billion dollar streaming service hired a number of noteworthy talents from the film and TV industries to produce their short fictions, including Steven Spielberg, Mary Harron, Sam Raimi and Tricia Brock, which hinted at a certain level of ambition within the restricted format.

One of the first original Quibi series was a peculiar and raunchy dramedy called *Dummy* (2020) in which an unlikely friendship develops between a young woman and her husband's sex doll. The director of this series, Tricia Brock, was known from television where she had worked on renowned drama series like *Breaking Bad* (AMC, 2008-2013), *The Walking Dead* (AMC, 2010-) and *Halt and Catch Fire* (AMC, 2014-2017), groundbreaking comedy series like *30 Rock* (NBC, 2006-2013) and *Community* (NBC, 2009-2015) and popular dramedies like *Girls* (HBO, 2012-2017). When detailing the production process on *Dummy*, it is interesting that Brock describes it within a conceptual framework known from TV. Though pointing to the unusual production process and the edgy content, she still describes it as a sort of TV series in direct lineage with her other work:

> *Dummy* was totally out of the box. The writing was so out there and so different, and I just loved it, and I admire Cody Heller so much. The fact that we didn't have to think of commercials or anything really helped. *Dummy* is, I don't know if raunchy is the word, but pretty edgy, so you could definitely not do that kind of show on network television. I'm sure you could on cable.
>
> It was daunting, in that we were the first show to shoot. We were Quibi's first scripted show that went into production, and I had a brilliant DP, an American woman who lives in London called Catherine Goldschmidt, and Catie just was a champ. She was so technologically astute, and she went and met with Quibi and worked out her own system where we had a grid on the monitor: It was taped off, so we could see what was in the frame, when it was vertical and horizontal. And once I knew she had it, I let go and focused on my work with the actors. Catie totally figured out the system for doing those shows, and then everyone after would call her to ask her how she did it. On set, when she was location scouting, she had this big monitor that she carried around with her. And she was always showing me - "If we do it this way, we'll lose this and this" - but most of the time I just shot it the way I wanted to shoot it, and if we had to make any concessions, we would. It didn't happen by magic. It happened because Catie was so good at organizing the shooting, but it didn't really interfere with my process.[151]

Ultimately, the radicality of Quibi and its insistence on an ultra-short mobile format aimed at a narrow demographic might have precipitated its demise, and in October 2020 the founders, Jeffrey Katzenberg and Meg Whitman, chose to shut down their streaming service due to its lack of traction.[152]

Finally, Catherine Johnson mentions a third category of online TV providers called *content natives*. These *content natives*, which are often overlooked in studies of internet-distributed television and modern TV series, have "extended content businesses in sectors as varied as sport, theater and charity into an online TV service."[153] Johnson specifically mentions Globe Player and Arsenal Player, two VOD services connected to the popular British theater and soccer team that offer filmed stage productions, interviews and behind-the-scenes footage. There are numerous similar examples across different countries (many of the larger sports teams in Europe and the US have similar online services, for example), and many *content businesses* are using audio-visual content as part of their business strategy, at times even branching out into serialized fiction. In this context, Johnson also distinguishes between *content businesses* and *technology businesses* where *content businesses* focus primarily on "the production, acquisition and delivery of audiovisual content to viewers", and *technology businesses* are "responsible for the technological infrastructures and devices needed to access online TV services."[154]

	TV natives E.g. BBC, DR, TV2 Play	Online natives E.g. Netflix, Amazon Prime	Content natives E.g. Globe Player, Ribe VikingeCenter
Business origins	TV networks (broadcast, cable and/or public service channels)	Online services or mobile video platforms	Content businesses from various sectors
Business objectives	Extend an existing TV service to the Internet or deliver channels online that are no longer viable as traditional flow-TV	Originate online or mobile TV service	Online TV service or transmedia universe builds on existing content business
Dependencies	Existing TV business	Existing online business (where relevant)	Existing content business

Fig. 5. TV natives, online natives and content natives. Modified version of Catherine Johnson's table in *Online TV* (2016, p. 56).

There are numerous examples of such *content natives* and a number of interesting hybrids where a *content business* has produced serialized fiction and/or documentaries for social media and (relatively) open-access platforms such as YouTube. In this context, video sharing platforms like YouTube and Vimeo, though also producers of original content in their own right (cf. *High Maintenance* and *Cobra Kai*), function as platforms for various *content businesses* who might link to the company's YouTube and Vimeo channels or embed the videos on their own company websites.

In Denmark, the museum called Ribe VikingeCenter has produced a historical series called *RIPA* (2016) about life in Ripa - the original name for the town of Ribe in western Jutland, which was founded in the Danish Viking Age - from 750 AD to 860 AD. Created for Ribe VikingeCenter's own website and

YouTube, *RIPA* was conceived in a collaboration between historians and curators from the museum and a production company called Malstrøm.

The series was launched as part of a larger transmedia universe, and it stars popular Danish actors like Rudi Køhnke. "The use of film for social media is a new way for museums and heritage centres to communicate often complex subjects," as the director Simon Lykke explains, and the managers of Ribe VikingeCenter, Bjarne Clement and Karen Nørgaard, have described the series as a good way to make their "living history interpretation [...] stand out."[155] In that sense, *RIPA* is a modern way of curating historical knowledge of the Viking Age, while becoming visible in a competitive market and attracting attention from different demographics as well as tourists (e.g. young people who might otherwise not visit the museum and foreigners who might be interested in the Viking Age but unaware of the specific town and museum).

A more popular example is *Margot vs. Lily* (2016), a charming Nike original starring Samantha Marie Ware and Brigette Lundy-Paine and produced for YouTube. *Margot vs. Lily* is an example of *branded content*, and both Nikewomen and YouTube are integrated into the story and structure of the series, often in creative and subtle ways. Margot (Lundy-Paine) and Lily (Ware) are sisters - a rather incongruous element, since one is African-American and the other Caucasian - and they have different issues and views on life. Lily has a popular workout channel on YouTube, but only has virtual friends and followers and no real social life. Margot, on the other hand, has numerous friends and has no respect for YouTubers or workout videos. Trying to prove their different points, Margot and Lily enter a competition, Lily attempting to gain actual, physical friendships, and Margot creating a workout channel on YouTube and trying to get a group of followers. In that way, Nike's brand is subtly introduced into the story (through the workout clothes and the focus on fitness and personal training), just as YouTube is overtly integrated into the narrative and the form (there are often captions and visual effects that mimic YouTube's functionalities). As Tricia Brock says:

> *Margot vs. Lily* was done for Nike as a form of branded content. I think it's a comedy, yet it's about these two sisters, and I love the fact that one is white and one is black, and we almost never refer to it - I think there was one reference to them being adopted. It was just a quirky little show, made by the same writer who wrote *Me and Earl and the Dying Girl*, and it felt more comedic than dramatic to me, but it had some emotional tugs, which I think is nice. If I were to pick, I would call it a comedy, but it could also be called a dramedy. It's one of those shows that fall between the cracks.
>
> It's much easier to maintain a comedic tone, when it's shorter. It's very hard to really keep that drama and tension going. In more dramatic pieces, you have to build tension in action, and that's very hard to sustain when you're chopping things up into episodes of six or eight minutes, so the more comedic pieces really lend themselves to short-form on platforms like YouTube and Quibi.[156]

Fig. 6-7: In 2016, the Danish museum Ribe VikingeCenter launched an online series called *RIPA*, which was meant to curate the early history of Vikings in Denmark and broaden the interest in national and regional history to younger Danes and international visitors (the series is subtitled in English and freely available online in all countries). Part of a larger transmedia universe, *RIPA* might be seen as a reaction to popular drama series like *Vikings* (History/Amazon Prime, 2013-2020), but it also illustrates a changing mediascape where *content businesses* in various sectors are beginning to produce serialized fiction. © *RIPA*, courtesy of Simon Lykke.

Thinking of different *content natives* and new players in the current mediascape, The Guardian's Andrew Marr has argued that we are witnessing a "wave of creative destruction overturning all traditional media,"[157] and, specifically mentioning *Margot vs. Lily*, the strategist Camilla Grey writes:

> Today's leading brands not only come armed with money and power, but also with creativity. Whether in-house or agency, brands have access to some of the most creative people in the world, enabling them to disrupt traditional media as much as traditional industries.[158]

Michael Curtis, Jennifer Holt and Kevin Sanson also argue that we are seeing a "veritable revolution" in the mediascape these days, and they moreover claim that "[w]hen looking to understand the current tumult in the media landscape, it is [...] clear that distribution networks and technologies are where the seeds of transformation have been sown."[159] While words like "revolution" or "disruption" might over-emphasize change (as opposed to continuity), it is fair to suggest that we are experiencing major changes in the media landscape due to new ways of distributing and consuming television. The question is whether, or to what degree, streaming services and potentials for *non-linear viewing* have resulted in extensive *cord-cutting* and *cord-shaving* and a general abandonment of *flow TV* and *linear viewing*.

Non-Linear Television and the Paradigm of Flexibility

The traditional TV landscape during the *three-network era*, claims Amanda D. Lotz, was governed by a *hegemony of linear norms* where viewers watched television in a broad sense or made appointments to watch specific TV programs at scheduled points (*appointment viewing*).[160] The idea and concept of *flow TV* goes back to an essay by Raymond Williams from 1974, in which he described the feeling of turning on a television set only to find, after a few hours, that he had become unable to distinguish between the different programs in the schedule.[161] Though Williams wrote his essay in the 1970s, just as American television was entering a new phase, he described a traditional *scheduling strategy* where programs are part of a larger TV schedule and where the announcer bridges the gaps between the different programs.[162] *Flow TV* and *appointment viewing* were both related to the concepts of broadcasting and scheduling. During the classic three-network and public service era, television was a mass medium, and viewers would generally watch the same programs at the same time, some programs becoming massive *watercooler phenomena* (i.e. programs that people debated by the watercooler at their workplace) or international events.

For example, 350 million viewers tuned in to find out who shot J.R. from *Dallas* (CBS, 1978-1991), and a session at the Turkish parliament was even suspended to give people the chance to go home and watch the episode.[163]

Time-Shifting and Binge-Watching

> Watch TV on your own schedule.
> – Netflix Quick Guide, May 2013.[164]

Before the premiere of the first original Netflix series, *House of Cards*, the showrunner Beau Willimon said in an interview that the goal was to "shut down a portion of America for a whole day."[165] This notion of shutting down a large portion of the country, due to them watching an entire season of a new series in one sitting, illustrates the differences between *linear* and *non-linear* television and different kinds of viewing behaviors. As mentioned earlier, *binge-watching* was not a new phenomenon as such in 2013, and the idea of *compressed consumption* goes back to DVD box sets (by 2005, the DVD sales of TV shows accounted for almost 20% of the entire DVD market) and the marathons that were frequently scheduled on different channels.[166] The Danish channel TV2 Zulu, for instance, launched a popular segment called *Seriesøndag*, in which entire seasons of popular TV series would fill the TV schedule on Sundays, allowing audiences to *binge* their favorite show while relaxing on the couch.[167]

Although it is a relatively new term, *binge-watching* (aka *binge-viewing*) is not a new phenomenon *per se*. Nor is the possibility for *time-shifting*, i.e. watching TV episodes outside of their scheduled time slots, a concept that goes back to the VCR (Video Cassette Recorder) and DVRs (Digital Video Recorder).[168] In a British survey from 2006, it was concluded that eight of the nine Sky+ households "had moved almost entirely to pre-recorded shows from the DVR," and some interviewees struggled to name the last TV show that they had watched on live TV.[169] In that sense, DVR, VCR and DVD pointed towards new viewing patterns - "from programmed flows to user-defined schedules" - and modern streaming channels such as Netflix have further nudged this change in viewing behaviors and modes of consumption.[170]

Even if Netflix did not invent *time-shifting* or *binge-watching*, it is fair to argue that they have had an effect on the current *on-demand* or *binge culture*, as Casey J. McCormick calls it, "promoting immersive viewing [and] complicat[ing] the assumed relationship between distribution methods and seriality."[171] The possibility of watching an entire season in one sitting goes against an intuitive understanding of what a TV series is (at least if we, like Jennifer Hayward, define a TV series as an "ongoing narrative *released in successive parts*").[172] And it makes it possible to skip *recaps* or *previously on*-montages and reduces the necessity for *intra-* and *extra-episodic cliffhangers* and *slow-paced redundancy* (often seen as staples of the *serial melodrama*).[173] In the words of Amanda D. Lotz:

> Streaming services are largely unconcerned with maintaining program norms that derived from scheduling - such as having programs that are exactly a particular length, produce a particular number of episodes, and often also dispense with characteristics of advertiser-support such as writing episodes with a structure of commercial breaks at certain intervals. This flexibility in storytelling structure, as well as opening up the marketplace to finite stories written as miniseries or limited series that reboot in each season (*American Horror Story*, *American Crime*, *True Detective*), has considerably expanded the range of stories conceived of as commercially viable in the US marketplace.[174]

In that sense, *binge-watching* might change the very construction of TV series, and it could facilitate narrative complexity and long arcs, as implied by Beau Willimon, Hagai Levi, Kelly Luegenbiehl and Ida Maria Rydén later in this book. As Mareike Jenner convincingly notes, Netflix, in their early marketing campaigns, promoted *binge-watching* and 'quality TV' as two central aspects, and this link between 'quality' TV and the possibility for *compressed consumption* was also seen in HBO's marketing campaign when they launched their DVD box sets.[175] If *The Wire* was made for DVD, perhaps *House of Cards* was made for streaming, both of them promoting, or even requiring, a different kind of consumption and engagement. As Jason Mittell writes:

> Compiling a serial allows viewers to see a series differently, enabling us to perceive aesthetic qualities traditionally used for discrete cultural works to ongoing narratives - viewing a DVD edition helps highlight the values of unity, complexity and clear beginnings and endings, qualities that are hard to discern through the incremental releases of seriality.[176]

As Michael Z. Newman and Elana Levine posit, DVD and streaming services are "cinematiz[ing] television," inasmuch as films and TV series are shelved alongside each other in video rental shops and online catalogues, making "the distinctions viewers make between film and television as media become thinner and thinner."[177]

Interestingly, however, *binge-watching* seems to connote a somewhat guilty viewing behavior, not unlike the traditional (critical) perception of television.[178] To binge something is to engage in an excessive behavior, and it is associated with an addict who consumes a given substance or product in large quantities (however unhealthy the substance or product). This metaphor goes back to the early years of television and the notion of TV as a bad habit, as seen in the writings of philosophers such as Theodor Adorno and Max Horkheimer, popular words like "idiot box" and critical comments by filmmakers and showrunners (e.g. David Simon who compared the act of watching television to "quiet masturbation"). "I hate television as much as I hate eating peanuts. I can't stop eating peanuts," as Orson Welles famously quipped.[179]

The term *binge-watching* has negative connotations and suggests an unhealthy viewing behavior (even if studies about the cognitive psychological effects of *binge-watching* have indicated both positive and negative effects).[180] Therefore, some producers and creators have argued that their series should not be binged, perhaps implying that 'true art' requires reflection and savoring. The Showtime executive David Nevins, for example, compared the new *Twin Peaks* (Showtime, 2017-) to "heroin," and co-creator Mark Frost argued that it would probably be unhealthy to watch it all in one or two sittings.[181] Similarly, the writer-director Derek Cianfrance argues that bingeing his series *I Know This Much Is True* (HBO, 2020) might not be a sound choice given its heavy and demanding subject matter:

> To watch it all at once, it could be a lot to take. You could get over-saturated. But by watching it a chapter at a time, it becomes a different experience. [...] Of course, two weeks from now the whole thing will be on HBO Go [HBO Max], and people can binge it till their hearts go out, but I really do think that this story in particular benefits from these longer moments of reflection and introspection.[182]

Following the same logic, Lindsay Zoladz of *The Ringer* has made "A Case For Savor-Watching," arguing that the streaming era is defined "by a constant, overwhelming feeling of excess," and today critics and scholars distinguish between many different viewing behaviors and types of engagement.[183] The question is whether these new options have made traditional *flow TV* and "linear" viewing patterns obsolete and to what degree they have changed the actual style, structure and storytelling of the TV series.

From Cord-Shaving to Cord-Cutting

After the launching of YouTube, Netflix and other streaming services, we have seen a change, not just in terms of distribution, but also in terms of consumption. Consumers today, as Rafaella Masoero writes, "are prepared to create a bundle of services, tailored to their particular viewing preferences which may include full pay-TV subscriptions ('cord-keepers'), a reduced or cheaper pay-TV service alongside other services ('cord-shavers') or may comprise a set of OTT packages with no pay-TV subscription at all ('cord-cutters')."[184]

The question is not whether there is a tendency towards *cord-shaving* and *cord-cutting*, but whether this tendency is as massive and unambiguous as many critics and media seem to imply. According to a report by Kagan, cable, satellite and telco multichannel providers lost a combined 1.8 million US subscribers in 2016, and the development accelerated in the fourth quarter of 2016 (with a decline of 460,000 subscribers). From the beginning of 2015 to the end of 2016, the amount of US households with pay-TV subscriptions had dropped from 81.3 % to 77.5 %.[185] In a report called "Tech in 2020: Standing on the Shoulders of Giants," Benedict Evans describes a similar development,

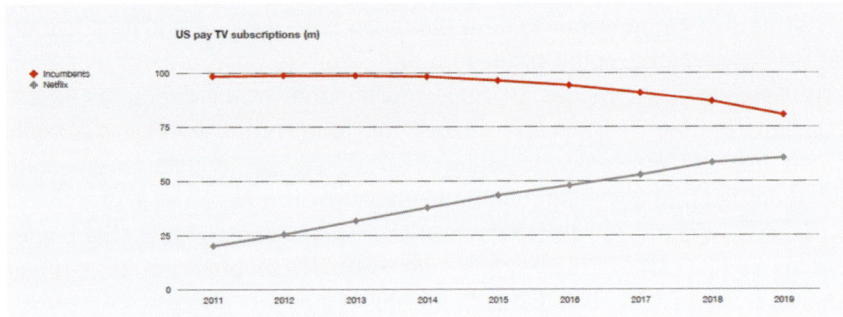

Fig. 8: Pay TV vs. Netflix subscriptions in the US from 2011 to 2019. Source: Benedict Evans 2020, "Standing On the Shoulders of Giants," p. 38.

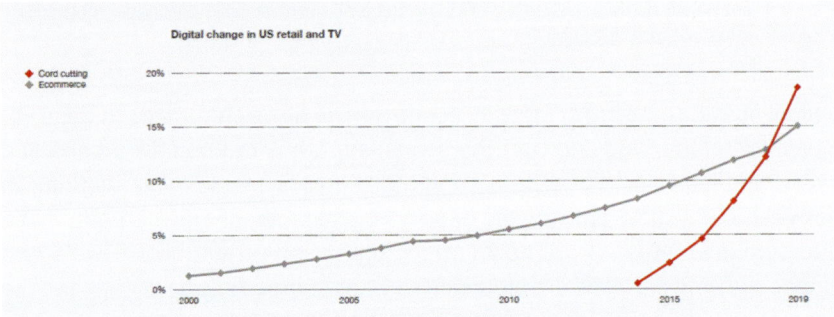

Fig. 9: Digital change in US retail and TV. US cord-cutting % has passed E-commerce % in just five years. Source: Benedict Evans 2020, "Standing On the Shoulders of Giants," p. 38.

noting a 20% drop in pay-TV subscriptions from 2011 to 2020 and an exponential growth in *cord-cutting* from 2014 to 2019 (cf. Fig. 8-9).

On a global scale, we are seeing a similar development, and a survey by Grabyo from 2019 (Fig. 10), covering almost 10,000 companies in Europe, the US and Australia, suggests that 65% of all consumers (globally) have chosen to replace their pay-TV subscriptions with OTT services (including SVoD).[186] As Grabyo CEO Gareth Capon says:

> Broadcasters, rights holders and publishers need to cater to an audience that is moving away from traditional TV. Flexibility, access and price are important to consumers, which means delivering a multiplatform video strategy that reflects these needs. The transition to cloud services will support this shift, but these changes need to accelerate.[187]

A central point in the JP Morgan report, cited by Benedict Evans, is that we can see a generational gap where especially young audiences (18-25 years) are turning to OTT, primarily using smartphones, smart TV and "streaming devices" like Chromast, Apple TV and Roku to watch their programs.[188]

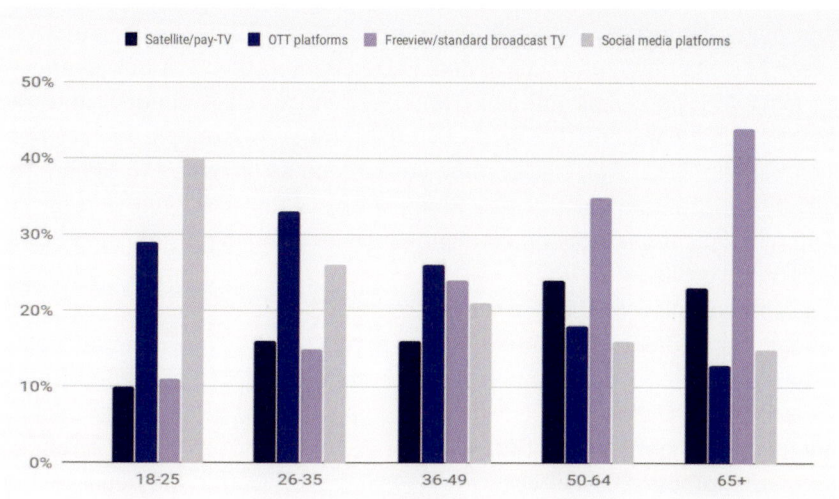

Fig. 10: Services used by different demographics (globally). Source: *Mir.dk*, 2020.

However, based on a survey of 13,000 respondents in various countries from Europe, North and Latin America, Grabyo suggests that older demographics are also gradually embracing OTT services, with 63% of the people over 65 saying that they subscribe to at least one platform. Globally, the report claims, the OTT penetration has surpassed pay-TV (55% vs. 50%), and a staggering 74% of all respondents plan on *cord-cutting* by 2025.[189]

Indeed, the market is changing, and the traditional TV networks are being challenged by various platforms and services. However, different surveys and reports give slightly different pictures of the current mediascape, and there are significant national differences and nuances that need to be noted. Focusing on a Danish context, for example, Jakob Isak Nielsen arrives at a different and somewhat surprising conclusion, noting that the percentage of households in Denmark with a TV subscription was 82 in both 2008 and 2018.[190] Referencing an article from 2017 by TV2's Anders Blauenfeldt and a report by Jacob Graff Hedebrink, presented at the *Copenhagen Future TV Conference* in May 2019, Nielsen challenges four myths concerning the current TV landscape in Denmark:

- Flow TV is dead
- TV subscriptions are dead
- TV as a 'family altar' is dead
- Danish television is dead.[191]

Though Danes are also *cord-shaving*, especially after 2013, Nielsen concludes that many Danes are still subscribing to traditional TV channels. Moreover, *linear TV* does not seem to be "dying" in Denmark; rather it largely seems to co-exist with *non-linear* options. The streaming services connected to the two major networks, DR (DR TV) and TV2 (TV2 Play), for example, include possibilities for "live" TV (in this context understood as an option to stream the respective programs as they are being aired), options for *time-shifting* (i.e. watching episodes back and catching up on last week's episode) and downloading for offline-viewing.[192]

In a broad sense, Netflix and other streaming services appear to have challenged the traditional TV networks, which has resulted in a general decline in pay-TV subscriptions and some noticeable infrastructural changes in the TV landscape. Nielsen's article, however, may serve as a cautionary tale, reminding us to look for counter examples, nuances and national differences. And in November 2020, it was revealed that even Netflix will begin testing linear offerings, giving viewers an option to watch Netflix programs in a way that is similar to traditional, scheduled television.[193]

As Michael Curtin, Jennifer Holten and Kevin Sanson noted back in 2014:

> Despite all of the "disruptive" innovations, most of the money being made today in film and television is still being made the old-fashioned way: in theaters, from ads on linear television, or from syndication deals. As such, some eyeballs are simply more important than others. For example, broadcast and cable television viewers continue to command exponentially higher advertising rates than those who view content on computers and mobile screens. At the same time, profound changes are taking place as taste-based algorithms and other emergent audience metrics are beginning to challenge measurement techniques and undermine the premium prices charged for conventional TV advertising. Audience engagement, rather than size, is the current zeitgeist.[194]

Peak TV: From Saturation to Vertical Integration

> Every new medium is accompanied by the perception of abundance. Most recently, digitisation and the web ignited a new wave of perceived abundance, as they provide an array of news, information and entertainment, networked connections, new ways of consumption and opportunities to become a consumer and producer of content.
> - Hilde Van Den Bulck & Hallvard Moe, media scholars.[195]

How much the TV landscape has changed in terms of production norms and viewing patterns - and to what degree these elements are affected by new distribution technologies - is subject to debate as well as national and industrial variations. In terms of the sheer amount of content, however, it seems evident that the TV landscape has, indeed, changed. In 2015, the chairman of FX Networks, John Landgraf, coined the term *Peak TV* to describe a critical tendency in the modern mediascape where a plethora of content has made for an almost saturated marketplace. According to Landgraf, the growth in scripted series in the US (and globally) has made it all but impossible for viewers to locate the good series, and this tendency, he felt, was "doing a noticeable disservice to networks and platforms" (cf. Fig. 11).[196]

Since the launching of FX's own *The Shield* in 2002, the number of scripted shows in the US has been steadily growing, hitting 495 in 2018 and reaching 532 scripted shows in 2019 (a 7% increase from 2018). This is a cause of concern for many TV creators. As Tom Fontana says in the introduction to this book, the problem concerning this plethora of content is that TV creators have to "make noise" in order to be noticed, and this might be detrimental to the 'smaller' TV series that deal with quotidian or everyday-like events.

Another interesting issue concerning the current mediascape has to do with the concentration of power and potential monopolization (behind the seeming de-centralization of the media landscape). From the sheer number of outlets and platforms one might naturally assume that the current TV landscape is more democratic and less monopolistic than the classic three-network era.[201] From the 1940s to the early 1980s, the American TV landscape was largely dominated by three broadcast networks, and Danish television was essentially defined by one public service channel (DR) up until the launch of TV2 in 1988. Compared to that era, the current TV landscape certainly looks more democratic, yet both Amanda D. Lotz and Jakob Isak Nielsen point to signs of *vertical integration* in today's streaming landscape, naturally coinciding with the general *conglomeration* in America.[202] "[T]he in-

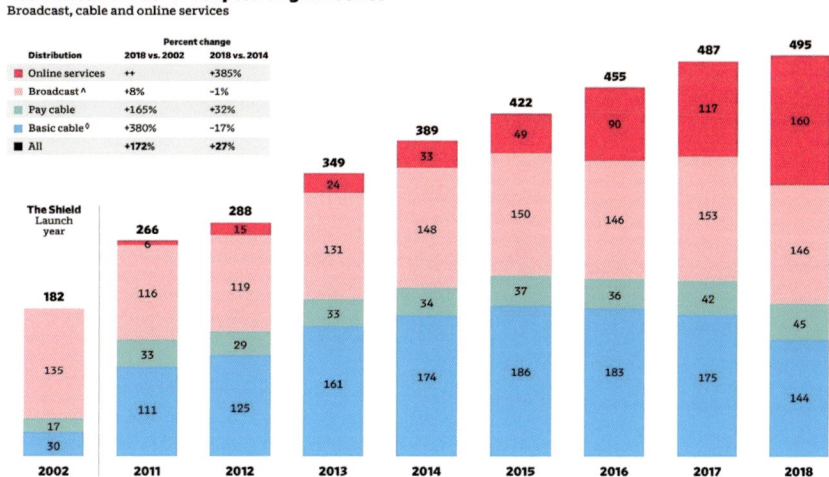

Fig. 11: Source: FX Networks Research, December 12, 2018. Some types of scripted series are not included in the FX chart, including *daytime dramas*, non-English series, children's programs and series with an episode length of less than 15 minutes.

TV creators and directors on the growth of content in America and changes in the global TV landscape

Michael Lannan (writer-producer): HBO showed everyone what's possible in terms of great storytelling. A lot of that is due to their model of subscription that let people pay directly for quality boundary-pushing stories instead of relying on the corporate advertisers who defined the American TV landscape until the cable explosion.

That's especially significant for queer stories because they often challenge the status quo, which typically isn't great for selling cars, etc. This is all an oversimplification of course, but it's part of it in my opinion.

A company like Netflix is kind of the next evolution of that process, letting people pay directly for a vast array of programming, which makes them capable of financing series for all kinds of niche audiences. It's an exciting time for sure, but also a complicated one with its own set of problems for creatives.[197]

Sam Levinson (writer-producer): I think we have more tools available and the scope of the stories can be bigger, although not necessarily better. I think we're at a point where there's such an over-saturation that it's hard to stay focused or to care. I think that's the biggest obstacle for filmmakers. How do you push the medium further? How do you show people something they haven't seen before?[198]

Tricia Brock (director): To get a show ordered or financed, my manager always says it has to be "noisy" because now the market is flooded, and you have to make yourself stand out, trying to find those things that aren't already in the marketplace which is completely saturated."[199]

Daniel Knauf (writer-producer): Once upon a time, the purpose of a show was to sell toothpaste and toilet paper. For HBO, the purpose of a show was to get subscribers, and now with Netflix the purpose is to produce a lot of content to constantly attract new subscribers and then move on.

Back when *Carnivàle* came out, 90% of everything was shit, and 10 percent was good. What I've noticed is that now, with the increase in series, it's almost more like 97 percent of everything is shit. There's so much garbage. The three percent is really good, but, consider this, I think there are more than 500 scripted shows on TV now, so if you say three percent of those shows are good, there are 10 or 15 stand-outs whereas before, in the old days, there might have been two or three stand-outs. So, the illusion is that we're in a golden age, but it's really just a law of numbers.[200]

troduction of new technologies is often accompanied by utopian promises of greater access, broader political participation, and increased choices," as Chuck Tryon writes. "But despite these promises, true choice and mobility are often greatly exaggerated."[203] Or as the independent film and TV producer Maggie Monteith provocatively puts it:

> We've created a class hierarchy within this new media landscape that replicates the class hierarchy that was there before with the studios at the pinnacle and a little humpty dumpty distributor from Peru at the other end.[204]

If we look at bandwidth consumption, Netflix has been the biggest application for a number of years, according to Sandvine, only recently dropping to 12.6% of downstream traffic worldwide (with HTTP media streaming accounting for 12.8%). In the Americas, Netflix has dropped from a share of 19.1% in 2018 to 12.9% in the first half of 2019, but this is still a large proportion given that the "HTTP media stream" category in Sandvine's report represents all the streaming services that they have not tracked individually (which they have done for YouTube and Netflix).[205] The relative decline for Netflix in 2019 coincides with the "growing popularity of piracy services," and the Sandvine report, though indicating some subtle shifts in power balance, still illustrates that the streaming landscape is dominated by only a few major players.[206]

In 2019, 85% of all US streaming subscribers subscribed to Netflix, and the US Netflix penetration hit 65%, whereas the global number of subscribers reached 167.1 million (further growing to 182.86 million in the first quarter of 2020).[207] These numbers and the Sandvine report both indicate a certain concentration of power, akin to the *vertical integration* of the American film industry in the classical Hollywood era where just a handful of majors controlled the production, distribution and exhibition of films. The numbers also indicate, however, that international subscribers of Netflix have "outpaced domestic growth," and this might be one of the explanations for *the global turn*, which I will explore in the following chapter.[208]

"Netflix is not just a player on the market," the journalist Rasmus Elmelund wrote in an article from 2018. "Netflix *is* the market."[209] Even if that was a journalistic overstatement, it spoke to the general tendency towards *conglomeration* and monopolization where a small number of companies supply most of the TV shows and "take in more than 85 percent of movie revenues" in the US.[210] In April 2020, the value of Netflix rose to 196 billion dollars, surpassing the American oil giant ExxonMobil, and scholars like Mareike Jenner have expressed concern about a future media landscape dominated primarily by American streaming services whose libraries consist mainly of American content.[211] Jenner's concern may be valid, but the fact that international subscribers of Netflix have outpaced American subscribers within the last few

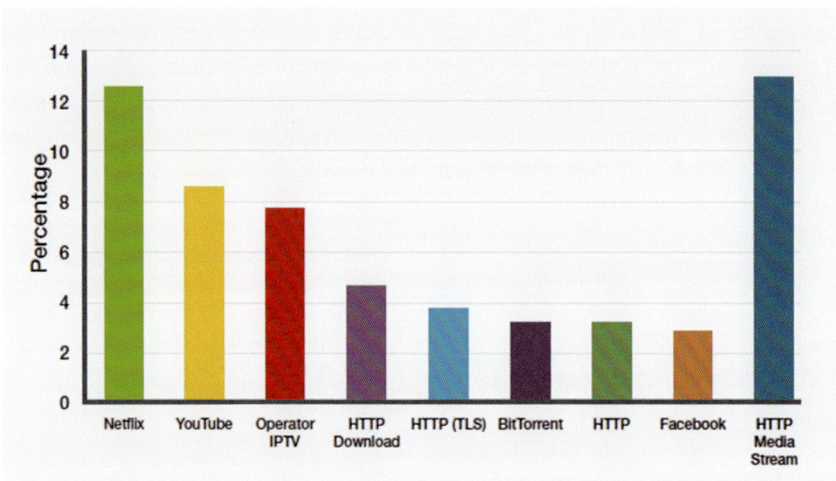

Fig. 12: Global Downstream Application Traffic Share. Source: Sandvine, 2019

years might point to a different picture, and, as we shall see, some American streaming services are, in fact, focusing on non-American content.

"Netflix taught its users to watch programming online," as industry scholar Cameron Lindsey writes. "It instilled users with the notion that television doesn't have to be watched on a TV."[212] As of yet, it is difficult to say exactly how the ever-changing TV landscape will look in 2025 or even at the end of 2021. Regulatory policies or increasing licensing fees, for example, might shift the power away from Netflix and other streaming giants to broadcasters and *TV natives* with vast catalogues (according to Lindsey, Netflix spends 1.3 million dollars per episode of AMC's hit series *The Walking Dead*).[213] As Michael Wolff writes:

> While Netflix and Amazon, the two leading *non-television* television platforms attempt to define themselves as alternatives to television and even a mortal disruption of it, they pay the traditional television industry more than $3 billion a year in licensing and programming fees.[214]

It seems evident that streaming services, related to both *TV natives*, *online natives* and *content natives*, have changed and widened the landscape as well as challenged traditional norms concerning TV production, content and storytelling (e.g. concerning preferred episode lengths, the use of *intra- and extra-episodic cliffhangers* and the use of recaps). Moreover, Netflix and other streaming services have prompted and promoted new viewing patterns, and they have shifted the general focus from schedules to libraries, from demographics and ratings (what Amanda D. Lotz calls *the hegemony of demographic thinking*) to audience engagement and "taste cultures."[215] Streaming services may be challenging the traditional broadcast networks and our understanding of what a "TV series" is, yet there is nothing to suggest, at least not at this point, that TV is dead. "The Internet, which was thought to be a TV killer, is turning out to be its wingman," as the TV critic Brian Stelter said in an article from 2014. In marketing campaigns, Netflix also described their original series as "the future of television," thus accepting its relationship to the TV medium and its historical connections to the "boob tube".[216] In the words of media scholar William Uricchio:

> Television's ongoing change seems endless - from tubes, or transistors, to chips; from cathode ray displays, to plasma, to projection; from broadcast, to cable, to Internet streaming; from dial-up, to remote-control, to algorithmic recommendation; from mass audiences, to niche audiences, to individuals.[217]

The first phase of the *multiplatform era* introduced new types of channels, storytelling, content and viewer engagement (through VCRs and DVD box sets). By the 2010s, this shift in American television grew into an even more complex and global landscape where the borders between different media, nations and industries began to erode. The major streamers might have changed the TV landscape, but at the cusp of a new decade they are introducing internet-distributed versions of *linear TV* and programs that share a lot of characteristics with "comfort TV" (what Anna McCarthy calls *ambient TV*).[218] If anything, the landscape is characterized by both continuity and change.

The Art of Bingeing: *House of Cards* as High-End Melodrama

In 2015, the former American president Barack Obama interviewed David Simon about *The Wire* and the war on drugs. While branding Obama as a hip president, attuned to 'new' media and popular TV series, it also lent an aura of legitimacy or cultural significance to Simon's series, which, according to the president, was "one of the greatest not just television shows but pieces of art in the last couple of decades."[219]

Similarly, Obama reacted to the growing popularity of the first original Netflix series, *House of Cards*, sending out an official tweet at the cusp of the second season: "Tomorrow: @HouseOfCards. No spoilers, please."[220] That tweet by Obama illustrates an interesting relationship or dialectic in Beau Willimon's series between 'bingeable' entertainment and cultural legitimacy, serial melodrama and high-end television reminiscent of cable dramas like *The Wire* and *The Sopranos*.

Ted Sarandos, the Chief Content Officer for Netflix, has said that there is "no such thing as a 'Netflix show'," implying that Netflix has a broader range than premium cable networks like HBO and their "not-TV" brands.[221] Nevertheless, *House of Cards*, an American re-adaptation of Michael Dobbs' novel from 1989, in many ways seemed to brand itself as more than traditional television. Instead of episodes, the different seasons were divided into "chapters," all of which were delivered at once. This choice of words, also seen in other Netflix originals such as *Stranger Things*, seemed to signify an almost novelistic quality, and, similarly, the different people behind *House of Cards* pointed to other and more legitimate media. The creator, Beau Willimon, was known primarily from theater, film and political communication; the director of the first two episodes, David Fincher, was a recognized auteur in American cinema; and the actors Robin Wright and Kevin Spacey were also associated with film. Thus, by pointing to other media and venues - literature, theater, cinema and the political scene - *House of Cards* was branded as more sophisticated and culturally relevant than most TV series, and, consequently, it has been referenced and discussed in numerous political debates and journalistic articles about American culture and politics.[222]

From Shakespeare to Serial Melodrama

> *Hamlet* isn't soap because Hamlet's problems are introduced, complicated and then ended by his death and the death of almost everyone else. End of story. In soap, there is no end of the story ever.[223]
> - Hilary Kingsley, TV scholar

> In a certain sense, the first real melodrama author was Shakespeare. There are some very soapy elements to Shakespeare.
> - Beau Willimon, creator/showrunner (House of Cards; cf. feature interview)

Apart from its most immediate ancestors (the novel by Michael Dobbs and the BBC adaptation from 1990-1995), *House of Cards* is lodged between the sophistication of Sophocles, Seneca and Shakespeare on the one side and one of the most traditional TV genres on the other: the soap opera. These points of inspiration are mentioned in the feature interview with Beau Willimon at the end of this chapter, and they are evident from the structure and composition of the series itself, however playful it is.

The basic story about Francis (Frank) and Claire Underwood (Kevin Spacey and Robin Wright), who strive to climb the political hierarchy by whatever means necessary, is noticeably similar to Shakespearean tragedies such as *Macbeth*, *Othello* and *Richard III*. Indeed, when Francis says to Claire in the pilot episode that they will have a lot of nights like this, "making plans, very little sleep," the motifs of treachery and sleep deprivation are eerily similar to *Macbeth*, most notably the sleepwalking scene in Act 5.[224] And as Claire calmly replies, "I expected that - it doesn't worry me," her likeness to Lady Macbeth is evident, something that is further emphasized by her surprise at Francis' lack of distrust and skepticism ("You don't usually underestimate people, Francis") and his self-reflexive response: "I know. Hubris. Ambition."

In that sense, *House of Cards* can be seen as a modern *tragedy of ambition* where the stories of hubris and treason are transported from Shakespeare's Britain to the political climate of modern America. The Shakespearean motifs and allusions give a sense of cultural legitimacy to Willimon's series, but they are playfully combined with elements from the *serial melodrama* - a traditional TV genre that is often associated with low production costs and low-brow entertainment.

As Jason Mittell writes, the soap opera was adopted from the radio in the 1940s and 1950s, and the first soap operas in American television were described as *daytime dramatic serials*, the term "soap opera" referring pejoratively to sponsors such as Procter & Gamble. "Soap operas are a derogatory moniker coined by commentators in the 1930s," as Mittell notes, "to mock the juxtaposition of high melodrama with low commerce, condescending the presumed audience of allegedly unsophisticated housewives."[225] As a genre, the melodrama can be seen as a modern version of the tragedy, both genres focusing on psychological and relational issues and strong emotions.

These elements, then, are central to the *serial melodrama*, but the "stigma of soap opera," as Mittell calls it, is presumably connected to its formal and stylistic qualities. Traditional soap operas, as Robert Allen writes, have a *high output* and *low production costs*, resulting in long seasons and multiple episodes per week.[226] Due to the low production costs and high output, soap operas are typically shot in a studio, often employing an efficient lighting and multi-camera technique akin to the *three-headed monster* known from traditional sitcoms.[227] Finally, soap operas often run for many years (ABC's *General Hospital*, for example, celebrated its 50th anniversary in 2013), making it necessary to avoid stability or finality and obeying a "logic of endlessly deferred conclusion."[228] Hence, Marsha Kinder describes the typical soap opera as "open-ended, slow-paced [and] multi-climaxed,"[229] and Jason Mittell argues that soap operas, being tailor-made for housewives who had chores around the house while watching their series, feature an overwhelming abundance of flashbacks and repetitions. "A soap opera might portray a key event," as Mittell writes, "but the event itself becomes less narratively important in its initial portrayal than in the chain of subsequent conversations about the event."[230]

Soap operas often include multiple *intra-* and *extra-episodic cliffhangers* where characters are caught in dire situations from which they seemingly cannot escape, or appear to die just as the credits are introduced. This narrative device, which is connected to commercial, serialized television in general and soap operas in particular, is also employed in *House of Cards*.

In Willimon's series, however, the cliffhanger is used in a somewhat surprising way, subverting the audience's expectations. Typically, an *intra-episodic cliffhanger* is introduced just before the commercial break, and *extra-episodic cliffhangers* are introduced at the end of an episode, most effectively at the end of a season (as is seen in the finales of seasons 1, 2 and 3 of *Stranger Things*). In *House of Cards*, though, one of the most widely debated cliffhangers was introduced in the beginning of the second season (Ep. 2:1) where Francis suddenly - and shockingly - pushes the young journalist Zoe Barnes (Kate Mara) out in front of a moving train. By killing off one of the central characters at the opening of a new season, Willimon exposes Francis' ruthlessness (as he also mentions in the feature interview) while subverting a traditional soap opera trope and toying with his audience.

Another typical feature in soap operas is the so-called *fake departure* where a character apparently dies or disappears, only to reappear at a later stage. This element is also used in Beau Willimon's series (in Chapter 26) where a character named Doug Stamper (Michael Kelly) appears to be killed with a rock (until he later returns). A related element is seen in the metaphorical reappearance of Peter Russo (Corey Stoll) and Zoe Barnes, as Francis talks in church to Peter's ghost - not unlike Macbeth who is haunted by the ghost of Banquo - and hallucinates about Peter and Zoe in Chapter 45. In this way, Willimon cleverly combines the Shakespearean trope of guilt with a soap operatic feature of repeated storylines and reappearing characters.[231]

House of Cards is about a causal string of events connected to the rise-and-fall template known from Shakespearean tragedies, but the conversations about the events are as important to the series as the actual events. In many episodes, Francis and Claire discuss the unfolding events and evaluate their plans, often while smoking cigarettes, and Francis even turns to the camera and involves the viewer in his thoughts and actions. These asides, again, could be interpreted as Shakespearean soliloquies (they were also used in BBC's original miniseries), and they could be described as an almost Brechtian form of *Verfremdung*, commonly associated with arthouse cinema and directors like Ingmar Bergman and Jean-Luc Godard.[232] Casey J. McCormick, however, notes that these kinds of asides differ from the Godardian and Brechtian devices used in modern theater and art cinema, and, instead of distancing the audience from the action, they draw the audience in, making them complicit in the violent actions.

In that sense, *House of Cards* seems aware of its medium and the way that audiences engage with it, exploiting the specific kind of intimacy that television and streaming can produce. In McCormick's view, we are dealing with a sort of *Skype ontology*.[233] Watching the main character address you directly, while you are on your tablet or mobile device, can feel almost like participating in a Skype call or a Zoom conference, and as Willimon implies in the feature interview later in this chapter, that sort of intimacy and alignment was an intended effect.

House of Cards is aware of its cultural heritage, not just in terms of Michael Dobbs' novel, Andrew Davies' miniseries and the references to canonical tragedies by Sophocles, Seneca and Shakespeare, but also in terms of its televisual roots. Playfully it (ab)uses some of the basic tropes known from the *serial melodrama*, often subverting the audience's expectations, and it situates itself in a twilight zone between tradition and actuality, high art and bingeable entertainment.

The style could not be further from traditional soap operas, David Fincher being extremely meticulous about the expressive use of lighting and the muted color palette (cf. the feature interview with Beau Willimon at the end of this chapter). Together with the evocative title sequence and mannered acting style, the colors and lighting contribute to a sense of coolness and artifice. At a narrative level, though, *House of Cards* seems to embrace its televisual heritage, and it is interesting to note that Willimon unapologetically describes it as a *serial melodrama*.

Many of the interviewees for this book describe their TV series (regardless of distribution technology) as modern versions of the soap opera, although that comparison is often regarded as stigmatizing. When talking about the popular zombie series, *The Walking Dead* (AMC, 2010-), the showrunner Angela Kang, somewhat surprisingly, agrees with George A. Romero's comment: "It's just a soap opera with a zombie occasionally."[234] Similarly, the Danish TV creator Maya Ilsøe, when talking about her Bergmanesque family melodrama *Arvingerne* (*The Legacy*, DR, 2014-2017), says that the crew, while working on the show, described it as an "arthouse soap," humorously acknowledging it televisual lineage. Aesthetically, however, Ilsøe worked with "a minimalistic set-up with only a few cameras and some stylistic dogmas in relation to the arena and the characters," and the main principle was to "push the style as far as possible without compromising authenticity or making it a pure genre piece."[235] Finally, when describing the modern cable classic *Six Feet Under* (HBO, 2001-2005), one of the main script writers Nancy Oliver uses the following words:

> I would describe the show, at this moment, anyway, as a sophisticated soap opera with the elements you mention (absurdity and surrealism) - and humor, of course! It was beautifully elevated by the quality of the work at every level: acting, writing, production design, direction, editing and cinematography. But at its heart, I feel it was a straight-up soap, which is part of its strength.
>
> For me as a writer, the emphasis on character was a perfect fit. I appreciate a good plot, but I'm not instinctively a plot person and find the generally linear nature of plot sometimes restrictive. Character and relationships are what interest me most in a story, as a reader and a writer.[236]

Like Kang, Ilsøe and Oliver, Beau Willimon also acknowledges his use of soap opera formulas, without using the terms "melodrama" and "soap opera" as *derogatory labels*, and *House of Cards* is also aware of its relation to modern media and the concept of bingeing. As McCormick insightfully notes, the characters often engage in different addictions - Peter being an alcoholic, Frank being addicted to computer games, and Frank and Claire smoking cigarettes in most of the episodes - and these elements seem to mirror the addictive qualities of bingeing.[237] Though not a streaming phenomenon as such, Netflix popularized the sort of consumption that had previously been possible only when watching marathons on TV or watching entire seasons on VHS and DVD, and they popularized the term *binge-watching*.[238] A central series in this context was *House of Cards*, and even President Obama noticed and commented on its bingeability.

From Exclusive Distribution Rights to Netflix Originals

Prior to *House of Cards*, Netflix was not, itself, a producer of TV drama. It was founded in 1997, began renting out DVDs by mail in 1998, and later started distributing films and TV series online. In February 2012, only a few weeks after its national premiere on NRK1 in Norway, *Lilyhammer* (NRK, 2012-2014) was distributed by Netflix as their first example of "exclusive content."[239]

Though not a Netflix original, Anne Bjørnstad and Eilif Skodvin's show was co-financed by Netflix, and its popularity across different cultures (with 998,000 viewers when premiering on NRK1 and numerous viewers watching it after its North American premiere) marked a potential for transnational collaborations, original Netflix series and non-American content. In Netflix terms, the word "original" has often meant "exclusive distribution rights," but *Lilyhammer*, albeit produced in Norway with minimal intervention from Netflix, was at its heart a transnational series about an American gangster, Frank Tagliano (Steven Van Zandt), who is relocated to the Norwegian small town Lillehammer. Bjørnstad and Skodvin's series combines different languages and traditions - a *Sopranos*-like gangster story with quirky local characters, subtle humor and a uniquely Nordic setting - and it paved the way for Netflix's first original series: *House of Cards*. In the feature interview below, Anne Bjørnstad, Eilif Skodvin and Beau Willimon talk about their respective series and the influence of Netflix and streaming on the current TV landscape.

After this double interview, I will turn my attention to the global and *glocal* tendencies in the current mediascape, using Bjørnstad and Skodvin's two series, *Lilyhammer* and *Beforeigners* (HBO, 2019-), as my points of departure.

Digital delivery widened the TV landscape, creating a sense of *platform mobility* and an "ongoing shift towards ubiquitous, mobile access to a wide range of entertainment choices."[240] Streaming services like Netflix, Amazon Prime and Quibi challenged our understandings of television, and they also held utopian promises of a more democratic mediascape. In reality, however, those promises or ideals involve "the continued efforts of major media conglomerates to develop better mechanisms for controlling where, when, and how content is circulated," and what looked like a general de-monopolization of the media landscape may, in fact, end in a new form of *vertical integration*.[241] As the editors for an upcoming anthology (*Unseen Television*) write in their call:

> With Disney+, Apple TV+, and NBC's Peacock joining Netflix, Amazon Prime, HBO Go [HBO Max], Hulu, Crunchyroll, ESPN+, and CBS All Access, industry observers and tech writers have declared that we now live in an era of "peak streaming TV." [...] Economically, Netflix's novel cost-plus business model has upended the traditional deficit financing model favored by studios. This model allows Netflix to produce a more diverse library, yet a shallower depth for its more cost-prohibitive original series. Additionally, the unique production model has contributed to a recent wave of vertical (AT&T-Time Warner in 2018) and horizonal (Disney-Fox in 2019) integration, resulting in bundling, vaulting, or selective windowing. Furthermore, such integration typically results in a narrowing of creative diversity.[242]

In the global streaming landscape, TV series are moving beyond TV in terms of distribution, and they are moving across national borders and connecting different industries. Following the feature interview below, I will explore the most essential qualities and issues of this global TV landscape and the most noteworthy tendencies - from transnational collaborations, international co-productions and *Europudding* to *local-language originals* and the questions of authenticity and national specificity.

Feature Interview #2

The Pioneers of Streaming: Interview with Anne Bjørnstad & Eilif Skodvin (*Lilyhammer*) and Beau Willimon (*House of Cards*)

In February 2012, *Lilyhammer* (2012-2014) premiered on Netflix, two weeks after it had premiered to record numbers on Norwegian national television. The Norwegian-American series, co-financed by NRK and Netflix and distributed in America exclusively by the latter, marked the beginning of a new strategy for Netflix and a new era in television history. Having been a curator of content, almost as an extensive library of films, Netflix now became an exclusive distributor and (co-)producer of serialized content and, one year later, in 2013, they produced their first ever TV series, *House of Cards* (2013-2018), where all episodes of the first season were launched at once. The creator Beau Willimon adapted his original Netflix series from a British miniseries trilogy (BBC, 1990-1995) and infused it with a different setting, style and tonality, much of which could be attributed to David Fincher, who directed the first two episodes and established the audiovisual style. Deeply interested in the 'game' of global politics, Willimon is currently developing a new series inspired by Hasbro's popular strategy game *Risk*.

In this double interview, the creators of *Lilyhammer* and *House of Cards* discuss their respective series and how streaming channels such as Netflix have affected, or even changed, the TV landscape.

From Norway to Netflix: *Lilyhammer*

How was your series conceived, and how did Netflix become involved?

Bjørnstad & Skodvin: We came up with the idea for *Lilyhammer* when we were working on a weekly satirical comedy show, not unlike Comedy Central's *The Daily Show*. For a programme like that you have to produce a high number of ideas from week to week for the different segments. So we were working hard to come up with fun and interesting ideas, when one day Eilif had an idea we got quite excited about: What if a New York Mafioso decided to go into witness protection in Lillehammer, after watching the 1994 Olympics on television? We were really enthusiastic about that idea, but it didn't fit the parameters of the show we were working on at all, so we put it in the drawer and thought we would maybe turn it into a book or maybe a movie script one day. A year or so later, Eilif had become head of development in the production company we worked for and was in charge of coming up with a drama series pitch. And then we started talking about that mobster/ immigrant idea that we really liked, and realized that it could serve as an interesting premise for a drama series.

We developed and produced the first season with NRK, and Netflix got involved when we were editing it. At the time, in 2011, few people in Norway had heard about the streaming service, so when we told people our series had been sold to Netflix, we had to explain - "it's like iTunes, only with television". Most people just shrugged and thought nothing of it.

So Netflix had little impact on the content of Season 1. In the subsequent seasons, they were also laid-back, and we never got notes. The most striking transition for us was the scope of the distribution. As soon as Netflix started streaming *Lilyhammer*, comments and tweets from very different parts of the world started pouring in. It was a highly unexpected and interesting experience. It turned out that the same things that worked in Norway, worked in the other territories. We had made a show about local issues, specific for a small town in Norway, and were surprised to see the response that it got and is still getting today.

***Lilyhammer* cleverly combines American and Norwegian elements, and the Norwegian landscape itself would probably have an exotic appeal for most Americans. Where did that idea (of combining a New Yorker and Lillehammer) come from?**

Bjørnstad & Skodvin: We are not sure exactly where the idea came from, but we were fans of gangster comedies and read a lot of books in that genre by authors like Elmore Leonard. We started talking about what it would be like if a character like Chili Palmer went to Norway instead of California, how much stronger the clash of cultures would be in a social democratic society like ours. About the same time we read somewhere that the Lillehammer Olympics, because of the Tonya Harding-Nancy Kerrigan conflict, was one of the most viewed TV moments in the States, and it dawned on us that it was plausible that a mobster could have watched it and thought "hey, that would be a nice little town for me to go to if I ever need to hide, because nobody would look for me there".

So what attracted us was to explore what would happen if a person like that, someone who is used to taking what he wants when he wants it, who is like a predator in his jungle, crashes into the security net of a social democracy, and is labeled as an immigrant in need of help.

The series is a charming combination of humor and gangster series. Could

you say a few words about the unique mix of genres and tonalities in the series?

Bjørnstad & Skodvin: We wanted to make a gangster comedy, because we are fans of that genre and it has hardly been made in Norway before. At the same time we wanted to explore different sides of social democracy and bureaucracy that are fun to see through the eyes of an outsider. So we had a hard-hitting protagonist and a satirical scope of the story, and that can balance out the comedy in an interesting way.

The main thing we learned from making three seasons of *Lilyhammer* is that a TV series can be anything you want it to be. You don't have to be constrained by genre, it is possible to have plot lines and scenes that cross over, that are unexpected and don't "belong". TV drama is a young and quickly evolving art form.

Why do you think that streaming channels like Netflix and now HBO Nordic are interested in these kinds of Scandinavian and even transatlantic co-productions? Is there a heightened awareness these days of the qualities of Scandinavian storytellers and an interest in the uniquely Scandinavian tone, style and setting?

Bjørnstad & Skodvin: There is a lot of high quality drama coming from Scandinavia these days, and the international audience seems to have a growing appetite for it.

Partly it has to do with streaming that the audience has been truly globalized. Now even parts of the American TV audience have discovered that it is possible to watch a subtitled series. Also, with the huge number of shows being produced now, the audience seems to be looking for something different, like an exotic snack every now and then.

We don't know how long the hype will last, hopefully for the rest of our lifetime.

After the success of *Lilyhammer*, you made another streaming series called *Beforeigners*, this time for HBO Nordic. *Beforeigners*, like your previous series, combined local or regional elements with qualities that we would naturally associate with American genre fiction. Where did the idea come from, and what prompted you to develop that series?

Bjørnstad & Skodvin: After *Lilyhammer* we wanted to do something different. We love low sci-fi stories like *The Leftovers* and *District 9*, and thought that a story in that genre would be interesting to create and also feel fresh in a Nordic context. But Norwegian broadcasters have been very skeptical of sci-fi, and also it is hard to come up with a concept that is strong enough.

We had been working on ideas for a show like that on and off for a couple of years, when we were invited to pitch for HBO Nordic, and we realized that this could be our shot at making a sci-fi series. About the same time, Eilif came up with an idea that we were immediately attracted to: What would happen if refugees started arriving, not from distant places, but from ancient times? What would that do to our society? How would nowadays folks react to "temporal refugees"? Also, what would these new/old-comers think of our world? Would they deem it progressed or decayed? Early on, we decided that we wanted it to be a buddy cop story about a contemporary policeman who is teamed up with the first police officer with an Old Norse background, the former shield maiden Alfhildr. But it started with a fascination for the world of *Beforeigners*. We spent a lot of time exploring it in great detail.

Lilyhammer and Beforeigners have come in the midst of a changing TV landscape. How would you describe the changes that have occurred within the last 25 years?

Bjørnstad & Skodvin: The TV business has been revolutionized by the new technology. The proliferation of channels and streaming services has pushed towards an extreme multitude of shows and a limitless consumption of TV drama. It is overwhelming and quite inspiring.

From Shakespearean Tragedy to Internet Sensation: *House of Cards*

House of Cards is an American version of a British miniseries trilogy as well as a re-adaptation of Michael Dobbs' political thriller from 1989, and although the two televisual versions have some similarities, they are also vividly different. What was the background for your series?

Willimon: I have a good deal of admiration for the BBC version that Andrew Davies conceived and made, but I think that version was a bit more tongue-in-cheek, veered more towards satire than ours did, in a way that was very effective. For our story and an American audience, chiefly to begin with - we ended up having a global audience, of course - I wanted to steer more towards drama. Not to get rid of satirical elements altogether, but to spend more time exploring the humanity and inhumanity of Frank Underwood and the other characters. Of course the British version only had 12 episodes in total, over three years, and our first season alone had 13 episodes, so we knew we had to dig a lot deeper into the narrative substance of our characters. And when you start veering more towards drama, away from satire, that will always change the tone. You're not necessarily approaching it with as much of a comedic sensibility, and if you watch the BBC version of *House of Cards*, it's not a comedy *per se*, but satire does certainly lend itself towards that.

In terms of the language, we were an American colloquial construct and idiom, so you're going to automatically see differences in terms of cadence, compared to the British version, especially since our lead character, we wrote him so that he would be from the South, which has its own sort of Gothic sensibility that's very different from England.

We developed the first episode over the course of about a year. We stole plenty of things from the BBC version, shamelessly, but more and more it became our own thing and pretty quickly departed from the BBC version within our first few episodes. The other thing is that I wanted to tell the story of a marriage between two people, who when they're working together are able to really amplify each other's power, and when they're working against each other are each other's worst threat.

Over time, I wanted the audience to root as much, if not more, for Claire than Frank. Here you've been following this guy who's been speaking to you for several seasons, and perhaps the more treacherous and effective of the two, Claire Underwood, in her own way, has come to the fore and has surpassed him as the protagonist.

In both the British version and your series, there are numerous examples of direct address, a stylistic element that might remind the viewer of European New Wave films from the 1960s and 1970s and Shakespearean soliloquies, but which was also seen in forgotten cult series like *The Strange World of Gurney Slade* (ITV, 1960). What was the idea and inspiration behind these 'asides'?

There's nothing revolutionary about breaking the fourth wall. But you're absolutely right. We lifted that from the BBC series that lifted it from Shakespeare who lifted it from the Greeks. It goes back to the earliest days of dramatic narrative. And, as you mention, it's been used in film for quite some time. You can see it in the *Nouvelle Vague* and in films like *La Jetée* - that moment where the eye opens, looking straight at the camera - and you can cite plenty of other examples prior to that. Maybe not as much in television, and perhaps the reason that it feels a little bit more shocking in television is because there's an intimacy to television. Most of the time people are watching it in their home, and they're not in a theater full of people to share that experience with, so when the protagonist turns and speaks to you, it feels quite personal, in a way that it might not as much in theater or in cinema. We absolutely used that every which way we could imagine, exploiting direct addresses to advance the story. And many of them never made it onto the screen. For every direct address that we see on screen, there's probably one that we got rid of. That's a very difficult thing to write because you are intentionally putting a pause on the dramatic action and threatening the viability or the suspension of disbelief, and yet if you do it right, it can actually accelerate both.

In terms of story and genre, you seem to draw a lot on William Shakespeare and perhaps even Greek and Roman tragedies. Is that the case?

Willimon: In terms of Shakespeare, all authors are constantly going back to that trough, and probably the three plays that we thought most about were *Macbeth*, *Richard III* and *Othello*. Of course there is plenty to be taken from all the other classics as well, but those were the three plays that I thought about consciously.

In a way, serial melodramas or soap operas can be seen as a televisual version of a theatrical and cinematic genre which is rooted in the old tragedies. Though obviously a political thriller, couldn't we describe *House of Cards* as a stylized serial melodrama which goes back to the roots of that genre?

Willimon: Melodrama is an interesting word. Some people use the word disparagingly, others not so at all. It is a modern term that is something of a double-edged sword in that it's used both disparagingly and, in some cases, as a form of praise. In a certain sense, the first real melodrama author was Shakespeare. There are some very soapy elements to Shakespeare, and you start to see melodrama occur when narratives become psychological because you're talking about people's feelings, their emotional states. For the Greeks, even though Medea or Electra is out there beating their chest in grief or anger or what have you, their audience is the Gods. In the performance of a Greek tragedy – as it was performed in Athens – the actors are quite literally standing on the stage speaking outwards to the audience as loudly as they can because they had to reach a lot of people with the power of their voice. The whole thing was direct address. Even when the actors were speaking to each other, they were facing the audience, and there wasn't a notion of subtext or emotional reality in a way that we conceive of it in modern drama – every story, every tragedy was really the same tale, which is that we are subservient to the Gods, and we are subjects to fate, and you can't escape fate.

And fate was external rather than internal. With Shakespeare you start to see the psychological emerge, but there isn't much subtext in Shakespeare. Most of what is felt is being said aloud, and part of that has to do with the stage. You can't have a quiet moment in the dialogue and still hear what was being said. But you did start to see the psychological appear. You could think about someone like Orson Welles, who had no issue with melodrama, or Tennessee Williams who is a great melodramatist.

In terms of melodrama vs. drama, I don't know how much of a useful axis that is to compare because I don't think there's been pure tragedy.

Perhaps you are right, and "melodrama" to me is not a negative word, nor is the word "serial melodrama". One of the most popular Danish film directors, Lars von Trier, is probably most widely known for his melodramas and his work in television.

Willimon: I have not seen his television work, but my favorite film of his is *The Five Obstructions* (*De fem benspænd*). The one he made with Jørgen Leth. I love that director, and I watch his film *The Perfect Human* (*Det perfekte menneske*) at least once or twice a year. It truly is perfect.

If not a serial melodrama in a traditional sense, *House of Cards* displays a form of heightened realism. It references political history but also introduces some extreme, if not hyperbolic, actions and forms of behavior. How do you toe the line between realism and exaggeration?

Willimon: Certainly, we can't look at *House of Cards* as pure naturalism. A guy is turning and speaking directly to the camera after all, and there are certainly these moments of exaggerated behavior which in real life - whatever real life is - would have been highly unlikely or overboard. And certainly, for some people, that did come across as a gimmick, a stunt or as unbelievable. But this is not conceived to be a story told through purely naturalistic behavior, ever. When you look at something like Shakespeare, you have incredibly heightened behavior happening in his tragedies – his comedies, as well – and I wanted a broad enough palette to be able to explore that. You could say that it's so unlikely as to veer towards the impossible. Which president would ever show up at a subway station and push somebody out in front of a moving train? Fine, I will not necessarily argue with you on that. But there's an essential truth to the character that is being dramatized in that moment: I wanted to tell that he was capable of doing that, that in his heart of hearts he was a person who was willing to murder in order to maintain power. I think many powerful people have that instinct within them, and certainly among authoritarian leaders you see quite a bit of murders. If you look at Putin, journalists are murdered frequently. Pushed out of windows, poisoned, shot. I think it's fair to say that Putin is a murderer. Is he doing it with his own two hands? No, but how different is it delegating it to someone and doing it with your own two hands?

So when it came to that scene, I just wanted to close the gap and show that impulse, that desire, that need to maintain power at all cost through his own physical behavior.

We had a sort of rule. Obviously, we were creating a kind of parallel universe. There had never been a president named Frank Underwood. But we didn't want to recreate history from scratch, so we had a rule that we could reference actual history up as far as Clinton, and from that point on we shifted into our parallel history. But it was important, if we're putting him in the actual White House, and that White House is filled with portraits of previous presidents, that it had to have some sort of connection to actual history. Hopefully, it would reinforce the story's poignancy for whatever the contemporary situation would be.

In any case, *House of Cards* is quite stylish, and the style and tone are already established in the iconic title sequence. What were your stylistic principles, and how was the style established?

Willimon: In terms of the title sequence, I have to give the credit entirely to David Fincher who used all of those tracking shots to show a sort of kinetic version of Washington D.C. Most of the images are actually odd angles or places in D.C. from the fringes or places you don't typically see. And then, later, he took out any evidence of human beings, so you have these kinetic landscapes that are devoid of anything human, which gives it this desolate, eerie feeling. There's activity, but not humanity. He worked with an expert in time-lapse photography to achieve that, and when he married the images with Jeff Beal's music, it created one of the more iconic title sequences.

The visual style and performative quality of the show was established by David Fincher, who directed the first two episodes. He really established the look of our show, and in terms of acting it aligned with all of his previous films. There's a dry, winking, almost forbidden nature to the way that his actors perform.

If you look at *Se7en* or *Fight Club* as being thrillers or dramatic, there's an element of humor or perversion to almost everything that he does, and that certainly could be said of Frank Underwood.

As I said, we wanted to do a drama, not a satire. But a drama utterly without humor would fall flat, so we certainly paid attention to extracting humorous

elements whenever we could, in the darkest way possible, of course.
Of course it was a reaction to the script, but it was also him pushing me and the script, and that created the foundation we used for every episode that followed.

Some staples of Fincher's aesthetic certainly found their way into the show. He established some stylistic principles, for instance that there would be no lens over 50 mm. Another rule was that there would be no Steadicam or handheld camerawork. Everything had to be on a dolly or a track. We didn't do unmotivated movement with the camera. The camera could only move, if it was motivated by the movement of a character or something within the frame. We also had a very limited color palette, which definitely veered toward neutral; no bright colors. Very rarely in *House of Cards* would we see a bright red or a bright yellow. So at times it had almost a black and white feel, black and white often being associated with drama, and bright colors often being associated with comedy.

There was also an interesting signature approach to lighting. He's very particular about lighting. Often when he was setting up a scene, he was instructing the DP and the lighting department exactly where the lighting elements would go. One example of his approach to lighting is on the stages we built. None of the rooms had ceilings. They all had a translucent screen above which was a lighting unit that would create a flat tone, a light that would pervade space, which meant that you had to rely on the practicals on the ground much less. You were infusing this overall light which allowed you, then, to make more subtle choices with the units on the ground. So all of these technical aspects, I think, contributed to a quite rigorous and specific visual style that Fincher had developed over years through his many films.

House of Cards was the first original Netflix series, and it became a vast streaming and Internet phenomenon. Even Barack Obama tweeted about it. How would you say that the TV landscape has changed with the advent of streaming?

Willimon: How have streaming channels changed the TV landscape? In some ways fundamentally and in some ways not at all. Fundamentally in terms of many aspects: One is the volume of production. There's more television shows being made now than any time before in television history – I think it's over 600 shows – so the amount of content, of stories being produced, is extraordinary. Two, you are now seeing shows that find a global audience instantly. It's not true of every show, obviously – the traditional model was a show created in a given territory and then sold internationally – but when you look at Netflix, Amazon or Disney+, you're seeing the total vertical integration of global streamers. You have shows that are reaching the entire world on the same day.

Of course - and this has been written about much, certainly in the first few years of *House of Cards* - there is the bingeing phenomenon, too. We were the first show to deliver an entire season at once. Now, bingeing existed before that. For example, I watched the first three seasons of *The Sopranos* within a week on DVD. I didn't watch them when they originally aired, but when I finally got around to watching *The Sopranos*, I watched the first three seasons all at once. So people had been bingeing with the use of DVD and VHS prior to streaming, but with streaming it became really a quite frequent and intended phenomenon. I don't know if that necessarily affects the storytelling *per se*. A story has to work regardless of whether it's being binged or not - not everyone binges, people might watch two episodes and wait a week, then watch three and wait two weeks and then watch another one - so it has to work both ways. But it does create the possibility for certain stories to function better in one or two sittings, being viewed almost like a very long movie, to have their place in the narrative landscape.

So what will be next? How do you think that the TV landscape will change in the coming years?

Willimon: I think you'll see more shows, you'll see them reaching greater audiences, and you'll see those audiences viewing those shows in different ways. I also think with the volume of work that's being created, you have the opportunity for stories that would not have ever made their way to traditional broadcasting on network television now have their day in court. There are smaller shows with smaller budgets that are more niche, that are odder, weirder and more experimental that get a chance. It's almost the equivalent of indie filmmaking in television, and what that has led to is a scenario where there is probably more experimental work done in television than there is in cinema, in terms of the amount of people that are niches and what people have access to. And I think that is why so many cinema directors, actors and writers have begun making the move to television because they actually have the opportunity to tell stories that the big film studios won't touch any more. Of course there is still great independent cinema being made - we've seen in the last few years some extraordinary independent films - but I think if you talked to screenwriters, at least in the US, they would say it's increasingly difficult to make those films. So those filmmakers either want to move into television or, in many cases, make their feature films for streamers who will actually fund the films that the big studios won't. These are important changes that have occurred over the last decade, even less than that. It feels like it's been a long time, but we've only really had seven years of streaming.

But in a way it hasn't changed at all. A story is a story. We were just referencing the Greeks, Shakespeare and Tennessee Williams. It's the same universal questions that we are confronting now that we saw in the works of those masters many decades and centuries ago. They are the same as they were when the first cave person got up in front of the other cave people and told a story for the first time. The format, the medium, the technique, the distribution model – all of those can evolve over time. But we are still human. We are still dealing with the same universal truths and questions, and that will never change. So the role of the artist, the role of the filmmaker remains the same which is to investigate ourselves and the world around us and then exploit whatever medium is available to him or her at a given time to communicate that to audiences.

I do think it's important to remember that über-historical perspective which is that cinema itself is not much more than a century old, and cinema was probably the primary art form of the 20th century. I can make the argument that video games will be the primary art form of the 21st century. We're still in the very early days of the 21st century, and in 1920 you wouldn't necessarily have predicted that cinema was going to be the primary art form. Charlie Chaplin was seen as a clown, as low art, if his work was seen as art at all. Novels and theater were still primary in the early days of the 20th century, but of course films ended up eclipsing them, and I believe that will probably be true of video games or hybrids – interactive storytelling – in the decades to come. But before cinema you had the theater. Photography itself wasn't even invented until the 1800s, and in the first few decades of photography it was not seen as an art form. In fact, most of the photographers that were working in any way artistically were just trying to recreate painterly images or tableaus. Using photography, they were still working within the language of painting. Prior to all of these, I would say in the 19th and 18th centuries novels and operas had supremacy and before that poetry.

Our mechanisms as artists for how we communicate to each other change over time, and often they're driven by technology. And artists tend to be on the vanguard of exploring and exploiting the technological evolution. But you can look at an opera from the 1700s, and you can look at a television show now in 2020 or a video game 30 years from now, and they're still going to be dealing with the same fundamental questions: Who are we? What is our purpose? How should we treat each other? What does it all mean? These will remain the constants.

Chapter 3

Beyond Borders: Transnational Television and Glocal Perspectives

> Contemporary television industries are now characterized by dense, overlapping palimpsests of technologies, markets, and viewing habits, none of which are easily contained within national borders. As a result, scholars are increasingly conceptualizing television as both a national and a transnational technology.
> - Ramon Lobato, media scholar[243]

> The most interesting development over the last years - and I think Netflix is pretty responsible for it - is that instead of adaptations we now watch regional series in their original language in a global distribution.
> - Hagai Levi, TV creator[244]

Though not a Netflix original *per se*, *Lilyhammer* was the first "exclusive" series on the streaming platform, a Norwegian-American gangster comedy set in the titular Norwegian town and starring the actor and co-writer Steven Van Zandt as an all-American mobster in a foreign environment. The premise of the series was essentially transnational, combining regional locations and aspects with traditional American tropes and genres. Even the title, an Americanized version of the Norwegian placename Lillehammer, reflected the transnational premise, and the series became a national success in Norway, where it was aired on NRK1, and a global phenomenon on Netflix.

Following their success with *Lilyhammer*, Anne Bjørnstad and Eilif Skodvin approached the Scandinavian streaming service HBO Nordic with an idea for a new TV series: *Beforeigners*. This series, again, would combine genre fiction (in this case science fiction) with regional aspects and Norse mythology, and HBO Nordic - which had never previously produced its own fiction, but only acted as a streaming outlet for HBO with added content from other networks - were open to Bjørnstad and Skodvin's vision. "Because of the sagas we know a lot about the Vikings and their way of life," as the creators explain.

> Their culture is incredibly fascinating and lends itself easily to drama. That being said, it was not our impression that HBO Nordic was looking for Viking themed or even historically themed shows. Their approach seems to be very open, and the only thing they have pushed for is that we should not be afraid to explore, as long as we stay true to our original vision.[245]

At a time when TV series about Vikings and Norse mythology are in vogue (cf. *Vikings*, *RIPA* and the Danish-Norwegian Netflix production *Ragnarok*), *Beforeigners* looks like an interesting and timely combination of Nordic history, mythology and language and a genre tradition, which is more broadly popular internationally than in Scandinavia. The basic premise is somewhat quirky, dealing with a group of people from the past (e.g. from the 1800s and the Viking Age) who suddenly show up in the present day as a sort of 'native immigrants'. These "beforeigners" ("fremvandrere" in Norwegian), who speak an older and more traditional language, struggle to communicate with their modern countrymen, and, in that sense, the series seems to reflect the current issues and policies concerning refugees and immigration in Scandinavia. As Bjørnstad and Skodvin put it:

> We thought it was fun to create a circumstance where no one can say, "Go back to where you come from," to the strangers. Because they were here first. In the *Beforeigners* universe, nobody cares about immigration anymore because these new refugees put the whole thing into perspective.
>
> We also like the notion that all human beings are time travelers. Our protagonist Lars is a modern man who has had his life turned upside-down by "timeigration". It has changed the city he lives in and his work, and his wife has left him for a man from the 19th century. So Lars, like the beforeigners, longs for the past, and his past is as inaccessible to him as the Viking or Stone Age is to the other characters.[246]

As implied by Bjørnstad and Skodvin, *Beforeigners* can be seen as a meeting point between a regional history and a global present, and in that sense the series, in terms of plot, language and distribution, reflects the current TV landscape. *Beforeigners* was envisioned as "an eclectic mix of elements, moods and styles," combining regional history and elements of *Nordic Noir* with an expansive mythology akin to *The Leftovers* (HBO, 2014-2017), and it illustrates a 'transgressive' tendency in the modern mediascape where TV series often transcend national territories while mixing different genres, cultural traditions and regional aspects.[247] The series is produced by the Norwegian company Rubicon for HBO Nordic, a streaming service connected to the American cable network HBO, and it is both Norwegian and international, consciously regional and potentially global.[248] The series was made available to European and North American viewers via HBO Europe, HBO Now and HBO Go, and it reflects an "authorial vision" from Bjørnstad and Skodvin, but also a strategic interest from the global streaming services in regional productions and non-English content.

In this chapter, I will explore some of the *glocal* aspects of the current TV landscape, from transnational co-operation and international co-productions to transnational remakes and local-language originals.[249] The chapter is not an exhaustive study of those interconnected phenomena, but an introduction to some perspectives and issues that are crucial to understanding television production in the *multiplatform era* and helpful when trying to understand the dialogic relationship between different cultural traditions and industries. The modern TV series is not just moving "beyond" television in terms of distribution. It is also moving across national borders, connecting

Fig. 13-14: *Beforeigners* (2019-), created by Anne Bjørnstad and Eilif Skodvin, is the first original TV series produced for HBO Nordic and illustrates an interesting tendency in the current TV landscape to mix regional language, history and traditions with international genre fiction and streaming services. © HBO Nordic, courtesy of Celine Ryel.

different industries and traditions in terms of storytelling, style and genre.

"For much of its history, television has been closely bound to a national territory," as Jean K. Chalaby writes.[250] This chapter explores how the ties to national territories have been loosened, just as the ties to broadcast media, TV schedules and the television set itself, resulting in a complex TV landscape and some interesting examples of *cross-influencing* and cross-cultural exchange.

Transnational Television

In his seminal book *Netflix Nations: The Geography of Digital Distribution*, Ramon Lobato argues that the current TV landscape is characterized by various strategies concerning internationalization, globalization and localization. "The history of broadcast television," as Lobato writes, "is closely tied to the nation-state," and the "nationwide distribution of television has shaped advertising markets, has propagated official language policies, and has established common frames of national discourse."[251] With new forms of distribution, however, those ties are being weakened, and the TV landscape is undergoing fundamental changes. Those changes, Lobato posits, can be traced back to the 1970s and 1980s with the advent of satellite and cable distribution and "successive waves of liberalization [sweeping] through the international TV system, leading to the privatization of state broadcasters, and the deregulation of infrastructure, advertising, and content control."[252]

Though we still do not have a single "world-wide television service," as Lobato writes, we do have a number of *transnational multiplatform television services*, from international news channels like CNN to subscription-based streaming services like Netflix and Amazon Prime and relatively open-access video sharing platforms like YouTube.[253] These are all transnational, albeit in different ways, and, according to Lobato, the concept of *transnational television* covers many different - interconnected - phenomena. These include:

- The cross-border *mobility* of television content, talent, and formats
- The *interaction* of international broadcasters, regulators and institutions
- The *cosmopolitanization* of television audiences, styles, and viewing habits.[254]

From Transnational Co-operation to International Co-Productions

Obvious examples of *transnational television* can be seen in the great variety of transnational collaborations and international co-productions. In itself a vast field, it is important, as Julia Hammett-Jamart, Petar Mitric and Eva Novrup Redvall note, to distinguish between different categories of transnational collaborations. In their anthology, *European Film and Television Co-Production: Policy and Practice* (2018), the editors distinguish between *transnational cooperation* and *international co-production* where the latter is characterized by "the involvement of two or more producers from different countries collaborating creatively and financially on a project." Moreover, they distinguish between *official* and *unofficial co-productions* - the former "occurring under auspices of formal intergovernmental agreements," and the latter "constituting the various types of joint venture that occur between producers of different countries on a private basis."[255]

The famous Scandinavian crime series *Bron/Broen* (*The Bridge*, DR/SVT, 2011-2018) - a series that, together with *Forbrydelsen* (*The Killing*, DR, 2007-2011), came to popularize the *Nordic Noir* genre - is an interesting example of an international co-production. The title refers to the bridge between Sweden and Denmark where a fictional murder takes place, and it also cleverly alludes to the transnational nature of the series itself. Co-produced by the Swedish and Danish broadcasters SVT and DR, and conceptualized by the Swedish and Danish writers Hans Rosenfeldt, Camilla Ahlgreen and Nikolaj Scherfig, *Bron/Broen* uses different languages (as evident in the title) and Danish and Swedish actors/characters (Sofia Helin as Saga Norén and Kim Bodnia as Martin Rohde), who humorously display some national differences and stereotypes. In that sense, *Bron/Broen* may be regarded as a clever attempt at involving different markets, exploiting different funds and pooling together resources from two major broadcasters in order to produce a series that can compete in a global TV landscape by combining regional qualities (e.g. the language, the tone and the locations) with an international budget.[256]

The transgressive nature of *Bron/Broen* is not only illustrated in its title, but also in its evocative title sequence (where the bridge is a recurring visual element) and the opening sequence where the corpse is located on the exact borderline between Sweden and Denmark. This motif is then re-used in the two transnational remakes of *Bron/Broen*: the FX series *The Bridge* (2013-2014), which takes place on the US-Mexican border, and the British-French co-production *The Tunnel* (Sky Atlantic/Canal+, 2013-2018), a so-called "subterranean adaptation" that takes place inside the Euro-Tunnel.[257] In a fascinating and inventive audiovisual essay, media scholars Janet McCabe and Catherine Grant convincingly illustrate the visual similarities (e.g. the use of lighting, *aerial shots* and visual motives) in the three versions of *Bron/Broen*, arguing that these particular series mirror the processes and issues connected with transnational television in general:

> In these transnational in-between spaces of somewhere and anywhere, where jurisdictions collide, otherness is encountered and cross-border cooperation demanded, it is a female fatality – with a body that quite literally splits in two before our very eyes – that conjures this imaginary transnational television space into existence.
> There is, of course, nothing particularly novel in the sight of a female cadaver; in fact a gendered, often sexually violated, corpse has long been a common generic feature of television crime. Such desecrated femininity speaks to a range of societal inequalities and discrimination, of inequities in power and wealth, told through the body's storytelling proximity from *inside* a national broadcasting territory; but a corpse split in two at the border creates a new visual language with a global reach and awakens different ideas and thoughts about injustice and inequities spilling across national territorial lines.[258]

The title and the visual motif may both allude to the transnational nature of the series itself, yet they also reflect the central themes of transgressive behavior and border-crossing crime. These elements, though major concerns in a globalized world, are not new to television, and *the dead girl show*, as Alice Bolin puts it, is something of a staple in American TV.[259] In the second part of this book, I will return to those elements and the connections between *Bron/Broen*, *Nordic Noir*, other national variations of crime and detective fiction and how they mutually cross-reference and cross-influence each other in the modern TV landscape.

Another TV series that deals with border-crossing crime is Stefano Sollima's Italian thriller *ZeroZeroZero* (2020-), which was produced for Sky Atlantic, Canal+ and Amazon Prime. A transnational collaboration, Sollima's series was co-financed by different companies and created by three writers (Sollima, Leonardo Fasoli and Maurizio Katz), but it is usually described as an Italian series, not an international co-production. The transnational aspects in Sollima's series are still evident, however, because it employs actors from America (Dane DeHaan), England (Andrea Riseborough), Ireland (Gabriel Byrne) and Mexico (Noé Hernández Álvarez) and directors from Argentina (Pablo Trapero) and Denmark (Janus Metz). Depicting the cruel and cynical international drug trade, *ZeroZeroZero* also takes place in various different cities, including Monterrey in Mexico, Gioia Tauro in Italy and New Orleans in the US, and it employs a vast variety of language, including English, French, Spanish, Italian, Calabrian, Wolof and Arabic (Fig. 15-17).

Fig. 15: The Danish director Janus Metz and the American actor Dane DeHaan on location in Mexico for the Italian series *ZeroZeroZero* (2020-), a transnational collaboration that depicts the international drug trade, using various different locations, languages and international talents. © Rosa Hadit, courtesy of Janus Metz and Rosa Hadit.

Fig. 16-17: Janus Metz on location in Senegal and Calabria for Stefano Sollima's TV series *ZeroZeroZero* (2020-). © Stefania Rosini, courtesy of Janus Metz and Stefania Rosini.

Described by *The New York Times* as a "globe-trotting thriller," *ZeroZeroZero* was unusual, even for an international collaboration with a big budget, inasmuch as nearly all the scenes are shot on location, despite the series taking place in various different countries and dangerous regions across many parts of the world.²⁶⁰ As the Danish director Janus Metz explains:

> They had seen *Borg/McEnroe* and thought that my directing style was a good fit for the series, so they asked me whether I wanted to follow Stefano and direct Episodes 3, 4 and 5. Then I read the project description, and I thought it was a really interesting script, and it was a fascinating challenge having to create a dialogue between all these different places, shooting the series in multiple different locations. It is very much a location-driven show, and almost all of the scenes are shot where we claim to be, even the ones that are shot in the mountainous villages where the mafia operates. We are the only ones who have ever been allowed to shoot in that area, and it adds a certain authenticity to the series. Nearly all the scenes in the show are shot on location, except those in Mali, which were shot in Morocco, because those regions in Mali are extremely dangerous; most of them are controlled by Islamic terrorist organizations.²⁶¹

The creator, Stefano Sollima, adapted the series from a docufictional book by Roberto Saviano, who had also made the story behind *Gomorra*, which Sollima produced for Sky Atlantic in 2014. The authenticity in Saviano's book is mirrored in the series via the use of location footage and authentic languages and dialects - elements that are reminiscent of Italian Neo-Realism and the televisual work of David Simon.²⁶² The same thing could be said of the kaleidoscopic nature of the narrative, shifting between different places, persons and perspectives. Stylistically, however, the series is closer to *film noir* than to Italian Neo-Realism and David Simon in its use of shifting lighting strategies (often with an expressive use of shadows and contrasts) and different color palettes (from mauve and dark blue to sandy browns and muted earth tones). Accordingly, Mike Hale of *The New York Times* characterizes it as an "operatically scaled gangster melodrama," and Metz describes it as a "symphony of different environments and worlds that converse with each other in complex ways."²⁶³ Generically, the series combines elements from the *noir* and gangster genres with a touch of road movie (connected to the two siblings who have to make sure that a shipment of cocaine travels from Mexico to Italy), and in many ways it reflects a global reality and mediascape. According to Janus Metz:

> It is a series about globalization, you could say, and how cocaine flows through global chains of commerce on the black market. You might describe it as a flip-side version of the global world: the illegal 'shadow economy' behind the 'white economy' that we all know with its flow of ideas, goods and people. And perhaps that 'shadow economy' is as important to the way the world works as the 'white economy', inasmuch as many people earn their living that way. If you follow Saviano's logic, cocaine is as important to the global economy as the production of coffee. In that way, *ZeroZeroZero* naturally reflects the current era with international terror organizations and international drug trafficking as some of the topical issues, and it would not have been the same story if it had been made 20 years ago.²⁶⁴

From Transnational Remakes to Local-Language Originals

> Imitation is the sincerest form of television.
> - *Television Comes of Age (CNN, 2013)*[265]

Transnational collaborations and international co-productions are a significant part of the current TV landscape, but TV series also travel in other ways, as is clear from the *transnational remakes* of non-American series and the international adaptations of various local formats.

The concept of remaking or recycling well-known formats and formulas is not as such new to television. In fact, Derek Kompare argues that American television, despite being associated with "liveness", has a historical predilection for repetition. Since the early days, Kompare argues, the television set has essentially functioned as "a machine of repetition, geared toward the constant recirculation of recorded, already-seen events."[266] Focusing mostly on reruns and syndication, Kompare also describes the American television industry more broadly as a *reproduction economy*, echoing the German philosophers Theodor Adorno and Max Horkheimer and their collective critique of the so-called *culture industry*.[267]

This *reproduction economy* is reflected in the airing of old Hollywood movies (a popular practice since the 1940s), the use of *clip shows* (i.e. TV episodes that mainly consist of previously aired material and flashbacks to earlier episodes) and the long tradition for syndication and reruns. Currently, this tendency is seen in the form of remakes and adaptations of popular series and formats from various countries (a tendency that is experienced across many television genres, from reality and game shows to comedy and drama series).[268]

Today, there are numerous popular examples of such transnational remakes and adaptations. From American remakes of British miniseries like *House of Cards* (BBC, 1990-1995) and Scandinavian *noirs* like *Forbrydelsen* (DR, 2007-2012) and *Bron/Broen* (DR/SVT, 2011-2018) to popular Latin-American *telenovelas* like *Yo soy Betty, la fea* (RCN Televísión, 1999-2001) and renowned Israeli drama series like *BeTipul* (Hot3, 2005-2008) and *Euphoria* (Hot3, 2012-2013).

In that sense, *remake culture* is a central part of TV history, and even though it is not a new phenomenon, *remake television*, as TV scholar Carlen Lavigne calls it, is a notable part of the modern media landscape. "Remakes are pervasive in today's popular culture," as he writes, "whether they take the form of reboots, 're-imaginings,' or overly familiar sequels. Television remakes […] have proven popular with producers and networks interested in building on the nostalgic capital of past hits or giving a second chance to underused properties."[269]

From Telenovela to Transnational Success: *Yo soy Betty, la fea*

Transnational remakes can be seen as an outgrowth of the American remake culture, but also as a way of adapting or translating regional stories to an American storytelling tradition. One of the most notable transnational successes is *Yo soy Betty, la fea*, a Colombian *telenovela* that was aired on RCN from 1999 to 2001 (in the very beginning of the *multiplatform era*), before appearing on one of the biggest Spanish-language networks in the world: Telemundo.[270] *Betty* was a massive success in the Spanish-speaking world, and the first season (335 half-hour episodes) was shown in Spain and all Latin-American countries with ratings that could rival the most popular Brazilian *telenovelas* in history (e.g. *A Escrava Isaura*, Rede Globo, 1976-1977).[271] Furthermore, *Betty* was dubbed in countries such as the Czech Republic, Hungary, Turkey, India and Indonesia, and, at the beginning of the new millennium, Sony was the first company in the world to acquire the adaptation rights. According to Marta Perotta and Lothar Mikos, Sony took advantage of RCN's lack of understanding of *Betty*'s potential, and within a few years the series was remade in numerous national variations.[272]

The premise of *Betty* is simple and deals with a skilled, but unpopular and unattractive young woman, Betty, who works at a fashion magazine where she falls in love with her boss. This basic premise has been kept in most of the different adaptations and remakes, but the first two transnational remakes, the Indian *Jassi Jaissi Koi Nahin* (*There's Nobody Quite Like Jassi*, SET, 2003-2006) and the Russian *Ne Rodis Krasivoy* (*Not Born Beautiful*, CTC, 2005-2006), are still considered to be most loyal remakes. Both of these remakes start out in virtually the same way: We begin with a *low-angle shot* of a fancy office building as seen from the outside (this is where the main character will be going to her interview). In the Indian version, the building is revealed through an upwards going tilt, but in the Russian version there is a downward moving tilt revealing an attractive business woman who looks directly into the lens with great disgust. Apart from that, the two opening sequences are similar. In both instances, we are dealing with a *point of view* technique, as indicated by the use of handheld camera, and we understand that the Russian business woman reacts with disgust to our main character (who, as the title indicates, is not born pretty). A minor difference between the two sequences is that the Indian version uses *elliptical cuts* and *jump-cutting* instead of showing people's reactions to our main character. As we move into the office building, it is still not clear, in the Indian version, whether the main character is beautiful, ordinary or unappealing (nor is this revealed in the title). In the Indian version, it takes 35 seconds before we get the first *reaction shot*, and here the negative reaction is emphasized by a close-up and a sudden sound cue. After two minutes, we see Jassi for the first time, and now we get an explanation for the critical reactions and disgusted faces. In the Russian version, we get the first *reaction shot* after less than 10 seconds, followed by another *reaction shot* from two young boys, who laugh and comment on the protagonist. Within the first 50 seconds, in fact, six people react to the main character, and she is almost denied entry at the door.

Despite these differences, the Indian and Russian remakes are both fairly loyal to the original series - even if the Russian series included more episodes than the original Colombian *telenovela* - and the similarities remain more striking than the differences. Nevertheless, the subtle differences may imply a few things concerning different cultural and national appropriations of the same text.

The media scholar Divya McMillin has used *Betty* as an entry point for examining the importance of beauty for young Indian TV viewers. Based on conversations with more than 200 young people in Bangalore, McMillin poses the question "How Ugly Can *Betty* Be in India?", and she concludes that the remake reflected "the best practices of a transnational television circuit as well as a robust Indian film industry from which television voraciously feeds." The Indian respondents reacted very differently to Jassi: Some respondents were happy to see a potential reaction to the beauty regime in Bollywood, while others were dismayed at the fact that a good series had such an unattractive main character.[273] But the series had many different purposes and reflected a variety of media strategies. The remake practice, in itself, could be seen as a strategic attempt on the part of SET to position itself in relation to Rupert Murdoch's media giant Star Plus. "To stay afloat," McMillin writes, "networks indulged in frenzied purchasing of programme format licenses that had proven successful in foreign markets."[274] But the remaking of *Betty* could also serve other functions, and, according to McMillin, it should also be seen in the light of media pedagogical tendencies in various countries and developing economies in Latin America, Asia and Africa from the 1960s to the 1980s. In programs such as *Hum Log* (Doordashan, 1984-1985), *More Time* (1993) *Twende na wakati* (The Entertainment-Education Network, 1993-), from India, Zimbabwe and Tanzania, the creators and producers tried to introduce pedagogical elements into the fictional worlds and create characters that could show young people how (not) to behave.[275]

Apart from the remakes in Russia and India, *Betty* became the object of numerous transnational remakes and adaptations, including the German series *Verliebt in Berlin* (Sat.1, 2005-2007), the Dutch series *Lotte* (Talpa/RTL Lounge, 2006-2009) and the popular American dramedy *Ugly Betty* (ABC, 2006-2010). The opening sequence of the American series is markedly different from both the Russian and the Indian remakes, inasmuch as it does not use *point of view* and handheld camera. Instead, it opens on a static close-up of Betty, upon which the title card is introduced. After the introduction of the title, we cut back to a *shallow focus* shot of Betty, followed by an *analytical cut* that reveals a couch in the reception of a hip office building. On the couch, Betty is talking to an attractive model who does not seem to notice her, and afterwards Betty is called in for an interview. This brief conversation is shot in a traditional *shot/reverse-shot* style, and here we get the first reaction to Betty and her looks.

This opening seems noticeably different from the original series and the other transnational remakes, and it neatly follows the principles known from classical Hollywood cinema. Classical Hollywood films often use *prompt character introductions* and various cutting techniques to focus the audience's attention on the main action, to create a sense of continuity and orientation (the use of *analytical cuts* and *shot/reverse-shot* editing are prime examples of this).[276] Subjective realism, as indicated in the use of *point of view* and subjective camera, is more closely related to art cinema. This could be a possible explanation for the differences between ABC's remake and the other transnational remakes of *Betty*, but the stationary camera and the use of *shallow focus* give the American remake a sense of 'quality' or high production value, as opposed to the jerky handheld camera and 4:3 aspect-ratio (known from traditional television).

Beyond the Bridge: Remaking Scandinavian Television[277]

When writing about transnational remakes of popular TV series, one immediately comes to think of Scandinavian export successes in the form of *Forbrydelsen* and *Bron/Broen*. Those two series in particular have been the object of much debate and numerous academic projects, and much has been written about *Nordic Noir* in general and Scandinavian TV series that travel.[278]

Søren Sveistrup's crime series, *Forbrydelsen*, about the killing of a young high school student, Nanna Birk Larsen, quickly became a notable success in Denmark and abroad. After the first two seasons, England opened their eyes to the phenomenon that was *Forbrydelsen*, and it suddenly became hip to watch TV series with subtitles while wearing Icelandic jumpers. "The Killing puts torchlight on subtitled drama," as it said in a British article from November 18, 2011.[279] From then on, the term *Nordic Noir* became a widespread designation and a well-known phenomenon. The term - though often used broadly as a collective name for all crime stories made in the Nordic countries - is used to describe the dark, melancholy tone of many Nordic crime series and their combination of mystery, eeriness, psychological realism and gloomy weather.[280] The DVD version of *Forbrydelsen* was just the starting point, and soon the American *basic cable* channel, AMC, purchased the rights to remake the series in an American context, whereas the rights to the Swedish-Danish co-production *Bron/Broen*, as mentioned above, were sold to various countries. Following the American and British-French remakes (*The Bridge* and *The Tunnel*), numerous other countries have secured the rights to adapt or remake *Bron/Broen*, including Germany/Austria, Russia/Estonia and Asia (where the action will take place on the border between Malaysia and Singapore).

The term *Nordic Noir* was popularized in 2011, and critics have highlighted the slow-paced realism, the strong female characters and the *noir*-like darkness as characteristics of many of the Scandinavian drama series.[281] Following shows like *Forbrydelsen*, *Broen/Bron* and *Den som dræber* (*The One Who Kills*, TV2/Viaplay, 2011-), Scandinavian crime series were beginning to travel overseas, both through licensing agreements and transnational remakes.[282] *Forbrydelsen* became an almost immediate international success, and in the wake of its success, DR began to look for new ways to employ external funding, apart from the funding coming from DR, media licence and regional programs such as *Film i Skåne*. These would include 'co-funding with external partners,' 'canned programme sales,' 'pre-sales of canned programmes,' 'format/remake sales,' and 'international funds'.[283] In other words, *Forbrydelsen* did not just introduce a new wave of Scandinavian crime series; it also changed DR's financial strategies and prompted other channels in Denmark to experiment with television drama and original programming.

In that sense, the *Nordic Noir* genre was undoubtedly influential, but it was, itself, influenced by American television shows from the 1980s and early 1990s. During the so-called "Golden Age" of Danish television drama, approximately stretching from Lars von Trier's *Riget* (*The Kingdom*, DR, 1994) and onwards, the Danish producer Sven Clausen looked to the United States for potential sources of inspiration.[284] Hoping to revive and reinvigorate Danish television drama, Clausen went on an "inspiration trip" to America in 1996 where he became smitten by the style and the production process behind realistic cop shows such as *Hill Street Blues*, *Homicide* and *NYPD Blue* (ABC, 1993-2005). "The production community behind the Danish TV series," writes TV historian Jakob Isak Nielsen, "has been actively engaged in invoking national specificity and Americanization to explain courses of action that led to [the] 'Golden Age' [of Danish television drama]."[285]

In that sense, Danish crime series like *Forbrydelsen* and *Bron/Broen* were inspired by American ancestors (I will expand upon this aspect in the second part of this book), yet they later became a point of inspiration for modern American television drama, travelling overseas as subtitled entertainment or in the form of transnational remakes. The showrunners behind the American remake of *Forbrydelsen*, Veena Sud and Elwood Reid, have described the Danish 'mother series' as a "beautiful poem" that they both wanted to present to the American TV audience, and the opening of *The Killing* is also relatively loyal to its Danish original.²⁸⁶ In the course of the first season, however, *The Killing* started digressing from its Danish source, perhaps due to the shorter season and episode lengths (AMC's remake consisted of thirteen 45-minute episodes, whereas *Forbrydelsen I* consisted of twenty 58-minute episodes). Two central consequences of this are: (1) That the pacing and tonality of the American version differ from the Danish original (there is more room for melodrama and realism in the Danish version), and (2) that the murderer is not revealed in the Season 1 finale of the American series.

In an article from *The New York Times*, "The Danes Do Murder Differently," Mike Hale also notes a few other variations, including the introduction of new side characters and side plots in the American version.²⁸⁷ The Danish producer Piv Bernth also finds significant differences between the Danish series and the American remake, especially concerning the atmosphere, the characters and the plot. "It becomes gradually more American," Bernth says, "with a faster pacing, more action and a tendency to explain things." *The Killing*, which was canceled after the first season and later resurrected by Netflix, is not markedly different or disloyal to its source material, however, and the introduction of Sofie Gråbøl as Dep. Attorney Christina Nielsen in the beginning of the second season looks like a nod to the original series. ²⁸⁸

Following DR, the Norwegian broadcaster NRK also started producing some notable TV series that, in different ways, began to travel across different media, platforms and nations. The most obvious example in this context is the modern teen drama *SKAM* (NRK, 2015-2017) that became a huge hit in Norway with more than 1.2 million viewers per week (in a country consisting of only five million people). *SKAM* became known as a *multi-medial, character-based* series that integrated social media where the fictional characters had Instagram profiles and where they, on a daily basis, published comments on the series' website (in the third season, more than 135 updates were published on the website, including 48 video clips).²⁸⁹ The success of *SKAM* led to various transnational remakes in seven different countries, and *SKAM France* (France.tv Slash, 2018-) and *SKAM Austin* (Facebook Watch, 2018-) have both premiered on new streaming services that are specifically tailored to young audiences. Most of the remakes follow the structure of Julie Andem's original series, with the exception of the French version (which expands the story by a few seasons) and the Spanish version (where Jente-Chris is the main character in the second season).²⁹⁰

Andem's series (cf. Fig. 18) became a transnational phenomenon, influencing teen drama and young adult fiction in numerous other countries, and that particular aspect will be explored in the second part of this book where I focus on new tendencies and approaches concerning style, storytelling and

Fig. 18: Julie Andem's SKAM (NRK, 2015-2017) became a global hit with its shifting perspectives and *multi-medial* approach, and it became the object of several transnational remakes. Photo: NRK.

genre.

In the context of cinematic remakes, the French critic André Bazin has described the American procedure as "cultural imperialism" or even "economic terrorism," arguing that Hollywood, by adapting films from different European and Asian countries, took some culturally specific stories, removed their cultural heritage and re-sold them to an American and international audience.[291] This critique, however popular and broadly circulated, fails to acknowledge the complex relationship that is at play in transnational remakes where different nations, industries and institutions are mutually - though not necessarily equally - dependent on each other. Moreover, the idea of *cultural* or *national specificity* is problematic in itself, due to the constant flow of different traditions, styles and storytelling practices and the elusiveness of cultural and national identity. "What makes a TV series uniquely 'American' or specifically 'Danish'," one might ask. Bearing in mind the potential pitfalls of *cultural essentialism*, it is possible to see how different televisual traditions influence each other in a global TV landscape through international co-productions, transnational collaborations and remakes as well as global distribution. And this exchange does not simply equal "Americanization," even if American streaming services seem to be defining global distribution.

Local-Language Originals and the Challenges of Localization

"The history of transnational television is full of [...] frictions between the global and the local."[292] Thus writes Ramon Lobato, citing the early attempts at localization for US-based channels such as National Geographic and Discovery in the 1980s and 1990s. When talking and writing about transnational television, we often focus on how TV series travel (i.e. how Danish crime series are sold or adapted in the US, how Latin-American *telenovelas* are remade across large parts of the world, or how Norwegian teen dramas become global phenomena). What we often forget is the aspect of *localization* and the interest from global streaming services in *local* content. Not necessarily because local content sells or travels (thus having *global potential*), but because local markets, in and of themselves, are interesting to global streamers like Netflix. As Amanda D. Lotz writes:

> Although television fiction has long reached multinational markets, it has typically prioritized a first domestic market, or markets in the case of co-production. In some cases, profoundly local original series developed by multinational streamers have proven very successful (*Narcos*, *13 Reasons Why*), which will perhaps discourage the development of 'Europudding' - or global pudding in this case - that has drawn criticism in previous efforts to tell stories for multinational audiences.[293]

As the Israeli TV creator Hagai Levi noted at the opening of this chapter, one of the most profound changes in the TV landscape, over the last decade, lies in the increased (strategic) focus on local content. And as the Danish TV creator Ida Maria Rydén says:

> I was at a worldwide conference for script writers and TV creators last year, and one of the major statements was "local is global." There was an intense interest in local series such as *La Casa de Papel* and *Sacred Games*.
> We have always talked about combining *identification* and *fascination* where arenas, such as the funeral home in *Six Feet Under*, can be fascinating. But now, in a global market, the different countries or local regions can be fascinating, and this is a new thing.[294]

In time, this shift might lead to a decline in transnational remakes, just as it might "discourage the development of 'Europudding'." That development is important and potentially challenging for local producers and national broadcasters, but it is likewise important and challenging in a global perspective, inasmuch as the flow and mobility of local content and talents invariably - though often in complex and elusive ways - affects American TV production and taste cultures. As the British producer Charlie Hanson (*After Life*, Netflix, 2019-) puts it:

> We used to make movies and TV and wait till somebody else did the remake, but we don't have to do that anymore because, basically, every little particular, local story, if it's particular and real, can resonate in any culture. [...] That is a major change for me in my career: That you can appeal to people across the globe and find an audience.[295]

That global streaming services like Netflix have begun focusing on local markets and content is evident, perhaps coinciding with the fact that the per-

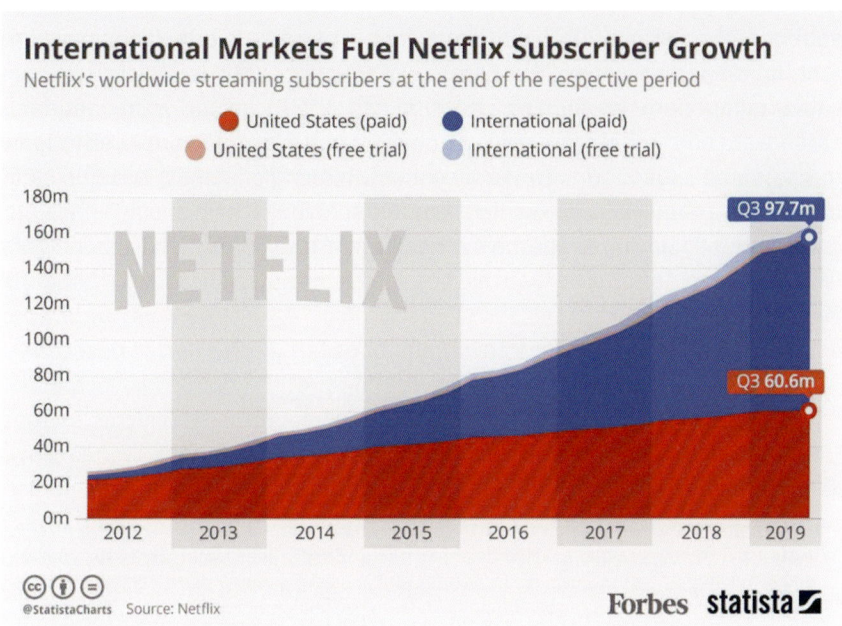

Fig. 19: National vs. International Netflix Subscribers. Source: Forbes, 2019.

centage of international subscribers to Netflix has now surpassed the number of national subscribers (cf. Fig. 19). This shift in focus has naturally led to certain challenges concerning localization, challenges that National Geographic and Discovery faced already in the 1980s and 1990s. According to Jean K. Chalaby, Discovery and National Geographic were initially "oblivious to local culture and market conditions" and "overestimated audience appetite for foreign programming," and the global streamers in today's TV landscape are looking to better understand local markets, taste culture and viewing patterns.[296] "Local expertise - including staff with a deep understanding of a country's media landscape - is necessary for success," as Ramon Lobato writes. "Tailored strategies and programming are needed for each market."[297]

The feature interview with Kelly Luegenbiehl at the end of this chapter illustrates that Netflix is well aware of these challenges, employing local experts in the hope of finding local talents and gaining a better grasp of different markets with "diverse tastes, income levels, languages, genre preferences, willingness to pay and other factors."[298] Luegenbiehl is the Vice President of International Content at Netflix, and her comments are naturally influenced by her position. What others might describe as an attempt to usurp national talent and monetize regional traditions and taste cultures, at a time when international subscribers are outnumbering the domestic subscribers, Luegenbiehl describes as a positive tendency. According to Luegenbiehl, we are seeing a global interest in regional content, and Neflix is providing local content, co-financing series like *Borgen* (DR/Netflix, 2022) and producing local-language originals such as *The Rain* (2018-2020), for the good of both local viewers and global audiences. Knowing that its future lies in international markets and subscribers, Netflix is cleverly looking overseas, and this *global turn* may also be a strategic way for Netflix to build their own international catalogue, not having to rely on expensive and fragile licensing agreements with the major American broadcasters. As the creator of *The Rain*, Jannik Tai Mosholt, puts it:

> From the beginning, Netflix have known that, in order for them to survive, they need to build a big library of original content, since other channels and companies might at one point remove their content from Netflix, especially if Netflix is becoming too big. Moreover, I think that Netflix may have seen the potential in branching out into different regions, producing local content in different territories, perhaps because it is cheaper to produce stuff abroad than in America, but also because they found out that even local stuff can travel and become global phenomena. Not as much as *Stranger Things*, perhaps, but still enough for Netflix to call it a success and a viable business model. Finally, they might have seen that it is smarter to position themselves in different local markets than it is to compete in the US where they are facing tough competition from national broadcasters and other major streamers.[299]

Whatever the motive, Netflix and other international streaming services are beginning to focus their attention on non-English content, and in shifting their focus to international markets they may in turn have prompted a change among American viewers (who are becoming more open to subtitled entertainment). The Israeli journalist, writer and TV creator Ron Leshem, who created the original version of *Euphoria*, argues that this change is facilitated by Netflix but also, perhaps, by the tendency towards *switch screening*, *second screening* and *multiscreening*. Using two or more devices at once or switching between different devices, Leshem says, may have prompted American viewers to watch TV series with subtitles instead of relying only on sound. This change in viewing habits, combined with Netflix's focus on international content, might have opened American audiences, who would not otherwise watch foreign films and TV series, to subtitled entertainment and TV series from other regions.[300]

That, of course, is only speculation, but there is an increased flow of non-English series in the US and, apparently, an increased openness towards foreign, subtitled content, at least when combined with recognizable genres and storytelling modes (cf. *Parasite*, which won the Academy Award for Best Picture in 2020, despite being a South Korean film). That particular aspect - the combination of local environments, storytelling traditions and genre preferences with universal storytelling qualities and recognizable formulas - is exactly what Netflix is looking to monetize.

From Nordic Realism to Dystopian Fantasy: *The Rain*

One example of this strategy is the dystopian series *The Rain* (2018-2020), which was conceived by the Danish writer Jannik Tai Mosholt. Combining elements of psychological realism, which is a popular tradition in Danish film and television, with a dystopian sci-fi story, Mosholt wanted to make a kind of series that you rarely see in Denmark. He had originally envisioned his story as a film and had never thought to ask DR about doing it as a TV series, given that Sunday dramas on DR have to attract a large share of the audience - something that is virtually impossible for sci-fi series and Americanized genre fictions. Fortunately, though, Netflix were scouting for talent and potential projects in Scandinavia at the time and were specifically looking for series that could combine recognizable genre elements and well-known storytelling formulas with regional aspects, narrative traditions and exotic locations (most of *The Rain* is shot on location in Copenhagen).

The combination of different genres and traditions is illustrated from the beginning of the series. The pilot episode begins *in medias res* in a high school where the central character Simone Andersen (Alba August) is running in the hall with a red Fjällräven on her back (a popular backpack in Scandinavia, often associated with hip or eco-conscious young people).[301] The non-diegetic music and the shallow depth of field are both reminiscent of popular American teen dramas, but the handheld camera, never static or fully at ease, is a feature that is associated with a more realistic tradition (from John Cassavetes in the US to the Dogme95 movement in Denmark). While adding a sense of 'Scandinavian realism', the handheld camera also functions as an omen, indicating that something dangerous is afoot.

Simone is all but ready to enter the group exam – the focus on groups and collectives rather than individuals and individuality is another phenomenon that is immediately associated with Danish culture – but her father suddenly shows up and pulls her away, saying that the situation is serious. "It is beginning to rain," he says to her, as we follow them out of the school building, and in the next shot we cut to the sky, subtly and almost subliminally introducing the dystopian elements before tilting down and revealing a normal Danish highway. The scene in the car looks like an average Danish TV series, using a handheld camera and a jarring cutting style to capture a typical family discussion, but the juxtaposition of this handheld aesthetic and the drone shots of the highway seems to illustrate the two traditions behind *The Rain*. The visual effects, the drone shots and the heavy use of dolly tracks and non-diegetic music are all reminiscent of American TV series, as are the supernatural or dystopian elements, yet the focus on everyday life and the use of handheld camera and discontinuity are typical of Danish television. The combination of realistic family (melo)drama and a strong external plot with a topical or ethical aspect – in this case the climate – also seems to reference DR and their focus on *double stories*.[302] Finally, the very premise of a deadly virus spreading through rain naturally seems to reference the typical Danish weather with an average of over 700 mm rain per year.[303]

The first season of *The Rain* had 30 million viewers, and even if ratings are not as important to Netflix as they are to traditional broadcast networks, these numbers illustrated the international or global potential in a mix of teen drama, psychological realism and dystopian science fiction set in the dark and rainy streets of Copenhagen. In an article called "Inside the Binge Factory," Josef Adalian of *Vulture* writes about the differences between Netflix and cable networks such as HBO, arguing that Netflix operate with different categories than most other channels (what they call "verticals") and use algorithms and "Big Data" to catalogue search and taste patterns.[304] Nevertheless, Netflix is also thinking in terms of traditional genres and how these can be combined in interesting and strategic ways with locally specific styles and storytelling traditions. And they are hardly oblivious to the number of viewers that their series attract (even if they are more concerned about gaining subscribers and producing *viewer engagement*).

Fig. 20: Jannik Tai Mosholt's *The Rain* (Netflix, 2018-2020) is a mix of psychological realism, teen drama and dystopian science fiction, cleverly combining elements from mainstream (American) cinema and television with storytelling traditions from Denmark and formulas from DR. At the end of 2020, it was revealed that *The Rain* was No. 2 on the list of most watched international series in the US, and Tea Lindeburg's *Equinox* (2020-) became the second Netflix original from Denmark. © Netflix, courtesy of Oliver Rawlins and Kim Stagmeier.[305]

Jannik Tai Mosholt (writer-producer) on *The Rain* as a Scandinavian Netflix Original

Production and pitching: We were the first ones in Scandinavia to make a Netflix series, and it all came about almost by accident. Christian Torpe, who has written *Rita* and numerous other series, was in the US, working on *The Mist*, so I helped him write Season 4 of *Rita*. And then he asked me whether I wanted to meet with someone from Netflix; they were in Scandinavia at that point looking for their first Nordic projects and talents. So I ended up having a meeting with a person from Netflix called Brian, and that meeting was basically just him asking me what I wanted to make, and when I left that meeting, I had the strange feeling of suddenly having a new potential project on my hands.

This project was conceived a few years earlier by myself and the director and animator Esben Toft, and it was basically a dystopian science fiction film. Upon writing that idea down, we quickly shelved it, though, knowing that we would never be able to make it in Denmark. That genre didn't exist in Denmark at that time. But when talking with Brian, I thought about returning to the idea and the possibilities of reshaping it into a TV series. That was basically what I did, so I talked to Esben and Christian Potalivo, the producer, about my idea, and then I wrote a 'Show Bible' of 20-25 pages, describing my ideas for the first season, the main characters and some of the major arcs. We included some visual material and sent it off to Netflix, and since I was going to Los Angeles to meet Torpe anyway, I asked Netflix whether we could have a meeting about the material we had sent them. Consequently, we had a meeting, and a week later they contacted me, saying that they wanted me to do it.

American genre fiction and Danish realism: I grew up watching American genre fiction, from sci-fi, fantasy and adventure films by Steven Spielberg and George Lucas to American horror movies. These were the kinds of films that Christian and I watched, and these were the traditions that formed us during our formative years. At the same time, though, we are formed by a cultural tradition and a Danish approach to storytelling. Even if we are making science fiction, not social realism, we inevitably stand on the shoulders of those Danish traditions and the film and TV creators that came before us. At the end of the day, though, our idea was to create a story that took place in a universe that was not our own world, something that wasn't as close to reality as most Danish films and TV series.[306]

Fig. 21-22: The Indian series *Sacred Games* (2018-) and the German series *Dark* (2017-2020) are examples of local-language originals that have become global successes, perhaps by combining regional traditions and traits with popular genres and modes of storytelling. In this context, one could also mention the popular French crime series *Lupin* (2021-), which was co-created by the French writer-director François Uzan and the British *Killing Eve* writer George Kay. © Netflix, courtesy of Oliver Rawlins and Kim Stagmeier.

Mosholt, himself, says that *The Rain* grew out of an interest in American genre fiction and the potentials of combining the colorful genre fiction known from Hollywood and American television with aspects and traditions known from Danish film and television. This will also be the case in his two upcoming Netflix series: *Nisser* and *Chosen*. Mosholt describes *Nisser* as as a Christmas-themed "family horror in the vein of *Gremlins*, *Jaws*, *E.T.* and *Stranger Things* combined with elements of Norse mythology," and he says that *Chosen*, which is inspired by "everything from *Close Encounters of the Third Kind* to *Buffy the Vampire Slayer*," has grown out of an interest to "to make something lighter and to explore the intersection between normalcy and absurdity."[307]

Among the local series that Netflix have produced or co-financed, there are numerous examples like *The Rain* where regional storytelling traditions and generic and stylistic preferences are combined with more universally recognizable features. An example of this is the Indian series *Sacred Games* (2018-), which is described by Kelly Luegenbiehl as a "Bollywood noir," juxtaposing a well-known Indian genre (known for its melodramatic, musical and romantic qualities) with a deeply American genre tradition (known for its dark and depraved characters, its fatalistic stories, tragic endings, expressive camerawork and low-key lighting). In this context, one could also think of the popular German series, *Dark* (2017-2020), which combines narrative complexity and a mythological universe, reminiscent of series such as *Twin Peaks* and *Carnivàle*, with German philosophy and elements of science fiction, teen drama and 1980s nostalgia akin to *Stranger Things* (2016-). I will return to *Dark* later in this book when analyzing and discussing new approaches to storytelling in the *multiplatform era*, including concepts such as *complex TV* and *transmedia storytelling*.

Between Heist and Heightened Emotions: *La Casa de Papel*

A notable case in this context is the popular Spanish heist series *La Casa de Papel* (2017-), which was created for Antena3 by Álex Pina and Vancouver Media before appearing on Netflix in 2019. From the very onset, Pina's series combines Spanish elements and icons with international genres and stylistic elements that are reminiscent of American series like *House of Cards*. The title sequence, for example, illustrates one of the predominant sites in the series (The Royal Mint of Spain) while mirroring David Fincher's montage from *House of Cards*. The sense of emptiness or hollowness is similar – the buildings in Washington naturally replaced with a central building and icon in Madrid – and even the color palette is similar. Apart from these aspects, however, *La Casa de Papel* has a flamboyant visual aesthetic and acting style that is a far cry from Beau Willimon's series.

The moral ambiguity of the main characters is in direct lineage with *House of Cards* and the most prominent series from the cable revolution (e.g. *The Sopranos*, *Breaking Bad* and *The Americans*). Yet, with *La Casa de Papel*, Pina wanted to create "a new TV genre" by mixing "black comedy, highly emotional thriller and action" with elements of narrative complexity (what he calls "time fragmentation") and visual motifs and locations associated specifically with Spain: the red color, the city names and the Dalí masks.

When it came to the visual style in particular, Pina and the cinematographer Migue Amoedo took a formalistic approach and looked to some visual points of reference that would immediately set it apart from American TV, thus acting as a visual counterpart to the American genre tradition. Like other local shows on Netflix, *La Casa de Papel* combines local traditions, history and preferences with American genre traditions and also with stylistic references from various other countries and sources. Brandon Katz notes that *La Casa de Papel*, from April 3 to April 5, 2020, was "31.75 times more in demand than the average series globally, beating out such perennial popular series as *Game of Thrones*, *The Walking Dead*, *Brooklyn Nine-Nine* and *Westworld*," and its popularity speaks to the global potential of local content.[308]

Álex Pina (creator) and Migue Amoedo (DP) on *La Casa de Papel* and the globalization of the TV landscape

Pina: Never before had such a solid emotional architecture been displayed in the action genre. The biggest change lies in the fact that the genre is essentially American. It is succinct, scientific, rational. We have made it more Latin. The characters' feelings are as important as the plot. Friendship, romance, father-son relationships are over-emphasized.

'Local' blows a fresh breeze in a world of fiction that has always been controlled by American or Anglo-Saxon models. The audience can sometimes watch over ten hours of fiction per week. As experts, they demand more stimulating products, and being different is stimulating. To stay local and reinvent a genre like the "perfect heist" is almost exotic. *La Casa de Papel* displays a Spanish essence connecting to *Don Quixote*, the quintessential Spanish novel. This novel talks of idealism, the combat between reality and ideal, but, at the same time, it connects to a black sense of humor used by some Spanish directors such as Berlanga. Hence, the series resorts to the use of tragi-comedy, even variety in some moments. We always try to feature elements of Spanish pop culture: folk music, paella, slang, and local uses and manners in characters such as Moscú. Spanish surrealism is sometimes at the service of humor; turning losers into heroes is a very Spanish trait as well. At the end of the day, our characters are misfits in search of the impossible.[309]

Amoedo: A very important conceptual reference is the book *From Caligari to Hitler* by Siegfried Kracauer. In Spain, we were coming out of one of the most devastating economic crises ever. The book claims that German Expressionism reflected, both formally and aesthetically, the collective subconscious, infested with insecurity and fear, and that led to the Nazi era a few years later. As we were developing *La Casa de Papel*, we seemed to be able to find fertile ground for that sort of idea. In fact, Leni Riefenstahl herself is another important reference. The technical innovations in her films promoted an epic feeling, which was conveniently used as propaganda at the time. At a merely aesthetic level, the cinema from other European countries was very important in the early years of the last century. In particular, Eisenstein's Soviet movies, praising the power of the masses, and Pudovkin's movies that focused more on individual feats.

The search for less-explored formal sources was intentional so as to differentiate ourselves from the American series, whose formal style is much more set within an already-established mode of representation.[310]

Fig. 23-24: *La Casa de Papel* (2017-) is a popular Spanish heist series that mixes a variety of different influences, from surrealism and American heist movies to Leni Riefenstahl and Spanish folk music. The uniquely Spanish elements, including the beautiful varieties of the language itself, became a part of its attraction, and in April 2020 it eclipsed popular shows like *Game of Thrones* and *The Walking Dead* in terms of viewer demand. In November 2020, it was revealed that Netflix are launching a Korean version of *La Casa de Papel*, clearly exemplifying the strategic focus on *localization*.[311] © Netflix, courtesy of Oliver Rawlins and Kim Stagmeier.

Shifting Perspectives and Complex Conflicts: *BeTipul* and *Our Boys*

As a final example, one could mention the work of Israeli TV creator Hagai Levi, who is known for employing shifting perspectives and points of view and for creating complex, kaleidoscopic depictions of real-world conflicts.

To American TV audiences, Levi is best known for having co-created *The Affair* (Showtime, 2014-2019) together with Sarah Treem, a series that Emily Nussbaum, somewhat sarcastically, described as "True Detective: For Her."[312] Levi established some of the main ideas behind the series, including the use of unreliable flashbacks, subjective narration and *Rashōmon effects* – something I will explore in Chapter 4 – but he wanted the series to revolve exclusively around the affair and its (inter)personal consequences and, therefore, left the show after only one season due to creative differences.[313]

Before conceptualizing *The Affair*, however, Levi had created one of the most influential Israeli TV productions – a TV series that has currently been licensed and sold for remakes in 15 different countries. That series, *BeTipul* (Hot3, 2005-2008), was an almost Bergmanesque chamber play, made on the smallest of budgets and using only one essential setting: a therapist's office. In that sense, Levi had taken what David Chase described as the foundation of television, "yak-yak-yak-yak," and made an entire TV series about it. Almost every scene in the Israeli series takes place inside the therapist's office, and in that sense the only true stylistic feature is *shot/reverse-shot* editing. But by confining the entire action to one space and one conversation, it transcends that formula and becomes an almost minimalistic or Talmudic exploration. By exploiting the traditional TV set-up and pushing it to its limits, *BeTipul* subverts traditional television, creating an almost existential and at times claustrophobic space. As Levi says:

> I was quite confident about what I was doing. I didn't think that a lot of people would watch it, but I was pretty certain that my kind of people would like to see it. The whole thing was quite natural for me because I like dialogue. It's the most amazing creation in the whole world, I think: dialogue between two people. I didn't come to cinema and television from a visual point of view; I grew up in a world consisting only of books. I grew up in a Jewish, religious environment where you don't have any exposure to images. I think I went to my first exhibition at a museum at the age of 25. So, for me, words were the thing and especially the idea of interpretation. The other thing was that I was looking for the greatest amount of creative freedom that I could have, and very early on in my life I understood that *the cheaper it gets, the more freedom you get*. It's a very simple equation.
>
> You could see psychological treatment portrayed in many different shows. You could see it in *The Sopranos*, for example, but I wanted to explore the thing in itself. That was also the case with *The Affair*: I didn't just want to use the affair as a narrative element, but to explore it to the end. And that was also what we were trying to do in *Our Boys*. You could describe it almost as an anatomy of a hate crime, exploring all the layers behind it. And you are totally right in saying that there is a Talmudic quality to my work because that was basically what I was doing till the age of 18: learning the Talmud from morning to night. You could say, in that sense, that psychoanalysis is a Talmudic concept in a way, dealing with theses and antitheses all the time.[314]

A somewhat surprising success in Israel, *BeTipul* was adapted and remade in many different countries, most famously in the US where it was given the succinct title *In Treatment* (HBO, 2008-2010). Levi, himself, functioned as a sort of executive consultant on most of the transnational remakes, helping the local crews adapt his story and explorative style to different cultural contexts. This was particularly difficult in various parts of Eastern Europe where psychotherapy had been banned for many years during the communist era.

The American version also differed from the Israeli original. Most significantly, the therapist Paul Weston, played by Gabriel Byrne, has a different status and authority (as seen in his clothing, his posture and the look of his office), and the relation between patient and therapist is different in the American version compared to the Israeli show. "One of the main things in *BeTipul* is the desire to cross the border," as Levi says. "Most of the time this is what the patients want to do, physically, while America is a place where boundaries are much more well perceived and executed, so you can see that the distance is bigger. And it was less blunt. The original is very blunt."[315]

Specific characters and backstories were also changed, as in the case of Alex Prince (Blair Underwood), an African-American fighter-pilot who is traumatized by a bombing mission in Iraq. That character was originally an Israeli soldier who bombed and killed children in Gaza and who carried with him an inherited trauma (his father being a Holocaust survivor). That inherited trauma was adapted into an American historical context through Alex and his African-American roots (his family having experienced segregation). As Levi puts it:

> In all the adaptations, there were two things we had to think about. The first one was: What would be the psychological heritage or ethos in that place because it differs from country to country. In Scandinavia, they often use CBT, and in America it is all about psychodynamics. The second main issue was the story of the pilot. That was actually the most local story, the one that very much made it an Israeli creation. We had to find two equivalents: Something that could represent the current trauma and something that could represent the past trauma.[316]

The current trauma for Alex in the American version is his experience in Iraq, and the historical trauma is his family's experience of the Jim Crow Laws and the dark history of racism in America. In the Eastern-European versions, the past trauma would often be represented by the communist policies, and in the French adaptation, which is set to air in 2021, the current trauma is represented by the terrorist attack at the Bataclan theater in November 2015.[317]

The different adaptations of *BeTipul* tell the same story in different cultural interpretations and with subtle stylistic and tonal variations. Given the restricted setting and minimalistic premise, most versions are similar in a stylistic sense, but the *mise en scène* and pacing differ widely from version to version, with the American remake being notably faster and more frenetic. "In the European versions we could afford more pauses, and pauses are almost a tradition of European cinema," as Levi says. "But in America, they talk much faster. I remember visiting the editing room at one point during the second season where I heard the director giving notes to the editor, and the first note was: 'Lose all the pauses'."[318]

A minimalist inspired by Ingmar Bergman, Levi focuses on characters, psychology and perspectives. Fittingly, Levi was approached by the Bergman family while he was in Sweden for a screening of *BeTipul* (in Sweden it was shown in its original, Israeli version), asking him to make a modern remake of *Scenes from a Marriage*.[319]

Following his transnational success with *BeTipul* and his international experience with *The Affair*, Levi returned to Israel where he created an original series for HBO. Perhaps inspired by Netflix and their focus on local-language originals, HBO has also begun focusing on regional content and transnational co-productions, and the American-Israeli miniseries *Our Boys* (2019) is a noteworthy example. A fairly complex series, *Our Boys* is a docufictional story about the kidnapping and killing of three Israeli boys, followed by an equally vicious retaliation. In that sense, Levi's series is a story about vengeance, but it is also a story about the potentials for dehumanization and inhumanity in the face of great adversity or trauma. Thus, the series, yet again, illustrates Levi's authorial focus on perspectives and layers, and this is already indicated in the title where the pronoun "our" can illustrate both the Israeli and the Palestinian boys. The title is written in English, but also in Hebrew and Arabic, further emphasizing the different perspectives on the complex conflict whose historical, territorial and religious roots are all but impossible to grasp for foreign audiences.

When it comes to actual storytelling and style, *Our Boys* also works with different perspectives, often using *rack focus* and switching attention between different characters in an Altmanesque fashion. Combined with the use of handheld camera and archival footage, this makes for a confusing and rather chaotic experience where it is difficult to fully understand the situation and distinguish between the archival elements and the fictional (but seemingly authentic) shots.

The series opens with an introduction describing it as "a dramatization of events that occurred during the summer of 2014 in the greater Jerusalem area" and ending with a disclaimer stating that characters, dialogues and events have been "fictionalized for dramatic purposes." Hence, from the very onset, Hagai Levi places the audience in an in-between space, and the sense of confusion – or of being in between – continues throughout the entire opening sequence. The text fades out, and on the soundtrack we now hear the ringing of a phone before seeing a screen displaying a sound wave. A voice is talking about being kidnapped, and suddenly we cut to a female news reporter saying: "We interrupt this broadcast with some breaking news." A male journalist in the television studio begins to explain the news story, as if speaking to a knowing audience, and after 1:17 minutes the camera tilts upward, revealing the news broadcast as coming from a young boy's computer. The young boy is seen in a tight *shallow focus* shot, and as we hear an off-screen voice saying "Muhammed, come on," a bearded man (Muhammed's father) is revealed in the background through the use of *rack focus*. The sound of the news reporter continues on the soundtrack, saying that the circumstances around the kidnapping are still unknown and, thus, illustrating the viewer's sense of confusion. Functioning as overlapping sound, the voice of the news reporter then explains that a terrorist organization could be involved, as we cut to a *four shot* of some Jewish boys seated in a restaurant – indicating the different perspectives and layers of religious and territorial conflict in the story. As we cut to a close-up of one of the Jewish boys, we now understand that he, like Muhammed, is a central character in *Our Boys*. The sequence continues to alternate between news footage, reconstructions and the different fictional characters who are listening to and watching the broadcast, before cutting to an office where we see a number of different people watching multiple screens and talking into headsets. The overlapping dialogue is accompanied by a chaotic visual aesthetic of handheld camera and constant *rack focus*. At this point, it is unclear whether we are in a police station or a newsroom, and the viewer is placed in a chaotic intersection of different people, voices and fragments (interestingly, there has been no establishing shot yet, but only a number of close-ups and medium shots in various locations). A new close-up reveals a third central character, though initially out of focus, and as the man leaves his house we follow him out into his car while we are also being served snippets of (what looks like) archival footage. The man, we later learn, is the Shin Bet officer Simon (Shlomi Elkabetz), and this five-minute sequence is probably intentionally confusing and chaotic in its introduction of a complex conflict with multiple different layers and perspectives. As Hagai Levi says:

> I always like to play with points of view. I did it in *The Affair*, and basically *In Treatment* was also about points of view because the patient would come in – this happened in every episode – and say this and this happened, and then the therapist would say: "We can look at it differently, from a different perspective." That would always be the essence of the story: "This is how you perceive this event, but could we look at it in a very different way? Can we give it a different interpretation and a different point of view?" That is the core of my dramas: a clash between different interpretations or points of view. It doesn't mean that there is no objective truth. There are facts and there is truth, but it is the way you look at it and the way you interpret the facts that makes the whole difference and creates the conflict.[320]

Based on a real-life tragedy following the kidnapping of Naftali Frenkel, Gilad Shaar and Eyal Yifrach, *Our Boys* combines documentary-like footage, hand-held camera and constant shifts in focus. Like *In Treatment*, it has been described as "challenging" and "uncomfortable," and, as Esther D. Kustanowitz of *The Jewish News* writes, it leaves the viewers with a frustrating question: "How much of this narrative, punctuated by actual news reporting and riot footage, is fact, and how much is fictionalized?"[321]

Much less flamboyant than many of the local-language originals by Netflix, *Our Boys* is a transnational co-production by Keshet and HBO, and it draws on staples of Israeli television – the thriller and espionage elements and the references to regional history and territorial-religious conflicts – while fitting Hagai Levi's oeuvre and HBO's 'quality' brand.

The former CEO of AT&T, Randall Stephenson, has famously described HBO as the "Tiffany" of streaming and Netflix as the "Walmart" of streaming.[322] But with its venture into local-language originals, Netflix is currently positioning itself in the global TV landscape and rebranding itself as a producer of original, regional content. With AT&T's takeover, it looks as if HBO is changing, too, and approaching the model of Netflix. HBO are still supposed to create award-winning drama series, but, according to AT&T's John Stankey, they are also supposed to produce more content, hoping to survive the competition from players such as Netflix and Disney.[323]

The battle for subscribers continues in the age of streaming where traditional broadcasters, *online natives* of the Netflix kind and various *content natives* try to position themselves in an uncertain landscape (e.g. by holding on to strong catalogues, by expanding their libraries or entering different local markets and producing regional content). The modern TV landscape is not just characterized by different distribution technologies and a plethora of content, but also by a blurring of the boundaries between different territories and national traditions. In that sense, television has begun moving beyond traditional forms of distribution and across national borders, and these changes are affecting the modern TV productions in complex ways.

In the feature interview at the end of this chapter, Kelly Luegenbiehl explains the strategy behind Netflix's local-language originals while reflecting on the current TV landscape. Following this, I move on to the second part of the book, where I will look at specific tendencies and approaches to storytelling, style and genre in the modern TV landscape and how these are affected by changes in the landscape itself.

Feature Interview #3

Local is Global: Interview with Kelly Luegenbiehl (Vice President of Local-Language Originals, Netflix)

Discussing some crucial aspects of the modern TV landscape, Kelly Luegenbiehl describes the general rise of regional or non-English content and, more specifically, the strategic focus on local series and *glocal* perspectives. In the interview, Luegenbiehl describes the strategic and executive level. But she also reflects upon specific TV series, from the popular German phenomenon *Dark* (2017-) to the Danish series *The Rain* (2018-2019), a combination of dystopian fiction, teen drama and psychological realism, as well as the Indian genre hybrid *Sacred Games* (2018-).

What is your role at Netflix exactly, and what is the scope of your work?

Luegenbiehl: My current role is overseeing the original productions for Europe, the Middle East and Africa - that small, compact group of countries (*laughs*) - which includes making scripted series, unscripted series and documentary series, stand-up specials, sketch comedy and live-action kids series. So really anything, even if it's a returning season or just a limited series, like this German series we just did, called *Unorthodox*, everything that's multi-episodic falls within our remit. We have teams in London, Paris, Madrid, Berlin, we're opening an office in Rome, and we're based in Amsterdam, so we have local content experts buying and making the content for each of the countries where we're working.

We just launched our first series for South Africa, called *Queen Sono*, and then we have another one coming called *Blood and Water*, which I love, which is a young adult soap set in Cape Town, and then we're also working on our first series for Nigeria right now.

When did Netflix start to show an interest in local-language originals or non-English content? Today, it is a rather important part of the Netflix brand, and there is also a broader, more general, tendency towards regional content, but when did it begin?

Luegenbiehl: It started a little before I joined, about five years ago. I've been at the company for about four and a half years, and it started with a series from Mexico called *Club de Cuervos*, which was our first original non-English language series in this kind of current iteration. And what we saw was that there's a huge appetite for local content, so from that we started investing in a small number of series in our very important territories and countries. So we had our first series for France, and then came Italy, Germany and Brazil. But as we were launching Spain - as we were launching that first slate - it was exciting to see that not only were the people from the countries where the shows were produced excited about them, but so, too, were people everywhere. And I think perhaps 3% in Brazil was the first one that opened that up for us, in that it was not a show we did marketing and publicity campaigns for in, for example, the US or the UK. But, organically, publications were finding it, writing about it, talking about the future of non-English language content. That was one of our early shows, and then the European slate started to roll out: *Dark*, *Suburra* and *The Rain*, and it just continued to grow from there.

It seems like local content is becoming increasingly popular these days, whether subtitled or dubbed, whereas it was more normal, not that many years ago, for American companies to buy foreign concepts and formats and remake them in the English language.

Luegenbiehl: Absolutely, there is an interest in subtitled, non-English content, and we have been working very hard on our dubbing qualities as well. That was an art form that was very well perfected in many European countries, but not so much in English speaking countries, like the US for example, so we've worked to increase the quality of that. But absolutely, even things with subtitles, with *Parasite* being able to win the Oscar, that's a huge indicator of the openness and the excitement that audiences are having for non-English language content.

A good example is the German hit series *Dark*, which is quite interesting in many ways. Could you say a few words on the conception of that series?

Luegenbiehl: The first pitch for that was made during my first week at Netflix, so I remember it very clearly. Bo, who is our director-showrunner, came in and brought a treatment, and that had really been born out of a number of conversations where the team, prior to my arrival, had started to talk with him as a filmmaker: "What would you like to do next? Do you have any series ideas?" From that, Bo and his partner Jantje had an idea that they had been working on for a feature film, which they ultimately decided would be a better series because there were so many characters. If they did it as a series, they could go much deeper with it.

They had just never imagined that there would be a platform where they could tell that version of a story as a series, so when we called them, this is what they came back with. It was really exciting, and I remember they were asking me when it started: "Do you think this could be a great series?" And I was like: "Well, in sci-fi it's always about who the writer is; do they have the theoretical and the emotional foundation, all of that tied together". I went to lunch with Jantje in Venice, and I'll never forget, it was like a three-hour long lunch, and she pulled out this giant leather bound notebook. She had all of the family trees, she had every element that she went deeper and deeper into, and I think, when you watch that series, you can tell that the makers knew from the beginning exactly the level of complexity, all the answers and how they would be planning and plotting it all out. So it really goes back to four and half years ago, when we started that conversation.

It may be difficult to pinpoint, but where do you see the regional aspects of that series or the specific "Germanness" of it, if such a thing as cultural specificity ever existed?

Luegenbiehl: I think there are a couple of elements that speak to that. The first is that German audiences love a great crime story, if you think back to the DNA of Season 1, there is a very strong mystery investigative through-line in that. Using that as a familiar aspect for German audiences, and then with the next level of the puzzle pieces being so unexpected, is what makes it satisfying. When you watch a typical crime story, at least for me, you are always trying to solve the mystery and put the pieces together, and I think German audiences have become very accustomed to doing that from the great tradition of crime series there. So *Dark* takes a bit of that idea and then expands upon it. I also think that - my father is a German philosopher, so I can say this - there is a very philosophical nature to the way Germans think. That's very common and acceptable, and that is definitely something that they tap into as well. That sort of nihilism and exploration of the human condition through the darkness of expression. All of that was what they were excited about doing, and nobody had really done that before in a series format. When you get into Season 3, there's even more of that what's-real-and-not-real element, asking those more existential questions.

The level of complexity in *Dark* was a very conscious choice for Bo and Jantje. They never wanted to dumb it down for the audience. They said: "The audience will go on this complex journey with us", and I think that people are being rewarded at the end of the series for that. But it has also been a very satisfying experience for them to have a series that keeps you on your toes in terms of thinking and engagement.

One might argue that streaming channels like Netflix make it easier for audiences to accept complex series such as *Dark* and non-English content in general, inasmuch as you can pause the action and watch episodes multiple times. Is that a fair assessment?

Luegenbiehl: I think that's right on a couple of different levels. The idea that you can stop a series, go back and start it again. You can watch it once with subtitles, once with dubs. You can watch the whole season again right before you start the new season. That flexibility and that freedom of how you want to consume content is something that makes Netflix really unique, but it also allows the audience to have ultimate freedom in terms of how to watch things, and I think it can change their level of engagement. Maybe I'll watch *Love is Blind* and have it on in the background because that's how I want to connect with it. But when it's something in another language, I'll need to be very immersed, so it is about figuring out what my mood is at any given moment, and that's the case for everyone who's at home watching Netflix.

What role do the local-language originals have for Netflix as a brand? Do you think that they will play a vital role in the future?

Luegenbiehl: In terms of our non-English language series, I would say, in general, that they are a huge part of our future in terms of expanding our connections to local audiences, but also just tapping into that next level of storytelling. Hollywood is not the be-all and end-all of great storytelling. When going into the Middle East and Africa, we are venturing into places that have these huge and very rich traditions of storytelling, and to be able to express those traditions to a global audience is a real opportunity for us as a company and also for our storytellers.

When talking about *The Rain*, the creator Jannik Tai Mosholt has said that he wanted to combine an American genre tradition that we rarely see in Danish television with an element of psychological realism, which is very popular in Denmark. Is that kind of combination between different genre traditions - and between universally accepted and culturally specific elements - what you are aiming for?

What you are hitting on in terms of what Jannik has said about tapping into the Danish realism is really important. And one of the things that we love to do - I am a huge fan of Danish content - is to be able to take the best of that storytelling tradition and give it a little bit of a twist. Jannik said to me, time and time again, that he would have never been able to make that story just in Scandinavia, and he and Christian are both huge fans of *E.T.* and *Goonies* and all of those kinds of young adult programs. For them to be able to take what they do very well at the highest level of Danish realism and combine that with genre fiction is something that they love. It was a great opportunity, and I think that combination is the reason why people got so excited about the show globally, because there was the 'recognizability' in the young adult element and the respect for Danish realism – and it was combined into something the viewers had never seen before.

Jannik Tai Mosholt also described how different the process was, making a series for Netflix versus making a series for Danish national television (DR). He claimed that it was a much smoother and more efficient process.

Luegenbiehl: We do have a bit of a bias for action: We love to make great stories, we don't love to just develop great stories. I think that's something that sets us apart as well: When we find somebody who has a great idea, we want to actually help the creators execute it, so it can be on the service. That's a bit unique. We quickly say: "Yes, let's make it". People are always a little surprised because it's not traditional, not quite what they're used to.

Why do you think that dystopian series like *The Rain* and *Dark* are so popular these days?

Luegenbiehl: I think there is a strong desire for escapism, and I think that you can see that in many of the series that we are showing, even a show like *The Witcher*. The world is hard right now, so that ability to remove yourself one or ten steps from the current reality is something that people are really tapping into. Not to say that we don't see the shows that portray real life also working really well – a show like *Unorthodox*, for example. But even a show like *La Casa de Papel* has an element of wish fulfillment added to the heist, and we've seen that capture the imagination of audiences all around the world, so there is that desire to escape and to connect with the characters and bring it all into a fun, enjoyable experience of watching.

A show like *Dark* is fun to watch. Even though it is very dark and heavy, there is a lot of fun to be had in putting all those puzzle pieces together and going on that ride. All of these shows have a bit of that "What if?"-quality to them: Could this happen? What would life be like? It's a sport for the imagination and one step outside of the current reality.

Both *Dark* and *The Rain* have been very successful, and what's exciting for us is that they are very popular in Germany and Denmark, respectively, in addition to being watched by many viewers outside of those countries. People focus very much on the idea that these shows travel, and that everyone in India, Korea and Brazil is able to watch them, but they've also been very important for Denmark and Germany. The impact that a great local show can have on a local audience is the most exciting thing for us.

The more authentic and specific we are to whatever country we're producing in, the more global it is. If we try to make something global, it's too watered down and it doesn't work. If we go deeper into that authenticity and specificity, that's where we see something becoming more global.

Which other series are worth mentioning in this context?

Luegenbiehl: I mentioned *The Witcher*, which I think everyone is watching these days. Another show that was quite transformative is *Sacred Games*, which was our first original for India and which really captured the zeitgeist for that country in a very unexpected way. The passion of the filmmakers and the quality of the storytelling, as well as having great star talent behind it, really opened people's eyes to what a streaming series could be. It even spawned its own kind of genre: *the Bollywood noir*, combining the best of what they do in Bollywood with elements from the noir crime drama. I've had people in the US call me up, saying that they liked it better than *The Wire*, so it's definitely one of those really hard-hitting crime dramas that you don't see on a regular basis.

It's about a cop and a gangster who, through a number of circumstances, are brought together one night, and then, moving forward, you follow the cop story, the police officer's story in the present day, and you flash back to the gangster story that's told over a number of decades, watching his rise to power. The two main characters are only really together in the first episode.

Part II

Beyond Traditional Television

New Approaches to Storytelling, Style and Genre

In the past 15 years, television's storytelling possibilities and practices have undergone drastic shifts in medium-specific ways. What was once a risky innovative device, like subjective narration or jumbled chronology, is now almost cliché. Where the lines between serial and episode narratives used to be firmly drawn, today such boundaries are blurred. The idea that viewers would want to watch – and rewatch – a television series in strict chronology and collectively document their discoveries with a group of strangers was once laughable, but is now mainstream. Expectations for how viewers watch television, how producers create stories, and how series are distributed have all shifted, leading to a new mode of television storytelling.
- Jason Mittell, TV scholar [324]

What a movie is and what a TV series is have changed. Television has become more sophisticated and challenging.
- Mary Harron, film and TV director [325]

Cable television, I say, is the new art house.
- David Lynch, film and TV director [326]

From Tradition to Experimentation

As seen in the previous chapters, the TV landscape has changed fundamentally within the last two decades. The introduction of cable distribution, satellite TV and new technologies such as VCR, VHS and DVD all contributed to this change, which was also facilitated by deregulation policies and the expansion of the Internet. With the advent of streaming, the shift became more profound – some critics and practitioners even describe it as a "disruption" or a "revolution" – and the *global turn* as well as the introduction of local-language originals have blurred the boundaries between industries, institutions and territories even further. As Trisha Dunleavy writes:

> Restructured by deregulation, conglomeration and globalization in the 1980s and 1990s, the television landscape was transformed after 2000 by the combined impacts of digitization and convergence, consequent multiplatform transmission and continuing inter-network competition.[327]

These changes are interesting from an industrial and infrastructural perspective, yet they are also relevant when exploring the modern TV series themselves, inasmuch as modern American TV series are affected by the general infrastructural changes, the *cross-border mobility* of content, talent and formats and the *interaction* between different institutions and media.

The infrastructural changes may not have any direct or immediately noticeable effects on modern TV series; it is, at least, difficult to establish a simple causal relationship between the two. Even so, many American TV series made within the last 15-20 years display new or experimental approaches to storytelling, style and genre, challenging traditional practices and modes of production. Typically, these series are also promoted as untraditional or innovative, and many of the creators, as we shall see, explicitly describe their series as "cinematic" or "unlike traditional television", often citing cinematic sources of inspiration and rarely mentioning any televisual precursors. As Elana Levine and Michael Z. Newman argue, TV creators and critics often describe TV series as "cinematic" as a way of legitimizing TV, as if the medium were not inherently legitimate.[328] In that sense, the "cinematizing of television" could be a general *trade story* among practitioners: a story that is told by people in the industry to legitimize their TV productions. But in many of the cases discussed in this book, the TV series have, in fact, been produced in a way that differs from traditional television, e.g. by avoiding typical set-ups or lighting strategies, by mixing the series in Dolby Atmos (even having a theatrical mix) and by employing a *cross-boarding technique* (historically associated with cinema).

The chapters in this part of the book explore some new approaches to storytelling, style and genre in modern television, focusing primarily on American TV. The point is to investigate how modern TV series experiment with the medium and challenge our traditional understandings of television, while drawing on televisual traditions and (ab)using established formulas. Though focusing on new and experimental practices, I do not argue that we are seeing a general and widespread change in television. Nor do I argue that experimentation is a new phenomenon in TV. I simply explore some new approaches to storytelling, style and genre in television – new approaches and forms of experimentation that seem to reflect a changing TV landscape and the *cross-influencing* between different industries and national traditions (what Nic Pizzolatto describes as "mirrored influences").[329] In that sense, we are not necessarily witnessing a shift "*from* tradition *to* experimentation," as the headline might indicate. What we are seeing is merely a number of modern TV series that approach style and storytelling in a new way by building on and subverting televisual traditions and conventions.

Referencing scholars like Jason Mittell, Trisha Dunleavy, Henry Jenkins and Marie-Laure Ryan, Chapter 4 looks at new approaches to storytelling in modern American television, focusing on the concepts of *complex TV* and *transmedia storytelling*. Narrative complexity and *transmedia storytelling* are not new phenomena as such, but they are, naturally, linked to the modern mediascape and differ notably from the self-contained stories and *episodic ideal* of the traditional American TV landscape.[330] The main cases in this chapter are *The Walking Dead* (AMC, 2010-) and *Twin Peaks: The Return* (Showtime, 2017-). But the chapter also explores the narrative complexity in American series like *Carnivàle* (HBO, 2003-2005), *The Leftovers* (HBO, 2014-2017), *The Affair* (Showtime, 2014-2019) and *American Crime* (ABC, 2015-2017), compared to European TV series such as *Dark* (Netflix, 2017-2019), *Our Boys* (HBO, 2019) and *Når støvet har lagt sig* (*When the Dust Settles*, DR, 2020). At the end of this chapter, there is a feature interview with the co-creator of *Twin Peaks*, Mark Frost, and the current showrunner of *The Walking Dead*, Angela Kang, discussing their respective approaches to storytelling and *world building*.

Chapter 5 deals with different examples of stylistic experimentation through reference to Kristin Thompson's concept of *art TV*. Moreover, the chapter looks at the concept of *TV auteurism*, specifically focusing on *limited series* and how they challenge our traditional understandings of *auteurism* in American television. Various examples are used to illustrate stylistic experimentation and innovation in television across different fields: from title sequence design, cinematography and editing to music and sound design. The most central cases are *Succession* (HBO, 2019-), *Stranger Things* (Netflix, 2016-), *Breaking Bad* (AMC, 2008-2013) and *Better Call Saul* (AMC, 2015-). At the end of the chapter, I explore *Twin Peaks: The Return*, *Alias Grace* (CBC/Netflix, 2017) and *I Know This Much Is True* (HBO, 2020) as three interesting instances of *art TV* and *TV auteurism*. This exploration is followed by a feature interview with Sabrina Sutherland, Peter Gould, Mary Harron and Derek Cianfrance. Sutherland, Harron and Cianfrance talk about style and new forms of TV production and *auteurism*, especially focusing on *limited series* and "limited event series" (which is the official description of *Twin Peaks: The Return*), and Peter Gould talks about the differences between *Breaking Bad* and *Better Call Saul* in terms of collaboration, style and authorship.

The final chapter of the book, Chapter 6, deals with new approaches to genre and the *cross-influencing* between different generic and cultural traditions. Specifically, the chapter focuses on three genres – teen drama, crime fiction and dramedy – exemplified by various series from different countries. The most central cases are *Euphoria* (HBO, 2019-), *True Detective* (HBO, 2014-2019) and *Transparent* (Amazon Prime, 2014-), yet these are compared with other examples and non-American series like *SKAM* (NRK, 2015-2017), *Normal People* (BBC Three/Hulu, 2020), *Luther* (BBC One, 2015-2019), *Forhøret* (Viaplay, 2019), *Ófærð* (*Trapped*, RVK, 2015-) and *After Life* (Netflix, 2019-). At the end of the chapter, there is a feature interview with three American TV creators. These creators, Sam Levinson, Nic Pizzolatto and Jay Duplass, talk about their respective series and the question of genre, and they all reflect on the changes in the TV landscape.

Experimentation is not a new thing in television, nor is it a general tendency across all TV productions in today's saturated media landscape. However, some TV series experiment with new approaches to storytelling, style and genre, and this experimentation may be linked to the infrastructural changes in the mediascape, including the introduction of new distribution technologies and platforms and the influx of TV series and talents from other countries and cultures.

Chapter 4

A Complex Affair: Transmedia Storytelling and Complex TV

[T]o call something complex is to highlight its sophistication and nuance, suggesting that it presents a vision of the world that avoids being reductive or artificially simplistic, but that grows richer through sustained engagement and consideration. It suggests that the consumer of complexity needs to engage fully and attentively, and such engagement will yield an experience distinct from more casual or partial attention.
- *Jason Mittell, TV scholar*[331]

I always demand a lot from my viewers. It is important that certain people will watch my work, and that my series create a discourse or have an impact on culture. But that does not necessarily come with large audience numbers. Not at all. It depends on *who* watches; who are the people that are going to talk about it and write about it. So, yeah, demanding is the word…
- *Hagai Levi, TV creator (The Affair and Our Boys)*[332]

Television has matured, and we now have all these complex stories and multi-layered, interesting characters that we used to see in mid-budget movies.
- *Lesli Linka Glatter, Producing director (Homeland)*[333]

When characterizing the modern TV landscape, many critics and scholars point to the element of narrative complexity as a crucial aspect, arguing that modern *high-end* TV series have become increasingly more serialized and narratively sophisticated.

Narrative complexity is not a new phenomenon as such. The word itself goes back to Aristotle and his concept of *peplegmenos,* and Jason Mittell traces its televisual roots back to the *serial melodramas* of the *three-network era.*[334] The serial melodramas were not complex in a way that is comparable to modern prestige series, yet they included long serial arcs, flashbacks, large ensembles and multiple interconnected storylines. Generally, though, TV series were more episodic during the *three-network era,* according to Mittell, and the serial melodramas included a fair amount of redundancy where flashbacks and conversations would often be used expositionally to recap the main plot threads and necessary pieces of information. According to film historian David Bordwell, narrative complexity requires a high degree of redundancy, and for the classical serial melodramas "slow-paced redundancy" was something of a dogma.[335] "Instead of treating repetition as a necessary evil, soaps raise it to an art form," as Mittell concludes.[336] The reason for that principle, according to Mittell, was that early serial melodramas were aimed at *erratic viewers,* who were doing other things while watching television and, therefore, could not direct their full attention at the TV set.[337]

The serial melodramas of the *three-network era* might have been an early ancestor of the complex serials in the modern TV landscape (what Mittell calls *complex TV*), but compared to their modern descendants the early serial melodramas looked more like an "ephemeral daily check-in" where you revisit some beloved characters and well-known conflicts.[338]

The kind of narrative complexity that we see in the modern TV landscape requires full attention and *comprehensive viewers*. "Complex dramas are not devised to be viewed casually," as Trisha Dunleavy writes; "instead, they offer their fullest readings and pleasures *only* to those willing to watch and listen closely."[339] Referring to *Mad Men* (AMC, 2007-2015), TV critic Matt Zoller Seitz has argued that AMC should change their slogan to "Short Attention Spans Not Welcome," and the Danish TV scholar Jakob Isak Nielsen has also used *Mad Men* as an example of the long arcs and *narrative memory* in modern TV series. As Nielsen writes, a close-up of Don Draper who puts his hand on top of Peggy's hand to comfort her is mirrored in a later episode, a few seasons after the original shot, where the roles have now been switched, and only the attentive viewer would notice this repetition and subtle variation.[340]

Complex serials "foreground serial form and narration," as Trisha Dunleavy writes, and they are also "*conceived* as serials." In that sense, the concept of *complex TV* is associated mainly with TV serials, not episodic series, and, despite their historical connection with soap operas, they are vividly different. Not only are they designed for *comprehensive viewing* and aimed at "well-educated viewers with higher levels of disposable income"; they are also meant to be experienced as serials with a beginning and an end (unlike soap operas that are designed to "endure indefinitely").[341] In characterizing the modern *complex serials*, Dunleavy points to four different features:

- The complex serials are grounded in serial form (as opposed to long-format dramas that are grounded in series form with strong episodic features)
- The complex serials "eschew the tried-and-tested institutions" (they are not arena-based shows that take place in police stations, hospitals, lawyer's offices etc.)
- The complex serials revolve around complex, morally ambiguous and "usually transgressive" primary characters.
- The complex serials incorporate "more explicit content" than is possible on broadcast television.[342]

Dunleavy convincingly identifies a central tendency in the modern TV landscape, yet she points to some criteria that are not specifically related to complexity or storytelling. She thereby characterizes a trend in cable and streaming television, but misses some interesting examples of narrative complexity in broadcast television (e.g. *American Crime*, ABC, 2015-2019). While explicit content is certainly a feature of many cable series (cf. Chapter 1), it is hardly connected to the potential complexity of those series. It is also debatable whether complex serials always have "transgressive" primary characters, but ambiguity in itself, including moral ambiguity, is often connected with narrative complexity. Modifying Dunleavy's model, we could instead point to the following parameters as indicators of narrative complexity:

- Ambiguity and uncertainty (e.g. moral ambiguity, uncertainty concerning the boundary between reality and fantasy, and questions concerning reliability)
- Subjective narration and shifting points of view
- Non-linearity (e.g. through the use of flashback, flashforward and time-collapsing editing)
- Cumulative plots and a vast narrative memory
- Long arcs and a lack of redundancy
- Fragmentation and a lack of causality
- Large ensembles and polycentric stories
- Multi-layered narratives including multiple settings, realms and/or timelines.

This list is not exhaustive, and the different parameters are neither necessary nor sufficient conditions in complex serials. Rather, they are different *potential* features of a complex serial or different *signs* of narrative complexity. On the following pages, I will explore some different examples of *complex TV* from streaming services, cable networks and traditional broadcasters, before turning my attention to the concept of *transmedia storytelling*.

The Viewer as Detective: Non-Linear Plots and Shifting Perspectives

A typical feature of complex serials is non-linearity. Most stories are non-chronological to some degree, yet in traditional or mainstream narratives there is a relative linearity and a natural coherence between the *fabula* and the *syuzhet*. The *syuzhet* is the actual structure of the narrative, i.e. the order of the plot, whereas the *fabula*, as David Bordwell writes, is "a pattern which perceivers of narratives create through assumptions and inferences. It is the developing result of picking up narrative clues, applying schemata, framing and testing hypotheses."[343] Whenever we are watching a TV series, we are making inferences and creating patterns, based on our previous experiences, our knowledge of television narratives and traditional formulas, and, thus, we are effectively co-creating the story. "The fabula can only be guessed at, but is not given," as Bordwell concludes with reference to Yury Tynyanov.[344] This constructivist or neo-formalist idea is well-established by now, but it is important to emphasize that all TV series involve inferences and mental work on the part of the viewer, and, therefore, there will always be a subjective element to the notion of complexity. Different viewers have different experiences and levels of exposure to TV narratives, tropes and formulas, and, hence, they will naturally have different perceptions of what a complex serial is. What is accessible to one viewer might be inaccessible to another.

To give a concrete example of this, we could think of *True Detective* (HBO, 2014-2019), a limited crime series that reboots with each season. In the first season, we follow two detectives, Rust Cohle (Matthew McConaughey) and Martin Hart (Woody Harrelson), who are trying to solve a mysterious, complex and occult case in the state of Louisiana. Combining elements of *noir* and Southern Gothic, the series alternates between different characters, arenas and timelines, following Marty and Rust at their homes, on the job and at an interview where they are being interrogated about the circumstances surrounding their investigation. Something happened on the case, we quickly understand, but the interrogation scenes conjure up numerous questions for the audience to ponder: What happened between Marty and Rust? What has happened to Rust in particular to make him drink and let himself go? And why are the two detectives being interrogated? These elements are part of the multi-layered puzzle of *True Detective* and add an element of complexity to the series, as many critics have noted. TV scholar Anthony N. Smith, for example, argues that *True Detective* creates a "pleasing" sense of uncertainty on both a generic and narrative level, and, similarly, Bronwen Thomas claims that *True Detective* "offers the viewer a pleasing sense of disorientation, disrupting expectations and introducing fantastical, supernatural elements to destabilize the show's generic identity."[345] The actor Michael Potts, who played Maynard Gilbough, one of the detectives interrogating Rust and Marty, also describes the series as "complex" and remembers being afraid that it would be too challenging or demanding:

> I was a little skeptical, honestly, just from the scope of the story, from what I had read, and once we finished I was skeptical that they'd be able to pull it together in a coherent way. Would an audience be able to follow it? This is very complex. How are they going to pull this off? I was a little skeptical, but I watched it like everyone else, and my jaw dropped. By the third episode, I was like: "Oh, my goodness. This is great. This is *great*!"[346]

An example of the non-linearity in *True Detective* is seen in the episode called "The Secret Fate of All Life" (Ep.1:5) where we cut between Rust and Marty at the interrogation and flashbacks of them trying to capture the presumed culprit. During the interrogation in 2012, the detectives ask Rust and Marty how they caught the presumed killer of Dora Lange, and they tell a story about them hunting the potential killer down at a remote and eerie farm. The sequence is constructed in a clever way, giving the audience a distinct feeling about the story itself being a clever and potentially unreliable construction. Rust begins to tell the story ("as soon as we backed off…"), but before ending his sentence, we cut to a medium shot of Marty who seemingly continues the story, gesticulating heavily, as if having planned and rehearsed the script. "Bam! Bullets cut through, right near Rust's head," as Marty explains, saying that the suspects had "high-velocity" weapons. As Marty mentions the weapons, he bangs his fist on the table, and we cut to a slow-motion flashback of Rust and Marty in the high grass. "I mean it was on," we hear Marty saying on the soundtrack, and then we hear the sound of a man imitating a machine gun, naturally assuming that the sound is coming from Marty, before cutting back to Rust (at his hearing) who is using his hands as fire arms while mimicking the sound of "high-velocity weapons." That sequence from the first season is a good example of the non-linear storytelling in *True Detective* and its appealing combination of a "gothic sensibility and narrative complexity."[347]

Interestingly, though, the creator Nic Pizzolatto does not think of his series as complex, and he even describes it as "linear" and broadly accessible, emphasizing that he did not want to "cheapen character or narrative" by using narrative tricks or introducing gimmicky elements of *puzzle plots* or narrative complexity. As he explains:

> *True Detective* is actually linear. It only moves in one direction; it's just that it tracks two stories in two different times concurrently. Or in the case of Season 3, three different times concurrently. […]
> The interrogation framing was something I'd wanted to do for a long time - having a situation where a character could just tell their story. I wasn't worried about people being able to follow it because it was my job to make sure they could. If they couldn't follow the story, it was my problem, not theirs. I'm not saying that's always the case, but this was populist entertainment with two major movie stars, and it should be broadly digestible.[348]

The discrepancy between Pizzolatto's understanding of *True Detective* as "broadly digestible" and the critical appraisal of his series as "complex" or "disorienting" is quite interesting, and it proves that complexity is not an objective designation. What Pizzolatto sees as "populist entertainment," other people, including professional TV critics, might describe as "challenging art," and *True Detective* is even mentioned as an example in the book *Impossible Puzzle Films: A Cognitive Approach to Contemporary Complex Cinema* (although the specific reference there is to the much maligned second season).[349]

Fig. 25: The actor Michael Potts (Maynard Gilbough) was afraid that *True Detective* would be too complex and challenging. The creator, Nic Pizzolatto, on the other hand, describes his series as "broadly digestible." This discrepancy illustrates the critical difficulty in trying to characterize and pinpoint narrative complexity. Photo: Lasse Lorenzen & Jan Oxholm, 2019.

Naturally, Pizzolatto's words could also be seen as a defensive response to a potential pigeonholing of his series. In any case, *True Detective* has often been mentioned as an example of narrative complexity, and Showtime's *The Affair* has often been regarded as a "feminized" version of Pizzolatto's series or a part of the same cycle, combining a whodunit structure with melodrama.[350]

The central plot in Sarah Treem and Hagai Levi's series revolves around an extramarital affair between the narcissistic author Noah Solloway (Dominic West) and the young waitress Alison (Ruth Wilson), who is dealing with the trauma of losing her young child in a drowning accident. The most essential part of the first season is centered on their affair and how it affects the people around them. The series also introduces a *whodunit* element, though, surrounding the mysterious death of Alison's brother-in-law Scott Lockhart (Colin Donnell), and in the course of the five seasons, we get elements from various genres, including crime show, prison show, disaster film and dystopian cli-fi. As the co-creator Hagai Levi explains:

> There was some pressure to make it more commercial or accessible by adding some things that were not in the original idea, including some crime elements and a lot of sex. More than the story required. And I don't know how to do that; I really don't know how to make a commercial television show in a good way. There are people who can do that and who can address bigger audiences, telling stories that use more formulas or devices to make it more engaging or digestible. I don't know how to do that, so it was very natural for me to go to Israel and do a much more radical show (*Our Boys*) where I had total creative freedom.[351]

As the main characters are interrogated about Scott's death, we get a non-linear structure that is reminiscent of *True Detective*, intercutting past and present. Furthermore, the episodes are split into sections or chapters, showing us the events from different perspectives or points of view. In that sense, it employs a so-called *Rashōmon effect*, inspired by Akira Kurosawa's groundbreaking crime film *Rashōmon* (1950) where various characters provide different, mutually conflicting stories about what happened. This technique introduces an element of subjectivity and potential unreliability into the series, which is also reminiscent of the lying flashback in Alfred Hitchcock's film *Stage Fright* (1949/1950), thus raising the level of complexity. How can we rely on the things we see and hear, if everything is told from a subjective point of view that is potentially self-serving and dishonest?[352]

Converging Destinies and Time-Collapsing Editing

> It's like nothing you've seen on ABC.
> – Verne Gay, "American Crime review"[353]

A similar thing is at play in ABC's drama series *American Crime*, which combines a *polycentric* story influenced by Robert Altman, topical themes of racism and re-segregation in the US and some experimental approaches to storytelling and style. Like *True Detective*, *American Crime* is a limited series that reboots with each season. It even has actors such as Felicity Huffman and Timothy Hutton appearing in different roles across the three seasons, and it uses a non-linear structure as well as a sort of *time-collapsing editing*. This type of editing is seen in dialogue sequences, in particular, where silent flashbacks and flashforwards are intercut, creating a general sense of subjectivity and temporal confusion.

In the first season of *American Crime*, we follow Barbara Hanlon (Felicity Huffman) and Russ Skokie (Timothy Hutton), the divorced parents of Matt Skokie, who was killed during a home invasion. Apart from Barbara and Russ, we follow a large ensemble of characters. These include Matt's brother and wife, Mark (David Hoflin) and Gwen Skokie (Kira Pozehl); a former Mexican gang member named Hector (Richard Cabral); a young Hispanic teenager called Tony (Johnny Ortiz), who lives alone with his father and sister; a young addict named Aubry (Caitlin Gerard) and her African-American boyfriend, Carter Nix (Elvis Nolasco), who is accused of murdering Matt. These are but a selected list of the regulars in *American Crime*, and part of the series' complexity lies in its constant switching between various characters while intercutting subliminal flashbacks, thus creating a narrative uncertainty concerning what actually happened. In Chapter 5, I will return to the experimental approach to staging, framing and editing in *American Crime* - an approach that is reminiscent of Nicolas Roeg's classic horror film *Don't Look Now* (1973), and which is similar to the unconventional editing strategies in *Big Little Lies* (HBO, 2017-2019), *Sharp Objects* (HBO, 2018) and *The Undoing* (HBO, 2020).

Further contributing to the complexity, John Ridley and the various episode directors use *disembodied voices* where snippets of a conversation are used across shots from different timelines, making the viewer doubt what s/he sees. When the voices are *disembodied*, it becomes unclear how they relate to the images (i.e. whether the images illustrate what actually happened, the characters' faulty memory, their disturbed mental constructions or intentionally dishonest stories). The French composer and film critic Michel Chion has written extensively about the art of "mute bodies" and "bodiless voices," describing this particular stylistic element as *acousmatic sound*.[354] It is important to emphasize, in this context, that we are not simply dealing with off-screen voices or voice-over, but dialogue snippets that are played asynchronously (e.g. to images of the character whose lips are not moving, or to different presumed flashbacks and flashforwards). This technique is seen across most of the episodes, for example in the sequence from Ep.1:2 where Aubry is talking with her foster-father and the sequence, later in the same episode, where she is showering while reflecting on her dire situation. In the sequences with Aubry, the *disembodied* voice often has a subjective effect, mirroring her drug-induced disorientation and detachment. But *time-collapsing editing, jump-cutting, disembodied voices* and overlapping sound are used throughout the series, not just with her, and this creates a much more profound sense of confusion on the part of the viewer.

American Crime revolves around a large ensemble, but the structure is not episodic, nor do the different episodes feel like "ephemeral daily check-ins." Going back to the earliest serial melodramas, it is normal for TV serials to include a vast ensemble and numerous character arcs. In *American Crime*, however, the different characters and arcs converge in a complex way. In Ep.1:9, a judge talks about "the tangled roots that this case has travelled," and that line certainly sounds like a self-reflexive description of the series' own narrative structure - a narrative structure that interweaves multiple different characters while gradually dissolving the line between reality and fantasy.

At her psychiatric evaluation in Ep.1:10, Aubry is asked whether she "willfully bend[s] the truth," and at the end of the first season that question resonates with the viewer, as Aubry escapes into her own fantasy and Hector apparently gets the job at an IT firm, despite having no relevant experience or education. In the final scene of Ep.1:11, we see Hector talking to his girlfriend about getting the position at the tech firm. The intensity of his delivery, however, makes it seem like a story or a mental construction and, as he is about to explain how this makes him feel, he is cut off in a way that is uncannily similar to the ending of *The Sopranos*.

Since it is a limited series (or a type of anthology series), the three seasons include different characters, settings and plots, yet there are some subtle crossover effects running through the different seasons that give an element of added value to the *comprehensive viewer*. For example, when Felicity Huffman's character in the second season (the principal Leslie Graham) says to Timothy Hutton's character (the school's basketball coach) that they "could have done better," it subtly references the failed relationship between Huffman and Hutton's characters in the first season. And in Ep. 2:8, when Coach Sullivan (Timothy Hutton) discovers that his daughter has sold drugs to a boy from school, resulting in a tragic homicide, it clearly echoes the first season where Hutton's deceased son turned out to be a drug dealer. Similarly, when we notice Richard Cabral as a secondary character in the second season - wearing glasses, working in IT and having a young and very recognizable daughter - we are immediately reminded of his character in the first season, Hector, and his dying wish to become an employee at a respectable IT company. Ironically, though, we discover that Sebastian (Richard Cabral) in the second season is a hacker (or an activist, as he calls it), referencing the shadiness of Cabral's character in the first season. In the first season, Cabral's character dreamed about wearing a shirt and getting a respectable job in an IT company. In the second season, Cabral's character wears a shirt and works in IT as a "white hat hacker" (a respectable hacker).

Similar correspondences are located across all the seasons and characters. For example, Tony's father (Alonzo Gutiérrez played by Benito Martinez) was critical of illegal immigrants in the first season, arguing that they make other people of color look bad, but in the third season Martinez, ironically, plays an illegal immigrant. And the young Canadian actor (Connor Jessup), who played Taylor in the second season, now plays a drug addict in the third season, tying in with the tragic drug-induced homicide from the end of Season 2. In that sense, the characters across the three seasons are different, yet they are played by the same actors, and the subtle repetitions and variations make us think of them as different potential paths for the same people. Or for the same kind of people.

Like any traditional broadcast series, *American Crime* opens each episode with a recap. Even so, the series matches the narrative complexity and stylistic innovation of many cable and streaming series, and, not unlike *ZeroZeroZero*, it reflects a modern global situation by dealing with border-crossing crime, taking place in both Sinaloa, Mexico and Modesto, California, and employing various languages and codes (including English, Mexican, Spanglish and bits of Arabic). There are even instances of un-subtitled Spanish meant to produce a sense of group identity and cultural pluralism.[355]

"The series aired on network TV, yet by all counts is more like a cable television drama," as Amy M. Damico and Sara E. Quay write, pointing to its "cinematic influences" and brazen "sociological" narrative that constantly switches between different points of view.[356] *American Crime* is a modern TV series made for a broadcast network, but its narrative complexity lends itself naturally to *compressed consumption* or the ability to go back and rewatch sequences and episodes (something that is facilitated by DVD, Blu-ray and modern streaming services). Moreover, the themes are topical and reflect a modern, digital and global world. The first and third seasons deal with racism, border-crossing crime and new forms of slavery, while the second season deals with the illegal sharing of private photos, hate crime and structural issues in the school system. "Nearly all the characters in *American Crime* struggle against societal structures," as TV critic Henrik Højer writes, and the combination of social critique and a *polycentric*, complex structure is reminiscent of David Simon.[357] In terms of style, however, *American Crime* is much more expressive and experimental. As the three seasons depict structural issues, polarization and lack of cohesion in the American society, they all employ a fragmented narrative and an obtrusive style unlike the seamlessness and continuity editing we naturally associate with American film and television. In Chapter 5, I will return to the stylistic experimentation in John Ridley's series, upon exploring some other instances of complex seriality.

From Dense to Vast Seriality

Inspired by Robert Altman, *American Crime* and *Our Boys*, the TV creators Ida Maria Rydén and Dorte W. Høgh made a Danish TV series called *Når støvet har lagt sig* (*When the Dust Settles*, DR, 2020), a series that was financially supported by SVT, NRK, RUV and YLE, and which is currently being sold in numerous different countries.[358] Like *American Crime*, the Danish series introduces a *converging destinies*-trope where various characters get involved in the same complex and horrifying situation. It begins with a *cold open*, akin to cable dramas like *Breaking Bad*, showing us some different people seated in a restaurant. In a fragmented style and with a layered sound design, we get a visceral sense of the place before everything suddenly erupts in a ferocious series of gunshots from an automatic weapon. Within 75 seconds, the viewers have been introduced to the central climax, a terrorist attack in the heart of Copenhagen, without understanding the full implications of what they have seen. This, as the viewer soon comes to understand, was a flashforward intended to give the audience an intense and fragmented hint at future events and how the seemingly unconnected characters and storylines will eventually converge. According to Ida Maria Rydén:

> We are used to making series that take place in well-known arenas, like the family or the workplace, and that employ tried-and-true formulas. We wanted to do something else structurally, and we were very inspired by Robert Altman's *Short Cuts*.
>
> We asked ourselves the question: "Why haven't we seen any true *multiprotagnist* series?" It is normal in a TV serial to cut between different characters and plotlines, but the characters are often naturally related in some way. The idea of cutting between different characters that are not immediately or clearly connected seemed new to us, and that is something we wanted to do in Danish. There aren't that many series like that, *American Crime* being a notable exception. But we were ambitious and wondered whether we would be able to pull that sort of complex TV serial off. Would it be possible to cut between eight different locations, using some of the formal techniques that you see in HBO series like *Sharp Objects* and *True Detective*? In those series you often jump between different locations and timelines, but that is not something you normally see in a Danish TV series.[359]

As Rydén explains, Danish TV series are known for their sense of intimacy, authenticity and psychological realism, often delving into "the unflattering private sphere" of the characters. These elements are also featured in *When the Dust Settles*, but the series stood out by taking on some of the stylistic and narrative aspects from high-end American drama series, e.g. the use of fragmentation and the extreme uses of close-ups, *shallow focus* and subjective sound. "Milad Alami, who was the conceptualizing director, had a fantastic collaboration with the cinematographer Christian Winterø," as Rydén says, "and they decided to use a lot of tight and intense close-ups because we wanted to strengthen *the subjective narrative*. We had so many characters, so it became important for us to be completely in-your-face in order to get close to the characters."[360]

Apart from its stylistic experimentation, *When the Dust Settles* introduced a complex form of *polycentric* storytelling that was not typical of Danish television. The characters are introduced gradually, a new character appearing and taking center stage in each episode, and at the end of the *limited series* the storylines collide and the different destinies converge. In that sense, *American Crime*, *When the Dust Settles* and the Turkish series *Bir Başkadır* (*Ethos*, Netflix, 2020-) exemplify what Jason Mittell calls *centrifugal complexity* where "the ongoing narrative pushes outward, spreading characters across an expanding *storyworld*." This type of storytelling differs from the *centripetal complexity* of shows like *Breaking Bad* where "all narrative expansions connect back to Walter White or his associate Jesse Pinkman."

In *American Crime* and *When the Dust Settles*, the complexity lies in the kaleidoscopic nature of the story and the general sense of de-centralization. In *Breaking Bad* – a series that I will explore in Chapter 5 – we have only a handful of central characters, but a vivid and at times confusing use of flashbacks and flashforwards. Shows like *The Wire*, *American Crime* and *When the Dust Settles* are about "broad systemic" issues, whereas *Breaking Bad* and *True Detective* are dense narratives that focus on "depth of characterisation, layers of backstory and psychological complexity."[361]

On a thematic level, *When the Dust Settles* was based on a lengthy research phase where the two creators wanted to learn more about concepts such as trust and happiness in Danish society. Reports show that Danes have a high degree of life satisfaction and that this level of satisfaction may be related to an overall trust in social structures, institutions and other people.[362] *When the Dust Settles*, therefore, ended up exploring issues connected to trust in modern Danish society - and how a terrorist attack at a local restaurant could challenge the social cohesion and the trust in the political system, the national institutions and other people in general. The issues concerning cohesion are explored through a narrative strategy of fragmentation where the different characters and storylines converge in a tragic event that ends up driving a wedge between different groups and people within Danish society.

Novelistic Approaches and Puzzle Plots

Series like *True Detective* and *The Affair* use multiple timelines, and series like *American Crime* and *When the Dust Settles* take an Altmanesque approach, using a non-linear structure to tell some topical stories about collisions, crises and lack of cohesion. Other series attain complexity by building a vast mythology, by tackling major philosophical questions and by taking a more "novelistic approach" (as Daniel Knauf calls it) with numerous parallel stories, timelines and/or realms. Examples of this include series such as *Carnivàle* (HBO, 2003-2005), *Lost* (ABC, 2004-2010), *Dark* and *Westworld* (HBO, 2016-).[363]

Daniel Knauf's series *Carnivàle* was an almost immediate success for HBO when it premiered in 2003, with its pilot episode attracting 5.33 million viewers. A niche-oriented series, *Carnivàle* was slow-paced and intricate, using parallel storylines of epic, almost Griffithesque proportions. Consequently, its ratings gradually declined, which eventually led to its cancellation after only two seasons; yet it garnered a cult following and an active fan base (who called themselves "Carnies").[364]

Each episode follows two distinct storylines that gradually converge into one complex, mythological story, and they revolve around the young farmer Ben (Nick Stahl), who seeks refuge among a group of "carnies" in a traveling carnival, and a mysterious preacher from California called Brother Justin Crowe (Clancy Brown). Set in Oklahoma and California in the 1930s, the series has a historical aspect, alluding to classic dust bowl-novels like *The Grapes of Wrath* (1939), and it also includes a mythological fight between good and evil as well as some surreal visions and dream sequences that echo the original *Twin Peaks* (ABC, 1990-1991). In the words of Daniel Knauf:

> Carnivàle was similar to Twin Peaks in a few ways. David Lynch is probably one of my biggest influences, and the pacing and the visual language - the way the show was presented - was very Lynchian. But there are also elements of John Steinbeck, Clive Barker, Ray Bradbury and Richard Matheson, and there's some Kubrick there, too. There's a mélange of influences.[365]

There are numerous influences and allusions in Carnivàle. At one point, for example, the tarot card reader Sofie (Clea DuVall) says "one of us," directly referencing Tod Browning's Freaks (1932).

What was more challenging about the series was the scope of the story, the narrative structure of the episodes and the complex mythology. Originally, the series was meant as a trilogy of "paired seasons," spanning the years from the New Deal to the explosion of the nuclear bomb and interweaving historical, fantastical and mythological aspects.[366] As Knauf explains:

> We had a very unique filmic grammar, and you had to watch intensely and try to be educated in the way we were using visions, flashbacks and things like that. We were using a sort of novelistic approach, in that we had two stories going on almost through the entire season, stories that didn't come together until much later. That type of narration is pretty standard in a novel, but it hadn't been done in television before. Remember, this was 2003, and everything back then on TV was doctors, cops and lawyers, and on HBO they were having a lot of success with urban dramas like The Sopranos. And then this came out, and it was so odd. A lot of people didn't know what to make of it, and HBO, at that point, were expecting bigger numbers for Carnivàle than they had with The Sopranos. I remember when I first heard that. It was well into production on the pilot, and they came back and said that they loved what they were seeing. They were very happy, and they thought that it was going to get bigger numbers than The Sopranos. I thought, "Oh, my God. We are so doomed", because it wasn't as accessible as The Sopranos. Carnivàle was quite different from other shows at the time. It essentially consisted of two different shows with none of the same characters, and they were telling two completely different stories, although they were on a sort of collision course.[367]

This combination of elements, together with the unusual and demanding narrative structure, made for a complex show that was widely debated and dissected on message boards. Before *transmedia storytelling* became a widespread phenomenon, and many years before AMAs on Reddit were ever a thing, Daniel Knauf would engage with the fans on the message boards and discuss the different mythological and narrative questions. With the advent of social media and the expansion of the Internet, that sort of creator-fan interaction has since become more accepted and widespread, and it is usually connected with complex and *drillable* series that require focused attention and collective dissection.[368] As Knauf says:

> I was someone who watched movies and TV, and I was a consumer of this product. I wasn't a maker or a manufacturer. I was very much into the Internet in the 1980s and back in the old AOL days, so I was used to interacting with fans about shows. So when Carnivàle came out, I was interacting with the fans in a way that most showrunners don't usually do, participating

in boards and answering questions. I remember being called to the mat by HBO, and they said: "What, are you 15 years old?"

There's this wall between artists in mass media and those people out in the dark. That existed from the beginning of, say, motion pictures. Those people out in the dark were a strange, capricious animal. You really didn't have any direct interaction with them. You knew they were out there, but the only way you interacted with them was through these odd, very controlled events: premieres and things like that. The Internet blew that up, and I thought, "Well, isn't this fantastic," because I like talking with the fans and having an ongoing back-and-forth between the artist and the audience.[369]

Before turning our attention to the concepts of *drillable texts* and *transmedia storytelling*, let us briefly return to *Dark* as a radical example of narrative complexity in modern television. The first German Netflix series, *Dark* tells the story of four families in a small German town and revolves around the uncanny disappearance of two local boys. This tragic event, as Lothar Mikos writes, "causes the façade of the supposedly intact world of these families to crumble," and soon the "dark secrets of the family members are revealed."[370]

As Kelly Luegenbiehl mentioned in the feature interview at the end of Chapter 3, *Dark* is a complex series due to its philosophical aspects and its radical non-linearity where different timelines - even alternative versions of the same timelines - are interwoven. Referencing *Back to the Future* (1985), *Twin Peaks* and *Donnie Darko* (2001), *Dark* begins with a concrete mystery, but gradually develops into an existentialist exploration of concepts such as 'time' and 'self'.

The trope of a young person disappearing in a small town is not in itself new, and it clearly resonates with American series like *Twin Peaks* and *Stranger Things*. All three series take place in dark and mysterious small towns (Twin Peaks, Hawkins and Winden), and all of them combine an element of nostalgia with collapsing timelines and a mythological story about confronting oneself. In the original *Twin Peaks*, Dale Cooper (Kyle MacLachlan) faces himself in The Black Lodge where he tries to escape his own Doppelgänger, and in *Dark* there is an actual quote from Friederich Nietzsche, which seems to address the same issue: "[I]f you gaze long into an abyss, the abyss also gazes into you."[371]

Dark also references Arthur Schopenhauer and other German thinkers, adding a philosophical or existential layer to the complex narrative. Moreover, it shares yet another aspect with *Twin Peaks*: the idea of time as a cyclical phenomenon. In *Dark*, this concept is depicted in the actual time-travel aspect, but also through allusions to the infinity symbol and the mythological character Ariadne, who in Greek mythology gave Theseus the ball of thread that could help him out of the Minotaur's labyrinth. In a universe consisting of different timelines and alternate realities, Ariadne's thread would be helpful, and the same thing is true of complex serials such as *Dark*, with their labyrin-

Fig. 26: *Dark* (2017-2020) is a complex series that involves multiple different characters, places and timelines that blend and overlap in cryptic and perplexing ways. The long-awaited TV adaptation of Isaac Asimov's book series, *Foundation* (Apple TV+), might be the next example in a long line of popular puzzle box series. © Netflix, courtesy of Oliver Rawlins and Kim Stagmeier.

thine narratives and captivating *puzzle plots*.

Describing such *puzzle plots* and complex stories, Anne Jerslev mentions four criteria: *non-persons*, *achronological plots*, *negation* and *reconstruction*.[372] Jerslev specifically addresses complex and 'deceiving' films like *Lost Highway* (1997) and *Fight Club* (1999), which often subvert the audience's attention through sudden twists or *reframing acts*. Still, many of her criteria are applicable to complex serials such as *Dark*. *Dark* is certainly *achronological* - as is evident from the recurring quote "Der Anfang ist das Ende, und das Ende ist der Anfang" ("The beginning is the end, and the end is the beginning") - and it requires a thorough mental *reconstruction* from the viewer in order for it to make sense. As mentioned earlier, all fictions require mental work from the reader/viewer, who makes inferences and locates patterns. But in *Dark* the amount of reconstructive work that is needed far exceeds a traditional TV series. Not only does the series jump continually between different years (e.g. 2019, 1986 and 1953), it also includes alternate realities and numerous examples of significant repetitions and subtle variations. *Dark* is narratively confounding, and from the first reveal in Ep.1:5 ("Wahrheiten"/"Truths") - where we learn that Mikkel was not only sent back to the 1980s, but also lived on from that point, eventually becoming Jonas' father - it becomes gradually more complex and dizzying. At one point we learn, for example, that Charlotte Doppler's daughter from the future gives birth to a daughter, who, upon being sent back in time, grows up as Charlotte Doppler.[373]

In a recent article, Kellie Herson argues that many series today tackle "The Big Mystery," and this wave of complex serials, which also includes *The Left-*

149

overs (HBO, 2014-2017), *Mr. Robot* (USA Network, 2015-2019), *The OA* (Netflix, 2016-2019) and *Watchmen* (HBO, 2019), are fittingly dubbed *puzzle box series*. These TV series are characterized by "carefully paced episodes that drop leading clues and execute disorienting plot twists," and they illustrate the popularity of complex serials in the modern TV landscape where global streamers like Netflix, cable networks like HBO and traditional broadcasters like ABC inspire each other to push the boundaries of TV storytelling.[374]

The Leftovers, for instance, has been praised by many critics but described by others as "nonsensical" due to its complex interweaving of different places, timelines and characters and its fluid boundary between dream and reality.[375] Created by Tom Perrotta and Damon Lindelof (*Lost*, *Watchmen*), *The Leftovers* can be seen as a complex exploration of loss and grief or an apocalyptic story of almost Biblical proportions that takes its viewers from Mapleton, New York, to Jarden, Texas and the Australian outback. The first season follows Perrotta's original novel, but in the second and third seasons, the series becomes radically more demanding, and the lines between fantasy and reality are all but dissolved. This is seen most evidently in the episode "International Assassin" (Ep. 2:8), which was inspired by the coma dreams in *The Sopranos* and Dale Cooper's journey through The Black Lodge in *Twin Peaks*.[376] In this episode, there is a palpable break with the seeming realism of the first season, as we follow police officer Kevin Garvey (Justin Theroux) through a Purgatory-like dream world. "You've got to stop thinking in such straight lines," as Virgil (Steven Williams) reminds Kevin before assisting him on his psychological and/or metaphysical journey. This reminder, offered to Kevin at a critical point in the second season, may also be a clue to the viewers, hinting at the radical non-linearity and complexity of *The Leftovers*.

Complex TV might be a more natural fit with subscription-based channels and services that care less about ratings than about subscriptions and viewer engagement. Also, the possibilities for bingeing and re-watching that viewers get with DVD, Blu-ray and streaming services are neatly suited for complex and demanding television. "Bingeing on DVD can highlight narrative redundancies designed for weekly viewers," as Jason Mittell writes, and Amanda D. Lotz also argues that there is "a profound difference in meaning available to those who watch a season or even an entire series over the course of a few days or even a month."[378] Nevertheless, complex serials can be located across many different channels and services, which illustrates that narrative complexity thrives in a complex TV landscape.

Jason Mittell claims that "transformations in industrial norms, viewing practices and technologies have helped give rise to new formal elements of television storytelling," but he specifically notes that 'complexity' is not a synonym for 'quality', the latter being a problematic, normative word. *Com-*

Tom Perrotta (writer/co-creator) on *The Leftovers* and complex TV

There's a place, a line, and if you cross it into twists for the sake of twists it becomes uninteresting. I was very conscious of not violating the integrity of the story. Damon is a much wilder storyteller than I am, so early on I was often trying to hold him back, and as we developed a sense of trust – he started to internalize my sense of "what's too much," and I started to internalize his sense of "let's press the boundaries" – we were able to expand what the story could do and expand the complexity. Even in something like "International Assassin" – that kind of dream world that we created – we were able to have some sort of internal logic and move back into the real world in a way that felt okay to me. I was the realist who always tried to ground the story, and Damon is an incredible fantasist. It was two very different sensibilities, and as a result it has a texture that's very different from other shows that are in the fantasy or sci-fi realm; they are not quite as grounded as *The Leftovers*.

The storytelling ground shifted when we left Mapleton in the first season. That part was related very much to the book, and the book's idea was: an apocalyptic thing has happened, but the world looks the same. All of the shock and transformation is internal and psychological. As we moved out to these more magical or apparently magical places like Miracle and the Australian outback, there was a sense that we were writing a modern-day Bible story. This allowed for a more mythic and larger-than-life storytelling element to come into it. It was an evolution over the three seasons.

Damon is a very restless storyteller. He really likes to bring in new elements and reset all the pieces on the table, and he knows how to make that work because he's full of ideas and storytelling energy. It can be a bit daunting to say: "Okay, we're going to pick up all of our storytelling elements and move them to a different place." And some of it seems so thought-out afterwards, but some of it happened for practical reasons. Part of the reason that we moved to a new place in Season 2 was that it was really hard to shoot the show in New York because it was a suburban show, but everybody was based in the city, so we spent a lot of time picking up the set and moving it from one place to another. We spent hours on the road every day, and it wore people down. And we had gotten to the end of that story, and we had this idea of a town called Miracle in Season 1. We thought that it might be an episode where the character Tom would move through there as part of his cross-country journey, and we couldn't quite fit it in. At the same time, there was a feeling that we should leave New York, and all of these different things led us to say that we should set all of Season 2 in this place, and when we had decided to do that, people started to say: "You can shoot it in Atlanta or Texas."[377]

plex TV is a term that covers different approaches to television storytelling that thrive in an era of streaming and *compressed consumption*. In that sense, *American Crime* might be similar to *The Wire* in terms of storytelling, yet the two series are significantly different in terms of style. *The Wire*, as Mittell writes, "embraces a 'zero degree style' that strives to render its storytelling techniques invisible," whereas *American Crime* has an obtrusive and experimental aesthetic, overtly playing with many of the conventions from mainstream film and television.[379] Similarly, TV series like *Twin Peaks*, *Carnivàle* and *Dark* represent a broader tendency within television storytelling, exploring intricate storyworlds, vast mythologies and complex philosophical questions, but they are vividly different in terms of style and pacing.

In the following section, I will delve further into *Twin Peaks* as an untraditional example of *transmedia storytelling*, comparing its approach to the *transmedia strategies* in AMC's *The Walking Dead*.

Seriality Across Media: Transmedia Storytelling

If *complex TV* describes a wide range of new approaches to television storytelling, then *transmedia storytelling* covers an even broader, almost ubiquitous, approach to storytelling *across* different media. *Complex TV* may be a tendency in modern television, closely but not exclusively connected to subscription-based channels and streaming services, but *transmedia storytelling* is a massive trend and strategy across various markets and industries. The *multiplatform era* is a period in TV history (from 2000 and onwards) where TV series are viewed on various platforms or include different media and platforms as part of their narratives. In this era, *transmedia storytelling* is an obvious strategy, and it might be the most visible sign of the modern mediascape. We could even say that *transmedia is everywhere*, referencing the popularity of the concept and the inherent qualities of *transmedia storytelling* as a strategy where *storyworlds* span multiple texts and media.

The term *transmedia storytelling* was originally introduced by media scholars like Henry Jenkins (2006), Christy Dena (2009) and Jason Mittell, and it is basically defined as "the flow of content through multiple media platforms" or "a narrative so large that it cannot be covered in a single medium."[380] Elsewhere, Jenkins gives a more nuanced and elaborate description of the concept, which has become almost ubiquitous in the field of Media Studies:

> Transmedia storytelling represents a process where integral elements of a fiction get dispersed systematically across multiple delivery channels for the purpose of creating a unified and coordinated entertainment experience. Ideally, each medium makes its own unique contribution to the unfolding of the story.[381]

In that sense, *transfictionality* and *transmediality* are terms used to describe *storyworlds* that span multiple texts and media, and, according to Marie-Laure Ryan, we can broadly distinguish between two different forms of *transmedia storytelling*:

- *Snowball transmedia* (defined as a transmedial story that grows from the success of a single primary text, snowballing into a large universe that spans different texts and media).
- *Transmedia franchise* (understood as a more strategic attempt to tell a large story and create an expansive *storyworld* across multiple different text, media and platforms.[382]

More specifically, Jenkins pinpoints seven different principles of *transmedia storytelling*, and the most central of these are *spreadability* and *drillability*, *continuity* and *multiplicity*, *immersion* and *extractability*, *performance* and *world building*.[383] The concept of *spreadability* refers to the level of participatory engagement that different texts produce. All texts invite their audiences to engage, but some texts, in a more direct sense, invite the consumers to participate by sharing information about the text as well as sharing and debating snippets from the text itself. This concept is connected to another term called *drillability*, which refers to the level of complexity in a given text and how much 'drilling' it requires from the fans. This notion is similar to Jason Mittell's concept of *forensic fandom*, describing a type of engagement, which is associated with complex texts that are difficult to penetrate. If a text is complex and multi-layered, it might invite fans to debate and dissect it collectively, perhaps even rewinding and re-watching previous episodes while taking notes (Jenkins describes this as "the yellow pad fan culture").[384] As Mittell writes:

> Complex television encourages forensic fans to dig deeper, probing beneath the surface to understand the complexity of a story and its telling. [...] Drillable engagement and forensic fandom are not entirely new phenomena, but rather have accelerated by degree in the digital era... [C]ontemporary examples are notable for both the digital tools that have enabled fans to collectively apply and share their forensic efforts and the demands that mainstream network programs make on the viewers to pay attention and connect the narrative dots.[385]

The terms *continuity* and *multiplicity*, then, refer to two different, but both necessary, qualities in *transmedia storytelling*. The sense of *continuity* across the different texts in *transmedia storytelling* is important for fans, and if there is a strong sense of *continuity* across media and texts, that may yield a larger sense of pay-off for the 'hardcore' fans who invest a lot of time engaging with every part of the story. *Multiplicity*, on the other hand, refers to the possibility for creative participation (what Axel Bruns calls *produsage culture*) through fan fiction and similar activities.[386] *Continuity* is about the coherence and cohesion *within* the transmedial story, whereas *multiplicity* is about the potentials for adding and contributing *to* the transmedial story. The terms *immersion* and *extractability* refer to the possibilities of stepping into the fictional universe itself (through theme parks and location tours) and to take home parts of the fictional world (via merchandise). Finally, the terms *performance* and *world building* describe ways in which the stories invite their audiences to engage with the diegetic world in a performative way (e.g. through *cosplay*) and how secondary and tertiary texts add to the overall universe.

Though a relatively new term, *transmedia storytelling* is hardly a new phenomenon, and a striking early example is *Star Trek* (NBC, 1966-1969), which was created by Gene Roddenberry in 1966, gradually developing into a massive *transmedia franchise* that covers a long line of films, multiple interconnected TV series and various forms of *tie-in* products and merchandise. The TV scholars Roberta Pearson and Máire Messenger Davies, in fact, see *Star Trek* as a paradigmatic example of the type of *transmedia storytelling* that naturally grows out of cult series with expansive and strongly defined worlds.[387] Cult series, Matt Hills also argues, often operate with "detailed, expansive, diegetic worlds (or even universes)," and, in that sense, there are many examples in TV history of series that begin as cult phenomena before developing into large and more strategic examples of *transmedia storytelling*.[388] Apart from *Star Trek* and *Twin Peaks*, one could point to a popular phenomenon such as the *Buffy* franchise, which includes a film from 1992, a well-known vampire series (The WB/UPN, 1997-2003), a *spin-off* series (*Angel*, The WB, 1999-2004), and various *tie-in* books, comic books and video games. Another noteworthy example is *The X-Files* (Fox, 1993-2002), which grew from a *Twin Peaks*-inspired cult series into a vast *transmedia franchise* consisting of two cinematic sequels (1998, 2008), a humorous *spin-off* (*The Lone Gunmen*, Fox, 2001) and a televisual continuation (2016).[389]

Hence, *transmedia storytelling* is not a new concept, and the connection between *transmedia storytelling*, expansive universes and cult series is also a well-known part of TV history. Nevertheless, there seems to be a clear tendency in the modern TV landscape towards a more strategic form of *transmedia storytelling* that involves different media, engages the fan base and taps into the fans' nostalgic yearning for familiar diegetic worlds. This is seen in series like *Westworld* and *Cobra Kai* (YouTube Red/YouTube Premium/Netflix, 2018-) that return to popular films, expand the fictional universes and exploit the interest among fans to dissect and debate the series and return to the worlds that they love. *Westworld*, for example, has been the object of many fan theories, whereas *Cobra Kai* consciously plays on the nostalgia of the viewers through numerous references and flashbacks to the original *Ka-*

rate Kid films, popular hits from the era and dedications to deceased actors in the credits.[390] Add to this the many recent examples of cinematic prequels, sequels and *spin-offs* that continue the story or expand the diegetic worlds of popular TV series, e.g. *El Camino: A Breaking Bad Movie* (Netflix, 2019) and the prequel to *The Sopranos: The Many Saints of Newark* (New Line Cinema/HBO, 2021). Not to mention the ever-expanding Marvel and *Star Wars* universes (cf. the metafictional Marvel series *WandaVision* [Disney+, 2021] and *The Mandalorian* [Disney+, 2019-], which connects aspects from the original *Star Wars* trilogy with elements from animated series like *Clone Wars* [Cartoon Network/Netflix/Disney+, 2008-2020] and *Star Wars Rebels* [Disney XD, 2014-2018]) or series connected to *Alien* (Noah Hawley, FX), *Game of Thrones* (Ryan J. Condal and George R.R. Martin, HBO Max), *Harry Potter* (HBO Max) and *The Lord of the Rings* (J.D. Payne & Patrick McKay, Amazon Prime). The multi-season prequel to *The Lord of the Rings* has a budget of 1 billion dollars, and the production company spent 250 million dollars on securing the adaptation rights from the Tolkien Estate.[391]

Undeads and Hybrids: *The Walking Dead* as Transmedia Franchise

According to film and TV historian Jeffrey Sconce, *transmedia storytelling* is a noticeable part of the modern mediascape, and he describes this tendency in the following way:

> U.S. television has devoted increased attention in the past two decades to crafting and maintaining ever more complex narrative universes, a form of "world building" that has allowed for wholly new modes of narration and that suggests new forms of audience engagement. Television ... has discovered that the cultivation of its story worlds (diegesis) is as crucial an element of its success as storytelling. What television lacks in spectacle and narrative constraints, it makes up for in depth and duration of character relations, diegetic expansion, and audience investment. A commercial series that succeeds in the U.S. system ends up generating hundreds of hours of programming, allowing for an often quite sophisticated and complex elaboration of character and story world.[392]

A popular example of *transmedia storytelling* is AMC's *The Walking Dead*, which was developed by Frank Darabont and based on the comic book series by Robert Kirkman, Tony Moore and Charlie Adlard. The original TV series, which is currently in its tenth season, is a post-apocalyptic horror series about a group of characters (most prominently Rick Grimes) that try to escape a zombie infestation and establish a new civilization by constantly moving to new frontiers and creating new (temporary) homes.[393] In that sense, the series does not have one particular location - it is originally set in Atlanta, Georgia, but the characters continually move to new locations in order to avoid zombies and other potential threats - and the characters are also disposable, constantly being killed off and replaced by new apparent regulars.

The protagonist is Rick Grimes (Andrew Lincoln), a traditional western-like hero who wears a broad-brimmed hat, rides a horse and acts instead of talking, and in the beginning he is contrasted by his friend Shane (Jon Bernthal). While Rick is stoic and introverted, Shane is charming and talkative, his name ironically alluding to George Stevens' classic western from 1953. This difference is central to an inter-relational conflict between Rick and Shane, before Shane eventually dies, and the series is best described as a *serial melodrama* that explores psychological and relational conflicts while evoking and exploiting various televisual formulas and genres. A typical trait in *blockbuster series* is the use of a multiethnic cast and genre hybridity, hoping to appeal to different audiences and demographics.[394] This strategy is also evident in *The Walking Dead* that includes generic elements and conventions from horror fiction, westerns, disaster movies and even *wuxia* films (a stylish brand of samurai films produced in China). When asked about the genre hybridity in *The Walking Dead*, the showrunner, Angela Kang, also describes it as a way to engage and connect with different audiences.[395]

The western elements are noticeable from the very first episode, both in terms of iconography and various genre conventions, and they are used throughout the series. The idea of frontiers, fences and borders, for example, may be a topical reference to American politics, but might also be a western trope where the hero moves to new frontiers to face his/her "uncivilized double" (in this case zombies, not Native Americans).[396] Referencing the episode "Clear" (Ep. 3:12), the director Tricia Brock talks about the intentional use of western conventions in *The Walking Dead*, including allusions to John Ford and Fred Zinnemann:

> Luckily, a lot of people reference that episode as being one of their favorite early episodes, and I shot it like a John Ford movie with all kinds of wide shots - big graphic wides without moving the camera too much - and that whole battle when they get into town, we treated that like it was *High Noon*.[397]

Other characters and episodes refer to other genres; the scenes with the zombie attacks often evoke elements from the horror and the action genres, and the scenes with Michonne Hawthorne (Danai Gurira) immediately evoke the *wuxia* genre (most evidently in Ep. 4:16 where she is described as a samurai). This element of genre hybridity is not necessarily connected to the *transmedia strategies* of *The Walking Dead*, yet the different genre conventions often - at times even explicitly - lend themselves to different types of video games and theme park activities. The POV shots of characters shooting zombies and the scenes in "Say the Word" (Ep. 3:5), where Rick kills zombies in the prison with a blade, have an aesthetic that is notably similar to first-person shooter games. This aesthetic is a staple in *The Walking Dead*, going back to the very first episode, "Days Gone By", where we share Morgan's point of view as he kills zombies from his window, struggling to shoot his undead wife. The same aesthetic is evident in the episode "Try" (Ep. 5:15), and many of the scenes with Michonne lend themselves neatly to action-based computer games, from which they have borrowed much of their style. In the feature interview at the end of this chapter, the showrunner, Angela Kang, describes how they try to avoid getting "too video-gamey," although admitting that she and Scott Gimple are both gamers and, thus, drawn to the video game aesthetic.[398]

What may be an incidental crossover where the aesthetic qualities of different media influence each other in complex ways, may also be an intentional strategy. In any case, the genre hybridity and aesthetics of *The Walking Dead* facilitated a *transmedia experience* where audiences were able to enjoy thrilling and immersive haunted-house attractions at Universal Studios or play video and computer games connected to the *storyworld*.[399]

Today, the *Walking Dead* franchise covers a vast array of texts, including AMC's *The Walking Dead Webisodes: Torn Apart*, created by Greg Nicotero and featuring a memorable character from the original series called "Bicycle Girl". "Bicycle Girl" is a part of the original comic book series, and in the TV series she is shot by Rick Grimes in an act of mercy, as she is helpless and poses no threat to him or anyone else. In that sense, the small collection of webisodes functioned as a sort of *fan service*, catering to the fans by giving them a fictional addendum to the original story about a minor, albeit memorable and quite beloved, character. Other expansions include the *spin-off* series *Fear the Walking Dead* (AMC, 2015-) that re-situated the action to Los Angeles, while creating many direct links and crossover elements to the original TV series. Where *The Walking Dead* focused on a post-apocalyptic society and characters that move to new frontiers and attempt to rebuild civilization, *Fear the Walking Dead* focused on the *decline* of civilization.

In 2020, a new televisual *spin-off* was launched (*The Walking Dead: World Beyond*), and the transmedial world of *The Walking Dead* also includes popular video games, e.g. the first-person shooter game *The Walking Dead: Survival Instinct* (Terminal Reality, 2013), the episodic video game *The Walking Dead* (Telltale Games, 2012) and the Pokemon Go-style AR game *The Walking Dead: Our World*, which was released for iOS and Android in 2018.[400] Telltale's episodic in-world game, which references popular characters like Glenn, has received a lot of attention due to its thrilling combination of point-and-click adventure and compelling storytelling. With more than 30,000 positive reviews on Steam, Telltale's *Walking Dead* game is an immersive narrative experience that uses *cliffhangers* and recaps like the TV series and expands the *storyworld* (at one point, for example, Glenn wants to leave the group and go to Atlanta, saying: "I've got friends there").[401] Part of a small bundle, Telltale also released some other in-world adventure games, including *The Walking Dead: Michonne* and *The Walking Dead: A New Frontier* (Telltale Games, 2016).

Apart from the different video games and graphic novels, AMC has even produced a live television aftershow called *Talking Dead* (2011-) where cast and crew members discuss the different episodes together with the host Chris Hardwick. The world surrounding *The Walking Dead* continues to expand across a variety of texts and media. At times, however, there are issues concerning the *continuity* between different parts of the *transmedia franchise*, as in the case of the Governor, who seems slightly different in the series from the character in Jay Bonansinga and Robert Kirkman's horror novel *The Walking Dead: Rise of the Governor* (2011). Still, *The Walking Dead* remains a significant and successful *transmedia franchise*, and the TV series is a popular entity in the current streaming age (even if ratings have declined since the impressive Season 5 premiere that attracted 17.3 million viewers).[402]

The TV series was described by George A. Romero as a soap opera with zombies - a description that the showrunner Angela Kang willingly accepts - and it does have evident similarities with traditional *serial melodramas*.[403] Apart from focusing on relational and psychological issues, it employs a host of *intra-* and *extra-episodic cliffhangers*, and it even features some noteworthy examples of *fake departures* (e.g. when Glenn seemingly dies). One of the most essential elements of a *serial melodrama* is its longevity, and that aspect is also seen in *The Walking Dead*. As in a traditional soap opera, the situation in *The Walking Dead* is never stable, and the characters continually move to new frontiers, hoping to find resources, safety and stability. As a transmedia experience, *The Walking Dead* is also a continuing story that constantly moves to new media and platforms. The series itself might not run indefinitely, but the *storyworld* has proven flexible and endlessly expandable, as if it were a zombie refusing to die.

"A Bigger Game": *Twin Peaks* and Transmedia

"When you see me again, it won't be me." Thus said The Man from Another Place (Michael J. Anderson) in the original *Twin Peaks* when it aired on ABC 30 years ago. And he was right, not only because Michael J. Anderson was replaced by an electric tree (!) when Showtime revived *Twin Peaks* in 2017, but also because the series, in itself, came back in a new and different iteration. If the original *Twin Peaks* was an example of *snowball transmedia*, then Showtime's continuation could be described as a more strategic type of *transmedia franchise*. The original series was a surprising success and spawned a host of *tie-in* books, prequels and paratexts, but already when launching their continuation, it was evident that Showtime were strategic and deft in the way they involved various media and engaged the fans who had taken an active part in trying to prolong and resurrect the series. In that sense, the new *Twin Peaks* was not just a 'return', but also a transformation, and Showtime tapped into popular tendencies of nostalgia, fan involvement and *transmedia storytelling*.

The original *Twin Peaks* was branded as the 'singular vision' of David Lynch, who had migrated from film to television (as Ingmar Bergman, Rainer Werner Fassbinder and Krzysztof Kieślowski had done in Europe). And the new series, to an even larger degree, promotes itself as an 'authorial creation'. This time, as the executive producer Sabrina Sutherland says, David Lynch has directed all 18 episodes (or parts), besides having been heavily involved in the editing and sound design, having played a central part in the series (as Gordon Cole) and having checked and sanctioned all the decisions that were made during production and post-production.[404] The new *Twin Peaks* promises to be an organic work of art, made by a recognized auteur, but at the same time it is an organized story that cleverly includes various media and engages the 'forensic' fan culture.

"Give *Peaks* a Chance": From Cancellation to Continuation

The original *Twin Peaks* became a reality because Robert Iger from ABC took a chance at the end of the 1980s. The big broadcaster had some lackluster ratings compared to its immediate competitors, NBC and CBS, and the channel with the lowest ratings was usually more willing to take risks and more open to experimentation.[405] Hence, the network scheduled a meeting between the script writer Mark Frost, the arthouse director David Lynch and their common agent Tony Krantz. As Krantz remembers:

> David was and is this brilliant visual stylist. He's got a mood, a world that he references with everything that he does. Mark's training was more classical, more structural. When he worked on *Hill Street Blues*, which was really the gold standard of television dramas, he brought that sort of storytelling rigor to this extraordinary artistic mood and directorial style that David Lynch brought. The two of them together, like Mick Jagger and Keith Richards or John Lennon and Paul McCartney, were great in that moment for what they brought to each other to create *Twin Peaks*. *Twin Peaks* could not have existed with just one of them. It really had to depend on both of them.[406]

Lynch and Frost pitched their series as a *whodunit* about the murder of a young girl in a fictional small town in the Pacific Northwest. Employing a traditional trope, known as *the dead girl show*, the premise for the series, as journalist David Bushman has noted, might have been based on an actual case: the unsolved murder of Hazel Drew in the early 1900s.[407] Lynch and Frost used the *whodunit* formula as a hook, but Lynch also famously spoke about the wind and the trees and drew a map of a rural town named Twin Peaks (a name that alluded to the motifs of doubling and duality in the series). These stories caught the attention of Iger and ABC, but as the central case began to recede into the background - a case that was seemingly solved by Tim Hunter's famous episode "Arbitrary Law" (Ep. 2:9) - the ratings began to decline. What began as a *watercooler phenomenon* ("If you miss it tonight, you won't know what everyone's talking about tomorrow," as it said in one of ABC's official ads), had gradually turned into a cult or niche-phenomenon before niche branding and *narrowcasting* had become a norm.[408]

The original series came during *the multi-channel transition* where new cable and satellite channels were entering the TV landscape and where *appointment viewing* and *demographic thinking* became household phenomena.[409] *Twin Peaks* was never intended as a niche-oriented series, however, and it was a broad success during its first season (34 million viewers tuning in to watch the pilot episode on ABC). But as the ratings dropped, it became a more exclusive phenomenon, and eventually, as the ratings dropped to seven million viewers, Iger and ABC had lost their patience. The fan group *COOP* (*Citizens Opposing the Offing of Peaks*) fought to get the series back to its original slot, using the slogan "Give *Peaks* a Chance," and as David Lynch went on David Letterman's *Late Show*, prompting the fans to write Iger, they flooded him with letters in the hope of prolonging their favorite show.[410] They succeeded, if only for a brief time, but in 1991 Robert Iger placed *Twin Peaks* and two other lauded ABC classics, *Thirtysomething* (ABC, 1987-1991) and *China Beach* (ABC, 1988-1991), on "indefinite hiatus."

Different Peaks: From Resurrection to Reformation

> Is the murder of Laura Palmer really the end or just the beginning? In any case, I am absolutely certain that the key to the solution to this riddle is hidden within this film.
> - Dale Cooper (Kyle MacLachlan) in a Japanese promo for Fire Walk with Me (1992)[411]

After the cancellation, there were some thoughts about resurrecting *Twin Peaks*. But Robert Engels' idea about a *graphic novel* continuation to *Twin Peaks*, created in collaboration with a graphic designer, was rejected by Lynch, and the idea about a third season was turned down by the network. With a mixture of expectation and skepticism, fans and critics watched the prequel, called *Twin Peaks: Fire Walk with Me*, when it premiered at the festival in Cannes in May 1992. The film was a harrowing portrayal of Laura Palmer, depicting her Persephone-like "descent into Hades" during the last week of her life with a combination of heavy expressionism, collapsing timelines, morbid humor and graphic horror.[412] The film began with a shot of a television set tuned to a dead channel, accompanied by a jazzy score by Angelo Badalamenti. The television set was soon destroyed, and what followed was a lengthy sequence in a small town called Deer Meadow. In that sense, the film hardly promised to be a linear and chronological prequel to *Twin Peaks*, even if it was promoted as such. In fact, it almost looked like a metaphorical disavowal of the TV series or network television in general. Apparently, however, many fans and critics had hoped for exactly that: a linear prequel to *Twin Peaks*, told in the same charming mix of quaint melodrama, compelling crime fiction and quirky humor that people knew from the TV series, and the reviewers were generally underwhelmed. The Danish critic Ebbe Iversen called it "a travesty," while the American film and TV critic Vincent Canby wrote that it looked like "the worst movie ever made."[413] And it *was* different with its explicit content, its relentlessly dark and depressing tone and its tough depiction of incest. Teresa Banks (Pamela Gidley), who is killed in the opening of the film, never sees BOB, but only Leland Palmer (Ray Wise), implying that BOB (Frank Silva), in this iteration of *Twin Peaks*, was nothing more than a representation of Leland's evil side or a psychological externalization.[414]

In any case, the film was not a simple addendum to *Twin Peaks* or a linear continuation, whose purpose was to add some enticing backstory to the transmedial *storyworld*. It was the 'inverted mirror' version of *Twin Peaks*, and that might have been the reason for its lukewarm reception at Cannes; yet, at the same time, this was the basis for its rediscovery and reappraisal many years later (when it was hailed as a great film and highlighted by film historian Mark Cousins as a crucial part of Lynch's oeuvre).[415] *Fire Walk with Me* did not simply continue the story of *Twin Peaks*; it added another layer to the already multi-layered, multi-medial story and expanded the universe that Lynch and Frost had created in 1989. It may have been criticized and maligned upon its release in 1992, but in 2017 *Fire Walk with Me* was elevated to a canonical status in the *Twin Peaks* universe, as seen in the many recycled characters, locations and shots from the film in *Twin Peaks: The Return*.[416]

From *Snowball Transmedia* to *Transmedia Franchise*

In that sense, *Fire Walk with Me* contributed to the expansive *storyworld* behind *Twin Peaks*, a diegetic world that spanned numerous different texts. These included audio books (*Diane...*); novels (*The Secret Diary of Laura Palmer* and *The Autobiography of F.B.I. Special Agent Dale Cooper*); Log Lady introductions made in conjunction with the syndication of *Twin Peaks* on the cable channel Bravo; Georgia Coffee commercials with their own fictional in-world narratives (made exclusively for the Japanese market); and a feature film that premiered at Cannes.[417] *Twin Peaks* had turned into a world of its own that audiences could delve into and become immersed in from multiple vantage points, each text adding a new layer to the mystery, the town and the characters.

In Scott Frost's book, *The Autobiography of F.B.I. Special Agent Dale Coop-*

er, readers learn that Dale Cooper met a BOB-like character in his early adolescence, and in the Log Lady introductions viewers heard Catherine Coulson's character talking about mirroring and characters that multiply into many different people. Even more than in the original series, these themes and motifs are a part of *Twin Peaks: The Return*, which has a fragmented narrative and style, and perhaps this fragmentation, as TV critic Jeff Jensen suggests, illustrates Dale Cooper's attempt to 'return' to Twin Peaks and become 'whole' again:

> To borrow again from "Purple Rain," maybe Agent Cooper's journey is about "reaching out for something new" and becoming something new. Cooper's odyssey to recover the fullness of his unique identity — or not — in an alien landscape filled with people who confuse him for being someone else or want him to be something else is compelling, in part, because it plays to, and with, our nostalgia. It's a metaphor for the new *Twin Peaks* itself, a show that, for now, wishes to behave more as a new life reincarnation than a reboot or revival of a dormant old one. Cooper contains the questions, ambitions and restlessness of its creators. What should *Twin Peaks* be in 2017? How to satisfy themselves and the audience? By mimicking the original? By being radically different?[418]

The new *Twin Peaks* has been called *The Return* by the cable network Showtime - a title that is not sanctioned by Lynch and Frost - but it does not look like the *Twin Peaks* that viewers left more than 25 years ago. The red curtains in "The Red Room" have a different shade and an almost artificial look, and this time they seem to blow in the wind. The series also alternates between color and black-and-white, as seen in the opening where Dale Cooper is told by The Fireman (Carel Struycken) to "listen to the sounds." The title sequence has also been updated, and now we can actually hear the diegetic sound of the waterfall. The characters have changed, too, and the ageing characters and the "broken beauty" of the worn-down sites (e.g. the saw mill) illustrate that *Twin Peaks: The Return* is not just a 'return', but, like *Fire Walk with Me*, a *new* version of *Twin Peaks*.[419] As the editor Duwayne Dunham puts it:

> It's a different kind of environment, and even the characters *within* the environment are different. It didn't have the consistency in terms of pacing that the original series had, but it certainly had its own.
>
> As David was shooting, I experimented and tried putting some of the music from the original *Twin Peaks* into the new series, and it was difficult. I couldn't figure out whether it was because of the different timelines or the tonal differences between the two series. But then David got back, and one day I heard him in the studio. Earlier, David had slowed down a piece of music and used it for Bad Cooper's arrival. A great piece of music and a really interesting piece. But what happened now was that David was in the studio with his mixer, Dean Hurley, and I could hear that they were literally trying to crash the "Bad Cooper music" and the original theme for *Twin Peaks* into each other. He was trying to figure out how to connect those two worlds, not just musically but thematically, and I remember saying to my assistant: "What David is doing is really interesting, and I bet that when we cut the title sequence, we're going to cut from the waterfalls and go straight into The Red Room." That's what he was trying to do. Not blend the two worlds together, but *crash* them into each other.[420]

We may have returned to Twin Peaks in the new series, but the town and the citizens have changed, and even in a literal, geographical sense it is difficult to go back. The series alternates between various locations (e.g. New York, Las Vegas, Buckhorn and Twin Peaks) and between a dreamy, associative style akin to *Eraserhead* and *Inland Empire* (2006) and a more campy and comical universe that is reminiscent of the soap opera parody in the original series (cf. the scene where Bobby [Dana Ashbrook] cries to the vision of Laura's portrait, or the scenes with Naomi Watts that directly reference *Mulholland Dr.* [2001]). The original series was also a hybrid, alternating between different genres, moods and tonalities, but the new series is closer to avant-garde cinema, and it consciously toys with the audience and their expectations.[421]

When Shelly (Mädchen Amick) says, "James has always been cool," for example, that line seems to reference or comment upon the criticism and ridicule that James has received in the fan environment. And when they hold back many of the popular leitmotifs from the original series while playing a "live" version of the song "Just You and I", referencing one of the most divisive moments of the original series, that certainly looks like intentional, metafictional teasing.[422] If fans wanted a nostalgic return, they got something else. If they wanted to go back to a place where "there's always music in the air," this time they were met by a totally different style and atmosphere that invited them to "listen to the sounds." As the executive producer Sabrina Sutherland puts it:

> I think a lot of the people who worked on the show didn't know what to expect, and certainly they wouldn't know what to expect anyway because we were shooting it out of order, and no one really quite knew how everything went together. And if they did read the script, there were only a couple of lines of description of certain things, so it's all in David's head... It was an amazing kind of revelation. It's just the sound and the picture, and you're going into this other world. And *Twin Peaks* – the world itself – was changed. A lot of people wanted that nostalgia and were upset because it wasn't like the original series, in a way, but it's 25 years later, and it does go more in depth. And I think it does have a lot to do with *Fire Walk with Me*. It's much more similar to *Fire Walk with Me* than the way *Twin Peaks* became – not slapsticky, but kind of cornyish in a way. Not a parody of itself, but it kind of went in a different direction. And this kind of brought it back to a more real-world edginess.[423]

Trailers, Intentional Errors and Fan Involvement

The campaign surrounding *Twin Peaks: The Return* was shrouded in secrecy, and Mark Frost's *tie-in* book, *The Secret History of Twin Peaks* (2016), was launched at a strategic time, but posed more questions than it answered, adding yet another layer to the transmedial story. In Frost's book, we learn that Major Briggs (Don S. Davis) might have been wrong, when he presumed that the message saying "The owls are not what they seem" was meant for Dale Cooper (it said COOPER/COOPER/COOPER). Maybe it was not meant *for* Dale Cooper, but as a warning *against* 'Evil' Cooper. More interestingly, though, the book included a number of factual 'errors', while telling a *polycentric story* from multiple different perspectives and vantage points. The publisher, Flatiron, had also created an audiovisual trailer to promote Frost's book, and that trailer likewise included some (presumed) factual errors and strange references. In these cases, Frost invited the *forensic fans* to dissect the texts and find and discuss the 'flaws' on sites such as *Lynchland, Welcome to Twin Peaks, 25YL* and *Reddit* as well as in podcasts like *Diane* and *Twin Peaks Unwrapped*.[424]

They would also naturally notice that the maiden name of Margaret Lanterman (The Log Lady) was actually Coulson, which, as fans would know, was also the surname of the actor who portrayed The Log Lady. These elements were intentionally included in Frost's book and its trailer, as is evident from the feature interview at the end of this chapter, and they also carried over into the new series where The Log Lady spoke about death and "the fear of letting go," referencing the fans' nostalgia and the actor's real-life situation. As the cinematographer Peter Deming puts it:

> She was supposed to travel to Seattle and shoot with us, but she was too ill. And there came a time when it was apparent that we had to get her on film right away. So we found a gentleman in Portland who could go to her house and shoot, and David directed, basically via Facetime. You know, he was there, talking to her and directing her through the scenes and feeding her the lines and all that.
> I remember, we had gone to shoot one morning outside of the Sheriff's Station set in Washington, and we had just gotten there, and it was the crack of dawn, and we looked above the front of the Sheriff's Station. Behind it was woods, and coming through the woods was the sun in through this mist. We thought: "Isn't this beautiful". We quickly got the camera. We shot it actually – it's in the show – and right at that moment David got the phone call that Catherine had passed away. And it was sort of, you know, her talking to us.[425]

Sabrina Sutherland agrees with Deming, saying that "it was almost as if it was Catherine Coulson, not The Log Lady, saying those words," and the fans reacted strongly to that particular sequence (one of many *diegetic eulogies* in the new series). A crowd-funded documentary about Catherine Coulson (*I Know Catherine, The Log Lady*), directed by Richard Green, will soon be released.[426] Fans also reacted to the aforementioned trailer and Frost's *tie-in* book, comparing notes and debating *continuity* issues and potential errors.

This involvement of the fan base has become more strategic in connection with *Twin Peaks: The Return*. This can also be seen in the clever recycling of lines from *tie-in* books like *The Secret Diary of Laura Palmer* (1990) and *Welcome to Twin Peaks: An Access Guide to the Town* (1991) and the intelligent remixing of lines, scenes and shots from the original *Twin Peaks*, the prequel *Fire Walk with Me* and David Lynch's other works.[427] And when the official Showtime documentary about *Twin Peaks* was released on Showtime

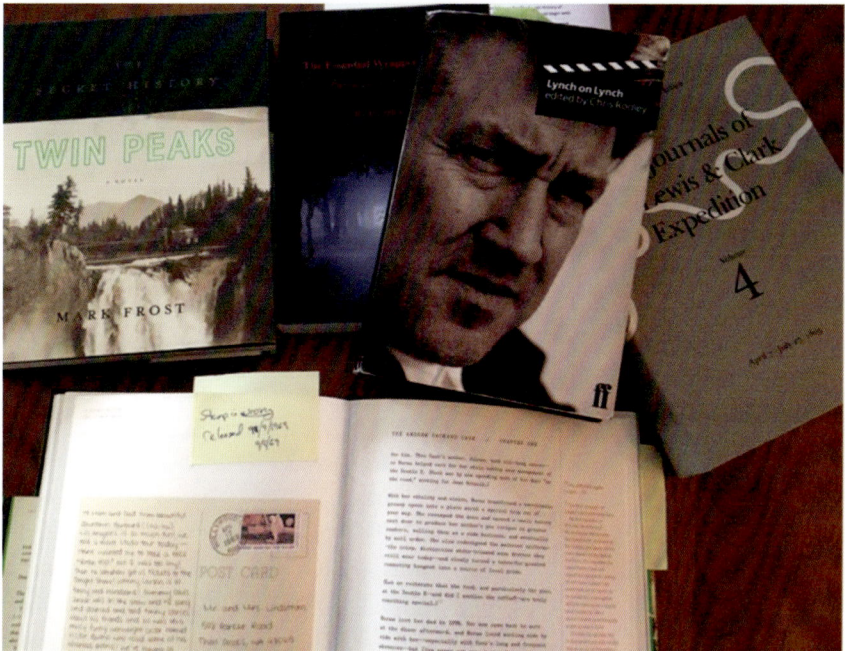

Fig. 27: The *aca-fan* John Thorne, who co-created the fanzines *Wrapped in Plastic* and *Blue Rose Magazine*, posted images on social media, upon having read Mark Frost's book *The Secret History of Twin Peaks*, about new potential interpretations and inconsistencies. Photo: John Thorne.

and YouTube, the company had chosen to use fans as experts, not critics, traditional scholars or well-known journalists. The recurring experts in the three parts were John Thorne (co-creator of the fanzines *Wrapped in Plastic* and *Blue Rose Magazine*), Pieter Dom (administrator of *Welcome to Twin Peaks*) and Brian Linss (who creates visual fan art). Fans, not scholars, can help promote *Twin Peaks*, and, therefore, they were a key to the more deliberate *transmedia strategy* surrounding the new series.[428]

This was also apparent in Showtime's 'fan art' campaign, which prompted fans to send in their individual fan art, giving them a sense of *official* connection to *Twin Peaks*, while exploiting their creativity and willingness to freely advertise Showtime and share their content. Showtime's campaign included a long list of guidelines, including some specific "dos" and "don'ts":

- Do create dark, quirky and authentic works directly related to TWIN PEAKS, a place both wonderful and strange full of small town charm, quirk and memorable characters. The series is the town, the characters, the music and the food.
- Do stay away from creating fan art that is too "cartoon-like."

- Do reference the Twin Peaks style guide, provided here.
- Do create strange yet beautiful designs from the classic TWIN PEAKS series as well as from the new RETURN season on Showtime that are "in world" and true to the series.
- Don't include any photographic character likeness.
- Don't mash up the old series with the new series, each design should stay true to its season and time.
- Don't mash up locations and themes that aren't true to the TV series storyline. Ex: don't include people in the Red Room who never appeared there during the series.
- Don't portray Kyle as a saint or use other religious references

(cf. help.redbubble.com/hc/en-us/articles/360028514471)

Brand Protection and Auteur Branding

Even in the teasers and trailers to *Twin Peaks: The Return*, fans were given small snippets to work with, and they were given fragments of a world they knew and loved ("Familiar Faces" and "Familiar Places"), without revealing anything. In fact, even David Lynch's negotiation with Showtime before the new season involved the fans via social media where some of the regular actors and the strong fan base gave Lynch the leverage to gain full creative freedom. This was seen in the video campaign "No Lynch, No Peaks!"[429] Indeed, David Lynch was the central reference point when promoting the original series, but this time there were explicit references and allusions to the works of David Lynch throughout the entire promotion campaign. In an early trailer, Lynch was seen in a strange *out of focus* shot (a Lynchian signature that is used in films such as *Lost Highway* and *Mulholland Dr.*), and in another trailer he was seen as Gordon Cole, slowly eating a doughnut. Finally, in an article from *Entertainment Weekly*, Lynch published one of the most cryptic (anti-)breakdowns of the new series that one could ever imagine.[430]

Showtime's David Nevins has said that Lynch had total freedom when creating his continuation to *Twin Peaks*, and there are, indeed, numerous references to Lynch's other works (I will return to this in Chapter 5). The new *Twin Peaks* claims to be an organic example of *auteur TV*, demanding a lot from viewers in terms of patience and attentiveness. This is neatly reflected in the scene from the new series where Norma (Peggy Lipton) is asked to change the name of RR Diner to "Norma's Double R", while using some cheaper products, becoming more business savvy and thinking more consciously about the potentials of "the brand" and "the franchise." Norma declines and gives a whole speech about organic produce and ownership, and that scene looks like a metaphorical reference to *Twin Peaks: The Return* itself as either an or-

Fig. 28: The actor Amy Shiels (Candie) makes a *photobomb*, while two fans are *cosplaying* and re-enacting a scene from *Twin Peaks: The Return* (Showtime, 2017) during the Twin Peaks UK Fest in 2017. There is a continual interaction between the people behind *Twin Peaks* and the fans, who have themselves become creative *produsers*. This is also seen in online campaigns, such as the #oneonenine campaign by Kenneth Phillips, and the fan-made films that expand the story(world) of *Twin Peaks* – from Thor Åmli's short film series about Leland Palmer's childhood (*The Summer House at Pearl Lakes*) to Cameron Cloutier's feature-length film about Annie Blackburn (*Queen of Hearts*). Photo: Emilie Declerck.

ganic piece of art or a strategic *transmedia franchise*.

The new *Twin Peaks* was fragmented, and this fragmentation mirrored Dale Cooper's attempt to find himself and return to *Twin Peaks*. It might also reflect the fragmentation of the TV audience that we have been seeing since the rise of cable. We are living in a *multiplatform era*, and some people might argue that *Twin Peaks: The Return* is not even a TV series. If HBO branded itself as something more than regular TV (via its slogan "It's Not TV. It's HBO"), Showtime was apparently doing the same thing with *Twin Peaks*, indirectly saying: "It's Not ABC's *Twin Peaks*. It's Lynch's *Twin Peaks*."[431]

During the second season, Agent Cooper said that he had begun focusing "out beyond the edge of the board. On a bigger game," and that entire monologue is an apt description of *Twin Peaks* and its expansive *storyworld*. It began as one original text in one particular and restricted medium, but grew into a curious example of *transmedia storytelling* that spans multiple different media, texts and paratexts.

Though vividly different from one another, *Twin Peaks* and *The Walking Dead* illustrate a common tendency in the current media landscape where series are distributed and consumed via multiple platforms and where stories often integrate various media, texts and platforms. As a series, *The Walking Dead* combines elements from *serial melodrama* with different formulas and conventions from other genres, and it employs a host of storytelling techniques that are traditionally associated with television (e.g. *intra-* and *extra-episodic cliffhangers*). Its integration of different media and platforms, however, is a more modern feature, even if there are historical precursors. By comparison, *Twin Peaks: The Return* is a much more niche-oriented TV series, dismissing many of the traditional tropes and formulas from television and even promoted as a "film" or "limited event series". Despite its evident differences from *The Walking Dead*, *Twin Peaks* is also an expansive *storyworld*, proving that *transmedia storytelling* is a broad phenomenon in the modern mediascape.

    The renowned TV scholar John Fiske has popularly distinguished between *primary texts* (i.e. the central media texts in a franchise), *secondary texts* (i.e. promotional texts and critical reception) and *tertiary texts* (i.e. fan-produced texts). But there are many types of *transmedia storytelling*, and in some cases the status of *primary text* might shift between different parts of the *transmedia franchise*, making it difficult to distinguish between center and periphery (this phenomenon could be described as *fluid transmedia*).[432] In the modern media landscape where the TV audience has become fragmented and where viewers can binge or rewatch their favorite series via DVD, Blu-ray or different streaming services, narrative complexity has become a more popular phenomenon, and that is also true of *transmedia storytelling*. These are not phenomena that are produced by a new TV landscape, but they are popular forms of storytelling in the current streaming age that gain from the kind of distribution and consumption that are associated with the streaming landscape. Television storytelling has not become more complex and more multi-medial in general, nor are the concepts of *complex TV* and *transmedia storytelling* as such synonymous with 'good' storytelling, as distinguished from traditional *serial melodramas* and more episodic forms. They are relatively new approaches to television storytelling that challenge the conventions of the medium, while relying on other well-known formulas and tropes, and they represent a growing interest in telling stories that span different media and engage different niche audiences across the globe.

Feature Interview #4

Building Worlds & Crafting Stories: Interview with Angela Kang (*The Walking Dead*) and Mark Frost (*Twin Peaks*)

Two completely different series, *The Walking Dead* (AMC, 2010-) and *Twin Peaks: The Return* (Showtime, 2017), premiered on separate channels, had very different formats and were produced under quite dissimilar circumstances. One is a long-running serial, produced for the *basic cable* channel AMC, and the other is a "limited event series" produced for the premium cable channel Showtime and used to promote their streaming services Showtime On Demand and Showtime Anytime.[433] However disparate, *The Walking Dead* and *Twin Peaks* are both examples of a general trend in the media landscape, a tendency towards telling expansive stories across various media and texts.

In this double interview, the co-creator of *Twin Peaks*, Mark Frost, and the current showrunner of *The Walking Dead*, Angela Kang, describe their respective approaches to storytelling and the universes connected to *Twin Peaks* and *The Walking Dead*. Angela Kang discusses genre hybridity, crossover aesthetics and *world building*, whereas Mark Frost talks about the mythology of *Twin Peaks* and the ways in which different secondary texts, including his own book *The Secret History of Twin Peaks* (2016), contribute to the overarching storyworld.

Collective Efforts & Consistent Storyworlds: *The Walking Dead*

The Walking Dead is an immense and very popular show, and it has grown into a massive *transmedia franchise*. When dealing with shows like that, it is very much about *world building* and about creating diegetic worlds that are both expansive and consistent at the same time. How much do you talk about that in the writers' room, and what do you as a showrunner do to maintain that consistency?

Kang: We talk about the *world building* aspect of the show in the writers' room all the time. It's one of the most satisfying aspects of writing a show like this, but also one of the most challenging. We have to be careful about anything we introduce into the show's mythology that has to be carried across *The Walking Dead* 'universe.' For example, early on in the show's run, it was established that the U.S. military bombed out major cities across the country in a failed attempt to contain the zombie threat. Years later, we still show images of that aftermath when we play storylines with a large city as the backdrop. We have a certain number of hard and fast rules to the universe that we abide by - mostly having to do with the zombies - and then it's a collective effort by the writers to keep track of anything we establish. Our Chief Content Officer, Scott Gimple, also keeps an eye on things across all the *TWD* shows and makes sure we're not wildly contradicting each other!

You have written numerous episodes since Season 2, and you have become the showrunner of the series. What are the main challenges as a showrunner when having to helm such a big and long-running serial?

Kang: The show is absolutely massive, but we don't have unlimited money or resources. A decade in, we still have to be clever and scrappy and adaptable when faced with challenges, but it's something I love about the vibe of the show. The hours are long, and there are many people and problems to manage and there is so much scrutiny that comes with a show like this. I feel a huge responsibility to the fans worldwide to be "true" to the show we've been writing for years, but also to continue evolving the characters and storylines. This is not a show where anyone can "phone it in." But I love playing in this sandbox, and everyone involved with the show pours their hearts and souls into it. I'm very lucky.

George A. Romero has referred to *The Walking Dead* as a "soap opera with a zombie occasionally." That is naturally a provocative description, yet there are elements of *serial melodrama* in *The Walking Dead*, just as there are elements of many other genres. How would you describe *The Walking Dead* in terms of genre, and how do the different genre elements contribute to *The Walking Dead* as a 'universe' and phenomenon?

Kang: George Romero was not wrong! One of the things I love about the comic book by Robert Kirkman is the mixing of genres with a healthy dose of relationship drama. I think it's part of what's allowed the show to reach a wide audience that's not necessarily all in it for the horror and gore. I personally love the horror and gore, but I've heard from a surprising number of fans that they close their eyes during the zombie attacks and just watch the character scenes.

I would probably call the show a thriller in the simplest sense, since thrillers often have that mixing of subgenres while being grounded in suspense, anxiety and formidable villains. My long answer is that it's a character-driven survival drama with a western vibe set in a horror universe.

Do you as a writer and showrunner ever take the other parts of the franchise into account (e.g. *Fear the Walking Dead* and the different video games)? It might be coincidental, but there are certainly scenes in the series that lend themselves neatly to computer games.

Kang: Because the other parts of the franchise are not in my realm, I don't particularly think about them much on a day to day basis, though of course I'm aware of them all and I'm interested in transmedia storytelling in general. I'm a gamer (as is Scott Gimple and some other folks that work on the franchise), so I suppose I'm drawn to that aesthetic at times, though we actually try not to get too video-gamey most of the time with our look on the show. Great games showcase beautiful cinematic work and people who work on films or TV series rip off visual inspiration from any and all sources, so I'm guessing more gaming 'language' will seep into TV over time. Also, sometimes there is a VFX aspect to why certain shots are chosen for the show. The same kind of digital modeling that's used in games is used for some of our zombie/battle work, so there may have been a cost-benefit to using a POV shot (which is often the case) vs. something else.

As is often the case with *transmedia storytelling*, there is a philosophy behind *The Walking Dead*, and it seems that you are generally exploring how human beings handle threats from the outside and the 'fine line' between civilized and uncivilized, human and zombie. How do you see it?

Kang: The "fine line" is my favorite place to explore as a storyteller. I think the philosophical aspects of the story are what make it most compelling to write in the long term. In the comic book and the show, the term "the walking dead" is used to describe *us* - the humans. *We* are the monsters. My favorite twist to zombie mythology from the comic is the idea that we are all already infected with the virus and can turn no matter how we die. That idea that we all have the capability for monstrosity within us and have to choose how to live is a foundational idea baked into the show and at the core of many of our characters' struggles. Our heroes have done dark things. Our villains have some redeemable qualities. I find it interesting to explore whether characters' actions are objectively heroic or villainous, or if part of it lies in the eye of the beholder. Every villain is the hero of their own story. From Negan's point of view, our heroes came into his house without personal provocation and murdered a bunch of his people when they were asleep; he merely killed two people in return to prove a point. Our heroes see Alpha and the Whisperers as barbaric; she thinks their idea of civilization is a ridiculous construct. We're over a decade into the apocalypse in the show's storyline and many of our characters operate in morally "grey" areas day to day. Some of them are deeply tormented by it, others are numb to it. And others fight the "slide" into the grey hard with every choice they make, even if it means putting themselves at terrible risk. But all that also feels real to me. As you and I are exchanging these thoughts, we're in the middle of a once-in-a-century pandemic, and we're seeing the best and the worst come out in people every day. Retreating into yourself can be a survival tactic. Aggressively taking what you need at the expense of others can be a survival tactic. Cooperating with others and helping "the village" thrive can be a survival tactic. We are seeing what people truly value and what they do when they feel backed into a corner. We are reading 'think pieces' about what we need as humans not just to survive, but thrive. A lot of people have been referencing our show when talking about what's happening now, and it's been a strange experience to see and hear. I always hope that what we're writing feels relevant. But it's also a bit sad and scary when it feels too close to home.

How do you deal with the challenge of having to discontinue or kill off regular characters (for various reasons), and how do you introduce new characters and still maintain a limited and familiar universe?

Kang: Honestly, it's really hard. As writers, we fall in love with these characters too because we have to live inside their fictional heads to craft their stories, and the actors are our colleagues and oftentimes become friends over the years. We've had to deal with some major characters leaving the show over the last couple of seasons (such as Rick and Michonne) and we tried to handle those exits by thinking about their character journeys and trying to give some sense of purpose to their lives and final moments. Introducing new characters at this point is an interesting challenge because long-time viewers don't necessarily connect to the newer faces as deeply right away, but we strive to populate our world with characters (and actors) who are memorable and bring something unique to the story.

Expanding the Mythology of *Twin Peaks*

Before the premiere of *Twin Peaks: The Return*, you wrote *The Secret History of Twin Peaks* in which you combine the grand history of American History, blending fiction, fact and myth, with the local, fictional story of Twin Peaks. What was the idea behind this addition to *Twin Peaks*?

Frost: I wanted to build or expand on the mythology of *Twin Peaks*, weaving in parts of what we believe to be facts. As for American history, I wanted to use the unifying elements that create the ties between them to blend them into a kind of historical myth. It's an attempt to create an American genre or version of magical realism. I like the whole Latin school of magical realism, and certainly we've had examples of that in American literature, but I wanted to make a version of that within a world that has become a part of popular culture. Something that has become almost an adjective in itself.

Are you arguing that history, or what we believe to be the factual history of America, includes fiction and myth?

Frost: That's clearly part of it. What we assume to be history, what we assume to be the rocks or the pillars under our democratic society may be more elastic than we care to believe. And these elements, unless tended to, can very easily be exploited. I think our current political history has made that evident.

Your book has already been dissected and debated in the fan community, and many fans have noticed some potential discrepancies and errors in your book. Are these errors intentional, and how much do you think about *continuity* and *consistency* across the different parts of the universe?

Frost: I think that aspect lines up with the tension that I line up in the book between mysteries and secrets. This was also one of the reasons I wanted a book that, in a sense, has multiple narrators – not just the archivist and the agent. I wanted the book to illustrate the fact that, while we can and must distinguish between fact and fiction, everyone's got a point of view and everyone has their own subjective experience. And that experience or understanding might include forgery and faulty memory. I intentionally have typos in the book in order to illustrate that idea.

   I wanted the book to mirror a greater verisimilitude – to remind us that life itself is a subjective experience. It may also be seen as a radio signal, and maybe our ability to receive the bandwidth is very narrow. Perhaps there are many different frequencies, and we are not able to receive or decode all of them. When it comes to storytelling in visual media, we're often assuming that what we see is real. We're rarely told to doubt the veracity of what we see and hear, but maybe that's not the whole story. And that was what I was trying to illustrate.

In your book, you introduce some of the characters from Twin Peaks that were minor or secondary in the TV series (e.g. Dougie Milford), thereby ex-

panding the universe and fleshing out the diegetic world.

Frost: Those were the people that in the pressure of weekly television – where you can only expect so much of the viewers and their attention spans – we did not have a chance to fully develop or flesh out. The chance to enhance your understanding of many of the characters that were not center stage was simply irresistible. I did want to go back through history and find those characters, those characters that might have been tangentially fascinating in the series, but who were worthy of more attention. I have long been interested in the idea of watching a movie of the 1930s and to see those characters that we all know and love, but I always find myself drawn to secondary characters, too. Sometimes I'll be drawn to extras, and I want to know their stories, too. It's a kind of interest in wanting an omniscient look, and as I let my own gaze wander along that landscape of Twin Peaks, and somebody says to me, "Hey, there's something over here that's interesting," I can go to that person in my book and delve into that story.

Dougie was part of the original series, but only for a short time, and then he died, and he was one of the characters that I thought was potentially interesting. He could be one of the most interesting characters in the world of *Twin Peaks*, perhaps, and I think that the book shows us that his story is, in fact, quite fascinating.

In television theory, people talk about a gradual shift in focus from *story* to *storyworld*, and scholars talk about different types of *transmedia storytelling*. Would it be fair to describe *Twin Peaks* as an example of that?

Frost: There's a design to all of it, and it is ultimately all tied together, but we're not going to spoon-feed anyone, wrapping it up nicely in a bottle. We are of course thinking about linking the different stories or texts, but you might learn that there isn't *one* cohesive explanation. There may be no *one* thoroughly objective story. But the notion that it's open-ended enough for people to draw their own conclusions is what fascinated me mostly, I think.

How did you see the mystery of your *tie-in* book in relation to the series and the other parts of the *storyworld*?

Frost: It was so much fun to write a book that bore resemblance to the show, that had a similar feeling or tone to it, but that had a very different message. And, then, you'll see and you'll decide for yourself. The interpretation should be up to the readers and the viewers. I guess you can more or less count on us not answering everything.

In the 1990s, there was talk about bringing back or continuing *Twin Peaks* in some form. But it did not happen, and ABC was not interested in prolonging the series. Do you feel that Showtime was a more natural home for *Twin Peaks*, and that they had a better understanding of your series and the universe behind it?

Frost: No question about that. Showtime feels like a more natural home for *Twin Peaks*. I think Showtime is much more forward-thinking, and they completely get the show and the world of *Twin Peaks*.

Chapter 5

The Art of Television: Stylistic Experimentation and TV Auteurism

> Art films form a sort of middle ground between mainstream commercial films and pure experimental cinema – the latter being the kind of personal, non-narrative films that screen mainly in museums and filmmaking cooperatives. [...] Can the same phenomenon occur in television? Can there be "art TV" that airs on mainstream networks?
> - Kristin Thompson, film and TV historian[434]

> Television is as capable as film of creating expressive richness in moments that are at once fleeting, demonstrative and dramatically declamatory, or seemingly inconsequential. [...] There are many television moments that strike us as compelling, extraordinary, haunting or distinctive.
> - Jason Jacobs & Steven Peacock, TV scholars[435]

Though a traditional part of Film Studies, style and aesthetics have not been a dominant part of Television Studies where scholars tend to focus on institutional and industrial aspects, technological and socio-cultural factors and elements concerning audiences, consumption and viewing patterns. Thalia Baldwin and Steven Peacock have even written about "the lack of attention to style" as a "worrying and widespread trend in TV Studies," and in 2006 Steven Peacock and Sarah Cardwell made a call, asking contributors to answer the questions: "What is good television?" and "Why are appreciation and evaluation so rarely tackled within television studies?"[436]

In this chapter, I will explore various examples of stylistic experimentation in the current TV landscape, combining textual analysis with insider perspectives concerning the different TV productions. In this context, I will also address the problematic and vague distinctions between film and television where the word "cinematic" is used loosely to connote a high level of sophistication, a high production value or a flashy audiovisual aesthetic which, by implication, is "better" than television. As we shall see, there are many different televisual and cinematic styles, and this chapter is not concerned with the potential differences between the two media, but with the diversity of audiovisual experimentation in the current TV landscape. There is no such thing as *one* traditional style in television, let alone *one* television aesthetic. There is a variety of television styles, even within the current TV landscape, just as there are different stylistic approaches – or different 'cinemas' – in the current film landscape.

Consequently, this chapter deals with experimental approaches to style in modern television and how different TV series and creators employ a distinctive style to differentiate themselves from other series in a saturated TV landscape and promote themselves as more than 'traditional' television (whatever that might be). This aspect is best explored by combining a neo-formalist approach to selected scenes and sequences with production-based interviews, revealing how the creators and craftsmen promote their stylistic approaches through references to arthouse films, distinctive *auteurs* and the film medium in general.

After a brief introduction to the concept of *art TV* and the question of *legitimation*, this chapter explores some specific examples of stylistic inventiveness across a range of fields (from title sequences and cinematography to editing, music and sound design). Various examples are provided as illustration, but specific attention is devoted to the audiovisual aesthetic in *Breaking Bad* (AMC, 2008-2013), *Better Call Saul* (AMC, 2015-) and *Twin Peaks: The Return*. At the end of the chapter, there is an explorative discussion about *art TV* and *TV auteurism* in the limited series, exemplified by *Alias Grace* (CBC/Netflix, 2017) and *I Know This Much Is True* (HBO, 2020) and followed by a feature interview with Sabrina Sutherland, Peter Gould, Mary Harron and Derek Cianfrance.

Art TV and the Legitimation of Television

As mentioned earlier, Television Studies has rarely focused on style and aesthetics, perhaps because television has always had a lower status in the *cultural hierarchy* than older and more recognized media such as film, theater and literature. As Jason Jacobs and Steven Peacock note:

> Historically, in Western culture, television has been perceived as a throwaway medium, a provider of information and entertainment, the latter easily devoured and dispensed with by the channel-hopping consumer. This scenario leads to thoughts on traditional forms of television broadcasting, of the image's live-ness, of a fixed schedule of air-dates and times, of groups within nations watching the same drama unfold at the same time.[437]

This general devaluation of television has led to widespread generalizations concerning television style and TV viewers. Early commentators like Jack Gould claimed that television was simply defined by a combination of "the close-up of the motion picture" with the liveness and spontaneity of the theater and the immediacy of the radio, and the French philosopher Roland Barthes has critically – and broadly – denounced television as 'the opposite of film'.[438] Similarly, John Caldwell and Jeremy Butler have referred to the traditional form of television as a *zero-degree style*, understood as a conventional and rather anecdotal form that is not heavily stylized or expressive.[439] According to John Ellis, the differences between film and television are even seen in the different types of consumption and viewing behavior:

> The regime of TV viewing is [...] very different from the cinema: TV does not encourage the same degree of spectator concentration. There is no surrounding darkness, no anonymity of the fellow viewers, no large image, no lack of movement amongst the spectators, no rapt attention. TV is not usually the only thing going on, sometimes it is not even the principal thing. TV is treated casually rather than concentratedly. It is something of a last resort ("What's on TV tonight, then?"), rather than a special event.[440]

Describing traditional television and viewing patterns, Ellis bemoans the "lower degree of sustained concentration," compared to cinema, and in that sense he gives a rather essentialistic understanding of the two media.[441] Both Ellis and Caldwell describe 'essential' TV styles and forms of consumption, but this sort of essentialism has always been questionable. As Noël Carroll has noted with reference to film, *medium specificity* is a problematic concept, as different art forms are not instruments with specific and readily defined purposes.[442] In the early days of cinema, however, there was a need to define film as a medium, and various theoreticians and practitioners pointed to different technical aspects as particularly cinematic. Sergei Eisenstein and Vsevolod Pudovkin pointed to *montage editing* as the essence of cinema, whereas Jean Epstein pointed to close-ups and *photogénie* as the most uniquely cinematic qualities, and André Bazin described *deep focus* and long takes as truly filmic.[443] The attempts to define cinema coincided with film being a new medium, having to differentiate itself from other media, describe its unique qualities and claim a certain status, and the same could be the case when people are trying to define the essence of television. "Theorists, still bent on pursuing the medium's essential qualities," as Caldwell writes, "tend to overlook the fact that television includes a great deal that comes from elsewhere."[444] Or as Brett Mills profoundly and thoughtfully puts it:

> The use of the term 'cinematic' not only simplifies cinema, its comingling with questions of quality and cultural hierarchies demonstrates its use in television studies is never innocent. In that sense, it may be the fact that the term 'cinematic television' is used at *all* that tells us most about television style; or, more accurately, the persistence of the term could be seen to represent an ongoing unease over the stylistic richness, diversity and specificities of the medium we say we study.[445]

Trisha Dunleavy might be right when arguing that television, since the beginning of the *multiplatform era*, has pursued new stylistic expressions and avenues, "reduc[ing] the remaining aesthetic distinction between television and cinema."[446] Dunleavy's comment, however, echoes the essentialism of Ellis and Caldwell and chimes with "the cultural denigration" of the TV medium (to use Elana Levine's words).[447] While I agree that we have seen a tendency towards stylistic experimentation and inventiveness in television since the early 2000s, perhaps coinciding with changes in the TV landscape, I will illustrate that we are not dealing with *one* modern aesthetic (as opposed to *one* traditional TV style). Rather, we are seeing a complex TV landscape characterized by a plethora of platforms and content and a remarkable stylistic diversity. In a saturated market, as Tom Fontana and Tricia Brock said, TV creators have to "make noise" or be "outrageous," and this may be one of the factors that have led to stylistic diversity where various TV series experiment with alternative approaches. From the obtrusive editing and noteworthy sound-level changes in *American Crime* to the slow-paced minimalism in *I Know This Much is True*; from the direct addresses and subjective lens-flare effects in *Halt and Catch Fire* and *Alias Grace* to the off-kilter framing and alternative mixing strategies in *Mr. Robot*; from the expressive use of angles and sound in *Breaking Bad* and *Better Call Saul* to the radical aesthetic of *Twin Peaks: The Return*.

Mills is right in claiming that the word "cinematic" is "never innocent" when referring to television, yet analogies are also a way for human beings to understand and describe concepts. Films by Terrence Malick are often called "painterly", and films by Chris Marker and Andrei Tarkovsky are often described as "poetic" or "lyrical". Such descriptions are rarely meant to denigrate the film medium, nor do they imply that cinema is not a valid art form. They are simply a shorthand for describing the type of films that Malick, Marker and Tarkovsky make, knowing full well that poetry and paintings are both broad media that include various different expressions and styles. Thus, when film and TV historian Kristin Thompson introduces the term *art TV*, comparing film and television, she is not arguing that television is becoming more "cinematic". She is describing alternative tendencies in film and television that differ from mainstream film and TV, without making any normative or evaluative distinction. Describing a typical art-cinema mode, David Bordwell mentions five different characteristics: *a loosening of causality, a greater emphasis on psychological or anecdotal realism, violations of classical clarity of space and time, explicit authorial comment and ambiguity*.[448] These are the qualities that Thompson also looks at when characterizing *art TV* as a modern tendency across different industries. Her main examples, *The Singing Detective* (BBC, 1986) and *Twin Peaks* (ABC, 1990-1991), are historical by now, but her term is still relevant, as the Danish scholar Henrik Højer also notes, and it is not simply a moniker for "good" TV or "prestige" television.[449]

The Art of Branding: Title Sequences and High-End Television

> A good title sequence is both an art form and a form of branding. It's about honoring the TV series and finding the most interesting vehicle for it.
> – Danny Yount, title sequence designer[450]

As mentioned in Chapter 1, Tom Fontana created the first original drama series on HBO and officially launched a new era in the American TV landscape. Though often forgotten in retrospective pieces about 'the cable era', *Oz* was lauded as a realistic prison show, following the popular prison documentaries on HBO, and it became known for its expressive use of wide lenses, saturated colors and direct address. Moreover, it introduced a symbolic and cinematic title sequence – a montage of close-ups hinting at the themes and gritty tonality of the show – and this type of title sequence would soon become something of a trademark for *high-end* series on cable networks like HBO.

At the most basic level, a title sequence is a sort of *paratext* or "liminal moment" that takes its viewer over the threshold to the given series. It is both an independent art form and a part of something else (the series) – sometimes introduced at the opening of an episode, but other times introduced after a *cold open* or as a 'breaker' or 'reflection point' deeper into the episode.[451] It serves many different functions and takes many different forms, but it usually gives a sense of genre, tonality, setting and characters, and it often serves, at least indirectly, as a marketing tool for the program and the network.

The traditional title sequence could be seen as an efficient way to frame and brand a specific TV series while directing the spectator's attention towards the screen. As mentioned earlier, many people in the traditional *three-network era* watched television in a broad sense, not for any particular program, and, in that sense, many viewers were *erratic*, not having the time or leisure to devote their full attention to the television set. Even if that is a somewhat crude description of viewing behaviors in the *three-network era*, it could still help describe a pragmatic function behind the title sequence and the main title theme: to swiftly introduce the series and catch the viewer's attention. "On our main title theme, it only took those three low guitar opening notes to get you excited, anticipating another emotional and outrageous program," as the composer Angelo Badalamenti says in relation to *Twin Peaks: The Return* and its nostalgic title sequence.[452]

Title sequences have many different qualities, however, and Pablo Ferro mentions three typical functions:

- Establishing a sense of tone, atmosphere and genre
- Establishing the main characters and the central environment
- Giving the viewers a strong sense of the brand.[453]

To those qualities, we could add various other aspects, e.g. the pragmatic functions of introducing the creators and the cast members, and the possibility of simultaneously saying something about *the specific series, the producers* and *the network* behind the given program. The title sequence to *Oz*, for example, could be a way to frame the series and entice the viewers while branding Tom Fontana as a writer-producer, *Oz* as a particular type of program and HBO as an edgy cable network and a provider of quality dramas. Michelle Dougherty, who created the title sequences for *Boardwalk Empire* (HBO, 2010-2014) and *Stranger Things*, agrees with Pablo Ferro, but adds a few other criteria:

> A good title sequence also evokes emotion and creates anticipation for the show or movie. Ideally it gives the audience another perspective and is so good that no one would want to be anywhere else than there watching it, absorbing it.[454]

Patrick Clair, who designed the main titles to *True Detective* and *Westworld*, introduces a similar poetics when it comes to title sequences, but he specifically points to the constant evolution of the art form and how different title sequences naturally fit different types of channels, platforms and environments:

> It's always evolving and always changing, but certainly during my career I've looked at the titles as having two functions. The first one is an aesthetic or a tonal function to welcome the viewer into the show, and that means doing so in an aesthetic that feels appropriate to the show in terms of the music, the colors, the pacing and the motifs we're using. But then I feel that a successful title sequence justifies its place in the show, as the show goes on, by capturing something fundamental about the characters and their journey. *Mad Men* is a great example, on an aesthetic level in terms of weaving through the symbiology of 1950s Manhattan, 1950s advertising and the world we're going into. But what's more interesting about it is the sense of a man in free fall, which speaks to something very fundamental about Don Draper's character. And that never really changes. It's just as fundamental to his character during the final episode as it is in the first episode.
>
> I think a good title sequence achieves that, in a way that works for the audience. It can change in terms of appointment weekly viewing; it can remind you, maybe on a subconscious level, what was fundamental about what you saw the week before. And in a streaming environment, it's almost like a space to think about what you've just watched. If you're binge-viewing, in a way title sequences become more important as a break between shows, than as an introduction to a show.[455]

Traditionally, title sequences can function somewhat like jingles, letting viewers know that their programs are 'on', but title sequences are not just about catching or holding the viewer's attention. There are many instances of complex and inventive title sequences in the modern TV landscape, and they often help promote the style and tone of the series and, by extension, the particular network or streaming service.

Elsewhere, I have distinguished, somewhat crudely, between two different types of title sequences: the *concrete-pragmatic title sequence* and *the abstract-metaphorical title sequence*.[456] Pointing to pivotal series from the *multi-channel transition*, like *Dallas*, *Hill Street Blues* and *ER*, I argue that many title sequences from that era alternated between various outtakes from the series and shots of the actors (in character) who turn and look to the camera, often ending in a *freeze frame*, as their names are introduced on the screen.

However, when HBO introduced their original dramas, starting with *Oz*, they experimented with title sequence design and came up with a more layered, abstract and stylized form of title sequence.

In her article "Is Quality Television Any Good?", Sarah Cardwell argues that a common trait in many of today's *prestige* series is a general proliferation of close-ups, abstract images and montage editing. "Fragmentation in the form of abstraction is commonly used," she writes, "allowing the focus to be narrowed to a small detail that is nevertheless connotatively rich and encourages work on the part of the viewer... This aesthetic is [...] clear in title sequences which also exhibit an 'art film' aesthetic."[457] The standard for an HBO title sequence became a short symbolic montage (often around 90 seconds long), which in metaphorical and often poetic ways would introduce the theme, tonality and style of the series.[458]

Like many of HBO's title sequences, the one for *Six Feet Under* (HBO, 2001-2005) was created by an external company (Digital Kitchen), and as the creator, Alan Ball, saw the finished piece, he was astonished, saying that it was "so elegant, so cinematic, so unlike TV."[459] This reaction to Danny Yount's work is telling of HBO and their "not-TV" branding. Thomas Newman's music in the title sequence to *Six Feet Under* subtly recalled the music from *American Beauty* (1999), and the use of a blue optical filter metaphorically hinted at the darkness and sadness of the show, while introducing two of the most predominant stylistic choices of the entire series. "With *ER* it was all about the turn-and-look style, and from the beginning I knew that I didn't want that. I didn't want to show the cast," as Danny Yount says:

> I didn't want it to simply be a marketing vehicle for the show and the cast. I wanted it to transcend that. I had Thomas Newman's music, which I found to be very ethereal, and the cello strings, to me, sounded very methodical. I wanted to tell a story without being too specific. It should be symbolic.[460]

Yount explains that they used different metaphorical references to death (e.g. the hands parting, the time-lapse of flowers that bloom and then decay, and the raven on the tombstone), and they even wanted the typography to illustrate the theme of death. "I tried to make it like ashes-to-ashes, but they didn't want that. Back then, that was a really nice effect. It was really hard to do."[461]

When *Six Feet Under* came out in 2001, the title sequence was an innovative combination of concrete and abstract elements, depicting the everyday-life of a mortician while using abstract symbolism and imagery to connote death (e.g. the raven, which was associated with Edgar Allan Poe and Gothic horror). The evocative use of symbolism, montage editing and optical filters also naturally mirrored the style in the series, and the implied themes of façades and

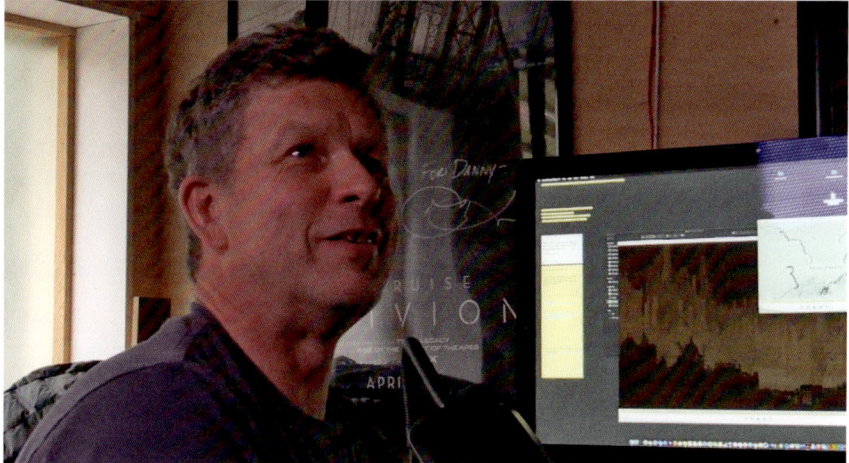

Fig. 29: The title sequence designer Danny Yount describes his work on *Six Feet Under* (HBO, 2001-2005), which became an early and almost iconic example of the 'HBO standard'. Photo: Jan Oxholm & Lasse Lorenzen, 2019.

repression also resonated with Alan Ball as an authorial figure. In that sense, it had some evident *art TV* qualities (ambiguity and authorial comment) while helping brand HBO as a producer of ambiguous and attention-demanding television drama.

From Authorial Concept to Collaborative Art: *True Detective*

Even more groundbreaking, the title sequence to *True Detective* was produced by Patrick Clair and the external company Elastic. Clair designed all the title sequences to the three independent seasons, and they could be seen as different variations on the same theme, recycling many of the same motifs and resonating with each other and the separate seasons in interesting ways. The title sequence to the first season begins on an extreme long shot of a desolate, fading landscape. The desaturated colors (muted greys and algae-like greens) give a sense of toxicity or lifelessness, and the moody theme, "Far From Any Road," gives a subtle sense of environment while establishing the atmosphere. The elements of Southern Gothic are indicated from the first shot, and the use of double exposure and superimpositions (where landscapes and faces bleed into each other) seem to imply that the environment is an unavoidable or even inescapable part of the characters. The characters are seen as hollow silhouettes, indicating a sense of existential malaise, and an ambiguous juxtaposition of sin and righteousness is introduced through a number of interesting superimpositions. At 0:27, a preacher is seemingly spiked by an inverted red cross; at 0:44 a bare-backed woman is sitting in an Ozu-like *low-angle shot* with spiked shoes; and at 1:13 a woman seems to be displaying lust while a crucifix is seen in the picture. These ambiguous juxtapositions and religious motifs are also connected to the central characters, as we see an attractive woman wearing a Stars-and-Stripes-themed bathing suit. The image of the 'All-American' woman is superimposed on top of Marty's face, subtly indicating his inner battles and extramarital affairs. Rust is particularly interesting in this case, in that his face is often double exposed with burning flames (as if to signal his own personal Purgatory while reiterating the complex religious motifs in the story). The hollow faces, existential and religious motifs and the toxic, empty landscapes – what Clair calls "petrochemical America" – combine into a condensed version of the entire series.[462] As Patrick Clair says:

> I really enjoyed the process of making that title sequence, and, as you say, it became something of an iconic piece. We got a little too much credit for it, though. Yes, we were doing double exposure, but that was floating around at that time. It was becoming a trend, I think. But the reason we used double exposure was not that it was trendy. It came from something which was really fundamental to the show. I remember very clearly the first time I had a conversation with Nic Pizzolatto. He was telling us what the show was about, and there was one phrase that leapt out at me: "We're using the exploited, poisoned landscapes of 90s Louisiana as a metaphor for broken, exploited, poisoned people." That idea of using the broken landscapes as a metaphor for broken people just immediately led to this other idea: "We need to make broken portraits from landscapes."
>
> It just came from this simple thing, but it was very much about the characters. And then what we did is that we started playing around with this design, using some of the material from the show, but also some of the source material they had given us. Photos of those landscapes from that era. Where I hope we were successful is on a thematic level by tapping into this really fundamental thing that the writer used to guide the building of his characters. It worked on that level, and then it maybe worked on an aesthetic level as well. It felt connected to the show because it was literally some of the photographic material that we had been given, inspiring the look and colors of the show. So there was this really great textual relationship between the two.[463]

Interestingly, Patrick Clair describes the title sequence as an authorial conception, supporting the idea of *True Detective* as an example of *art TV* created by the 'singular' vision of writer-producer Nic Pizzolatto. Pizzolatto, himself, paints a similar picture, as we can see in the feature interview at the end of Chapter 6. As Pizzolatto says, the title sequence was based on "some very specific ideas," taking their point of departure in landscapes that Pizzolatto knew personally. The writer-producer ends up crediting Patrick Clair for creating a title sequence that is "its own piece of art" and that "exceeds the conception," but there is no doubt where the "conception" came from.[464]

The title sequence to *True Detective* was remarkable when it came out, and it came to represent a strand of *art TV* series produced by cable networks like HBO. This is supported when looking at the three title sequences comparatively, whereby recurring motifs, authorial signatures and subtle variations become evident. The use of double exposure and superimpositions – techniques that are rooted in French Impressionism from the 1920s – is experienced across all three title sequences. In the title sequence for *True Detective 2* (HBO, 2015), the color palette is slightly different, though, emphasizing the warm reds and yellows. The warmer colors are combined with sandy earth tones and hints of turquoise, subtly introducing the juxtaposition of Sunny California and LA Noir. The theme song, Leonard Cohen's "Nevermind," adds a sense of fatalism to the images, and the deep tone of Cohen's voice hints at the masculinity and gender issues in the second season. Finally, the blending of roads and faces – a motif that was also used in the first season – seems even more salient here, mirroring the labyrinthine nature of California and the plot itself.[465] According to episode director Janus Metz:

> What I found interesting about Season 2, compared to Season 1, was that their stories had almost opposite trajectories in terms of the relationship between man and nature. Whereas Season 1 dealt with the nature inside human beings – and it was shot in the swamps of New Orleans, giving us the feeling that the swamps and the decay existed *inside* every one of us and threatened to destroy us – then Season 2 had a different trajectory. That season is about a natural disaster. It's about the damage that we as human beings cause to the world that surrounds us – as if we were germs or bacteria. In this season, *we* are the destructive element, *we* are the ones that destroy the nature around us.[466]

The title sequence to the third season employs some of the same stylistic trademarks, though again using a slightly different color palette (this time closer to a bleached version of *orange and teal*) and a different theme song (a beautiful rendition by Cassandra Wilson of the Delta Blues classic "Death Letter"). The change from bluegrass to blues, in Seasons 1 and 3, could represent the different depictions of race in these two seasons. And the repeated motifs and subtle variations across all three title sequences could illustrate a shift in environment - from Louisiana to California and the Ozarks - while emphasizing that the three title sequences, just like the three seasons, are part of *one* cohesive and authorial exploration.

The title sequences to *Six Feet Under* and *True Detective* are typical of the *art TV* aesthetics promoted by HBO, and in that sense they exemplify what Catherine Johnson calls *telebranding* (branding TV programs and networks at one and the same time).[467]

A more recent trend, however, is the use of short title sequences and ultra-brief "title cards". The so-called "title cards" are often used in connection with comedies, dramedies and short-format series like *Girls*, *SKAM* and *Atlanta* (FX, 2016-), perhaps representing a hip alternative to the lengthy title sequences on HBO or an attempt to keep the young viewers engaged in the story in an era of *second* and *multi-screening*. In some cases, the titles are used as pauses or *spaces for reflection*, and that strategy is exemplified by the notably lengthy mid-episode titles in *I Know This Much is True*. These titles are similar to the brief "title cards" by simply combining words and non-diegetic music, yet they are markedly different in terms of pacing and function (due to the intensity and gravity of the series). As the writer-director Derek Cianfrance puts it:

> There was a very conscious choice behind the title sequence. I actually wrote into all of the scripts that titles would be over black, no images, and I wrote the prologue to every episode and then wrote into the script: "Titles happen here. Titles happen over black." One of my favorite films of all time is Lars von Trier's *Breaking the Waves*, and I have always been amazed by his use of title cards in that movie. I've always thought that his title cards, while setting the mood, allowed for the audience to reflect on what they'd just seen. That was my big inspiration. Obviously, I'm not doing it the same way that von Trier did, but the feeling I got from *Breaking the Waves* was what I tried to replicate in my title sequence.[468]

The Art of Imitation: *Stranger Things*

In an era of *binge-watching*, Netflix has famously created an option to 'skip the intro', yet there are Netflix Originals that have some rather intriguing and innovative title sequences, however simple and skippable they might seem. Apart from the title sequence to *House of Cards*, which has been discussed earlier in this book, the opening to *Stranger Things* (Netflix, 2016-) is also interesting in this context.[469] Deceptively simple, the "intro" to *Stranger Things* introduces the title in capital red letters, accompanied by an evocative theme by the synth band Survive. The main theme (as many of the other leitmotifs in the series) was composed by Kyle Dixon and Michael Stein, and the music gives an immediate sense of mystery. A flickering light seems to illuminate the letters in the title, and the typography, the synth music and the flickering light (a motif that is used in the series to connote the interconnectivity between the real world and the Upside-Down) create an unmistakable 1980s vibe. Though not an obvious example of *art TV*, the seemingly simple title sequence to *Stranger Things* is actually quite intricate, and it contributes to a strong sense of authenticity and 'filmicity' in the Netflix series by mimicking an analogue title-sequence technique that was typical of cinema in the 1980s. The same thing could be said of Saskia Marka's elegant title sequence to *Babylon Berlin* (Sky 1/Das Erste, 2017-), which mirrors the time period, Germany in the 1920s and early 1930s, through reference to prominent films from that era (e.g. *Berlin, die Sinfonie der Großstadt* by Walter Ruttmann and *Ballét Mecanique* by the experimental filmmakers Fernand Legér and Dudley Murphy).[470]

The influences for the title sequence to *Stranger Things* were almost all cinematic, illustrating that TV creators often look to cinema when attempting to create *high-end* series. Critics and scholars might evoke other media when debating television, consciously or inadvertently denigrating the TV

Michelle Dougherty (title sequence designer) & Natalia Dyer (actor) on the Nostalgia of *Stranger Things*

Dougherty: When working on the *Stranger Things* title, I looked at old films from that time period, and I was like an investigator trying to find any inconsistencies or interesting "mistakes" that appeared on film. Additionally, at the very beginning of my career we still would film out our main titles, so I was familiar with that process and with some of the "mistakes" one could cause. Probably because I made them myself. Thank goodness I could finally put them to good use!

We also called around to a few places because we wanted to see if we could film out this sequence just like they might have done at that time. We weren't able to find someone that could, but then we just recreated them. I think the Duffer Brothers said once that we geeked out on this, and it's true, we did because we wanted for it to feel authentic.

We tried many typefaces at the beginning, and then the Duffer Brothers said that they had a logo they liked that had been made for them. When we saw the typeface, we knew it screamed the 80s because it used a very popular typeface from that period: Benguiat. We took it and altered it by outlining it in red and added the bars on top and bottom and adjusted some of the sizing, so it felt like this strong compact logo that was reflective of our early designs.

The Duffer Brothers had become familiar with Richard Greenberg, a title designer. Richard worked on some very iconic titles such as *Altered States*, *Superman*, *The Dead Zone*, *Alien*, just to name a few. He had a simplicity about his work that was memorable and a unique way he used typography to communicate. Once they referenced him, I knew what direction they were giving me, since I had admired Richard's work all of my career.[474]

Dyer (Nancy Wheeler): The Duffer brothers do a really good job of paying a lot of meticulous respect to that era, but also making it feel quite appealing in modern times.

We definitely got some homework, of course there were movies to watch. I had to watch scary movies like *A Nightmare on Elm Street* – there are a lot of references to horror films and books from the 1980s – and I also watched things again like *Goonies*, *E.T.* and *Close Encounters of the Third Kind*.

I also bought a perfume that was very popular at the time. It's called Charlie. People do that sometimes to get into character – they'll smell a certain way – but I couldn't do it. It was so strong. Everyone cares so much for the 80s on this show. Everyone behind the scenes, everyone from the art-side of things, and they do a lot for us in a way.[475]

medium. But TV creators also allude to films and mention "cinema" when describing their inspiration for specific series or sequences, and many of the interviewees for this book have explained how executives and producers urge them to make their work "more cinematic".[471] That is also the case for the title sequence to *Stranger Things*, which was indirectly inspired by the title sequence to *Bullitt* (1968) and directly influenced by Richard Greenberg.[472]

Title sequences continue to change and evolve, as Patrick Clair says, and there are various competing trends and tendencies within title sequences, corresponding to the many different channels, platforms and providers. Channels have different brands, and the title sequences reflect and introduce specific series, but often they also reflect the channel or streaming service that produced the series and the way in which audiences are supposed to engage with the series. A common denominator, however, is that title sequences have become an art form in and of itself, reflecting different artistic ideas and endeavors in television. From *the art of symbolism* (*True Detective*) and *the art of reflection* (*I Know This Much is True*) to *the art of authenticity* (*Stranger Things*) and *the art of brevity* (*Girls*), title sequences are more than a simple addendum or a throwaway element. In that sense, TV scholar Angelina Karpovich may be right when assuming that title sequences are "conceptually [...] the most complex moments in film and television programs."[473]

From Aesthetic Anonymity to Visual Inventiveness

Apart from introducing the setting and the central characters, title sequences can convey a sense of tonality and genre, and they can function as an *audiovisual signifier* of the artistic ambitions behind the given series.

A more typical element to mention, when it comes to *art TV* and visual experimentation, is the cinematography itself. Identifying a traditional use of cinematography and visual staging is an almost impossible task, but when it comes to mainstream film and television, scholars often point to the typical staging of dialogue scenes, using *masters*, *coverage* and *shot/reverse-shot* editing, and the general principle of *inconspicuousness*.[476] These principles relate to both visual and sonic aspects of film style, aspects that I will explore individually before turning my attention to the general audiovisual design behind series such as *Breaking Bad*, *Better Call Saul* and *Twin Peaks: The Return*. In this section, then, I will look at some alternative and experimental approaches to staging, cinematography and editing, focusing on two elements: (1) the conspicuous use of cinematography and editing in modern series like *Boardwalk Empire* and *Halt and Catch Fire* and (2) the alternative staging of dialogues in series like *American Crime* and *Succession*.

In his seminal book, *Mise en Scène and Film Style: From Classical Hollywood to New Media Art* (2014), Adrian Martin introduces some different approaches to *mise en scène* and film style. According to Martin, classical films are often characterized by an *aesthetic anonymity*, as opposed to the more conspicuous and *excessive* nature of art films (to Martin this distinction is not connected to any value judgment, however, and he has, in fact, defended *the seamless style* on many occasions).[477] David Bordwell, Janet Staiger and Kristin Thompson also reference the typical understanding of mainstream cinema and Hollywood *classicism*, reiterating some standard ideas about mainstream films that are often mentioned in the industry itself (e.g. that "unity is a basic attribute of film form" and that "the Hollywood film strives to conceal its artifice through techniques of continuity and 'invisibility'").[478] Many of the series mentioned in this section break the 'rule' of *aesthetic anonymity*, potentially breaking the narrative illusion and distancing the viewer. The series are rarely *excessive*, though, and the stylistic choices, however overt and conspicuous, often serve an expressive function. In that sense, the examples below are closer to mainstream cinema than to art films, but they employ stylistic techniques that we naturally associate with art films and that, therefore, form a sort of middle ground between the expressiveness of mainstream film and television and the conspicuousness and stylistic excess of art cinema.

Conspicuousness and Lyricism in *Halt and Catch Fire*

An interesting example of *stylistic conspicuousness* is found at the end of AMC's *Halt and Catch Fire*, a character-based period drama that revolves around a group of tech people in the 1980s. Lauded by many critics, *Halt and Catch Fire* had mediocre ratings and was discontinued after only four seasons.[479] It was rarely flashy or overtly experimental, but in Tricia Brock's episode "Who Needs a Guy" (Ep. 4:7) there is a touching and artful sequence where one of the main characters, Gordon, played by Scoot McNairy, suddenly dies. Using *lens flare* effects and a moving camera, the sequence differs markedly from the general style of the series, dissolving time and space in an almost Bergmanesque form of *abstract lyricism*.

Though dealing with the tech industry in the 1980s, *Halt and Catch Fire* could best be described as a *serial melodrama* about a small group of colleagues, competitors and friends, and the action – moving at a leisurely pace – takes us from Dallas to San Francisco and upstate New York. The series is about friendship, love and ambitions – and about *almost* making it despite marital problems, professional challenges and sudden health issues. These themes are all commonplace, but when death finally strikes in *Halt and Catch Fire*, it does so in a heartrending and harrowing way that forever changes the tonality of the series. As opposed to *Breaking Bad* where Walter White's cancer diagnosis functions as a threatening "Sword of Damocles", the viewer naturally forgets Gordon's health issues in *Halt and Catch Fire*. It is rarely mentioned or highlighted in the series, and there are no evident set-ups or omens, leading us to suspect his tragic departure. Even the title of Tricia Brock's episode seems to reflect this ambiguity and subtlety: Is it meant as a sneering question ("*Who* needs a guy?") or an unfinished sentence ("… who needs a guy"), and who does the relative pronoun, in that case, refer to?

This kind of ambiguity is telling of the series, and it is also reflected in the poetic death sequence that comes after half an hour into Brock's episode. Death has been depicted in various ways in American television – from the morbid prologues and the poetic montage in the finale of *Six Feet Under* to the *Taxi Driver*-like *aerial shot* at the end of *Breaking Bad* – but few death sequences are as striking and poetic as the one in *Halt and Catch Fire*. Over the course of four seasons, the viewers have come to love Gordon – the quiet computer 'geek' who had his prime in the 1970s and has had his share of problems with disloyal business partners, divorce and lack of recognition – and when he finally leaves the show, it is almost unbearable.

The sequence begins with a tracking shot, the camera slowly closing in on Gordon who is standing by the mirror and adjusting his pants. The intimate *over the shoulder shot* gives us a feeling of being close to Gordon, and the noticeable lack of *non-diegetic* sound adds a sense of gravity to the situation and functions as a subtle omen (silence being a typical metaphor for death).[480] After the *countershot* of Gordon, who looks directly into the camera (the mirror), we hear an *off-screen* sound of a door being opened. The *disembodied sound* naturally makes you think that this is a sort of *ellipsis*, but the "bodiless sound" could also be a sign of Gordon's imminent demise (he is already leaving his body). It then cuts back to an *over the shoulder shot* of Gordon, who turns to see where the sound came from, and now we see Donna (Kerry Bishé) coming in through the door. The inattentive viewer might not notice it, but here we have a gradual blurring of the lines between dream and reality, and this is emphasized when we get a *countershot* of Donna, who passes Gordon without noticing him. Gordon turns to look at his ex-wife, and a conspicuous *lens flare* effect gives the sequence a poetic and unnaturalistic quality. As if it were a technical glitch in the camera or the projection system.

The effect becomes more overt as Donna leaves the frame, and suddenly it looks as if Gordon is standing by a projector that is projecting images of Gordon's life on a big screen outside of the frame. His life is literally flashing before his eyes, and the sequence seems to mirror the opening of Ingmar Bergman's *Persona* (1966), albeit in a less radical form. "Donna, what are you doing here?", Gordon asks, as the camera follows him in a moving *over the shoulder* shot, trying to catch up to Donna. From this point on, the sequence alternates between *over the shoulder* shots and close-ups of Gordon, and the *lens flare* effects become gradually more overt and conspicuous, as if to illustrate the liminal space that Gordon has found himself in. Gordon's in-betweenness is illustrated by the radical use of *lens flares*, whereby a seeming technical error is turned into a lyrical illustration of death.

Gordon follows Donna into the living room and repeats his question, without getting any reply, and now he hears the words "Mommy, mommy," apparently coming from another room. At this point, the *lens flare* effects are accompanied by a discrete piece of *non-diegetic* music, indicating that Gordon is dying and that these were all glimpses from Gordon's memory bleeding into the last minutes of his waking life. Donna leaves the room to attend to their child, and Gordon follows her with a puzzled look on his face. The *non-diegetic* music is intensified, and the light, spherical tones add an almost angelic or dreamy quality to the scene.

When we see the children, it is evident that they are not the right age, and at this point the viewer knows that Gordon is either dreaming or dying. The beautiful *non-diegetic* music and Donna's lullaby (Donna is a trained classical musician) are slowly being distorted, as if the signal were fading or getting weaker, and as we follow Gordon into the bedroom, we see Donna holding their baby in her arms. This sequence, we now understand, was a mental journey to the beginning of Gordon's marriage and fatherhood – to the starting point of the relations and the life he created – just as the last shots of his inner movie are flickering by. The sequence ends on a shot of Gordon, looking toward the lens, bathed in light, before cutting to a *countershot* of Donna with a quiet sadness in her eyes.

Fig. 30: Evans Brown (DP) talks about the poetic death sequence from *Halt and Catch Fire* (AMC, 2014-2017), a sequence that used *lense flare* and direct address to startling effect.

Tricia Brock (director) & Evans Brown (director of photography) on the death sequence in *Halt and Catch Fire*

Brock: It is a Bergmanesque thing. I wish I could take complete credit for it, but it was on the page like that – that he went back in time. That's how we experience it, as if he's going back in time. It was really that thing you hear of, of life flashing before you. That was on the page. I have to give all the credit for the initial vision to the brilliant writer of that episode Lisa Albert. But then I would like to think that, visually, I was so inspired by what she wrote, and then in collaboration with Evans Brown we went after it.

It was handheld, without being too jerky, in order to keep it intimate. We wanted the feeling that we were with him, that we *were* him, we were inside him. In fact, I just saw Scoot McNairy recently in New York City, and we were talking about that scene, and I told him that I don't think I have ever experienced something else like that in my career. People who saw that are just so knocked out by it. It's one of my favorite things I've ever done.

Evans was using all the filters, and I had Glenn Brown on Steadicam, and he's now become a DP himself. Evans was standing there holding the lights with the filters himself, as we were moving, because a lot of it was one take. We let Scoot pass through, and then Evans would run from behind him around the house and then into the kitchen, while we were shooting – we never stopped – to be ready for the next part as he passed from room to room. Evans was standing there, holding the lights to get those lens flares. It was magic.[481]

Brown: The way they approached Gordon's death is some of the best writing I've ever read. The way that it was handled. The fact that we didn't see him die, the fact that we didn't really know what happened, but you are just kind of following along and you figure out: "Oh, my God, he died."

I pitched to Tricia: "Let's shoot this vision." Let's call it that because I can't call it a flashback. I don't know what it is. And we had a conversation about it because Gordon is kind of a hum-head, he's kind of like a ham radio guy, he's an electrical engineer and stuff like that.

It's like trying to tune in to a station on the ham radio, and then Tricia said that to me: "What can we do that's like tuning in, like Gordon-is-this-electrical-engineer thing"? And I was like: "That's interesting. How do we visually show that?" So the thing that came to mind was lens flares, and I said: "Well, what's the best lens flare in the world but with an anamorphic lens?" So, we shot that little sequence in a 16:9 center extraction with an old 1970s Hawk 50 mm lens. And basically all those shots were all done on Steadicam and me following the camera out of frame with a flashlight, flaring the lens when I felt the moment.[482]

The Art of Yak-Yak: Alternative Dialogues in *Succession* and *American Crime*

Trying to characterize traditional television, David Chase famously described the medium as a "prisoner of dialogue" – as mentioned earlier – and he argued that most TV series were dominated by traditionally staged dialogues consisting of *masters* and *shot/countershot* editing (aka *shot/reverse-shot* editing). Though a provocative generalization, Chase's comment still pointed to a crucial element of narrative film and television and a conundrum for modern TV creators who wish to brand their series as something other (or more) than traditional television. In modern examples of *art TV*, then, we often see two ways of approaching this conundrum:

- Reducing the relative amount of dialogue scenes
- Staging dialogues in unconventional ways.

As we shall see later in this chapter, *Twin Peaks: The Return* is an evident example of the first strategy, reducing the amount of traditional dialogue scenes and putting more emphasis on wordless (in)action, whereas *American Crime* and *Succession* (HBO, 2018-) exemplify the second strategy.

As mentioned in the previous chapter, *American Crime* uses *time-collapsing editing* as part of its complex narrative structure. This editing technique, however, is also a part of the interesting and unusual ways in which it tackles *the dialogue conundrum*. A dialogue-centric series, *American Crime* goes to great length to avoid a conventional paradigm. Throughout the three seasons, the series employs various strategies to stage dialogue sequences in an alternative way, including:

- Avoiding *countershots*;
- Intercutting *flashbacks*, *flashforwards* and *imaginary shots*, thereby fragmenting the dialogue scene;
- Using *disembodied voices* to make it unclear when and where the voices come from;
- Using off-kilter framing, e.g. placing characters on the outer edges of the frame or hiding the faces of the people who talk.

These techniques are used frequently in *American Crime*, and it therefore seemed natural for the creator, John Ridley, to contact the British director Sam Miller and make him part of the show. Miller was known for directing various British TV series, including the globally popular and influential crime series *Luther* (BBC, 2010-2019), which was one of the four top-rated shows on BBC America in 2011.[483] One of the things that critics and industry people noticed when watching *Luther* was the off-kilter framing and the unconventional staging of dialogue scenes – elements closely linked to Miller's directorial style.

Miller came on to *American Crime* during the first season where he directed Ep.1:7, and if we take a stylometric approach to that episode, the results are quite interesting; 20 out of the 23 sequences in that episode are dialogue-centered sequences, yet only seven of these are traditional dialogues. In this context, a traditional dialogue is understood as a scene that uses a *shot/countershot* technique where all the dialogue partners are seen, and where the voices are not *disembodied*. Three of the dialogue sequences are crafted as *two-shot* dialogues with elements of non-linearity, and in one dialogue scene Tony's father is talking to the police who are standing in the foreground of the shot with their backs to the camera. In another scene, Barb (Felicity Huffman) is talking to her son's fiancé, Richelle, who is positioned in an unconventional way, covering Barb's face as she is talking. In some of the more conventional scenes (e.g. during Hector's testimony), the traditional set-up is accompanied by a disjunctive use of *jump-cutting*, making the general aesthetic seem conspicuous and potentially jarring.

Miller's episode is fairly close to Chase's description of traditional television, inasmuch as most of the sequences revolve around dialogues and words. The actual staging of these dialogues, however, is far from conventional, and in that sense the series might be dialogue-centered, but it is not *verbocentric*. The French film critic Michel Chion writes about traditional film and television as being *voco-* and *verbocentric*, focusing primarily on human voices and words. According to Chion, this is a natural tendency in film and television, inasmuch as it mirrors the human perception. In a sonic environment, we immediately notice and focus our attention on the human voice, trying to hear and understand the words.[484] In that sense, there is nothing peculiar about TV series focusing on dialogue as a central form of human interaction and an efficient expositional tool. It is rather unconventional, though, when dialogues are shot and edited in a way that distracts or confuses the audience, making them notice the style and staging itself, sometimes even at the expense of *intelligibility*.

This is the case in the second season where scenes between Taylor and his counselor at the school are staged in an alternative fashion. During the conversation, the sound levels change abruptly, and these changes make it difficult for the viewer to catch and understand the counselor's words.

The abrupt changes, like the off-kilter framing and conspicuous cutting patterns might seem strange to the viewer, potentially breaking the illusion. But they often serve an expressive and narrative function (the changes in sound levels may mirror Taylor's lack of focus and attention, and the

Sam Miller (director) on his approach to dialogue scenes in *Luther* and *American Crime*

I often try to resist shots that feel like they're staged. On a film set, that can be kind of tricky because of course they're staged. Of course you're staging dialogue, and actors are standing a certain way, so they can be filmed. But I like it when actors don't make it too easy for me to film them. I like it, when the camera has to work a little bit harder. There's something strange with where you put the camera. There's a million places you can put the camera, and we try to whittle out the right one for this particular sequence to find a way that it hasn't been done before. But if you become too self-conscious about it – if you begin to do the off-framing too self-consciously – it doesn't hold up. But occasionally, if you find it, and you go for the off-framing – you go for the short side, or you put the actor in the bottom of the frame – it becomes interesting. If it's forced, if it's intellectual, it doesn't work for some reason. It's a perfect gut feeling about how shots are put together; how actors stand in a space, and how the camera interacts with that. You try not to let it become soft. There's a tradition for actors to turn out slightly, when they're talking to each other, to allow you to come over their shoulder. I don't want that. We're trying to iron the TV-ness out of it.

Sometimes it's about choosing a situation that isn't that film-friendly that forces you into a certain shot. It's like the old cliché of everything being shot in a loft space where there's loads of room for the camera to move and get up behind everyone. I quite like to shoot in awkward and uncomfortable spaces where there's only one place you can put the camera. There's a truth about it. I also quite like shooting actors up against a wall or something like that. I like shooting flat and not have a lot of depth behind the actors because it feels real to the audience instead of these perfectly staged and perfectly lit dialogues.[486]

jump-cutting seemingly illustrates Aubry's drug-induced detachment). The audiovisual style is conspicuous, but not excessive. It is inventive and experimental, but still within a narrative paradigm and closely connected to the classical principle of "unity", however fragmented and disjunctive it seems.

In that sense, *American Crime* is similar to *Mr. Robot* which, as director Tricia Brock says, "had a very definitive visual style: very low angles, lots of headroom, wide graphic frames, and the camera never tilted or panned."[485]

From "Filmed Theater" to "Photojournalism": *Succession*

A similar kind of visual experimentation is seen in HBO's recent series, *Succession*, which depicts a family-run media conglomerate in New York and the dysfunctional relationship between the different family members and in-laws. Known for its Aaron Sorkin-like use of snappy, overlapping dialogue, the series is also interesting from a technical point of view, especially when it comes to the many dialogues. Like *American Crime*, *Succession* is a dialogue-centric series, but the roaming, handheld camera makes for a very unconventional and slightly more authentic and chaotic experience. In an article for *No Film School*, Jason Hellerman claimed that *Succession* "will change how we shoot and edit," its cinematography and editing "elevat[ing] it to one of the best on TV."[487] Though a sweeping and somewhat ahistorical statement, Hellerman's comment touches upon an important and often overlooked aspect of *Succession*.

Drawing on various cinematic references, from Jonathan Demme to *Direct Cinema*, *Succession* tries to create a sense of realism, and this is achieved through an untraditional and more liberal approach to dialogue staging. As the cinematographer Patrick Capone says:

> I agree that it's a different style of shooting and editing. It's not the first that has done it. I think you can reference some of Adam McKay's earlier films. Things like *The Big Short*, and one I like to reference is Jonathan Demme's *Rachel Getting Married*. When I talk with people about *Succession*, I call it almost a *photojournalistic* way of telling stories. The operators have complete freedom to follow the story within the cast, as they hear and see it. We do not do traditional masters, over-the-shoulder single coverage. We try to be a fly on the wall and document this beautiful performance that this ensemble is doing. And, yes, it *is* a different way of doing it. It doesn't work for every narrative, but for this particular script and narrative, I think it does work.
>
> It's also very much about the reactions of the other people in the room. You hear the "yak-yak", but you don't have to see it. In traditional television, you have to cover every line, and every line has to be equally covered by each cast member, whereas we can equally cover it by watching the reaction of Shiv looking at Roman listening to Kendall off camera. And that is far more powerful than sitting on Kendall talking. Sometimes we will do several takes, and every take is completely different with all of the cameras because they are getting different things.[488]

When Dogme95 was launched at the Odéon Theatre in Paris in 1995, it introduced a set of principles that were meant to make films more realistic and less opulent. The stylistic ideas (including avoiding non-diegetic music, using handheld camera and shooting in 4:3) were reminiscent of older strands of realism, but the idea was to create a more liberal and authentic expression by going against traditional cinematic conventions. As a positive side effect, these principles or dogmas also made for cheaper and more efficient filmmaking.[489] In a similar way, Patrick Capone explains, *Succession* proliferated a realistic style that also made for more efficient filmmaking, the scenes at the Thanksgiving dinner and the yacht being shot in only a dozen takes. "We did a ten-page scene in half a day," as Capone says.[490]

As a young man, Capone dreamed of becoming a photojournalist or a concert, rock-n-roll photographer, inspired by Annie Leibovitz, before eventually studying photography and going to film school. As a professional, Capone then worked on a number of feature films (e.g. *The Mosquito Coast* and *Philadelphia*) before going to television, and he eventually brought that photojournalistic *ethos* with him when working on Jesse Armstrong's series.[491] An interesting example of the series' combination of stylization and documentary-like realism is seen in the final sequences of the different episodes, sequences that are often punctuated by visual "exclamation points" (as Capone calls it). At the ending of "I Went to Market" (Ep.1:5), there is a beautiful *wide-lens* shot of Logan's brother that echoes the use of wide lenses in *Miami Vice*, and at the ending of "Austerlitz" (Ep.1:7) there are some aesthetic singles of Kendall (Jeremy Strong) outside in the sun. Even more noteworthy, the ending of "Safe Room" (Ep.2:4) depicts a troubled Kendall who walks towards a glass window and presses his head against the glass, effectively punctuating the episode with a stunning *mirror motif*. As Capone says:

> We don't plan it, and Jeremy doesn't like to rehearse. So we just said: "Jeremy, you do what you want to do. We'll just follow you." We followed him, and he slowly walked closer and closer to the glass, and my operator just got tighter and tighter with him and found that final frame. We didn't know that he was going to put his head against the glass. That's the documentation, that's the photojournalism. As if we were still photographers in a war zone thinking: "What image tells the story?" It was so organic. We said "cut", and we all thought: "Where the hell did that come from?"[492]

As opposed to *Sex and the City* (HBO, 1998-2004) and *Billions* (Showtime, 2016-), *Succession* is not intent on showcasing the glamor of New York or using the location as an attraction in itself. Though showing us Manhattan from the sky, when following the central characters in a helicopter, we rarely have traditional *establishing shots* of iconic places or emblematic parts of the city. In fact, the camera crew had a set of dogmas while shooting the series, hoping to avoid the controlled and glamorous look of many urban TV series:

> We wanted the characters to enter into uncontrollable situations. They can control a lot of things in life, but they can't control what everybody has to deal with: the weather, their health and things like that. There are things that even money can't control. There are many scenes that others would go to cover and shoot inside, but we say: "Fuck them. They are billionaires, and they have to walk in the rain like the rest of us."
>
> We do a lot of location stuff. Even the car scenes are shot realistically. The cars are driving with a camera operator. We don't do towing shots or put the car on a flatbed and drive it around Manhattan. And they drive around in traffic. We try to keep it as realistic as we can.
>
> We are having this discussion constantly at work: "Are we making it 'too cinema', or is this the reality of where we are?" And when we find ourselves getting too cinematic, we back off a little bit and keep it as realistic as possible – and yet make it look good. So we take that reality and try to be as genuine as we can, especially in the business part of it, and add to that this genuine language.[493]

Like the Danish series *When the Dust Settles*, *Succession* is based on extensive research, employing ten different people (e.g. travel experts and legal experts) whom they could contact if they needed information.[494] The research was meant to add an element of authenticity to the series, and the same thing could be said of the alternative, Dogme-like approach to cinematography. As the cinematographer and director Andrij Parekh puts it:

> We didn't want to do filmed theater. That was a big part of it – that we weren't going to do traditional coverage. The camera would be constantly moving, roaming, almost like a character in itself.
>
> Jesse Armstrong has made a new *King Lear*, combining the best of Shakespeare with the best of Chekhov, and what we did camerawise was to almost do a sort of provisional in-camera editing, cameras panning a lot, picking up moments. I began as a cinematographer on the series and then became a director, and what I said to the operator was: "Imagine that this is the only camera angle of the entire scene and try to capture everything that you can in the scene with one shot."
>
> We never felt beholden to the dialogue and to make sure that everyone that was speaking was on camera, and I think that kind of looseness became the style of the show.[495]

It is interesting to notice that the different filmmakers talk about some aesthetic conventions they were trying to avoid or go against when making *American Crime* and *Succession*, although referencing different media. Sam Miller talked about "iron[ing] the TV-ness out" when working on *Luther* and *American Crime*, whereas Patrick Capone talked about not becoming "too cinematic," and Andrij Parekh talked about avoiding "filmed theater". These comments are interesting because they illustrate that the different series and TV creators are all trying to differentiate their work from certain cinematic and televisual conventions, perhaps hoping for their series to be noticed in a saturated media landscape, but they are not denigrating any specific medium. In that sense, phrases like "filmed theater" and "TV-ness" might reference the same thing – a conventional way of staging scenes and dialogues – and the word "cinematic", though often used as a positive adjective to connote an artful style or high production value, is also used as a shorthand for "conventional" or "artificial".

Fig. 31-32: Director Andrij Parekh on the set of *Succession* (HBO, 2018-) with lead actors Brian Cox and Jeremy Strong. Before becoming an episode director on Jesse Armstrong's series, Parekh was one of the main cinematographers who introduced the show's unconventional visual aesthetic. Courtesy of Andrij Parekh.

Jesse Armstrong (creator) on the genre, style and authenticity of *Succession*

Style and authenticity: In terms of authenticity, we did and do a lot of research to make sure all our business, media, financial and political stuff is right.

Adam McKay shot the pilot, and since then Mark Mylod has been my closest collaborator as a director. My comic pitch of the show when I took it to HBO was that it would be "*Festen* meets *Dallas*," so some of that Dogme sensibility appealed to me, and I think we watched *Festen* again when we were preparing to shoot the pilot. But Andrij Parekh and Adam McKay, and subsequently Mark Mylod, have evolved a look for the show that nods towards the effects of the restrictions of Dogme – that documentary sense of real life captured – but also allows them to do basically whatever the hell they want stylistically in any given scene.

Genre and tonality: I wouldn't object, if people called the show a drama, a comedy or a satire. They're all applicable. I guess it's not so useful to think about from the inside out, the specific categorization. There are a few over-arching principles for stuff that can be in the show and stuff that can't.

To be in the show it has to be related to our central family, and it has to have a relationship to things that have or could happen in the real world.[496]

A similar thing is seen in *Euphoria* (HBO, 2019-), which, as Sam Levinson says, generally avoids *over the shoulder shots* in dialogue scenes in order to create a more subjective and radical aesthetic (this is not the case in the first "Corona special", though, which consists almost entirely of *shot/reverse-shot* editing).[497]

The same *anti-traditional credo* is reflected in Sidney Wolinsky's description of working with Martin Scorsese on the pilot episode of *Boardwalk Empire* - a transgressive period drama that depicts the illegal selling of alcohol during the Prohibition Era in the 1920s. As the editor remembers:

> In the beginning of the pilot, there's a shootout at a road at night, and I got this series of cuts: wide, close, closer. So I cut it in the traditional way where you cut from the wide shot to a POV to a closer shot to a POV, you know to emphasize. And Marty (Martin Scorsese) looked at it, and he said: "No, no, no. I want you to just go in, in, in. In *Yojimbo* or maybe it's *Ikiru*, there's a scene..." And I said; "Okay, I'll get those films and take a look at them, and I found the series of shots which just goes bang, bang, bang, and I replicated it. And when I left, he actually gave me, as a Christmas present, the complete Criterion Collection of Kurosawa which I thought was very wonderful and generous.[498]

Wolinsky's anecdote illustrates the affinity for arthouse cinema in modern TV series, in this case Japanese films from the 1950s and 1960s, but, more importantly, it illustrates what Scorsese was trying to avoid: the traditional *master shot technique*.

The series mentioned in this section all exhibit *signature styles*, conspicuous aesthetic choices and *explicit authorial comments*, and they all favor ambiguity and psychological realism over conventional principles of cinematography and editing. They could be described as *oppositional styles* by differentiating themselves from established aesthetic norms, but many of these norms are not uniquely related to TV and were, in fact, established many decades before the birth of television.[499]

Stranger Sounds and Musical Peaks: Sonic Strategies in Modern TV

> When I got my nomination for *Game of Thrones*, and it was my fifth nomination, I was nominated as a sound designer, but I was demoted by the Academy because they didn't recognize the title. So many people are sonically illiterate, and I think they should recognize it. It's funny how long it's taken for it to take hold because of people's sonic illiteracy.
> - Paula Fairfield, sound designer[500]

In recent years, we have seen some interesting examples of stylistic experimentation within title sequences, cinematography and editing. Similar tendencies can be located if we turn our attention to the sonic aspects of television. The traditional principles of *aesthetic anonymity* and *seamlessness* also guide the typical use of sound and music in mainstream film and TV, and the most cited theories concerning film sound and film music specifically reference these ideas. According to Theodor Adorno and Hanns Eisler, traditional film sound and music must be *unobtrusive* and *inconspicuous*, and Claudia Gorbman has famously noted that film music in mainstream cinema should be *inaudible*.[501] Much has been written about that particular term, but Gorbman's point is essentially that classical film music is "subordinate to narrative form [and the human voice]", often functioning as an "unnoticed" element that accentuates narratively important details and otherwise stays in the background.[502] This idea is echoed in various books about film music and sound, and Michel Chion also writes about a *sonic hierarchy* and the general concern with *intelligibility* in narrative film and television: Since the human voice is considered more important than other sonic aspects, dialogue must never be compromised by other parts of the soundscape.[503]

Many of these ideas have been challenged, both theoretically and practically, and in the so-called *Dolby Era* we are seeing some interesting examples of complex and compact sound designs and a more conspicuous or noticeable use of sound and music.[504] In this section, I will explore those elements of modern TV series, focusing more narrowly on the use of *sonic superfields*, *conspicuous sound* and *musical moments* in modern series like *Stranger Things* and *Twin Peaks: The Return*.

Sensory Complexity and the Superfield

The term *sound designer* was coined in the 1970s when people like Walter Murch, Ben Burtt, Richard Portman and Alan Splet pioneered a new approach to film sound. According to Murch, a film should have a sonic design, just as it has a general visual design, and all of the sonic elements should reflect a general *sound strategy* in the given movie. This approach was used in films like *The Godfather* (1972), *American Graffiti* (1973), *Star Wars* (1977) and *Eraserhead* (1977).[505] Since then, there have been many technological advances in television, and TV series are beginning to approach sound in new and more experimental ways, just as sound designers and re-recording mixers are migrating from film to television. One example of this tendency is Craig Henighan, who was known as a recognized sound designer in American cinema and a recurring collaborator of directors such as Darren Aronosky and Wes Anderson (on films like *Black Swan*, *Noah* and *Moonrise Kingdom*), before becoming the leading figure on the vast sound team behind *Stranger Things* - a team that includes 90 (!) people. As Henighan says:

> The big television buzz word is "cinematic." The onus is usually on the sound designer to really pull rabbits out of hats time and time again. They tend to work long hours to achieve cinematic sound for television. The irony is that most people watch it on a smartphone or tablet. It's an odd time with technological advances in sound (Dolby Atmos, IMAX, DTS-X etc.), but the final delivery device is smaller and smaller.[506]

In 1994, Chion introduced the word *superfield* to describe "the space created, in multitrack films, by ambient sounds, city noises, music, and all sorts of rustlings that surround the visual space," and today this type of space is seen (or heard) in both film and TV series and across various platforms.[507] Other scholars have described the same phenomenon as *post-classical film sound* and *compact sound spaces*, pointing to the invention of new sound technologies in the 1970s as an essential factor in this development.[508]

A televisual example of this trend is seen in the intriguing and bleak miniseries *The Night Of* (HBO, 2016), which was based on the British series *Criminal Justice* from 2008. A *noir*-like series, *The Night Of* has garnered a lot of attention for its intense performances and expressive lighting strategies, yet its sound design is a good example of the *sensory complexity* that Chion writes about. In the series, we follow Naz (Riz Ahmed) who settles into Rikers Island, a well-known prison in New York, and much of the action takes place in that dark and claustrophobic space. For that reason, some critics have also described it as a *prison show*, in line with cable and streaming classics like *Oz* and *Orange Is the New Black* (Netflix, 2013-2019), yet the style and tone in *The Night Of* differ widely from its popular precursors.[509] A central part of the claustrophobic feel and the visceral experience of moisture and wetness comes from the complex and layered sound design. We hear the sound of water dripping and running, body bags being opened, footsteps echoing in the hallway, and rings being removed from corpses and placed in noisy plastic bags. These are all part of a larger and quite complex design, which in style and tone is closer to David Lynch (*Eraserhead* and *The Elephant Man*) or Joel Schumacher (*Falling Down*) than to modern-day blockbusters with their sensory overloads and sonic density. According to sound designer Ruy Garcia:

> I worked with John Turturro on the movie he did right after that, and we were talking about the show, and he described it in the way of working with the director that he would do the same thing on the set. That he would have like a glass in the scene, and he would be like, "Do it like this, do it like that", and by the tenth take he would say, "That's the take." He did that with everything – he did it with the production design, with the music. It's a very precise show, and if you see all the sessions – the amount of tracks we had… I remember he came and sat and wanted to hear like every sound of ambience, of backgrounds, and we started talking. We both said, "It's kind of like *Eraserhead*", and we both said it at the same time. I was like, "Thank you. That completely gives an idea of what we want".[510]

Musical Moments in Modern Television

The use of popular music is not a new concept in film and television, yet popular music, in the form of pop or rock-scores and actual *compilation tracks*, is associated, more specifically, with the new cinemas of the 1960s and 70s. In the early stages of conglomeration, film and music companies saw the possibilities of *cross-promoting* films and popular music, selling soundtracks in massive quantities to a group of new moviegoers who wanted something less antiquated and opulent than the big, symphonic scores of the classical era.[511] Following *Easy Rider* (1969) and *American Graffiti*, movies began to feature modern tunes or popular tracks from the past, and if film music had ever really been "inaudible", it would now become increasingly audible, urging audiences to hum and sing along to their favorite songs and using lyrics to comment on the action.[512] "I don't know that it's true that film sound goes unnoticed," as the re-recording mixer Adam Jenkins puts it. "It is true that in certain cases it is best practiced as an unnoticed art, but there are places in a TV series where the sound carries the show, whether it be sound effects or music."[513]

Writing specifically about the differences between classical score music and the use of popular music in recent films and TV series, Rick Altman points to a set of significant, albeit general, differences:

Classical film music	Popular music
Muteness	Linguistic dependence
Indeterminacy	Predictability
Inconspicuousness	Singability
Quiet listening and mental involvement	Active physical involvement

Fig. 33: Classical Film Music vs. Popular Music. Source: Altman, Rick (2001), "The Sound of Sentiment," pp. 23-25.

As Altman notices, the use of popular music in film goes back to the early years of cinema where live versions of evergreens like "Auld Lang Syne" were used as part of collective *sing-along happenings* in movie theaters.[514] The more general and strategic use of popular music in film and television is a more recent phenomenon, though, involving various questions concerning use, licensing and legality. When acquiring music for a modern series, the producers have to purchase two separate licenses: *matter use license* (where the producers pay a sum of money to the record company for the music) and *synchronization license* (where the producers pay a sum of money to the creators and publishers of the music allowing them to use it in an audio-visual context).[515]

In that sense, using and showcasing popular music in a TV series is an expensive and tricky endeavor, and in recent years TV series have begun to use music supervisors to find suitable songs for different moments in the series and clear the rights for the music. According to music supervisor Thomas Golubić:

What's interesting about how television operates is that it's essentially like a well-orchestrated army that's doing a choreographed dance with a lot of landmines around them. So the idea is that there has to be precision to every player, and because the time frame is so tight and the budgets are so high, it's really important for everybody to play their part really well. And when you're dealing with a very ambitious show - and I'd say that *Breaking Bad* and *Better Call Saul* are extraordinarily ambitious - everybody is delivering such extraordinarily, highly precise results, which means that every choice is there for a reason. I have my own team, including a music editor and a composer, and we're all working very closely together. We're very practiced in how to know what our part is and how to work efficiently with each other, and because we have enormous respect for each other, it becomes a really efficient machine.[516]

Working as a music supervisor on shows like *Six Feet Under*, *Breaking Bad* and *Halt and Catch Fire*, Golubić tries to figure out ways to "tell the story with music" by "build[ing] playlists for each of the characters" and selecting the "music that informs their journey."[517] In that sense, popular music is an integral part of modern TV series from the earliest stages of conceptualization to the final mix and the way that audiences engage with the series. According to music and media scholar Mathias Bonde Korsgaard, we have seen a number of *musical moments* in modern TV series where popular music takes center stage for several minutes in order to tell the story, to create a heightened emotional reaction or to suspend and punctuate the narrative.[518] These *musical moments* are often seen at the end of episodes or seasons, as in the final sequence from *Halt and Catch Fire* where Joe McMillan's move to upstate New York is underscored by Peter Gabriel's popular track "Solsbury Hill" or in the refrain-like ending montages from David Flebotte's *I'm Dying Up Here* (Showtime, 2017-2018). Not to mention the symbolic use of Joy Division's "Love Will Tear Us Apart" and the chilling combination of cross-cutting and Leonard Cohen's "Treaty" in Ep. 1:3 of *Your Honor* (Showtime, 2020), an American version of the Israeli series *Kvodo* (Yes, 2017-), to illustrate the emotional dilemma of the young man Adam (Hunter Doohan) and his father, Judge Desiato (Bryan Cranston), who is desperately trying to remove all signs of his son's accidental wrongdoing. "When I first did that sequence, I was concerned the producers might not like it," as the editor Michael Ruscio says. "But everyone did, and it stayed."[519]

Another example is seen in Ep. 4:8 of *Halt and Catch Fire* where the remaining characters mourn the loss of Gordon. The sequence opens on a shot of Cameron (Mackenzie Davis) trying to select the most fitting song for the situation. She picks an album by Dire Straits (*Brothers in Arms*) and looks at Gordon's ex-wife, Donna, saying: "Sorry, nothing feels right." But Donna quickly replies: "This is perfect," and, consequently, Cameron puts the record on the turntable. Thus, the popular music is used to frame the entire sequence, and it is even highlighted as a perfect fit for the moment, making the audience conscious of the musical track ("So Far Away") that underscores the emotional montage. In the words of Thomas Golubić:

> When that album came out, for Gordon as a character, you get a sense that it was really satisfying, that he would have had an individual relationship with each of those songs. [...] It captures, in the life-line of our story with him, a moment when he viewed the world in a really positive way, from a band that was maybe fundamentally a 70s band, to a certain degree. So I think that it kind of comes from a comfort zone, but it shows the sense of a 'New Spring', and I think that is why that album felt so right.
>
> "So Far Away" is not a sad song, but it has such depth of feeling to it. It has a sense of bitter-sweetness. The lyrics are talking about absence, but in a way that has a kindness to it. I think that's the way we view Gordon in that moment.[520]

A more canonical example is found at the end of *Six Feet Under* where Claire (Lauren Ambrose) drives off in her Prius. The Russian filmmaker and theoretician Vsevolod Pudovkin has written about a form of montage editing that he calls *leitmotif* where a thematic montage at a crucial point in the film reiterates the central themes and, thus, functions almost like a musical *leitmotif*.[521] The final sequence of *Six Feet Under* fits Pudovkin's description neatly, using montage editing and Sia's popular song "Breathe Me" to illustrate the main themes of death and grief in a poetic way. As Claire drives off, we cut to a lengthy montage of images that take us from the present day to the deaths of the different characters at various points in the future. The entire sequence is underscored by Sia's music, and the relative absence of diegetic sound (we only hear small snippets of diegetic sound, e.g. of Claire sobbing) makes it look and feel like a music video. The ending to *Six Feet Under* has been the object of much debate, and some critics describe it as one of the most iconic moments in TV history, whereas others argue that it becomes too conspicuous.[522] The staff writer Nancy Oliver, for example, did not like "having everything wrapped up and spelled out" and "fought it in the writers' room."[523] Eventually, though, she was outvoted, and it became a memorable sequence and an evident example of the *musical moments* in the modern TV landscape.

Other interesting examples include the clever and contrapuntal use of "In the Air Tonight" in the pilot episode of *The Americans* (FX, 2013-2018), through reference to *Miami Vice*, and the extensive and diegetic use of Led Zeppelin in *Sharp Objects* and various popular acts from the 1970s in the period drama *Vinyl* (HBO, 2016). Portraying the music industry of the 1970s, and co-created by Mick Jagger, Martin Scorsese, Rich Cohen and Terence Winter, *Vinyl* is full of popular music and *musical moments*. According to the re-recording mixer, Tom Fleischman, Scorsese's approach to sound is "really straightforward," but he has pioneered the use of "pre-lapping sound and sharp sound effects to make awkward cuts work," and he often flaunts popular music. "Music plays a big part in his productions," as Fleischman concludes, "and it's almost like another character."[524] The references to the 1970s are interesting, since that was the era where popular music became an overt part of the film landscape. And the intertextual reference to *Miami Vice* in *The Americans* is also striking, inasmuch as *Miami Vice* was a prominent precursor for modern TV series like *Six Feet Under* and *The Americans*.

Thomas Golubić (music supervisor) and Michael Ruscio (editor) on the final sequence from *Six Feet Under*

Golubić: We actually pitched "Breathe Me" for a video. It was a music video that was done for the season. A lot of people don't remember this. But the song was actually used in a special music video that HBO had done to promote the final season of *Six Feet Under*.

At the same time we had production doing stuff that was way outside of their comfort zone. I think it's fair to say that they were not experts in doing futuristic art direction and design, make-up wasn't really a huge part of our show – we were doing major ageing make-up – and the actors are not really in the position of doing old versions of themselves. They never had a chance to develop an old version – like what would Rico feel like when he's in his 70s and about to keel over on a cruise ship? The actor had never actually set up how he would be old, so it was pure guesswork what would work. So we had all these elements that were really challenging in a very long sequence that was incredibly ambitious with a song that was not really designed for this sequence. It was just one that we were trying to adapt to the very ambitious goals. And we all thought, when we saw the first cut of it, that we literally had jumped the shark. This was going to be the time when we jettisoned all of our credibility as a TV series. And everybody was nervous about it.

And then there was a little bit more work, a little bit more tinkering, a little bit more effort. There was some really subtle work done with color correction and changing the settings of it, and it evolved into what became a really iconic moment in television history.[525]

Ruscio: You understand that it's the finale, as you're watching it. And then you get to that moment where she's in the Prius, and you have the inserts of the little shifter, and she has the CD - which weirdly is a CD that Ted, the straight conservative guy, gave her - and she puts that into the CD player. And you wouldn't expect that song to come out of it.

Right away, you sort of know that you're in for this ride, and that, when she gets on the freeway, you sort of have her in the Prius, counterbalanced. And then we did the *speed ramps* and the *time-lapse* with the Prius going faster, uphill, downhill and whatnot, and interspersed with it you just know that you are on this journey. So the music drives it, along with the imagery.

On *Six Feet Under*, they hired directors who had films at Sundance: Rodrigo García, Nicole Holofcener, Lisa Cholodenko, Michael Cuesta. People who came from indie films began to gravitate towards TV. The other thing is that it was *appointment television*. People couldn't wait till next week, and people *had* to wait, so you had all these *watercooler moments*.[526]

Joel Fields (executive producer) and Ken Hahn (re-recording mixer) on authenticity, sound and music in *The Americans*

The Americans is a period drama that takes place in the 1980s. In the series, which champions an intense and *noir*-like use of *mirror motifs*, *low-key lighting* and *cucoloris*, we follow Elizabeth and Philip Jennings (Keri Russell and Matthew Rhys), two Russian spies who live in America as next-door neighbors to an FBI agent. The series has been described as *family noir*, in that it deals with the construction and tragic disintegration of a family. Featuring solid plot arcs and strong cliffhangers, *The Americans* is proud of its "TV-ness", as Matt Zoller Seitz says, and the different episode directors, according to Charlotte Sieling, were permitted a great deal of "aesthetic freedom", even if a producing director, Chris Long, oversaw the entire production and used lighting, recurring motifs and *musical moments* to create a sense of aesthetic continuity. Critically, the series has been lauded for its authenticity and its use of lengthy montages featuring popular music from the era, often underscoring emotional crescendos at the end of episodes. From the contrapuntal use of "In the Air Tonight" and "The Chain" to the emotional use of "Don't Dream It's Over" and "Goodbye Yellow Brick Road", tragically foreshadowing Philip and Elizabeth's return to Russia, *The Americans* has become known for its combination of popular music, parallel montages and emotional close-ups, and in the finale of Season 6, the most harrowing twists are accompanied by lengthy versions of "Brothers in Arms" and "With or Without You". Below, the executive producer Joel Fields and the re-recording mixer Ken Hahn talk about the use of sound, music and authenticity in the series.[527]

Fields (on the development of the series): John Landgraf and FX came to us and essentially said to me and Joe Weisberg: "How long do you think this story goes? Do you want it to be four, five or six seasons?" And then Joe and I were able to take a series of walks around Gowanus, Brooklyn and pitch out different versions. By that point, we had the story written, pretty much, so we talked about what shape it would fall into, and by coming to us early, the network allowed us to build towards that ending. Joe and I started to write out what we called "the master document" where we would put in all of the story for each of the characters. It was broken down by character, and it had all of their stories written in bullet point form, and when we had ideas, they would go in there. Sometimes we would surprise ourselves and find out that the story went in a completely different direction than we had expected, but other times we found that the story unfolded the way we had originally thought. We weren't bound by it, but we knew we had a direction.

Keri is such an amazing actress, and it was wonderful to see her bringing that character to life on set. I would quibble with the idea of calling her an antihero, though. Part of the bedrock of the show is that they are actually *not* antiheroes. They actually were heroes in their own eyes. If you look at Walter White or Tony Soprano, those were antiheroes. They were bad guys, and they knew it. But Philip and Elizabeth were soldiers, doing what soldiers do. They weren't on our side, but they were on *one* side, and, in fact, they made incredible sacrifices for their ideals. You can't look at those characters and say that they were acting out of selfishness. They were trying to make the world better in their own way. In the background, I have a poster that I was given by Steven Levenson, with whom I made *Fosse/Verdon* (FX, 2019). That's the Polish poster for *All That Jazz* (1979), and next to it there is a poster for the Cole Porter musical *Can-Can*. Those are also flawed characters. You think about the genius that David Chase did with *The Sopranos* and this creation of the antihero genre. It was transformative and paved the way for so much great television, and at the same time, if we talk about William Shakespeare, why is Richard III so interesting? Basically, Walter White is Richard III; it just takes him a little longer to get there. Ultimately, it's our flaws that make us interesting. It's our flaws that make us human, and those are the things you want to explore in television. There's another show I'll mention, which is *Hill Street Blues*. Think about what Steven Bochco did with *Hill Street Blues* and how he changed the cop show. Up until that point, you had cops like Columbo who solved crimes, and Bochco started to create *human* stories, and that was a pivotal part of this journey too. How television changed.

Fields (on authenticity and music): We always envisioned the story as its own real story in a real universe, so what we tried to do was to tell the story in a way that was most authentic and truthful. We would never try to bend that authenticity to make it more dramatic. We talked about authenticity a lot. Obsessively. Joe and I were both in high school in the 1980s, so we had a vivid memory of that. You'd remember how much those football games were a part of your life and how David Copperfield made The Statue of Liberty disappear. When I grew up during The Cold War, we all thought we were going to die all the time, and the episode that had *The Day After* in it reflected that fear. That was not a crazy high-concept movie; it was a serious movie about the nuclear apocalypse that was aired without commercial interruptions and followed by a round-table news discussion.

The balance was trying to have all of that appear as part of the fabric of the show without it ever being at the forefront because when one is living through a period, one is not thinking of what is unique to that period. You're just living in it. The same was the case with wardrobe. It's easy to do a show set in a particular time frame and have all of the wardrobe from that time frame, but if you look closely people would still be wearing clothes from the 50s, 60s and 70s.

I can tell you a great story about the McDonald's scene at the end of the series. We so wanted to do that scene, and we reached out to McDonald's. They came back to us, and we showed them the script, and they said: "It's fine, but we have one concern about authenticity. We have a McDonald's Museum and a McDonald's Archive, and if you're doing everything in a period, we want it to be just the way it was in that period." And we said: "Oh, my, you are singing our song."

Television is at its core such a collaboration. Ken Hahn and his team are just a perfect example of those people who do incredible artistic work that is experienced, but not consciously. And if it is consciously experienced, it means that it hasn't been done well. You talked about the music, and of course the songs were a big part of the show, but the composed music was huge too, and Nathan Barr is just a genius. He literally created instruments for the show, so the title theme is played on what he calls a "butchered piano," which is a piano that he created to make the music for Elizabeth's theme. I think he cut a piano in half and restrung it, and I think Philip's theme is made on an instrument that he invented called "the sympathetic drone cello". One thing we always talked about with Ken Hahn and his team, Nathan Barr and his team on the composing side, and P.J. Bloom and his team in terms of music choices, was that we never wanted music to lead the viewers towards emotion. We wanted it, as subtly and imperceptibly as possible, to support what was going on, so we found ourselves very often pulling music back, quieting it, taking out cues. We always tried to be very responsible from a production standpoint, but by the time we got into the fifth season, shows like *Game of Thrones* had come out, and there was a different expectation in terms of what a TV series would look and sound like. You could see and hear that, also in terms of music, but in a way the scope never changed. One nice thing about making television these days is that you are not making it for a 14-inch box. It is essentially a cinematic experience.[528]

Hahn (on sound and authenticity): All if it – the sound, the score, the popular music and the silences – is like one great composition where we play with tension and release and different perspectives. The series takes place in an analogue world. It's not a clean, crispy sound. For instance, the cars all suggest it. Think of Philip's car, for instance. I know what an 8-cylinder Camaro sounds like, and my effects mixers certainly weren't around back then, and I just had to force them, saying: "I know what it should sound like. People in my generation know what it would sound like, and I'm trying to evoke that sensation."[529]

"Toastering" and Musical "Touchstones" in *Stranger Things*

Musical moments and conspicuous sound are also a crucial part of *Stranger Things*, a TV series that was created for Netflix by the Duffer Brothers and which has come to be known for its blatant and nostalgic references to the 1980s.[530] *Stranger Things* takes place in the fictional small town of Hawkins, Indiana in the 1980s, and it introduces the ambiguous combination of different moods and genres - fantasy, sci-fi, horror, comedy and teen-drama - through overt allusions to artists like Stephen King and Steven Spielberg. As one of the main actors, Natalia Dyer (Nancy Wheeler), says:

> Most of us were not born in the 1980s. We rely on those classic movies that the show references a lot. But everybody – the costume department, the art department, hair and make-up – most of these people did experience the 80s, and they have a passion for it. There is such a care and a passion for that time period from everyone that works on the set. You can go through your set room, and it's so specific - each little detail in the clothing is so specific, and you see yourself in the clothing, and when your hair is done, and you are in your make-up and surrounded by hundreds of extras dressed in 80s clothing, you lose yourself in that world.[531]

The most interesting element in this context is the use of popular music - something that often establishes a sense of ambiguity on many different levels. One example of this is the scene from the second season where the new guy in town, Billy (Dacre Montgomery), is introduced. This scene begins with a *point of view shot* where Nancy notices Billy - to the seeming dismay of her boyfriend Steve (Joe Keery) - after which we cut to a *low-angle shot* of the car, as Billy opens the door and lets his boots hit the gravel. On the soundtrack we hear the first notes of the 1984-classic "Rock You Like a Hurricane" - a track that, like the band Scorpions, *seems* harder than it actually really is. As the camera tilts upward, slowly revealing Billy, the music becomes louder, and as he turns to the camera, he is immediately underscored by the line "Here I am," pointing to the performative nature of his "toughness." Billy, who looks like a copy of Rob Lowe in *St. Elmo's Fire* (1985), is putting on an act, and the musical choice seems to mirror this act by playing on the nostalgic coolness of "Rock You Like a Hurricane" and the campy correspondence between Billy's looks and the lyrics of the song. In many ways, this scene is reminiscent of a sequence from *Terminator 2: Judgment Day* (1991) where Thorogood's "Bad to the Bone" is used to simultaneously accentuate and debunk the toughness of Arnold Schwarzenegger's character. The boots, the sunglasses and the tilt all seem to indicate that "Arnie" is tough, but as the music says the words "I'm bad to the bone… b-b-b-bad," it becomes an *ironic double-accentuation* of his toughness, as Birger Langkjær writes.[532]

The reveal of Billy also reminds the viewer of the way Jane or Eleven (Millie Bobby Brown) was introduced in the beginning of the first season, thus connecting the androgyny of Eleven's character to the pseudo-masculinity of Billy. This point is later emphasized in the scene where Billy is told off by his father while listening to Metallica's "The Four Horseman" - a thrashy, hard-hitting track that some people would associate with young aggression and others with stereotypical notions of masculinity.

Stranger Things often employs popular music to create a sense of ambiguity, and other examples include the wonderful scene from the pilot episode where Nancy and Steve are making out in Nancy's bed to the nostalgic and slightly corny sound of Toto's "Africa." A track that neatly emphasizes the cuteness of the situation, but with a hint of irony, using the line "It's gonna take a lot to drag me away from you" to illustrate the romantic relationship between Nancy and Steve, and using the word "rain" as a transitional cue.

Also, we could point to the use of "Should I Stay or Should I Go?" - a song that serves as a popular *leitmotif*, connecting Will (Noah Schnapp) and his brother, Jonathan (Charlie Heaton), while lyrically indicating Will's in-betweenness. As Will is stuck in an intermediate space between the real world and the Upside-Down, The Clash fittingly ask, "Should I Stay or Should I Go?" As Craig Henighan says:

> "Should I Stay or Should I Go?" was in one of the earliest cuts. The ideas were cut out early on, and when you then put the sound design around it, it becomes great. Those songs are integral to those guys. It's almost like *Baby Driver*. To me, it was always about working around those touchstones, and they're paying for those songs, so – and that's the other side of the business – I get out of the way. They're not paying for my sound effects or my sound design. But those songs, in a way, make the other sequences with my sound design even more noticeable.[533]

Finally, there is an interesting example of this ambiguity at the end of the second season, during the dance at the high school. This sequence begins in a cute romantic tone, underscored by The Police, whose hit "Every Breath You Take" is often used at weddings and anniversaries to signal devotion and life-long commitment. As a romantic ballad, "Every Breath You Take" is nonetheless quite ambiguous and it has also been read as a song about stalking. This other potential meaning is then illustrated at the end of the sequence, as the camera pulls out and we see The Mind Flayer watching ominously over the school, underscored by a faint, reverberant version of the aforementioned Police track.

Immersion, Reflexivity and Performance

The popular music in *Stranger Things* often comments - at times overtly or even ironically - on the action. When Jane/Eleven goes to Chicago in the second season, running away from her substitute father (Hopper, played by David Harbour), she is underscored by Bon Jovi's track "Runaway". This music has been criticized as being too "on the nose," with the lyrics clearly alluding to Jane's situation, but the conspicuousness of the music seems conscious and intentionally campy: "She's a little runaway / Daddy's girl learned fast / All those things she couldn't say."[534]

Elsewhere, the popular music has a similar conspicuousness to it, as in the examples with Toto and Bon Jovi. This is the case, for example, in the self-reflexive use of Madonna's "Material Girl" in Season 3 - in what looks like a *Pretty Woman*-montage in 1980s clothing - and the diegetic and contrapuntal use of Don McLean's "American Pie" in Ep. 3:3, as Heather (Francesca Reale) hits her father on the head with a wine bottle. The most conspicuous and popular example, however, is seen in the last episode of the third season where Dustin (Gaten Matarazzo) finally connects with his girlfriend Suzie (Gabriella Pizzolo), who asks him to perform a duet with her of Limahl's "NeverEnding Story" in exchange for her giving him Planck's constant and, thus, helping him save Hawkins. In the sequence that follows Suzie's request, we see Dustin and Suzie in *singles* and *split-screen* performing Limahl's song, and *reaction shots* from the other characters are intercut as part of the performative montage. The sequence became a viral hit, and it resulted in an Instagram challenge called #NeverEndingChallenge where people reenacted the sequence, and a renewed interest in Limahl's popular song. Within days, the viewership of the original music video on YouTube had increased by 800%, and Spotify noted an 825% increase in stream requests for the original song.[535] When Limahl performed his track on the Danish version of *X Factor* (Feb. 28, 2020), he talked about the renewed interest in his music, following the use of "Too Shy" and "The NeverEnding Story" in *American Horror Story* (FX, 2011-), *Black Mirror* (Channel 4/Netflix, 2011-2019) and *Stranger Things*, and he gave a brazen message to the contestants: "I hope you get a multi-million dollar hit like me. It's a good feeling."

These examples illustrate the elaborate strategy behind the overt use of popular music in *Stranger Things*, and a similar conspicuousness governs the use of sound and sonic transitions. Normally, *match-cutting* is seen as a way of creating seamless transitions between shots, scenes and sequences, but in *Stranger Things* the *match-cuts* are often quite noticeable. In Ep. 3:3, there is a humorous *match-cut* between a set of binoculars and a surveillance camera, and in Ep. 2:7 there is a Hitchcockian *match-cut* between a merry-go-round and an eye, seemingly referencing the famous shower scene from *Psycho* (1960). These matches are not seamless but consciously perceptible, and the same thing could be said of the sonic transitions between different scenes and sequences (a technique that the sound crew described as "toastering"). As the re-recording mixer Adam Jenkins puts it:

Fig. 34-35: Craig Henighan (above) is a recurring sound designer on *Stranger Things* and a central part of the vast sound team behind the series' complex design. Here we see him at his Icon Console. Adam Jenkins and Joe Barnett (below) have also been part of the team, and here they are seen during the final mix of Season 1. Photo: Rodrigo Ortiz. Courtesy of Henighan and Jenkins.

> Working with Matt and Ross Duffer on *Stranger Things* was a personal and professional pleasure. They write their scripts with not only visual cues, but with audio cues. They are thinking about the sound for a scene as they are creating the scene.
>
> One sequence had us starting with the sound of a truck leaving a driveway, the camera shot pushing into an exterior air intake duct, down the duct, out through giant fan blades, across a busy room, past the Rift, and finally coming to rest on a large winch being lowered and then bolted to the floor. The exaggerated reverberant sound of the air hammer turning the bolts to the floor then carried us out of the room and into the next exterior scenes. Like the picture, the sound of the truck tyres, motor and gravel faded into the sound of the duct, which then faded into the sound of the fan blades, which then faded into the sound of the room with the unique sounds of the Rift as we passed it, and then over to the winch being lowered and bolted to the floor. It helped tell the story, move the plot forward and was done in a fashion that needed no dialogue.
>
> *Smash cuts* were the exact opposite. In one of the earlier episodes, we cut from the quiet end of a scene to a close-up shot of some Eggos popping out of a toaster. The picture cut was nothing out of the ordinary, but by highly exaggerating the sound of the toaster, we made an effective, unusual cut. That was done in one of the earlier episodes, and from then on, when we did a *smash cut* with sound, it became known as "toastering" a cut.[536]

As the bold use of popular music and *musical moments*, so the use of exaggerated sound effects and "toastering" created a sense of audiovisual conspicuousness. In that sense, *Stranger Things* provided the possibility for different types of engagement - from immersion and immediate excitement to a more reflexive or even performative form of engagement.

Even more than *Stranger Things*, *Twin Peaks: The Return* uses musical interludes, alternative scoring principles and a complex sound design consisting of multiple tracks and layers of organic and inorganic sounds. If *Stranger Things* is conspicuous and self-aware, resulting in an almost performative form of engagement, *Twin Peaks: The Return* is radical and excessive, creating a musical and sonic sense of *defamiliarization*.

"Listen to the sounds": The Radical Sound of *Twin Peaks*

> A lot of directors will say, "I really love sound." David Lynch actually means that. David is the one guy who will actually sit there with you and who will get involved in the sound design from start to finish.
> - Ronald Eng, re-recording mixer[537]

> I worked with George Lucas for seven years, and he taught me how to build a box. I worked with David Lynch for seven months, and he taught me how to take the lid off.
> - Duwayne Dunham, editor[538]

Since its original release in 1990, many critics have talked about *Twin Peaks* as the series that "changed television history."[539] While co-creator Mark Frost has disputed this common argument, saying that *Twin Peaks* did not change television "one iota," most people seem to agree that *Twin Peaks*, if nothing else, was at least groundbreaking in terms of style.[540] Network television might be "impervious to change, for the most part," as Harley Peyton has put it, but even within the confines of commercial, broadcast television *Twin Peaks* was different from most other TV series.[541] It had a different mood, a different pacing, a different look and a different *sound* than most TV series at the time.

Even more so, Showtime's continuation, *Twin Peaks: The Return*, has a distinct and expressive use of sound, and the sound design seems to illustrate that this is not ABC's *Twin Peaks*, nor is it comparable to traditional TV.

Counterpoint and Ambiguity

One of the most recognizable features in David Lynch's productions is the use of counterpoint to create a sense of uncanniness and uncertainty, both in terms of mood and in terms of the spatial and temporal relations. Lynch often combines score music, ominous silences, expressive bursts of noise and popular tracks from the 1950s and 1960s. Using popular tunes by the likes of Bobby Vinton, Roy Orbison and Glenn Miller, David Lynch creates an audio-visual ambiguity where different moods and registers collide, often placing the audience in an *emotional and temporal in-betweenness*. This technique is used repeatedly in his films, from Bobby Vinton's theme song in *Blue Velvet* (1986) to the use of Elvis and Glenn Miller in *Wild at Heart* (1990) and the eerie use of "The Loco-Motion" at the end of *Inland Empire* (2006).

In *Twin Peaks: The Return*, this technique is particularly striking in two different instances. In the first of these scenes, we see Shelly's daughter, Becky Burnett (Amanda Seyfried), sitting in a car with her dubious husband Steven (Caleb Landry Jones). Becky gets high, and as she turns on the car radio, there is a sudden and noticeable reframing just as the first lines from The Paris Sisters' "I Love How You Love Me" (1961) are heard on the soundtrack. The innocence of the song collides with the sad and eerie content of the scene, and the line "I love how you love me" seems to act as a verbal counterpoint to the tragic relationship between Becky and Steven. The song has a nostalgic vibe, longingly pointing to an innocent past that is no longer there. But the scene also reminds the viewer of a scene in the car between Bobby and Shelly from the original *Twin Peaks* (also featuring diegetic music from the car radio), thus pointing to the repetitive nature of the situation. Becky seems to repeat her mother's pattern, and the close-up of her 'happy' face eerily recalls the ending of *Fire Walk with Me* (1992).

In a similar way, Lynch uses contrapuntal music in the scene where Johnny Horne is forced to witness the horrifying assault on his mother (by her own grandson). The opening of the scene, mirroring elements from the Lynch animated series *Dumbland* (2005), illustrates Johnny's catatonic state and the dubious attempt to help or heal him. The mechanical voice of the teddy bear, repeating the line "Hello, Johnny. How are you today," becomes increasingly

217

uncanny, and the quiet melody on the soundtrack, "Charmaine" (1926), changes from soothing to contrapuntal as Sylvia is attacked and beaten in front of her own son. This song was likewise used in Miloš Forman's *One Flew Over the Cuckoo's Nest* (1975) during the famous "medication time" scene, and through this intertextual reference Lynch reminds the viewer of the fluid boundary between sanity and insanity. The clash between sound, music and images is used to create an eerie sense of uncertainty, juxtaposing innocence and decay, nostalgia and horror. This technique is used often in *Twin Peaks: The Return*, and the use of "Charmaine" recalls the uses of "The Surrey with the Fringe on Top" (from *Oklahoma*), "What a Wonderful World" and "Pennsylvania 6-5000" in the original series.

Push-Pull Mechanisms

The scene with Richard, Johnny and Sylvia might allude to *One Flew Over the Cuckoo's Nest*, yet it plays out like the controversial rape scene from Stanley Kubrick's *A Clockwork Orange* (1970). What Kubrick introduced in his films was a vivid use of push-pull mechanisms, where the viewers were often drawn into the action of a scene while, suddenly, being alienated from the action through bursts of noise, musical counterpoints and strange *Verfremdung effects*.

In *Twin Peaks: The Return*, Lynch and Frost make use of a similar kind of push-pull logic, toying with the audience and their expectations. The audience will wait for almost 16 hours to see Dale Cooper as his own recognizable self. And they are treated to ritualistic repetitions of scenes from the original series that many fans disliked, while having to wait impatiently for motifs and songs that are either withheld or cut short (cf. the use of "The World Spins" and the surprisingly short appearance of Julee Cruise in Part 17). The cyclical repetition and creative recycling in *The Return* are counteracted by the brutal fact of unrecognizability and the baffling changes in color palette and soundscape.

While holding back many of the famous *leitmotifs* by Angelo Badalamenti, Lynch chooses to repeat the song "Just You" from the original series – one of the most maligned scenes of the entire show. In the original series, the song seemed strange and artificial (we hear bass guitar and percussion without ever seeing those instruments). This was never coincidental, though, and the artifice served to catch the viewer off guard as the scene suddenly changed and BOB appeared from behind the couch. "It became odd, otherworldly and cute in a way," as James Marshall puts it, "and then you had these girls doing this terribly cliché background-singeresque thing, as if all of a sudden we're doing this musical. Don't get me wrong, Sheryl and Lara did a good job, but the whole scene felt somewhat corny. And then BOB comes out, and it truly fucks with the audience."[542] Even more so, the cyclical repetition of "Just You" in *The Return* seems artificial, and the entire scene, where James plays the song "live" at The Roadhouse, comes across as radically unnatural and unrealistic, creating a sense of uncertainty within the viewer. Are they, in fact, playing the song "live" at The Roadhouse? Would the audience really respond to this track in that particular way, and why is there absolutely no sense of liveness to the recording?[543] Mentioning that particular song and Rebekah Del Rio's track "No Stars" from Part 10, some people have criticized the unnatural or artificial sound in those scenes, noting that the lip-syncing is too evident and that it is too obvious that we are dealing with mechanical reproductions. I would argue, however, that this artifice is exactly the point, and we are, indeed, supposed to notice the unnatural and mechanical nature of the music, never knowing what is real and what is not.

The same thing could be said of the strange replaying of "Audrey's Dance" in Part 16, which, this time, is introduced *as* "Audrey's Dance" (as if that were the title of the song in the diegetic world and not just the official title of the track on Badalamenti and Lynch's soundtrack). In the original scene from Ep. 2, Audrey (Sherilyn Fenn) refers to the music as "dreamy." Now, as the song is repeated, her sensual dance takes on a new and slightly more tragic vibe, and as we suddenly cut to a shot of Audrey in front of a mirror in a white room, cued by a sudden change in the sound, we cannot help thinking that this might, indeed, have been a "dreamy" scene. Was this all just a dream or a fantasy within Audrey, imprisoned in her own mind?

The cyclical nature of *Twin Peaks* is a well-known element, and the sampling of Sarah's voice at the end of the new series seems to indicate a Moebius strip-like structure akin to *Lost Highway* (1997).

Physicality and Sensory Complexity

As mentioned earlier, the new series begins with a title sequence that re-employs the main theme and many of the visuals from the original show. More importantly, however, the new title sequence, in a subtle way, introduces the *newness* of the new *Twin Peaks*. Angelo Badalamenti's theme is heard on the soundtrack. But this time we also hear *diegetic* sounds of air and the waterfall, as if to indicate the change from the spherical and romantic music of the original series to the sheer physicality of the new series (dominated by a rich sound design and a *compilation score* of many different kinds of music).[544]

"David seems to like sounds that are organic," as re-recording mixer Ronald Eng puts it. "He likes the sounds of wind, fire and water – things that occur in nature. That being said, he also loves the sound of electricity."[545] David Lynch creates a rich world of different sonic textures (organic sounds and inorganic sounds, sounds of old technologies and sounds of new media), and noises often produce an eerie sense of suspense while serving different narrative functions (the sound of electrical noise and short-circuiting, for example, seems to illustrate that we are "between two worlds").[546]

Nowhere is this physicality more evident than in Part 8 where a Woodsman (Robert Broski) crushes the skull of a receptionist at a radio station in the 1950s, contrapuntally underscored by The Platters' 1956-hit "My Prayer" (one of the early members of the vocal group, The Platters, was, in fact, named David Lynch). The grating sound of Broski's voice and the visceral sounds of brains and blood illustrate the *sensory complexity* that, according to Chion, is a typical part of the modern film and TV landscape. "*Twin Peaks* was one of the first projects of my career where we actually had enough time," says Eng. "David had time to mix, to go back and listen and to get everything just right. I just hope people will like it because it is so *different*. It is not formulaic, and it will make you think."[547] As the actor/musician Chrysta Bell (Tammy Preston) puts it:

> When watching a David Lynch production, you're forced into something that is so far away from your realm of experience, but at the same time so familiar. It's so familiar, yet so uncomfortable. It's discomforting, yet we're putting ourselves through it on purpose. [...] Recently, David Nevins compared Lynch to heroin, and I get it. You're drawn to his art, curious about your own discomfort, and then you're drawn to the characters, the music and the mood. It's so addictive.[548]

Like Dr. Amp (Russ Tamblyn), who employs both old and new technologies, *The Return* combines old *leitmotifs* and themes with new sonic elements. The dreamy performances of Julee Cruise in the original series are replaced by some strangely *unhinged musical performances* at the end of most episodes in the new series – performances that often seem artificial and almost look *extra-diegetic* (in a way that reminds me of the string sections in Jean-Luc Godard's *Prénom Carmen* [1983]). The musical performances have often been compared to *Beverly Hills 90210* (Fox, 1990-2000), but here they serve a totally different function (apart from promoting different bands), often suspending the action and functioning as a kind of pause or an intermezzo in an opera. The five-minute track by Nine Inch Nails in Part 8, for example, serves to punctuate the action just before a lengthy montage that includes abstract imagery akin to Man Ray's *La Retour à la Raison* (1923, *Return to Reason*), American experimental films by Jordan Belson (*Samadhi* [1967] and *Chakra* [1972]), Bruce Connor (*Crossroads*, 1976) and Stan Brakhage (*Stellar*, 1993), modern classics like Stanley Kubrick's *2001: a Space Odyssey* (1968) and Lynch's own *Eraserhead*.

There are numerous instances in *The Return* where popular music is performed or played for long stretches of time, in scenes that seem strangely *excessive*. A striking example of this type of *defamiliarization* is found in Part

7 where we see a man sweeping the floor (in one shot of 2:17 min.) while listening to Green Onions. In this context, the music and slowness make for an almost *transcendental style* – a radical sensibility that Paul Schrader associates mainly with modernism and art cinema.[549] As the editor Duwayne Dunham says:

> I've been guilty over the years of saying: "David, we need to cut this down." I don't use the term "it's too long", but is it really holding our attention?
> I think David has heard that his whole career – and I think part of it is *he could do it, and he did* – and, so, the scene with that guy sweeping the floor goes on for a very long time. If you were to cut that down, it wouldn't work. This is sometimes what I think is the mentality of a studio, always trying to guess the ants in the seat of the audience's pants: "They'll never sit for this." Well, trim it down. Then it means nothing, then you might as well throw it out. But if it goes on and on like that did, you, the audience, now become engaged, and you're saying: "Wait a minute. What's going on here?[550]

At times, the sound design seems as alien and un-*Twin Peaksy* as the changing color palette. The opening of the new series is sonically closer to *Eraserhead* and *Inland Empire* than to the original series, and the convenience store sequences at the end of Part 8 are both visually and musically reminiscent of *Lost Highway* (using audiovisual glitches to great sensory effect). All of these elements are connected to David Lynch as an auteur, and just as he is credited for having pushed the boundaries for television sound back in 1990, he is lauded for having changed the parameters with *The Return*. "Music and sound are a big part of his productions," as the performer Rebekah Del Rio says. "David has an amazing ear, and he is the master of strange."[551]

Duwayne Dunham, Jonathan P. Shaw (editors) and James Grixoni (actor) on the *transcendental style* of *Twin Peaks: The Return*

Dunham (about the slow pacing and the ending): David's not afraid to take things to the limit and beyond... At the end of the story with Cooper picking up Carrie Page, I said to him: "David, are we going to drive in real time from Texas to Twin Peaks? I mean, come on, man." And he just said: "I like it, make it longer." He's earned that right, to make it exactly the way he wants it, and I think that's part of it. But David does like for things to move at a more leisurely pace.

Shaw (about the slow pacing and "The Sweeping Scene"): As an editor, you're working with your own internal clock, and in other TV shows you might cut it differently and have a faster pacing. For me, it's a tonal thing because you're sitting there as an audience member, and because there is so little action - or such a sense of inaction - it makes you reflect, it makes you study the character more, and it makes you think: "Why am I in this situation for so long?" It's spiritual in a way, almost like a prayer, and it has a great tonality to it.

I've done a lot of editing for MTV, and all they want is for you to cut faster. That was the style back then. But that's not David Lynch's style. There's a whole aesthetic that comes along with all of David's material. If you're going to watch a film or a TV show by David Lynch, you know what you're in for, and the people who hire and fund him know that too. And it's really great to work with somebody like that who has a very specific style. He doesn't do it for somebody else. It's his stuff.

Grixoni (about the pacing in *Twin Peaks: The Return*): I believe *The Return* fits into television history in the sense that it's suited for the last fragment of human attention. In a world where our attention span only lasts a minute and a half, this show challenges the viewer. If you are going to watch this show, you are going to need attention, you are going to need to be engaged, and that was what film was essentially all about. We live in a world where movies are about explosions - superficial stimulation. When the original *Twin Peaks* came out, it was like an antidote, and with *Twin Peaks: The Return*, David has come back to re-instill that antidote. He is re-instilling an antidote into a culture of media that - at least a lot of it - is mind-numbing. In an age of the same formula in entertainment, along comes David Lynch to totally throw that formula out and to re-introduce his own formula. And in today's entertainment that is what we need.[552]

New Approaches to Scoring

A central part of the radicalism in *Twin Peaks: The Return* is its alternative approaches to scoring. The collaboration between Lynch and Badalamenti differs quite radically from traditional scoring principles, and in *Twin Peaks: The Return* the music was often used as a foundation for the pacing and editing of a scene and, at times, even functioning as a sort of sound effect.

One particular sequence from Part 6 illustrates the Leone/Morricone-like collaboration between Lynch and Badalamenti. Here, a boy is tragically killed by a truck, and the graphicness and sheer physicality of the sequence are quite different from the style that you would usually associate with Lynch and Badalamenti. In the words of Badalamenti:

> There's a scene in one of the episodes where a mother is holding her boy, who then releases from the mother and runs into the street and gets hit by a truck and gets killed. The mother screeches and runs after the boy, goes over and hugs him, but he's dead on the ground. "He's dead on the ground, and the mother is just in this pain and sorrow, and she picks him up, and then his soul is moving up to heaven, and you can see his soul moving up to heaven." That's what David tells me, and I start playing this thing. I start building a tempo, and the speeding truck is coming. I pick up the tempo, and as I reach a climax, I hit an abstract chord, and you hear the mother scream. She sees the boy being hit by the truck, and she cries. She goes out, and she starts hugging him, and it goes on for a long time, this incredible, emotional music – the mother over her child – and she turns her head up after this music has played, and the boy's soul is moving up to heaven.
>
> Now, here's what's fantastic. It's mind-boggling, and it's so different from what you usually do with music and a director: Every note that I played, I recorded that. I just played it, improvised what he had described. David took the track that I played, improvised from his words, and used the track for the whole scene and edited his film to match that music.[553]

Twin Peaks: The Return is radical in its use of music and sound, and it establishes a general physicality and *sensory complexity* across its 18 parts, combining abstract music, popular songs and various noises. These qualities are often ascribed to David Lynch, and a similar *authorial reading* is presented by the crew when describing the audiovisual style and design of *Breaking Bad* and *Better Call Saul*. In the following section, I will look at these two series in terms of both visual aesthetic and sound design, before rounding off the chapter with an explorative discussion of *TV auteurism*.

Angelo Badalamenti (composer) on David Lynch and *Twin Peaks: The Return*

On the collaboration between Badalamenti and Lynch: Like Leone and Morricone, David and I have been lucky to have a great creative relationship. In terms of the process, I did *Blue Velvet* in the traditional way, which is where a director shows you a mostly edited film and then you score it, but on every project since we have talked about it before we even started shooting. And a lot of the music for *Twin Peaks* was done before we started filming. David would even play the demos and have the actors move to the tempo of the music. It's a marriage made in heaven. Let's face it, very few times have a director and a composer really hit it off like a team. It's like Danny Elfman and Tim Burton, Alfred Hitchcock and Bernard Herrmann or Sergio Leone and Ennio Morricone.[554]

On the process and music behind *Twin Peaks: The Return*: We basically had three sessions together. After he shot all his episodes, he needed music. He already took a lot of music from Seasons 1 and 2 of *Twin Peaks* and *Fire Walk With Me* – whatever we had that would work for this – and a lot of that music is spotted in various places in *Twin Peaks: The Return*.

David Lynch was in LA, and I was here in my studio house in New Jersey, and we did Skype. So on the weekend – on a Saturday – we did six hours from 11 a.m. till 5 p.m. of him talking to me through Skype. We were both recording everything – not only everything I played on the keyboard, but everything that we said to each other, so we could always check whatever we had done. That was great, and all he did was describe things. He would say one-word things like: "Angelo, play electricity". "Okay." And I would start playing electricity. I would do about six minutes of electricity. "Okay, Angelo. Now play electricity and make it build and make it more intense, make it more intense, and go into high, abstract electricity. Let it scream." And then I would do another six to eight minutes of this description of electricity. "Okay, Angelo. That's great, but play me a ghost wind." "Okay". And I would sit – whatever that was – and play six or eight minutes of that. He had maybe eight or ten different one-word things. That's all. And I would play his one-word notes. Improvised.

He finished shooting the series and needed one extra piece of music. I got a message on my machine: "I need you to do me a favor. I need you to write the most beautiful melody. I want it to be Pucciniesque but still Badalamenti-like. I want you to tear the hearts out of everyone that hears it. I need a piece, and here's my problem: I need it for tomorrow morning." So I wrote that "Heartbreaking" theme, and later I got a new message: "Angelo, this is the most beautiful song I have ever heard in my life. It's tearing my heart out."[555]

Fig. 36-37: Angelo Badalamenti (above) explains his use of music in *Twin Peaks: The Return* from his home in New Jersey (photo: Lasse Lorenzen). Badalamenti's score is a central part of the alternative sound in David Lynch's productions, but Lynch himself is often credited as sound designer. In the picture below, we see him with musician and actor Chrysta Bell. The picture was taken by Dean Hurley, who created the sound of *Twin Peaks: The Return* together with Ronald Eng, Angelo Badalamenti, David Lynch and various musical acts. Courtesy of Chrysta Bell and Lasse Lorenzen.

Better Call Gilligan: Audiovisual Artistry in *Breaking Bad* and *Better Call Saul*

In 2008, Vince Gilligan created a TV series that would, if not change the face of television, then at least teach audiences to watch and hear TV drama in a new way. A veritable film and television buff, Gilligan teamed up with writer-producer Peter Gould, cinematographers Arthur Albert, Michael Slovis and Marshall Adams, composer Dave Porter, sound designer Edmond J. Coblentz, music supervisor Thomas Golubić and supervising sound editor Nick Forshager. Together they would design the look and sound of *Breaking Bad* and *Better Call Saul* (which Gilligan created together with Gould, who later became the sole showrunner).

In this section, I will explore the sound design, music and cinematography of *Breaking Bad* and *Better Call Saul* before discussing the concept of *TV auteurism* in the modern TV landscape.

Big Sound on the Small Screen: *Breaking Bad*

It has been a long day. Working two jobs, trying to support his family and to make ends meet, he is stuck at a garage, doing over-time. And then it happens. A car arrives, and in the background of the shot we see an attractive woman from his *point of view* and, as we cut back to him, the sound seems to indicate that something is wrong. Is he attracted to her? Will this be the beginning of an extramarital affair? The viewer immediately conjures up a number of theories and hypotheses, but as the man collapses, we realize that something else is going on, something else entirely. This scene, at Bogdan's garage, is an iconic part of the pilot episode from *Breaking Bad*, and what follows is sonically one of the most striking scenes ever to be experienced on the small screen. The man, Walter White (Bryan Cranston), is brought to a hospital, and the camera now tilts upwards, slowly revealing Walter's situation and whereabouts. Walter is at the hospital, and as the camera tilts upwards, the muffled sound of the doctor gives us an immediate sense of Walter's state of mind. The scene proceeds to show us a dialogue between Walter and the doctor, but the doctor's words are inaudible, slowly giving way to a high-pitched, tinnitus-like sound. The doctor, gradually becoming more intelligible, looks at his patient. "You understood what I just said to you," he asks, and in a detached, almost robotic manner Walter replies: "Yes. Lung cancer. Inoperable."

"The pilot started, obviously, with Vince Gilligan's vision of the thing," Nick Forshager says, "and he had a very clear-cut idea from the script of what it was going to look and sound like." And he continues:

> So when I came, it had a very detailed description in the script – some detailed descriptions of the flapping pants in the beginning and the different signature sounds of the show, including the tinnitus sound which we used for Walt. It starts with Vince's vision, and then we try to create sounds and images that will fit his vision.
>
> I thought this would be like any other regular show where they'll put the music on, and that is it, but he said "no," and we built the sound design very organically. Vince is very open-minded. If you come in with an idea and you can express it, he is open to it, so it becomes very collaborative. It's great with someone who has a vision, but it is also great to have a showrunner who is willing to listen and collaborate, and Vince is like that.[556]

The tinnitus-like sound was created by sound designer Edmond J. Coblentz, and, as he explains, they wanted it to be a dynamic sound that could illustrate Walter's sense of detachment and his inability to deal with his diagnosis:

> That was designed by me specifically for Walter. When we did that particular scene, we talked about the MRI machine, about the sounds inside the scene. But what we came up with more importantly was what Walt was feeling. And it shouldn't be music. The tinnitus sound came from a combination of elements – some were from the library – and I think I might have had three stereo pairs and played them with one mono pair to get that sound you hear. We used a tuner, and somehow we came up with that sound. It wasn't a simple mono sound; there was some fluctuation in the frequency. It's an interesting sound.[557]

Sonic Expressionism and Subjective Sound

Having seen both *Breaking Bad* and *Better Call Saul*, the viewer will immediately notice the recurring use of subjective sound in both series. Apart from the tinnitus sound in the pilot episode, an expressive compilation of noises is used to illustrate Hank's state of mind in the episode "Negro y azul" (Ep. 2:7), as he, Walter's brother-in-law, sees a severed head on a tortoise and experiences a kind of shell shock. That scene is sonically reminiscent of *Saving Private Ryan* (1998), and it illustrates Gilligan's predilection for expressive and subjective sound while exemplifying the amount of sonic detail and variation in the series.

In the first few seasons of *Better Call Saul*, we encounter a character named Chuck (Michael McKean) who experiences a number of panic attacks, and to illustrate those attacks, Gilligan uses *SnorriCam*, subjective camera and subjective noise, in yet a new variation. As Forshager puts it:

> Walt always had that tonal tinnitus thing when he was injured or something like that. We always came back to that tinnitus thing which we heard at the doctor's office in the pilot. And then there is an episode where Hank experiences shell shock, and we had to do it in a different way which would fit Hank, and which would make it different from the signature tinnitus sound that we used for Walt. And when Chuck experiences a similar thing in *Better Call Saul*, it is much more electronic because of Chuck's fear of electricity. Especially in the second season where Chuck is in the printer room, it took on a different and very electronic sound. It is interesting that you mention that it seems as if the electronic sounds mirror Chuck who is, himself, short-circuiting because that is exactly what Peter Gould said. He said that Chuck is short-circuiting, he is coming undone, and we wanted the sound to illustrate that.[558]

Sonic Motifs and Audiovisual Contrasts

> One of the many decisions I made early on was to not try to create recurring motifs for the different characters.
> - Dave Porter, composer[559]

As seen above, the use of subjective sound is prevalent in *Breaking Bad* and *Better Call Saul*, and Gilligan, Coblentz and Forshager use different kinds of subjective noise for the characters, thus hinting at their different personalities. The composer, Dave Porter, intentionally decided against using musical *leitmotifs* in the series, since "the series was not a genre series with expected results" and because "the characters all change far too much far too quickly to have made that possible."[560] Instead of *leitmotifs* in a traditional, Wagnerian sense, *Breaking Bad* and *Better Call Saul* use a form of *sonic motifs* and an intricate sound design where sound effects, ambient noise, score and popular music intermingle in complex ways.

In the episode called "… And the Bag's Out of the River" (Ep. 1:3), there is a sequence where Walter White kills Krazy 8 in his basement, in what looks like an almost Freudian motif. In that sequence, different noises are used in a highly suspenseful way. We have the close-up sounds of a plate in the beginning, as Walter recognizes that a part of the plate is missing and that Krazy 8 might be planning to kill him, and there are lengthy stretches of what Hitchcock would call *ominous silence*. Walter descends into the dark cellar, and the scene suddenly erupts into a series of close-up sounds and shuffling noises, as Walter chokes his hostage with a bicycle lock. Afterwards, there is a brief blackout before we cut to a bright day where we can hear sprinklers on the lawn and birds chirping. "The house and the sprinklers were important to give us a contrast," as Edmond J. Coblentz says. And he continues:

> We tried, on a daily basis, to get that contrast. We were trying to give the audience a crescendo of fear, and then, suddenly, as we cut, the sun comes up and the fear is gone. We wanted to illustrate the double-life that Walter is leading and the difference between the beautiful surface and the dark underbelly.[561]

Interestingly, the idea was for the sequence to create a suspenseful and dark atmosphere, but also sonically to mirror Walter's double-life. Originally, though, the studio wanted the sequence to include *non-diegetic* music, as Nick Forshager says, but realizing the suspenseful and psychological potential of the sound itself, they ended up accepting the original mix *without* music. As Forshager puts it:

> That is one of my favorite sequences, and that was when we knew that we were doing something other than regular television. There is a kind of backstory to that sequence. Vince works in a different way, in that he does not use *temp music*.

So we heard that sequence, and we got to see it stripped down, and there was actually a lot of suspense in there already. Therefore, we decided that we wanted to build suspense without using music, but using pauses and small sounds. The basement would have this ominous sound, and we wanted more rumble and tension as we went along, especially with the clanging sound of the bicycle lock. We ended up using my mix, and Vince loved it.[562]

Compressed Titles and Compact Symbolism

The title sequence of *Breaking Bad* was striking in its intense, symbolic brevity, and, as Dave Porter explains, it was meant to mirror Walter White and his personal journey over the course of the five seasons. "The main titles are designed to be arresting, aggressive and assertive in a way that Walter White certainly is NOT at the beginning of the series," as Porter says, "but is a reminder at the beginning of every episode that no matter the route it may take to get there, he will eventually become a very different Walter White."[563]

Even more striking and experimental, the title sequence to *Better Call Saul* was also meant to reflect the main character (Jimmy McGill, played by Bob Odenkirk). Full of visual glitches that differ from episode to episode, the opening of *Better Call Saul* ends abruptly, in the middle of a musical note. It seems sloppy and unfinished, but the look and sound constitute a conscious aesthetic choice by Vince Gilligan and Peter Gould who wanted the title sequence to illustrate Jimmy McGill and his tendency towards cutting corners. In the words of Thomas Golubić:

> We were trying to figure out the main title. We knew that the images would change each week, and the song would stay the same. We had pitched a few different ideas - Dave Porter had also presented ideas - and one of the songs we presented was by a band called Little Barrie, who are essentially a blues-rock outfit out of the UK. So I reached out to Barrie Cadogan and found out that he was available. He did a series of demos for us, and we spoke together every day over Skype, talking about the demos. And he did another set of them - he must have done 17 or 18 different versions - and they found one that really captured the show.
>
> And the cutting off, which was Vince's idea, was such a stroke of genius. I remember Barrie reached out to me and said: "Hey, super excited about this. Love the way it sounds. I think they made a mistake though. They cut off the last note." And I said, "No, that's actually intentional," and it makes me laugh every single time because it's very much a sloppy Saul Goodman-kind of thing. He would clip off the last moment, and in a weird way it just captures the character in a very efficient and elegant way.[564]

Visually, the title sequence was supposed to look grainy and imperfect, as the cinematographer Arthur Albert puts it, illustrating the work and style of the charismatic would-be-lawyer Jimmy McGill. In Albert's words:

> I know Vince Gilligan and Peter Gould loved the look of old tube-TV with the bars and where the colors are bad. They wanted the title sequence to be reminiscent of the first color TV shows that were made in the early days of television drama. And they wanted the visual style to fit Jimmy.[565]

It is interesting that Gilligan and Gould wanted the title sequence to look like a traditional network show because that approximation of a traditional TV aesthetic would naturally be different from the rest of *Better Call Saul*, thus illustrating its 'not-TV-ness'. In that sense, the title sequence could mirror Jimmy's sloppiness, but it could also illustrate a conventional aesthetic that *Better Call Saul* is trying to transcend.

Montage Editing and Counterpoint

Apart from the use of suspenseful sound, sonic contrasts and subjective noise, *Better Call Saul* and especially *Breaking Bad* are known for their vivid montages that often include contrapuntal, *non-diegetic* music and raw, punctual noises. A particularly noteworthy example is taken from the episode "Gliding Over All" (Ep. 5:8) where we see Walter White looking at his wrist watch, waiting for different people – potential threats – to be killed off by some hired hands. The montage is reminiscent of the Russian filmmaker Vsevolod Pudovkin who, when trying to describe the potential functions of montage editing, uses a hypothetical example with a watch. The watch, in both Pudovkin's example and the episode from *Breaking Bad*, gives us a sense of *parallelism*. All of the killings take place within a short time frame, and that illustrates the growing cynicism on the part of Walter.[566] The montage includes different shots of prisoners being killed in various clinical and morbid ways, and the use of high-contrast imagery and *low-angle shots* clash with the slow tempo and *low-key* lighting of the opening (where Walter is looking at his wrist watch) and the mellow *non-diegetic* song "Pick Yourself Up", as performed by Nat King Cole. As Forshager says:

> We try not to do the same thing over and over again. There are times when we have a montage, where I think we don't need sound here. And then there are examples like this one where it's kind of a symphony, and my job was to be the in-between, somewhat like a percussion instrument, so we added these bits of sound. We picked up these small sounds – a stab, a fall, a watch – that could help tell the story, so it became punctuations in a way, and the music would be a contrast that would make the images look even more heinous. That is one of my favorite montages of the entire show with all those small sounds and the music that just adds this great contrast to the picture. It's very Scorsese-like, in a way. We can find many references like that, but Vince will always do it in his own way. When he comes up with something, it might look like something we have seen before, and he might borrow different elements from other films, but he turns it into his own.[567]

Or as Golubić poignantly puts it:

> When you're calibrating irony or counterpoint, it's very important to do it in just the right way. It's very easy to oversteer or to become smug or clever. One of the things we try not to be is clever. Often people try to be clever with music choices, and that's an insult to the work. You don't want it to be clever, you want it to be smart. For Walt with his stopwatch, he is ticking down the moments of him having done one of the most extraordinary things of

his entire career. He is setting up his own future. He is showing both his ruthlessness and his capacity for survival. He is in many ways doing a point of no return. We could have played that darkly, we could have played that aggressively and in many other ways. Vince wanted to play it with something that had a sense of the bright future that he's moving towards.[568]

From Art TV to Avant-Garde

When thinking of *Breaking Bad* and *Better Call Saul*, we often recall the montages, the contrapuntal music, the high-contrast imagery, the weird *point of view* shots and the expressive sound work. But, in fact, the most radical episode in *Breaking Bad* (Ep. 3:10: "The Fly") is characterized primarily by its *lack* of music, expressive colors and noise. In that episode of *Breaking Bad*, nothing much happens, and the rapid editing and unusual choices of framing and angles that we usually associate with the show give way to a style consisting of long takes, long stretches of quietude and inaction (what the *Nouvelle Vague* directors would called *temps mort*). According to Nick Forshager:

> When they brought that to my attention – that there'd be an entire episode of a fly – I was scared, and I don't think there's *any* music in that episode. There's the sound of the fly and the lab. You don't even have the sounds of the machines or the music. What we ended up having to rely on was the fly sound, having enough of it that it would annoy the audience, and then we would build suspense using small sounds of ladders etc. It was conceptually very difficult to make, it was a real challenge. And then story-wise it didn't really say much – it moved forward one little ounce in 40 minutes, but that move was huge in a way – and I think we pulled it off. It was difficult to do, having to rely on the sounds of the lab, the fly and different objects to create enough suspense to make it interesting. Some people hated that episode, but I am happy they did it, and I think it was a testament to how different this show was from regular television
>
> The nature of television has changed a lot over the years. There have been pockets of shows in the past that were very cinematic, *Twin Peaks* and *The Sopranos* for example, but *Breaking Bad* was one of the first shows to be told from beginning to end in a highly cinematic way. Now, we are used to a totally new type of television – television telling stories in a very different, cinematic way, and it's really exciting. We see that in shows like *Stranger Things* and *Mr. Robot*, just like in *Fargo* and *Better Call Saul*.[569]

As Peter Gould mentions in the feature interview at the end of this chapter, "The Fly" is a so-called *bottle episode*, and its radical style could be attributed to budgetary considerations (they had to make the episode on a small budget, limiting the amount of potential sets and actors).[570] Ironically, though, the budgetary concerns made for a more experimental episode, not unlike the minimalistic strategies and inventiveness of Carl Th. Dreyer, Robert Bresson and the Dogme95 movement. By contrast, the most radical part of *Better Call Saul*, "Bagman", is an expensive location-driven episode where we follow Jimmy McGill walking through the desert. If "The Fly" is extreme in its minimalistic strategies due to budgetary limitations, then "Bagman" is radical for its slow pacing, its location-driven action and its cinematic *wide shots* akin to David Lean's *Lawrence of Arabia* (1962).

From Stylistic Differentiation to Integration

The sound work in both *Breaking Bad* and *Better Call Saul* is quite expressive, and it uses a lot of counterpoints and contrasts. Visually, the shows are also full of contrasts and clashes: There are saturated colors and toned down black-and-white sequences, beautiful *high-key* lighting counteracted by *noir*-like *chiaroscuro*, close-ups versus *extreme long shots*, and jerky handheld camera and compact montages as opposed to lengthy, static tableaus.

Being a prequel to *Breaking Bad*, *Better Call Saul* is stylistically linked to the original show, and framing-wise and sonically there are many similarities. However, the two series are also vividly different, inasmuch as Gilligan and Gould wanted *Better Call Saul* to relate to the 'mother show' without inheriting an established look and tone. According to Arthur Albert:

> When Vince and I met on *Better Call Saul*, I asked him whether he wanted the same look as in *Breaking Bad*, and he told me: "No, I want it to look like nothing you have ever seen on television." First of all, we wanted Saul to be in the worst possible place he could be, for us to see how far he has fallen, so the opening sequence had to convey that.
>
> Stylistically, one of the things we wanted to do was to move away from the handheld style of *Breaking Bad*. *Breaking Bad* used a lot of handheld camera, which gave it this nervous feel. *Better Call Saul* is much more static, and it has a much more 'old' style, unlike most television shows where cameras will often move in order to create a certain dynamic. I was inspired by Ozu in his use of angles and static camera. When the camera moves in *Better Call Saul*, it moves *with* the characters. We did not want movement for the sake of movement.
>
> The other stylistic departure was Vince's approach to comedy. I have shot a lot of comedy shows, and they usually want to show the viewers everything, the actors and their punchlines, and we did not want to use that style in *Better Call Saul*, even though it is a comedy. Vince Gilligan would often say: "We know who the characters are. We don't need to see them all the time," so the characters' faces would often fall into half-light or silhouettes. Something you would rarely see on traditional television where they often want us to see the stars. The story in *Better Call Saul* is a comedy, but it also has *noir* elements, particularly introduced by the character Mike, so it is a blend of *noir*-like style and comedy. Vince really encourages you to push the limits: There are entire scenes shot in long and extreme long shots, and you very rarely get encouraged to do that in television.[571]

Albert points to the shift in style from *Breaking Bad* to *Better Call Saul*, specifically in terms of lighting choices and pacing, and he refers to the opening sequence where we see Jimmy McGill working at a Cinnabon and going home to his lonely and quiet living room. The use of black and white is a stylistic choice, as Albert says, meant to differentiate *Better Call Saul* from *Breaking Bad*, but it is also a playful choice in terms of narration because we naturally think of it as a flashback, even though it is a flashforward. What looks like a flashback to where Jimmy started is, more likely, a glimpse of his tragic future.

Visually, one of the most striking choices in *Better Call Saul* is the extreme use of angles, pacing and lighting. The scenes at Chuck's house, for example, are much darker than you would naturally expect from a TV series. In those scenes we are closer to the visual design of classical *noir films* like *The Big Combo* (1955) or *neo-* and *future-noirs* like *Blade Runner* (1982), and, in fact, *Blade Runner* is one of the primary stylistic influences on the show. As Albert says:

> The brother's house was very difficult to shoot because there's no electrical light. Usually you would hard-light everything in those scenes. But we did not do that. Most of the night scenes are lit only by the moonlight or a street light, so it's the lamp in the scene – we made our own LED lamp because it is too dangerous using a gasoline lamp – that lights the characters. Nothing else. They wanted it to look like *Blade Runner*. Had I known that before we started shooting, I would have asked for a building with tall windows. But I used *Blade Runner* as my inspiration when doing the scenes at Chuck's house. That lighting technique could not have been done in the old days of television. The transition from analog to digital was huge. In the analog days, every TV set was different, so you had to play it safe and make it brighter, otherwise many people wouldn't be able to see anything. With digital it is much sharper with a better dynamic range, and it will come across the way you want it to on most people's TV sets.[572]

In terms of music, Gilligan also wanted *Better Call Saul* to differ from *Breaking Bad*, but gradually, as the timelines of the two series meet, they will also be visually and musically more similar. As Dave Porter says:

> At the beginning of *Better Call Saul*, I was encouraged to be dramatically different from *Breaking Bad*. That was hard to do - after all, the plot was occurring in the same universe - and what we had done for *Breaking Bad* had been pretty successful. But it quickly became clear that it was a very different animal, and, as a result, the score in the first few seasons of *Better Call Saul* is, indeed, very different. And the importance of this became ever clearer to me as we moved along because, of course being a prequel, the further we got, the closer we got to the world we created for *Breaking Bad* and the more of the musical influences we would need to incorporate. So by starting from a very different place, it has given me the ability to really explore Jimmy's universe first, before slowly incorporating it into *Breaking Bad*'s universe. I have taken that journey trying to stay very much in the moment, and reflect as best I can where characters are in their evolution, and in doing so, the score has naturally progressed alongside them.
>
> Unlike the two series, *El Camino* followed the story of just one character, Jesse, and, if you think about it, we covered at least a season's worth of screen time for him in one continuous film. This gave me a unique opportunity to be singularly focused on this one character and storyline.[573]

Finally, *Better Call Saul* differed from *Breaking Bad* by having a slower pacing and an artsy use of silence and pauses, and it introduced some other tonal and generic elements (e.g. legal drama and a romantic Hepburn and Tracy-like quality connected to Jimmy and Kim Wexler). According to Golubić:

> We had much longer stretches without music. If you look at *Breaking Bad*, the montages are generally very tight and very compact. *Better Call Saul* takes its time, and what I love so much is that it really changes the way we play the game. We're a bit looser, and we have to figure out: When is it going to be score, when will it be a song, when is it going to be silence, and when does Nick take the lead in using sound to help build the palate. We're working with silences in a very specific way.[574]

From Artistry to Auteurism

Gilligan and Gould exploited new techniques and technological possibilities when creating *Breaking Bad* and *Better Call Saul*, and they are recognized as very specific and detail-oriented showrunners. On most of the episodes, Edmond J. Coblentz says, they used 32-48 tracks, and Gilligan would spot the show with the sound crew describing exactly how he wanted things to sound:

> What we did was to spot the show with Vince Gilligan, and as we spotted the show, he would describe the sounds – what Walt's car, Krazy 8's low-rider or the inside of the house with the bathtub would sound like – and every time we had liquids or something burning or acid falling on the floor we were asked to do it over and over again. It had to be very specific for Vince. He didn't want boiling water to sound like boiling water. He wanted to sell that these guys were cooking drugs. It should not sound like your mom cooking in the kitchen. It should be more dramatic and evil, in a way.[575]

The same thing could be said of the visual design, and Arthur Albert vividly recalls the first meeting with Vince Gilligan and Peter Gould about *Better Call Saul*. At that meeting, Gilligan and Gould showed Albert some stills from old movies to illustrate that they wanted a cinematic look on the show and that they had some very specific thoughts on the visual design, both in terms of what it should look like and what the template should be:

> It's funny. I've always loved Vittorio Storaro. I've always loved his work, his unique visual aesthetic. And when I sat down with Vince Gilligan and Peter Gould to talk about *Better Call Saul*, they showed me some stills for inspiration. Some stills were from Kubrick, especially his vanishing point perspective shots. And, I mean, who isn't a fan of Kubrick? But some of the stills were from *The Conformist* where they showed me some strange and untraditional off-balance compositions. And I was thinking that they were showing me images from some of my favorite cinematographers. But then I asked Vince Gilligan, "You want it to look like *The Conformist*, so why are we not shooting in Rome?" We were not shooting in Rome. In fact, we were shooting in Albuquerque, which is one of the ugliest cities that I have ever had the misfortune of visiting, and we did our best to make it look as aesthetic as possible.
>
> Gilligan is a brilliant writer and showrunner. One reason for the success of *Better Call Saul* and *Breaking Bad* is Vince's almost obsessive attention to detail. From time to time, that makes it difficult to work on his shows because he is so involved in everything, but that is also the reason why it is so cohesive and distinctive. It is his vision.[576]

Even when it came to the final sequence of *Breaking Bad*, Gilligan chose the music and the final shot – an expressive *aerial shot* that was inspired by the evocative and ambiguous ending of *Taxi Driver* (1976). The combination of the *God's eye view* and Badfinger's song take us out of the series on a poetic note, lyrically commenting on the moral degeneration and tragic fate of Walter White: "Guess I got what I deserved." As Thomas Golubić says:

> Another one of Vince's pulls was the closing song in the series: Badfinger's "Baby Blue". That song, in a way, is so truthful to the character because it is the love song of *Breaking Bad* for the makers of *Breaking Bad*, for the team that did it, for Vince himself and for Walter White and his love of chemistry. Having a warm song playing up against that final sequence

> just adds a perfect bed for it and allows the audience to see things that are extraordinarily violent while taking the edge off and creating a little bit of distance. It makes it palatable. That's the dance we did with *Breaking Bad* in many ways: We allowed things that were quite extraordinarily dark and at times really brutal to be given just enough context to let the audience take in the brutality and recognize it for what it is. We seduce you to go further into Walter's story and not just dismiss him as a monster.[577]

It would be fair to argue that *Breaking Bad* broke the mold of American television drama, but *Better Call Saul* managed to be cohesive with its 'mother show' while breaking new ground. Both series were visually and sonically innovative, employing a range of different techniques – *low-key* lighting, high-contrast images, montage editing, contrapuntal sound, subjective noise, conspicuous *point of view* shots, low angles and long, static takes – but they employed all of these elements in a way that seems strangely organic. Both series, it seems, are about the contrasts of American society (as mentioned by Barack Obama in his recent appraisal of *Better Call Saul*), and they illustrate that theme through nuanced, complex characters, audiovisual contrasts and counterpoint and, as Golubić says, "a playing with tone and sense of humor".[578]

Tonally and stylistically, there are evident differences between *Breaking Bad* and *Better Call Saul*, but gradually, as the timelines and characters meet, the two series begin to overlap. An almost Shakespearean tragedy in five seasons, *Breaking Bad* encourages viewers to identify with Walter White up until the point where his cynicism has made him all but unrelatable. *Better Call Saul* deals with a different story and a different dynamic between the two main characters, Jimmy and Kim (Rhea Seehorn), and as the show develops, it becomes less clear whose tragedy we are witnessing. Both shows are visually and sonically striking, however, while alluding to films by Ozu, Hitchcock, Lean, Friedkin, Bertolucci and De Palma (cf. the Hitchcockian close-up of Kim's eye at the end of Season 5 or the Palmaesque gurney scene at the opening of Ep. 4:1).

The question is whether we should attribute this experimental *signature style* to the writer-producers Gilligan and Gould. In the final part of this chapter, I will explore and discuss this question with a particular focus on *limited series* and the shifting understandings of *auteurism* across different formats.

The Artistic Vision and the Collaborative Medium

> [B]eautiful Art is only possible as a product of Genius...
> – Immanuel Kant, philosopher[579]

> I ... reject the definition of style as the mark of the individual genius on a text.
> – Jeremy Butler, TV scholar[580]

The question of authorship goes back to the Romantic ideal, which was introduced by philosophers like Immanuel Kant at the cusp of the 19th century, and it has been looming in film and TV criticism for decades. In the 1940s, the French filmmaker and critic Alexandre Astruc wrote an essay called "Le Camera-Stylo" (1948), in which he claimed to be witnessing the birth of a new avant-garde in French film connected to directors who were using their cameras as an author would use his/her pen and a painter his/her paintbrush.[581] A few years later, in 1954, François Truffaut wrote a polemic essay bemoaning "a certain tendency" in French cinema to make impersonal films, adapted from literary classics and created in close collaborations between the directors and the screenwriters.[582] The discussion that Astruc and Truffaut had initiated was a debate over artistic merit, authorship and, as Andrew Sarris writes, "the tension between a director's personality and his material."[583]

The idea of assigning authorship to a film director was not new in the 1940s, and some scholars see traces of *auteurism* in the early 1900s connected to directors such as D.W. Griffith.[584] In the last few decades, however, the concept of auteurism has been rejected by many film and TV scholars due to the evaluative nature of the *auteur theory* and the collaborative nature of film and TV productions. "I reject the notion that the next logical step after identifying beauty is to invoke the spectre of the auteur," as TV scholar Deborah L. Jaramillo writes. "We can successfully connect beauty to the talent involved in creating it as well as to circumstances that enable and sometimes impede that talent."[585]

In film criticism, authorship is often assigned to the director, but television is typically described as a "producer's medium" where the writer-producer is seen as the creative visionary or manager of his/her series.[586] This understanding of *TV auteurism* is also reflected in various sections of this book. In relation to *The Wire* and *Show Me a Hero*, the actor Michael Potts talks about 'David Simon coming in' and changing the American TV landscape with his visionary form of storytelling, and in relation to *Treme*, the sound mixer Bruce Litecky talks about Simon's intense involvement in the sound design. These two stories represent some typical authorial narratives among various practitioners and craftsmen, and they could be described as *stories of singular visions* and *stories of strong involvement*. Examples of such *trade stories* abound in this book. Adam Sawelson, for example, says that David Chase was "very involved" in the process of mixing *The Sopranos*, and Ronald Eng claims that David Lynch is "the one guy" who will get involved with the sound process from the early pre-production phase to the final stages of post-production. Similarly, the graphic designer Patrick Clair describes how his title sequence to *True Detective* was inspired by Nic Pizzolatto's vision and photos he had given him during a 'prep meeting', while Arthur Albert explains how

Vince Gilligan and Peter Gould showed him pictures from various films as direct sources of inspiration for his cinematography in *Better Call Saul*. Especially when it comes to *Breaking Bad*, *Better Call Saul* and *Twin Peaks*, the cast and crew talk about their work as a logical consequence of the creator's vision, and that authorial reading of *Twin Peaks: The Return* is also reflected in the interview with executive producer Sabrina Sutherland at the end of this chapter.

Another interesting example is seen in Tim Hunter's description of his work on *Mad Men* and *Breaking Bad*. On *Mad Men*, the showrunner, Matthew Weiner, had a preferred visual aesthetic with a slight low angle and some headroom over the actors, and this aesthetic was part of a *signature style* that the episode directors had to follow. Consequently, Tim Hunter, who has a predilection for *slow reveals* and camera movements, could only have 2-3 crane shots per episode, and he was urged to stay within the given parameters. As Hunter says:

> Matthew Weiner had shot the pilot, which Alan Taylor directed, and set a style for the thing. It was a fairly simple style: clean lines, geometrical framing. Matt didn't like people cut off in the forehead; he wanted a certain amount of room above everybody's head, and the *wide shots* had to look composed. [...] The style was probably meant to mirror films from that era. Beyond whatever personal preferences Matt had in terms of framing, I think that they did want a classical look for the thing that evoked the period. Of course styles change – perhaps you could peg it to the advent of widescreen and the wider frame ratios where you have more width of the frame, so in order to get more in, you cut the heads a little tighter and frame just on the hairline or across the forehead or something. That has become a more modern way of doing things.[587]

Weiner had a strong authorial presence and a personal style that he wanted episode directors to imitate, although he allowed small elements of variation and experimentation. More aggressively, however, Vince Gilligan wanted Hunter to stick to the *signature style* of *Breaking Bad* - a style that was dominated by static *wide shots* and wide lenses. According to Hunter:

> I did that episode of *Breaking Bad* which became the Season 1 finale, and it went very well. For years, people talked about that episode, to me, as being a stand-out episode, but they never brought me back on *Breaking Bad*, and I never could figure out why. I have a friend who is a producer, and who was working several years later with one of the *Breaking Bad* producers, and I said: "Would you ask this person why they never brought me back?" And the answer came back that Vince Gilligan thought that I moved the camera too much on the show. [...]
> Generally, the producers want more production value today. They want it to be more like a feature film. They want more action, more production value, and they put much more pressure on you to give it a "feature look".[588]

These narratives seem to come from the cast and crew rather than the creators themselves. In that sense, they may reflect the natural hierarchy of a TV production where creators talk about *the collaborative aspects* behind a given TV series, and where the technical craftsmen talk about *assisting the showrunner's vision* or, in the case of Tim Hunter, about having to renounce his own creative preferences in order to follow the creator's *signature style*.

Though also talking about their visions, the creators and showrunners often stress the complex and collaborative efforts behind their TV productions. Beau Willimon readily credits David Fincher when describing the audiovisual style of *House of Cards*, even if Fincher was only involved in the early stages of the series, and Nic Pizzolatto immediately points to the collaborative nature of the TV medium. "The show is conceptualized on the page, then realized through the efforts of a large crew and the expertise of the individual departments," as he emphasizes.[589]

Although it is also an art form, television has often been seen as an industrial and commercial production - something that is "*produced* rather than *authored*," as Jason Mittell puts it - and this understanding of television goes back to Adorno's idea of *the culture industry*.[590] As Mittell acutely says:

> Given the intensely collaborative nature of the production process, [traditional] understandings of authorship, even in its managerial conception, oversimplify the creative process and threaten to deny agency to the array of contributors who help make television.[591]

Mittell describes different understandings of authorship - *authorship by origination*, *authorship by responsibility* and *authorship by management* - and argues that the role of the producer in television has "transformed significantly" over the years. In the early stages of TV history, the producers were often stars in their own productions (such as Lucille Ball and Desi Arnaz in *I Love Lucy*). Later, the producers were often directors-turned-producers (like Michael Mann and David Lynch), and in recent years the executive producer has become a mostly organizational or managerial figure (for example Sabrina Sutherland).[592] The production process itself is undeniably Fordistic, especially in American television where the crews are larger and the budgets are bigger. Still, it is possible and justifiable to look at authorial qualities in a TV series, as long as we do not forget the collaborative aspects and the industrial nuances. As John Caughie notes:

> [T]he tendency to reject *auteurism* because it is 'hopelessly romantic' lends itself to an over-reaction in which the author appears as 'nothing but' an effect of the text, failing to elaborate what the text does ... and the way he is used in the cinephile's pleasure.[593]

A significant point in Mittell's book is that "every television series has its own particular organization and division of duties," and, consequently, different TV series have different types and degrees of *auteurism*. As the Danish TV creator Jeppe Gjervig Gram says:

> The *showrunner model*, as it is employed in America and Denmark, has emerged out of sheer necessity. On long-running series (i.e. a TV series with 10 or more episodes per season) it is virtually impossible for a director to have a leading role, simply because s/he cannot be on set *and* in the *writers' room* at one and the same time. And you have to be present in the *writers' room*, if you are supposed to deliver episodes on a regular basis. You lay the foundation of a series in the *writers' room*, and that is the reason why writer-producers are often the leading figures. That has been the rationale in Denmark, at least, where films are often director-driven. In Hollywood, where it is normal to hire a writer on a film production before attaching a director, it is probably less surprising to think of the writer-producer as the captain of the ship. On *limited series* or series that only have one season, it is more normal to see a director in a leading capacity because all the scripts can potentially be finished before the beginning of the shooting phase (something that you do not see on long-running series).[594]

As we shall see in the feature interview at the end of this chapter, there are tendencies towards a more director-driven kind of television in limited series like *Alias Grace* and *I Know This Much Is True*, as opposed to longer-running series like *The Walking Dead* that employ shifting showrunners and episode directors. In *The Walking Dead*, the showrunner's role, as Angela Kang says, is to *manage* a large *storyworld* across various media, to keep track of the general story and to avoid inconsistencies. In shorter formats, the mode of production and degree of authorial control are often different, but there are numerous approaches to TV production and ways of authoring and managing a series. For example, the showrunner on *Homeland* (Showtime, 2011-2020), Lesli Linka Glatter, is a so-called *producing director* who helms the show while directing many of the episodes. As Glatter says:

> As a producing director, I love being involved with the whole novel, the whole big picture of the season, as well as the individual chapters. There's an overall look and feel and tone to each season, and I also get to direct four of the 12 episodes. We have other amazing directors who come in, and that creates energy and brings in a different point of view, yet it fits into the whole, overall storyline and feel of the season.[595]

The Limited Series and the Singular Vision

In Denmark, during the first phase of the so-called *Golden Age* in the 1990s and early 2000s, the miniseries was often seen as a more experimental and director-driven format. Series such as *Riget* (DR, 1994), *Charlot & Charlotte* (DR, 1996), *Edderkoppen* (DR, 2000) and *Forestillinger* (DR, 2006) were all created by renowned Danish directors (Lars von Trier, Ole Bornedal, Ole Christian Madsen and Per Fly), and a similar tendency can be detected in other countries, including the US.

One example of this is *Alias Grace*, a Canadian series that was produced for CBC Television and co-financed by Netflix. Adapted from a novel by Margaret Atwood, the series was written by Sarah Polley and directed exclusively by Mary Harron. When talking about *TV auteurism*, we often refer to creators and showrunners, yet Harron, as a film and TV director, has a relatively distinguishable style and brand, and she can add a certain pedigree and aura of art when being brought onto a television show. Without being overly stylized or having an immediately recognizable *signature style*, Harron often employs a set of stylistic devices that fit her preferred themes in various interesting, yet often subtle, ways. Exploring the inner battle between sanity and lunacy, Harron often uses *mirror motifs*, and when illustrating the conflicts in society between normalcy and perversion, she often uses popular music and symbolic compositions.

Those recurring themes and trademarks are also seen in *Alias Grace* which, like the popular show *The Handmaid's Tale* (Hulu, 2017-), is based on a novel by Margaret Atwood. Atwood's historical novel behind *Alias Grace* was also made into a telefilm in 1974, but Harron's televisual adaptation cleverly transcends the limits of the historical setting and the short format. The story deals with the notorious 1843 murders of Thomas Kinnear (Paul Gross) and his housekeeper Nancy Montgomery (Anna Paquin) and the feelings and inner turmoil of the wrongly (?) convicted Grace Marks (Sarah Gadon).

"I will confess to having a wicked thought," says Grace in the opening of the first episode (perhaps referencing the abuse she endured in her youth), and the entire miniseries reflects upon those issues: Where are the lines between vice and virtue, sinner and saint, sanity and insanity? Using abrupt montages, *low-key* lighting and flashback narration, Harron creates an ambiguous story and a multi-layered character that keeps the viewer guessing. The title character herself reflects on issues such as sin and sanity, but the fragmented flashbacks and the ambiguous narration are reminiscent of Edgar Allan Poe and his unreliable narrators and charming, Byronic heroes. Grace is likeable, and she is both clever and charismatic, but what should we make of her many comments on sin and suffering? "There are some that take pleasure in the distress of a fellow mortal," she says, "and most especially if they think that fellow mortal has committed a sin, which adds an extra relish. But which among us has not sinned?" That question, from the first episode of the six-part miniseries, seems like a Harronesque motif, questioning the lines between the sinners that are convicted and the societies that convict them. In line with Friederich Nietzsche, who wrote extensively about the ascetic moral and the strangely perverted types of punishment that were used for so-called perverted and sinful behavior, Mary Harron is interested in the mental processes of *those who commit* and *those who are committed*.[596]

Flashbacks, montage editing and *sound hooks* are employed to illustrate the hidden world beneath the would-be orderly society, and the miniseries seems to allude to a classic motif in literature called *The Madwoman in the Attic*. As Sandra Gilbert and Susan Gubar argue in their 1979-book of the same title, female characters have often been depicted as either "angels" or "monsters", but women writers from the 19th century, in subtle ways, began to probe and question that dichotomy.[597] *Alias Grace*, too, looks like a reflection and a subtle debunking of that binary, and, according to Mary Harron, that was part of the reason for her coming on board:

> Sarah Polley said that she was first attracted to it because of the idea of women being who they're asked to be. All the expectations of women and all the prejudices, which was what the opening scene was about: "People say I'm an innocent girl, people say I'm a terrible harlot. I'm this and I'm that". You know it's all the expectations and ideas that people have about women and whether women try to live up to them or how they affect their lives.[598]

Grace herself ponders that binary opposition by referring to the strange term "murderess", a feminized equivalent of the word "murderer". "I'd rather be a murderess than a murderer, if those were the only choices," as she says, arguing that the word "murderess" has a gentler and less harmful ring to it. That remark looks almost like an authorial comment, questioning the strange dichotomies that are created and repeated in phallocentric societies where women are thought to embody qualities such as gentleness, purity and harmlessness.

There are many aspects of *Alias Grace* that could be seen as directorial trademarks, even if Harron attributes most of the stylistic choices to Sarah Polley. The direct address in the final shot of the series, for instance, clearly echoes the breaking of the fourth wall in many of Harron's works - from *I Shot Andy Warhol* (1996) to *American Psycho* (2000) and *The Expecting* (Quibi, 2020). The same thing could be said of Harron's recurring motif: the lonely, complex woman who often falls victims to societal demands and judgement. In *Alias Grace*, the societal judgement of women is a central theme, and in the short horror series *The Expecting* it is illustrated through Trier-like aerial shots of the female lead, Emma (AnnaSophia Robb), and allusions to films like *La passion de Jeanne d'Arc* (1928), *Rosemary's Baby* (1968) and *Alien* (1979).

In terms of production, *Alias Grace* was *cross-boarded* and treated like a film, and that could also be said of Derek Cianfrance's HBO-series *I Know This Much Is True*. Both productions are adapted from acclaimed novels and created as limited series, akin to BBC's renowned miniseries from the 1970s and 1980s. Wally Lamb's novel behind Cianfrance's series is an epic story of 928 pages, and there have been multiple unsuccessful attempts at making it into a film. As Cianfrance explains, he saw the possibility of adapting Lamb's story into a *Godfather*-like miniseries, and the result is an interesting combination of Bergmanesque chamber play, Cassavetes-like intimacy and a complex interweaving of different timelines. The intimate use of close-ups and handheld camera was inspired by John Cassavetes' *Faces* (1968), but also echoed the cinematic work of Cianfrance himself (especially *Blue Valentine*), and the title sequence and heavy emotionality were both inspired by Lars von Trier's *Breaking the Waves* (1996).

One reviewer has argued that the complex narration is reminiscent of Terrence Malick, but Cianfrance's series never seems interested in creating a *puzzle plot* or in engaging the viewer in a game of sense-making.[599] At the most basic level, the story deals with two brothers, Dominick and Thomas Birdsey (both played by Mark Ruffalo), who struggle with psychological issues, inherited trauma and the psychiatric system in America, while learning of their family's story through the sordid and unflattering writings of their grandfather.

Chronicling a working-class family that travels from Italy to America, *I Know This Much Is True* is a story about the Birdseys, but it is also a microcosmic story of America as an immigrant nation. Most evidently, this aspect is seen in the final part of the series where the Birdseys learn that their biological father is a Native American, despite their grandfather's outspoken racism. As Dominick says at the end of the series, upon learning about his mixed-race heritage:

> I'm not a smart man, particularly. But one day, at long last, I stumbled from the dark woods on my own, and my family's and my country's past, holding in my hands these truths. That love grows from forgiveness. That from destruction comes renovation.

Like *The Godfather* trilogy is a saga about American history, told through a non-linear chronicle of an Italian-American family, *I Know This Much Is True* is a saga of epic proportions, telling the story of an ordinary American family with extraordinary psychological problems and tragic experiences.[600] Combining working-class realism (visually illustrated in the muted colors and the handheld camera), complex narration and an almost impressionistic use of close-ups, it looks and feels like a New Hollywood film or a Swedish miniseries by Ingmar Bergman. In that sense, it is an overt example of *art TV*, evidently alluding to arthouse films and employing an attention-demanding style and narrative. Apart from Bergman and Cassavetes, the series refers to films like *One Flew Over the Cuckoo's Nest* (1975), *Dead Ringers* (1988) and *Adaptation* (2002). The idea of having one actor play two identical twins is reminiscent of David Cronenberg and Spike Jonze's films, and the idea of combining a microcosmic story about mental illness and the psychiatric system with a story about racial and structural issues in America is similar to Miloš Forman's adaptation of *Cuckoo's Nest*. There are also more specific references to Forman, as in the scene where Thomas is forced to go to Hatch. This scene immediately echoes the scene in *Cuckoo's Nest* where Charlie Cheswick (Sydney Lassick) is dragged off to shock therapy, frantically repeating the words:

"No, I won't."

I Know This Much Is True is adapted from an epic novel and inspired by various cinematic sources, but it is also based on a lengthy research phase. As part of the preparation phase, Cianfrance contacted NAMI (National Alliance on Mental Illness), and he chose to cast actors who all had experiences with mental illness, adding a level of empathy and authenticity to his piece. In her review for *RogerEbert.com*, Sheila O'Malley claimed to experience an element of "compassion fatigue" when watching the series, but the repetitive and heavy nature of the narrative and the unflattering personality of Dominick naturally seem to mirror the story of two brothers who are struggling to deal with each other and their individual and collective traumas.[601] Thomas is a paranoid schizophrenic, and through Dominick's voice-over the audience learns about their complex and ambiguous relationship - an ambiguity that is reflected in the narrative and the identification structure itself.

In 2015, Ryan Lattanzia wrote an article in *Indiewire*, arguing that American television was experiencing a "new wave of auteur TV," and whether or not we dismiss the concept of *auteurism* as normative, the industry itself promotes many of their series as the products of singular visions and strong involvement.[602] *Art TV* is not a new phenomenon as such, neither is the idea of a visionary creator, but in the modern TV landscape many series have an experimental and conspicuous approach to style and some evident trademarks of different showrunners and directors. From the *musical moments* in *Stranger Things* to the radical slowness and *sonic complexity* of *Twin Peaks* and the alternative approaches to cinematography and staging in *Succession*, *American Crime* and *Mr. Robot*. Not to mention the use of counterpoint, montage editing and overt angles in the series by Gilligan and Gould. We could speculate about these individual and conspicuous styles - whether they represent a general "cinematizing" of television or an attempt from TV creators to stand out in a saturated marketplace. Certainly, the use of *musical moments* in *The Americans* and *Stranger Things* lends itself neatly to a new media landscape where audiences engage with TV series in a new way, and the off-kilter framing of *Mr. Robot* and *American Crime* and intimate close-ups of *I Know This Much Is True* and *Normal People* make the series immediately recognizable, even when watched on a smartphone.

Whether *auteurism* actually exists in a medium as collaborative and Fordistic as television is debatable, but it certainly exists as a *trade story*. The roles of the producer and the director differ from production to production. But there is a certain tendency towards a more director-driven paradigm in the limited series, and this tendency is perhaps facilitated by new media. In their respective Quibi series, Mary Harron and Tricia Brock have directed all the episodes, and like *Alias Grace*, *I Know This Much Is True* and *Twin Peaks:*

The Return, they were all shot and produced like films. "*Twin Peaks: The Return* was more like a gigantic film, a TV show in a feature film format," as the editor Jonathan P. Shaw puts it. "It is unlike anything I had ever worked on in television." A similar point is made by writer-director Ole Christian Madsen (showrunner on *Banshee*, Cinemax, 2013-2016). "Some series, like *True Detective*, are very creator-driven and have a homogeneous style across the different episodes," as he says. "On a series like *Banshee*, on the other hand, the different episode directors, who were brought in from the independent film circuit, were encouraged to bring their own directorial style and to treat their episode as a small feature film. Limited series that have a strong authorial touch are popular these days, perhaps because the viewers in today's TV landscape are demanding. They want personal works of art."[603] Or as the director Tricia Brock says with reference to her work on limited series like *Dummy*:

> That the director has a bigger role on limited series makes sense to me. The next project, which I am working on, is a series by Soderbergh called *The Gater and the Egg*. If that series is picked up, I will direct all of the episodes in the first season. He directed all of *The Knick*, and he very much is in favor of a single voice.[604]

Twin Peaks: The Return, which was described by Showtime as "a limited event series," was mixed for various platforms (e.g. a theatrical mix and a sound mix that was suitable for home viewing). The first two episodes were screened at Cannes together with Jane Campion's *Top of the Lake: China Girl*, and the entire series was even exhibited at MoMA. As TV series are moving into movie theaters and art museums and onto smaller, portable devices - all at once - they are beginning to exhibit some new and more conspicuous approaches to style that will also make them stand out in a flooded market.

In the following feature interview, Sabrina Sutherland, Peter Gould, Mary Harron and Derek Cianfrance reflect upon the questions of authorship in modern American television in relation their respective TV series: *Twin Peaks: The Return*, *Breaking Bad*, *Better Call Saul*, *Alias Grace* and *I Know This Much Is True*. Following this cluster of interviews, I will explore some new approaches to genre - specifically crime series, teen dramas and dramedies - to round off my exploration of the modern TV landscape. As we shall see, the modern examples of these genres (e.g. *Normal People*, *Euphoria* and *Transparent*) also display some interesting signature styles, and Jay Duplass (*Togetherness*, *Transparent*) may be regarded as a clear example of the authorial tendency in the limited series and the short format, often producing, writing, directing and even starring in his own series. In his case, the director *is* the star.

Fig. 38: The executive producer Sabrina Sutherland argues that *Twin Peaks: The Return* was mostly a David Lynch production and describes how the series was *cross-boarded* and produced in an unusual way. Most people from the cast and crew express a similar authorial reading and ascribe most of the series radical 'otherness' to David Lynch. Mark Frost, however, describes the process as quite collaborative, saying that he would provide the narrative foundation and allow Lynch to do "jazz solos within that composition" (Bushman 2020, p. 276).

More precisely: "This time, the immersion in writing was deeper and undivided. We were working closely together, and we divided our attention, him focusing on directing and me focusing on writing parts of the show and writing the book. But we are both contributing things in every department. It is very much a collaboration" (Author interview, May 18, 2017).

Currently, David Lynch is rumored to be working on a new series for Netflix, perhaps related to *Twin Peaks*, *Mulholland Dr.* (2001) or one of his previously unproduced projects, and once again Sabrina Sutherland is attached as executive producer.

Feature Interview #5

Artists and Tele-visionaries: Interview with Sabrina Sutherland (*Twin Peaks: The Return*), Peter Gould (*Breaking Bad, Better Call Saul*), Mary Harron (*Alias Grace*) and Derek Cianfrance (*I Know This Much Is True*)

Lauded for their artistic endeavors, *Twin Peaks: The Return* (Showtime, 2017), *Breaking Bad* (AMC, 2008-2013), *Better Call Saul* (AMC, 2015-), *Alias Grace* (CBC, 2017) and *I Know This Much Is True* (HBO, 2020) were all promoted as visionary creations and groundbreaking television.

    David Lynch was already known as the creator of art films and abstract paintings when he made the original *Twin Peaks* in collaboration with the seasoned TV writer Mark Frost. But when Showtime produced their continuation of the series, Lynch directed all 18 episodes and fought the cable network to make it as long, abstract and personal as he wanted. That, at least, is the authorial narrative that surrounds *Twin Peaks: The Return*, and the executive producer, Sabrina Sutherland, reiterates and reinforces that narrative. A similar narrative surrounds *Breaking Bad* – a show that Vince Gilligan struggled to sell, until AMC finally picked it up. Today, *Breaking Bad* and *Better Call Saul* are lauded as great examples of *art TV* that reflect the shared vision of Vince Gilligan and Peter Gould.

    Though surrounded by fewer myths and mysteries, Mary Harron and Derek Cianfrance were also known as visionary filmmakers, like David Lynch, before creating *Alias Grace* and *I Know This Much Is True*, and these two series illustrate different artistic approaches and *signature styles*. In this compilation of interviews, Sutherland, Gould, Harron and Cianfrance discuss their respective series and the concepts of *art TV* and *TV auteurism*.

"It's All His Vision": *Twin Peaks: The Return*

Ben Travers posted a question in *Indiewire*, pertaining to *Twin Peaks: The Return*: "How much impact [can] a TV show make if virtually no one is watching?" It would probably not be considered a success in terms of *ratings* on *linear TV*, but it was received positively by the critics. Matt Zoller Seitz even described it as "the best series on TV," and it was included in *Cahiers du Cinéma*'s list of the best "films" of the decade. How do you see it,

and would Showtime describe it as a success? [605]

Sutherland: Thinking in terms of ratings is the old way of defining success, and I think that TV is starting to change from that. Remember, television is antiquated. And even cinema, unfortunately, is struggling. The arthouses are almost gone. You'll go for these tent-pole things or you'll have very indie-indie things, but for the most part, things are moving toward the Internet and towards a new way of doing things, and so I think this helps bridge that. You'll look at it and think 'maybe we don't have to do that traditional thing anymore'. And I think with Showtime wanting to have a streaming service, which is something new, more people watch *Twin Peaks* on the streaming service and you're watching it multiple times, so it's not just one show and that's it. You want to see it over and over because you want to understand it, and because it's so long and because it's a film, you kind of have to go back and rewatch some things because we didn't do recaps. David didn't want to do recaps, he wanted every show to be a surprise. That's why there was so much secrecy in terms of the scripts, the non-disclosure agreement and the promos that didn't give anything away.

He wants everyone to experience it for themselves. He wants you to allow yourself to go into a dark room, have great sound and great picture and to just watch it and have your own emotional response and interpretation of it. You may not understand it, but it should generate something in you, hopefully, like art does. So I'm hoping it was a success for Showtime. I think to some degree it was definitely a success. If you look traditionally at it, maybe not, but I think we are moving away from that traditional and limited understanding of success.

You describe the new series as "a film". Why do you use that term?

Sutherland: David and Mark wrote the entire series, the new season of *Twin Peaks*, and they made it into one script. So it was one giant script. We didn't know how many episodes there would be. It was just one feature film, and that's how we approached it when we started shooting in 2015. Everything was scheduled based on location and actor availability, so it was just a giant puzzle piece like a feature film. So it's definitely different from the original series, which was shot like a television show.

Your title is executive producer, but that title has various meanings in today's TV landscape. What was your role on *Twin Peaks: The Return*?

Sutherland: There are some ideas that David wants to get across through the pictures and the sound. Without saying what those ideas are, he will say what he wants on the screen, and if I can help facilitate that or make that happen, I do what I can. Remember, I am more of a concrete knots-and-bolts person, so I have to translate his vision into something concrete. It takes time to figure out what's up here and understand it. He'll explain to me exactly what he would like to see, and then I will try to get that through and to have the different department heads create that image or audio for him. I try to understand and translate his vision, while thinking about the budget. "Well, we can't do or afford this, but he wants something like this. What can you do?" Essentially, I am a kind of translator for him, just making sure that whatever he wants is there. I am not looking at the bigger picture (what he wants to say), but everything we get on the screen (what he wants to show). We're not trying to theorize or make sense of it.

The new *Twin Peaks* recycles and remixes various elements from the original series, from *Fire Walk with Me* and the *tie-in* books. When and how did that idea arise?

Sutherland: I think David had it all in his head as he was writing. I remember, we're back at the time when he was doing the deleted scenes for the Blu-ray box, and we were going through and looking at the original series and *Fire Walk with Me*, so he had all of the scenes fresh in his head as he met up with Mark and started writing.

Because he was working with it and creating the deleted scenes and looking back at that, at the time when he was writing the new season, that's how it was interwoven. It wasn't thought of later. He actually had ideas that grew out of that, so he was able to meld in some of the old stuff and to make it work. He'd say exactly what he wanted. He knew the scenes he wanted to be in there, so it was just a matter of going back and finding that old material, to look through the old material and find the clips he wanted, and then to find out exactly how he could use them. Some clips were altered, some were not, but he wanted to put them into the script he had written. We knew up front, before we even started pre-production, that these clips were going to be necessary, so we had two years to work those in. And it took us two years.

It was all David. He had all of that in his head and knew what he wanted, and it was all about translating that vision. Taking that video material, sometimes having to use visual effects, was necessary in order to create the world he had envisioned. We had to figure out how to do it, so it was a challenge, but David knew exactly what he wanted. In terms of editing, for example, Duwayne Dunham and the other editors assembled the material in the order that they saw it, and then David went through it and looked at everything, and he would change things or edit things on his own after those guys left. David continued editing for six months after the whole editing team left. So he was there, working on everything together with a couple of assistants who were very integral to the process. But it's all David's idea, it's all his vision, it's all him looking at every frame. I'm not kidding, every frame, and making sure that every shot, every sound and every visual effect – that all of it works. He checked everything both with picture and with sound. Dean and Ron worked and got all of the things, and David would go through every mix and make sure that everything was there or create them himself or have Ron and Dean create what he wanted. Everything was done according to David's instructions, and everything was checked and approved by David at the end, so, seriously, it is David's film from start to finish

What made Showtime produce a series as abstract, slow-paced and potentially alienating as *Twin Peaks: The Return*? Did they see it as an *auteur* series?

Sutherland: I think it all goes back to giving the respect and the creative control to David. And when Showtime understood that this was going to be a film, and we didn't know how long it was going to be – it was just going to be a journey and David's vision – they were 100% behind it. So even Duwayne with editing, he would have things cut short. He had cut some of the scenes in a somewhat normal way where you cut out images of people walking, for example, but David wanted to include that. "No. That's what I want," he would say. He wants that pace. It's all part of his vision. He wants to explore and to experiment, and that was the pace he had set, and he wanted to see that through. And he's like: "I can do what I want to do. I'm happy with it, and that's the aim." He doesn't want to be constricted or to compromise in any way, and my job is to work within the boundaries that are set – the monetary boundaries and whatever rules Showtime have set up – and to get David's vision within those boundaries. Each part, for example, could be 52 to 58.30 minutes, or something like that, and it was my job to try to make sure that each part would fit within that time frame. That was how we edited them, and my job is to try to get David's vision on screen.

That's probably why he likes to work with me because, as a producer, usually you're not really the director's person. I am the director's person. And, thankfully, Showtime was so wonderful. After I explained to them that this is what David wants, and if you want it to be "David's *Twin Peaks*," this is what he needs, they were 100 % on board. That allowed the creativity and the artistic intent to be there. Showtime were willing to take a chance on something, and you have to give them credit for that. I hope that, in the future, maybe more artistic, *auteur*-driving productions can get through.

Apart from the new series, David Lynch has said that he mainly likes the pilot episode and *Fire Walk with Me*. The episodes that he directed from the second season are quite interesting, though, and they seem very Lynchian, as if he were coming back to put his authorial stamp on a series that he was losing touch with. Is that a correct assumption?

Sutherland: Exactly! And so, when he wasn't there, those episodes were either trying to emulate what he had done with *Twin Peaks* or the ideas that Mark Frost, Harley Peyton and Bob Engels had of the way to go with *Twin Peaks*. When David directed his episodes, he would go back to what *Twin Peaks* was in his head. I have the idea that people working on the second season of *Twin Peaks* weren't in the same vein as David, so you can see that his episodes are different because that is how he views *Twin Peaks*, and the other ones are how other people view *Twin Peaks*. That is why the new *Twin Peaks* is so interesting to me because he directed all of them and was able to put his spin or creative vision on the whole thing, and that, to me, is what makes *Twin Peaks* *Twin Peaks*. David has a clear vision, and that, to me, is what art is. And from the very beginning of his career, when he first went into filmmaking, that was exactly what he wanted to do: make moving pictures. Art.

"Visual Storytelling": *Breaking Bad & Better Call Saul*

You began as a writer on *Breaking Bad*, before becoming an executive producer and co-creator of *Better Call Saul*. Today, you are the sole showrunner of that show. Could you say a few words on the development of *Better Call Saul* and the collaboration between you and Vince Gilligan?

Gould: I was a working writer before *Breaking Bad*, but I had never worked on a TV series, so the first time I was in a *writers' room* was literally Season 1 of *Breaking Bad*. It was a transformational experience. After years of working by myself, getting to be in a room with other writers while we figure out the story and then getting to write an episode on my own was just wonderful.

   Vince Gilligan, from the beginning, ran his show in a very decent way. Not everybody in the business is as decent and generous as he is. There's no question that *Breaking Bad* was his baby and his creation, but I like to think that we all contributed to it. We had a great time working together, and I was lucky enough in Season 2 to write the episode that introduced Saul Goodman, which was probably the most difficult and stressful work that I had done in television.

I was worried whether or not the tone in that episode would work for *Breaking Bad*. At that point, we had done a season and a half, and I was still trying to understand what the show was. But Vince had a vision for a drama that could include a lot of comedy, and that is right up my alley. I'm not really a comedy writer. That's a very specific skill, and working with Bob Odenkirk I've learned more and more what that skill entails. But I also think that drama works better when there's sometimes a lightness of touch to it. So I got to write that episode and introduce Saul and Bob to this world, and pretty soon after that we used to joke in the writers' room about *The Saul Goodman Show* that we would do next. We knew that *Breaking Bad* would end, but it seemed too good to be true that we could make a show about Saul Goodman. My experience from working in the industry is that a lot of shows don't get produced, so it just seemed too delightful to think about another show with Vince. Then, as *Breaking Bad* was winding down, Vince and I started to talk about it some more, and we decided that there was a show there. But we didn't know what the show was, and it's a very different experience for a writer in show business to try to figure out what a show is going to be, when there's already an appetite for it. There was a lot of interest, but what was the show going to be? That was our struggle, and one of the things I was focused on was that it shouldn't be too similar to *Breaking Bad*.

We had a lot of ideas about doing the show as more of a comedy, maybe as a half-hour show, and then we gravitated towards doing an hour show because that's really the tool set that both Vince and I have. And we started to work together on the show – it was a pretty smooth transition – but there's a difference between working *with* someone and working *for* someone. Having said that, Vince makes it almost invisible in some ways because when you work with him, you want to please his artistic sensibility. We had a wonderful time, the first two seasons, and then Vince left the show for seasons 3, 4 and 5. And I was in the position of taking over, which was very stressful, but we had the best group of people working together, and we kind of had a momentum going at that point.

Initially, *Better Call Saul* differs quite evidently from *Breaking Bad*, but gradually, as the timelines meet, the two shows become more similar in terms of style. How would you describe the stylistic transition from *Breaking Bad* to *Better Call Saul*, and did you have any aesthetic principles when developing *Better Call Saul*?

Gould: We thought a lot about trying to make the shows look and feel different. *Breaking Bad* had a handheld look to it. It was inspired a lot by William

Friedkin's *The French Connection*, which was shot by Owen Roizman. With *Better Call Saul*, we decided that we wanted the camera to be more static, a little bit heavier. But the thing that makes to two shows different is the different personalities of the main characters. It all grows from that. Where Walt is in a marriage that's had its better days, Jimmy in *Better Call Saul* is in the beginning of a romantic relationship. But both Jimmy and Kim are adults. Kim has her own personality, and she's not going to bend herself around to make the relationship work, at least not at first. Those are the things that make it most different. The visuals certainly play a role, but the truth is that a lot of it comes from the same team, so there's a lot of constancy between the two shows also.

For the first couple of seasons, we did a *look book*, and a lot of it was from *The Conformist* (*Il conformista*), although there were a lot of other movies there too. We weren't saying to Arthur Albert: "Duplicate this." We were saying: "Let's use this for inspiration to tell the story visually."

One of the things that excites me about television today is that we have an opportunity to do much more visual storytelling. I think the audience is more attuned to the visual side than, perhaps, they were in the past. Historically, at least in the US, television came from radio – all the television networks were radio networks – so it was sort of a radio model that started it. We're in a position now where people have such wonderful screens and such an ability to see, and we also have audiences that are willing to pay attention, which is not something you can take for granted.

There are some evindent allusions to canonical films in *Breaking Bad* and *Better Call Saul*, from *Psycho* and *Lawrence of Arabia* to *film noir* and Frank Capra, and some of the episodes are fairly radical and "ballsy" in terms of style and pacing (I am thinking of episodes like "Fly" and "Bagman", for example). What were your main stylistic influences, and were you ever worried that your style was too demanding?

Gould: It's unnerving to do long scenes without dialogue or scenes that are very quiet. There's always a fear that the audience is not going to stay with us. But if it's "ballsy" – and I love that you use that phrase – I think our courage has increased over the years, as we see that people are willing to stay with us. There's a little bit of a feedback loop with the audience. It's a slow one because we start working on a season that doesn't come out for a year or more. But when something worked last season, why not push it? And by the way, if you're playing it safe – if you know for sure that something's going to work – it's probably not worth doing.

We're in a very special position in American television where we have a tremendous amount of freedom, and certainly Vince earned that over the seasons of *Breaking Bad*. There are a lot of constraints in terms of time and money, but creatively we've been given a lot of freedom. And if you're given that freedom, if you have that room to operate, it will be unforgivable to play it safe.

We would do more episodes like "Fly" and "Bagman", if the story allowed it. Part of the reason why we did "Fly", the episode from *Breaking Bad*, was that there was a constraint. We were a little over budget, and we had promised to do what's called a *bottle episode*, which is an episode that takes place only on sets. So that was part of the origin for that episode. "Bagman", on the other hand, may well have been the most expensive episode of either show, simply because the locations were so difficult, and it was so hot. We had to really do our best to take care of our cast and crew, and it was a very complicated episode that took a little longer to shoot than most episodes. We weren't economizing there. That's for sure.

We're all movie buffs in the *writers' room*. We love movies, and we talk about movies and television all the time, so there are, inevitably, references to some keystones that we have. Those things don't necessarily shape the story, but they might shape how we tell the story, and I agree about the wonderful compositions in "Bagman" and the David Lean feel to it. Obviously, the pandemic has taken a huge toll, and one thing that has made me a little sad is that we used to be able to show our episodes on the big screen in Los Angeles a few times. No one has seen "Bagman" on the big screen in a theater, except for those of us who have worked on the show.

In the beginning of Better Call Saul, it seems as if Jimmy McGill is the only protagonist, and in the first few seasons we follow him and his brother Chuck. Later, though, the series develops into a show about Jimmy and Kim Wexler, and Kim turns out to be a very nuanced character. Was it always your intention that Kim should be a central character, and how much would you say that the characters in Breaking Bad and Better Call Saul inform the style and tonality of the two shows?

Gould: It's a great example of one of the special properties of the medium we work in: serialized television. Things can change organically. People often expect us to have figured out every aspect of the show from day one, but the truth is that there's an evolution. We're constantly reevaluating what we've done and what comes next. There's an improvisational aspect to it, though it's very highly structured. And one of the wonderful things about that is that we get to watch the show too, to see what interests us and to understand what's important to us. We got very interested in Kim, and the more we worked on the show, the more important she became. The fact that she's not a part of *Breaking Bad* gives us a lot of freedom. A lot of these characters have their fate set in concrete already, but not Kim.

I thought of Jesse Pinkman as very important to *Breaking Bad*, partly because Aaron Paul is a brilliant actor, but, as you mention, it becomes hard to root for Walter White or identify with him completely. He is fascinating, you can't take your eyes off him. I'm so proud to have been part of the creation and evolution of that character, but he is not someone you'd want to have in your life. Jesse sort of took over that role, and you knew that Walt was going to die. But what was Jesse Pinkman's fate going to be?

The shows are very different, but there are rhymes between them, and as we go on we get more and more worried about what's going to happen to Kim Wexler. Not just because she's a victim because I don't think Kim is a victim. For better or for worse, she is the architect of her own fate. Some of it is just watching Rhea Seehorn and Bob Odenkirk together, and it reminds me a little bit of someone like Mike Leigh. He has a very different approach to filmmaking, one that we don't use in television or in the US very much at all: He works with the actors for months or even years, develops their characters and then brings them together and makes a series of improvisations. In a weird way, there's a similarity between that approach and *Better Call Saul*, even though everything is scripted. We get to watch the actors and see the possibilities in the characters that maybe we didn't even realize when we were talking about them in the writers' room and take that back to the writers' room. So you see a character like Kim Wexler, and you realize that this is a person who's always going to be the captain of her own ship, but maybe that wasn't obvious to us when we first started the show. In Season 1, Jimmy and Kim never get together. It's a little bit ambiguous what their relationship is, and it doesn't become romantic until Season 2. There was a particular moment where we realized that. At the end of Season 1, Jimmy finds out that his brother has sabotaged his career, and he's also gone home and visited his good friend Marco who dies in his hands. Kim has set him up for a job interview, and he's going to go to the job interview, and then he changes his mind. He tells Mike, "I know what stopped me... It's never stopping me again," and when we started Season 2, we thought that maybe he was going to be Saul Goodman. He's going to open the crazy office and buy the Cadillac. And the more we thought about it, we thought: "Kim set up this job interview for him. Did he just walk away from that? Shouldn't he have called her and told her?" That made us think about what his obligation is to her and what he wants from her, so it was literally at the beginning of Season 2 that we started digging in to that relationship.

The theory that we're running under is that *what* happens isn't as interesting as *how* it happens. You can summarize anyone's life in three sentences, but it's the twists and turns of life that make it interesting. Also, there's something to be said for paradox, so when you meet Jimmy, he's not Saul Goodman as an egg. He's somebody else. So the question becomes: How does this guy, who has a core of decency, become the Saul Goodman we know on *Breaking Bad*. For many seasons, we didn't understand that at all. When we were working on Season 5, the curtains parted a little bit, and we saw how that would go, but now the question is: What happens to Kim?

A Certain Pedigree: *Alias Grace*

You are best known as a director of independent films like *I Shot Andy Warhol* and *American Psycho*, but you have worked as an episode director on quite a few series. One of the first major series you worked on was *Homicide*. How did you get into the business, and how would you describe the transition from film to television?

Harron: I worked on one of the later seasons of *Homicide*, and I had my first movie out the year before, so I think my agent had put me up for it. My agent at the time, I think, knew that I needed to work.

It's interesting. I never had any prejudice against television. Some film directors look down on TV, and I never did because I had spent my teenage years and early 20s in Britain, and I had grown up with the Golden Age of British television drama. Things like *Play for Today*. Great television drama and really interesting TV comedy. And great actors like Judi Dench would be on a TV show, and nobody would think: "Oh, she's doing TV". It was normal to do TV and theater. There wasn't that much of a film industry in the UK at that point, so most of the great actors, directors and writers worked in television. The early Dennis Potter stuff had started, for example. So I didn't have any problem with TV or the idea of doing TV.

I had just had my first child, and my older daughter was five months at the time, so I remember I was very nervous about going back to work, which I think happens with women right after they've had a child. You go into this other place, and the idea of going back into directing was quite frightening to me. I remember going through the scripts and writing a lot of notes, and when I got on set, I thought, "Oh, this is fine" because it was all handheld. You can't really plan ahead.

My husband came out - we had to go to Baltimore - and my mother and sister flew out to be with me in Baltimore because I didn't know how I was going to work with my baby. So I had all this family support. My husband would bring me my daughter, Ruby. Nobody in Baltimore had seen anyone with a Babybjörn, you know. My husband would come to visit me on set, and I would nurse the baby during lunchtime. I would use a breast pump. The first AD put a little room aside for me, and I would go and pump milk, if I couldn't actually be with the baby. So it was just a little crazy, but it was a fun and very interesting episode.

I had a fair amount of freedom on that one. I had much more freedom on that show in terms of casting than I had on most of the later shows I worked on. Obviously, the episode is about racism, but I didn't want someone who was an obvious, aggressive, militant Black Power guy. I wanted someone who seemed kind of intellectual - more of an inwards person - so I think I brought that to it, casting someone who was not an obvious choice. I felt like this character had an analysis and was an intellectual hoot who had driven himself a little mad, like Valerie Solanos, dwelling on the injustices, and had gone over the edge.

How would you characterize the work of an episode director, and do you think that you have been chosen on series like *Homicide* and *Oz* because you have a certain pedigree?

Harron: The one thing in television is that you get the script that you are given, so in a way it's serendipitous that it suited me so well, but, at the same time, when they choose which episode to give you, they give you something that's right based on your previous work. In some ways that also reinforces things. People ask me sometimes, "Why do you always do things that are violent?", and then I answer: "Well, that's what I'm asked to do". People, especially in America, tend to give you things to do based on your previous work.

Why do you think that many independent film directors have migrated to television, which is usually known as a "producer's medium"?

Harron: A lot of independent directors ended up making their careers in television, although in some way that stopped their film careers because they ended up having great careers in TV. And as great as television is, and as exciting as the shows are, you don't have as much creative freedom as you do on your own movies.

But one reason is that television has become visually sophisticated, therefore attracting people from the film industry. Another reason is that it has become very difficult to make mid-budget movies. *Very* difficult.

In *Alias Grace*, you are the director on all episodes, and there are some sty-

listic elements that look almost like trademarks of yours. The story was written by Margaret Atwood, however, and the script was crafted by Sarah Polley, so how would you describe your role?

Harron: What is interesting with doing someone else's script, which is what has happened to me, mainly in television, is that it pushes you to do things which you don't necessarily want to do, and then you discover something in the process of doing them.

Sarah Polley was working on the scripts for years, and then she decided at one point that she didn't want to direct them, and she told me that she had started to write them, at some point, for me to direct. With me in mind. And she never told me this even though I know her, and after the scripts were done - we share the same manager - he rang me up and said: "We have these six scripts for you to read". I was going on vacation and read these 300 pages of scripts which were amazing, and I felt like, when I started reading: "Oh, this is perfect for me". As soon as I started reading it, I felt like this really could have been done for me because it had a lot of things that I am interested in: It's historically based, but it's also ambiguous, and it's about madness and sanity and identity.

What came from Margaret Atwood's book and is maintained in Sarah Polley's script is a very strong and accurate historical touch. It's very accurately a woman in that period who thinks in a way a young working-class Irish girl from the 19th century would, although her writing and voice-over are more eloquent and poetic, probably, than it might have been. It's a different vocabulary, but the thoughts, the prejudices and the fears are very rooted in the life of a woman in the 19th century. On the whole, I don't like these very ahistorical things that basically put modern characters in period clothes. This really was an exploration of one thing that has always interested me: Women in history. What a woman's life was like at a particular time.

One thing that seemed indelibly Harronesque is the final shot where Grace looks directly into the lens. You have similar camera addresses in *I Shot Andy Warhol*, *American Psycho*, *The Notorious Bettie Page* and even *Oz* (though that was an inherited style). Was that a signature of yours?

Harron: It's interesting because that last shot in *Alias Grace*, which I love - and Sarah Gadon is such a brilliant actress that she brings so much to that shot - was written into the script. A lot of the stylistic things in the script, I have to say, were in the directions in the script that Sarah Polley wrote. She had a very strong idea of certain things she wanted. She wanted *tracking shots* through the empty farmhouse where the murder took place, and I didn't know whether they would work or if they would look too hokey. But when we did them, they looked fantastic. So there were certain things that were in the screen directions, and I was glad that I did them because it was her script, and I didn't realize how right they were until I actually did them, including the opening scenes. My two favorite things in *Alias Grace* are the opening shot of Grace where she's looking in the mirror and the hypnotism scene, and with both of those scenes I thought: "This isn't going to work".

The way it was written, she is looking in the mirror, and she physically transforms; she became taller, thinner and differently dressed. But then I realized that Sarah Gadon was such a great actress that she could do it just with her face, so it became a more contained thing of a woman looking at her real self in the mirror and then her changing expression. But I have to say that it was a great idea of Sarah Polley's, and there were things in it that might look like they're authorial choices, but they were actually Sarah Polley's directions, so I can't take all the credit for it.

For the hypnotism scene, when I first read it, both of us thought: "How are we going to do this?" She has a veil on her head. It's like a twenty-minute scene, and she has a veil over her, and she's talking in this weird voice. I thought: "How are we going to make this work?" But we had the right actress, and she made it work.

Alias Grace is a miniseries or a limited series. Does that make a difference for the way you create and produce the series, and does it change the relationship between the writer, producer and director?

Harron: Now they call them limited series. I grew up on miniseries. BBC did a ton of great miniseries like *The Six Wives of Henry VIII* or series that were self-contained. Adaptations of great novels and that kind of thing, and that was very much a BBC tradition. They'd do *Nicholas Nickleby* and other adaptations of classics as miniseries. So I think, in doing *Alias Grace*, the CBC and Netflix were doing that in that tradition. When Sarah initially asked me to direct them, I said to her: "Why don't we both direct them?" One person doing all six of them seemed like a big project, and it would make more sense if we split them. But she was adamant. She said: "One person *has* to direct them all".

And after I was done shooting, I realized that it made perfect sense because, in fact, you can't divide them into discrete episodes when you're filming them. You have to shoot it like one very long movie - do it with a 65-day or 13-week shoot - it was pretty long, pretty intense. By the way, she had just seen *Top of the Lake*, which had been a big success artistically, and that influenced us, too. That seemed like one long movie, although it had two directors. Sarah felt that *Alias Grace* had to have only one director. It had to be consistent, so it was shot exactly like a movie, in that it was *cross-boarded*, meaning that you divide the shoot by location. So all of the scenes at the farmhouse are shot at the same period, and all of the scenes in the prison are shot at the same time, and that is how you would do a movie: shooting by location. And because I was doing it all, working with the designer and the DP, then it had the consistency that a movie would have. And I would say, since doing *Alias Grace*, that my favorite way of doing television is to do a limited series because then I have the resources of television but the control that a director has on a film.

Are you saying that a director of a limited series has almost the same role as a film director? Is the director becoming a more central person in television or in the limited-series format?

Harron: I'm in one of the Directors Guild counsels, and I've been pushing them for a couple of years now to make stronger creative potentials for directors doing limited series because at the moment you are still catering - you still have the same rights as a director as when you're doing an episodic show. Once you do a limited series, I think, the director is a more influential person. That's something that's interesting to look at in terms of the television landscape.

In some ways, the great era, the Golden Age of television of the last 15 or 20 years now, has been the rise of the writer/showrunner. People like David Chase, who also sometimes directs, obviously, or Vince Gilligan, Matthew Weiner and David Milch. In some ways, I think that they were all very tough. They would fight the network or fight the cable channel to get what they wanted, and they all made these great shows that came out of people who were writer-producers. The director, I think, has had less power in episodic television, and the limited series is a place for the director to have a stronger authorial role. It's still a collaboration between writer and director, but the director also has to get some of the power back because they need to control the cast and a lot of the creative choices to give it a personal aesthetic. It's much easier, if the director has also written some of it, like Jane Campion did with *Top of the Lake*.

"Battling the Scale": *I Know This Much Is True*

You migrated from film to television in order to write, produce and direct *I Know This Much Is True*. How would you describe that move and the shift

from one medium to another?

Cianfrance: When I first came to HBO, and they said that they were going to do it, there were a lot of questions from them - "Well, you've never done a TV series before" - and a lot of questions as to whether I understood the TV medium. What I told them was that this is just storytelling and that I didn't see it as anything other than an extension of the films that I had been making. And in the films I have made, I have often come into a situation where I would be battling the scale: The scale of my ambition vs. the scale of the movie screen. In *The Place Beyond the Pines*, for instance, I had always envisioned - and I even wrote it into the script - that there would be an intermission. And I had a naïve belief that people would go see that movie: They would see the Ryan Gosling section, the Bradley Cooper section, and then there'd be a card that came up and said "Intermission". Then they could go out, get popcorn, go to the bathroom, and when they would come back, 15 years would have passed in the story on the screen, and we would be with the kids. And I believed that right up till the point of editing the movie. My financiers had put a condition on it, saying that it should be under two hours and twenty minutes, so that "Intermission" card became a "15 Years Later" card.

Then I found out, when I was making *The Light Between Oceans*, that I was in the third act and trying to catch up to time, and I just felt that everything I was doing was servicing plot, not necessarily character. And the things that I love in a movie are characters and moments. John Cassavetes is a huge influence to me. I feel like he captures these moments that can never be replicated, and I always set out, when I'm shooting a film, to find those moments that can only happen once. Moments that can never be rehearsed, recaptured or replicated - like Halley's Comet. When I was a kid, I saw Halley's Comet, and I know I'll never see it again, and that's what I think of with the moments I try to make in my movies: That they are once in a lifetime. That's the bar that I raise for myself.

With this series, *I Know This Much Is True*, I did it exactly the same way I would make a movie. I shot it on film stock over 116 days: That's about 19 days per episode, and if one episode is an hour, that's about 35-40 days to shoot a two-hour movie, which is a very healthy movie time frame. HBO understood that. I got rid of some excess baggage that I didn't need - that would have cost more money - but I just shot it the way I would have shot a movie. Never once did I think that I was shooting anything other than a movie, except for the fact - and this isn't to disparage television - that television and movies are obviously different mediums.

Did you see it as a film, and did you consider the viewing situation and the

intimacy connected to television as a medium?

Cianfrance: What I thought I could do was to give people the experience of watching a movie in their homes that had a television format to it where we would have these hour-long chapters. And I think it's really been beneficial to this story in particular because it's so intense and so heavy and because there's so much drama in it.

The experience of watching a TV show can bring cinema closer to the experience of literature because when you're reading you can take pauses, you can have moments to reflect. A chapter ends, and you go make dinner, you go for a walk or you go to bed, and you think about the things you've seen. And that's what's been a real gift and something that I was really excited about with television: This idea of *audience reflection time*.

Why do you think that limited series are popular these days, and does the shorter or more limited format change the role of the director?

Cianfrance: I think the limited series is coming back because there are a lot of filmmakers like me who want to expand their story, their characters and their ideas, when their ideas don't necessarily include caped crusaders, superheroes and franchisable universes. In the Hollywood system, the only way I can really tell an expansive story, the only way I can tell a six-hour epic, is if I put it in outer space or if I make it some sort of franchisable universe. But to tell a story about the people my story is about - blue collar people, ordinary people with their issues that are so small that nobody would care about them except for the people who are in their orbit - those stories would never be able to make it on the big screen. This story, for instance, is adapted from a 1000-page book, and they tried for 16 years to make it into a movie, but it could never be made as a two-hour movie. And, at the same time, no Hollywood studio in their right mind would put up the money to tell this story the right way and make a multi-part movie out of it. *The Godfather Part I* and *Part II* don't exist anymore.

There's a whole world of possibilities in television and streaming. I'm not going to say that it's not there in movies, but it seems to me that movies are having a hard time, and the two kinds of movies that really function well these days are the massive *Avengers*-type of movies or the independent *Moonlights* of the world. And *Moonlight* is every bit as big of a movie as *Infinity War*. Culturally, cinematically and in every other way.

As you say, the series is about ordinary people, and I would probably describe it as a character-driven series. Is that a fair description?

Cianfrance: It *is* a character-driven series, and I think that's what I could do with this medium. With more time, I didn't have to let the plot drive anything. It could just be about these characters and how they respond to the lot that they have been given in life. Part of what I learned from working on documentaries was that I could learn from people who are professionals, so when I cast a cop, for example, I will often cast a real cop instead of casting an actor to play the cop. For this, I cast people who had a certain quality for the character, but I also cast people who understood mental illness. Almost all the cast in this 'movie' has experienced mental illness very close to them. I've been doing some conversations with NAMI (National Alliance on Mental Illness), and they told me that one in five people suffers from mental illness. Because we all knew it or had close experiences with it, we were able to empathize with it and not treat it like a diagnosis. We just had to find the human side of things.

Chapter 6

Unboxing Television: Hybridity and New Approaches to Genre

> Genres do not operate by following [...] clear nesting categorizations, but rather through cycles of evolution and redefinition. Boundaries between genres and subgenres are too contingent and fluid to carry across different historical and cultural moments - what is a subgenre today might easily become tomorrow's genre through more widespread circulation (like teen drama's evolution out of family dramas) or a forgotten category relegated to television's archives through the waning of a generic cycle.
> - Jason Mittell, TV scholar[606]

> Every true work of art has violated some established [genre] and upset the ideas of the critics, who have thus been obliged to broaden the [genre], until finally even the broadened [genre] has proved too narrow, owing to the appearance of new works of art, naturally followed by new scandals, new upsettings and - new broadenings.
> - Benedetto Croce, philosopher[607]

The concept of genre is a vast and vexing issue in film and TV history, and the current media landscape, with its endless circulation of texts across various territories, industries, media and platforms, has only made it more perplexing. TV genres have never existed in a vacuum; they have always appeared, changed and mutated across different media and cultural contexts. Hence, it might make more sense, as Mittell writes, to look at "the cultural circulation of *television genres* rather than *genre television* to understand how genres evolve, change and disappear."[608]

According to John G. Cawelti, genres evolve from different *formulas*, and these formulas are understood as a-historical and a-cultural 'ur-genres' that exist across various cultures and historical eras. Cawelti mentions a handful of formulas, including *mystery, adventure, romance, alien beings and states* and *melodrama*, and these formulas represent different *moral fantasies*.[609] By focusing on an enigma that is solved at the end of the story, a *mystery* might reassure the audience that the world is knowable. A *romance* story, on the other hand, might reassure the reader that 'there is someone for everyone'; and an *adventure* story, through its quest structure, strong hero and reassuring resolution, might teach the viewer that problems can be overcome through action and brute force. From these formulas modern genres develop, according to Cawelti, and they do so by combining *invention* and *convention*.[610]

Cawelti's formulas are possibly the roots of modern TV genres, yet genres continually develop, blend and dissolve due to a multiplicity of factors, so they are hardly fixed categories. As Rick Altman writes, genres serve different functions for producers, distributors, audiences and critics. For producers, they are a sort of "blueprint" that can be used to minimize risk, and for distributors, they are "labels" used to communicate the genre and sell the film or TV series. For audiences and critics, on the other hand, genres are seen as "contracts" (a set of criteria that a given TV series has to live up to in order to satisfy the viewer) or "structures" (for the critic to study).[611] In that context, it is also worth noticing that producers, distributors, audiences and critics may have totally different conceptions and definitions of a certain genre, while TV channels and streaming services often introduce their own specific categories.

In this chapter, we will meet different creators and producers talking about genres in many different ways - some may speak of teen dramas, while others call it *youth series* or *young adult fiction*, if not rejecting the category altogether - and these conflicting terminologies illustrate the ongoing negotiation and redefinition of TV genres.

In 1974, the film critic Andrew Tudor wrote a seminal essay in which he mentioned the so-called "empiricist dilemma," and this dilemma continues to haunt genre studies in relation to both film and television. What Tudor noticed was that critics and scholars often analyze a pre-selected list of *genre films* when trying to categorize and describe a certain genre, thereby essentially, but perhaps inadvertently, pre-determining the outcome of their analysis.[612] The examples in this chapter are not random or unbiased either, but have been chosen to illustrate the diversity and cultural fluidity of different TV genres.

The first section deals with a popular and traditional TV genre - crime fiction - in various modern iterations, and it explores the complex relationship between different traditions from America, England and the Nordic countries. The most central case in this section is *True Detective*, its relation to American traditions, such as *Southern Gothic* and *film noir*, and its potential non-American influences. *True Detective* was influenced by various traditions, and it in turn came to influence crime series from different parts of Europe, and these "mirrored influences" (as Pizzolatto calls them) are also mentioned in the feature interview with Nic Pizzolatto, Sam Levinson and Jay Duplass at the end of this chapter.

The second section of this chapter deals with teen drama and *young adult fiction*, focusing particularly on Sam Levinson's *Euphoria* and its relation to the American teen drama tradition, its Israeli ancestor and Scandinavian teen dramas like *SKAM*. This section looks at new tendencies within teen drama and *young adult fiction* across different platforms and territories, including the use of *transmedia storytelling* and experimentation with new forms of distribution (cf. *SKAM* and *No Filter*) and the tendencies towards bleakness,

Kategorier				
Action	Anime	Anmelderrost	Blockbustere	Dansk
Dokumentarer	Dramaer	Familiehygge	Fantasy	For børn og voksne
Gyser	International	Komedier	Krimi	Musik og musicaler
Nordisk	Reality	Romantik	Sci-fi	Standup
Thrillere				

Fig. 39: Netflix operates with *verticals*, *taste clusters* and individualized genre categories. These include nation- or area-specific categories like "Nordic Fiction" ("Nordisk") and "Danish Film and TV" ("Dansk"), more traditional film and TV genres like "Horror" ("Gyser"), "Romance" ("Romantik") and "Fantasy", and broad reception-based categories like "Critically Acclaimed Films and TV series" ("Anmelderrost"). Screen shot, March 2020.

radical experimentation (*Euphoria*) and a more intimate realism (cf. *Sex* and *Normal People*). Most importantly, this section explores the crossroads between various national tendencies and the cross-cultural exchange between teen series such as *SKAM*, *Eagles* and *Euphoria*.

The final part of this chapter is devoted to the dramedy genre, which has become increasingly popular since the advent of the genre in the 1970s (with series like *M*A*S*H*, CBS, 1972-1983). In this section, I focus on the popularity and flexibility of dramedies and the short format in *the multiplatform era*, and I delve into the thematic, tonal and generic in-betweenness of series such as *Looking* (HBO, 2014-2016) and *Transparent* (Amazon, 2014-2019) and the influence of British series like *Fleabag* (BBC Three, 2016-2019) and *After Life* (Netflix, 2019-). More explicitly than many other genres, the dramedy thrives in the new media landscape and exhibits an impressive flexibility in terms of platform, tonality and format. From short and raunchy series like *Dummy* (Quibi, 2020, 10 min. per episode) and commercial phenomena like *Margot vs. Lily* (YouTube/Nikewomen, 2016; ca. 5-8 min. per episode) to experimental series like *Transparent* (20-30 min. per episode) and harrowing experiences like *After Life* (ca. 25-31 min. per episode).[613]

At the end of the chapter, Nic Pizzolatto (*True Detective*), Sam Levinson (*Euphoria*) and Jay Duplass (*Transparent* and *Togetherness*) reflect on their respective series and questions concerning genre, and that triple-interview is followed by a short epilogue, wrapping up the most essential tendencies and the most recurring *trade stories*. This book is about changes in the TV landscape and new approaches to storytelling, style and genre in modern television (especially American drama series and dramedies), but also about the potential relation between the infrastructural and aesthetic changes and ways in which industry people *talk* about those changes and tendencies.

The Mystery of Mirrored Influences: Cross-Cultural Tendencies in Modern Crime Series

> I remember watching *NYPD Blue* and *Homicide*, when they first came out, and becoming aware of the psychological aspects of those series. There was an understanding of therapy and different character types, which was probably missing in our world at that stage, and I guess that crept over on our side and became a part of our language as well. It's really interesting how TV series from different cultures travel and blend.
> - Sam Miller, director (*Luther* and *American Crime*)[614]

> Even if our references were from American TV, we took this to Denmark and maybe made our own look out of it.
> - Bo Tengberg, cinematographer (*Forbrydelsen*)[615]

A modern descendant of the *mystery formula*, crime fiction has a long televisual tradition that goes back to the earliest stages of *the three-network and classic public service era*. Crime fiction is an 'umbrella-term' covering a wide range of different crime-related genres (from gangster dramas to detective series and police procedurals), but the most traditional examples of crime fiction were established by authors such as Edgar Allan Poe, Arthur Conan Doyle and Agatha Christie. Poe's stories about the clever and arrogant detective C. Auguste Dupin and Doyle's serialized fictions about the eccentric mastermind Sherlock Holmes introduced some traditional tropes and characters. Doyle's stories were published as a literary serial in the monthly *Strand Magazine* (between 1891 and 1930, *The Strand Magazine* published a large number of Holmes stories, and later these were also published as newspaper serials in other countries), and the focus on deductive and inductive reasoning became a central part of the traditional *whodunit*.[616] Like its literary ancestors, traditional detective series follow a strictly Aristotelian logic, in which a problem is introduced at the beginning, developing into a conflict in the middle, and eventually arriving at a solution. In that sense, detective series typically present *two stories*, as Tzvetan Todorov writes: (a) the criminal act, which often precedes the actual plot, and (b) the detective work, which ultimately leads to a solution. As such, traditional detective series have a *teleological structure*, steadily moving toward a clearly defined goal (*telos*). As Todorov puts it: "The whodunit par excellence is not the one which transgresses the rules of the genre, but the one which conforms to them."[617]

Historically, *whodunits* have been a popular form of crime fiction in film and television, and on the 'small screen' they have often been seen in the form of episodic, self-contained series and *locked room mysteries*. This tendency is reflected in the American series about Jessica Fletcher (*Murder, She Wrote*, CBS, 1984-1996) and the British TV series about *Taggart* (STV, 1983-2010) and Hercule Poirot (*Agatha Christie's Poirot*, ITV, 1989-2013). The popular procedural *Columbo* (NBC, 1968-1978/ABC, 1989-2003) follows a similar episodic form, but shows the culprit "execut[ing] his or her dirty deed" before showing the viewers how Columbo (Peter Falk) puts the pieces together, using his wit and rationality. The TV critic Elisabeth Vincentelli has described *Columbo* as "comfort viewing" and "formulaic in the best possible way," and the so-called *murder of the week*-formula has been a staple in American and British television almost since the birth of the medium.[618] As Jason Mittell writes:

> Prior to the 1940s, the most common crime films and fiction were detective stories, focusing on a mystery solved through the rational skills of detectives like Sherlock Holmes.[619]

In the 1940s and 50s, however, a new strand of crime films emerged in America, often produced as B-movies in the *double feature* system and existing in the periphery of classical Hollywood cinema. These films were described as *film noir*, and they came to be known for their use of *low-key* lighting, flashback narration, expressive camera angles, gritty urban settings, treacherous and double-sided characters and fatalistic endings. According to film scholar Forster Hirsch, the classical *noir* was born at the beginning of the 1940s (with films like *The Maltese Falcon* and *Citizen Kane*), and it gradually faded out by the end of the 1950s (with films like *Kiss Me Deadly* and *Touch of Evil*). The *noir* had its heyday from 1944 to 1950 - a period that was framed by two Billy Wilder productions (*Double Indemnity* and *Sunset Boulevard*) - and the term was used to describe a broad and diverse tendency in American film.[620] According to Paul Schrader, the traditional era can be subdivided into three phases:

- *The wartime period* (1941-1946) where many *noir* films drew their main inspiration from *hardboiled detective stories* by Raymond Chandler, Dashiell Hammett and James M. Cain and focused on the private eye and the lone wolf.
- *The post-war realistic period* (1945-1949) where *noir* films began to focus more on crime in the streets and political corruption.
- *The period of psychotic action and suicidal impulse* (1949-1953) where *noir* films began to delve into the darker abysses of the mind and the bleaker aspects of life and society.[621]

The *noir* film was inspired by *hardboiled crime* stories, German Expressionism, French Poetic Realism and gangster films from the 1930s, and it was the result of numerous different factors (from the aftermath of the Depression to the horrors of World War II and the wave of immigrants coming from Germany to America).[622] The *noir* films formed an alternative to classical Hollywood by rejecting the happy ending, questioning the nuclear family as an institution and focusing on dubious or morally ambiguous characters. As such, the *noir* films of the 1940s and 50s all but "reinvented Hollywood," as film historian David Bordwell puts it, and this strand of crime fiction has also come to influence modern television across a variety of countries and cultures.[623]

Before becoming a visible part of the modern TV landscape, however, the *noir* was an influential part of American cinema, and, ironically, television might have been one of the factors that led to the demise or dissolution of the classical *film noir*. According to film and TV director Tim Hunter:

> Mid-budget movies can no longer compete in the mass marketplace. By the time you make a mid-budget movie, if it doesn't have a mass-appeal, and you still have to double that budget to market it, you're going to lose money on it. That's why the drama or genre pictures that used to be the staple of Hollywood no longer exist, except as television or independent film. I think a lot of it, historically, started with television, which basically wiped out the B-picture, wiped out the western, wiped out the *film noir*. All of that ceased to exist when the *double feature* ceased to exist. You used to have the big releases and then you had the B-pictures or the smaller films, and they would have their first run, say, in downtown Broadway or in the main theaters, and then they would fan out to the neighborhood theaters for an extended run as part of a *double bill*. Television wiped all that out. Not only are there no neighborhood theaters with *double features* anymore, there are no smaller films. There's no second run for a feature anymore. It makes most of its money on the first weekend, and then it's a question of how badly it falls and how many weeks they can sustain it, and that's it.[624]

Film Noir and Its Legacy: From *Bosch* to *True Detective*

The *noir* genre was initially a cinematic phenomenon and would not become a central part of the American (and global) TV landscape until the 1990s. There were some interesting televisual precursors, however, and Jason Mittell points to *Dragnet* (NBC, 1951-1970/Syndication, 1989-1991/ABC, 2003-2004) as an early example of two different tendencies in American television:

- *The tough thriller*, which focuses on "an independent male detective solving a crime relying more on his masculinity and physical endurance than deductive detection skills, while painting a cynical representation of urban America."
- *The semi-documentary police procedural*, which was a "distinctive film cycle in the 1940s, commencing with *The House of 92nd Street* (1945)," and which was inspired by the *true crime* stories that were published in magazines like *True Detective* (1924-1995).[625]

Many of the influential TV series from the 1980s and 1990s had elements of the two brands of crime fiction that Mittell mentions. *Hill Street Blues*, *Homicide* and *NYPD Blue* had elements of the *semi-documentary police procedural* by using location footage, handheld camera, journalistic research methods and real-life stories. As mentioned earlier, *Homicide* was based on real crime stories and the journalistic chronicles of David Simon, and the camera style on *Hill Street Blues* was inspired by the American documentary *The Police Tapes* (1977), which was produced for public television and later aired on ABC.

Twin Peaks later combined *serial melodrama* with a traditional American crime trope (*the dead girl show*) and a *noir*-like aesthetic consisting of *mirror motifs*, *low-key* lighting, expressive camera angles and deep focus. The original *Twin Peaks* had an outspoken stylistic diversity, though, where the different episode directors were given a large amount of freedom. One of the recurring directors, Tim Hunter, introduced a combination of many styles in his episodes and drew his aesthetic inspiration from directors such as Douglas Sirk, Yasujirō Ozu, Fritz Lang and Sam Peckinpah. In his most famous episode, "Arbitrary Law" (Ep. 2:9), Hunter begins with a *wide shot* of Dale Cooper, Sheriff Truman (Michael Ontkean), Hawk (Michael Horse) and Albert Rosenfield (Miguel Ferrer) and a *slow reveal* moving down from the tree branches, before going into an intense, *noir*-like dialogue between Dale Cooper and Albert. As Hunter says:

> David Lynch and Mark Frost, unlike modern shows today that are really run much more tightly by the numbers, were willing to give directors a fair amount of overtime, if they needed it. And I believe that overtime came out of their producer fees, so they put their money where their mouths were. In general, they gave directors the room they needed for the episodes to breathe.
>
> On shows in general, depending on the show and the genre, I'm often reminded of scenes in movies, and I love old movies. So when I'm doing a soap opera, I can often reference a Sirk or a Minnelli, and when you're doing *noir* – *noir* comes fairly naturally to me - my classical defaults tend to head towards Hitchcock, Otto Preminger and Fritz Lang. So occasionally I'll do a shot that recalls a traditional move by one of those guys: A low-level sweeping crane shot from Preminger, a camera pull-back from Fritz Lang, and the kind of sequence building and cutting that we know from Hitchcock.
>
> That *wide shot* was inspired by Peckinpah, but the off-angle stuff was inspired by *film noir*: Siodmak and directors like that. Fritz Lang never used much off-angle stuff, neither did Otto Preminger, and those are my favorites, but I did it for *Twin Peaks* because it seemed right. The show gave you the freedom to do those kinds of angle shots. Today, it would be rare for anybody to get that kind of freedom.[626]

Inspired by both of these traditions, Michael Connelly and Eric Overmyer created a series called *Bosch* (Amazon Studios, 2014-), which was adapted from Connelly's book series about the charismatic LA police officer Harry Bosch (Titus Welliver). Bosch is named after the Dutch artist Hieronymus Bosch, who is known for his macabre and nightmarish paintings, and, on the surface, the series might look like a typical *LA noir*. It takes place in LA - mostly in the dark alleys and the unattractive backside of the city - and it uses *mirror motifs* and *low-key* lighting to startling effect. From the very opening of the series, we see Harry Bosch on a stakeout saying: "It's gonna rain like a bastard tonight... We need it to wash all the shit away." This line, along with the extreme *low-key* lighting, the dark blue filter and the gravelly voice of the main character, gives the scene an unmistakable *noir*-like quality, clearly echoing Martin Scorsese's *Taxi Driver*. The title sequence - a good example of the abstract and symbolic title sequences in modern TV series - also has a *noir*-like quality by employing a *mirror effect* where different parts of LA are mirrored against themselves. This effect, perhaps inspired by Hieronymus Bosch and his famous *triptychs* (e.g. *The Garden of Earthly Delights*), illustrates LA as a city of contrasts, and it indicates that this series will be about different parts and versions of Los Angeles.[627] As episode director Tim Hunter says:

> *Bosch* was much more of an LA location show, so by comparison it was easier to give *Bosch* an authentic LA look with Southern California vibes and *California noir* iconography than it was to give *Mad Men* a specific New York look because *Mad Men* was so set-bound. In *Bosch*, we're dealing with an adaptation of Michael Connelly's novels. They're not *noir* in the way that one thinks of *Out of the Past*, *Detour* or *Gun Crazy*. They have a *noir* edge to them, but they're fairly realistic police procedurals, and there's a lot of attention given to the lives and emotions of the different characters.[628]

Aesthetically, *Bosch* is similar to *film noir*, and the main character "solves crimes by working outside social norms rather than following strict procedures," yet he is not a traumatized *noir* detective or an abusive and corrupt antihero akin to Orson Welles' Hank Quinlan from *Touch of Evil* (1958).[629] He is haunted by the death of his mother, and he is an "independent male detective" who has a definite issue with authorities, yet he is also sympathetic and satisfied with his job situation. As the producer, Henrik Bastin, puts it:

> He's a complex character. He has a lot of baggage and all of that, but he's a happy cop. He's happy, even when he gets into fights with his superiors or has to tell Chief Irving to "go fuck himself". Even then, he just loves his job. He's passionate about it. He's not – and that would be my one critique on some of the Scandinavian stuff that I do like, but they're all so depressed and so moody. Harry Bosch *loves* his job, and nothing will stop him. He only cares about serving justice. He is prepared to cut some corners to do that, but he's always on the right side of the fence.
>
> *Bosch* is a throwback to classic back-in-the-days cop shows like *Hill Street Blues*. At the same time, it's very present day because it's set in a realistic version of LA. Not a fake LA. We only see the Hollywood sign once over six seasons, and that is in the pilot episode, in the very opening. That's the only time. Otherwise, we're in the parts of LA that you don't necessarily see in traditional cop shows or LA shows.[630]

Bosch is an interesting example of different crime traditions, drawing on both *film noir* and traditional police procedurals, while adapting some of the realistic sensibilities of modern American and Scandinavian crime series and consciously veering away from the melancholy and existential malaise of *Nordic noir*. Bastin was born in Stockholm and produced TV programs for TV4 and Kanal 5 in Sweden, before moving to Los Angeles in 2010, and in that sense he represents the *cross-border mobility of talent* that, according to Ramon Lobato, is a central part of the modern mediascape. He specifically mentions

Fig. 40: The producer Henrik Bastin (Fabrik Entertainment) talks about *Bosch* (Amazon Studios, 2014-) and its relation to traditional cop shows and modern tendencies of crime fiction in America and Scandinavia. *Bosch* represents a modern combination of police procedural and *film noir*. The same thing could be said of HBO's stylish reimagining of *Perry Mason* (2020-), which references the original legal drama with Raymond Burr (CBS, 1957-1966) but adds a modern touch, a sense of moral ambiguity, and an unmistakable *noir*ish flavor. Photo: Lasse Lorenzen & Jan Oxholm, 2019.

both American and Scandinavian series when promoting *Bosch*, arguing that it combines elements of American cop shows like *Hill Street Blues* and *The Shield* with qualities from *Forbrydelsen/The Killing* and hints of *The Wire*.[631]

Bastin has described *Bosch* as "the next binge experience," and the release of the sixth season on April 16, 2020 was followed by a five-day #BoschStakeout marathon and live tweet during the COVID-19 pandemic.[632] In that sense, *Bosch* is promoted as a mediator between different trends and traditions: It is both deeply American (taking place in LA and echoing the works of Chandler and Hammett) and global (by opening itself up to external influences like *Forbrydelsen* and Hieronymus Bosch). It is both traditional (by drawing on *hardboiled crime stories* and well-known cop shows) and modern (by utilizing new media). It is both *high-end* television (by associating itself with *The Wire* and *Forbrydelsen*) and 'bingeable' entertainment (by inviting its viewers to watch entire seasons in one sitting and interact with the creators).

Between Southern and Urban Gothic: *True Detective*

> Setting shapes the people who live there, who in turn shape their setting.
> - Nic Pizzolatto, creator (*True Detective*)[633]

As mentioned earlier, the original *True Detective* was a complex combination of different tropes and types of crime fiction: from *whodunit crime* and *dead girl show* to *Southern Gothic* and a *noir*-like character-study of two masculine detectives in the desolate landscapes of Louisiana. A gifted thinker with a traumatic past, Rust could be seen as a realistic and troubled version of the Holmesian detective, and Marty - a competent, active cop who embodies his profession while disconnecting from his wife and family - could be seen as the apotheosis of American masculinity and *hardboiled detection*.

The two detectives and the sordid case (with its underpinnings of religion, mysticism and incest) were all linked to the environment: the dilapidated homes, the lifeless vegetation, the eerie sense of remoteness and the intense combination of heat and humidity. As seen in the feature interview at the end of this chapter, Nic Pizzolatto regards the setting as a central part of the story and atmosphere in *True Detective*, and the actor Michael Potts mentions how the environment also affected the cast while they were shooting the final episode:

> When people think of New Orleans, they naturally think about Mardi Gras and food – the creole culture there. But you also have voodoo, vodon, so you have all those kinds of things, too, because of the African influence in New Orleans. It's always been a mysterious place. You have swamps and whatever images that conjures for you – swamps and alligators.
>
> When we were shooting the final episodes of *True Detective*, we experienced this ourselves. The poor camera guy was being eaten alive by bugs, and we had to have an alligator wrangler on the set.[634]

The complex story of *True Detective* fittingly ends at a strange and maze-like fortress called Carcosa - a place that has long seemed mysterious or even mythical (cf. Fig. 41-42). The maze-like structure of the ruins and the wild vegetation (the fort is surrounded by a moat and overgrown with plants and branches) reflect the narrative structure of the series and the mythological aspect of the ending: Is this where Rust will finally confront not only the culprit, but also himself? The camera follows Rust, creating a vivid and ominous sense of disorientation, and a sudden *aerial shot* of the fortress makes it seem infinite and impossible to escape from. As Micah Conklin writes:

> The majority of the scenery depicted in *True Detective* was familiar to those who have experienced Louisiana's landscape: open fields, oil refineries on the river, small town churches, and shacks on the bayou filled the show's beautifully filmed scenes. However, one "place" mentioned several times in the series — Carcosa — kept viewers mystified and confused throughout the episodes, ever since the eerie, tattooed killer Reggie Ledoux told Rust Cohle, "You're in Carcosa now."[635]

In the second season of *True Detective*, the uncanny and bewildering landscape of Louisiana is replaced by the *noirish* asphalt jungle of California with its winding roads and intricate web of places and people. And this time we follow four different characters: the villain Semyon (Vince Vaughn) and the

Fig. 41-42: In the opening of *True Detective* (HBO, 2014), a young woman is found naked and dead by a majestic tree in Louisiana (at Oak Alley Plantation). This scene is the beginning of an unusual combination of *dead girl show* and *Southern Gothic* where the eerie and treacherous landscapes play a vital role. The setting is also an important part of the final episode where Rust finds himself in Carcosa (Fort Macomb), an uncanny and labyrinthine fortress where he will meet his opponent and his *shadow self*. Photos: Lasse Lorenzen & Andreas Halskov, Louisiana, 2019.

detectives Velcoro (Colin Farrell), Woodrugh (Taylor Kitsch) and Ani Bezzerides (Rachel McAdams) - a name that fittingly alludes to the famous *noir* author A.I. Bezzerides (e.g. *Kiss Me Deadly*, 1955) and the Greek tragedy *Antigone* where the titular character defies the king despite the consequences she may face ("Ani" is short for Antigone).

On the surface, *True Detective 2* is a *whodunit*, much like the first installment, but the intricate puzzle eventually develops into a psychological exploration of the dubious criminals and the damaged detectives. Bezzerides, with her inability to establish and maintain emotional relationships, is probably the most obvious example of a *hardboiled* detective akin to the *noirs* of the 1940s and 50s. Woodrugh, in contrast, is a veteran and carries both physical and psychological scars, and Velcoro is pathetic in his uncontrollable aggression and unhinged behavior. A narcissistic vigilante, a wounded divorcée and a traumatized alcoholic, Velcoro switches between self-pity and self-loathing. When he, in a sad attempt to defend his own son, threatens a 12-year-old boy and forces him to watch, as he beats his father with brass knuckles, the line between good and evil is blurred. And it becomes even more *hardboiled* at the end of the sequence where Velcoro grabs the boy by his neck and says: "If you ever bully or hurt anybody again, I'll come back and butt fuck your father with your mom's headless corpse on this goddamn lawn."

The thin line between good and evil is also reflected in the main theme where Leonard Cohen sings "You're of their kin / You're of their kind," and these lines are reminiscent of *Touch of Evil* and *Chinatown* (1974) and their depictions of fluid morality and corruption in the political system and in the police force.

That *True Detective* is obsessed with psychology and inner conflicts is portrayed, most vividly, in the opening of the episode "Maybe Tomorrow" (Ep. 2:3), which features an expressive use of lighting, colors and sound and an almost Lynchian sensibility. The episode opens on a *long shot* of a male singer, dressed in an Elvis costume and drenched in a dreamy blue light, reminiscent of the "Slow Club" scenes in *Blue Velvet* (1986). On the soundtrack, we hear the first notes from Bette Midler's title song to *The Rose* (1979), as performed by the aforementioned Elvis-impersonator. The noticeable lack of ambient sound makes the scene strangely artificial (almost like the famous Club Silencio scene in *Mulholland Dr.*), and as we cut to a *medium shot* of Velcoro, we see him sitting in a half-empty bar with a performer singing or lip-synching in the background. The scene becomes even stranger and more artificial, though, as we cut to a *medium shot* of Velcoro who turns and looks directly into the camera, potentially confusing the viewer or breaking the illusion. Is he looking at the audience, or is this just another audiovisual cue telling us that we have entered a mental space or a possible dream state?

We then cut to a *point of view* shot of Velcoro talking to his father while the "live" music is playing unobtrusively in the background: "Maybe you lacked grit," his father says. "I see you. Running through the trees. You're small. The trees are like giants. Men are chasing you... You step out of the trees, you ain't that fast. Awh, son... They kill ya. They shoot ya to pieces." The music is intensified, and we now cut to a *medium shot* of the singer from Velcoro's *point of view*, before he turns to his father and asks: "Where is this?" "I don't know," he replies. "You were here first." At this point, the music takes over, and as the sound levels change, we cut to a new scene where a *tracking shot* slowly reveals a radio (playing "The Rose") and a wounded Velcoro lying on the floor. This sequence, with its fluid boundary between reality, dream and fantasy and its potentially confusing transition between different scenes and planes, illustrates the complexity and the focus on inner turmoil in *True Detective*. As the director, Janus Metz, puts it:

> In the scene, we see Ray talking with his father in a sort of 'realization space', and the scene is part of a central story for Ray: the inherited brutality within him and whether and how he can contain that brutality in relation to his own son, who might not even be his own flesh and blood, but the result of a rape. At the same time, the scene also functions as an omen, foreshadowing Ray's personal fate. We staged it like a death scene. The lighting seems unreal, and both he and his father address the camera directly, so it almost looks like a confessional where the characters are giving their confessions directly to us, the audience. At that point, the series breaks its own grammar; at no other point in the series do the characters break the fourth wall. The sequence is a tribute to David Lynch, in a way, by adding a metaphysical or spiritual quality to the series.[636]

True Detective has become something of a touchstone in modern American television, and it is an evident source of inspiration for *Sharp Objects* (HBO, 2018), which follows an alcoholic reporter (Camille Preaker, played by Amy Adams) who has recently been discharged from a psychiatric institution and suddenly finds herself in the middle of an uncanny situation. The story takes place in the fictional small town of Wind Gap, Missouri, and it combines *Southern Gothic* with themes concerning gender and sexuality and a *time-collapsing* form of editing akin to *American Crime*. Apart from cutting up sequences in a chaotic, non-chronological way, the series also uses a *post-credit sequence* at the end of the final episode, visually solving the puzzle in short fragments and shocking flashes and mirroring Camille Preaker's psychological lability (she is a cutter). "The post-credit sequence and non-chronological cutting style were not new," as the editor Justin Lachance says. "Similar techniques had been seen in *Westworld* and in the Marvel movies, but it worked well in our show."[637]

The term *noir* was originally introduced by the French critic Nino Frank in 1946 to describe a cycle of post-Depression movies in America, yet the bleak urban stories, the *hardboiled characters*, the non-linear narration and the expressive use of lighting, angles and deep focus have since become an integrated part of American television.[638] In *True Detective*, it is combined with elements of *Southern* and *Urban Gothic* to create a dark atmosphere and to stylistically echo the ambiguous, conflicted characters and the complex, labyrinthine narratives, and in *Bosch* it is used as a stylistic "edge" (as Tim Hunter says) to an otherwise fairly straight and realistic cop show.

In some cases, the *noir* elements are used as a general tone or atmosphere in a series that cannot easily be classified in terms of any one genre. This is the case with *Twin Peaks: The Return*, especially in the scenes with Mr. C (Kyle MacLachlan) and in the lengthy black-and-white sequence from Part 8. In those sequences, the atmosphere is similar to old *noir* films - the black-and-white sequence from Part 8, in fact, bears a striking resemblance to *noirs* and *neo-noirs* like *Kiss Me Deadly* (1955), *Invasion of the Body Snatchers* (1956) and *Carnival of Souls* (1962) - but the series, as a whole, transcends generic classification. David Lynch has often used *low-key* lighting and *noir* motifs in his work - from the expressive use of *chiaroscuro* in *Eraserhead* (1977) to the *noir*-like characters and lighting strategies in *Blue Velvet* and *Twin Peaks* and the visual aesthetic in his *Sunshine Noir Trilogy* (*Lost Highway*, *Mulholland Dr.* and *Inland Empire*).[639] When working on his LA films, he and cinematographer Peter Deming tried to create a visual mood, using *film noir* as a template, and they pushed the envelope in terms of darkness and contrast. As Deming says:

> David and I never really talk about lighting; we talk about mood mostly. I'll talk with David about the mood of the scene, and he'll give me some very broad ideas, saying "today it's sunny out" or something like that, and it's really all about mood. When doing *Mulholland Dr.*, we sort of had a short-hand from *Lost Highway* as to how dark it could be. There's "dark", there's "next door to dark", there's "*dark*" and there's "darker than dark".
>
> As far as shooting the new *Twin Peaks*, there was never a discussion whether this was appropriate or not for television. But David is a special case here, and he has always been a special case. Going back to the original version of *Mulholland Dr.* – when it was a pilot meant for television – we were forced into a different aspect-ratio, and that was okay, since it was the standard of television back then, but in terms of lighting and composition David did not adhere to any standards or norms of television.[640]

Other TV series employ an extreme or radicalized form of *noir* aesthetic, and this is the case in Nicolas Winding Refn's *Too Old to Die Young* (Amazon Studios, 2019), which combines *LA noir* with Mexican cartels and elements of Japanese *yakuza films*. As in his popular, Melville-inspired 'synth-*noir*', *Drive* (2011), and his Lynchian *box-office* failure, *Fear-X* (2003), *Too Old to Die Young* is a cool and artsy remixing of different references and styles, and it has been described by one reviewer as "13 hours in purgatory."[641] *Too Old to Die Young* may be an extreme case, yet it illustrates the ubiquity of *noir* aesthetics in the modern TV landscape and the diversity of its application. From a small stylistic "edge" in *Bosch* and a general atmosphere in *Twin Peaks: The Return* to a more thorough implementation in *True Detective* and a radical form of stylization in *Too Old to Die Young*. Film noir originally referred to a strand of American crime films made by European immigrants in the 1940s and 50s, but it has since become part of the global TV landscape and is seen in various cultural incarnations. In the following section, I will turn my attention to the *Nordic noir* genre (also known as *Scandi noir*) and how this genre draws on American traditions while, in turn, influencing modern American TV series through *transnational remakes* and a more general stylistic or tonal appropriation.

Follow the Money: **Nordic Noir and Beyond**

As mentioned earlier, the Danish TV producer Sven Clausen travelled to America in the 1990s, visiting the production of some of the most prominent cop and crime shows of that era. After returning to Denmark, Clausen employed many of the techniques from *Hill Street Blues* and *NYPD Blue* on shows like *Taxa* (DR, 1997-1999), and new writers, for instance Søren Sveistrup (*Forbrydelsen*) and Nikolaj Scherfig (*Broen/Bron*), would draw heavily on the work of American showrunners like Steven Bochco, David Lynch and Mark Frost. "When *Twin Peaks* came along," Scherfig has said, "I felt as if there was finally something for me and my generation. Many of the Danish writers and directors, who were educated at the Danish National Film School, were hugely inspired by David Lynch and Mark Frost. *Forbrydelsen* was clearly linked to *Twin Peaks*, and *Bron/Broen* was also inspired by it, albeit in a slightly more subconscious way."[642]

That prominent series like *Bron/Broen* and *Forbrydelsen* were influenced by American crime shows is well-documented by now, and the Danish film and TV historian Jakob Isak Nielsen has described this strategic combination of American formulas and culturally specific sensibilities as "The Danish Way to Do It the American Way."[643] Interestingly, though, modern crime series from the Nordic countries are beginning to veer away from the *Nordic noir* brand and adopt stylistic qualities and sensibilities from other regions. As American and British series are beginning to adopt the tonal characteristics and psychological realism of *Nordic noir*, Nordic TV creators are turning away from the global *Nordic noir* brand and looking to other countries, including England and America, for inspiration or making crime stories with a lighter touch (what is sometimes called *Nordic Bright*).[644] One example of this trend is *Bedrag* (*Follow the Money*, DR, 2016-2019) - a limited series which is formally similar to *True Detective* but thematically closer to *The Wire* and *Breaking Bad* (especially in the third season). The creator of *Bedrag*, Jeppe Gjervig Gram, began his official TV career in 2005. But his actual training started in 2000, when he worked as a consultant for DR, deciding which American TV series to acquire.

After applying to the Danish Film School, Gram and his friend Tobias Lindholm came up with an idea for a TV series, and they were scouted by the aforementioned producer, Sven Clausen, who thought that they might become the next stars of Danish television drama. Afterwards, Gram worked as a writer on series like *Borgen* and *Sommer* (DR, 2008) – a family-melodrama with echoes of *Six Feet Under* – before creating the first season of *Bedrag*.

The first two seasons (20 episodes) of *Bedrag* dealt with the same financial plots, but with each their own seasonal arc. They did not follow an episodic *murder of the week* formula, but each season had a new case and some new character arcs, even if they essentially dealt with the same fiscal complexities. Over the course of the three seasons, we follow the young criminal Nicky (Esben Smed) and his *rise-and-fall* template, ending in a devastating final sequence at the end of Season 3, but otherwise the first two seasons deal with bankers, business people and boardrooms, tying in with topical issues of whitewashing and financial crisis. In that sense, *Bedrag* combines archetypal characters and traditional American formulas (Nicky is reminiscent of Jesse Pinkman, and the bank manager, Anna Berg Hansen from the third season, looks like a feminine version of Walter White) with DR's formula about *the double story* (i.e. that the plot needs to have a topical and ethical underpinning). But the third season essentially reboots the entire series and stands out as the most intense and successful combination of American crime formulas and Danish public service television. From its wide format to its inventive title sequence (which changes with each episode) and its almost prophetic reflection of the money-laundering scandal at Danske Bank, the third season excelled in many respects.

The clear difference between the third season and the two previous seasons was reflected in the introduction of bank manager Anna Berg Hansen. The four scenes that were meant to introduce her were done as *one long take*, hoping to add an element of bravura and authenticity to the series. "That shot raised the bar, and it became the reference point for all of the directors. This was what they wanted to achieve or to outdo. We ended up prioritizing that kind of bravura shot in the production schedule, making room for signature scenes like that."[645] Another noticeable difference was the title sequence. The first two seasons had employed an abstract and symbolic title sequence akin to the cable classics of the early 2000s, but the title sequences for the third season are done as *sequential montages* depicting an object (e.g. money, drugs or a gurney) that travels from person to person.

Bedrag deals with whitewashing, corruption and police detectives and bank managers with private and psychological issues. However sympathetic, the investigator Alf (Thomas Hwan) is a tragic case who takes illegal pills

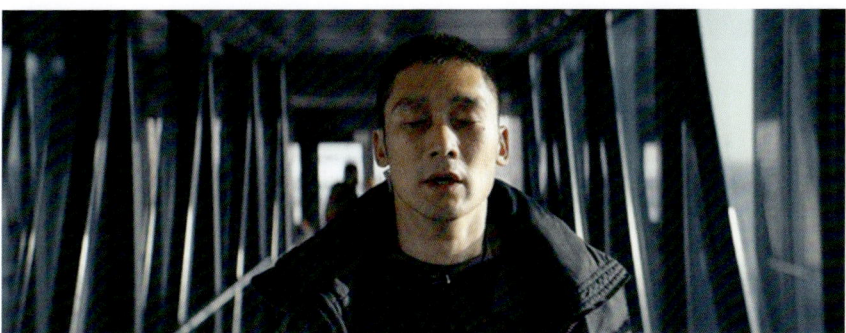

Fig. 43: The inner struggle of police officer Alf (Thomas Hwan) is a central part of *Bedrag 3*, but the series is closer to *The Wire*, *Breaking Bad* and *semi-documentary police procedurals* than to *Nordic noir* and traditional *whodunits*. Likewise, the critically acclaimed crime series, *Alfa* (TV2 Zulu, 2020), created by the Avaz brothers, has looked to America for inspiration in an attempt to renew and reinvent Danish crime fiction. © DR.

on the job and physically assaults his colleague in an act of frustration. Those elements may be similar to traditional *noirs*, but the style and tone of *Bedrag* differ markedly from *Nordic noir* series like *Bron/Broen* and *Forbrydelsen*, and there is an authentic rawness in *Bedrag* that does not look like other Scandinavian crime series. The documentary-like quality was also seen in the casting of former gang member Nedim Yasar, who was tragically shot after the production of the series before he had been able to watch himself on the 'small screen'.[646]

Bedrag looked to America for inspiration and consciously looked away from the *Nordic noir* brand, which had become globally popular by the 2010s. The same thing could be said of Christoffer Boe's *Forhøret* (Viaplay, 2019-) which combines a *dead girl show*-formula with a heavy stylization and a fairly radical concept where each of the episodes essentially follows the main character (the policeman Bjørn played by Ulrich Thomsen) in one location with one other person. Like *In Treatment*, *Forhøret* takes the dialogue-centric nature of television to extremes and, thereby, deconstructs traditional television and interrogation-based crime fiction. The writer-director Christoffer Boe began his career as an arthouse director inspired by Godard (in *Reconstruction*, 2003) and Tarkovsky (in *Allegro*, 2005), but in recent years he has begun focusing on a stylized form of genre fiction (e.g. *Journal 64*, 2018). "I have always been interested in genres and how they work," as Boe says, "but back in the day I often tried to deconstruct different genres. Now I try to understand *why* and *how* these genres work, and I work within the genres and explore their conventions."[648]

As Boe explains, *Forhøret* is a fairly clear-cut *whodunit*, but its generic title might be slightly deceptive, and as the series progresses, it evolves into a

Jeppe Gjervig Gram (writer/creator) on *Bedrag* (*Follow the Money*)

Moving to television: Before I applied to film school, I dreamed about becoming a director and making my own movies. But through my job as a TV consultant, I fell madly in love with American TV series, and I realized that, even before HBO entered the stage, there was a 'Golden Age' in American television. TV series like *Homicide*, *The West Wing* and *The Sopranos* became my artistic canon, and, instead of directors, my heroes became writers like Sorkin, Milch and the hyper-productive 'TV genius' David E. Kelley, who was like the Mozart of network television.

Reinventing *Bedrag*: As we were reinventing the series, we could see that the changes were so profound that we might as well have been making a new series, a *spin-off* like *Better Call Saul*. We also realized that we needed a radical change in terms of storytelling, characters, arena and even style. It was not possible to shoot the series in the streets of Nørrebro and maintain the classical aesthetic of the first two seasons. It would seem overly aestheticized. Therefore, we chose to shoot it *on location* in Nørrebro, and the bank and the police station were built in old industrial buildings in the Northwest. The *conceptualizing director* (Søren Balle) and the *conceptualizing cinematographer* (Laust Trier-Mørk) had created many of the episodes from the first two seasons, so they knew what had worked - and what we wanted to go against this time. Stylistically, the third season was not meant to approximate the style of the first two seasons, but to have its own unique aesthetic. It might sound easy, but it's not. We had to question everything, and it also meant that we changed the staff. We ended up with the following creative dogma: *If something feels right or natural, we must do something else.* It was an oath of bravery. As you can see from the series, we looked a lot at *The Wire*'s loose, almost documentary-like aesthetic, but the most important stylistic inspiration was *Sicario*, both in terms of color and *mise en scène*.

If you are interested in social structures, *The Wire* is an inevitable source of inspiration, and we drew on that from the first season. At the same time, we knew that we could not make a narrow, anthropological series for a public service broadcaster like DR. But it was a big source of inspiration, also because it follows both cops and criminals. It is not a *whodunit* where detectives track down an enigmatic culprit.

Instead of making yet another *Nordic Noir*-whodunit at a time when everybody in the world wanted nothing but *Nordic Noir*, we created a series about complex financial issues. And we were the first ones to really delve into that subject. The financial crisis made it possible for us to make our series, even if many producers thought that it was too difficult, and DR gave us a chance.[647]

stylized, psychological exploration of the investigator himself with a radical use of colors and contrast that seems notably different from series like *Forbrydelsen* and *Bron/Broen*. And this type of experimentation and stylization may have been possible precisely because *Forhøret* is not a Danish broadcast series, but a streaming series made for Viaplay (the same streaming service that is currently co-producing Season 3 of Lars von Trier's *Riget*). As Boe explains:

> My work has always been oppositional. There are always things *out there* that I like, but in terms of Danish film and television, I often try to make something that is different. It's a natural impulse for me. There are many good things about *Nordic noir*, and *Journal 64* belongs to that category, even if I also tried to do some new things in that one, but with *Forhøret* I wanted to see how far I could go in terms of integrating the style of my original films in a crime series. It is basically just two people talking in a room - and that's as artsy as you can get - but by using the *whodunit* as a frame, I thought that it was possible to combine the investigatory impulse with the minimalistic conversation. At the same time, I wanted it to have a very tight concept and design: Crime fiction has a strong narrative drive, but it also had to vibrate and mirror the psyche of the main character. The locations and *mise en scène*, for example, are meant to mirror the main character in an almost expressionistic way; they are not part of a social realistic setting, as we often see in Danish television.[649]

From the discovery of the body, it is evident that *Forhøret* is inspired by international films and TV series, clearly echoing the opening sequences of *River's Edge* (1986) and *Twin Peaks*. From that point, it develops into a psychological character study of the professional investigator who is suddenly involved in an unprofessional and emotional way, as he realizes that the dead girl is his own daughter Christina (played by the actor's daughter, Alma Ekehed Thomsen) and that her tragic fate may be linked to his professional detachment. In the course of the action, Bjørn learns that his daughter had become a prostitute, and this knowledge leads him to track down and kill the culprit, physically eliminating the external reason for her death while repressing his own role in her tragedy.

A final example in this context is Baltasar Kormákur's series *Ófærð* (*Trapped*, RVK, 2015-), which is the most expensive Icelandic series of all time with an estimated budget of 6,500,000 Euro. Kormákur's TV series is a fairly traditional *whodunit* with a slight postcolonial aspect, dealing with the trafficking of African women to Iceland (on a boat with a devious Danish captain played by Bjarne Henriksen). In many popular media, the series has been described as *Nordic Noir*. The Danish critic Lone Nikolajsen, for example, argues that it employs a "*Nordic Noir* recipe" while using the majestic, exotic landscapes of Iceland as a sort of "landscape porn".[650] However positive, that review seems to miss the central qualities of Kormákur's series, and by describing it as a typical example of *Nordic Noir*, it reduces the term *Nordic noir* while also overlooking the specific qualities of *Ófærð* and the narrative functions of the

Fig. 44-45: Christoffer Boe directs the actors in his new crime series *Forhøret* (Viaplay, 2019-) which combines radical elements of art cinema and heavy stylization with traditional tropes and formulas from American crime fiction. Photo: Henrik Osthen. Courtesy of Henrik Osthen and Christoffer Boe.

landscape. There is a definite sense of isolation and melancholy in the series, and the characters (especially the chief of police, Andri Ólafsson) are not traditionally attractive. These qualities, however, do not amount to *Nordic Noir*, and Kormákur is intent on explaining how the series reflects an Icelandic experience, not a Nordic one:

> We started with the idea of a claustrophobic winter situation, them being stuck inside the village with a murderer, and then it developed into *Ófærð*. Basically, we wanted to use the nature as one of the central characters in creating a suspense thriller, taking on, through a smaller society, the whole country and the themes of corruption and collapse. So we wanted to deal with both the political situation and the experience of living in that kind of nature.
>
> To me, "landscape porn" is when you use landscapes without having a real purpose - only to show the beauty of it - but what we are trying to do here, and I do it in my films as well, is to use nature as a storytelling device. It's a character in the story and in this case it's also part of the plot. You have this huge range of mountains around the village, and then you have those claustrophobic villages which are stuck in the valley.[651]

The sense of claustrophobia is a central part of *Trapped*, as reflected in the English title - not just in terms of the characters being trapped in blizzard, but in many other ways, too. The characters are stuck in the small village due to a natural phenomenon, but the protagonist, Andri, is also stuck in his life both physically and geographically (living in the same house as his in-laws). According to Kormákur, this sense of isolation and claustrophobia speaks directly to the Icelandic experience where you have to accept the overwhelming powers of nature. This is also reflected in the poetic title sequence which combines *aerial shots* of Iceland and extreme close-ups of the human body to illustrate the juxtaposition of man and nature in Iceland, accompanied by the beautiful classical theme by Jóhann Jóhannsson, Hildur Gudnadóttir and Rutger Hoedemakers. "If you fly high, the rivers feel like veins in a body, and the earth and the human body start to look the same," as Kormákur explains. "The closer you get to the body and the further away you get from the earth. It's all like one big organism."[652]

A central difference between *Nordic Noirs*, such as *Forbrydelsen* and *Bron/Broen*, and *Ófærð* is seen in the environment and the characters. *Forbrydelsen* and *Bron/Broen* take place in urban Scandinavian environments, whereas *Ófærð* takes place in a snowy Icelandic village (more similar to *Twin Peaks* than to any of its Scandinavian ancestors). And where Martin Rohde in *Bron/Broen* is a goofy, jovial cop - a humorous contrast to the socially awkward but much more professional attitude of his Swedish counterpart, Saga Norén - Andri is a pensive and brooding man with an imposing physique but a quiet personality. In the words of Kormákur:

> I wanted Andri to look a certain way. He's an unusually big lead actor - and I had to defend that to some of our partners because the German TV stations, for example, would rather have an attractive lead character for the female audiences. It was important to me that he

looked that way, that he was like a pro. He's a part of the mountain, a part of the landscape. And on the other hand you could describe his female partner almost as an elf. I wanted to portray them in the same way that I portray the landscapes. It is about people in landscapes and landscapes in people.

Also, I didn't want to create this kind of typical *noir* character who's drinking or taking pills. We wanted a warmer character. He's actually nice to his children. He wants to be a good father, and he wants to be involved in their lives. Normally, the cop has left his wife because he devotes himself to his work, but in this case she has left him, not because of his work, but because their relationship wasn't good anymore. And now he's living with his in-laws in her village.

What I was conscious about with *Forbrydelsen* and *Bron/Broen* was the stylishness of those shows. I didn't want that. I didn't want them drawing their plans on glass or something like that. I wanted it to be raw and to present a small-town element. I wanted to give it a provincial, western feel, also because the lead actor has this stoic, Clint Eastwoody quality. But, then, there's also a bit of Agatha Christie with the *locked room mystery*. You would not confuse this show with any of the *Scandinavian Noirs*. When you were watching it, you would say: "Oh, that's the Icelandic one."[653]

Torfinnur Jákupsson (creator) on *TROM* (KVF, 2021) as a Nordic crime series and a local phenomenon

Over the past few years, the Nordic brand of crime fiction has become broader and more inclusive, welcoming inspiration from both American and British crime series, and TV creators from smaller countries like Iceland and Faroe Islands have introduced some new types of crime stories that are indelibly local.

In 2021 the first Faroese crime series, *TROM*, will premiere on KVF, and it has already been pre-sold to ZDF/Arte for Germany and France. Below, the creator Torfinnur Jákupsson comments on *TROM* as a uniquely Faroese crime drama, and like Baltasar Kormákur and Nic Pizzolatto he points to the local landscape as a central part of the tone and atmosphere in his series. Like *Ófærð*, *TROM* is related to the *Nordic Noir* genre, but it is also, specifically, colored by the Faroese country and people.

Jákupsson: *TROM* is a contemporary crime series with an environmental angle that touches on some of the themes that affect us all as human beings today.

When I was three, I almost drowned. Ever since then, I've had a fascination with the ocean and the idea that what keeps us alive can just as quickly become our biggest threat. In the Faroes, we are very closely connected to nature as well as each other, and that works as a framework for the series – the landscape itself affecting and molding our characters as much as the other way around. To a certain extent, the Faroes are our main character. The islands are among the safest places in the world, and our series reflects that for better or worse. It offers a lot of fun contrasts. When you come to the Faroes, it's like stepping back in time. But it's a highly modern society. The whole of the Faroes is like a small town, but also a sort of modern wild west in the middle of the North Atlantic. The Faroese are a people with their own strong identity, but at the same time we're part of the Danish kingdom. We have a very dark sense of humor and don't take things too seriously, but at the same time we may often seem like very serious people.

Many of these cultural things are interesting to play around with in the series. We are attempting to create an iconic series, but that is a big challenge in itself. Nothing's new under the sun. Not to mention the fact that it's set in the Faroes where no such series has ever been produced before. It's challenging but also extremely exciting. *TROM* is hopefully just the beginning of something much bigger.[654]

From Holmes to Hercules: New Traditions and Hybrids

An interesting example of the "mirrored influences" in modern crime fiction is found in the British crime series *Luther*, which combines elements of the traditional *whodunit* with a darker, more melancholy tone akin to *Nordic noir* and a grittier sense of realism reminiscent of the American *hardboiled* tradition. *Luther* takes place in London and follows a *whodunit* structure, but it is a creepier and more *noir*ish version of London than the thriving, homely cityscape that audiences know from the modern adaptation of *Sherlock* (BBC, 2010-2017). The use of *time-lapse* photography and traditional signposts such as the London Eye in the title sequence to BBC's *Sherlock* creates a sense of safety and familiarity that fits the lighthearted music, the emblematic detective and the largely episodic structure. In *Luther*, on the other hand, we are dealing with a bleaker and less attractive version of London. Not the iconic detective and the tourist attractions, but the hidden, seedy underbelly. As the main director Sam Miller puts it:

> I was drawn to *Luther* because I liked how intricate and sophisticated the writing was, but what was magical about the series was the presence of Idris Elba because he turned the character into a superhero. What Idris brought to it was something bigger, something grander - an almost Homeric or Greek dimension to the character - and that also made it play differently in America because he felt almost like a character from the Marvel universe. There's something Herculean about Luther: The world is on his shoulders, and he has to go through and endure all these tasks. But there's a resoluteness to his character that makes you feel safe with him and allows the series to be extremely violent, even sexually violent and gory. Each form of crazy or psychotic madness that he has to encounter, he meets with a sense of resoluteness and order.
>
> The series became a love-song to London, especially the East End. It was about the lee of the city, the lee of the citadel, sheltering in the shadows of the towers. That was where the series lived, and it was a part of the city that was close to both mine and Idris' heart. Idris grew up in that area, and Neil Cross had a connection to that area as well, and that kind of rooted the series in the real architecture and fabric of the city. It was not a deliberately flashy use of London. It was scrappy and punky, kind of what Brooklyn is (or used to be) to New York. There's something kind of windswept, bleak and dangerous about it.[655]

When conceptualizing *The Sopranos*, David Chase was adamant about making a gangster series *outside* of New York. It should be rural and take place in an environment (in New Jersey) that we rarely see in television, and the same thing could be said of *Luther* (which depicts an often un-seen part of London).

A native of London, Idris Elba brought a certain pedigree to *Luther*, also because he played a prominent part in *The Wire* (the drug mogul Stringer Bell). In that sense, Elba may have contributed to *Luther's* transnational success, and, as mentioned earlier, it was one of the top-rated series on BBC America. The success of *Luther* moreover made people notice the directorial flair of Sam Miller, who brought his alternative approach to staging and dialogues when working as an episode director on *American Crime*. Commuting between England and America, Miller also co-directed the *Nordic Noir*-inspired thriller *Fortitude* (SkyAtlantic, 2015-2018), starring *Forbrydelsen*'s Sofie Gråbøl (who also had a cameo in AMC's *The Killing*), and this illustrates the *cross-cultural mobility* of talent, trends and traditions.

Like Sam Miller, the Danish director Susanne Bier exemplifies the *cross-cultural mobility* of talents in today's TV landscape, and HBO's most recent crime series, *The Undoing* (HBO, 2020), thrives on a combination of Bier's directorial trademarks – a moving, restless camera, out-of-focus shots and extreme close-ups of eyes – with David E. Kelley's efficient writing style and their mutual respect for classical genre fiction. The popular HBO series by Kelley and Bier has been described, somewhat pejoratively, as "lifestyle porn," yet it has also garnered attention for its interesting *whodunit* structure where the main suspect, a narcissistic doctor played by Hugh Grant, almost succeeds in convincing the audience that he is innocent. The strangely inauthentic acting style of Grant cleverly reflects the character's constant role-playing, and the series has been described, by Grant himself, as "a *Scandi noir* thriller with a massive and, I hope, successful *whodunit* element."[656]

Like Susanne Bier, Tobias Lindholm has become a famous Danish film and TV director, lauded for his raw and realistic sensibility in films such as *R* (2010) and *Kapringen* (*A Hijacking*, 2012), before migrating to the US to work as an episode director on *Mindhunter* (Netflix, 2017-). Though employing a cool and expressive audiovisual style, *Mindhunter* is a good example of the realistic tendency in modern crime fiction in that it explores true crimes and historical serial killers in a fictional format.

True Detective adapted its title from the popular *true crime* magazines, but since the premiere of Pizzolatto's series, we have witnessed a regular boom of *true crime* series that use *True Detective*-like *drone shots* and suspenseful music to reconstruct and dramatize real-life crime stories (cf. *The Jinx* [HBO, 2015] and *Making a Murderer* [Netflix, 2015-2018]).[657] At the same time, we have seen a number of modern crime series that explicitly reference real crime stories, but within a fictional format (cf. Tobias Lindholm's TV2 series, *Efterforskningen*, about the brutal killing of the Swedish journalist Kim Wall).

Crime fiction is an old and broad genre with a long cinematic and televisual history and a wide range of subgenres and tropes.[658] Traditional *whodunits* are often episodic, employing a *murder of the week*-template, but in the global TV landscape we are now seeing an ongoing exchange between different cultural traditions and tendencies: from Holmesian and episodic *whodunits* to different types of *noir* and more realistic sensibilities. Even the more traditional crime series, like *Bosch* and *Sherlock*, are adapted to a modern context by utilizing various platforms and employing modern forms of audience engagement. *Bosch* invited its viewers to binge the sixth season during COV-

Susanne Bier on *The Undoing* and different genre traditions

My work has always existed in a sort of intermediate space between traditional genre films and art cinema. Even *Hævnen* (2010) and some of my other Danish films combine elements of arthouse cinema and traditional genre films. I come from a state-funded film tradition in Denmark, so when I make big, international TV series, they are born out of a combination of an aesthetic language, which I have refined over the course of many years, and a general respect for genres. I began making genre films, and I have always happily existed in that space between genre films and arthouse cinema.

Before Dogme95, Danish films had often tried to imitate American films, but when Dogme95 came along, Danish films became more interesting because they could only focus on the story and the characters. We have always had a strong literary tradition, and suddenly it seemed as if Danish films began to tap into that tradition. In that sense, it does not seem strange, when looking at *high-end* miniseries and drama series like *Succession*, that they look to Dogme95 or John Cassavetes for inspiration.

Playing with Style: *The Night Manager* (BBC One/AMC, 2016) and *The Undoing* were both *cross-boarded*. When you direct the whole series and shoot it like one long film, you effectively have the executive artistic vision, and I would not have agreed to simply direct one episode. I need to work in close collaboration with the writer and take over the responsibility for our shared vision when directing the series. The style in a TV series is not just a matter of visual preferences. There is a musicality to it that cannot simply be emulated, and, therefore, the idea of inheriting a style seems problematic to me.

It is funny that you should mention not just my use of handheld camera and extreme close-ups, but also my use of *rack focus*, because people almost never notice that aspect. Those elements are definitely aesthetic preferences for me, and I am very conscious about it. You can of course use *rack focus* in a traditional way, but I love to use it in an irrational way where we suddenly focus on the "wrong" thing. It is not coincidental at all, but there is an element of *Verfremdung* to it. That is also the case when it comes to the handheld camera and the extreme close-ups, which have always been a part of my aesthetic. It might be difficult to explain why, but you are never fully at ease when watching the series. And that was my intention.

We absolutely try to toy with the audience. Part of it can be ascribed to Hugh Grant and his abilities as an actor. At one point he seems 100% sincere and authentic, and then, suddenly, he seems strangely unbelievable. He gave us different levels of authenticity while playing Jonathan, and then we tweaked it in post-production.

ID-19 and interact with the creators. Even more interactive, *Sherlock* uses snappy intertextual comments (e.g. references to the first Sherlock Holmes film, *Sherlock Holmes Baffled* [1900], and subtle allusions to Doyle's *The Adventure of the Naval Treaty* [1893]) as well as ultra-swift visual *cues* that invite the *forensic fans* to pause the action and look for clues to the mystery.[659] Different environments and cultural traditions may function as visual attractions in the global TV landscape, but they are cross-influencing each other in complex ways and merging into new mysterious hybrids that, like the crimes they depict, transgress borders, territories and platforms.

Media Literacy and the (Un)mediated Self: Teen Drama in the *Multiplatform Era*

> My biggest concern was reaching the target audience. I was not sure I would be able to, knowing how critical and flaky they are. Creating something they seemed to like felt like a huge achievement.
> - Julie Andem, TV creator (SKAM)[660]

> We haven't had a *Skins* or a *SKAM*. But we've always had a hard time treating the inner worlds of young people with the emotional depth that they deserve.
> - Sam Levinson, TV creator (Euphoria)[661]

Crime fiction, in its various iterations and mutations, is a traditional genre that has existed in television since the advent of the medium. Teen drama, on the other hand, is a relatively new genre in film and television, and in American TV it is often described as an outgrowth of the *serial melodrama*.[662] Traditional *serial melodramas*, e.g. *Days of Our Lives* (NBC, 1965-) and *The Young and the Restless* (CBS, 1973-), often deal with problems connected to the entire family.[663] Teen dramas, by comparison, focus on young ensembles and teenage problems and often cater to young, media savvy audiences through popular music, references to modern media, stylistic playfulness and "frequent intertextual references."[664]

As opposed to crime series, which are defined by a set of formal, narrative and stylistic qualities, a teen drama is not only defined by dealing with issues and rites connected to adolescence, but also by appealing to a young demographic. Thus, as Sharon Marie Ross and Louisa Ellen Stein argue, the term "teen television" refers to the on-screen characters, the thematic concerns and the central arenas of the given series, but also - and perhaps more importantly - to the target audience.[665] In accordance with the Danish media scholars Kirsten Drotner and Anders Lysne, we might describe teen dramas as TV series 'about', 'made for' and/or 'consumed by' young audiences.[666] But there is nonetheless a complex relationship between *teen dramas* and their audiences, as Catherine Driscoll notes, and "the 'teen audience' is not confined to teenagers."[667]

In this context, some critics distinguish between *teen series* and *youth series*, and this distinction is also reflected in the shifting terminologies across different industries, cultures and practitioners (even among the interviewees for this book). In Scandinavia, for example, the term "ungdomsserie" (*youth series*) refers to a broad genre that depicts and targets young people, but without focusing exclusively on teenagers, and this genre is an integral part of Scandinavian *public service* channels like SVT, NRK and DR. But even in America, *teen drama* is something of an elastic term, and Driscoll argues that critics should accept this fluidity instead of complicating matters through unnecessary distinctions and a rigid, biological understanding of the word "teenager":

> [S]eparating 'teen' and 'youth' film obscures the importance of their shared discourse on adolescence. Some films emphasize the institutionally framed world of dependent adolescence, and others the refusal or struggle with that framing, but a vast number of films explore their interdependence.[668]

Or as Adrian Martin cogently puts it:

> [T]he teen in teen movie is itself a very elastic, bill-of-fare word; it refers not to biological age, but a type, a mode of behaviour, a way of being... The teen in teen movie means something more like youth.[669]

This fuzziness is even reflected in the actual ages of the actors and actresses. The noticeable, at times blatant, discrepancy between the character's age and that of the actor in a teen drama reflects the vagueness of the concept itself, and is also a legal or financial matter. "If they cast teens with actors who are their real age, then due to child labor laws they are limited to how much time they're allowed to work and also need a teacher to keep schooling up - and that teacher would have to be paid," as casting director Johanna Ray (e.g. *Beverly Hills 90210*) says. "So it would cost more money and less time on the set."[670]

In this section of the book, I will explore teen dramas in the *multiplatform era*, with a particular focus on Sam Levinson's American series *Euphoria* and its different sources of inspiration (from the Israeli 'mother series' by Ron Leshem to the different European influences, e.g. François Truffaut and Julie Andem, and the biographical aspects). There are significant variations in teen drama across different industries and cultures, and a detailed account of all these industrial particularities and cultural traditions is beyond the scope of this book. What is of interest here is the *cross-influencing* between different traditions and series and the ways in which modern teen drama - perhaps more so than any other genre - reflects a global TV landscape by depicting the *mediatization* of life and society and by engaging their audiences through multiple media and platforms. Teen dramas deal with "the historically changing experience of adolescence," and, as Driscoll writes, they often follow a set of narrative conventions:

> The youthfulness of the central characters; content usually centered on young heterosexuality, frequently with a romance plot; intense age-based peer relationships and conflict either within those relationships or with an older generation; the institutional management of adolescence by families, schools, and other institutions; and coming-of-age plots focused on motifs like virginity, graduation, and the makeover.[671]

Many of those themes and conventions also emerge in the examples used in this book, including the central case, *Euphoria*. But modern teen dramas, I will argue, often deal with issues concerning *intimacy*, *privacy* and *mediacy* in a more explicit way, thereby reflecting a global media landscape where young people interact through various new media and platforms without confining themselves to any one territory or tradition.

Beverly and Beyond: A Historical Introduction

The term *teen drama* might be relatively new in the context of film and TV history, but it has complex roots and noteworthy precursors going back to the early years of cinema. In his seminal book *Teen Movies: American Youth on Screen* (2005), Timothy Shary traces its roots back to one of the earliest *attraction films* by the Lumière Brothers: *L'arroseur arrosé* (*Tables Turned on the Gardener*, 1895). In that film, we see a gardener and a young, naughty boy. The young boy steps on the garden hose, and as the gardener checks his hose to see what has happened, the young boy removes his foot, resulting in a humorous sprinkling 'mishap'. The gardener eventually discovers the boy and punishes him for his tomfoolery, either by hosing him down or spanking him. That film, which was part of the first official Lumière screening in December 1895, can hardly be characterized as a teen drama, but it illustrated an early interest in generational conflict and "youth at play."[672] Following that, in the 1920s, a number of films were released in America that dealt more explicitly with young people, often in the guise of flappers and juvenile delinquents.[673] These films, including *The House of Youth* (1924), *Campus Flirt* (1926) and *Our Dancing Daughters* (1928), often portrayed young people as a potential menace to society, but the young men and women were an evident part of the cinematic attraction. *Harold Teen* (1928), for example, was promoted as a "peppy collegiate musical," and this description illustrates two things: (1) That young people were part of the attraction, and (2) that teen drama or *youth film* was not yet a generic category in its own right. Rick Altman has argued that we often use nouns to describe well-known and well-defined genres (e.g. *teen drama*), whereas we often use adjectives to describe new or less recognized genres, often combined with a "broader established category" (e.g. *collegiate musical*).[674]

In the 1930s, the number of youth-oriented films increased rapidly, and the young star Deanna Durbin, through films like *Three Smart Girls* (1936) and *That Certain Age* (1938), helped save Universal from potential bankruptcy.[675] The first boom of the genre was in the 1950s, however, coinciding with the emergence of the word "teenager" to describe a new group of filmgoers with actual purchasing power. The word "teenager" dates back to the early 1900s, but it was not broadly used until the 1950s where J. Edgar Hoover warned Americans of "an appalling increase in the number of crimes that will be committed by teenagers in the years ahead."[676] If there had been films about naughty boys and juvenile delinquents since the earliest days of cinema, we now saw an actual wave of *juvenile delinquency films* (e.g. *The Delinquents* from 1957), and they often featured attractive young men and women and cool popular music (cf. the innovative use of "Rock Around the Clock" in *Blackboard Jungle* [1955]). Films like *The Wild One* (1953) and *Rebel Without a Cause* (1955) became early touchstones of the genre, and they were followed by a series of youth-centric films made during the New Waves of the 1960s and 70s (e.g. *Les quatre cents coups/The 400 Blows* [1959], *Le souffle au cœur/Murmur of the Heart* [1971], *The Last Picture Show* [1971] and *American Graffiti* [1973]) and often featuring catchy pop and rock scores.

From the 1970s, teen movies became a central part of the Hollywood system. New directors with a teen movie pedigree started to emerge (e.g. John Hughes), and the genre began to merge and mutate into different hybrids. From *teen horror* (e.g. *Friday the 13th* [1980] and *A Nightmare on Elm Street* [1984]) to *teen comedy* (e.g. *Animal House* [1978] and *Fast Times at Ridgemont High* [1982]) and even *teenage sci-fi* (e.g. *Bill and Ted's Excellent Adventure*, 1989).[677]

During this era, teen dramas also became a more visible part of the TV landscape, starting with the Canadian series *Degrassi Junior High* (CBC/PBS, 1987-1989) and its American and Australian descendants: *Beverly Hills 90210* (Fox, 1990-2000) and *Heartbreak High* (Network Ten/ABC TV, 1994-1999). These series, sometimes described as *teen-soaps*, followed the basic structure of a traditional *serial melodrama* where each episode featured a new self-contained dilemma and functioned as an *ephemeral daily check-in*. The educational aspects were evident, as the episodic dilemmas often dealt with issues like drug and alcohol abuse (e.g. when Dylan in *Beverly Hills 90210* falls off the wagon or when David starts doing drugs to keep him awake for the night shift on the radio), homosexuality (e.g. when Kelly discovers that her date, Kyle, is gay), teen pregnancy (e.g. when Brenda fears that she is pregnant) and inequality in terms of race and class (e.g. when Brandon crashes into his African-American neighbor Sherice, or where he is schooled by the Latina girl, Karla, about life in East LA). The structure of these series was largely episodic, but they also had longer arcs connected to the characters and their shifting relationships, and they often featured intertextual references and hip popular music. *Beverly Hills 90210*, for example, used REM's "Losing My Religion" as a sort of *leitmotif* for the stormy relationship between Brenda (Shannen Doherty) and Dylan (Luke Perry), and numerous acts performed "live" at the local café-turned-club: Peach Pit After Dark.[678] The intertextual elements were also evident - from the *implicit allusions* to Marlon Brando's *The Wild One* and James Dean's *Rebel Without a Cause*, via Brandon and Dylan, to the *explicit references* to series like *Twin Peaks*, films like *Casablanca* (1942) and cinematic waves like *cinema vérité* and *Nouvelle Vague*. As the Danish media scholar Karen Klitgaard Povlsen argues, *Beverly Hills 90210* was an early example of the intertextuality and media-reflexivity that we often see in modern teen dramas, but it had an anonymous audiovisual style.[679] In fact, Tim Hunter has said that he was discontinued on *Beverly Hills 90210* after using some of his stylistic trademarks in the pilot episode (e.g. a *slow reveal* of Brandon lying in his bed that recalled the slow tilting camera from the opening of *River's Edge*). The visual experimentation and conspicuousness in the pilot episode did not sit well with Aaron Spelling, and, indeed, there is a clear stylistic shift between the pilot and the second episode.[680]

Media Literacy and the Modern Teen Drama

In the 1990s and early 2000s, the genre blossomed in American television, and channels like The WB and The CW emerged, focusing primarily on teenagers and young adults and bringing in fresh talents from the film industry. According to Jamie Kellner (former CEO of The WB):

> The people executing our shows have not come out of the same pool of talent as other networks have looked at. J.J. Abrams (*Felicity*) hadn't done TV before, Kevin Williamson (*Dawson's Creek*) hadn't done TV before. And we weren't getting the 'A' showrunners anyway because those folks were getting enormous payouts. So we had to look elsewhere, at film.[681]

In this period, American teen dramas began to hybridize, just like the teen movies had done a few decades earlier, and we saw a surge of different types of teen series. These included popular *teen horror* and vampire series like *Buffy the Vampire Slayer* (The WB/UPN, 1997-2003), *Vampire Diaries* (The CW, 2009-2017) and *Teen Wolf* (MTV, 2011-2017), stylish *teen-noirs* like *Veronica Mars* (UPN/The CW/Hulu, 2004-2019) and self-reflexive *teen-soaps* and mature youth dramas like *Felicity* (The WB, 1998-2002), *Dawson's Creek* (The WB, 1998-2003) and *One Tree Hill* (The WB/The CW, 2003-2012). At the same time, we saw a wave of raw and more transgressive teen dramas, inspired by the films of Larry Clark and Harmony Korine. These included the British series *Skins* (E4, 2007-2013) and its short-lived American remake (MTV, 2011) that dealt with mental illness and adolescent sexuality in a way that you could not see on American broadcast television.

When casting the title role for *Felicity*, a large number of potential actors were considered, as the agent and producer Tony Krantz remembers, and they ended up choosing Keri Russell because she was the only one who could pronounce the word "preface".[682] A curious anecdote, this story says something about the sophistication in modern teen dramas that are often centered on intelligent or bookish characters and that often feature intertextual references and metafictional elements that require a certain amount of *media literacy* (as Jeffrey Sconce calls it).[683] This was also reflected in *Dawson's Creek*, which, despite being a fairly straight *teen-soap*, included explicit references to *The Last Picture Show*, *Breakfast Club* and The French New Wave and numerous metafictional puns and in-jokes (e.g. about the use of *cutaways* in love-making scenes). Even more so, intertextuality and metafiction were a part of *Veronica Mars*, and it is a noticeable and playful element in *Riverdale* (The CW, 2017-) - a conspicuously stylish *teen-noir* that features actors from *Twin Peaks* and *Beverly Hills 90210* (Mädchen Amick and Luke Perry) and lifts its episode titles from significant films and precursors such as *Blackboard Jungle* and *River's Edge*. Perhaps Tim Hunter was hired as an episode director on that series precisely because of his history from independent film, but this time he was not asked to make it stylistically anonymous and inconspicuous. Quite the contrary:

> I didn't cast Luke Perry for *Beverly Hills 90210*, and, in fact, I didn't work with him until years later when I did an episode of *Riverdale* where he plays Archie's father. We had a good laugh over the fact that I did the pilot of *90210*, and then he entered the show afterwards. He said: "I always say that you directed the pilot, and I directed the other 300 episodes."
>
> Every episode of *Riverdale* has the name of a classic movie, and the title of the pilot was *Chapter One: River's Edge*, so, yes, I think they hired me because of *River's Edge*. I don't know what they thought. The ending of my episode was pretty interesting. They wanted it creepy, and I got it and cut it that way, and that was exactly the way it wound up in the show, but I haven't heard much from them. I tend to think that they felt I was not stylish enough on that episode, that maybe they wanted me to push it even further. They push the visuals more broadly on that show, and I may have shot my episode very specifically. I captured all of the nuances of that episode, but I think, in retrospect, that they had wanted me to go broader to a more conspicuous and showy visual style.[684]

Teen dramas have often employed popular music, intertextual references and metafictional in-jokes, but in *the multiplatform era* we are seeing a high degree of media reflexivity and a notable stylistic diversity: from the overt use of colors and lighting in *Riverdale* and *Euphoria* to the intimate use of close-ups and *shallow focus* in *SKAM* and *Normal People*. Teen dramas are still dealing with issues connected to adolescence. But as the lives of young people have become *mediatized*, modern *teen dramas* reflect (on) the interconnected problems of early adulthood and new media: issues concerning intimacy, privacy and mediacy.

New Media and Mediatized Problems: SKAM

The themes and issues connected to adolescence are relatively universal, and many of the problems that modern teen dramas explore are the same as in the popular teen dramas of the 1980s and 1990s. Young people are still struggling with peer pressure, ostracism and harassment connected to race, sexuality and religion. Many of these issues have become intensified by new media, however, and as the media scholar Stig Hjarvard argues, we are experiencing a rampant *mediatization* of life and society.[685] The lines between the public and private spheres have become blurred, and digital media are now a central part of our social lives and interactional space. Some scholars even describe the current era as a *media-saturated society*, arguing that digital media, in complex ways, contribute to and intensify the social and psychological issues of young people.[686] This is also reflected in modern teen dramas that often deal explicitly with the connection between traditional 'teen issues' and modern media.

As mentioned earlier, *Margot vs. Lily* concerns issues of loneliness and isolation, albeit in a humorous tone, through its story about a popular YouTuber who struggles to find lasting relationships outside of the virtual world. Similarly, but in a more sincere and melodramatic way, Julie Andem's *SKAM* focuses on pressing issues among young people today. An important difference between *SKAM* and many traditional teen dramas is that the main themes and dilemmas in the series were based on surveys and feedback from Norwegian adolescents. As Andem says:

> The title is very random. During auditions, we had the teens giving suggestions to what the title could be. *SKAM* was the only suggestion nobody in the production hated.
>
> The topics were chosen after doing research with the target audience. The goal was to try to create a show where the teens felt represented in an honest way. Not in the way grown-ups would like them to be, but the way they really are. We tried to create something for Norwegian teens that they could relate to and identify with, and if people from all over the world relate to that, I guess it just tells us that we are not that different?
>
> We wanted to create a concept that could go on for a while, but still feel fresh every season. Being a public broadcaster, NRK always has to think about how it can serve the public more than just entertain. Doing research for *SKAM*, it became apparent that teenagers today struggle with the pressure to perform in every aspect of life. We wanted to try to create a show that could take some of that pressure off. One of the ways we tried to do that was by showing how everyone you meet is fighting their own battle. I guess we tried to teach them patience with each other.[687]

Not unlike the British series *Skins*, *SKAM* revolves around issues to do with race and religion (as seen in Season 4, which focuses on the Muslim girl Sana and her efforts to be accepted), sexuality (as seen in Season 3 where Isak struggles to open up about his homosexuality) and mental illness (connected to Even and his bipolar disorder). Especially intense and topical is the depiction of sexual assault in the second season where we follow the beautiful girl Noora (Josefine Frida Pettersen). Noora and her boyfriend William (Thomas Hayes) have relationship issues, and she comes over to patch things up with him. William is not there, though, and instead his older brother, Nikolai ("Niko"), invites her into the apartment where they are having a party, only to tell her that William is aggressive, manipulative and unfaithful. Heartbroken, Noora takes a glass of wine, and what follows is a harrowing depiction of sexual assault where different shots of Noora and the other partygoers are connected in a non-linear montage, interrupted by lengthy *blackouts* and *out-of-focus shots* that illustrate Noora's inebriated state of mind. The following episode (Ep. 2:9) then begins with a series of uneasy close-ups of Noora who is lying naked in bed next to Niko and another young woman, and in the following days she is confused and ashamed (*SKAM* means "shame") about what has happened. She isolates herself from her peers and messages Niko, hoping that she simply fell asleep. At first he reassures her that nothing happened, but then suddenly he sends her a naked photo of her with the following comment: "Just found this picture on my phone, and then remembered EVERYTHING! You were so horny. Haha! Behaved like a little whore."

Sexual assault is not a new problem, and it has been a part of teen dramas since *Degrassi* and *Beverly Hills 90210* (Paige was date raped in *Degrassi*, as was Kelly in *90210*). In *SKAM*, though, the consequences of the sexual assault are intensified and prolonged by new media, as Niko not only assaults Noora, but takes pictures of her without her consent and uses them afterwards, in an attempt to blackmail her. The educational aspect is a central part of *SKAM*, as it was in traditional teen dramas, but Andem focuses more on the psychological consequences of sexual assault than the ethical and legal aspects in themselves. This is illustrated in the use of *jump-cuts*, handheld camera and tight close-ups, creating an intense and claustrophobic space around Noora, and it is particularly evident in Ep. 2:10, which opens on a three-minute long (!) close-up of Noora, who is texting with William and trying to deal with the impact of Niko's abuse while isolating herself from her boyfriend and her roommates.

In reference to *soap operas*, the TV scholar Tania Modleski has written that "close-ups provide the spectator with training in 'reading' other people, in being sensitive to their (unspoken) feelings at any given moment," and that seems to be the point in this and many other scenes from *SKAM*.[688] Andem champions the use of tight close-ups and *mute texts* throughout her series, and the intimacy and emotional impact of these close-ups become even stronger when viewers watch the series on their smartphones. As the Norwegian scholar Gry Rustad writes:

> Just as the close-up was well-suited for the small older television screen, the close-up is perfect for the smartphone screen. The close-up becomes even more intimate when watched on the phone because [...] for many of the young viewers the smartphone is their most personal belonging, it is what they first see when they wake up and the last thing they check when they go to bed.[689]

According to Casey J. McCormick, the direct camera addresses in *House of Cards* were particularly effective due to the intimacy of the viewing situation. McCormick argued that Beau Willimon created a sort of *Skype ontology* in his series, and similarly we could describe the style of *SKAM* as a sort of *smartphone ontology*, exploiting modern media to create an intimate or even personal space.

In Andem's series, viewers are often invited into an intimate space and asked to reflect upon issues like peer pressure and exclusion in the context of modern media. In the fourth season, for example, Sana (Iman Meskini) has taken a photo of Isak's private chat with a girl named Sara, who is doing her best to exclude Sana. Sana creates an Instagram profile and posts the hideous comments by Sara, in a dubious attempt to let everyone know how shallow and untrustworthy she is. But the plan backfires, and soon everybody begins to write about the anonymous Instagrammer. This example has been described by one reviewer as "preachy," but it portrays the psychological effects of *cyberbullying* in a convincing way, and the season is more about Sana's fear of exclusion than about *cyberbullying* as a moral issue in a *media-saturated society*.[690]

The same thing could be said about Isak's story in the third season, a story that does not deal with the social consequences of coming out, but with the fear of social stigmatization and exclusion. The trailer, which was launched ahead of the third season, humorously hinted at the themes of homosexuality and fear of disapproval through references to Brian De Palma and his famous Stephen King adaptation *Carrie* (1976). In the trailer, we see Isak (Tarjei Sandvik Moe) in the school's locker room, gazing at the other half-clad boys. The boys are playing around with a water bottle, and the use of *super slow motion* and not-so-subtle eroticism are immediately reminiscent of the opening to *Carrie* (where the girls are showering in *slow motion*). In the trailer, Andem alternates between *point glance* shots of Isak leering at the other boys or shamefully looking down, and *low-angle shots* of the semi-naked boys, focusing explicitly on their groin area. Isak's friend, Jonas (Marlon Langeland), grabs a box of milk and throws it against the wall right behind Isak, whose face is soon covered in milk (almost like Carrie whose face is covered in blood at a crucial point in De Palma's film).

Andem wrote and directed all the trailers herself, and the coming-out scene where Isak reveals his homosexuality to Jonas was inspired by the experiences of a real Norwegian boy. As Andem says:

> It was based on an interview I did with a 17-year-old gay boy: He told me that he came out to two of his best friends in a Messenger group chat, and the way he did it was to have them guess who he was interested in. He would give them more and more clues and the last clue was "it's not a girl". He described their reaction as "disappointingly undramatic". I thought that was a sweet story and went with it.[691]

SKAM soon became a global phenomenon, and it was the most popular streaming sensation in all of Scandinavia.[692] Many people noticed its intimate close-ups and relatable stories, but it was particularly innovative in terms of distribution and engagement (even if some scholars have questioned the quantity and quality of the fan engagement via Facebook groups like Koseg-ruppa).[693] Not only were the plots based on real-life stories from Norwegian adolescents, they were also distributed in a modern way that utilized multiple media and platforms. Small clips and conversations from social media like Instagram and Facebook were published in real-time (as indicated on the screen in capital yellow letters), which were then combined into episodes that were released on a weekly basis on NRK's website and then on *linear* TV. "The show packs a punch and is leading the way in exploring multi-platform storytelling," as Simon Fuller has put it, and some people have even described it as "the future of storytelling."[694] As Andem explains:

> At NRK we have been creating transmedia shows like *SKAM* since 2008 (*SARA*, *Mia*, *JENTER*), but always for a younger audience (10-12 years old). *SKAM* was an experiment to see if that kind of show could work for an older audience. Everything was pre-planned, the social media drops were planned as soon as the scripts were done. One of the most important measures of success in these kinds of shows is fan activity and engagement. We always tried to come up with new ideas for how to engage the fans in the show, and the community around the show.[695]

When The WB was launched in America, it was meant to target a previously neglected demographic (females aged 12-34), and it did so through popular teen dramas and "frilly pink bedroom shows."[696] Similarly, *SKAM* targeted young people, especially young females, and as the Norwegian scholar Vilde Schanke Sundet writes, it was quite successful. At the end of the second season, a survey by NRK showed that 98% of young Norwegians (15-29 years) knew about *SKAM*, and 70% had seen the series.[697] The reason for its popularity might have been its thorough research among Norwegian adolescents, but it might also have been its focus on teen problems in a *media-saturated society*, its smartphone-friendly aesthetic and its innovative use of new media and multiple platforms.

Fig. 46: Julie Andem's *SKAM* is based on meticulous research among Norwegian teens, and it utilizes new media and multiple platforms to tell an authentic and engaging story about real issues for teenagers in a *mediatized* society. In this picture, we see Jonas (left) and his friend, Isak (right), who is the central character in the third season. Photo: NRK.

Un-Shaming Teen Drama: From *Eagles* to *No Filter*

An interesting hybrid of *SKAM* and popular American teen dramas, the Swedish series *Eagles* (SVT, 2019-) was inspired by the creator Stefan Lindén's own upbringing in the provincial small town of Oskarshamn. The series deals with the former NHL star Mats Kroon (Per Larsson) who returns to Oskarshamn from Boston with his adolescent children Felicia (Alva Bratt) and Elias (Edvard Olsson). From there, the series develops into a fairly traditional teen drama about star-crossed lovers, rivalry and trying to fit in while living up to both parental and social expectations. The basic premise is similar to American teen dramas (cf. episode titles like "Homecoming"), and the visual likeness to *One Tree Hill* and *The O.C.* (Fox, 2003-2007) is also evident, especially in the use of *lens flare* effects and *Steadicam shots* in the hockey matches, recalling the football matches and the moving camera in *Friday Night Lights* (NBC, 2006-2011).[698]

Even if American teen dramas were popular among Scandinavian teens, there was no broad interest in doing, let alone commissioning, Americanized teen dramas in countries like Sweden, when Lindén first started pitching his idea. In fact, neither SVT nor C More wanted it. This all changed after the success of *SKAM*, however, and soon Lindén and the producer Sanne Övermark began doing research among young Swedish audiences and fleshing out the idea for *Eagles*.

Like *SKAM*, *Eagles* was based on a lengthy and thorough research phase, and it also dealt with typical teen issues in a *media-saturated society*, as illustrated in Felicia whose role as a popular influencer becomes the center of both psychological and social conflicts. In a narrative and stylistic sense, though, *Eagles* is closer to an American tradition, and perhaps this, along with the portrayal of sports and small-town life, is the reason for its surprising popularity and fan base in countries like Russia, Ukraine and Indonesia.[699]

Series like *SKAM* and *Margot vs. Lily* reflect a modern society where digital and social media function as central tools and arenas for young people. Some critics and philosophers describe this *mediatized* social sphere as a substitute or *simulacrum*, while other media scholars describe it as an "*augmentation* of social reality."[702] Modern teen dramas reflect both understandings of digital and social media, and they often thematize teenagers' reliance on modern media while utilizing social platforms and digital media as part of their distribution and marketing campaigns.

A radical case in this context is the Finnish Instagram series *No Filter* (Yle, 2019), which was created by Janne Lankoski and Hyppe Salmi. Before working on *No Filter*, Salmi had a strong background in youth-oriented programming at the Finnish public service channel Yle and had commissioned the series *Karma* (2017) from a small independent company called Ryöväri. *Karma* was one of the first series produced for Instagram Stories, and with *No Filter*, Lankoski and Salmi wanted to experiment with creating a series meant for both Instagram and Yle's VOD platform Areena. As Salmi says:

> We wanted to create an immersive, authentic and even a bit terrifying series of all the possible ways your real life could be revealed by your phone as opposed to the way the target group usually use their phones to make themselves look good in social media. The teens and young adults have their mobiles with them all the time, even in the bed and the bathroom. They have everything on their phones: the pictures, the chats, the secrets.
>
> For the series, we created seven fictional social media stereotypes, one protagonist for each of the episodes, and made them use the fictional application NOFILTER. It was sort of an inside joke, as we all know that some of the real-life influencers use #nofilter in their posts, even if it's easy to see that there are filters.
>
> When the viewer is holding his/her own phone in his/her own hand and watching NOFILTER, it is as if s/he were holding the phone of the main character. In each episode, the viewer is able to see both the posts the influencer is making for the social media – posh, shiny, partially false – and everything else that is happening in or around the phone in their real life. The viewer can see through the cameras of the phone, hear the audio or the phone calls, see the chats or the browsing in other platforms. It is extremely immersive, as if it were happening to you![703]

Using Instagram Stories, Lankoski had to shoot the series vertically with a smartphone, but Lankoski and Salmi took advantage of the development in Instagram Stories since the release of their previous series *Karma*. From 2017 to 2019, the medium had changed dramatically, now allowing Lankoski and Salmi to take content out from Instagram, add production value in post-pro-

Stefan Lindén (writer/creator) and Sanne Övermark (executive producer) on *Eagles* and modern teen dramas

Lindén: In my early teen years, I started watching a lot of teen dramas, mostly American. *Dawson's Creeks* that was the first one about a small-town movie nerd, kind of like me. The second one was *One Tree Hill*. That was about basketball and love in a small town, and I played basketball. The third one was *O.C.* and was nothing like my life, but what all of them had in common was that the characters of the series lived lives that I, in a way, wanted to live. *Eagles* was born from my interest in the genre and my only relationship to the genre was through American shows. The American way of storytelling has a broader potential to reach larger audiences because it works with universal themes that a larger audience can relate to and take in. That belief became kind of my niche when I entered the industry, and it was always very clear to me that *Eagles* would carry that same anatomy as an American teen drama.

Our research process consisted of me, Anton Nyberg and Alexandra Thönnersten travelling to small towns in Sweden with a strong hockey connection to make hour-long interviews with high school students, hockey players, influencers and artists to get a grasp of what their lives looked like. In addition, we did surveys with teenagers where we mapped out their dreams for the future, how they pick TV shows, what genres and themes interest them, what they watch and what they think of it. We must look beyond what we believe audiences want and ask them; only they can tell us.

The creation of a 50/50 *writers' room* created both female and male characters that were interesting. That and a *mood reel* of American teen dramas became our pitch. In March 2018, we were commissioned for production.

To me personally, *SKAM* meant everything. There would be no *Eagles* if it wasn't for *SKAM*. I don't mean that the idea wouldn't have been there, but no broadcaster would have dared to commission it, if it hadn't been for *SKAM*.[700]

Övermark: *SKAM* opened the door and made the broadcasters realize that if we only have good content and relevant series, the teens will come (to visit at least). There is a huge need for content, and the teens are the ones with the most time to spend on streaming, and they are the best in terms of viral marketing in many ways. We try to add lines or details sometimes that refer to comments, ideas or hashtags that the fans used. We add relevant details that went viral in the target groups and so on. But we have also used their fears or hopes in the characters to build them for the next seasons. Some will become happy, some will not. But at least it will be emotional.[701]

Fig. 47: Alva Bratt getting in character as the young influencer Felicia Kroon in Stefan Lindén's *Eagles* (SVT, 2019-), which combines biographical aspects, meticulous research and elements from American teen dramas like *Dawson's Creek* and *One Tree Hill*. Courtesy of Stefan Lindén.

Fig. 48: The moving camera in the hockey matches became a visual signature of *Eagles*, recalling the camera work and high production value in *Friday Night Lights*. Courtesy of Stefan Lindén.

duction and save the content in "Highlights".[704]

Like *SKAM* and *Eagles*, *No Filter* was based on research and a fruitful interaction with young viewers and followers, and Salmi had, in fact, experimented with multiplatform storytelling and social media accounts for fictional characters years before Julie Andem revolutionized the teen drama genre in Norway. "We made a 'skam' years before *SKAM*," as Salmi cheekily puts it. "However, *SKAM* has been a game-changer. I just loved how it was able to scale the real-life challenges and breathe in the same rhythm with the audience. Also, it was an inspiring example that great content can travel, even if it is not in English but some weird Scandinavian language."[705]

In *No Filter*, the characters are hacked by the application NOFILTER, and this is the beginning of the nightmarish story about the flipside of digital media and digitized lives. The Danish series *Doggystyle* (DR3, 2018-) is less radical and more difficult to fit into a generic category. Often described as teen drama or *young adult fiction*, the series follows a young woman in her early twenties (Asta played by Rosemarie Mosbæk), who reluctantly moves back to her small hometown in Odsherred, a Danish equivalent to Oskarshamn. The creator, Anna Emma Haudal, rejects the term teen drama or *youth series* to describe *Doggystyle*, even if the series is often classified as such and even if it airs on DR3, an online service aimed at young audiences. As Haudal puts it:

> *Girls* and *Transparent* were my main points of inspiration when making *Doggystyle*, and like *Girls* it does not easily fit the label of *youth fiction* or *young adult fiction*. I do not really see it as a *youth series*. I never thought of it that way, and I do not think that there are that many similarities between *Doggystyle* and *SKAM*. It has young people in it, but it is not a *teen drama* as such, and from what I hear it seems to appeal to many different people, across different ages.
>
> When I developed *Doggystyle* for DR3, I always thought of it as *digital first*, and I used the web series format to let the stories dictate the episode lengths. Not the other way around.[706]

The title of the series refers to the main character who initially "seeks love and recognition in a submissive way," using Instagram and other social media to connect with people from the big city and hoping to please and become part of the in-crowd.[707] In the first season, Asta is adamant about going back to Copenhagen, instead of staying in her birth town together with her parents and her disabled sister. But as the story progresses, Asta begins to grow accustomed to the rural homeliness of Odsherred, and Odsherred becomes a more accepted and visible part of her. Interestingly, this change also affects the style and tone of the series: from a swift and vibrant editing style in the first season, showing and approximating the staged and digitized life of the main character, to a more mellow and slow-paced style in the second season. If the first season felt like a teen drama - unsettled and uneasy - the sec-

Fig. 49: The Finnish Instagram series *No Filter* (Yle, 2019) is a radical experiment with interactive, multiplatform storytelling and a clever reflection of the fluid boundaries between *frontstage* and *backstage* for modern, digitized teens. Courtesy of Hyppe Salmi.

Fig. 50: The tonal shift in *Doggystyle* (DR3, 2018-) illustrates a change in the central character, who comes across as an unsettled and unsatisfied post-teen in the first season, before maturing and settling down in the second season. Like its main character, *Doggystyle* is in-between, and it does not easily fit any traditional generic label. Photo: DR.

ond season feels like a mature and muted small-town drama about a character who is settling down in a peripheral and often forgotten part of Denmark.

Modern teen dramas and *youth series* often reflect a *media-saturated society* and young people who struggle with traditional issues like heartache, peer pressure and the fear of exclusion, but in a modern and *mediatized* form. Digital media and platforms have become an integral part of adolescent lives, and they have also become a natural part of the distribution and interactive marketing campaigns of modern teen dramas. This is seen in a radical form in series such as *No Filter* and *Centrum* (YouTube, 2020) - a no-budget production created by Jonas Risvig and various young people on the basis of input from followers via social media - and in a less extreme form in popular series like *SKAM*, *Eagles* and *Doggystyle*. Though dealing with traditional 'teen problems', many of these productions also reflect a modern, digital society where everything is mediated - experienced through different media and filters - and the yearning for an unfiltered form of intimacy and *immediacy*.[708]

The Private Sphere and the Intimate Lens: *Normal People*

Issues of intimacy and privacy are closely connected to adolescent life and have always been a part of teen dramas. The same thing is true of tight close-ups, heightened emotions and *mute texts* - elements that are inherited from the *serial melodrama*. Tim Hunter, for example, remembers an emotional scene from the ending of the pilot episode to *Beverly Hills 90210* where Brenda admits to having lied about her age in order to get a date with a young lawyer (Jason, played by Maxwell Caulfield). The emotional crescendo takes place in a car between Brenda and Jason, and as he asks her whether it was "fun playing grown-up," we cut to a close-up of Brenda with teary eyes, accompanied by an emotional piano piece on the soundtrack. "My feelings didn't change, just because I'm a few years younger than you," Brenda replies. This line and the shallow, misty-eyed close-up function as the climax to the scene, and Tim Hunter remembers how the producer Aaron Spelling moved up to him, as he was directing the scene, grabbed him by his shoulders and started yelling: "Make her cry, Timmy baby! Make her cry!"[709]

Close-ups, intimate scenes and strong emotions are all staples of the genre, in that sense, but in recent years we have seen a wave of teen dramas that explore an even more intimate space, using tight close-ups and extreme *shallow focus* in an almost impressionistic and intrusive way. As if we, the viewers, were intruding on a private and very intimate affair.

The most radical and popular example of this tendency is the Irish drama *Normal People* (BBC Three/RTÉ One/Hulu, 2020), which was adapted from Sally Rooney's eponymous book and produced by Element Pictures. *Normal People* follows the sweet and tumultuous relationship between Marianne (Daisy Edgar-Jones) and Connell (Paul Mescal), who begin as secondary school students in Sligo, before moving to Trinity College in Dublin to study English, History and Politics. In that sense, the series is a close study of two young people - both academically gifted, but with different psychological, social and relational issues - while exploring, in a subtle and nuanced way, the differences between Dublin and rural Ireland.

Though a quiet depiction of love and everyday life in Ireland, *Normal People* quickly became a global sensation, and it gave BBC Three its best week ever on iPlayer, "surpassing more than 12.6 million requests in its first week."[710] It was especially popular among the young demographic (16-34 years old), and with 301,000 streams on RTÉ Player it became the most popular opening of a drama series on that particular service. Some critics hailed it for its bold and explicit display of sex and intimacy, while others described it as "inappropriate" and "immoral", but it was impossible to miss the visual aesthetic created by the two directors Lenny Abrahamson and Hettie Macdonald.[711] The series is divided into 12 episodes, and Abrahamson functioned as a sort of *conceptualizing director*, who created the audiovisual template of the series in the first six episodes before handing over the baton to McDonald. There is a minor visible difference between their respective directorial styles - McDonald has a slightly more conspicuous approach to dialogues and staging, reminiscent of Jean-Luc Godard and the Coen Brothers, whereas Abrahamson has a more subtle and intimate style akin to John Cassavetes - but the overall aesthetic is dominated by close-ups, *shallow focus* and handheld camera. This aesthetic is evident from the very beginning of the series, and it is reflected in the scene where Connell and Marianne share their first kiss. Upon first glance, the scene is a rather traditional *shot/reverse-shot* dialogue, but the somewhat uneasy camera and the tight framing give the scene a more intimate feel, as if we had invaded their private space. "It would be awkward, if something were to happen between us," Connell says, but as Marianne replies, "No one would have to know," we get an extremely tight *countershot* of Marianne, framed around Connell's ear and chin, and the shallow *depth of field* makes the two characters slide in and out of focus in an almost impressionistic manner. The difference between this and many other kissing scenes might be almost unnoticeable, but it is made evident by the sudden stylistic change as Connell's mother calls his name from another room, immediately followed by an *American shot* of the two characters with a lot of headroom and space around them. It is almost as if Connell's mother breaks the spell, forcing Connell and Marianne to leave their subjective space and enter collective reality. In any case, the scene invites the viewers into a private and intimate space in a way that can feel both strongly engaging and slightly invasive. According to Lenny Abrahamson:

> As a young filmmaker, Cassavetes' film *Faces* was very influential on me. He uses those big close-ups, which I think are extremely interesting. That kind of quality of intimacy is fascinating. It has to do with putting the audience in a very particular kind of relationship with the action. It is hard to describe. It's something you have to feel your way towards, but it's about creating a concentration of attention and bringing people close while holding something back at the same time.
> When I decided to direct *Normal People*, I thought it was an opportunity to do something quite different in television, in comparison to what we are seeing in many *teen dramas*.

> There was an era where the BBC took television seriously - I think back on some of the Mike Leigh films which were done for television, for example, and Alan Bennett's monologues - but now, especially when dealing with teens, television is extremely glossy. Particularly the international streamers, and everybody is trying to emulate Netflix. Everything is very glossy and high concept, and when it comes to teenagers there's either a sort of nihilism, focusing on dysfunction in a kind of sexy way, like *Euphoria*, or a sort of delicious fantasy as in *Sex Eductation*. It's a teenage dream where America meets Britain.
>
> I thought that it would be interesting doing something, which in its essence is quite naturalistic, and when I was pitching it, I said that I thought it would stand out because it would precisely *not* do the things that are generally being done. But I didn't, oddly, think that it would be successful because I probably accepted the common wisdom that people are addicted to the sugar. They're addicted to the rush of pleasure that they get from the current television output. But I'm reading the reactions that some people have to *Normal People* on social media - young people without, I would suspect, a history of watching arthouse cinema - and it's almost as if, without knowing it, they felt something of the power of that sort of storytelling, and it really affected them.[712]

Connell's story is particularly fascinating, and in the second part of the series, after the popular Gaelic football player has moved to Dublin to study English at Trinity College, he experiences a deep-seated sense of alienation and loneliness that eventually turns into an actual depression. "He's a little bit like a character I studied in a film called *What Richard Did*, and he's quite interesting," as Abrahamson says. "Rural Ireland, traditionally, was a place of very quiet, taciturn men. There's a very interesting book, which was written in the 1970s, called *Saints, Scholars and Schizophrenics*. It's a book by an anthropologist about mental illness in small Irish towns. That resonates with Connell, I think."[713]

The most pivotal scene in this context is when Connell chooses to see a therapist. Like the kissing scene from the beginning of the series, the therapy scene initially looks like a typical *shot/countershot* dialogue, but it soon develops into something quite different and atypical. In the first few shots, we cut between the therapist and Connell, as one would expect from a therapy session on TV (cf. *In Treatment*). But as Connell starts opening up about his problems saying, "I thought I'd meet more like-minded people," the camera stays on him for more than two minutes, lingering on a close-up of his sad, despondent face.

Talking about *The Handmaid's Tale*, the TV critic Evan Puschak has said that "super shallow depth of field has become a cliché in indie filmmaking…, a crutch to create that cinematic look."[714] Even if that is a correct assessment, the use of *shallow focus* and tight close-ups is more than a visual look and a marker of *art TV* in *Normal People*; it serves various narrative functions and creates an intimate space around the two characters and the (young) viewers.

The series has become known for its bold portrayal of intimacy and male nudity - something which is rarely seen on television - and these elements

Fig. 51: *Sex* (TV2, 2020-) feels authentic and loose, even if the episodes are quite short. The audiovisual aesthetic is reminiscent of John Cassavetes and films like *La vie d'Adèle - Chapitres 1 & 2* (2013). The most striking thing is not its intimate close-ups and sex scenes, however, but the portrayal of inner conflict and pensive moments rather than heightened external drama. In the photo we see Asta Kamma August (Catherine) and Jonathan Bergholdt Jørgensen (Simon) during the shooting of the first season. Courtesy of Amalie Næsby Fick.

are also a noticeable part of the Danish low-budget series *Sex* (TV2, 2020-), which was produced by Profile Pictures and TV2 and co-funded by the Danish Film Institute (it was screened at the Berlin Film Festival). The episodes in *SKAM* and *Normal People* have varying lengths, and both series employ a flexible and short format which is well-suited to the modern streaming landscape (as I will illustrate in the next chapter about modern *dramedies*). That is also the case with *Sex*, whose first season comprises six episodes of nine to fifteen minutes. The series, which was created by Clara Mendes and directed by Amalie Næsby Fick, revolves around the young woman Cathrine (Asta Kamma August), who lives with her boyfriend, Simon (Jonathan Bergholdt Jørgensen), in Copenhagen and works at a hotline where young people can call in and pose questions about everything connected to sex and intimacy. In that sense, sex is a central part of the series both in terms of Cathrine's job, her relationship with Simon and her blooming interest in her vivacious and artsy, female colleague Selma (Nina Terese Rask). As Amalie Næsby Fick says:

> Clara was introduced to the sex hotline when she was a teenager, and she and her friends would prank call the hotline, perhaps because there was something that they were curi-

ous about or wanted to know, but were afraid to ask. That was where the idea came from, and then TV2 had a call for short-format series. Clara sent in the idea, and it got picked up.

We wanted it to feel authentic. The acting style should be naturalistic, and I also talked with the cinematographer about the audiovisual aesthetic. How to make it authentic without making it look cheap (and it *is* a low-budget series). It's authentic and handheld, but at the same time it's quite choreographed, and it was a dogma for me that we couldn't have any white walls in the series. It is shot on different locations, and much of it takes place in their apartment, but it should not look like a low-budget series made in a normal apartment with white walls. We also thought about how to portray sex and nudity. How do we make it intimate, especially in the sex scenes, without crossing the line or making it uncomfortable?[715]

The visual style in *Sex* is similar to *Normal People* with its tight close-ups, *shallow focus* and handheld camera. Even more strikingly, the two series are similar in terms of tonality and pacing, and it is interesting that *Sex* feels relaxed and jazzy in its depiction of real-life occurrences, conversations between friends/lovers and steamy sexual encounters with charismatic co-workers, even as the episodes are very short and compressed. "There has been a tendency for short formats to also be 'quick' or 'light' formats," as Fick says. "We wanted to steer away from that. We wanted to have a relatively slow pacing within the short format and make it feel as if we are a part of these young people's lives."[716] The slow pacing and quotidian feel in *Sex* is evident in the scene where Cathrine tries to attract the attention of her bass-playing boyfriend and, even more so, in the scene where she is sitting on the steps in front of her apartment building, pondering her situation while eating a shawarma. That scene was originally done as a seven-minute one-take, and it retained a sense of looseness and emotional authenticity despite being cut down.

The Art of Appropriation: *Euphoria* as Modern Teen Drama

> Haven't you heard: There's a new revolution.
> – Ali (Colman Domingo), *Euphoria*

Upon its release in June 2019, *Euphoria* was met with critical acclaim, intense interest from global audiences and heated debate on social media. Critics almost unanimously lauded the "dizzying high school drama" for its "raw and unpolished" style, and some reviewers argued that it "raise[d] the stakes for teenage transgression" to the point where it made *Skins* look "positively Victorian."[717] Mostly, the reviews were positive - with the exception of a few critics who found it too bleak and "unrelenting in its depiction of dangerous behavior" - and the reviewers often compared *Euphoria* to traditional American teen dramas and popular local representatives of the genre.[718] Rebecca Nicholson of *The Guardian* compared it to *Skins*, the influential British teen drama; the Danish reviewer Sarah Gerlach Madsen saw it in light of popular Scandinavian phenomena like *SKAM* and *Doggystyle*; and Mike Hale of *The New York Times* compared it to transgressive American hit series like *13 Reasons Why* (Netflix, 2017-2020). Though mentioning other comparable series or older and more traditional formulas, the reviews of *Euphoria* rarely focused on the different influences behind *Euphoria*, and few of the reviewers even mentioned the Israeli 'mother show' from which Sam Levinson and HBO had adapted their series. It is interesting that many critics (e.g. Ben Travers of *Indiewire* and Benjamin Lee of *The Guardian*) neglect to mention the Israeli ancestor, but it is just as interesting that the reviewers who actually recognize the Israeli heritage behind Levinson's series, do so without comparing the two series or even reflecting upon *Euphoria* as an adaptation.

In this section, I will focus on that neglected aspect of *Euphoria*, i.e. the different influences behind Sam Levinson's series, and how it appropriates different cultural and televisual traditions while adding biographical elements and cinematic references. *Euphoria* is interesting in its own right, but I will argue that it is particularly noteworthy as an amalgam of various trends and traditions and an example of the *transgressive tendency* in modern teen dramas. Modern teen dramas, for instance *Euphoria*, are not just transgressive by showing edgy and potentially explicit content, but by transcending the borders between different territories, cultures, media and platforms. This aspect, though not as catchy and immediately noticeable as the graphic nudity, is precisely what makes *Euphoria* interesting and illustrative of the modern TV landscape.

"Edgy Mainstream": *Euphoria* as Adaptation

The story in Sam Levinson's *Euphoria* revolves around the depressed 17-year-old Rue Bennett (Zendaya), her complicated relationship with her family and her charming friend Jules (Hunter Schafer), and her battles with mental illness and drug abuse. Although focusing mostly on Rue and Jules, the series also follows other characters, each with their own set of insecurities and *mediatized* issues (from stories about illegal sharing of private photos to abuse, sexual solicitation and even *sextortion*). Many of these stories were created specifically for Levinson's series, inasmuch as Levinson used his own personal experiences with drug and alcohol abuse. Levinson also crafted the character of Jules specifically for the American version of *Euphoria*, using Hunter Schafer's personal story and status as a famous LGBTQIA+ rights activist to color her fictional character in the series - a warm-hearted trans person who is initially introduced, simply, as the "new girl" in town.[719]

The basic premise, however, was adapted from the Israeli series *Euphoria* (Hot3, 2012-2013), which was created by Ron Leshem as an alternative to traditional teen dramas and typical Israeli "thrillers about terrorism and espionage."[720] Before creating *Euphoria*, Leshem had worked as a writer and a TV executive, and as the cinematic adaptation of his novel *Beaufort* (2007) was nominated for the Academy Award, he decided to put all of his energy into producing original TV dramas and exportable formats.

Upon making *Euphoria* in Israel, Ron Leshem went to the US and tried to pitch an American adaptation of his series. The different companies turned down his idea, though, and when he finally found a producer, the networks, including HBO, were afraid that the producer and the company he represented would not be able to produce the series in a manner that would be stylish enough to fit their brand.

After a few years, however, HBO showed a renewed interest in the project, and Sam Levinson was brought in to create, write and direct the series, taking elements from Leshem's original version while updating its content to a rapidly changing media age, abandoning some of the characters and stories from the original series, and introducing new characters and biographical aspects. The intense focus on digital media and media-based interactions and issues was part of Leshem's original series. Leshem had also crafted an emotional *character arc* about an overweight girl who uses new media in her journey towards sexual liberation, and he had created a 13-year-old drug dealer based on a real-life story from Israel. Those characters and arcs also became part of Levinson's adaptation, but Leshem insists on calling it an adaptation, not a remake, since it mostly uses the original series as a template or a general source of inspiration. "Even the American version of *Homeland* had its own DNA," as he says, "but with *Euphoria* it truly is the creation of Sam Levinson. He had total freedom to fashion his own show as the writer, director and artist who crafted the entire creation here. The original show was a kind of initial inspiration for him to launch his journey."[721]

Ron Leshem (creator) on *Euphoria*, transnational remakes and televisual traditions in Israel

Series that travel: I was Head of Content at Keshet TV, and at that time we started exporting drama series and drama formats abroad. The remakes and adaptations are a part of globalization, and this industry is globalized in a good way. It's a small community. Basically, we know all the executives from Australia and Europe to North and South America. We are sharing ideas, and when you have something that is a proven idea or format, it's worth exploring as an adaptation. This is a global phenomenon. But what I can say about the Israeli side of things is that we are making series that travel, and there are many reasons for this. Part of it has to do with the Israeli audience. On the one hand, they get bored so easily, so you must create something edgy, but at the same time you have to make it mainstream, because in Israel a series is a failure if you don't get 20-25% in ratings. If you succeed on both accounts, you have created something that we call *edgy mainstream*. Another thing is that the Israeli government forces the Israeli networks to produce *high-end* drama, even if the networks know that *high-end* dramas are not profitable for them. You just lose money on that, so you have to look outside of Israel. While you are creating a show, you are more aware of the potential for your series to be adapted or remade. A final reason is that Israeli series often break the rules. Israel is such a mess, and people don't obey the rules. Most of the time it's a bad thing, but in TV it's something that helps you create cross-platform storytelling and makes you think outside the box.

Creating and adapting *Euphoria*: I had been running around with the idea of doing it in America since 2012, and we were trying to convince everyone to give this show a chance. But practically everyone said "no" to it, and we said "no" to every executive who said: "Let's make it a *Skins*-type teen drama" or "let's soften it and bring comedy into it."

Years have passed since *Skins*, and being a teenager is something that changes every year. It evolves so quickly, even if you compare Sam Levinson's version of *Euphoria* to our show from 2012. In our version, we had characters who were hooking up through a kind of Tinder app, but Tinder didn't exist at the time. We just figured that one day teenagers would look for sex through an app. When we made it, people said that it was all in our heads. It was just a fantasy. Young women would never use an app like that. But the things that were imaginary in 2012 are now a reality, and tomorrow they're history, so of course we knew that anyone who would make an adaptation of our show would need to reinvent it and bring an American soul into it. The best thing that could happen was someone who could bring *himself* into it.[722]

Fig. 52-53: Some of the ideas from Ron Leshem's *Euphoria* (Hot3, 2012-2013) would also become part of Sam Levinson's American adaptation. However, Levinson's version is radically different from the original series, and it was updated in its depiction of social media and digital dilemmas, relocated to an unspecified suburb in California and mixed with personal and biographical stories. Leshem's vision was to create "*Trainspotting* for kids" in order to emphasize that "adolescence" had become a different and more fluid concept.

When Leshem originally pitched his series in America, HBO said "no". But a few years later Casey Bloys had taken over, and he remembered the show and the original pitch. Bloys and Francesca Orsi struck a deal with Leshem, who sent his tape to the writer-director Sam Levinson. Levinson was fond of Leshem's series and was given full freedom to create his own version. Photos: Courtesy of Ron Leshem.

No Shame in Stealing: *Euphoria* as Appropriation

It begins with a trip. The first seven minutes of Sam Levinson's *Euphoria* are a subjective and stylized entry into a world of teenage depravity and depression, but with an ironic tone akin to Chuck Palahniuk and an almost Godardian sense of playfulness. It opens with a birth montage and a self-deprecating voice-over, reminiscent of the beginning to Spike Jonze's *Adaptation* (2002):

> I was once happy. Content. Sloshing around in my own private, primordial pool. Then one day, for reasons beyond my control, I was repeatedly crushed over and over by the cruel cervix of my mother, Leslie. I put up a good fight, but I lost, for the first time, but not the last.

The narrator tells the audience that she "was born three days after 9/11," and her words are accompanied - in a detached manner - by an archival image of a plane crashing into the Twin Towers. As the plane penetrates the innocent tower, it cuts, in an almost symbolic, Eisensteinian fashion, to the birth of a crying baby, as if to imply that Rue is born from a modern American tragedy. "Grief gave way to numbness," the narrator continues, and as she mentions her "middle-class childhood in an American suburb," we cut to a swift montage of different suburban homes. The use of still-photography, *planimetric* shots of houses and a deadpan delivery are all reminiscent of Wes Anderson, and the humor suddenly becomes morbid, as we cut to Rue's mother telling her that other famous people have struggled with similar psychological issues. The birth montage, which was associated with 9/11, now gives way to a death montage that is strangely lighthearted. As the mother mentions Vincent van Gogh and Sylvia Plath, we cut to a *long shot* of a man who shoots himself and a *low-angle shot* of a woman kneeling ominously in front of an oven. And when the mother, somewhat surprisingly, mentions Britney Spears, we cut to an archival image of the singer, who has chosen to shave her head, and an off-screen voice yelling: "She is completely bald!" This montage follows an almost joke-like structure by juxtaposing two tragic examples of artists who (apparently) committed suicide due to mental issues and a contemporary American singer who was described as a "tragedy" by *Rolling Stone* magazine, without bearing any major resemblance to Plath or van Gogh.[723]

As the sequence continues, Levinson constantly introduces new stylistic elements: from conspicuous re-framings and camera movements to radical changes in colors and lighting and, suddenly, a direct address where Rue looks at the camera and says: "I didn't build this system, nor did I fuck it up," as if trying to convince the audience. This comment is followed by a dizzying crane shot that mirrors Rue's drug-induced state of mind and a short, non-causal sequence that is fittingly underscored by Labyrinth's "When

I R.I.P.": "Feel the morning on my face / Ain't a pill I didn't take." The audio-visual aesthetic gets even more conspicuous, as Levinson introduces strobe effects, extreme color palettes (from saturated blues and purples to warm browns and reds) and noticeable shifts in terms of sound. From the diegetic party noise, Levinson cuts to an abrupt moment of silence, as the narrator says, "all I wanted was two seconds of nothingness," and some sudden musical transitions (e.g. when Andy Williams' "Can't Get Used to Losing You" segues into Beyoncé's "Hold Up", just as the title is introduced on the screen).

The opening of *Euphoria* illustrates Levinson's conspicuous and saturated aesthetic, and it also illustrates the eclectic nature of the series by remixing archival footage and references to various (pop) cultural figures, art films and teen dramas. The use of direct address is often connected to directors like Ingmar Bergman, François Truffaut and Jean-Luc Godard, and the camera address in *Euphoria* could naturally be a reference to Bergman's *Sommaren med Monika* (*Summer with Monika*, 1953) or the accusatory camera address at the end of Truffaut's *The 400 Blows*. Levinson specifically mentions Truffaut in the feature interview at the end of this chapter, but the combination of voice-over and cheeky camera addresses also echoes the British youth drama *As If* (Channel 4, 2001-2004).

The idea of casting Hunter Schafer and letting her draw on her own personal experiences is reminiscent of the research behind *Eagles*, *SKAM* and *No Filter* (*No Filter*, for example, thematizes the pitfalls of sugar dating, and the female character is played by a young feminist and gender activist from Finland).[724] More specifically, the story about Nate (Jacob Elordi), who uses naked photos of Jules in an attempt to blackmail her, immediately echoes the story about abuse and sextortion from the second season of *SKAM*. And as many critics have noted, the beautiful underwater kiss between Jules and Rue, which directly references *Romeo + Juliet* (1996), also resonates with a beautiful scene between Isak and Even (Henrik Holm) from *SKAM*. The heterosexual love scene in Baz Lurhmann's film is re-envisioned as a same-sex romance in *SKAM* and a non-binary scene about love and friendship in *Euphoria* (their complex relationship is further explored in the two radical specials).[725]

Finally, there is a touching scene at the end of Ep. 1:1 of *Euphoria* where Jules rides away from a conflict-ridden party with Rue on the back of her bicycle. Though hardly a rare sight in teen dramas, this bicycle scene seems to echo a touching moment from Ep. 3:4 of *SKAM* where Even and Isak ride away from a party, also in slow motion, to the sound of "Head Over Heels" by Tears for Fears. The scene from *SKAM*, in itself referencing *Donnie Darko* (2001), is an example of the *musical moments* that we often seen in modern TV series, especially in teen dramas, and the heavy use of popular music in

SKAM was one of the reasons that it could not simply be exported to the US. As Vilde Schanke Sundet writes, there are more than 200 popular tracks in SKAM, and the producers would have to buy new licenses when airing the series outside of Scandinavia or cut out the music (which would be virtually impossible, inasmuch as the popular music is an integral part of the series).[726]

The French Connection: *Euphoria* as Artification

When interviewed for this book, Levinson mentioned *Skins* and *SKAM* as prominent examples of modern teen dramas, but he also mentioned the American series *My So-Called Life* (ABC, 1994-1995) as an important precursor to *Euphoria*.[727] Interestingly, and perhaps more surprisingly, Levinson also specifically referenced Truffaut and Louis Malle as sources of inspiration when making his series, and when looking at *Euphoria* more carefully, you cannot help but notice the echoes of the French New Wave.

A very concrete and visible example of this is seen in Ep. 1:4 of *Euphoria* where Kat (Barbara Ferreira) is on a ride at a local carnival. Ferreira is a well-known advocate of body positivity, and her character in *Euphoria*, which was directly lifted from the Israeli original, finds sexual liberation and confidence through digital media, but still struggles with self-doubt and problems concerning love and intimacy. In the fourth episode, she is at a carnival with a male friend, and as they enter a ride, Levinson makes an explicit homage to a similar scene from *The 400 Blows* where the ride spins around rapidly before taking us into the next scene. In Truffaut's film, Antoine Doinel (Jean-Pierre Léaud) is dizzy from the ride, and in *Euphoria* the dizzying effect also mirrors the characters while, once again, making the audience aware of the technical craftsmanship behind his series. Similarly, the use of direct address in the first episode looks like a nod to Truffaut or Godard, and the use of silence in the opening sequence from the first episode (upon Rue's request for a few "seconds of nothingness") is an *implicit reference* to Godard's *Bande à part* (*Band of Outsiders*, 1964).[728]

In many ways, *Euphoria* fits the term *art TV*, as used by Kristin Thompson, in that it often *violates classical clarity of time and space* while using a conspicuous audiovisual style and overt *authorial comments*. In that sense, it is an evident example of modern television and teen drama, and it echoes important precursors from France, England, Scandinavia and America while referencing new media and *mediatization* as a premise for young people today. When the boys are trying to convince Chris McKay (Algee Smith) that his girlfriend Cassie (Sydney Sweeney) is a liberated young woman, for example, they show naked photos and videos of her without her consent, and the narrator immediately reacts upon this by scolding both the boys and the older generation:

> Here's the fucking thing that pisses me off about the world. Like every time someone's shit gets leaked, whether it's J. Law or Leslie Jones, the whole world's like: 'Well if you don't want it out there, don't take the nudes in the first place.' I'm sorry. I know your generation relied on flowers and fathers' permission, but it's 2019, and unless you're Amish, nudes are the currency of love, so stop shaming us. Shame the assholes who create password-protected online directories of naked, underage girls.

In an interesting and eclectic way, *Euphoria* combines social commentary and topical issues (as when Ali comments on polarization and aggressiveness in the world today or when Rue gives a humorous lecture on dick pics) with references to old films, historical personalities and real-life celebrities. Somewhat like *Skins* or *Easy* (Netflix, 2016-2019), the different episodes of *Euphoria* focus on different characters, and the style seems to change from episode to episode. Ep. 1:1 is characterized by montage editing, direct addresses and a symbolic, trance-like use of popular music, while Ep. 1:3, which focuses on Kat and her fan fiction, uses match-cutting and a vivid combination of live-action and animation (akin to Japanese *anime*). Compared to the heavy stylization of those episodes, the first of the two "Corona specials" ("Trouble Don't Last Always") seems almost radically minimalistic, consisting mainly of *shot/reverse-shot editing* and a lengthy dialogue between Rue and her would-be therapist Ali who, in a blatant reference to *It's a Wonderful Life* (1946), tries to convince her not to commit suicide.

Crossing Borders: Teen Drama in the Global Age of Streaming

Euphoria references the *multiplatform era* and how digital media have intensified some of the traditional issues that young people face. Modern teen dramas are a good example of the changes in television drama and the TV landscape, by utilizing multiple platforms and by reflecting on issues connected to new media and *mediatization*. This is seen in different ways: from multiplatform stories such as *SKAM* and *No Filter* to series like *Euphoria* that exploit new approaches to style and storytelling while reflecting the *mediatized* problems of young people. Some series focus on old media and an analogue era (cf. *Stranger Things* and *I Am Not Okay with This*), perhaps implying that modern media have robbed the young generation of their innocence, or catering to older audiences who remember their adolescence with a hint of nostalgia.[729] Other series focus on normal adolescents and normal lives without commenting explicitly or critically on new media (in *Normal People*, for example, Skype functions as a positive or even therapeutic link between Marianne and Connell, when they are apart). Some teen dramas are intense and stylized (cf. *Riverdale* and *Euphoria*), while others are more intimate and realistic (cf. *SKAM* and *Normal People*) or even bleak and transgressive (*Euphoria* and *13 Reasons Why*), but they all deal with issues concerning intimacy, privacy and mediacy, and they mutually influence each other.

In 2006, the film and TV critic Roz Kaveney wrote the following about modern teen dramas:

> Through films and television, and most especially through the teen genre of the last two decades, many of us are acquainted with an adolescence that has nothing in common with anything we actually experienced. The boys are all handsome, the girls are all beautiful, even the ones who wear glasses and talk of themselves as geeks and losers - many of them appear oddly physically mature for their years. They watch American football from the bleachers, with illuminated scoreboards and scantily clad cheerleaders jumping up and down and chanting their hearts out. They go to homecoming, or their senior prom, looking oddly dignified in tuxedos and evening dress; they sign each others' year books and endlessly vote for each other to be Student Body President, or Homecoming Queen, or Person Most Likely to Succeed. They inhabit an entire sequence of ritual years which has little or nothing to do with the lives of anyone outside the United States of America.[730]

While painting a picture that most TV viewers would recognize, Kaveney overlooks a crucial aspect of modern teen dramas - an aspect that has become more evident since the publication of her book. As I hope to have illustrated, the modern teen drama is no longer an insular phenomenon, and American series like *Euphoria* are as influenced by European precursors as European TV series (e.g. *Eagles*) are by American teen dramas. Like modern TV series in general, modern teen dramas try to stand out by drawing on various sources of inspiration or perhaps differentiating themselves from certain series and tendencies. Anna Emma Haudal emphasized that her series, *Doggystyle*, is nothing like *SKAM*, and Lenny Abrahamson argued that *Normal People* was meant to differentiate itself from the glossiness of traditional teen dramas and the "nihilism" of *Euphoria* (though emphasizing that he likes Sam Levinson and his popular series).[731] If anything, this illustrates that modern teen dramas are not created in a vacuum. Rather, they draw on televisual traditions and cultural tendencies from different countries while using modern media and multiple platforms to tell stories about young people in a *mediatized* society. Even when it comes to promotion, social media and platforms are being utilized, as was the case when Zendaya announced on her private Instagram profile that two special episodes of *Euphoria* would drop on December 6, 2020, while audiences were eagerly awaiting the second season.[732]

Many of the problems are the same today as in the 1980s and 90s, and modern teen dramas still exploit popular music and intertextual references (perhaps even more so). But adolescence is not a fixed concept, and modern teen dramas reflect the changes in society and technology as well as the ways in which these changes affect the lives of young people and the viewing behavior of young and mature audiences.

Teen dramas are increasingly popular in today's mediascape, as seen in modern hybrids like *Shadowhunters* (Freeform, 2016-2019), *Class of Lies*

(Snapchat, 2018-) and *When the Streetlights Go On* (Quibi, 2020) and youth-related streaming channels like Brat TV (a channel that attracted attention from young audiences upon signing the Tik Tok star Dixie D'Amelio).[733] Teen dramas are more than speculative entertainment, though, and the genre is beginning to attract attention from renowned creators and young talents who push the boundaries in terms of style, storytelling and production, transcending generic conventions and traditional forms of distribution.

Blurred Boundaries and Flexible Formats: Prestige Dramedies in the Digital Age

> I said "traumedy" once, and it kind of caught on. I said it as a joke, but maybe it's not a good word for what I do. There's not a good word for a lot of stuff we do. People like things to be easily understood. Do we make comedies, or do we make dramas?
> - Jon Lewis, Amazon Prime Executive[734]

> *Fleabag* would have been sold as a comedy, but it started as a theater piece, and it was very much a drama, and I now get scripts that are definitely dark-humored dramas, and I'm thinking: "This could go both to the drama and the comedy department." If it's half an hour, I might send it to the comedy people, but call it a dramedy. Equally, if it was an hour, I would send it to the drama department, but drama departments are looking for dramas with humor. It has become blurred, and the competition is less clear. It was probably clearer, when they used to make half-an-hour sitcoms in front of a studio audience. We still make those in both the UK and America, but they are less common everywhere else, and mostly we have single-camera shows. The line between comedy and drama has become blurred.
> - Charlie Hanson, TV producer (*After Life*)[735]

Crime fiction is an old and broad genre, rooted in the stories of canonical authors like Poe, Doyle and Christie and seen in various audiovisual iterations. Teen drama, on the other hand, is a more recent phenomenon - an outgrowth of the *serial melodrama* which is defined not only by *semantic* and *syntactic* qualities, but also in terms of the targeted audience. A third type of genre is the so-called dramedy, which is a hybrid of drama and comedy that usually inhabits a short 30-minute format. This genre, however, exists within a thoroughly fluid and flexible area - a televisual twilight zone that troubles both critics and craftsmen. In the industry, we have seen a host of different terms to describe this hybrid, and the fact that *Orange Is the New Black* (Netflix, 2013-2019) was placed in the drama category at the Emmy Awards, whereas *Better Call Saul* (AMC, 2015-) was placed in the comedy category, illustrates how dramedies challenge traditional categories and televisual formats.

The TV scholars Julia Havas and Maria Sulimma have written about this "hybrid televisual format," arguing that "the increased interest in commissioning mainly half-hour prestige dramedies signals television companies' efforts to secure industry status by linking two intertwined textual practices."[736] Similarly, I will argue that dramedies are a popular phenomenon in the modern TV landscape due to their flexibility in terms of tone and format. In other words, they illustrate a form of *flexible seriality* that is particularly suited to a modern *multiplatform era* where audiences watch television in different contexts and circumstances and on various different platforms.

The Danish media scholar Helle Kannik Haastrup has distinguished between four different types of dramedies (*the subjective lifestyle dramedy, the moral dramedy, the satirical dramedy* and *the crisis dramedy*), and the TV critic Steffen Moestrup has written about *existential dramedies* like *Louie* (FX, 2010-2015) and *Derek* (Channel 4, 2012-2014).[737] Following their investigations, I will explore tales of ambiguity, fluidity and in-betweenness in modern *prestige dramedies*, focusing on the American series *Looking, Transparent, Togetherness* and *Mrs. Fletcher* (HBO, 2020) and popular British *sadcoms* like *Fleabag* and *After Life*. It is a central argument that the hybridity of the format reflects the thematic focus on in-betweenness and intersectionality in the series and the flexibility of the modern mediascape. It might not be a new phenomenon *per se*, but the dramedy genre seems ideally suited for the *multiplatform era* and modern debates concerning identity and hybridity.

From M*A*S*H to McBeal: The Birth of a Genre

> Is it a comedy or a drama?
> Or is it a genre-bending dramedy?
> I say, as long as it's good, does it matter?
> - Neil Landau, screenwriter/critic[738]

Though a visible and important part of the modern TV landscape, the dramedy genre is not a new invention. Following Glen Creeber, Havas and Sulimma describe dramedies as a hybrid of *serial melodrama* and comedy that focuses on both communal aspects and private issues concerning identity and sexuality. The roots of the modern *prestige dramedies*, according to Havas and Sulimma, can be traced back to the mid-1990s and the launching of series like *Ally McBeal* (Fox, 1997-2002) and *Sex and the City*.[739] Similarly, Helle Kannik Haastrup points to *Sex and the City* as a crucial precursor to the modern dramedies, and the TV critic Iben Albinus Sabroe has even argued that *Sex and the City* "changed the world."[740] Combining humorous conversations on love, sex and friendship with a melodramatic story about the writer Carrie Bradshaw (Sarah Jessica Parker) and her various love interests, most notably Mr. Big (Chris Noth) and Aidan (John Corbett), *Sex and the City* might have changed the world of series, but it was hardly the first notable dramedy in TV history. Still, it is a strong and revivable property for HBO Max.

When talking about *St. Elsewhere* and its combination of medical show and comedy, Tom Fontana mentioned *M*A*S*H* as a prominent source of inspiration, in the sense that it "transcended the half-hour 'sitcom' form and showed us how you can reinvent your show on a weekly basis."[741] Industry critic Neil Landau instead points to Normal Lear's popular sitcoms (e.g. *All in the Family*, CBS, 1971-1979) as important precursors to modern dramedies due to their focus on serious problems and sincere emotionality.[742] And Adrian Page mentions *Moonlighting* (ABC, 1985-1989) as a central piece, with its combination of mystery, comedy and romance, though also pointing to *Ally McBeal* and its influential mix of "sitcom, soap opera, courtroom drama and MTV."[743] The combination of drama and comedy is not a new concept in film and television (Ernst Lubitsch, in fact, criticized the established Hollywood formulas of "drama with comic relief and comedy with dramatic relief" already in 1942).[744] But modern dramedies, as Page concludes, are not just a mix of different genres and tonalities, but also a blend of structural elements connected to the episodic series and the long-running serial.[745] As Landau puts it:

> [A dramedy] may serve up a wholly serious episode, followed by a more broadly comedic one. There's less of a consistent comedic or dramatic tone, and more of the creator's sensibility. Authenticity trumps easy laughs. Subtext and nuance are mined for maximum cringe and relatability. If traditional sitcoms are about likably flawed characters getting into and out of trouble, then dramedies are more about coping with the ongoing hardships and moral complexities of relationships. [...] Dramedies are generally much more ambiguous, and their characters tend to be self-involved, self-destructive, and while forgiveness and love are still the currency required to solve a dilemma, dramedies don't offer up easy answers.[746]

In an attempt to define the genre more precisely, Leah Berg and Helle Kannik Haastrup argue that modern dramedies use different formats (both the short format known from traditional sitcoms and the long format known from traditional drama series) while avoiding the *status quo*-structure and the stylistic techniques that we traditionally associate with sitcoms (e.g. laugh-tracks and multi-camera set-ups).[747] Many critics have pointed to elements of intertextuality and metafiction in modern dramedies and so-called *smartcoms*, and some scholars have pointed to the radical variation in terms of genre and tonality across different episodes of the same dramedy.[748] The Italian TV scholar Luca Barra argues that this tendency towards dramedies may well be a natural result of the saturated TV landscape:

> "Dramedy" is the usual umbrella term for a slew of shows that find their own way of balancing drama and comedy, typically by stressing the dramatic at the expense of the comic. In contemporary US cable and on-demand comedies, then, and sometimes the network ones, too, the jokes, puns, funny situations, and more generally the light-hearted approach typical of classic sitcoms are thinned out or almost even expunged. Unable to achieve affect, these titles avoid laughter, too. The shift towards dramedy, or at least a semi-dramatic narrative, is at once a creative and stylistic choice and a necessity: there is no longer enough time to develop affect and familiarity, and the shows are no longer part of viewers' everyday routines, so other passions are needed, and drama is quicker than comedy at rousing them.[749]

Havas and Sulimma describe modern *prestige dramedies* and their *cringe aesthetics* as a cable phenomenon, and Barra also points to a potential connection between modern dramedies and the subscription model that we naturally associate with cable channels like HBO and Showtime and subscription-based streaming services like Netflix and Amazon Prime. This associative connection makes sense, when listing some of the most prominent American dramedies of the last two decades. From *premium cable* series like *Sex and the City* (HBO, 1998-2004), *Californication* (Showtime, 2007-2014) and *Barry* (HBO, 2018-) to *basic cable* series like *Atlanta* (FX, 2016-) and *Better Things* (FX, 2016-) and streaming series like *Master of None* (Netflix, 2015-2017), *Orange Is the New Black* (Netflix, 2013-2019), *Transparent* (Amazon Prime, 2014-2019) and *Easy* (Netflix, 2016-2019).[750]

Haastrup identifies four types of dramedies that, according to her findings, are typical of the American TV landscape. The first of these categories is called *the subjective lifestyle dramedy*, and this type of dramedy (e.g. *Ally McBeal* and *Sex and the City*) is characterized by having a protagonist who guides the entire story, often through point of view editing or voice-over narration. Another type of dramedy is the so-called *satirical dramedy*, which uses the combination of drama and comedy to satirize famous people, institutions or social constructs (as seen in *Entourage*, which satirizes Hollywood). The *moral dramedy*, then, focuses on moral and existential issues, often connected to the intimate sphere (as seen in *House, M.D.*), and *crisis dramedies* revolve around characters who struggle with life and identity crises (as seen in *Nurse Jackie* and *Glee*).[751] Haastrup's categories are not mutually exclusive, and her list is not exhaustive, but they serve as a good starting point when investigating the complex field of *prestige dramedy*. Synthesizing the different points, we can describe the dramedy genre as a type of televisual fiction that

- merges elements from serials and episodic series;
- blends comedic aspects and various dramatic formulas (e.g. *serial melodrama*);
- employs tonal shifts or an overall tonal ambiguity;
- focuses on both communal and private aspects, such as identity, sexuality and (inter)personal crises;
- includes morally ambiguous characters, transgressive elements and/or awkward situations (*cringe aesthetics*).

Keeping it Together: Tonal Shifts and Ambiguity in *Togetherness*

As Landau notes, dramedies often explore the "ongoing hardships and moral complexities of relationships," and these themes are reflected, quite profoundly, in the "domestic dramedy" *Togetherness* (HBO, 2015-2016), which was created by the Duplass Brothers and Steve Zissis.[752] In 1996, Mark and Jay Duplass founded an independent production company, Duplass Brothers Productions, and from 2015 they began creating and producing original TV productions, focusing primarily on dramedies and limited series. Already in 2003, the Duplass Brothers had created a short film called *This Is John*, and that short film, as Jay Duplass says in the feature interview at the end of this chapter, taught the brothers about their unique sensibility and tonal ambiguity. *This Is John* is neither a straight comedy nor a traditional horror film, but it produced a lot of laughs when it premiered at Sundance, and it also had audiences sighing and recoiling in horror. This generic and tonal in-betweenness is typical of the Duplass Brothers, and since the airing of *Togetherness* and *Transparent* (which stars Jay Duplass as Josh Pfefferman), they have become famous for their playful approach to the dramedy genre and the short format. "The siblings have become masters of creating neuroses-laden indie dramedies on modest budgets," as Alex Nino Gheciu puts it.[753]

Togetherness is a dramedy about a group of friends and relatives - the aspiring actor Alex (Steve Zissis), his friend Brett (Mark Duplass), Brett's wife Michelle (Melanie Lynskey) and her sister Tina (Amanda Peet) - and their struggles to keep it together as individuals, couples and friends. Though not as a conscious premise, *Togetherness* is about *the things that threaten to pull us apart but eventually bring us together.*[754] Brett and Alex are geekily preoccupied with Frank Herbert's *Dune*, hoping to adapt his story into an independent theater production, and this preoccupation destroys Alex's relationship with his girlfriend Christy (Ginger Gonzaga). In the meantime, Michelle has become infatuated with a man named David (John Ortiz) who, like her, is interested in creating an alternative charter school that reflects society. Brett's neurotic interest in *Dune* makes him lose sight of Michelle and widens the gap between them, just as it destroyed the relationship between Alex and Christy. Ironically, though, *Dune* is exactly what saves Brett and Michelle (who is able to trick some local parents into thinking that their set for *Dune* is part of her creative charter school), and it becomes a potential opening for Alex and Tina to get together.

That is the basic premise of *Togetherness*, but while it might illustrate the dramatic arcs and the melodramatic qualities in the series, it hardly explains the unique combination of different genres and tonalities. An example of the tonal shifts in *Togetherness* is found in a car scene from Ep. 1:3, which is both touching and quite humorous. In the sequence leading up to the aforementioned car scene, Alex and Tina have been to a wrap party for a film that Brett has worked on (Brett is a sound editor/recordist). At the party, the attractive and charming Tina persuades Alex to introduce himself to the producer, Larry (Peter Gallagher), who is famous for having worked with Tom Hanks and having produced numerous independent films. Awkwardly, Alex bumps into Larry at the restroom, and as Larry sees Alex and Tina outside, he finally approaches Alex and asks him whether he might be an actor. Alex admits to having stalked him for professional reasons and proceeds to amuse him with funny anecdotes and impressions of Jimmy Stewart. It turns out that Alex and Larry agree on the current state of cinema and television, both of them bemoaning the 'death' of the mid-budget movie (as mentioned by Tim Hunter and Lesli Linka Glatter in this book). But Larry was apparently more interested in Tina, and they drive off together while leaving Alex behind. At this point, Alex calls his friend, Brett, who fetches him in his car, and as Alex enters the car, saying that he feels "really embarrassed", Brett gives him a touching and slightly quirky pep talk:

> This song is called 'Tom Sawyer', and it is about a magical, amazing and inspiring person, who lifts the spirits of everyone around him by the very nature of who he is. Tom Sawyer never needs to be embarrassed. Okay?

During Brett's pep talk, we cut between close-ups of Brett and *reaction shots* of Alex, in a classic *shot/countershot* fashion that emphasizes the emotionality of the scene. And as Brett suddenly punctuates his monologue by asking, "Are we doing this or what?", the diegetic music is intensified and the scene changes into a humorous *musical moment* between two geeky friends who sing along and airdrum to the 1976-hit "Tom Sawyer" by the progressive rock band Rush. What began as a touching and somewhat quirky scene about friendship suddenly evolved into a humorous situation, akin to the *musical moment* in *Wayne's World* (1992) where the two main characters lip-sync to "Bohemian Rhapsody" (1975).[755]

There are numerous other scenes like that, and the series abounds with the kind of *musical moments* that, according to Mathias Bonde Korsgaard, have come to define modern television drama. The final sequence of the first season, for instance, is a suspenseful and emotionally intense moment, underscored by James Blake's "The Wilhelm Scream", where we cross-cut between Michelle, who considers having sex with David, and Brett who is driving to Michelle's hotel in an attempt to rectify their relationship. Elsewhere, the musical moments are more comedic and often combined with slow motion. When Brett and Alex, for example, go to a club in Detroit, the Red Hot Chili Peppers' track "Blood Sugar Sex Magic" is used, in conjunction with slow motion, to illustrate their feeling of coolness, as they enter the room, sporting matching white suits and sunglasses. A similar scene is located in the pilot episode where a family trip to the beach is accompanied by slow motion and a non-diegetic version of "Otherside" by the indie band Family Portrait. At one point in the humorous sequence, which recalls the opening of the Spanish film *Manolo, la nuit* (*Manolo by Night*, 1973), we cut between two young men with sculpted bodies who are wooing Tina, and the less attractive Alex, who is looking at her from the water.

The combination of humor and (melo)drama is a central part of *Togetherness*, and the scenes exhibit different types of humor and emotionality. When Brett is recording bird sounds, for example, a sudden reframing makes him look laughable in a way that recalls traditional sitcoms and *pull-back-and-reveal humor*. But when the director makes fun of Brett's authentic coyote sounds at the wrap party, it is awkwardly funny and almost sad. The series also employs *cringe aesthetics*, as seen in the sequences where Brett and Michelle are trying to have sex, despite having become too familiar with each other's quirks and routines, and sometimes it is almost side-splittingly funny. When Alex, for example, says to Larry that he lost his virginity to one of his films, as a somewhat strange way of praising his film work, Tina makes a snappy follow-up: "It was last week."

Trading Places: *Mrs. Fletcher* as Topical Dramedy

Like *Togetherness*, Tom Perrotta's *Mrs. Fletcher* (HBO, 2020) is a *domestic dramedy* that focuses on different issues concerning family, love and friendship. Often billed as a comedy, *Mrs. Fletcher*, which is based on Perrotta's eponymous book, follows the lives of Eve Fletcher (Kathryn Hahn) and her teenage son Brendan (Jackson White). Brendan is off to college and Eve, a single mother, is on a journey towards self-discovery and sexual liberation. In that sense, Perrotta's *limited series*, which ends in a *cringy* and amusing cross-cutting sequence where Brendan discovers his mother in a threesome with a female friend and one of Brendan's old high-school aquaintances, is more than simply a comedy about a mother and her son: It is an astute reflection of issues concerning gender, sexuality and generational gaps that switches, rather seamlessly, between different moods and tonalities. As Perrotta says:

> One thing that *The Leftovers* taught me was how much story you need to sustain a one-hour drama. I mean, we burned through the book of *The Leftovers* in Season 1. If you have eight hours of TV, you often need some kind of genre component to keep the audience hooked and create a constant dramatic pressure. So once I realized that and I started seeing shows like *Atlanta* that were doing really wonderful, complicated things in the space of half an hour. *Girls* was also inspiring. It's an uneven show, but the great episodes are *great*. There were a number of other shows that also inspired me: *Search Party* is more satirical, but I also thought that was a good show, and it started to seem like that was a better way to go for something that was more character-driven, that did not have a really deep storytelling engine. We could focus more on moments and slow evolution of the characters. I like how *Atlanta* would take something like "Earn gets a haircut" and turn that into a whole story. It was not an incredibly complicated narrative. It was more like: "Let's put our characters in a situation and watch them interact with each other and some new people."[756]

Perrotta had written the novel in 2017, but when turning it into a limited series, he teamed up with a set of renowed women directors in order to tell the story of a woman's sexual awakening in a more authentic way:

> Kathryn Hahn was very interested in working with women directors, and the show was going into production just as the #MeToo movement was happening, and there was a feeling then – and I think it's even stronger now – that women should tell women's stories, and people of color should tell their own stories. There's a sense that it can be a little bit invasive if a man tells a woman's story. I had written the book already, and Kathryn loved the book, but there is a certain politics of collaboration that made me aware that I needed to bring in as many women's voices as I possibly could. And we found such a great group of directors. Gillian Robespierre, for example, is a great indie director. I love *Obvious Child*, and I feel a great kinship with that kind of dramedy vibe, which is why I think it's so funny that I'm associated with *The Leftovers* when my own personal inclination is in that space between drama and comedy.[757]

Mrs. Fletcher has not received the same critical awareness and hype as other modern dramedies (e.g. *Girls*, *Orange Is the New Black*, *Transparent* and *Atlanta*), yet its combination of everyday issues, low-key drama and cringe-like humor make for an interesting *domestic dramedy* that, quite profoundly, reflects the time of its inception. "*Mrs. Fletcher* is reflective of its time, a time where women are becoming empowered and men are getting a come-uppance," as Perrotta says, "and it's very strange to see that play out in a story of a mother and her son, an older and a younger person. A whole bunch of hierarchies are getting flipped over."[758]

"Funny and Emotional": the In-Betweenness of *Looking*

That *Sex and the City* has been influential for the modern dramedies can be seen from the many TV series that follow its basic template (about a small group of friends who talk about sex and relationships) while adding a progressive edge and an artistic twist. When Lena Dunham created *Girls* (HBO, 2012-2017), for example, her tentative title was *Degradation and the City*, inasmuch as her series was envisioned as a more realistic and less flattering depiction of young women living in New York.[759] Despite its many qualities, *Sex and the City* seemed glossy and inauthentic (would a young column writer be able to live like Carrie Bradshaw in an expensive city like New York?), and it soon became a formula, akin to *Beverly Hills 90210*, for writers to adopt and tweak. Dunham's series, in itself, became an influential piece, known for its thoughtful and provocative portrayal of body positivity, gender issues and sexual abuse, and in one of the major Danish newspapers it was chosen as the best series of the decade by a panel of Scandinavian TV creators. "It had the half-hour format that we traditionally knew from pure sitcoms, but it was a mix of comedy and drama," as one of the panelists said. "So it was a new way of telling stories which paved the way for a modern type of series that some would call *traumedies* or *sadcoms*."[760]

Though not the first of its kind, *Girls* became a touchstone for modern dramedies, and Michael Lannan's *Looking* (HBO, 2014-2016) was soon categorized as "the gay *Girls*", even if it was adapted from Lannan's own film, *Lorimer* (2009), which premiered three years ahead of Dunham's show.[761] Like *Sex and the City* and *Girls*, *Looking* revolves around a group of friends - in this case a group of openly gay friends living in San Francisco. There were earlier LGBT-centric TV series (e.g. *Queer as Folk* and *The L Word*), but the combination of an intimate roaming camera and a series about openly gay men that combined humor and *serial melodrama* was something of an anomaly in American television. Detailing its conception, Lannan emphasizes the biographical elements and the generic and tonal ambiguity in his series:

> The show really began in a long, messy Word document I kept of personal experiences and anecdotes that I heard from friends, at parties, etc. Like a lot of my friends, I came out post-AIDS crisis but pre-Grindr. It always felt like there was something significant about that. It wasn't as shameful to be gay anymore, but it wasn't exactly a breeze either. I wanted to create a show that captured this weird, funny feeling of in-betweenness. Also, so many queer stories in film and TV back then still tended to be either deeply tragic or completely comedic. I wanted to find a world that was funny and emotional at the same time.
>
> My day job was working as an assistant in film and TV production in the mid-late 2000s. I knew that I didn't have the clout to pitch a TV show, especially the way the industry was back then. So I wrote a feature film script that was very simple about three friends rambling around New York (where I lived during that period) and I took it to indie/queer film producers. I spent years submitting, getting rejected and spiraling into depression about it. I gave up many times, but I would always come back to it and rewrite it again. At one point, I made a short film of a few of the scenes from that script and it ended up making the rounds on the LGBT circuit. That didn't directly help me get the show made, but it was the first time I ever saw anything I wrote and directed play for an audience. That was a huge shift of mindset for me like: "wow, this didn't exist before I willed it into existence, and now everyone is watching it in a legit movie theatre and having a reaction to it." It definitely reaffirmed the feeling that I was onto something and helped me keep going. About a year later, thanks to a friend, my feature script ended up in the hands of an HBO executive who responded to the characters and the sensibility. We had a kind of lightning in a bottle meeting where we just really clicked on the opportunity to create a show with gay characters in the leads. We agreed that it should feel like it could only be made in that moment. The world had changed a lot since the American *Queer as Folk* and *The L Word* went off the air a few years earlier. Obama had been elected, the gay marriage dominoes were falling in the US. A lot of people's lives had changed so crazily fast. So it felt like there was a lot to explore. I took the three main characters from my script and adapted them into a half-hour pilot. The show just kept rolling from there.[762]

One of the major arcs in *Looking*, a love triangle between the main character Patrick (Jonathan Groff), a Mexican-American man called Richie (Raúl Castillo) and Patrick's boss, Kevin (Russell Tovey), might echo the melodramatic arcs of *Sex and the City* and *Girls*. But *Looking* is also markedly different from *Sex and the City* and *Girls*, both in terms of style and setting, and HBO was adamant about situating the story in San Francisco, not New York. As Lannan says:

San Francisco was critical to the birth, production, and the storylines of the show. I had lived there for a few years right after college and had some very formative experiences there. Then there was a point in development where HBO wanted to move the show out of New York for various reasons, and we had to figure out where to take it. At first I thought San Francisco was too on-the-nose. But then they sent me there on a reconnaissance trip. I came back to NYC and did a draft of the script set in SF, and everything kind of fell into place in this magical way. I changed very few words in the script, but the characters, the story, and the world all seemed to take a leap forward in this unexplainable way. Maybe because it's a very atmospheric and visual city. It's also a crucible of the rapid social and political changes taking place in the world. Tech booms, gay marriage, food culture, class and race conflicts... All of those things are in sharp focus in SF and inspired stories for our characters. And maybe the most important thing for the show was the backdrop of queer history. We shot in a lot of historically significant places, and I think the imagery of SF created a tension between past and present that somehow raised the stakes of Patrick's journey. Patrick is both a fully modern American boy and also subject to the legacy of shame and fear that decades of homophobia and the HIV crisis created. I think having the city as an ever-present backdrop captured some of that "in-betweenness" that I wanted the show to express.[763]

In terms of style, *Looking* employed a moving and intimate camera that was reminiscent of John Cassavetes - and which might have inspired modern teen dramas like *SKAM* and *Normal People* - and the roaming, voyeuristic camera seemed to mirror the title of the show. Not only was the series about people cruising and looking for dates via social media; it was also about presenting an image to the world and about getting a closer look at the relatively normal lives of people who are rarely represented in mainstream media. In Lannan's words:

When Andrew Haigh signed on to direct the pilot, he focused in on the idea of making this a show about intimacy, and driving the show with a close study of characters and relationships rather than hard plot. He deepened the emotional lives of the characters and made the show focus more on the love stories. We wrote the show toward his directorial style, which is very much oriented around finding the detail and beauty in everyday human interaction. We decided very early on to have no coming out stories. We wanted the show to feel like we were dropping in on lives in progress, not people discovering what it means to be gay for the first time or facing obstacles specifically related to sexual identity in the ways we are already familiar with from other movies and shows. Also, I recently read something about how Elena Ferrante's novels are so radically feminist because they are about female character journeys being witnessed and described by other female characters. I think there was some principle of that in the show too. We wanted these gay male characters to witness each other's lives and drive the show that way. Rather than having to always be defining themselves against the normative world.

I've been really lucky to have lots of incredible friends in almost every period of my life. So, in a way, this show is really a love letter to friendship, and the way friends can help you frame and understand other kinds of intimate connections. As far as TV, the British *Queer as Folk* was an original inspiration for me. When that first came out, it was so unlike anything I'd ever seen. It was a great portrayal of friendship, sex and relationships between gay men that was both funny and dramatic. The original *Tales of the City* was a huge inspiration too. It has this really strange and wonderful combination of queer melodrama and realism that's very unique. It's weird that both of those shows were born and aired primarily in the UK and we also ended up with a UK director/writer/producer, Andrew Haigh. The Brits know how to do gay stuff well, apparently. Andrew's elegant visual language brought that layer of what you call the New Wave quality.[764]

Due to lackluster ratings and a lack of "awards attention", *Looking* was discontinued after only two seasons and a short *tie-in* movie, and it has not been the object of intense critical scrutiny like other prolific dramedies of its era (e.g. *Girls, Orange Is the New Black* and *Atlanta*).[765] The use of handheld camera, tight close-ups and vibrant location shots, however, gave the series an intimate feel that was inspired by innovative British productions and which would come to inspire and influence popular TV series from both America and Europe.

Though mostly a dramatic series, the lighter and more comedic aspects are also an integral part of *Looking*. The scene where Patrick performs the first lines from the *Golden Girls* theme as a farewell comment to his friend Agustín (Frankie J. Alvarez), who is moving out of their shared apartment, is an example of that combination of sweetness and humor. That particular moment, as Lannan says, happened because Andrew Haigh's partner "would be watching *Golden Girls* reruns when he came home from a hectic shoot day," and, in that sense, even the lighter and intertextual moments had their roots in biographical stories and real-life experiences.[766]

The Moving Target and the Restless Camera: *Transparent*

> Before *Transparent*, Amazon was a place to buy toilet paper.
> - Jay Duplass (Josh Pfefferman)[767]

If *Looking* was interesting for its use of a moving, intimate camera and its honest depiction of LGBT-characters in San Francisco, then *Transparent* (Amazon Prime, 2015-2017) was a radical rejection of all binaries and a vibrant portrayal of an alternative family. Like *Looking*, *Transparent* is a biographical series, and the central coming-out story where Jeffrey Tambor's character (Maura Pfefferman) opens up to her family about identifying as a woman, is based on the creator Joey Soloway, whose biological father also opened up about identifying as a woman. Like *Looking*, *Transparent* employs a handheld aesthetic, but in Soloway's series the restless camera seems to illustrate the fluidity and uneasiness of the characters, who are constantly trying to find or make peace with themselves, and the use of light and filters (often blue filters) create a cool and distant atmosphere that counteracts the intimate close-ups.

In an early episode, Maura explains to her daughter, Ali (Gaby Hoffman), that she is "riddled with anxiety," and Ali's brother, Josh (Jay Duplass), admits to being "fucked up all the time". The title might refer to Maura, but it also relates to two other aspects in the series. First of all, *Transparent* is about characters who are constantly in transition. People who are searching for themselves and who are enveloped, at times narcissistically, in their own existential journeys. But secondly, the series is about characters who, in searching for themselves, are constantly performing and putting themselves on display. It is hardly coincidental, in this respect, that the title sequence mirrors the silkscreen paintings of Andy Warhol and the video cover for the British New Wave film *Performance* (1970). Though referencing the family's history, through old media and media expressions, the title sequence may also allude to queer art and performance.

A particularly interesting example is found at the opening of Ep. 1:10 where a wedding photographer is planning to take a traditional and beautiful photo. During the scene, the Pfeffermans move chaotically in and out of the frame, and the restless film camera (which approximates the photographer's point of view) anxiously tries to capture the family. The moving *sequence shot* continues for 3:45 min., and the duration of the shot in itself makes it a noteworthy example of *art TV*, according to TV critic Henrik Højer.[768] Højer is correct in assuming that long takes are more readily associated with art cinema and different types of realism, but what makes this scene so interesting is the double staging.[769] The characters are trying, unsuccessfully, to come across as a 'picture perfect' family in front of the photographer, but their continual movement makes it impossible. And when the photographer misgenders Maura, by using the wrong pronoun, chaos ensues. This entire scene is captured by the restless film camera, which seems to mirror the characters and their inability to stand still.

Transparent is about restless and anxious characters, but it is also about love and acceptance. This is seen, for example, in the sweet moments when Josh sings in the car and when he and Ali dance at the end of Ep. 1:4, and it is seen, most crucially, in the reactions to Maura from her children (who call her "Moppa") and her ex-wife Shelly (Judith Light). In the feature interview at the end of this chapter, Jay Duplass distinguishes between "hard comedies" and dramedies, arguing that studios still, to a large extent, think in the binary terms of 60-minute dramas and 30-minute "hard comedies". Executives did not know exactly how to market or define *Togetherness*, and that was also the case with *Transparent*, but Soloway's dramedy had the support of a new *online native* (Amazon) and a "marquis issue" that gave it an air of cultural significance and gravitas.[770] Before creating *Transparent*, Solloway had worked on acclaimed drama series such as *Six Feet Under* and *Tell Me You Love Me* (HBO, 2007) and edgy dramedies like *The United States of Tara* (Showtime, 2009-2011). *Transparent* can be seen as the natural next chapter in the meta-story of American television. *Six Feet Under* depicted homosexuality in a groundbreaking way, and *The United States of Tara* thematized mental illness while debunking the traditional understandings of normalcy and nuclear families. In *Transparent*, then, Soloway challenges our conceptions of family, gender and sexuality while rejecting the binary notions that have dominated Western culture and American television, including the televisual opposition of drama and comedy.[771]

The TV scholar Maria San Filippo sees *Transparent* as a debunking of the *Father Knows Best*-formula and the "ingrained conservatism" of the American sitcom genre, arguing that Maura's transition illustrates the symbolic fall of the patriarchy and the rejection of conventional formulas and labels in modern television.[772] And some scholars even see *Transparent* as a core example of the general fluidity in the current mediascape. Referencing *Transparent* and other shows like it, TV scholars Michael Goddard and Christopher Hogg have used the term *trans TV* as a name for the modern TV landscape which is defined by its fluid boundaries in terms of genres, formats, tonalities and types of engagement as well as its transgressive content and non-binary characters (this term is also associated with Lena Waithe and Ryan Murphy).[773]

"Tragedy Plus Time": *After Life* and the Modern *Sadcom*

In an episode of *It's Garry Shandling's Show* (Showtime, 1986-1990), a short-lived sitcom known for its metafictional aspects and breaking of the fourth wall, Gilda Radner appeared as herself. And as the host in the fictional show within the sitcom (Shandling) asked Radner, who was fighting ovarian cancer, why she had not been on television for a while, she snappily replied: "Oh, I had cancer. What did you have?" Radner died within a year of appearing on *It's Garry Shandling's Show*, and that short, autofictional exchange was an early example of how serious topics and tragic components, including illness and death, have begun to creep into the sitcom genre.

In 1993, the TV scholar Gerard Jones published a seminal study of the sitcom genre, arguing that sitcoms were "a mass consumption commodity, designed like a Sedan, to be constructed decade after decade on the same safe, reliable pattern, yet allowing enough surface variations to be resold as a new product every few years."[774] That statement was somewhat unsubstantiated already in the 1990s where series like *It's Garry Shandling's Show* and *Archie Bunker's Place* (CBS, 1979-1983) had shown that even sitcoms could deal with tough and tragic subject matters. But thirty years later, Jones' comment seems vividly reductive, as the line between comedy and drama has become thoroughly blurred, resulting in a multitude of dramedies and *sadcoms* that deal with heavy issues such as trauma, death and depression, while including extreme tonal shifts.

A significant example of this tendency is the British series *Fleabag*, which tells a tragic story about death and guilt through a clever use of flashbacks, while generating humor through Roy Andersson-like tableaus, playful camera addresses and shocking comments about intimate and private issues. Phoebe Waller-Bridge created the series, which was produced in collaboration between BBC Three and Amazon Studios, and she also plays the central character, Fleabag, who uses her humor as a coping mechanism to deal with the tragic loss of her friend. What began as *comic relief* gradually turns into *tragic realization*.[775] Other examples include *Baskets* (FX, 2016-2019), *Better Things* (FX, 2016-), *Horace and Pete* (louisck.net, 2016) and *BoJack Horseman* (Netflix, 2014-2020).[776]

An equally interesting example is Ricky Gervais' latest series *After Life* (Netflix, 2019-), which deals with the trauma of losing one's partner and the existential questions and emptiness that come with such trauma. Before *After Life*, Gervais had been lauded for his single-camera sitcoms and mockumentaries that often featured tragic characters, incongruous moments and *cringe aesthetics*. These elements were already a part of *The Office* (BBC, 2001-2003), but Gervais honed his craft while working with the producer Charlie Hanson on series like *Extras* (BBC Two/BBC One/HBO, 2005-2007), *Life's Too Short* (BBC Two/HBO, 2011-2013) and *Derek* (Channel 4, 2012-2014). On these shows, Gervais looked to Monty Python and Garry Shandling, but he drew his main inspiration from quirky people and situations he had experienced in real life. As Charlie Hanson says:

> I was a big fan of Garry Shandling and his shows: *It's Garry Shandling's Show* and *The Larry Sanders Show*. I was a fan of both of those shows, and I can clearly see the similarities. Ricky was definitely a fan of *Larry Sanders* as well.
>
> *Derek*, like the previous shows we had done, was filmed in a documentary style. Although more sincere, it was still filmed as if it were a documentary. It was important with *After Life* to make it more of a drama and not have the gimmick of characters looking to camera.
>
> My background was in drama and theater, and then I accidentally took a side step into comedy. I sometimes say to people who send me these scripts that are just knockabout farcical, almost silly comedies: "That's not me. My comedy has to be character-driven, I have to believe in the characters, I have to believe in the relationships." People don't realize how difficult good comedy is. You've got to get the drama right, you have to get the plot, the characters, the relationships, and you have to make the story work, and, on top of that, get some laughs along the way. That's why it's been so wonderful to work with Ricky because he's naturally so funny. He can get the laughs, but he can also draw on the emotions and reality of real people. He has a vast memory of people he's met over the years that he draws on. In every piece he's made, there are interesting people in there, and it's often triggered by people he's met where he remembers this one quirky thing about them that he is able to encapsulate into a character.[777]

After Life is a sweet and fairly straight *sadcom* about Tony (Ricky Gervais) who has lost his wife to cancer and who tries to get back to life. The title neatly illustrates Tony's attempt to come back to life after having lost his wife and best friend, and it also refers to the videos that Tony's wife has left him where she speaks to him (and the viewers) from beyond the grave.

The French philosopher Albert Camus has famously said that the most existential question is whether or not to commit suicide.[778] That question is central to *After Life*, looming as a dark shadow over every episode, and it also serves as a plot twist at the end of the second season (where Tony is about to take his own life, just as the doorbell rings). As Hanson explains:

> There is a sort of quick happy ending where people might have thought: "Oh, my God, he's not going to…" I think there was a suspense to that moment, people expecting the worst, and then they're kind of relieved when the doorbell rings. The reactions to *After Life* have been, clearly, that everybody has been moved by it. We've all had someone in our lives that has died, if not a husband or a wife, then our parents, a grandmother or a relative. Everyone's been through grief, but not necessarily to the extent that Tony is experiencing where it's a very immediate thing and it's very moving. In the first season, there were some brief flashbacks to home videos of the wife that he was looking at, but when we came to the second season, we made those flashbacks less momentary. We made them almost like parallel stories, in the sense that we knew the audience accepted them. And that is probably what makes the second season much more emotional because seeing them being happy together is also what makes people cry.[779]

Like Gervais himself, many of the actors in *After Life* began as comedians, and Hanson explains that Gervais prefers working with comedians and trying to teach them how to act, instead of having to teach comic sense and timing to a professional actor. According to the producer, Gervais surrounds himself with the same set of performers, almost like "repertory theater where you have the same group of actors who come back," and in that sense there is a clear link between his stand-up career and his TV work.[780] The relation is two-sided, though, and the surprising global success of *After Life* (which fared well in countries like Turkey, Russia and Chile) has changed the structure and venues of his upcoming comedy tour.[781]

The boundaries between comedy and drama have become blurred, and in the *multiplatform era* we have seen a group of *prestige dramedies* and *sadcoms* that combine elements of different genres and tonalities, while integrating structural components from both serials and episodic series. As Vanessa Thorpe puts it:

> Television comedy has a bad case of the blues – and yet it seems to be revelling in the gloom. The rise of such dark "dramedies", or comedy dramas, has been swift. Writers and performers who have established their careers in comedy or in sitcoms are now opting, almost en masse, to tackle serious subjects and to reject easy gags in favour of saying something that matters.[782]

The dramedy genre was not born with the *multiplatform era*, and its roots can be traced back to – at least – the 1970s. The genre has become increasingly popular with the advent of streaming, though, perhaps because of the short and flexible format that can draw audiences in through relatable characters and engaging stories without demanding the time and investment of

Fig. 54-55: Ricky Gervais stars as Tony in the touching dramedy *After Life* (Netflix, 2019-), which tackles major existential issues and questions, including death, grief and suicide, without wallowing in bleakness or backing down. *After Life* was created by Ricky Gervais, and it was produced by Charlie Hanson (cf. Fig. 55), who had worked with Gervais on productions like *Extras*, *Life's Too Short* and *Derek*. The themes of loss and grief are also central to *Fleabag* and the popular teen dramedy *Never Have I Ever* (Netflix, 2020-). © Netflix, courtesy of Charlie Hanson.

longer formats and long-running dramas. This may be the reason for the genre's popularity; it crops up across various channels and platforms - from cable channels like HBO (cf. *Looking* and *Togetherness*) to subscription-based streaming channels like Amazon Prime, Netflix and Quibi (cf. *Transparent*, *After Life* and *Dummy*) and relatively open-access video platforms like YouTube (cf. *Margot vs. Lily*). It might have happened without big drama, but the dramedy genre has become a prolific part of the *multiplatform era*, and it has changed the TV landscape dramatically. In 2020, for example, Michaela Coel's dramedy *I May Destroy You* (BBC One/HBO), about a woman who tries to get back on her feet after a rape, is widely recognized as one of the most important series of its time, and genre-bending shows like *Atlanta*, *Insecure* (HBO, 2016-) and *Master of None* (Netflix, 2015-2017) are often described as potential game-changers in today's mediascape. The ambiguity of Coel's series is neatly reflected in the title (both "I" and "you" could refer to different people, including both the rapist and the victim), and Darren Star has even described it as "*Sex and the City* for now," acknowledging its modern sensibility and its potentially influential status.[783]

In this chapter, I have explored some new approaches to TV genres and hybrids, focusing particularly on crime series, teen dramas and dramedies. These genres are markedly different from each other - one is a traditional genre rooted in literature from the 19th and early 20th centuries, and the others are relatively new mutations and hybrids. But the examples that I have analyzed all reflect the tendencies towards "circular influences", hybridization and *multiplatform storytelling* in the modern TV landscape, and they all illustrate the *global turn* in television where talents, formats and influences travel between different countries and produce new and interesting amalgams.

Feature Interview #6

Beyond the Generic: Interview with Nic Pizzolatto (*True Detective*), Sam Levinson (*Euphoria*) and Jay Duplass (*Togetherness, Transparent*)

Despite working in different genres and having different approaches to style and tone, the creators Nic Pizzolatto, Sam Levinson and Jay Duplass have at least two things in common. They have all created modern TV series that are interesting and innovative in terms of genre, and they are all known for making 'authored' series. Not only have they created their respective series, they are also writers and directors.

Pizzolatto created *True Detective*, which broke new ground for crime and detective fiction by blending different traditions and adding a unique and very personal tonality – and which also popularized the limited series. Similarly, Levinson wrote and directed a very personal adaptation of the Israeli series *Euphoria*. Levinson's *Euphoria* may have been an adaptation, but it combined elements from the Israeli original with biographical aspects and various artistic influences in what became a playful and transgressive reinvention of the American teen drama. Like Pizzolatto and Levinson, Duplass is deeply involved in all aspects of his productions, and together with his brother he has founded an independent production company that has made some of the most prolific dramedies and anthology series of the *multiplatform era*. In this triple interview, Pizzolatto, Levinson and Duplass talk about their respective series in terms of genre, format and tonality, and they reflect upon genres and formats in the modern TV landscape.

Venturing into New Landscapes: *True Detective*

How would you describe *True Detective* in terms of genre? It has been described as *noir* and *Southern Gothic*, but how do you see it?

Pizzolatto: I guess I would hope it's a character drama within the trappings and mechanics of pulp detective films and stories. Its tone and aesthetic always begin as expressions of character, but it's like landscape, tone and character could each be emanations of the other.

True Detective is known for its characters, and I particularly like the way that the environment mirrors the characters: from the swamps in Louisiana to the asphalt jungle of Vinci and the eerie Ozarks. Could you say a few words on the interplay between characters and environment in the three seasons of True Detective?

Pizzolatto: Everything emanates from character, for me - tone, style, incident, dialogue, etc. - and landscape has always been a character for me. Setting shapes the people who live there, who in turn shape their setting. The character of a place - not just its aesthetic and history, but its energy, its network of relationships and the things they create. A lot of the time it seems like character and landscape are each emanations of the other.

Rust Cohle from the first season of True Detective became something of an iconic character. From his existential monologues to his traumatic past, Rust becomes a complex avenue for the viewers. Some have described him as a *noir*-like antihero, while others have seen him as a sort of existential detective with Holmesian qualities. How did you envision him, and did you always think of Matthew McConaughey in that role?

Pizzolatto: I knew I wanted a man I could believe had a life behind him, and was traditionally masculine in his physicality and bearing, strong - not what Hollywood considered shorthand for an "intellectual", which is where the initial casting was trying to go - for a more bookish, less physical candidate. I thought Matthew could do it, and I really wanted him for it. But I don't think of Rust as an antihero; he's more or less a hero, to me. And he lacks any of Sherlock Holmes' deductive powers or intellectual genius. Rust is decently smart, but mostly an exceptionally hard worker and given to obsessive fixation. It's more the case that he'll outwork everybody else, rather than he possesses some kind of superior intellect. And he'll throw a toolbox in your face.

True Detective is also interesting in terms of pacing and tonality. It is slow-paced, and it uses some quite lengthy shots (some of them are several minutes long). What were your thoughts in terms of pacing and tone?

Pizzolatto: The pace was certainly always very deliberate, and I generally edited toward the same pace as the script. There was a very specific cadence and rhythm I felt where the first three and a half episodes of Season 1 were meant to be like a slow, deep drum, like a funeral dirge, until all this coiled energy the series had built up erupts into a *neo-noir* action film that collapses the narrative, compresses time, and starts to unify the story's structure.

How would you describe your process? You are known as a very precise and detail-oriented showrunner.

Pizzolatto: I think my writing process is somewhat an extension of the life process, an extension of a lot of thinking and observation coupled with irregular bursts of writing. I try to avoid it, but writing is the only way I know how to find out what's really going on in a story – to write it and listen back. Once I have the scripts I want, it's just about working with the actors, department heads, directors and my producing partner to realize a shared goal. I am very detail-oriented, because so many things are so specific – so many details, so many shots – but in the main you hope your work attracts talented people who understand the intention and can become inspired and end up executing a vision better than you could have hoped.

True Detective **is a modern crime or detective series, and you have also written a few episodes of another crime series, AMC's** *The Killing***. That series, as you know, is adapted from the** *Nordic Noir* **series** *Forbrydelsen***. What was that experience like, and how would you describe the Scandinavian tradition of crime fiction compared to the American tradition? Are the two traditions beginning to influence each other to a larger degree these days?**

Pizzolatto: I think the mirrored influences are kind of interesting, the way the Scandinavian tradition is influenced by the American *noir* and its aesthetic, which had been almost entirely abandoned by American film and TV. Then the Americans hear how successful these Scandinavian shows are, and start trying to make *noirs* like they do. I also think it's kind of funny - you would think from the entertainment it generates that Scandinavia was far and away the global capital of serial killers. I don't think their population could support the sheer amount of serial killers that appear to be dwelling in that region of the world, which is a region I love.

Modern Teen Dramas & Emotional realism: *Euphoria*

Back in the 1980s and 1990s, teen drama on television was a different and slightly more "low-brow" genre. TV series like *Degrassi* and *Beverly Hills 90210* had many qualities, and many of the episodes were directed by skilled directors, but they were more episodic and often educational in nature. This seems to have changed in both America and other countries. What has happened within the genre of teen drama or *youth series* in the last two decades, as you see it?

Levinson: The one outlier I can think of was *My So-Called Life*, the Winnie Holzman show. It wasn't episodic or moralistic or even that plot heavy. I was young when it came out, but I distinctly remember the feeling of watching that show and seeing my own insecurities and thoughts mirrored in Angela's. It's a testament to the respect that Winnie Holzman had for the inner lives of young people. Not to mention, the show had certain cinematic flourishes that were unusual at the time, particularly in its transitions.

With that said, I think the teen genre has undergone the same change that all of television has gone through, which is a slow implementation of the ideas of cinema from a technical perspective but also from a poetic one.

***Euphoria* deals with some very topical issues – illegal sharing of private photos, abuse and the search for identity in a complex, late modern society – yet it never seems moralistic. What were you going for?**

Levinson: It never occurred to me to write it any other way. I try to create characters that I love and whose eyes I can see the world through, and I let them do whatever they want to do. And naturally, the things they do change them, but I never look at it through a moral lens, just an emotional one.

The main thing I wanted to do was tell a story about being a teenager that was rooted in an extreme emotional realism but dealt with the complexities of modern life – which is less about depicting the internet itself and more about depicting how the internet has changed us. And that ultimately became the concept behind the visual language of the show. The emotional realism would be countered by a world that reflects how the characters wish they could be seen — in many ways mirroring social media. Which allows us to create a persona that projects how we wish the world could see us. From the pictures we post, to what we say matters, artistically or politically or emotionally… It's a narrative we're trying to sculpt, a story we're trying to tell and in many ways a wish. Who we are and who we wish to be.

As far as I know, part of your series is also autobiographical. Is that something that you can talk about, or is it too personal?

Levinson: Growing up, I struggled with pretty severe drug addiction, and I wanted to unpack that. To tell a story from the addict's perspective that dealt with the cycle of guilt and addiction. The wish to get better but failing over and over. And just how fucking long and debilitating and brutal that journey can be, not just for you, but for everyone in your life.

The style in *Euphoria* is quite interesting, and it combines a *Fight Club* or *Nouvelle Vague*-like breaking of the fourth wall with some very subjective camera movements and a quite expressive use of colors and music. In many ways, the expressive and at times hypnotic style seems to mirror the mental state of the main character. What were you going for stylistically, and did you have any concrete frame of reference?

Levinson: In terms of the style of the world from a visual perspective, I think the central idea was that almost everything would be an extension of an emotional reality, from the lighting to the production design to costumes and make-up, and music. But yes, it's definitely extreme subjectivity from a cinematic and lighting perspective, mixed with montage as story, mixed with a strict adherence to emotional realism... If that makes sense!

We used a lot of techniques to create that subjectivity. We primarily shot with one camera and one lens, which helped us create a coherence in terms of visual space. We also shot almost every scene inside the axis. There weren't any *over the shoulder shots* and maybe a total of four or five masters in the whole series. We wanted to make it feel like we are always inside the conversation, the world, the emotional sphere. And never outside of it. We didn't use steadicam, instead almost always dolly on tracks, because we wanted to feel that there was a certain rigid trajectory to the movement that was propelling it forward. We had to adjust all light to camera, not camera to light, which meant that we were never relying on "unreal" color correction in post-production. We also used as little VFX as possible. All of this created a consistent visual language.

The particular reference points for *Euphoria* are all over the place. I think there was a percussive nature to Chuck Palahniuk's *Fight Club* that I was drawn to. I know that book and movie made a big impact on me when I was younger. Obviously, French New Wave, in terms of montage as story and certain coming of age pieces, such as *The 400 Blows* and *Murmur of the Heart*. And at the same time, I think I was drawing on the rhythm of the internet, the tonal shifts, the way we scroll through twitter feeds and hop from one emotion to another. I think Todd Hido's photographs of suburban landscapes were a big influence on Marcell Rév and myself. Other points of reference were Vincente Minnelli, in terms of color, lighting and transitions, *One from the Heart* by Coppola, *Magnolia* by Paul Thomas Anderson, *Time Stands Still* by Peter Gothar, *Three Colors* and *The Decalogue* by Kieślowski

There are some interesting surprises in the show, specifically concerning Jules. Still, the show never seems to be that interested in twists and sur-

prises for the sake of throwing off the audience. The surprise regarding Jules quickly moves into the background, and the viewer begins to engage with her character and her friendship/relationship with Rue. Were you intentionally trying to play with the viewer and his/her preconceived ideas?

Levinson: I try to write characters that I see myself in. While there's certainly an undercurrent of anxiety and danger that runs through the entire series, I think it's representative of how uncertain the world feels when you're younger. But as far as twists and things of that nature, I'm not interested in toying with the audience.

Could you say something about the casting of Hunter Schafer and Zendaya and why you chose them for the roles of Jules and Rue?

Levinson: If you watch *K.C. Undercover*, Zendaya is brilliant in it. She has a stronger sense of physicality than almost any modern actor that I can think of. That extends both dramatically and comedically. But after I had written the first couple of episodes, I just knew that she was Rue. I had even put her on a mood board that I presented to HBO. I just didn't think that she would do it because it was so different from her previous work. But she read the scripts and wanted to sit down and talk and that was that. I will say, I think the longer this process goes on the more and more grateful I've become to have her in the lead of this show. Coming back to it and writing a second season for an actor as gifted as her is a real joy because the possibilities of where Rue as a character can go are endless.

With Hunter Schafer, I had heard her name from a couple of different people and she had come in to audition with our New York casting director. It was a longer process. I had already written the first four episodes but I wasn't sure how it was all going to conclude. So I sat down with Hunter and had a six hour conversation. She has such a boundless and creative spirit. We just started rattling ideas back and forth about the possibilities of Jules. And in many ways that started to bleed into that character's trajectory, specifically in some of the conversations she has with Anna in Episode 7.

There is some debate about the environment of *Euphoria*. Most people argue that it takes place in California, yet it is never made explicit in the series. Was it intentional that we should not be able to associate the show with one specific zip code (like *Beverly Hills 90210*)?

Levinson: Yes. I had always written it and envisioned it as a place that exists outside of reality. There's palm trees but there's also mountains with snow.

There's mid-century modern houses and cities nearby. I wanted it to mimic our sense of nostalgia through the films we watched about growing up in America and move away from specific individual experience. I didn't want it to be a specific location or set in a particular town because I didn't want people to dismiss the characters' problems for any socio-economic or political reasons. I didn't want it to be an acute study or to play into any kind of distant, intellectual, bullshit debates about authenticity.

Euphoria is adapted from an Israeli series (as is the case with a few American series these days). Do you think that the TV landscape has become more global, and what was particularly interesting about the Israeli show?

Levinson: It certainly has become more global because people are watching shows with subtitles, which five years ago they never did. In terms of the original *Euphoria*, what I liked about it was how raw it was and how much it respected its characters.

Do you feel that teen dramas have begun to feature 'real' people instead of generic archetypes (like the jock, the nerd, the princess etc.)?

Levinson: Not really. But I think shows stick to certain archetypes, not for audiences, but for critics. Because you're only showing a couple of episodes to critics, those archetypes give them a sense of security in vouching for a series because they know how it's going to end. So if your show strays from that they get nervous because they don't want to say they love something that then disappoints them or the rest of the internet. I think that fearful mentality has infected the development process in the sense that the note behind the note is always: "I just want to know that the characters are going to be okay."

Flexible, Fluid And Adaptive: *Togetherness*, *Transparent* and the Modern Dramedy

Something that characterizes dramedies like *Togetherness* and *Transparent* is their use of tonal shifts. Is that something that you and your brother work with intently and consciously?

Duplass: All of that originates from Mark's and my personality and just how we are in the world. In 2002, we made a sort of accidental piece of art called *This is John* about a guy who's trying to perfect the personal greeting of his answering machine and fails and has a nervous breakdown. That was a three-dollar movie that got us into Sundance, and it was very different from everything else we had made prior to that. It was all we had to offer at that point. We only had three dollars and that shitty camera, an apartment and my brother and me, so I filmed it, and he acted in it. We later figured out that that kind of humor, tension, awkwardness and terror was sort of what we uniquely had to offer the world, which is ultimately what you're trying to get at as an artist. In the early days, we were trying to be the Coen Brothers, and we love them, but we're not them. We're just very different. And the tone you're talking about is the nugget of that. There are two parts to it: One is that that's how Mark and I are in the world. We're sad and desperate and a little bit funny - the things that we do are funny to the people around us - and we've learned that it's our job to sort of mine that level of comedy and desperateness. But the other side of it is how you execute it in the making of a show, and we've gotten better at that along the way. When we showed that tiny film called *This is John* at Sundance, the thing that was so amazing was that we would watch audiences that were watching our short, and half of them were like terrified, and the other half were laughing hysterically, as if it were *Dumb & Dumber* or some ridiculous comedy. And there were some audiences who were recoiling and giggling, and we were thinking: "Wow, this is something that we've accidentally hit upon, but we can think about what this is."

In terms of the curation of how we've sharpened that tool over time, I think that, particularly on set, we always encourage our actors to play scenes fully dramatically. We are not interested in them trying to make laughs. We're pushing them to be as committed and driven as possible, and usually, what we will do is to give them things to do or say that we think are funny within that context. And we do talk a lot about things like: "Will this joke break the dramatic realism?" We're trying to make it as funny as we can, basically, but within a 100% context of realism, and that's tailored, also, in editing. Our primary editor, Jay Deuby - we also used Nat Sanders on the show, and he's famous for doing *Moonlight*, but like Jay Deuby he is a hilarious person - so they understand our ethic of wanting to make it as funny as possible. And then, going beyond that, we even test our movies and shows on our closest colleagues. We'll ask them specifically: "Was this a little much? Did it take you out of the realism?" That's the trick, I think. Some jokes become self-conscious or are made just to make someone laugh, but what we've found is that as long as the comedy is situated within the realism of the show, it not only doesn't take away from the emotional experience, it generally adds to the emotional experience.

A good example of these tonal shifts is seen in your use of slow motion and

non-diegetic music in *Togetherness*, for example in the scene where Brett and Alex are going to a club in Detroit. That seems like a comedic use of music and slow motion.

Duplass: We normally only experience that combination of slow motion and music in serious moments or in über-cool situations, like in a Scorsese movie, but we do employ that for fun and for laughs. But the truth is that the guys in the sequence you're talking about, who go to Detroit and out on the town, they are experiencing Scorsese-like moments in their heads. But we know that it is far from that. There's something sweet about it, and I think it's a perfect example of how the comedy, hopefully, is earned because it's true to them. It's 100% true to them and how they're seeing themselves and perceiving the world.

In *Togetherness*, it is almost as if the thing that threatens to tear them apart ends up bringing them back together. Was that a conscious thought on your part?

Duplass: I don't think I ever had that conscious thought, but what I've learned is that when you focus incredibly intently on the small things, and you can align yourself to the channels that open - open to the mystery of what the piece of art wants you to do with it - those things happen. So, for instance, with that tiny movie, *This Is John*, we were trying to be the Coen Brothers, and we had a lot of 'film schooly' ideas, trying to make movies from concepts, and they never worked out because they were too heady, and then finally we just made a ridiculous short film about a guy battling an answering machine. The press wrote things like: "It's an epic struggle of man versus technology as a proxy for himself." They were saying these huge things that we had never thought, but that do emanate from the film. What we did know is that there is incredible potential energy in this battle between this guy and this machine, in a super funny and real way. I think that Mark and I knew, on some level, that this was a modern, middle-class *Don Quixote*.

Those kinds of things, I guess when you obey them and go into them, they reveal larger allegorical truths that you weren't even aware of. I appreciate you saying it.

During the first phase of the *multiplatform era* - the so-called *cable revolution* - we witnessed a slew of interesting and innovative drama series in the long format. But these days it seems as if some of the most interesting experimentation is happening within limited series and the shorter formats. How do you see it?

Duplass: I agree with you 100%, but the industry doesn't see it that way as much, not just in terms of buying things, but in terms of awards. It's super interesting. My perfect model is the 30-minute dramedy, but the metrics of television viewership pushes for 60-minute dramas and 30-minute hard comedies. It was the same thing with both *Togetherness* and *Transparent* - and *Transparent* won a lot of awards because it had a marquis issue that was elevating it to something that was important culturally for all of us in the world. But we still had a lot of voters coming up and telling us: "It's hard to compare a show like *Togetherness* with a show like *Silicon Valley*" because *Silicon Valley*, pound for pound, is just way more laughs. Or bigger laughs. So that's a little bit tricky because the industry is not as financially rewarding for studios to make blends and hybrids in that way, but I think it's the most interesting stuff. Luckily, with *Transparent* we had the trans issues, which put it on the map, on a whole new level. Also, *Transparent* was one of the first shows on Amazon, and the shows that were concurrent with us on Amazon had no viewership, compared to what we were doing. So we had the full backing of a titan that was ready to blast onto the scene. Before *Transparent*, Amazon was a place to buy toilet paper.

Compared to *Togetherness*, *Transparent* is more dramatic and less comedic, but again it explores that fluid area between comedy and drama, and it uses an uneasy camera, as I see it, to mirror the fluidity and restlessness of the characters. How would you describe the style in that series?

Duplass: I agree with that, and I think it's all due to the director of photography, Jim Frohna. Almost everyone on the show regarded him as the witness of what was happening because that was a super intense show, and we sort of became that family on some level. And we really are that way. Gaby and Amy are my sisters in real life now. I text and talk with them almost every day, and we are a very tight-knit group. And in terms of the camera style, Jim would usually just hold the camera to his body and allow the action to lead him. So he was working in a very intuitive way, almost as if he were an actor, and I think that it worked on some level because the feedback that we got from a lot of fans was that they felt as if they were a part of that family.

And I think there is something very interesting about the fact that all the characters are so hard and challenging because I think that's how we all feel in our own families. They're all so challenging, and you feel consternation and a sense of unrealized potential, and there's that feeling of: "Are we moving towards healing? Are we going to get there? Are we going anywhere?"

Everything on *Transparent* was very fluid. There was an enormous amount of improvisation and an enormous amount of rewriting on set. The creator really gave us a tremendous authority over our characters. There was a tremendous amount of chaos on set that was allowed, which is hard. It's hard to live in that chaos, but it also made it very life-like. You have this sense, when you're watching the show, that this is not controlled. Shit is off the rails, and anything can happen in this moment. And that was true of the experience.

Transparent deals with people who are in transition or who reject traditional binaries, and in itself it is a series that almost rejects classification and which is not made for traditional American television. It seems like we are seeing quite a few shows like that, especially within the dramedy genre?

Duplass: What's great about internet distribution is that you don't need a quarter of your country to watch the show to make the show viable. All you have to do is hit a corridor of hardcore fans. And it's worldwide now. It used to be that shows were made mostly in the US, and then they would get syndicated to other countries, if they were good enough. Now, with Netflix, Amazon, HBO, Hulu and all these other great providers, things can get more specific, and they don't need to fit into a traditional category. You can have a 30-minute drama or a 60-minute dramedy. A series like *Fleabag* has really opened the door to thinking that maybe a miniseries can be two or three seasons. It's interesting because *Togetherness* is two seasons, and it got "canceled", but for me, when I originally envisioned it, I had those two seasons in mind. I didn't have anything beyond that. I'm sure that we would have tried to go beyond that just because people loved it, and we were getting paid, and we loved the actors, and it was a good show to make. But that box set of those two seasons feels like *one* arc to me. I was able to express everything that I wanted to express with that show, even to the point where I'm ready, at least for now, to move on from the family dramedy or the very internal, domestic dramedies.

Some people argue that the directors have a different role on limited series than on long-running serials and that the degree of authorship is different. How do you see it?

Duplass: A lot of people look at the limited series as a way to make a big movie, and as a showrunner you can attract A-level feature film directors, if you have a miniseries. If they can start and finish it and call it a piece of art that they are responsible for, it's way more interesting for them than just doing the pilot or coming and going. Because once a show is up and running, for you to come in and direct it, you're really just helping people to move through set in an inspired and comfortable way. You're not really authoring that episode that much. And especially for a writer-director who wants to be involved in the writing and shaping of the show, a limited series is definitely more suited for that. Very few shows are good after three seasons. It is very rare for a show not to go downhill, and shows that push six, seven, eight, nine years... The impetus behind that is not usually to make the best piece of art that you can make. The impetus behind that is usually to make a shit ton of money, having fun and continuing to work with people that you love. I don't think that anybody who is doing the same show after five or six years thinks: "This is fulfilling me on my deepest levels creatively." To get a show up and running, usually you have been working hard for two years before that pilot even airs, so you're talking eight or nine years for somebody.

You have created, produced and directed a lot of dramedies and limited series, and you have also co-created *Room 104*, which is a so-called *anthology series*. That genre was popular during the early days of American television, but it seems to have come back within the last few years. Why do you think that is?

Duplass: My brother and I had this idea ten or twelve years ago. My brother is a brilliant producer in terms of modelling things that can be made, reverse engineering things that can be made, in a super efficient and cost effective way, so that you can maximize creativity and exploration. That's his brilliance, and I think it was ultimately his idea to start with, but we had always talked about something like that. I used to live by a hotel that is exactly like the one in the show, and we always talked about getting into that hotel and start shooting. The way we talked about it in the early days was: "We'll shoot ten episodes in ten days. We'll rent this room and the one next to it for ten days, and we're going to have a whole season of TV." This was before anybody was making TV independently, but that was our thought because it's so efficient, and everyone has had an experience in a motel room. Anything can and will and does happen in a motel room. People, when they're on vacations, tend to "try on" different personalities. So for us it just started as something fun and easy and as a way to explore.

We love championing up-and-coming directors, we've grandfathered a lot of directors into the Directors Guild because it was their first studio job. It was a way for us to help people, whom we felt were super exciting, to write or direct an HBO show. A lot of the time for writers and directors, when they're working in TV, they have to really sublimate themselves into the show as it is and become someone else. And that's the opposite of what we wanted for *Room 104*. The credo was "get as weird and as *you* as you can get" because what we actually need is for your episode to differentiate itself from the other episodes. It seemed very exciting and encouraging of the exploratory process in terms of making art. We didn't expect it to be so *Twilight Zoney* at the very beginning, but it turns out that mystery, intrigue, thriller or horror works better for a one-off 20-30-minute piece of art because it's really hard to get people to emotionally invest deeply in that short period of time. So it started to spin more and more that way. That was where the fans were, and it gave us an opportunity to go to a place that we hadn't explored before. We shot most of those episodes in two days.

When you start to see productions by regional artists, people of color, women and LGBTQ filmmakers, you are essentially democratizing not just who gets to make art, but also what kind of art that gets to be released to the public. That's ultimately a good thing, when television becomes representative of the way the world really is, and if we can be a part of that process, that's what we want to do.

What are the most profound changes in the TV landscape, as you see it?

Duplass: I try to work as an adaptive person because everything is going to change. Constantly. A few years ago, people were mourning the death of the movie. It wasn't exactly the death of movies, but I think we can all acknowledge that two years ago television series became the dominant art form of our time. Movies had the title for almost a hundred years, but now it's television series. They've taken the title. You could be sad about that, but the truth is that there are storytellers and people who receive stories, and if you can be flexible about what those stories need to be or how they need to be told, it is a good thing. Now TV series are starting to shorten up a little bit, and you no longer need to be committed for seven years. Networks are no longer looking for seven years. They are looking for two or three years, and then we'll see where we are.

In one way, the fact that you can reach a niche audience, and you don't have to reach so many people, is very advantageous. But in another way it's disadvantageous because, for instance, if you have a decently made *young-adult vampire series*, it's going to get greenlit, and in a way that hedges the need for it to be great. If you can check a few genre boxes or audience category boxes, you can sort of make art by numbers. But I'm not sure that it's different from the way that TV used to be because before, when you had NBC shows that had to reach everybody, there was a blanket of generic, acceptable comedies and dramas. I'm not sure that it's any different. It might just be a different form.

Epilogue: Television in the *Multiplatform Era*

In the introduction to this book, I argued that we are living in the midst of a transition. Later, however, I discussed the use of words like "revolution" and "disruption" as a potential simplification of the current TV landscape that might over-emphasize the changes, which have occurred since the early 2000s, while overlooking or under-emphasizing the elements of continuity.

Over the course of six chapters, I have looked at TV production in the *multiplatform era* - an era characterized by TV series that are consumed on various platforms and that sometimes utilize different media and platforms as part of their storytelling. In the first part of the book, I explored the changes in the TV landscape from the advent of cable and DVD to the introduction of streaming and the so-called *global turn*. As Trisha Dunleavy writes, the cable revolution of the late 1990s and early 2000s could be seen as the first phase of the *multiplatform era*, and I argue that media akin to VCR and DVD allowed for a new type of engagement (what Amanda D. Lotz calls *compressed consumption*), and that cable series such as *Oz*, *The Sopranos* and *The Wire* exploited the possibilities for *compressed consumption* and new types of engagement to create complex stories with large ensembles and longer arcs. These series were used as flagships in HBO's "not-TV" branding strategy, and creators like David Chase and David Simon talk about this period in American television as a formative or transitional phase where television "matured" (to use Simon's word).

The second chapter focuses on the expansion of the Internet and the so-called streaming era. Netflix was founded in 1997, but the effects of streaming on the TV landscape were not felt until the 2010s, when Netflix began producing original series (e.g. *House of Cards*, *Orange Is the New Black* and *Stranger Things*). Since then, other players have entered the market, and we are now dealing with a complex TV landscape where *TV natives*, *online natives* and *content natives* are competing for the same customers - or vying for different demographics in a fragmented media landscape. Critics and scholars have debated the streaming era intensely since the launching of *House of Cards* in 2013, and journalists often focus on the so-called *streaming wars* while eulogizing the 'death' of *linear TV* or television altogether. While the TV landscape is, indeed, changing, such obituaries are premature and reductive. We *are* seeing tendencies towards *cord-shaving* and *cord-cutting* in the current mediascape, but people are still watching television (at least *non-linear television*), and it is difficult to say, with any degree of certainty, that streamers like Netflix are outcompeting the big networks. Talking about Netflix as the only player in today's TV landscape, as some critics have done, seems like a simplification of the complexity that characterizes the modern mediascape. But the notions of free competition and free choice might also be an illusion. As mentioned in Chapter 2, there are clear tendencies towards *vertical* and *horizontal integration* where we have a large group of channels and platforms, but where the power is concentrated on a few *media conglomerates* and powerful streamers like Netflix. As industry critic Julia Alexander writes:

> Over the last year, if an entertainment conglomerate hasn't announced a shift to focus on streaming, does it really count as an entertainment conglomerate? With the end of the year in sight and the entertainment industry crowded with options, legacy companies are making big bets on their new services, using public executive shake-ups and declarations of digital-first importance to make their point heard. Streaming isn't just a part of their businesses; it's *their future*. Over the last several months, Disney, NBCUniversal, WarnerMedia and ViacomCBS have restructured their teams to makes streaming a primary focus. Long-time executives have been fired, others have stepped down (aka fired), and departments merged in an effort to compete with the biggest competition in the room. The lingering question is will it work for every player in the game? How much of it is too little too late?[784]

That the American (and global) landscape has changed dramatically is beyond doubt, but streaming does not precipitate the death of television, and it is too early, at this point, to describe streaming series as an independent form with its own set of storytelling practices and viewing behaviors. Certainly, *binge-watching* has become a broader and more noticeable phenomenon after the premiere of *House of Cards*, and some creators and producers, for instance Beau Willimon and Henrik Bastin, may even encourage the viewers to binge their series. But *binge-watching* is not a new form of consumption, and series like *Lilyhammer* and *House of Cards* illustrate that modern streaming series rely on televisual traditions just as they try to transcend or debunk them.

Amanda D. Lotz cleverly distinguishes between television as a medium and television as a distribution technology. Following that distinction, I argue that TV series are being distributed in new ways today, but many of the series that are made for *online natives* and *content natives* have a lot in common with the traditional form of seriality and mode of storytelling that we know from regular television. Films can also be consumed in different venues and via different distribution technologies, but that does not alter the conceptual status of the different productions and the terminology with which we describe them. *Marriage Story* is still a film, even if we stream it via Netflix and watch it on our smartphones, and *Die Hard* (1988) is still a movie, even if we watch it on *linear TV* as part of the Christmas schedule.

The advent of streaming has changed the TV landscape quite profoundly, and it has also changed television from an insular phenomenon, bound to different industries, territories and nation states, to a global one. While focusing primarily on American TV and the American TV landscape, I argue that new media and platforms have created a *global turn* in television where it is difficult to see American television as an isolated phenomenon. Inspired by Ramon Lobato, I illustrate how talents migrate from industry to industry and how TV series travel, in the form of transnational adaptations and remakes and international collaborations and co-productions. A more recent trend in this context is the focus, from global streamers like Netflix, on regional productions and *local-language originals*. This trend may be seen as a natural consequence of the *global turn*, and it might also be seen as a strategic way to branch out and monetize different territories and cultural traditions.

The first part of the book deals with changes in the American (and global) TV landscape, and the second part of the book explores the changes in modern American TV series - in terms of style, storytelling and genre - and how these aspects reflect the general changes in the TV landscape. In the fourth chapter, I look at new approaches to storytelling, focusing particularly on *narrative complexity* in modern television (as in series like *True Detective*, *American Crime* and *Dark*) and *transmedia storytelling* (as in *The Walking Dead* and *Twin Peaks*). These tendencies are described as new approaches to storytelling that reflect a modern TV landscape where audiences consume television in different ways and where producers seek to utilize different media and platforms to create transmedial and immersive *storyworlds*.

In Chapter 5, I describe some new and alternative approaches to style in American television, and, with reference to Kristin Thompson, I explore the concept of *art TV* and how this is reflected in modern television. Modern American series, I argue, often try to stand out in a saturated media landscape by employing *signature styles* and elements of experimentation and conspicuousness. This is seen in the alternative approaches to dialogues and staging in series like *American Crime*, *Succession* and *Euphoria*, and it is seen in the use of *lens flare*, off-kilter framing and *musical moments* in series like *Mr. Robot*, *Better Call Saul*, *Twin Peaks: The Return* and *Stranger Things*. At the end of Chapter 5, I discuss the concept of *TV auteurism* and how practitioners evoke the "spectre of the auteur" when describing the artistic qualities of a given series and trying to legitimize television as an art form. There are many examples of alternative and conspicuous approaches to style in modern American television, just like multiple different TV productions vie for the attention of the fragmented audience, but I argue that the new and/or alternative aspects of these series often go hand in hand with traditional, televisual qualities. *American Crime* has an alternative approach to dialogue staging and editing, for example, but these experimental approaches may be necessary in order to make the series stand out, given that it consists almost exclusively of dialogue scenes. This is also the case with *Succession*, which takes a traditional component of American television - the dialogue scene in a confined space - and stages it in a new and less controlled fashion. Even

Twin Peaks: The Return, which uses long takes, lengthy *musical moments* and a conspicuous audiovisual style, includes traditional markers of seriality at the end of each episode, despite being promoted as an 18-hour film and screened at arthouse cinemas and art museums like MoMA.[785]

The final chapter of the book, then, explores some modern approaches to genre and forms of hybridization in American television, focusing on three specific genres: crime fiction, teen drama and dramedy. In this chapter, I argue that modern crime series are colored by various cultural traditions that circulate and intermix in complex ways, through *transnational remakes* and "circular influences" (as Nic Pizzolatto says). American crime series such as *True Detective* and *The Killing* draw their inspiration from both American and Scandinavian traditions (e.g. *Southern Gothic*, film noir and *Nordic Noir*), and modern crime series from Denmark (e.g. *Bedrag* and *Forhøret*), Iceland (*Ófærð*) and England (*Luther*) combine elements from American and British traditions with culturally specific locations and tonalities.

The same thing is true of modern American teen dramas like *Euphoria* that are inspired by various cultural traditions and productions - from French youth films like *Les quatre cents coups* to edgy Israeli productions and British, Scandinavian and American teen dramas like *Skins*, *SKAM* and *My So-Called Life*. Teen dramas are a modern outgrowth of the *serial melodrama*, and they often include young people as their main characters while thematizing issues and problems connected to adolescent life and targeting a young demographic. This was also the case for traditional teen dramas like *Degrassi* and *Beverly Hills 90210*, but in modern teen dramas, digital and social media are often a part of the problems and their potential solutions. The lives of young people have become *mediatized*, and modern teen dramas reflect this *mediatization* by exploring issues such as cyberbullying, sextortion and unsolicited sharing of private photos and by utilizing multiple media and platforms as part of their storytelling.

The final section of Chapter 6 deals with the dramedy genre as a relatively new hybrid between drama and comedy and a form of television that is particularly suited for the *multiplatform era* with its short, flexible format and its combination of humor and emotional engagement. Analyzing *Togetherness*, *Looking* and *Transparent*, I argue that modern dramedies often explore a televisual twilight zone between different formats, genres and tonalities while thematizing and, in some cases, debunking the traditional binaries in terms of gender and sexuality.

Television production has changed in the *multiplatform era*. Many productions, especially limited series, are *cross-boarded* and shot like movies, and they frequently utilize different media as part of their storytelling and engagement structures. American TV series have also changed, and the practitioners themselves argue that film and television have moved closer to each other in various ways. A recurring *trade narrative* is the so-called *maturation story*, which claims that American television has evolved and matured since the advent of cable and streaming. Another recurring narrative is the so-called *saturation story*, which argues that modern American TV series are becoming more "outrageous" and edgy because of a saturated media landscape and a vast array of content. These narratives are also, at times, combined with a *sophistication story*, which argues that TV series and audiences have become more sophisticated. TV series, they posit, have become more complex and "cinematic", as viewers have become more *media literate*. As the film and TV director Jennifer Lynch poetically puts it: "Bravery happened. Respect for the intelligence of the audience happened. Storytellers turned the 'idiot box' into a set of open palms and offered the world things they could receive and evolve with."[786]

The renowned author and TV creator Tom Perrotta describes a similar development from the advent of cable television to the current streaming age, arguing that TV has changed due to multiple different factors:

> *Twin Peaks* may have been the outlier, but things really began to change two decades ago. *The Sopranos* started this so-called "Golden Age", and it's hard to remember how rigid TV was before that. Part of it was that there was no way to *binge*, so if you were out the day when Episode 4 was aired, you'd have to miss it, and you couldn't catch up on it. So it meant that the storytelling couldn't be serialized in the same way. Cable allowed for serialization, and writers just went for it, and this was even before libraries like HBO Go [HBO Max] or streaming services existed.
>
> But that, I think, was the big leap: When writers felt that they could tell long, serialized stories over the course of, at that point, thirteen hours. And especially for novelists it turned out to be very recognized: TV series became much better vehicles for adapting a novel than a film which is 90 minutes or two hours. I certainly experienced that with *Little Children*. I loved working with Todd Field, and I think we made a really cool movie, but there were just chunks of the book we couldn't fit. We actually wrote a very long script, and we did pitch it to HBO. I think we could have done a great six-part miniseries of *Little Children*; it would have been better, and that was one of the reasons that I moved to TV with *The Leftovers*.
>
> That technology of allowing people to watch very complicated eight or ten-hour seasons created the potential for writers to tell really complex, deep stories. And HBO, back then, was not very concerned with ratings. They would stick with a show like *The Wire*, when nobody was watching, and now that's a treasure, a landmark show. And they allowed *The Leftovers* to go on for three seasons, when nobody was watching except for the critics who were saying that it was an amazing show. I'm really grateful for that moment that opened up the possibilities for storytelling and relaxed the economic pressure on writers to find a mass audience. And the idea that drama was one thing and comedy was another started to fall apart. TV didn't respect that distinction as much, at least not high-quality TV. Watch *The Sopranos* now, and it's as much a comedy as it is a drama.[787]

Finally, there is a narrative that we could call the *liberation story*, arguing that television and audiences have been liberated by the globalization of the TV landscape and the introduction of new media, platforms and outlets. Many of the interviewees for this book talk positively about the introduction of new media and channels, and there is an almost unanimous positivity concerning the *global turn* and the introduction of *local-language originals*. A few interviewees (e.g. Beau Willimon and Maggie Monteith) question that narrative, however, pointing to signs of *vertical integration* and cautiously arguing that the interest in regional productions and *glocal* aspects might lead to exoticism and inauthenticity.

American television *has* changed in the last twenty years, and this book has hopefully provided plenty and plausible data to support that conclusion. The American TV landscape has changed radically since the advent of cable and DVD in the late 1990s, and American TV is no longer an insular phenomenon. American TV series today are formed by various televisual and cultural traditions, and they are informed by a changing media landscape and new modes of production and distribution. With almost 200 million subscribers, Netflix is a behemoth in the ever-changing TV landscape. But their focus on broadly popular series (like Tiger King, Emily in Paris and The Queen's Gambit), *ambient TV* and linear offerings harks back to television in the pre-streaming era, and other giants like Amazon, Disney (especially after acquiring Hulu) and HBO Max challenge their position in the mediascape. In 2021 alone, Netflix, HBO and Disney are spending a combined 120 billion dollars on content, illustrating their fierce competition and their intense focus on original content.[788]

Despite the many stories of *maturation*, *sophistication* and *liberation*, American TV has hardly moved "beyond" television. Many critics and practitioners talk, jubilantly even, about the "cinematization" of television, and modern series (e.g. Twin Peaks: The Return and Top of the Lake: China Girl) are frequently screened in cinemas and added to listicles about the best "films" of the decade.[789] Creators and producers will readily tell you that their TV series was shot or conceived as "one long movie" and crafted by people who had their primary experience from the film industry. But modern American TV series, albeit experimental and innovative, are still televisual, even if audiences watch them in a movie theater or on their smartphones, in only one or two sittings. We have not moved "beyond" television, but modern TV series are challenging the traditional and limited understandings of television as a medium, and as TV series are stretching the conventional formats and moving outside of "the 14-inch box" (as Joel Fields says), they are finally being recognized as an art form worthy of critical examination and close scrutiny (cf. Steve McQueen's anthology series Small Axe [BBC One, 2020], which harks back to the first golden age of TV while effectively being a series of films). Television is not everything, but it seems to be everywhere. We are seeing it in many iterations and watching it on multiple platforms in various different ways. We might not be living in a "golden age", but there is plenty of "precious metal amid the dross", as Harley Peyton says, and television is far from dead.

Bibliography

Adalian, Josef (2016), "How Amazon Became a Major Player in Half-Hour Television," *Vulture*, October 6. vulture.com/2016/10/amazon-became-a-major-player-in-half-hour-tv.html.

Adalian, Josef (2018), "Inside the Binge Factory," *Vulture*, June 11. www.vulture.com/2018/06/how-netflix-swallowed-tv-industry.html.

Adams, Sam (2016), "*The Night Of* Is More Than a Crime Thriller. It's Also a Great Prison Drama," *Slate*. August 10. slate.com/ulture/2016/08/the-night-of-is-more-than-a-crime-thriller-it-s-also-a-great-prison-drama.html.

Adelborg, Jeppe Kondrup (2019), "'Girls', 'Game of Thrones' og 'Chernobyl' satte standarden for tv-serier i 10'erne," *Politiken*, December 19. politiken.dk/kultur/film_og_tv/art7559746/Girls-Game-of-Thrones-og-Chernobyl-satte-standarden-for-tv-serier-i-10erne.

Adorno, Theodor & Hanns Eisler (1947), *Composing for the Films*. London: The Athlone Press

Adorno, Theodor & Max Horkheimer (1991), *Kulturindustri*. Oslo: Cappelen.

Agger, Gunhild (2012), "Thrillerens kunst: *Forbrydelsen I-III*," *16:9* 10(48), November. www.16-9.dk/2012-11/side08_feature1.htm.

Agger, Gunhild (2020), "Dream a Little Dream of Me," *Kommunikationsforum*, December 1.

Akass, Kim & Janet McCabe (2018): "HBO and the Aristocracy of Contemporary TV Culture: affiliations and legitimating television culture, post-2007", *Mise au point*, 10 | 2018, January 15, 2018. journals.openedition.org/map/2472 ; DOI : 10.4000/map.2472.

Albrecht, Michael Mario (2016), *Masculinity in Contemporary Quality Television*. New York: Routledge

Alexander, John (1993), *The Films of David Lynch*. London: Letts.

Alexander, Julia (2019), "Can HBO Now survive HBO Max", *The Verge*, September 27.

Alexander, Julia (2020a), "Quibi is already locked in a legal battle over its rotating video tech," *The Verge*, March 11. www.theverge.com/2020/3/11/21173981/quibi-eko-lawsuit-turnstyle--technology-jeffrey-katzenberg-streaming-interactive.

Alexander, Julia (2020b), "Streaming was part of the future – now it's the only future," *The Verge*, October 28. www.theverge.com/21536842/streaming-disney-hbo-max-peacock-cbs-all-access-warnermedia-viacom-nbcuniversal.

Allen, Robert C. (1985), *Speaking of Soap Operas*. Chapel Hill, NC: University of North Carolina Press.

Altman, Rick (2001), "Cinema and Popular Song: The Lost Tradition," in Wojcik, Pamela Robertson & Arthur Knights (eds.). Durham: Duke University Press, pp. 19-30.

Altman, Rick (2012 [1984]), "A Semantic/Syntactic Approach to Film Genre," in Grant, Barry Keith (ed.), *Film Genre Reader IV*. Austin: University of Texas Press.

Andersen, Kim Jong (2019), "*Too Old to Die Young* - 13 timer i skærsilden," *P.O.V.*, June 26. pov.international/too-old-to-die-young-13-timer-i-skaersilden.

Andersen, Tore Rye (2019), *Serier*. Aarhus: Aarhus Universitetsforlag.

Astruc, Alexandre (1948), "The Birth of a New Avant-Garde: La Camera-Stylo," in Vincendeau, Ginette & Peter Graham (eds.) (2009), *The French New Wave: Critical Landmarks*. London: Palgrave.

Baker, Djoymi (2017), "Terms of Excess: Binge-Viewing as Epic-Viewing in the Netflix Era," in Barker, Cory & Myc Wiatrowski (eds.), *The Age of Netflix: Critical Essays on Streaming Media, Digital Delivery and Instant Access*. Jefferson, NC: McFarland & Co.

Barra, Luca (2017), "*Master of None*, *Atlanta* and Audience Engagement in Contemporary US TV Drama," *16:9*, November 19. www.16-9.dk/2017/11/master-of-none.

Bastholm, Søren Rørdam (2014), "I mørket findes frelsen," *16:9*, August 15. www.16-9.dk/2014/08/i-moerket-findes-frelsen.

Bastholm, Søren (2018), "Interview med Jannik Tai Mosholt - hovedforfatter på *The Rain*, den første danske Netflixserie," *16:9*, April 17. www.16-9.dk/2018/04/interview-med-jannik-tai-mosholt-showrunner-paa-the-rain.

Bastholm, Søren Rørdam (2019), "Tænk på Fincher - *Mindhunters* titelsekvens," *16:9*, August 10. www.16-9.dk/2019/08/mindhunters-titelsekvens.

Baudrillard, Jean (1994 [1981]), *Simulacra and Simulation*. Translated by Sheila Faria Glaser. Michigan: The University of Michigan Press.

Bazin, André (1952), "Remade in USA," *Cahiers du Cinéma* #11.

Bazin, André (2004 [1967]), *What is Cinema?* Berkeley & Los Angeles: University of California Press.

Beck, Jay (2016), *Designing Sound: Audiovisual Aesthetics in 1970s American Cinema*. Rutgers University Press.

Bendtsen, Johan Varning (2018), "DR laver ny sæson af drama-succes med afdøde Nedim Yasar på rollelisten," *Politiken*, December 12. politiken.dk/kultur/film_og_tv/art6913752/DR-laver-ny-s%C3%A6son-af-drama-succes-med-afd%C3%B8de-Nedim-Yasar-p%C3%A5-rollelisten.

Berg, Leah R. Vande (1991), "Dramedy: Moonlighting as an Emergent Generic Hybrid," in Berg, Leah R. Vande & Lawrence R. Wenner (eds.), *Television Criticism: Approaches and Applications*. New York & London: Longman, pp. 95-109.

Bertelsen, Diana (2016), "RIPA - a new Danish Viking Series on the social media," *RibeVikingeCenter*, February 15. www.ribevikingecenter.dk/de/aktuelles/ripa-new-danish-viking-docudrama.aspx.

Bianculli, David (1992), *Teleliteracy: Taking Television Seriously*. New York: Continuum

Bianculli, David (2016), *The Platinum Age of Television: From* I Love Lucy *to* The Walking Dead, *How TV Became Terrific*. New York: Doubleday.

Bigsby, Christopher (2013), *Viewing America: Twenty-First Century Television Drama*. New York: Cambridge University Press.

Blair, Iain (2018), "Showtime's *Homeland*: Producer/director Lesli Linka Glatter", *Randi Altmans postPerspective*, June 18. postperspective.com/showrunner-lesli-linka-glatter-showtimes-homeland.

Bloodsworth, Adam (2020), "How *I May Destroy You* Should Open the Door for More Groundbreaking TV Shows," *Huffpost*, August 19.

Bogdanovich, Peter (2000), *Interview with David Chase*, featurette on the DVD release of *The Sopranos*, Season 1 (HBO, Region 1).

Bojalad, Alec (2017), "Stranger Things: In Defence of Nostalgia," *Den of Geek*, November 2.

Bolin, Alice (2018), *Dead Girls: Essays on Surviving an American Obsession*. William Morrow Paperbacks.

Bordwell, David (1979), "The Art Cinema as a Mode of Film Practice," *Film Criticism* 4, No. 1.

Bordwell, David (1985), *Narration in the Fiction Film*. Madison: University of Wisconsin Press.

Bordwell, David (1986), "Classical Hollywood Cinema: Narrational Principles and Procedures", in Rosen, Philip (ed.), *Narrative, Apparatus, Ideology*. New York: Columbia University Press.

Bordwell, David (2006), *The Way Hollywood Tells It: Stories and Style in Modern Movies*. Berkeley: University of California Press.

Bordwell, David (2017), *Reinventing Hollywood: How 1940s Filmmakers Changed Movie Storytelling*. Chicago & London: The University of Chicago Press.

Bordwell, David et al. (1985), *The Classical Hollywood Cinema: Film Style & Mode of Production to 1960*. New York: Columbia University Press.

Bronwen, Thomas (2016), *Narrative: The Basics*. London: Routledge.

Brown, Barry & Louise Barkhuus (2006), "The Television Will Be Revolutionized: Effects of PVRs and Filesharing on Television Watching", conference paper, *CHC 2006*. Montréal, Québec: Canada, April 22-27.

Bruns, Axel (2008), *Blogs, Wikipedia, Second Life and Beyond*. Peter Lang.

Bruun, Hanne (2014), "Eksklusive informanter. Om interviewet som redskab i produktionsanalysen," *Nordicom-Information* 36, pp. 29-43.

Bushman, David (2020), *Conversations with Mark Frost: Twin Peaks, Hill Street Blues, and the Education of a Writer*. Columbia, Ohio: Fayetteville Mafia Press

Butler, Jeremy G. (2010), *Television Style*. New York: Routledge.

Caldwell, John T. (1995), *Televisuality: Style, Crisis, and Authority in American Television*. New Brunswick: Rutgers University Press.

Caldwell, John T. (2008), *Production Culture: Industrial Reflexivity and Critical Practice in Film and Television*. Durham & London: Duke University Press.

Camus, Albert (1991), *The Myth of Sisyphus*. Translated by Justin O'Brien. Alfred A. Knopf.

Canby, Vincent (1992): "One Long Last Gasp for Laura Palmer", *The New York Times*, August 29.

Cappelen, John (2020), "Nedbør og sol i Danmark," *DMI*, January 31. www.dmi.dk/klima/tema-forside-klimaet-frem-til-i-dag/nedboer-og-sol-i-danmark.

Cardwell, Sarah (2007), "Is Quality Television Any Good? Generic Distinctions, Evaluations and the Troubling Matter of Critical Judgement," in McCabe, Janet & Kim Akass (eds.), *Quality TV: Contemporary American Television and Beyond*. London: I.B. Tauris.

Cardwell, Sarah & Steven Peacock (2006), "Introduction," in Cardwell, Sarah & Steven Peacock (eds.), "Good Television?", *Journal of British Cinema and Television* 3:1.

Carr, David (2014), "Taking Back Your TV, Incessantly," *The New York Times*, March 14. www.nytimes.com/2010/03/15/business/media/15carr.html.

Carroll, Noël (1996), "The Specificity of Media in the Arts," in *Theorizing the Moving Image*. Cambridge: Cambridge University Press.

Carter, Bill (2011), "'Sopranos' Sets Ratings Record with Season Finale," *The New York Times*, May 22.

Caughie, John (1981) (ed.), *Theories of Authorship: A Reader*. London: BFI.

Cawelti, John G. (1976), *Adventure, Mystery and Romance*. Chicago: The University of Chicago Press.

Cawelti, John G. (2001), "The Concept of Formula in the Study of Popular Literature," in Harrington, Lee & Denise Bielby (eds.), *Popular Culture. Production and consumption*. Oxford: Blackwell Publishing.

Chalaby, Jean K. (2005), *Transnational Television Worldwide: Towards a New Media Order*. London: I.B. Tauris.

Chaney, Jen (2015), "Damon Lindelof on 'The Leftovers' Finale, the Show's Future and his Afterlife Obsession," *The New York Times*, December 7. www.nytimes.com/2015/12/07/arts/television/damon-lindelof-on-the-leftovers-finale-the-shows-future-and-his-afterlife-obsession.html.

Chavez, Mercedes (2019), "Twin Peaks S3 EP1 & Twin Peaks S3 EP2," *Cinemetrics*, January 19. cinemetrics.lv/movie.php?movie_ID=23613.

Chion, Michel (1994), *Audio-Vision: Sound on Screen*. Translated by Claudia Gorbman. New York: Columbia University Press.

Chion, Michel (1999), *The Voice in Cinema*. Translated by Claudia Gorbman. New York: Columbia University Press.

Chitwood, Adam (2014), "*The Walking Dead* Season 5 Premiere Shatters Ratings Records with 17.3 Million Viewers," *Collider*, October 13. collider.com/the-walking-dead-season-5-premiere-ratings.

Christensen, Jørgen Riber (2018), "Troper i krimiserier," *16:9*, November 14. www.16-9.dk/2018/11/troper-i-krimiserier.

Christie, Thomas A. (2009), *John Hughes and Eighties Cinema: Teenage Hopes and American Dreams*. Crescent Moon.

Codero, Rosy (2019), "The NeverEnding Story theme singer Limahl celebrates newfound interest thanks to 'Stranger Things', *Entertainment Weekly*, July 9.

Collins, Sean T. (2018), "The Ten Best Musical Moments in *The Americans*," *Vulture*, May 31. www.vulture.com/article/the-americans-10-best-musical-moments.html.

Conklin, Micah (2014), "Fort Macomb and True Detective," *Deep South Magazine*, March 17. deepsouthmag.com/2014/03/17/fort-macomb-and-true-detective.

Corkin, Stanley (2017), *Connecting The Wire: Race, Space, and Postindustrial Baltimore*. Austin, TX: University of Texas Press.

Cousins, Mark (2014), *The Story of Film*. BCA/Pavilion Books.

Croce, Benedetto (1929), *Aesthetic*. Trans. Douglas Ainsley. London: Macmillan.

Curtin, Michael et al. (2014), "Introduction," in *Distribution Revolution: Conversations About the Digital Future of Film and Television*. California: University of California Press

Cusumano, Katherine (2018), "Rising Model Hunter Schafer Is Fighting for the Future of Trans Individuals On and Off the Runway," *W*, March 21. www.wmagazine.com/story/hunter-schafer-model-bathroom-bill.

Dane, Benjamin (2020), "For 30 år siden vendte ét afsnit op og ned på tv-landskabet: Her er historien om Twin Peaks, der måske ændrede modern tv for altid," *Børsen*, May 31.

Davis, Glyn & Kay Dickinson (2008), "Introduction," in *Teen TV - Genre, Consumption and Identity*. London: BFI.

Dawson, Max (2012), "Defining Mobile Television: The Social Construction and Deconstruction of New and Old Media," *Popular Communications* 10.

Debnath, Neela (2020), "Walking Dead season 11: Has Maggie changed amid time-jump? Star drops cryptic clue," *Express*, June 23. www.express.co.uk/showbiz/tv-radio/1299810/Walking-Dead-season-11-Maggie-Rhee-time-jump-Lauren-Cohan-AMC-series.

Dibdin, Emma (2006), "Is *Six Feet Under*'s final episode the best TV finale of all time?", *Digital Spy*, March 6. www.digitalspy.com/tv/ustv/a663836/is-six-feet-under-the-best-tv-finale-of-all-time/-

Dom, Pieter (2017), "David Lynch's Personal Recommendations on How to Watch *Twin Peaks* Properly," *Welcome to Twin Peaks*, June 23. welcometotwinpeaks.com/news/david-lynch-how-to-watch-twin-peaks-recommendations.

Dornbush, Jonathan (2015): "25 Years Later: The 5 Ways *Twin Peaks* Changed TV," *Entertainment Weekly*, April 8.

Dreier, Troy (2017), "Pay TV Lost 1.8M Subscribers in 2016 as Cord-Cutting Accelerates," *Streaming Media*. www.streamingmedia.com/Articles/News/Online-Video-News/Pay-TV-Lost-1.8M-Subscribers-in-2016-as-Cord-Cutting-Accelerates-116888.aspx.

Driscoll, Catherine (2011), *Teen Film: A Critical Introduction*. Oxford & New York: Berg.

Dunleavy, Trisha (2009), *Television Drama: Form, Agency, Innovation*. Basingstoke: Palgrave Macmillam.

Dunleavy, Trisha (2018), *Complex Serial Drama and Multiplatform Television*. London: Routledge

Eisenstein, Sergei (2009 [1988]), "Film Form: Beyond the Shot & The Dramaturgy of Film Form," in Braudy, Leo & Marhsall Cohen (eds.), *Film Theory & Criticism*. Oxford: Oxford University Press, pp. 13-40.

Ellis, John (1992 [1982]), *Visible Fictions: Cinema, Television, Video*. London & New York: Routledge.

Ellis, John (2000), *Seeing Things: Television in the Age of Uncertainty*. London: I.B. Tauris

Elmelund, Rasmus (2018), "Netflix er ikke bare en spiller på markedet, Netflix ER markedet," *Information*, May 25. www.information.dk/kultur/2018/05/netflix-bare-spiller-paa-markedet-netflix-markedet.

Elsaesser, Thomas (2012), "Actions Have Consequences: Logics in the Mind-Game Films in David Lynch's Los Angeles-Trilogy. Paper presented at *The Art of the Real: An Interdisciplinary International Conference* in Berlin (Roter Salon, Volksbühne), June 28-30. lynchconference.hbk-bs.de/actions-have-consequences-logics-of-the-mind-game-film-in-david-lynchs-los-angeles-trilogy.

Engelstad, Audun (2011), "It's Not TV – or Is It?", *16:9*, February. www.16-9.dk/2011-02/side11_in-english.htm.

Epstein, Jean (1993 [1924]), "On Certain Characteristics of *Photogénie*", in Abel, Richard (ed.), *French Film Theory and Criticism: A History/Anthology, 1907-1939: Vol.1: 1907-1929*. Princeton University Press.

Evans, Benedict (2020), "Tech in 2020: Standing on the Shoulders of Giants," February 2020. www.ben-evans.com/presentations.

Every Little Thing (2017), "The Voices Hiding in Your Favorite Movies", Dec. 4, 2017.

Fawell, John (2008), *The Hidden Art of Hollywood: In Defense of the Studio Era Film*. Westport, CT & London: Praeger.

FCC (1934), *Communications Act of 1934*. transition.fcc.gov/Reports/1934new.pdf.

Ferguson, Latoya (2020), "'The Lord of the Rings': Everything You Need to Know About Amazon's Big Money Adaptation," *Indiewire*, July 6. www.indiewire.com/gallery/amazons-lord-of-the-rings-explained-plot-cast/the-lord-of-the-rings-the-fellowship-of-the-ring-2001-2.

Fienberg, Daniel (2020), "'ZeroZeroZero': TV Review," *The Hollywood Reporter*, March 6. www.hollywoodreporter.com/review/zerozerozero-review-1282768.

Filippo, Maria San (2016), "Transparent Family Values: Unmasking Sitcom Myths of Gender, Sex(uality), and Money," in Dalton, Mart M. & Laura R. Linder (eds.), *The Sitcom Reader*. New York: SUNY Press, p. 306

Fiske, John (1987), "Intertextuality," in *Television Culture*. London: Routledge.

Flitterman-Lewis, Sandy (1992), "Psychoanalysis, Film, and Television," in Allen, Robert C. (ed.), *Channels of Discourse, Reassembled*. London: Routledge.

Foutch, Haleigh (2017), "The 'Twin Peaks' Revival Will Be 'Pure Heroin,' Says Showtime Boss," *The Collider*, January 9. collider.com/twin-peaks-season-3-david-lynch-showtime.

Frater, Patrick (2020), "Netflix to Launch Korean Version of 'Money Heist' Hit Spanish Series," *Variety*, November 30.

Freuendal, Jakob (2020), "'ZeroZeroZero': Ambitiøs narkoserie på HBO Nordic er et kludetæppe af tilfældigheder," *Soundvenue*, February 18. soundvenue.com/film/2020/02/zerozerozero-ambitioes-narkoserie-paa-hbo-nordic-er-et-kludetaeppe-af-tilfaeldigheder-397663.

Frost, Scott (1991), *The Autobiography of F.B.I. Special Agent Dale Cooper: My Life, My Tapes*. New York: Pocket Books.

Frost, Vicky (2011): "*The Killing* puts torchlight on subtitled drama," *The Guardian*, November 18. www.theguardian.com/tv-and-radio/2011/nov/18/the-killing-torchlight-subtitled-drama.

Fry, Naomi (2020), "'The Undoing' Is Empty Life-Style Porn," *The New Yorker*, November 9

Garner, Ross (2017), "What We Learned from Sam and Tracey: Does the New *Twin Peaks* Differ from Contemporary Quality TV," *CST*, May 27.

Gay, Verne (2015), "American Crime review," *Newsday*, March 3.

Geertz, Clifford (1990), "Deep Play: Notes on a Balinese Cockfight", in Mukerji, Chandra & Michael Schudson (eds.), *Re-Thinking Popular Culture*. Berkeley: University of California Press.

Gemzøe, Lynge Stegger (2018), *The Showrunner Effect: System, Culture and Individual Agency in American Remakes of Danish Television Series*. PhD dissertation, Institut for Kommunikation og Kultur, Aarhus Universitet.

Genette, Gérard (1997), *Palimpsests: Literature in the Second Degree*. Lincoln: University of Nebraska Press.

George, Diane Hume (1995), "Lynching Women: A Feminist Reading of *Twin Peaks*," in Lavery, David (ed.), *Full of Secrets: Critical Approaches to Twin Peaks*. Detroit: Wayne State University Press.

Gheciu, Alex Nino (2018), "Why the Duplass Brothers Are Done Directing (Unless It's the Next 'Star Wars' Movie)," *Sharp*, May 17. sharpmagazine.com/2018/05/17/why-the-duplass-brothers-are-done-directing-unless-its-the-next-star-wars-movie.

Giannetti, Louis (2002), *Understanding Movies*. 9th Edition. Upper Saddle River, New Jersey: Prentice Hall.

Gilbert, Sandra & Susan Gubar (1979), *The Madwoman in the Attic: The Woman Writer of the Nineteenth-Century Literary Imagination*. Yale University Press.

Gilbert, Sophie (2018), "*The Rain* Is a Taut Dystopian Thriller," *The Atlantic*, May 3. www.theatlantic.com/entertainment/archive/2018/05/the-rain-review-netflix/559439.

Gilbert, Sophie (2020), "The Teen Dramas That Reject Modernity," *The Atlantic*, March 4. www.theatlantic.com/culture/archive/2020/03/netflix-new-teen-nostalgia-i-am-not-okay-with-this-sex-education-stranger-things/607366.

Gjelsvik, Anne & Jørgen Bruhn (2011), "Listen carefully – The Wires opgør med politiserien", Nielsen, Jakob Isak et al. (eds.), *Fjernsyn for viderekomne - de nye amerikanske tv-serier*. Aarhus: Turbine, pp. 115-129.

Goddard, Michael & Christopher Hogg (eds.) (2018), "Trans TV Dossier 1: Platform Television, Netflix and Industrial Transformations," *Critical Studies in Television* 13(4).

Goldberg, Lesley (2020), "'Emily in Paris' Creator Darren Star Responds to French Critics and Gives Update on 'Younger' Spinoff," *The Hollywood Reporter*, October 22.

Gooden, Tai (2019), "The Song Dustin & Suzie Sing in 'Stranger Things' from 'The Neverending Story' Was an Epic Choice for the Teen Coule," *Bustle*, July 4.

Gora, Susannah (2010), *"You Couldn't Ignore Me If You Tried": The Brat Pack, John Hughes, and Their Impact on a Generation*. New York: Three Rivers Press.

Gorbman, Claudian (1987), *Unheard Melodies: Narrative Film Music*. Bloomington: Indiana University Press.

Gorman, Bill (2011), "'Doctor Who', 'Top Gear,' & 'Luther' Lead BBC America to Best Ratings Quarter Ever," *TV By the Numbers*, October 14.

Grabyo (2019), "Grabyo OTT Video Trends Report 2019". about.grabyo.com/ott-video-trends-2019.

Granild, Dorte Schmidt (2020), "*Crime Spree*: Om true crime-bølgen og *The Jinx*," in Nielsen,

Jakob Isak et al. (eds.), *Streaming for viderekomne: Fra* Doggystyle *til* Black Mirror *og* The Jinx. Aarhus: VIA Film & Transmedia, pp. 140-160.

Grater, Tom (2020), "Netflix Unveils Its Most-Watched Series and Films in America: 'The Platform' & 'Barbarians' Top Lists Also Featuring 'Cuties', 'Money Heist', 'Dark'," *Deadline*, December 10. deadline.com/2020/12/netflix-most-watched-international-series-films-america-the-platform-barbarians-cuties-1234653658.

Greene, Andy (2013), "How 'Lilyhammer' Changed the TV World: 'Netflix is opening a whole new golden era of television,' says Steve Van Zandt. Plus: Can the E Street Band play forever?", *Rolling Stone*, December 5.

Grego, M. (2002), "Feared, Yet Respected," *Variety* (Special on HBO), November 4, A1-A2, A5.

Grey, Camilla (2016), "Branded content review: Nike's web series *Margot vs. Lily*", *Medium*, February 17. medium.com/@camillastore/branded-content-review-nike-s-web-series-margot-vs-lily-2171036db449.

Grigoriadis, Vanessa (2008), "The Tragedy of Britney Spears," *Rolling Stone*, February 21. www.rollingstone.com/music/music-news/the-tragedy-of-britney-spears-rolling-stones-2008-cover-story-254735.

Grimes, William (1991), "Television; Welcome to Twin Peaks and Valleys," *New York Times*, May 5.

Grusin, Richard & Jay Bolter (1999), *Remediation: Understanding New Media*. MIT Press.

Haastrup, Helle Kannik (2011), "Dramedien som genre," in Nielsen, Jakob Isak et al. (eds.), *Fjernsyn for viderekomne - de nye amerikanske tv-serier*. Aarhus: Turbine.

Hale, James (2020), "Brat Brings in TikTok Star Dixie D'Amelio to Front New Series 'Attaway General'," *Tubefilter*, February 17.

Hale, Mike (2012), "The Danes Do Murder Differently," *The New York Times*, March 28. www.nytimes.com/2012/04/01/arts/television/comparing-the-killing-to-the-show-forbrydelsen.html.

Hale, Mike (2019), " 'Euphoria' Review: HBO Raises the Stakes on Teenage Transgression," *The New York Times*, June 14.

Hale, Mike (2020), "Missing 'Gomorrah'? Watch This," *The New York Times*, March 5. www.nytimes.com/2020/03/05/arts/television/review-gomorrah-zerozerozero.html.

Hallam, Lindsay (2018), *Twin Peaks: Fire Walk with Me*. Devil's Advocate. Auteur.

Halskov, Andreas (2011), "*Carnivàle* - støvskålens magi," *16:9 books*. www.16-9.dk/fjernsynforviderekomne/carnivale.htm

Halskov, Andreas (2013), "*Girls* - Degradation and the City," *16:9 Books*. www.16-9.dk/fjernsynforviderekomne/girls.html.

Halskov, Andreas (2014a), *Paradoksets kunst - om David Lynch og hans film*. Aarhus: Turbine

Halskov, Andreas (2014b), "'The worst movie ever made': en revurdering af *Twin Peaks: Fire Walk with Me*," *16:9*, May 29. www.16-9.dk/2014/05/the-worst-movie-ever-made.

Halskov, Andreas (2014c), "Indledningens kunst: Den moderne titelsekvens," *16:9*, www.16-9.dk/2014/04/indledningens-kunst-den-moderne-titelsekvens.

Halskov, Andreas (2014d), "The Sound of Silence: Stilhed på film," *16:9*, August 28. www.16-9.dk/2014/08/the-sound-of-silence-stilhed-paa-film.

Halskov, Andreas (2015a), *TV Peaks: Twin Peaks and Modern Television Drama*. Odense: The University Press of Southern Denmark.

Halskov, Andreas (2015b), "My Least Favorite Life," *16:9*, June 18. www.16-9.dk/2015/06/my-least-favorite-life.

Halskov, Andreas (2015c), "What's the Frequency, David? Noise and Interference in the Films of David Lynch," *16:9*, August 16. www.16-9.dk/2015/08/whats-the-frequency-david.

Halskov, Andreas (2016), "16:9 Talks: Peter Albrechtsen," *16:9*, October 24. www.16-9.dk/2016/10/peter-albrechtsen.

Halskov, Andreas (2017a), "No Place Like Home: Returning to *Twin Peaks*," *16:9*, May 30. www.16-9.dk/2017/05/returning-to-twin-peaks.

Halskov, Andreas (2017b), "Fra Lucy til Louie: smarte sitcoms til smarte seere," in Nielsen, Jakob Isak et al. (eds.), *Helt til grin: Moderne audiovisual komik på tværs af medier*. Aarhus: VIA Film & Transmedia, pp. 118-144.

Halskov, Andreas (2017c), "Komedieserien er ikke længere sjov," *Soundvenue*, March 6.

Halskov, Andreas (2018a), "'En frygtelig kvinde' benytter et velkendt greb: Disse seks film og serier bryder den fjerde væg," *Politiken*, January 12. politiken.dk/kultur/film_og_tv/art6287478/Disse-seks-film-og-serier-bryder-den-fjerde-v%C3%A6g.

Halskov, Andreas (2018b), "Echoes of the Past: Popular Music and Nostalgia in Modern Television Drama," *16:9*, May 28. www.16-9.dk/2018/05/nostalgia.

Halskov, Andreas (2018c), "*BoJack Horseman* og situationskomedie," in Agger, Gunhild et al. (eds.), *TV-analyse*. Universitet. Aarhus: Systime, pp. 251-268.

Halskov, Andreas (2019), *Remakes, sequels og serialisering*. København: Samfundslitteratur

Halskov, Andreas & Højer, Henrik (2011), "Kunsten ligger i nichen: 'The HBO Playbook'," *Kosmorama* #248, pp. 37-46, video.dfi.dk/Kosmorama/magasiner/248/kosmorama248_037_artikel2.pdf.

Hammett-Jamart, Julia et al. (2018), "Introduction: European Film and Television Co-Production," in Hammett-Jamart, Julia et al. (2018), *European Film and Television Co-Production: Policy and Practice*. London: Palgrave Macmillan.

Hammond, Michael & Lucy Mazdon (eds.)(2005), *The Contemporary Television Series*. Edinburgh: Edinburgh University Press.

Hans, Simran (2019), "Does it matter if a television show tops the best-film lists?", *The Guardian*, December 12. www.theguardian.com/commentisfree/2019/dec/12/best-film-twin-peaks-cinema-tv.

Havas, Julia & Maria Sulimma (2020 [2018]), "Through the Gaps of My Fingers: Genre, Femininity, and Cringe Aesthetics in Dramedy Television," *Television & New Media* 21:1.

Hayward, Jennifer (1997), *Consuming Pleasures: Active Audiences and Serial Fictions from Dickens to Soap Opera*. Lexington: University of Kentucky Press.

Hellekson, Karen (2014), *Forbrydelsen, The Killing*, Duty, and Ethics," in Lavigne, Carlen (ed.), *Remake Television: Reboot, Re-use, Recycle*. Lanham: Lexington Books, pp. 131-140.

Hellerman, Jason (2019), "HBO's 'Succession' Will Change How You Shoot and Edit," *No Film School*, August 23. nofilmschool.com/succession-hbo-technical-specs.

Henderson, Rik (2018), "The Walking Dead Pokemon Go-Style AR Game is out now for iOS and Android," *Pocket-lint*, July 12. www.pocket-lint.com/games/news/pokemon/143939-the-walking-dead-our-world-ar-game-is-pokemon-go-for-zombie-lovers.

Herbert, Daniel, Lotz, Amanda D., & Marshall, Lee (2019), "Approaching media industries comparatively: A case study of streaming," *International Journal of Cultural Studies*, 22(3), pp. 349-366.

Hersko, Tyler et al. (2020), "Quibi to Shut Down – Here's What Went Wrong," *Indiewire*, October 21. www.indiewire.com/2020/10/quibi-shuts-down-post-mortem-failed-mobile-streaming-service-1234588080.

Herson, Kellie (2019), "The biggest mystery on TV is how every show became a puzzle box," *Culture*, March 25. theoutline.com/post/7242/puzzle-box-television-shows-westworld-true-detective-the-good-place.

Herzog & Company (2013), "Television Comes of Age", from the documentary series about *The Sixties*, CNN.

Hills, Matt (2005), "Cult TV, Quality, and the Role of the Episode/Programme Guide," in Hammond, Michael & Lucy Mazdon (eds.), *The Contemporary Television Series*. Edinburgh: Edinburgh University Press.

Hirsch, Forster (1999), *Detours and Lost Highways: A Map of Neo-Noir*. New York: Limelight.

Hjarvard, Stig (2013), *The Mediatization of Culture and Society*. London: Routledge.

Hochscherf, Tobias & Heidi Philipsen (2017), *Beyond the Bridge: Contemporary Danish Television Drama*. London: Tauris Academic Studies.

Hodsdon, Barrett (2017), *The Elusive Auteur: The Question of Film Authorship Throughout the Age of Cinema*. Jefferson, North Carolina: McFarland & Co.

Hooton, Christopher (2014), "House of Cards: Barack Obama calls for halt on Season 2 spoilers on Twitter," *Independent*, February 14. www.independent.co.uk/arts-entertainment/tv/news/barack-obama-please-no-house-of-cards-season-2-spoilers-9128013.html.

Hopewell, John (2020), "'When the Dust Settles': Dorte W. Høgh, Ida Maria Rydén Drill Down on the New DR Series," *Variety*, January 24. variety.com/2020/tv/global/when-the-dust-settles-dorte-w-hogh-ida-maria-ryden-drill-down-new-dr-series-1203478542.

Højer, Henrik (2011), "Det er da tv? Den amerikanske tv-series udvikling fra antologi-tv til ikke-tv," in Nielsen, Jakob Isak et al. (eds.), *Fjernsyn for viderekomne - de nye amerikanske tv-serier*. Aarhus: Turbine, pp. 16-35.

Højer, Henrik (2015), "Family Noir", *16:9*, June 10. www.16-9.dk/2015/06/family-noir.

Højer, Henrik (2017a), "It's Not TV. It's Art-TV," *16:9*, February 21. www.16-9.dk/2017/02/its-not-tv-its-art-tv.

Højer, Henrik (2017b), "Transmedia Storytelling," in Linnebjerg, Mette & Michael Højer (eds.), *Det nye mediefag: Et inspirationsmateriale*. København: Medielærerforeningen.

Højer, Henrik & Andreas Halskov (2009), "It's Not TV... (Part 2)", *16:9* #34.

Højer, Michael (2011), "Teen Noir - *Veronica Mars* og den moderne ungdomsserie," in Nielsen, Jakob Isak et al. (eds.), *Fjernsyn for viderekomne - de nye amerikanske tv-serier*. Aarhus: Turbine.

Internet World Stats. www.internetworldstats.com/emarketing.htm.

Iqbal, Mansoor (2020), "Netflix Revenue and Usage Statistics," *Business of Apps*, June 23. www.businessofapps.com/data/netflix-statistics.

Iversen, Ebbe (1992), "Tomme mysterier", *Berlingske Tidende*, October 9.

Jacobs, Jason & Steven Peacock (2013), "Introduction," in Jacobs, Jason & Steven Peacock (eds.), *Television Aesthetics and Style*. New York & London: Bloomsbury.

Jaramillo, Deborah L. (2013), "Rescuing Television from the 'Cinematic'," in Jacobs, Jason & Steven Peacock (eds.), *Television Aesthetics and Style*.

Jensen, Jakob Linaa (2009), "Fra onlinefællesskaber til onlinenetværk: Facebook som augmentering af den sociale virkelighed, *Mediekultur* #46, pp. 86-99.

Jensen, Jeff (2017a), "*Twin Peaks* Recap: *The Return* Parts 3-4," *Entertainment Weekly*, May 28.

Jensen, Jeff (2017b), "*Twin Peaks*: David Lynch Breaks Down the First Four Episodes," *Entertainment Weekly*, May 26.

Jenkins, Henry (2006), *Convergence Culture: Where Old and New Media Collide*. New York: New York University Press.

Jenkins, Henry (2007), "Transmedia Storytelling 101," *Confessions of an Aca-Fan*, March 21. henryjenkins.org/blog/2007/03/transmedia_storytelling_101.html.

Jenkins, Henry (2009), "The Revenge of the Origami Unicorn: The Remaining Four Principles of Transmedia Storytelling," *Confessions of an Aca-Fan*, December 12. henryjenkins.org/2009/12/revenge_of_the_origami_unicorn.html.

Jenner, Mareike (2018), *Netflix and the Re-Invention of Television*. Basingstoke: Palgrave Macmillan.

Jensen, Mikkel (2017), "'From the Mind of David Simon': A Case for the Showrunner Approach," *Series*, Vol. 3, No. 2, Winter.

Jensen, Mikkel (2020), "'Our future is in the city': Storbyens udfordringer i David Simons tv-serier," *16:9*, March 7. www.16-9.dk/2020/03/david-simons-tv-serier.

Jensen, Pia Majbritt et al. (2016), "When public service drama travels," *The Journal of Popular Television*, January 1.

Jensen, Troels Peter Mourits (2019), "Serieverdenens populære flagskibe: Et blik på underholdningsværdien i *bottle episodes*," *16:9*, March 10.

Jerslev, Anne (1993), *David Lynch i vore øjne*. København: Frydenlund

Jerslev, Anne (2001), "Vildledninger: Den overrumplende dramaturgi,"*Ekko* #9, September.

Jerslev, Anne (2017), "Twin Peaks peaker," *Kommunikationsforum*, May 24.

Johnson, Catherine (2012), *Branding Television*. London: Routledge.

Johnson, Catherine (2019), *Online TV*. London: Routledge.

Jones, Gerard (1993), *Honey, I'm Home! Sitcoms, Selling the American Dream*. Grove, PR.

Kael, Pauline (1994), *For Keeps*. New York: Dutton.

Kant, Immanuel (1892 [1790]), *The Critique of Judgement*. Translated by J.H. Bernard.

Karpovich, Angelina (2010), "Dissecting the Opening Sequence," in *Dexter - Investigating Cutting Edge Television*. London & New York: I.B. Tauris.

Katz, Brandon (2020), "Why Netflix's 'Money Heist' Is the Most In-Demand Show in the World," *Observer*, April 9.

Kaveney, Roz (2006), *Teen Dreams: Reading Teen Films and Television from* Heathers *to* Veronica Mars. London: I.B. Tauris.

Kellison, Catherine et al. (2013), *Producing for TV and New Media: A Real-World Approach for Pro-*

ducers. 3rd Edition. New York & London: Focal Press.

Kelly, Emma (2020), "'It's what you'd see in a porno': Normal People 'immoral' sex scenes spark major debate on Irish radio," *Metro*, May 1.

Kelly, J.P. (2017), *Time, Technology and Narrative Form in Contemporary US Television Drama*: London: Palgrave MacMillan.

Kelly, J.P. (2020), "Current Affairs or Comfort TV?: VOD Offerings in the Age of Covid-19," CSTOnline, November 27.

Kerins, Mark (2011), *Beyond Dolby (Stereo): Cinema in the Digital Sound Age*. Indiana: Indiana University Press.

Keslassy, Elsa (2019), "'The Intouchables' Helmers to Direct French Adaptation of 'In Treatment'," *Variety*, November 15. variety.com/2019/tv/news/the-intouchables-helmers-to-direct-french-tv-adaptation-of-in-treatment-1203405971.

Keslassy, Elsa (2020), "Netflix Picks France to Test First Linear Offering," *Variety*, November 6.

Kildebæk, Morten (2020), "'I Know This Much Is True': Ny HBO-serie med dobbel Mark Ruffalo rammer hårdt og nådesløst," *Soundvenue*, May 11.

Kingsley, Hilary (1989), *Soap Box: The Australian Guide to Soap Operas*. Melbourne: Sun Books.

Kirschbacher, Felix & Sven Stollfuß (2015), "Lost in TV: Überlegungen zur Fernsehserie." lost-in-tv.de/about-us.

Kiss, Miklós & Steven Willemsen (2017), *Impossible Puzzle Films: A Complex Approach to Contemporary Complex Cinema*. Edinburg: Edinburgh University Press.

Klein, Paul L. (1971), "Why you watch what you watch when you watch," *TV Guide*, July 24, pp. 6-9

Koepnick, Lutz (2002), *The Dark Mirror: German Cinema Between Hitler and Hollywood*. Berkeley: University of California Press.

Kompare, Derek (2005), *Rerun Nation: How Repeats Invented American Television*. New York: Routledge.

Kompare, Derek (2006), "Publishing Flow: DVD Box Sets and the Reconception of Television," *Television and New Media* 7(4).

Korsgaard, Mathias Bonde (2020), "'Musical Moments' i nyere serier," in Nielsen, Jakob Isak et al. (eds.), *Streaming for viderekomne: Fra* Doggystyle *til* Black Mirror *og* The Jinx. Aarhus: VIA Film & Transmedia, pp. 196-216.

Kristensen, Pernille Kjeldgaard et al. (2019), "Seriesøndag: Hvad sker der i din krop, når du bruger hele weekenden på sofaen?", DR.dk, March 3. www.dr.dk/nyheder/viden/kroppen/serie-soendag-hvad-sker-der-i-din-krop-naar-du-bruger-hele-weekenden-paa-sofaen.

Krüger, Steffen & Gry C. Rustad (2019 [2017]), "Coping with Shame in a Media-saturated Society: Norwegian Web-series SKAM as Transitional Object," *Television and New Media* 20:1.

Kustanowitz, Esther D. (2019), "'Our Boys' will make you uncomfortable, which is exactly why you should watch it," *The Jewish News of Northern California*, August 29. www.jweekly.com/2019/08/29/our-boys-will-make-you-uncomfortable-which-is-exactly-why-you-should-watch-it.

Ladingkær, Lars (2019), "Disse DR-kanaler lukker per 31/12", October 29, Recordere.dk. www.recordere.dk/2019/10/disse-dr-kanaler-lukker-per-31-12-19.

Landau, Neil (2016), *TV Outside the Box: Trailblazing in the Digital Television Revolution*. New York & London: Focal Press.

Landau Neil (2018), "Blurring the Lines: Redefining TV Genre and Tone in the Dramedy," *Creative Screenwriting*, June 13. creativescreenwriting.com/blurring-lines-redefining-tv-genre-tone-dramedy.

Landekic, Lola (2018), "Babylon Berlin", *Art of the Title*, April 24. www.artofthetitle.com/title/babylon-berlin.

Langkjær, Birger (2000), *Den lyttende tilskuer: Perception af lyd og musik i film*. København: Museum Tusculanums Forlag.

Lauridsen, Palle Schantz (2014), *Sherlock Holmes i Danmark*. København: Rosenkilde & Bahnhof.

Lauridsen, Palle Schantz (2016), "Audience Involving Strategies," *16:9*, January 28. www.16-9.dk/2016/01/audience-involving-strategies-in-sherlock.

Lattanzio, Ryan (2015), "Lynch, Fincher, 'True Detective' and the Unknowable Future of Auteur TV," *IndieWire*. August 11. www.indiewire.com/2015/08/lynch-fincher-true-detective-and-the-unknowable-future-of-auteur-tv-184757.

Lavigne, Carlen (2014), "Introduction," in *Remake Television: Reboot, Re-use, Recycle*. Lanham: Lexington.
Lavik, Erlend (2014), *Tv-serier:* The Wire *og den tredje gullalderen*. Universitetsforlaget.
Law School Case Brief (1977): "Home Box Office, Inc. v. FCC - 185 U.S. App. D.C. 142, 567 F.2d 9 (1977). www.lexisnexis.com/community/casebrief/p/casebrief-home-box-office-inc-v-fcc.
Lee, Benjamin (2019), "*Euphoria* review - dizzying high school drama is one of the year's best," *The Guardian*, June 14.
Lee, Benjamin (2020), "Quibi review - shortform sub-Netflix shows aren't long for this world," *The Guardian*, April 6. www.theguardian.com/tv-and-radio/2020/apr/06/quibi-streaming-review-short-form-tv.
Lee, Mark (2007), "Wiseguys: A Conversation between David Chase and Tom Fontana," *Writers Guild of American*, west, May.
Leszkiewicz, Anna (2017), "Eleven's 'Stranger Things 2' Punk Revamp Is Corny But That's the Point," *Vice*, November 2. www.vice.com/en_us/article/vb33m3/eleven-stranger-things-2-episode-7-lost-sister-punk.
Leverette, Marc (2007), "Introduction: The Not-TV Industry," in Leverette, Marc et al. (eds.), *It's Not TV: Watching HBO in the Post-Television Era*. London: Routledge.
Levine, Elana (2008), "Distinguishing Television: The Changing Meanings of Television Liveness," *Media, Culture & Society* 30:3.
Licklider, J.C.R. (1967), "Televistas," in Carnegie Commission of Educational Television (ed.), *Public Television: A Program for Action*. New York: Harper & Row, pp. 201-205.
Lindsey, Cameron (2016), "Questioning Netflix's Revolutionary Impact," in McDonald, Kevin & Daniel Smith-Rowsey (eds.), *The Netflix Effect: Technology and Entertainment in the 21st Century*. New York & London: Bloomsbury.
Lirette, Christopher (2014), "Something True about Louisiana: HBO's *True Detective* and the Petrochemical American Aesthetic," *Southern Spaces*. August 13. southernspaces.org/2014/something-true-about-louisiana-hbos-true-detective-and-petrochemical-america-aesthetic.
Lobato, Ramon (2019), *Netflix Nations: The Geography of Digital Streaming*. New York: New York University Press.
Lotz, Amanda D. (2006), "Rethinking Meaning Making: Watching Serial TV on DVD, *Flow* 4.12. www.flowjournal.org/2006/09/rethinking-meaning-making-watching-serial-tv-on-dvd/#fn2.
Lotz, Amanda D. (2007), *The Television Will Be Revolutionized*. New York: New York University Press.
Lotz, Amanda (2014), *Portals: A Treatise on Internet-Distributed Television*. Michigan Publishing/Maizebooks.
Lotz, Amanda D. (2018), *We Now Disrupt This Broadcast: How Cable Transformed Television and the Internet Revolutionized It All*. Cambridge, MA & London: The MIT Press.
Lotz, Amanda (2020), "Storytelling in the World of Streaming," in Nielsen, Jakob Isak et al. (eds.), *Streaming for viderekomne: Fra* Doggystyle *til* Black Mirror *og* The Jinx. Aarhus: VIA Film & Transmedia.
Low, Elaine (2020), "Disney Lays Out Multi-Billion Dollar Plan to Dominate the Streaming Wars," *Variety*, December 10. variety.com/2020/tv/news/disney-plus-investor-day-streaming-star-wars-marvel-pixar-1234850905/?fbclid=IwAR0CGSL8A14zQo_LoNGH8574IRchhgViF3_pkg-3IIC6GoMMYHR1fZm0T00.
Ludvigsen, Jacob (2015), "Dramaseriens guldalder kan være slut," *Soundvenue*, August 10.
Ludvigsen, Jacob (2020), "Fra Netflix til TV2 Play: Vi vurderer de otte største tjenester efter streamingkrigens første år," *Soundvenue*, December 28. soundvenue.com/film/2020/12/fra-netflix-til-tv-2-play-vi-vurderer-otte-tjenester-efter-streamingkrigens-foerste-aar-435993.
Lynch, David et al. (1991), *Welcome to Twin Peaks: Access Guide to the Town*. New York: Pocket Books.
Lynch, Jennifer (1990), *The Secret Diary of Laura Palmer*. London: Penguin.
Lysne, Anders (2013), "At forstå en teenager," *16:9* #52. www.16-9.dk/2013-09/side04_feature1.htm.
Madsen, Sarah Gerlach (2019), "Fucking råt for usødet: *Euphoria* taler et helt andet sprog," *Kom-*

munikationsforum, September 24.

Malkinson, Agnes (2016): " 'Damn Fine Coffee' Advertising: David Lynch's TV Commercial Adaptation of *Twin Peaks*," *Senses of Cinema*, #29, July. sensesofcinema.com/2016/twin-peaks/26839.

MarBelle (2020), "How Lenny Abrahamson Transformed Sally Rooney's Best Selling Novel Into the Record-Breaking TV Event of the Year," *Directors Notes*, July 27. directorsnotes.com/2020/07/27/lenny-abrahamson-normal-people.

Marr, Andrew (2016), "The loss of the independent means the loss of a community," *The Guardian*, February 13. www.theguardian.com/media/2016/feb/13/the-independent-gave-me-some-of-the-most-exciting-times-of-my-career.

Martin, Adrian (1994), "Teen Movies: The Forgetting of Wisdom", in *Phantasms*. Ringwood, Vic: McPhee Gribble, pp. 66-67.

Martin, Adrian (2014), *Mise en Scéne and Film Style: From Classical Hollywood to New Media Art*. New York: Palgrave Macmillan.

Martin, Brett (2013), *Difficult Men: Behind the Scenes of a Creative Revolution: From* The Sopranos *and* The Wire *to* Mad Men *and* Breaking Bad. New York: The Penguin Press.

Masoero, Raffaella (2016), "The rise of cord-shaving and cord-cutting", *Accenture*. www.accenture.com/us-en/~/media/pdf-30/accenture-the-rise-of-cord-shaving-and-cord-cutting.pdf.

May, Austin (2019), "Trump's national emergency is straight out of 'House of Cards'," *The Sunflower*, February 26. thesunflower.com/36463/opinion/may-trumps-national-emergency-is-netflixs-intellectual-property.

McBride, Joseph (2006), *What Ever Happened to Orson Welles? A Portrait of an Independent Career*. Lexington, Kentucky: University of Kentucky Press.

McCabe, Janet & Kim Akass (eds.) (2007), *Quality TV: Contemporary American Television and Beyond*. London: I.B. Tauris.

McCabe, Janet & Catherine Grant (2019), "Bodies at the border: Transnational co-produced TV drama and its gender politics in the pilots of 'Bron/Broen' and adaptations 'The Bridge' and 'The Tunnel'," *Necsus*, May 27. necsus-ejms.org/bodies-at-the-border-transnational-co-produced-tv-drama-and-its-gender-politics-in-the-pilots-of-bron-broen-and-adaptations-the-bridge-and-the-tunnel.

McCormick, Casey J. (2016), "'Forward Is the Battle Cry': Binge-Viewing Netflix's *House of Cards*," in McDonald, Kevin & Daniel Smith-Rowsey (eds.), *The Netflix Effect: Technology and Entertainment in the 21st Century*. New York & London: Bloomsbury.

McFadden, Kay (1999), "WB Hitting the Mark with Target Audience," *Chicago Tribune*. January 13. www.chicagotribune.com/news/ct-xpm-1999-01-13-9901130071-story.html.

McHugh, Maura (2017): *Twin Peaks: Fire Walk with Me*. PS Publishing.

McLuhan, Marshall (2001), *Understanding Media*. London: Routledge.

McMillin, Divya (2013), "How Ugly Can Betty Be in India?", in McCabe, Janet & Kim Akass (eds.), *TV's Betty Goes Global: From Telenovela to International Brand*. London: I.B. Tauris.

McNeil, Kenneth (2011), "*Friday Night Lights* - imellem amerikansk drøm og virkelighed," in Nielsen, Jakob Isak et al. (eds.), *Fjernsyn for viderekomne - de nye amerikanske tv-serier*. Aarhus: Turbine, pp. 286-301.

Mejia, Paula (2017), "Charting the Vast Musical Universe of *Twin Peaks*," *Vulture*, July 27.

Mikanowski, Jacob (2014), " 'True Detective': Down the Bayou (Far From Any Road)," *Los Angeles Review of Books*, March 8. lareviewofbooks.org/article/bayou-far-road.

Mikos, Lothar (2020), "Streaming Services and the Changing Nature of Drama Series Production in Germany - The example of *Dark* and *You Are Wanted*, in Nielsen, Jakob Isak et al. (eds.), *Streaming for viderekomne: Fra* Doggystyle *til* Black Mirror *og* The Jinx. Aarhus: VIA Film & Transmedia.

Miller, Liz Shannon (2015), "'Looking' Canceled by HBO After 2 Seasons, Though the Story Isn't Over," *Indiewire*, March 25. www.indiewire.com/2015/03/looking-canceled-by-hbo-after-2-seasons-though-the-story-isnt-over-248092.

Mills, Brett (2009), *The Sitcom*. Edinburgh: Edinburgh University Press.

Mills, Brett (2016), "What Does It Mean to Call Television 'Cinematic'?", Jacobs, Jason & Steven Peacock (eds.), *Television Aesthetics and Style*. New York & London: Bloomsbury, pp. 64-65.

Mitchell, Keith B. (2008), "Until the Fat Man Sings: Body Image, Masculinity, and Sexuality in *The*

Sopranos," in Fahy, Thomas (ed.), *Considering David Chase: Essays on* The Rockford Files, Northern Exposure *and* The Sopranos. McFarland & Company.

Mittell, Jason (2004), *Genre and Television: From Cop Shows to Cartoons in American Culture*. New York & London: Routledge.

Mittell, Jason (2006), "Narrative Complexity in Contemporary American Television," *The Velvet Light Trap* #58, Fall.

Mittell, Jason (2013), "The Qualities of Complexity: Vast versus Dense Seriality in Contemporary Television," in Jacobs, Jason & Stephen Peacock (eds.), *Television Aesthetics and Style*. New York: Bloomsbury.

Mittell, Jason (2015), *Complex TV: The Poetics of Contemporary Television Storytelling*. New York: New York University Press.

Modleski, Tania (2003), "The Search for Tomorrow in Today's Soap Operas," in Jones, Amelia (ed.), *The Feminism and Visual Culture Reader*. London & New York: Routledge

Moestrup, Steffen (2017), "Lena, Louie og Derek: et blik på den eksistentialistisk dramedie," in Nielsen, Jakob Isak et al. (eds.), *Helt til grin: Moderne audiovisuel komik på tværs af medier*. Aarhus: VIA Film & Transmedia, pp. 145-164.

Moestrup, Steffen (2020), "Interview with Michael Højer," in *Film:syn - den om ungdomsserier*, DK4. www.dk4.dk/item/6231/filmsyn-den-om-ungdomsserier.

Molloy, Tim (2018), "Twin Peaks' Origin Story 'Blonde, Beautiful and Dead' Optioned by Part2 Pictures (Exclusive)", *The Wrap*, d. 19. november. www.thewrap.com/twin-peaks-origin-story-blonde-beautiful-and-dead-optioned-by-part2-pictures.

Monggaard, Christian (2020), "Det er Netflix' verden - vi bor bare i den," *Information*, April 29, Section 1.

Moore, Frazier (2008), "What Does 'Watching TV' Mean in the Post-TV Age?", *Associated Press*, June 19.

Mosco, Vincent (2004), *The Digital Sublime: Myth, Power, and Cyberspace*. Cambridge, MA: MIT Press.

Murray, Noel (2017), "'Twin Peaks' Season 1, Episode 1: Wrapped in Plastic," *New York Times*, April 20. www.nytimes.com/2017/04/20/watching/twin-peaks-recap-season-1-episode-1.html.

Ndalianis, Angela (2005), "Television and the Neo-Baroque," in Hammond, Michael & Lucy Mazdon (eds.), *The Contemporary Television Series*. Edinburgh: Edinburgh University Press, pp. 83-101.

Netflix (2013a), "Netflix Quick Guide: What is Streaming and Why is It Better?", *YouTube*, posted by Netflix, May 21.

Netflix (2013b), "Netflix Original Series – The Future of Television is Here," *YouTube*, posted by Netflix, September 3, 2013.

Newcomb, Horace & Robert S. Alley (1983), *The Producer's Medium: Conversations with Creators of American TV*. New York: Oxford University Press.

Newman, Michael Z. & Elena Levine (2012), *Legitimating Television: Media Convergence and Cultural Status*. Abingdon: Routledge.

Newman, Sydney (2020), "The Walking Dead Attraction closes at Universal Studios Hollywood," *Inside Universal*, March 4. www.insideuniversal.net/category/universal-studios-hollywood.

Nicholson, Rebecca (2019), "*Euphoria* review – so explicit it makes *Skins* look positively Victorian", *The Guardian*, August 6.

Nielsen, Jakob Isak (2011a), "Broadcastnetværk," in Nielsen, Jakob Isak et al. (eds.), *Fjernsyn for viderekomne - de nye amerikanske tv-serier*. Aarhus: Turbine, pp. 241-253.

Nielsen, Jakob Isak (2011b), "Rundt om *Mad Men*," in Nielsen, Jakob Isak et al. (eds.), *Fjernsyn for viderekomne - de nye amerikanske tv-serier*. Aarhus: Turbine, pp. 202-223.

Nielsen, Jakob Isak (2012), "Solen må aldrig skinne, og Sofie må aldrig smile: Interview med Piv Bernth," *16:9* 10(48), November. www.16-9.dk/2012-11/side06_interview3.htm.

Nielsen, Jakob Isak (2013a), "Netflix: Paradoksernes holdeplads", *16:9* #51, June. www.16-9.dk/2013-06/side03_leder.htm.

Nielsen, Jakob Isak (2013b), "The Oscars og den klassiske Hollywoodfilm", in Højer, Henrik et al. (eds.), *Guldfeber – på sporet af Oscarfilmen*. Aarhus: Turbine.

Nielsen, Jakob Isak (2013c), "Blockbuster TV," conference paper delivered at the conference *Bestseller & Blockbuster Culture* conference at Aalborg University.

Nielsen, Jakob Isak (2015), "Camera Movements in Narrative Cinema," *16:9*, February 2. www.16-9.dk/2015/02/camera-movement-in-narrative-cinema.

Nielsen, Jakob Isak (2016), "The Danish Way to Do It the American Way," *Kosmorama*, May 13. www.kosmorama.org/en/kosmorama/artikler/danish-way-do-it-american-way.

Nielsen, Jakob Isak (2020), "Streaming i det danske medielandskab", in Nielsen, Jakob Isak et al. (eds.), *Streaming for viderekomne: Fra* Doggystyle *til* Black Mirror *og* The Jinx. Aarhus: VIA Film & Transmedia-.

Nielsen, Jakob Isak et al. (2020), "16:9 Podcast: Streaming for viderekomne," *16:9*, March 25. www.16-9.dk/2020/03/podcast-05.

Nietzsche, Friedrich (1872), *Zur Genealogie der Moral* (*On the Genealogy of Morality*). Translated by Carol Diethe. Cambridge: Cambridge University Press.

Nietzsche, Friedrich (2013 [1886]), *Jenseits von Gut und Böse: Vorspiel einer Philosophie der Zukunft*. JiaHu Books.

Nikolajsen, Lone (2016), "Storslået landskabsporno i islandsk krimiserie," *Information*, December 16. www.information.dk/kultur/anmeldelse/2016/12/storslaaet-landskabsporno-islandsk--krimiserie.

Nikolajsen, Lone (2017), "Der var gråd, og det var fantastisk, indtil antimobbekampagnen tog over," *Information*, June 3. www.information.dk/kultur/anmeldelse/2017/06/graad-fantastisk-indtil-antimobbekampagnen-tog.

Nochimson, Martha (2019): *Television Rewired: The Rise of the Auteur Series*. Austin: The University of Texas Press.

Nordstrøm, Pernille (2004), *Fra Riget til Bella - bag om tv-seriens golden age*. København: DR.

Nussbaum, Emily (2014), "Small Differences: He-said, she-said on 'The Affair'," *The New Yorker*. December 8. www.newyorker.com/magazine/2014/12/15/small-differences.

Nye, David (1990), *Contemporary American Society*. København: Akademisk Forlag.

Nystrøm, Camilla Gyldendal (2017), "The Leftovers er fyldt med mening", *EKKO*, October 13. www.ekkofilm.dk/artikler/leftovers.

Nørgaard, Thomas (2011), "Tv-auteurs", *16:9* #40.

O'Donnell, Bryan (2019), "Everything Comes Full Circle in *The Wire* Series Finale," *25YL*.

O'Halloran, Joseph (2020), "74% set to stop paying for pay-TV within five years," *Rapid TV News*, March 4. www.rapidtvnews.com/2020030458161/74-set-to-stop-paying-for-pay-tv-within-five-years.html#axzz6Uq5qvJrA.

O'Malley, Sheila (2020), "I Know This Much Is True," *RogerEbert.com*, May 8. www.rogerebert.com/reviews/i-know-this-much-is-true-movie-review-2020.

Oxholm, Jan (2014), "Se på mig - nedbrydningen af den fjerde væg," *16:9*, June 5. www.16-9.dk/2014/06/se-paa-mig-nedbrydningen-af-den-fjerde-vaeg.

Oxholm, Jan (2019), "*Sharp Objects*: Det dystre dukkehus," *16:9*, August 18. www.16-9.dk/2019/08/sharp-objects.

Parks, Lisa & Starosielski, Nicole (2015), "Introduction", *Signal Traffic: Critical Studies in Media Infrastructures*.

Page, Adrian (2005 [2001]), "Post-Modern Drama," in Creeber, Glen (ed.), *The Television Genre Book*. London: BFI Publishing.

Paskin, Willa (2015), "What does 'peak TV' really mean?", *Slate*, December 23. slate.com/culture/2015/12/what-does-peak-tv-really-mean.html.

Paterson, Richard et al. (1980), *Coronation Street*. London: BFI: Television Monograph.

Pearson, Roberta & Máire Messenger Davies (2014), *Star Trek and American Television*. Berkeley: University of California Press.

Pedersen, Peter Ole (2018), "Dette er vandet, dette er brønden," *Passage* 33:1, pp. 77-88.

Perrotta, Marta & Lothar Mikos (2011), "Traveling style: Aesthetic differences and similarities in national adaptations of *Yo soy Betty, la fea*," *International Journal of Cultural Studies* 15(1).

Petersen, Brian (2017), "Gådefuldt spild af tid", *EKKO* #76. www.ekkofilm.dk/artikler/gadefuldt-spild-af-tid.

Povlsen, Karen Klitgaard (1999), *Beverly Hills 90210 - Soaps, ironi og danske unge*. Aarhus: Klim.

Pudovkin, Vsevolod (2009 [1958]), "Film Technique [On Editing]," in Braudy, Leo & Marhsall Cohen (eds.), *Film Theory & Criticism*. Oxford: Oxford University Press.

Puschak, Evan (2017): "The Handmaid's Tale Won Emmy Best Drama," *Nerdwriter*, August 31.

Rankin, Selja (2020), "Barack Obama on the pop culture (and more) that inspired A Promised Land," *Entertainment Weekly*, December 15. ew.com/books/barack-obama-a-promised-land-interview.
Ramsay, Debra (2013), "Confessions of a Binge-Watcher," *Critical Studies in Television*, October 4.
Raskin, Richard (1997), "Camera Movement in *Wings of Desire*," *P.O.V.* #4, December. pov.imv.au.dk/Issue_04/section_1/artc5A.html.
Reay, Pauline (2004), *Music in Film: Soundtracks and Synergy*. London: Wallflower Press.
Redvall, Eva Novrup (2011), "Dogmer for tv-drama: Om brugen af *one vision, den dobbelte historie* og *crossover* i DR's søndagsdramatik," *Kosmorama* # 248.
Redvall, Eva (2013), *Writing and Producing Television Drama in Denmark. From "The Kingdom" to "The Killing"*. Basingstoke: Palgrave Macmillan.
Reeves, Jimmie L. et al (1996), "Rewriting Popularity," in Lavery, David et al. (eds.), *Deny All Knowledge: Reading The X Files*. Syracuse, New York: Syracuse University Press, pp. 22-35.
Roman, James (1998), *Love, Light and a Dream: Television's Past Present and Future*. London: Westport, CT: Praeger.
Romano, Nick (2021), "Just four creators are tied to nearly a fifth of all LGBTQ representation on TV," Entertainment Weekly, January 14.
Ross, Sharon Marie & Louisa Ellen Stein (2008), *Teen Television: Essays on programming and fandom*. Jefferson, NC: McFarland.
Rowles, Dustin (2020), "Review: HBO's Insanely Watchable 'Beforeigners' Combines 'The Leftovers' with 'Travelers'," *Pajiba*, February 21.
Rustad, Gry (2016), "Producing feminist teen television," paper presented at the Console-ing Passions Conference at Notre Dame University.
Ryan, Marie-Laure (2013), "Transmedial Storytelling and Transfictionality," *Poetics Today*, 34(3), pp. 361-388.
Ryan, Marie-Laure (2014), "Story/Worlds/Media: Tuning the Instruments of a Media-Conscious Narratology," in Ryan, Marie-Laure & Jan-Noël Thon (eds), *Storyworlds across Media: Toward a Media-Conscious Narratology*. Lincoln: University of Nebraska Press, pp. 25-49.
Sabroe, Iben Albinus (2010), *Da Sex and the City ændrede verden*. København: Sabroe & Sabroe.
Salt, Barry (1983), "The Early Development of Film Form," in Fell, John L. (ed.), *Film Before Griffith*. Berkeley & Los Angeles: The University of California Press, pp. 284-298.
Salt, Barry (1992), *Film Style and Technology: History and Analysis* (2. Ed.). London: Starwood
Salvati, Andrew (2020), "Call for Contributions to Edited Collection, *Unseen Television: Privililege, Power, and the Archive*," CST Online.
Sammond, Nicholas & Chandra Mukerjo (2001), "'What Are You? ... I Wouldn't Eat': Ethnicity, Whiteness and Performing 'the Jew' in Hollywood's Golden Age," in Bernardi, Daniel (ed.), *Classic Hollywood, Classic Whiteness*. Minnesota: University of University Press.
Sandvig, Christian (2015), "The Internet as Anti-Television: Distribution as Culture and Power," in Parks, Lisa & Nicole Starosielski (eds.), *Signal Traffic: Critical Studies of Media Infrastructures*. Urbana, Chicago: University of Illinois Press.
Sandvine (2019), "Netflix falls to second place in global internet traffic share as the other streaming services grown,"*Sandvine*, September 12. www.sandvine.com/inthenews/netflix-falls-to-second-place-in-global-internet-traffic-share.
Santopietro, Tom (2012), *The Godfather Effect*. St. Martin's Press.
Santos, Avi (2007), "Para-Television and Discourses of Distinction," in Leverette, Marc et al. (eds.), *It's Not TV: Watching HBO in the Post-Television Era*. London: Routledge.
Sarris, Andrew (2009 [1962]), "Notes on the Auteur Theory in 1962," in Braudy, Leo & Marshall Cohen (eds.), *Film Theory & Criticism*. Oxford: Oxford University Press, 9th Edition.
Schaal, Eric (2020), "Why David Lynch Would Rather Make a TV Series Than a Feature Film These Days," *Showbiz CheatSheet*, April 20.
Schepelern, Peter (2003), "Filmen ifølge Dogme: Spilleregler, forhindringer og befrielser," in Toftgaard, Anders & Ian Halvdan Hawkesworth (eds.), *Nationale spejlinger: Tendenser i ny dansk film*. København: Museum Tusculanums Forlag.
Schneider, Michael (2016), "Watch My Show: *Bosch* Is 'The Next Binge Experience,' Says Henrik Bastin," *TV Insider*, April 19. www.tvinsider.com/86432/watch-my-show-bosch-is-the-next-binge-experience-says-henrik-bastin.

Schrader, Paul (1972), "Notes of Film Noir," *Film Comment* 8:1, Spring, pp. 8-13.

Schrader, Paul (2018 [1972]), *Transcendental Style in Film: Ozu, Bresson, Dreyer*. University of California Press.

Sconce, Jeffrey (2002), "Irony, Nihilism and the New American Smart Film," *Screen* 43:4, pp. 349-369.

Sconce, Jeffrey (2004), "What If? Charting Television's New Textual Boundaries," in Spiegel, Lynn & Jan Olsson (eds.), *Television after TV: Essays on a Medium in Transition* Durham, NC: Duke University Press.

Seale, Jack (2021), "The last broadcast: as streaming takes over, are TV channels doomed?", *The Guardian*, January 12.

Seitz, Matt Zoller (2017), "The Best Show on TV Is Twin Peaks: The Return," *Vulture*, July. www.vulture.com/2017/07/vulture-tv-awards-best-show-twin-peaks-the-return.html.

Seitz, Matt Zoller & Alan Sepinwall (2016), *TV (The Book): Two Experts Pick the Greatest American Shows of All Time*. New York & London: Grand Central Publishing

Seitz, Matt Zoller & Alan Sepinwall (2019), *The Sopranos Sessions*. Harry N. Abrams.

Sepinwall, Alan (2012), *The Revolution Was Television: The Cops, Crooks, Slingers, and Slayers Who Changed TV Drama Forever*. Touchstone.

Sergi, Gianluca (1998), "A cry in the dark: The role of post-classical film sound," in Neale, Steve & Murray Smith (eds.), *Contemporary Hollywood Cinema*. New York: Routledge, pp. 156-165.

Sergi, Gianluca (2004), *The Dolby Era: Film Sound in Contemporary Hollywood*. Manchester: Manchester University Press.

Shary, Timothy (2005), *Teen Movies: American Youth on Screen*. London & New York: Wallflower.

Short, Sue (2011), *Cult Telefantasy Series: A Critical Analysis of The Prisoner, Twin Peaks, The X-Files, Buffy the Vampire Slayer, Lost, Heroes, Doctor Who and Star Trek*. London: McFarland & Company.

Silver, Stephen (2017), "Twin Peaks Revival Draws Record Showtime Signups & Soft Ratings," *Sceen Rant*, May 22. screenrant.com/twin-peaks-revival-season-3-showtime-subscribers-streaming.

Sitney, P. Adams (2016), "A Cinema of Resistance: The Films of Jean-Marie Straub and Danièle Huillet," *Artforum*, May. www.artforum.com/print/201605/a-cinema-of-resistance-the-films-of-jean-marie-straub-and-daniele-huillet-59535.

Skinner, Jessica E. (2020), "Bosch Season 7: Release Date, Cast, Plot, And All the Latest News", *NewsreaderWeb*, July 16. www.newsreaderweb.com/bosch-season-7-release-date-cast-plot-and-all-latest-news.

Smith, Jeff (1998), *The Sounds of Commerce: Marketing Popular Film Music*. New York: Columbia University Press.

Smith, Murray (1999), "Gangsters, Cannivals, Aesthetes, or Apparently Perverse Allegiances," in Plantinga, Carl & Smith, Greg M. (eds.), *Passionate Views: Film, Cognition, and Emotion*.

Snider, Mike (2018), "AT&T CEO Says HBO is 'Tiffany' to Netflix's 'Walmart'," *USA Today*, December 14. eu.usatoday.com/story/money/business/2018/09/13/randall-stephenson-att-ceo-netflix-walmart-hbo-tiffany/1288253002.

Snider, Zachary (2016), "The Cognitive Psychological Effects of Binge-Watching," in McDonald, Kevin & Daniel Smith-Rowsey (eds.), *The Netflix Effect: Technology and Entertainment in the 21st Century*. Bloomsbury.

Somanader, Tanya (2015), "President Obama Interviews the Creator of 'The Wire' David Simon," *The White House*, March 27. obamawhitehouse.archives.gov/blog/2016/08/18/president-obama-interviews-creator-wiredavid-simon.

Somoma, Serena (2019), "What Trans Teens Are Saying About Jules on 'Euphoria'," *Teen Vogue*, August 5. www.teenvogue.com/story/euphoria-jules-trans-teens.

Spangler, Todd (2019), "Netflix Bandwidth Consumption Eclipsed by Web Media Streaming Applications," *Variety*, September 10. variety.com/2019/digital/news/netflix-loses-title-top-downstream-bandwidth-application-1203330313.

Spencer, Samuel (2020), "'Euphoria' Cast and Crew Tease 'Special COVID Episode' Before Season 2", *Newsweek*, September 23. www.newsweek.com/euphoria-season-2-release-date-filming-special-hbo-zendaya-1533839.

Sperling, Nicole (2020), "Jeffrey Katzenberg Blames Pandemic for Quibi's Rough Start," *The*

New York Times, March 11. www.nytimes.com/2020/05/11/business/media/jeffrey-katzenberg-quibi-coronavirus.html.

Spiegel, Lynn (2004), "Introduction," in Spiegel, Lynn & Jan Olsson (eds.), *Television After TV: Essays on a Medium in Transition*. Durham, NC: Duke University Press.

Split Screens TV (2018), "Split Screens 2018 presents THE AMERICANS Debriefing with Showrunners Joe Weisberg and Joel Fields" (interviewer Matt Zoller Seitz), June 8. www.youtube.com/watch?v=u8rdiU1NSV4&t=136s.

Statt, Nick (2020), "Quibi adds Chromecast support for watching shows on a big screen," *The Verge*, June 9. www.theverge.com/2020/6/9/21285760/quibi-google-chromecast-support-feature-launch-apple-airplay-tv-shows.

Steam. store.steampowered.com/app/207610/The_Walking_Dead.

Stelter, Brian (2013), "New Way to Deliver a Drama: All 13 Episodes at Once," *The New York Times*, January 31. www.nytimes.com/2013/02/01/business/media/netflix-to-deliver-all-13-episodes-of-house-of-cards-on-one-day.html.

Strangelove, Michael (2015), *Post-TV: Piracy, Cord-Cutting, and the Future of Television*. Toronto: The University of Toronto Press.

Sundet, Vilde Schanke (2017), "'Det er bare du som kan føle det du føler - emosjonell investering og engasjement i nettdramaet SKAM," *16:9*, June 25.

Sundet, Vilde Schanke (2020), " 'Will it Translate?': SKAM som remake," in Nielsen, Jakob Isak et al. (eds.), *Streaming for viderekomne: Fra Doggystyle og Black Mirror til The Jinx*. Aarhus: VIA Film & Transmedia.

Svensson, Henrik & Pontus Möller (2019), *The conherency between Fjällräven's brand identity and brand image*. Jönköping University, Jönköping International Business School, Master's Degree Project.

Syme, Rachel (2017), "The Trouble with Our 'Golden Age' of TV," *The New Republic*, November 21.

Tally, Margaret (2016), *The Rise of the Anti-heroine in TV's Third Golden Age*. Newcastle upon Tyne: Cambridge Scholars Publishing

Tay, Jinna & Graeme Turner (2010), "Not the Apocalypse: Television Futures in the Digital Age," *International Journal of Digital Television 1*, pp. 31-50.

Telecommunications Act (2008), Paragraph 1. Retrieved from fcc.gov.

Tercek, Robert (2015), "The Rumored 'Death of TV' Is Really About Transforming Brand Identity and Advertising," *Medium*, May 6. medium.com/id-in-the-iot/the-rumored-death-of-tv-is-really-about-transforming-brand-identity-and-advertising-c051b63ec203.

The Take (2017), "*House of Cards* Explained: Shakespeare, History & Guilty Pleasure," YouTube, June 1. www.youtube.com/watch?v=dNAFTJ_Blg8.

Thompson, Derek (2018), "A Brief History of Teenagers," *The Saturday Evening Post*, February 13. www.saturdayeveningpost.com/2018/02/brief-history-teenagers.

Thompson, Kristin (2003), *Storytelling in Film and Television*. Cambridge, MA & London, England: Harvard University Press.

Thompson, Robert J. (1996), *Television's Second Golden Age: From* Hill Street Blues *to* ER. New York: Continuum.

Thorpe, Vanessa (2019), "Seriously funny: why we fell in love with dramedies," *The Guardian*, May 11. www.theguardian.com/tv-and-radio/2019/may/11/why-we-fell-in-love-with-dramedies.

Thurm, Eric (2017), "Farewell to *Halt and Catch Fire*, the best show that nobody watched," *The Guardian*, October 16. www.theguardian.com/tv-and-radio/2017/oct/16/farewell-to-halt-and-catch-fire-the-best-show-that-nobody-watched.

Todorov, Tzvetan (1977), *The Poetics of Prose*. Cornell University Press.

Travers, Ben (2017), "'Twin Peaks', New Ratings, Facing Off with 'Game of Thrones,' and What It All Means for the Future of TV," *Indiewire*, July 12. www.indiewire.com/2017/07/twin-peaks-ratings-2017-season-4-game-of-thrones-1201853930.

Travers, Ben (2019), "'Euphoria' Review: Zendaya's HBO Series Is a Teens-in-Crisis Horror Show," *Indiewire*, June 4.

Truelove, Thom (2016), "Amazon's *Bosch*: Echoes of Black", *Criminal Element*, March 18. www.criminalelement.com/amazon-bosch-echoes-of-black-harry-bosch-amazon-prime-michael-connelly.

Truffaut, François (1954), "A Certain Tendency of the French Cinema." soma.sbcc.edu/users/

davega/FILMST_113/Filmst113_ExFilm_Movements/FrenchNewWave/A_certain_tendency_tr%23540A3.pdf.
Truffaut, François (1967), *Hitchcock*. New York: Simon and Schuster.
Tryon, Chuck (2013), *On-Demand Culture: Digital Delivery and the Future of Movies*. New Brunswick: Rutgers University Press.
Tudor, Andrew (1974), *Theories of Film*. Viking Press.
Twin Peaks: Fire Walk with Me, Japanese Promo from 1992. www.youtube.com/watch?v=Molt-YM2EW7s.
Ulrich, Lise (2021), "Netflix, Disney og HBO kaster vanvittigt beløb efter din underholdning i 2021," *Soundvenue*, January 13.
Uricchio, William (2014), "Film, Cinema, Television ... Media?" *New Review of Film and Television Studies*, 12(3).
Van den Bulck, Hilde & Hallvard Moe (2018) "Public service media, universality and personalisation through algorithms: mapping strategies and exploring dilemmas," *Media, culture, and society* vol. 40,6, pp. 875-892.
VanDerWerff, Emily Todd (2012), "*Looking* reaches beyond simply being "the gay *Girls*," *AV Club*, January 17. tv.avclub.com/looking-reaches-beyond-simply-being-the-gay-girls-1798179204.
Vincendeau, Ginette (2019), "How the French birthed film noir," *Sight and Sound*, May 7. www.bfi.org.uk/news-opinion/sight-sound-magazine/features/deep-focus/french-film-noir.
Vincentelli, Elisabeth (2020), "Comfort Viewing: 3 Reasons I Love 'Columbo'," *The New York Times*, July 24. www.nytimes.com/2020/07/24/arts/television/columbo-watch.html.
Waade, Anne Marit & Claus Toft-Nielsen (2015), "Harry Potter som transmedia storytelling - franchise, fantasy og fans," in Lauridsen, Palle Schantz & Erik Svendsen (eds.), *Medieanalyse*. København: Samfundslitteratur.
Watson, Amy (2020), "Number of Netflix paying streaming subscribers worldwide from 3rd quarter 2011 to 2nd quarter 2020 (in millions)," *Statista*, July 17. www.statista.com/statistics/250934/quarterly-number-of-netflix-streaming-subscribers-worldwide.
WBUR (2020), "HBO's 'Beforeigners' Presents Sci-Fi Spin on the Refugee Crisis," March 6.
Weis, Elisabeth (1985), "The Evolution of Hitchcock's Aural Style and Sound in *The Birds*," in Weis, Elisabeth & John Belton (eds.), *Film Sound: Theory and Practice*. New York: Columbia University Press, pp. 298-311.
White, Brett (2014), "New 'Twin Peaks' Episodes Aren't Meant to Be Binge-Watched, Co-Creator Says," *CBR*, October 7. www.cbr.com/new-twin-peaks-episodes-arent-meant-to-be-binge-watched-co-creator-says.
Williams, Linda (2014), *On The Wire*. Durham, NC: Duke University Press.
Williams, Raymond (1974), *Television, Technology and Cultural Form*. London: Fontana.
Williams, Rebecca (2016), "'No Lynch, No Peaks!': Auteurism, Fan/Actor Campaigns and the Challenges of *Twin Peaks'* Retur*n*(s)," *Series*, 2:1, Spring, pp. 5-19.
Wolff, Michael (2015), "Michael Wolff: Television has Outgrown Nielsen," *The Hollywood Reporter*, May 12. www.hollywoodreporter.com/news/michael-wolff-television-has-outgrown-794419.
Wolk, Alan (2015), *Over The Top: How The Internet Is (Slowly But Surely) Changing The Television Industry*. Wolk.
Yacowar, Maurice (2003), *The Sopranos on the Couch: Analyzing Television's Greatest Series*. New York & London: Continuum.
Zoladz, Lindsay (2017), "The Case for Savor-Watching," *The Ringer*, May 26.

Notes

1. Strangelove, Michael (2015), *Post-TV: Piracy, Cord-Cutting, and the Future of Television*. Toronto: University of Toronto Press, p. 13.
2. Despite a general consensus, some scholars disagree with this statement. Cf. Tay, Jinna & Graeme Turner (2010), "Not the Apocalypse: Television Futures in the Digital Age," *International Journal of Digital Television* 1, p. 34.
3. Dunleavy, Trisha (2018), *Complex Serial Drama and Multiplatform Television*. London: Routledge.
4. Author interview, May 14, 2020.
5. Author interview, May 14, 2020.
6. Author interview, April 19, 2020.
7. Author interview, May 5, 2020.
8. Cf. Nielsen, Jakob Isak et al. (eds.)(2011), *Fjernsyn for viderekomne - de nye amerikanske tv-serier*. Aarhus: Turbine, and McCabe, Janet & Kim Akass (eds.)(2007), *Quality TV: Contemporary American Television and Beyond*. London: I.B. Tauris.
9. Herbert, Daniel, Lotz, Amanda D., & Marshall, Lee (2019), "Approaching media industries comparatively: A case study of streaming", *International Journal of Cultural Studies*, 22(3), pp. 349-366.
10. Author interview, April 28, 2020.
11. Geertz, Clifford (1990), "Deep Play: Notes on a Balinese Cockfight", in Mukerji, Chandra & Michael Schudson (eds.), *Re-Thinking Popular Culture*. Berkeley: University of California Press, p. 266.
12. Caldwell, John T. (2008), *Production Culture: Industrial Reflexivity and Critical Practice in Film and Television*. Durham & London: Duke University Press, pp. 38-39.
13. Ibid., p. 3.
14. Ibid., p. 37.
15. Cf. Bruun, Hanne (2014), "Eksklusive informanter. Om interviewet som redskab i produktionsanalysen," *Nordicom-Information* 36, pp. 29-43.
16. Cf. Lobato, Ramon (2019), *Netflix Nations: The Geography of Digital Streaming*. New York: New York University Press, pp. 73-106.
17. Quoted in Grego, M. (2002), "Feared,Yet Respected," *Variety* (Special on HBO), November 4, A1-A2, A5.
18. *Telecommunications Act* (2008), Paragraph 1. Retrieved from fcc.gov.
19. Kelly, J.P. (2017), *Time, Technology and Narrative Form in Contemporary US Television Drama*: London: Palgrave MacMillan, p. 59.
20. Ibid.
21. Kompare, Derek (2006), "Publishing Flow: DVD Box Sets and the Reconception of Television," *Television and New Media* 7(4), p. 341.
22. Catherine Johnson (2012, p. 6) fittingly describes this as "the thorny problem of periodization".
23. Cf. Halskov, Andreas (2015a), *TV Peaks: Twin Peaks and Modern Television Drama*. Odense: The University Press of Southern Denmark, pp. 19-52.
24. Thompson, Robert J. (1996), *Television's Second Golden Age: From* Hill Street Blues *to* ER. New York: Continuum, pp. 20-35.
25. Ibid., pp. 59-140.
26. Cf. Højer, Henrik (2011), "Det er da tv? Den amerikanske tv-series udvikling fra antologi-tv til ikke-tv," in Nielsen, Jakob Isak et al. (eds.), *Fjernsyn for viderekomne - de nye amerikanske tv-serier*. Aarhus: Turbine, pp. 16-35.
27. Thompson, Robert J. (1996), *Television's Second Golden Age*, pp. 13-15 and Bianculli, David (1992), *Teleliteracy: Taking Television Seriously*. New York: Continuum.
28. Albrecht, Michael Mario (2016), *Masculinity in Contemporary Quality Television*. New York: Routledge, p. 6-7. See also Tally, Margaret (2016), *The Rise of the Anti-heroine in TV's Third*

Golden Age. Newcastle upon Tyne: Cambridge Scholars Publishing, p. 8. Following the same logic and a similar terminology, David Bianculli has described the current TV landscape as *The Plantinum Age of Television*.

29. Cf. e.g. Ludvigsen, Jacob (2015), "Dramaseriens guldalder kan være slut," *Soundvenue*, August 10, and Syme, Rachel (2017), "The Trouble with Our 'Golden Age' of TV," *The New Republic*, November 21.
30. The interviews with Tom Fontana and David Simon are included in the first feature interview called "The Cable Vanguard", a triple interview with Fontana, Simon and David Chase. For more on Orson Welles and his often forgotten TV pilot, see McBride, Joseph (2006), *What Ever Happened to Orson Welles? A Portrait of an Independent Career*. Lexington, Kentucky: University of Kentucky Press, p. 124.
31. Quoted in Halskov, Andreas (2015a), *TV Peaks*, p. 35.
32. Ibid., pp. 31-32.
33. According to sound creator Joe Foglia, Don Johnson provided a great deal of creative input when it came to sound, whereas Michael Mann spent more energy on the editing process. Author interview, September 11, 2016.
34. Author interview, August 26, 2016.
35. Mark Frost has also described this tendency to (a) overemphasize David Lynch's role on *Twin Peaks* and (b) overestimate the level of consciousness and intentionality behind his aesthetic decisions: "[People] make assumptions about his work and tend to be more than charitable about his contributions and what they assume he's going after. He's, unqualified, a brilliant director. My experience is that his process as a writer is not as consciously directed as they assume. It's more inchoate and often as mysterious to him because he's anti-intellectual." Cf. Bushman, David (2020), *Conversations with Mark Frost: Twin Peaks, Hill Street Blues, and the Education of a Writer*. Columbia, Ohio: Fayetteville Mafia Press, p. 280.
36. Author interview, May 18, 2017.
37. As music editor Lori Escher Frystak says: "I remember how David Lynch, at the last minute, would add these little sound effects. He would say: 'Open om the mic, guys', and, like when Audrey flicks her cigarette into the sink at the high school bathroom, he just went 'psst'. You could hear it, but it sounds like a cigarette hitting the water." Author interview, April 16, 2019. Similarly, the supervising sound editor Douglas Murray has explained that David Lynch used his mouth to create a spur-of-the-moment wind sound for a central scene in the pilot episode where James (James Marshall) and Donna (Lara Flynn Boyle) are looking at Laura's empty chair in the classroom. In what looks like a reference to Fritz Lang, the hollow wind sound illustrates Laura's absence. Author interview, January 21, 2015.
38. Author interview, May 4, 2020.
39. Even when it comes to the use of sound design, many practitioners mention Ingmar Bergman as a source of inspiration. As Fred Judkins, the supervising sound editor on *Tell Me You Love Me* (HBO, 2007), says: "We took the European approach, inspired by people like Ingmar Bergman. European filmmakers think about using surreal sounds to illustrate how a character feels, and we tried to do the same thing on *Tell Me You Love Me*. It was all subtle – the way a dishwasher sounds or the sound of a small ticking clock used to illustrate the unhappiness of a wife. It's subtle, but it's letting the audience in on the unhappiness of the wife. We used multitrack recording, many channels, and we cut backgrounds focusing on specific sounds. It was done in a very cinematic way, and we tried to create a sort of European sensibility." Author interview, September 9, 2016.
40. Author interview, June 8, 2020.
41. Cf. Gunhild Agger's comment in Halskov, Andreas (2015a), *TV Peaks*, p. 198 and Redvall, Eva Novrup (2011), "Dogmer for tv-drama: Om brugen af *one vision*, den dobbelte historie og crossover i DR's søndagsdramatik," *Kosmorama # 248*.
42. Ellis, John (2000), *Seeing Things: Television in the Age of Uncertainty*. London: I.B. Tauris, pp. 1-5.
43. Ibid., p. 1.
44. Cf. Reeves, Jimmie L. et al (1996), "Rewriting Popularity," in Lavery, David et al. (eds.), *Deny*

45. *All Knowledge: Reading The X Files*. Syracuse, New York: Syracuse University Press, pp. 22-35.
45. Jenner, Mareike (2018), *Netflix and the Re-Invention of Television*. Palgrave Macmillan, pp. 13-14.
46. Cf. Lotz, Amanda D. (2007), *The Television Will Be Revolutionized*. New York: New York University Press, p. 55 and Nielsen, Jakob Isak (2011a), "Broadcastnetværk," in Nielsen, Jakob Isak et al. (eds.), *Fjernsyn for viderekomne – de nye amerikanske tv-serier*. Aarhus: Turbine, pp. 241-253.
47. Lotz, Amanda D. (2018), *We Now Disrupt This Broadcast: How Cable Transformed Television and the Internet Revolutionized It All*. Cambridge, MA & London: The MIT Press, p. 9.
48. Ibid., p. 7.
49. Lotz, Amanda D. (2007), *The Television Will Be Revolutionized*, p. 55.
50. Redvall, Eva (2013), *Writing and Producing Television Drama in Denmark. From "The Kingdom" to "The Killing"*. Basingstoke: Palgrave Macmillan, pp. 63-67.
51. Author interview, September 11, 2016.
52. Author interview, April 19, 2020.
53. Author interview, May 11, 2020.
54. Cf. Halskov, Andreas (2015a), *TV Peaks*, pp. 112-137.
55. Author interview, April 19, 2020.
56. Interestingly, *Riget* has also been said to initiate a "Golden Age" in Danish television.
57. Roman, James (1998), *Love, Light and a Dream: Television's Past Present and Future*. London: Westport, CT: Praeger, p. 63.
58. Dunleavy, Trisha (2018), *Complex Serial Drama and Multiplatform Television*. London: Routledge, p. 14n.
59. Klein, Paul L. (1971), "Why you watch what you watch when you watch," *TV Guide*, July 24, pp. 6-9
60. *FCC* (1934), *Communications Act of 1934*. transition.fcc.gov/Reports/1934new.pdf.
61. *Law School Case Brief* (1977): "Home Box Office, Inc. v. FCC - 185 U.S. App. D.C. 142, 567 F.2d 9 (1977). www.lexisnexis.com/community/casebrief/p/casebrief-home-box-office-inc-v-fcc.
62. For more on this, see Halskov, Andreas & Højer, Henrik (2011), "Kunsten ligger i nichen: 'The HBO Playbook'," *Kosmorama* #248, pp. 37-46, video.dfi.dk/Kosmorama/magasiner/248/kosmorama248_037_artikel2.pdf, and Højer, Henrik (2017a), "It's Not TV. It's Art-TV," *16:9*, February 21. www.16-9.dk/2017/02/its-not-tv-its-art-tv.
63. Cf. Hammond, Michael & Lucy Mazdon (eds.) (2005), *The Contemporary Television Series*. Edinburgh: Edinburgh University Press; McCabe, Janet & Kim Akass (eds.) (2007), *Quality TV*; Leverette, Marc et al. (eds.), *It's Not TV: Watching HBO in the Post-Television Era*. London & New York: Routledge; Nielsen, Jakob Isak et al. (eds.) (2011), *Fjernsyn for viderekomne*.
64. Akass, Kim & Janet McCabe (2018): "HBO and the Aristocracy of Contemporary TV Culture: affiliations and legitimatising television culture, post-2007", *Mise au point*, 10|2018, January 15, 2018. journals.openedition.org/map/2472 ; DOI : 10.4000/map.2472.
65. Cf. Dunleavy, Trisha (2018), *Complex Serial Drama and Multiplatform Television*, p. 25.
66. Author interview, April 19, 2020.
67. Author interview, April 19, 2020.
68. Sepinwall, Alan (2012), *The Revolution Was Television: The Cops, Crooks, Slingers, and Slayers Who Changed TV Drama Forever*. Touchstone, pp. 26-27.
69. Engelstad, Audun (2011), "It's Not TV – or Is It?", *16:9*, February. www.16-9.dk/2011-02/side11_inenglish.htm.
70. Leverette, Marc (2007), "Introduction: The Not-TV Industry," in Leverette, Marc et al. (eds.), *It's Not TV: Watching HBO in the Post-Television Era*. London: Routledge, p. 13.
71. Lotz, Amanda (2003), "Why Isn't It TV? Post-Network Television Economics and Evaluating HBO Texts,", quoted in Santos, Avi (2007), "Para-Television and Discourses of Distinction," in Leverette, Marc et al. (eds.), *It's Not TV*, p. 33.
72. Author interview, May 5, 2020.

73. Ibid.
74. *The Sopranos* is one series in a five-way tie for best TV series of all time, together with *Cheers* (NBC, 1982-1993), *The Simpsons* (Fox, 1989-), *The Wire* (HBO, 2002-2008) and *Breaking Bad* (AMC, 2008-2013), in Matt Zoller Seitz and Alan Sepinwall's *TV (The Book)*. Its high ratings were especially impressive due to the fact that only 32 million people in the US had access to cable at that time. Cf. Seitz, Matt Zoller & Alan Sepinwall (2016), *TV (The Book): Two Experts Pick the Greatest American Shows of All Time*. New York & London: Grand Central Publishing, pp. 21-52, and Carter, Bill (2011), "'Sopranos' Sets Ratings Record with Season Finale," *The New York Times*, May 22.
75. Quoted in Bigsby, Christopher (2013), *Viewing America: Twenty-First Century Television Drama*. New York: Cambridge University Press, p. 1.
76. Quoted in Biskind, Peter (2007), "An American Family," *Vanity Fair*, April.
77. Cf. Højer, Henrik (2017a), "It's Not TV, It's Art TV", *16:9*, February 21. www.16-9.dk/2017/02/its-not-tv-its-art-tv.
78. Author interview, May 5, 2020.
79. Cf. Højer, Henrik (2017a), "It's Not TV, It's Art TV"; see also Kael, Pauline (1994), *For Keeps*. New York: Dutton, p. 684 and Nielsen, Jakob Isak (2015), "Camera Movements in Narrative Cinema," *16:9*, February 2. www.16-9.dk/2015/02/camera-movement-in-narrative-cinema.
80. Lee, Mark (2007), "Wiseguys: A Conversation between David Chase and Tom Fontana," *Writers Guild of American*, west, May.
81. Author interview, May 11, 2020.
82. Bogdanovich, Peter (2000), *Interview with David Chase*, featurette on the DVD release of *The Sopranos*, Season 1 (HBO, Region 1).
83. Author interview, May 5, 2020.
84. Author interview, May 5, 2020.
85. Cf. *Split Screens TV* (2018), "Split Screens 2018 presents THE AMERICANS Debriefing with Showrunners Joe Weisberg and Joel Fields" (interviewer Matt Zoller Seitz), June 8. www.youtube.com/watch?v=u8rdiU1NSV4&t=136s. The term *apparently perverse allegiances* derives from Murray Smith's essay "Gangsters, Cannivals, Aesthetes, or Apparently Perverse Allegiances", in which he writes about the different levels of engagement and how audiences often come to identify with a dubious and amoral character despite his/her moral fallibility. The central point in Smith's essay is that the engagement is created through some sort of access to a character's inner thoughts (e.g. via voice-over and screen time), positive or likable qualities within the main character (e.g. wit and intelligence) and moral relativity (where the antihero is contrasted by other characters who are even more morally dubious or questionable). Cf. Smith, Murray (1999), "Gangsters, Cannivals, Aesthetes, or Apparently Perverse Allegiances," in Plantinga, Carl & Smith, Greg M. (eds.), *Passionate Views: Film, Cognition, and Emotion*. For more on the antiheroes in modern American television, see Martin, Brett (2013), *Difficult Men: Behind the Scenes of a Creative Revolution: From* The Sopranos *and* The Wire *to* Mad Men *and* Breaking Bad. New York: The Penguin Press.
86. Cf. Yacowar, Maurice (2003), *The Sopranos on the Couch: Analyzing Television's Greatest Series*. New York & London: Continuum, p. 25.
87. Author interview, May 5, 2020.
88. For more on this, see Mitchell, Keith B. (2008), "Until the Fat Man Sings: Body Image, Masculinity, and Sexuality in *The Sopranos*," in Fahy, Thomas (ed.), *Considering David Chase: Essays on* The Rockford Files, Northern Exposure *and* The Sopranos. McFarland & Company, p. 186.
89. Cf. Weis, Elisabeth (1985), "The Evolution of Hitchcock's Aural Style and Sound in *The Birds*," in Weis, Elisabeth & John Belton (eds.), *Film Sound: Theory and Practice*. New York: Columbia University Press, pp. 298-311.
90. Author interview, September 11, 2016.
91. Author interview, May 5, 2020.
92. For more on this, see Raskin, Richard (1997), "Camera Movement in *Wings of Desire*," *P.O.V.* #4, December. pov.imv.au.dk/Issue_04/section_1/artc5A.html, and Halskov, Andreas

93. Author interview, April 15, 2019.
94. Cf. Bordwell, David (1986), "Classical Hollywood Cinema: Narrational Principles and Procedures", in Rosen, Philip (ed.), *Narrative, Apparatus, Ideology*. New York: Columbia University Press.
95. Nørgaard, Thomas (2011), "Tv-auteurs", *16:9* #40.
96. Jensen, Mikkel (2017), "'From the Mind of David Simon': A Case for the Showrunner Approach," *Series*, Vol. 3, No. 2, Winter, p. 32.
97. Mittell, Jason (2015), *Complex TV: The Poetics of Contemporary Television Storytelling*. New York: New York University Press, p. 115.
98. Author interview, February 12, 2019.
99. Author interview, October 7, 2019.
100. Ndalianis, Angela (2005), "Television and the Neo-Baroque," in Hammond, Michael & Lucy Mazdon (eds.), *The Contemporary Television Series*. Edinburgh: Edinburgh University Press, pp. 83-101.
101. Robert Altman's use of overlapping dialogue was created in collaboration with location sound recordist Jim Webb and the late re-recording mixer Richard Portman, who is famous for his work on films by Mike Nichols, Hal Ashby and Robert Altman. For more on David Simon's use of background voices, see *Every Little Thing*, "The Voices Hiding in Your Favorite Movies", Dec. 4, 2017.
102. Halskov, Andreas (2016), "16:9 Talks: Peter Albrechtsen," *16:9*, October 24. www.16-9.dk/2016/10/peter-albrechtsen.
103. Author interview, September 5, 2016.
104. Cf. Sitney, P. Adams (2016), "A Cinema of Resistance: The Films of Jean-Marie Straub and Danièle Huillet," *Artforum*, May. www.artforum.com/print/201605/a-cinema-of-resistance-the-films-of-jean-marie-straub-and-daniele-huillet-59535.
105. Gjelsvik, Anne & Jørgen Bruhn (2011), "Listen carefully – The Wires opgør med politiserien", Nielsen, Jakob Isak et al. (eds.), *Fjernsyn for viderekomne*, pp. 115-129.
106. Cf. Kelly, J.P. (2017), *Time, Technology and Narrative Form in Contemporary US Television Drama*, p. 64.
107. Ibid., p. 62.
108. Lavik, Erlend (2014), *Tv-serier: The Wire og den tredje gullalderen*. Oslo: Universitetsforlaget.
109. Seitz, Matt Zoller & Alan Sepinwall (2016), *TV (The Book)*, p. 37.
110. Author interview, February 12, 2019.
111. Cf. Jensen, Mikkel (2017), "'From the Mind of David Simon'", p. 34, and O'Donnell, Bryan (2019), "Everything Comes Full Circle in The Wire Series Finale," *25YL*.
112. Apart from Erlend Lavik's book, scholars such as Stanley Corkin and Linda Williams have written monographs about *The Wire*, and Martha Nochimson uses David Simon as one of the most essential cases in her book *Television Rewired*. Cf. Corkin, Stanley (2017), *Connecting The Wire: Race, Space, and Postindustrial Baltimore*. Austin, TX: University of Texas Press; Williams, Linda (2014), *On The Wire*. Durham, NC: Duke University Press; Nochimson, Martha (2019), *Television Rewired: The Rise of the Auteur Series*. Austin: The University of Texas Press.
113. Jensen, Mikkel (2020), "'Our future is in the city': Storbyens udfordringer i David Simons tv-serier," *16:9*, March 7. www.16-9.dk/2020/03/david-simons-tv-serier.
114. Quoted in Bigsby, Christopher (2013), *Viewing America: Twenty-First Century Television Drama*. New York: Cambridge University Press, p. 1.
115. Lotz, Amanda (2020), "Storytelling in the World of Streaming," in Nielsen, Jakob Isak et al. (eds.), *Streaming for viderekomne: Fra Doggystyle til Black Mirror og The Jinx*. Aarhus: VIA Film & Transmedia, p. 27.
116. Author interview, June 8, 2020.
117. Landau, Neil (2016), *TV Outside the Box: Trailblazing in the Digital Television Revolution*. New York & London: Focal Press.

118. Cf. *Internet World Stats.* www.internetworldstats.com/emarketing.htm and www.business-modelsinc.com/exponential-business-model/netflix.
119. Moore, Frazier (2008), "What Does 'Watching TV' Mean in the Post-TV Age?", *Associated Press*, June 19.
120. Spiegel, Lynn (2004), "Introduction," in Spiegel, Lynn & Jan Olsson (eds.), *Television After TV: Essays on a Medium in Transition*. Durham, NC: Duke University Press, p. 3.
121. Cf. Kirschbacher, Felix & Sven Stollfuß (2015), "Lost in TV: Überlegungen zur Fernsehserie." lost-in-tv.de/about-us; Tercek, Robert (2015), "The Rumored 'Death of TV' Is Really About Transforming Brand Identity and Advertising," *Medium*, May 6. medium.com/id-in-the-iot/the-rumored-death-of-tv-is-really-about-transforming-brand-identity-and-advertising-c051b63ec203; Tay, Jinna & Graeme Turner (2010), "Not the Apocalypse: Television Futures in the Digital Age," *International Journal of Digital Television 1*, pp. 31-50; Strangelove, Michael (2015), *Post-TV: Piracy, Cord-Cutting, and the Future of Television*. Toronto: The University of Toronto Press, p. 4; Seale, Jack (2021), "The last broadcast: as streaming takes over, are TV channels doomed?", *The Guardian*, January 12.
122. Nielsen, Jakob (2020), "Streaming i det danske medielandskab", in Nielsen, Jakob Isak et al. (eds.), *Streaming for viderekomne: Fra* Doggystyle *til* Black Mirror *og* The Jinx. Aarhus: VIA Film & Transmedia, p. 21.
123. Strangelove, Michael (2015), *Post-TV: Piracy, Cord-Cutting, and the Future of Television*, p. 7.
124. Akass, Kim & Janet McCabe (2018): "HBO and the Aristocracy of Contemporary TV Culture: affiliations and legitimatising television culture, post-2007"
125. Sandvig, Christian (2015), "The Internet as Anti-Television: Distribution as Culture and Power," in Parks, Lisa & Nicole Starosielski (eds.), *Signal Traffic: Critical Studies of Media Infrastructures*. Urbana, Chicago: University of Illinois Press, p. 232.
126. Ibid., p. 233.
127. Ibid.
128. Licklider, J.C.R. (1967), "Televistas," in Carnegie Commission of Educational Television (ed.), *Public Television: A Program for Action*. New York: Harper & Row, pp. 201-205, 202.
129. I am indebted to Data Scientist Kim Bøg Brandt for introducing me to this analogy.
130. Lotz, Amanda (2020), "Storytelling in a World of Streaming," p. 27.
131. Cf. Bazin, André (2004 [1967]), *What is Cinema?* Berkeley & Los Angeles: University of California Press, and Carroll, Noël (1996), "The Specificity of Media in the Arts," in *Theorizing the Moving Image*. Cambridge: Cambridge University Press.
132. Dawson, Max (2012), "Defining Mobile Television: The Social Construction and Deconstruction of New and Old Media," *Popular Communications* 10, p. 255
133. Lotz, Amanda (2014), *Portals: A Treatise on Internet-Distributed Television*. Michigan Publishing/Maizebooks, p. 4.
134. This phrase is inspired by Marshall McLuhan, who coined the popular phrase, "the medium is the message," in his seminal book *Understanding Media*. Cf. McLuhan, Marshall (2001), *Understanding Media*. London: Routledge.
135. As Mittell writes: "Economic strategies privileged the episodic form for prime time programming - in large part, serialized content posed problems for the industry's cash cow, syndication. Reruns distributed by syndicators might be aired in any order, making continuing storylines an obstacle to this lucrative aftermarket." Cf. Mittell, Jason (2015), *Complex TV*, p. 32.
136. Cf. Lotz, Amanda D. (2020), "Storytelling in the World of Streaming," pp. 30-31.
137. Parks, Lisa & Starosielski, Nicole (2015), "Introduction", *Signal Traffic: Critical Studies in Media Infrastructures*, p. 1.
138. Herbert, Daniel et al. (2019), "Approaching media industries comparatively: A case study of streaming", *International Journal of Cultural Studies*, 22 (3), pp. 349-366.
139. Ibid., pp. 350-352.
140. Lotz, Amanda (2020), "Storytelling in a World of Streaming", p. 32.
141. Cf. Johnson, Catherine (2019), *Online TV*. London: Routledge, p. 31. It should be noted, however, that Lotz mentions YouTube as a relatively open-access streaming service, thus

acknowledging the issues that arise from focusing only on subscription funded streaming channels in America. Cf. Lotz, Amanda (2020), "Storytelling in the World of Streaming", p. 28.
142. Johnson, Catherine (2019), *Online TV*, p. 57.
143. Ibid., p. 61.
144. Ladingkær, Lars (2019), "Disse DR-kanaler lukker per 31/12", October 29, *Recordere.dk*. www.recordere.dk/2019/10/disse-dr-kanaler-lukker-per-31-12-19.
145. The interactive video developer Eko alleges that Quibi have stolen their technology and used it to market and promote its own mobile video platform. Cf. Alexander, Julia (2020a), "Quibi is already locked in a legal battle over its rotating video tech," *The Verge*, March 11. www.theverge.com/2020/3/11/21173981/quibi-eko-lawsuit-turnstyle-technology-jeffrey-katzenberg-streaming-interactive.
146. Sperling, Nicole (2020), "Jeffrey Katzenberg Blames Pandemic for Quibi's Rough Start," *The New York Times*, March 11. www.nytimes.com/2020/05/11/business/media/jeffrey-katzenberg-quibi-coronavirus.html.
147. Lee, Benjamin (2020), "Quibi review - shortform sub-Netflix shows aren't long for this world," *The Guardian*, April 6. www.theguardian.com/tv-and-radio/2020/apr/06/quibi-streaming-review-short-form-tv.
148. Author interview, May 17, 2020.
149. Cf. Statt, Nick (2020), "Quibi adds Chromecast support for watching shows on a big screen," *The Verge*, June 9. www.theverge.com/2020/6/9/21285760/quibi-google-chromecast-support-feature-launch-apple-airplay-tv-shows.
150. This point is based on the interviews with Mary Harron and Tricia Brock, who directed some of the first Quibi shows. Author interviews, May 11 and 14, 2020. *Cross-boarding* simply means that multiple episodes are shot at once (shooting by location instead of by episode). It is an efficient way to shoot a series, but it requires that all the scrips are available at the same time, and this has not historically been the case in television (at least not in long-running serials). Cf. Kellison, Catherine et al. (2013), *Producing for TV and New Media: A Real-World Approach for Producers*. 3rd Edition. New York & London: Focal Press.
151. Author interview, May 14, 2020.
152. Hersko, Tyler et al. (2020), "Quibi to Shut Down – Here's What Went Wrong," *Indiewire*, October 21. www.indiewire.com/2020/10/quibi-shuts-down-post-mortem-failed-mobile-streaming-service-1234588080.
153. Johnson, Catherine (2016), *Online TV*, p. 56.
154. Ibid., p. 64.
155. Bertelsen, Diana (2016), "RIPA - a new Danish Viking Series on the social media," *RibeVikingeCenter*, February 15. www.ribevikingecenter.dk/de/aktuelles/ripa-new-danish-viking-docudrama.aspx.
156. Author interview, May 14, 2020.
157. Marr, Andrew (2016), "The loss of the independent means the loss of a community," *The Guardian*, February 13. www.theguardian.com/media/2016/feb/13/the-independent-gave-me-some-of-the-most-exciting-times-of-my-career.
158. Grey, Camilla (2016), "Branded content review: Nike's web series *Margot vs. Lily*", *Medium*, February 17. medium.com/@camillastore/branded-content-review-nike-s-web-series-margot-vs-lily-2171036db449.
159. Curtin, Michael et. al (2014), *Distribution Revolution: Conversations about the Digital Future of Film and Television*, California: University of California Press, p. 2.
160. Lotz, Amanda (2020), "Storytelling in a World of Streaming", p. 29.
161. Raymond Williams describes flow as "the defining characteristic of broadcasting, simultaneously as a technology and as a cultural form." Cf. Williams, Raymond (1974), *Television, Technology and Cultural Form*. London: Fontana, p. 86.
162. Cf. Nye, David (1990), *Contemporary American Society*. København: Akademisk Forlag, p. 161.
163. Rettenmund, Matthew (1996), *Totally Awesome 80s: A Lexicon of the Music, Videos, Movies,*

TV. St. Martin's Press, p. 143.
164. *Netflix* (2013a), "Netflix Quick Guide: What is Streaming and Why is It Better?", *YouTube*, posted by Netflix, May 21.
165. Stelter, Brian (2013), "New Way to Deliver a Drama: All 13 Episodes at Once," *The New York Times*, January 31. www.nytimes.com/2013/02/01/business/media/netflix-to-deliver-all-13-episodes-of-house-of-cards-on-one-day.html.
166. Especially after syndication, cf. McCormick, Casey J. (2016), "'Forward Is the Battle Cry': Binge-Viewing Netflix's *House of Cards*," in McDonald, Kevin & Daniel Smith-Rowsey (eds.), *The Netflix Effect: Technology and Entertainment in the 21st Century*. New York & London: Bloomsbury, p. 102.
167. Unsurprisingly, an article was published on dr.dk (a website connected to DR, the main rival of TV2) about the mental risks associated with *binge-watching* and segments like *Seriesøndag*. Cf. Kristensen, Pernille Kjeldgaard et al. (2019), "Seriesøndag: Hvad sker der i din krop, når du bruger hele weekenden på sofaen?", DR.dk, March 3. www.dr.dk/nyheder/viden/kroppen/seriesoendag-hvad-sker-der-i-din-krop-naar-du-bruger-hele-weekenden-paa-sofaen. For more on *binge-watching* as a concept and its relation to *Seriesøndag* on TV2 Zulu, see Nielsen, Jakob Isak (2013a), "Netflix: Paradoksernes holdeplads", *16:9* #51, June. www.16-9.dk/2013-06/side03_leder.htm.
168. The idea of getting all episodes at once is described by industry critic Alan Wolk as *the Lilyhammer effect*. Cf. Wolk, Alan (2015), *Over The Top: How The Internet Is (Slowly But Surely) Changing The Television Industry*. Wolk, pp. 34-35. For more on *time-shifting* in relation to Netflix, see Lindsey, Cameron (2016), "Questioning Netflix's Revolutionary Impact: Changes in the Business and Consumption of Television," in McDonald, Kevin & Daniel Smith-Rowsey (eds.), *The Netflix Effect: Technology and Entertainment in the 21st Century*. New York: Bloomsbury, p. 174.
169. Brown, Barry & Louise Barkhuus (2006), "The Television Will Be Revolutionized: Effects of PVRs and Filesharing on Television Watching", conference paper, *CHC 2006*. Montréal, Québec: Canada, April 22-27.
170. Kelly, J.P. (2017), *Time, Technology and Narrative Form in Contemporary US Television*, p. 68.
171. McCormick, Casey J. (2016), "'Forward Is the Battle Cry'," pp. 101-102.
172. Hayward, Jennifer (1997), *Consuming Pleasures: Active Audiences and Serial Fictions from Dickens to Soap Opera*. Lexington: University of Kentecky Press, p. 3.
173. McCormick, Casey J. (2016), "'Forward Is the Battle Cry'," p. 102.
174. Lotz, Amanda D. (2020), "Storytelling in a World of Streaming," p. 30.
175. Jenner, Mareike (2018), *Netflix and the Re-Invention of Television*. Basingstoke: Palgrave Macmillan, pp. 140-141.
176. Mittell, Jason (2010), "Serial Boxes," *Just TV*. justtv.wordpress.com/2010/01/20/serial-boxes.
177. Newman, Michael Z. & Elena Levine (2012), *Legitimating Television: Media Convergence and Cultural Status*. Abingdon: Routledge, p. 136.
178. Debra Ramsay has also noted that we have no official words such as "binge-listening" or "binge-reading", and in that sense the word "binge-watching" may imply "a vague distaste for the medium itself." Cf. Ramsay, Debra (2013), "Confessions of a Binge-Watcher," *Critical Studies in Television*, October 4.
179. Quoted in Martin, Brett (2013), *Difficult Men: Behind the Scenes of a Creative Revolution – From The Sopranos and The Wire to Mad Men and Breaking Bad*. London: Penguin, p. 23.
180. According to Zachary Snider, *binge-watching* "recalls the type of problem-solving skills that cognitive psychology associates with collaborative forms of 'active participation'," but *binge-watching* a complex series such as *Orange Is the New Black* can also be exhausting and "negatively affect one's otherwise healthy mental stasis." Cf. Snider, Zachary (2016), "The Cognitive Psychological Effects of Binge-Watching," in McDonald, Kevin & Daniel Smith-Rowsey (eds.), *The Netflix Effect*, pp. 118-121.
181. Cf. Foutch, Haleigh (2017), "The 'Twin Peaks' Revival Will Be 'Pure Heroin,' Says Showtime Boss," *The Collider*, January 9. collider.com/twin-peaks-season-3-david-lynch-showtime

and White, Brett (2014), "New 'Twin Peaks' Episodes Aren't Meant to Be Binge-Watched, Co-Creator Says," *CBR*, October 7. www.cbr.com/new-twin-peaks-episodes-arent-meant-to-be-binge-watched-co-creator-says.
182. Author interview, June 8, 2020.
183. Zoladz, Lindsay (2017), "The Case for Savor-Watching," *The Ringer*, May 26. www.theringer.com/2017/5/26/16044678/the-case-for-savor-watching-8c76446ac5aa.
184. Masoero, Raffaella (2016), "The rise of cord-shaving and cord-cutting", *Accenture*. www.accenture.com/us-en/~/media/pdf-30/accenture-the-rise-of-cord-shaving-and-cord-cutting.pdf. An OTT (over-the-top) media service is offered directly via the Internet.
185. Cf. Dreier, Troy (2017), "Pay TV Lost 1.8M Subscribers in 2016 as Cord-Cutting Accelerates," *Streaming Media*. www.streamingmedia.com/Articles/News/Online-Video-News/Pay-TV-Lost-1.8M-Subscribers-in-2016-as-Cord-Cutting-Accelerates-116888.aspx.
186. *Grabyo* (2019), "Grabyo OTT Video Trends Report 2019". about.grabyo.com/ott-video-trends-2019.
187. Quoted by O'Halloran, Joseph (2020), "74% set to stop paying for pay-TV within five years," *Rapid TV News*, March 4. www.rapidtvnews.com/2020030458161/74-set-to-stop-paying-for-pay-tv-within-five-years.html#axzz6Uq5qvJrA.
188. Cf. Evans, Benedict (2020), "Tech in 2020: Standing on the Shoulders of Giants," February 2020. www.ben-evans.com/presentations.
189. Cf. O'Halloran, Joseph (2020), "74% set to stop paying for pay-TV within five years."
190. Nielsen, Jakob Isak (2020), "Streaming i det danske medielandskab," p. 17.
191. Ibid., p. 14.
192. Ibid., pp. 15-20.
193. Keslassy, Elsa (2020), "Netflix Picks France to Test First Linear Offering," *Variety*, November 6.
194. Curtin, Michael et al. (2014), "Introduction," in *Distribution Revolution: Conversations About the Digital Future of Film and Television*. California: University of California Press, p. 3.
195. Van den Bulck, Hilde & Hallvard Moe (2018). "Public service media, universality and personalisation through algorithms: mapping strategies and exploring dilemmas." *Media, culture, and society* vol. 40,6, pp. 875-892.
196. Quoted in Paskin, Willa (2015), "What does 'peak TV' really mean?", *Slate*, December 23. slate.com/culture/2015/12/what-does-peak-tv-really-mean.html.
197. Author interview, May 17, 2020.
198. Author interview, April 6, 2020.
199. Author interview, May 14, 2020.
200. Author interview, February 17, 2020.
201. Vincent Mosco describes this utopian idea as the "digital sublime," and Chuck Tryon notes that many critics and viewers had the same expectations of cable television. "Viewers were offered a wide array of channels and an escape for the 'oligopolistic' stranglehold of the major broadcasters," as Tryon writes, but "cable television eventually became central to television's commercial interests, with most cable channels being owned by one of the major media conglomerates." Ct. Mosco, Vincent (2004), *The Digital Sublime: Myth, Power, and Cyberspace*. Cambridge, MA: MIT Press and Tryon, Chuck (2013), *On-Demand Culture: Digital Delivery and the Future of Movies*. New Brunswick: Rutgers University Press, p. 4.
202. Cf. Nielsen, Jakob Isak et al. (2020), "16:9 Podcast: Streaming for viderekomne," *16:9*, March 25. www.16-9.dk/2020/03/podcast-05, and Lotz, Amanda D. (2017), *Portals*, p. 13.
203. Tryon, Chuck (2013), *On-Demand Culture*, p. 3.
204. Author interview, May 14, 2020.
205. Cf. Spangler, Todd (2019), "Netflix Bandwidth Consumption Eclipsed by Web Media Streaming Applications," *Variety*, September 10. variety.com/2019/digital/news/netflix-loses-title-top-downstream-bandwidth-application-1203330313.
206. *Sandvine* (2019), "Netflix falls to second place in global internet traffic share as the other streaming services grown," *Sandvine*, September 12. www.sandvine.com/inthenews/netflix-falls-to-second-place-in-global-internet-traffic-share.

207. Cf. Iqbal, Mansoor (2020), "Netflix Revenue and Usage Statistics," *Business of Apps*, June 23. www.businessofapps.com/data/netflix-statistics/ and Watson, Amy (2020), "Number of Netflix paying streaming subscribers worldwide from 3rd quarter 2011 to 2nd quarter 2020 (in millions)," *Statista*, July 17. www.statista.com/statistics/250934/quarterly-number-of-netflix-streaming-subscribers-worldwide.
208. Cf. Iqbal, Mansoor (2020), "Netflix Revenue and Usage Statistics."
209. Elmelund, Rasmus (2018), "Netflix er ikke bare en spiller på markedet, Netflix ER markedet," *Information*, May 25..
210. Tryon, Chuck (2013), *On-Demand Culture*, p. 7. The process of *conglomeration* goes back to at least the 1960s, and today the American media landscape is dominated by a small group of *media conglomerates* and powerful streamers. Cf. Halskov, Andreas (2019), *Remakes, sequels og serialisering*. København: Samfundslitteratur, pp. 49, 95 and 105.
211. Cf. Monggaard, Christian (2020), "Det er Netflix' verden - vi bor bare i den," *Information*, April 29, Section 1, pp. 14-15.
212. Lindsey, Cameron (2016), "Questioning Netflix's Revolutionary Impact," in McDonald, Kevin & Daniel Smith-Rowsey (eds.), *The Netflix Effect: Technology and Entertainment in the 21st Century*. New York & London: Bloomsbury, p. 179.
213. Ibid., p. 178.
214. Wolff, Michael (2015), "Michael Wolff: Television has Outgrown Nielsen," *The Hollywood Reporter*, May 12.
215. Cf. Lotz, Amanda D. (2020), "Storytelling in a World of Streaming," p. 30.
216. Cf. Carr, David (2014), "Taking Back Your TV, Incessantly," *The New York Times*, March 14. www.nytimes.com/2010/03/15/business/media/15carr.html and *Netflix* (2013b), "Netflix Original Series – The Future of Television is Here," *YouTube*, posted by Netflix, September 3, 2013.
217. Uricchio, William (2014), "Film, Cinema, Television ... Media?" *New Review of Film and Television Studies*, 12(3), p. 275.
218. Kelly, J.P. (2020), "Current Affairs or Comfort TV?: VOD Offerings in the Age of Covid-19," CSTOnline, November 27.
219. Somanader, Tanya (2015), "President Obama Interviews the Creator of 'The Wire' David Simon," *The White House*, March 27. obamawhitehouse.archives.gov/blog/2016/08/18/president-obama-interviews-creator-wiredavid-simon.
220. Cf. Hooton, Christopher (2014), "House of Cards: Barack Obama calls for halt on Season 2 spoilers on Twitter," *Independent*, February 14. www.independent.co.uk/arts-entertainment/tv/news/barack-obama-please-no-house-of-cards-season-2-spoilers-9128013.html.
221. Quoted in Adalian, Josef (2018), "Inside the Binge Factory," *Vulture*, June 11. www.vulture.com/2018/06/how-netflix-swallowed-tv-industry.html.
222. One example is the Danish debate program *Deadline* (with Martin Krasnik), which on March 4, 2013 was devoted to *House of Cards* and how (realistic) its portrayal was of contemporary American politics. A more recent example is Austin May's article about Donald Trump's national emergency where *House of Cards* is used as a popular analogy. Cf. May, Austin (2019), "Trump's national emergency is straight out of 'House of Cards'," *The Sunflower*, February 26. thesunflower.com/36463/opinion/may-trumps-national-emergency-is-netflixs-intellectual-property.
223. Kingsley, Hilary (1989), *Soap Box: The Australian Guide to Soap Operas*. Melbourne: Sun Books, pp. 1-2.
224. This motif is also seen in Chapter 23 where Frank, in one of his many soliloquies, turns to the camera and says: "I've always loathed the necessity of sleep. Like death, it puts even the most powerful men on their backs."
225. Mittell, Jason (2015), *Complex TV*, p. 234.
226. Allen, Robert C. (1985), *Speaking of Soap Operas*. Chapel Hill, NC: University of North Carolina Press, p. 142.
227. Cf. Mills, Brett (2009), *The Sitcom*. Edinburgh: Edinburgh University Press, p. 39.

228. Quoted in Modleski, Tania (2003), "The Search for Tomorrow in Today's Soap Operas," in Jones, Amelia (ed.), *The Feminism and Visual Culture Reader*. London & New York: Routledge.
229. Ibid.
230. Richard Paterson has a similar description of the soap opera: "Its narrative is constructed of multiple short segments, with continual repetition of narrative information, but no overall dramatic coherence in any episode. In part, this structure reflects its place in the schedule: continual viewing has to be ensured even though meal times and other domestic interruptions might make it impossible to follow a coherent narrative". Cf. Paterson, Richard et al. (1980), *Coronation Street*. London: BFI: Television Monograph #13, p. 82.
231. McCormick, Casey J. (2014), "'Forward Is the Battle Cry'," p. 111 and *The Take* (2017), "*House of Cards* Explained: Shakespeare, History & Guilty Pleasure," YouTube, June 1. www.youtube.com/watch?v=dNAFTJ_BIg8.
232. Cf. Oxholm, Jan (2014), "Se på mig - nedbrydningen af den fjerde væg," *16:9*, June 5. www.16-9.dk/2014/06/se-paa-mig-nedbrydningen-af-den-fjerde-vaeg/ and Halskov, Andreas (2018a), "'En frygtelig kvinde' benytter et velkendt greb: Disse seks film og serier bryder den fjerde væg," *Politiken*, January 12. politiken.dk/kultur/film_og_tv/art6287478/Disse-seks-film-og-serier-bryder-den-fjerde-v%C3%A6g.
233. McCormick, Casey J. (2014), "'Forward Is the Battle Cry'," in McDonald, Kevin & Daniel Smith-Rowsey (eds.), *The Netflix Effect*, p. 106.
234. Author interview, May 19, 2020.
235. Author interview, April 30, 2020.
236. Author interview, March 2, 2020.
237. McCormick, Casey J. (2014), "'Forward Is the Battle Cry'," pp. 106-110.
238. Ibid., p. 103.
239. Greene, Andy (2013), "How 'Lilyhammer' Changed the TV World: 'Netflix is opening a whole new golden era of television,' says Steve Van Zandt. Plus: Can the E Street Band play forever?", *Rolling Stone*, December 5.
240. Tryon, Chuck (2013), *On-Demand Culture*, p. 4.
241. Ibid.
242. Cf. Salvati, Andrew (2020), "Call for Contributions to Edited Collection, *Unseen Television: Privililege, Power, and the Archive*," CST Online.
243. Lobato, Ramon (2019), *Netflix Nations: The Geography of Digital Distribution*. New York: New York University Press, p. 52.
244. Author interview, April 28, 2020.
245. Author interview, March 24, 2020.
246. Ibid.
247. Ibid.
248. It has already received favorable reviews and commentary by international TV critics, being described as "insanely watchable" by Dustin Rowles and characterized as an ambitious Norwegian combination of sci-fi, crime fiction and personal drama by *NPR*'s Eric Deggans. Cf. Rowles, Dustin (2020), "Review: HBO's Insanely Watchable 'Beforeigners' Combines 'The Leftovers' with 'Travelers'," *Pajiba*, February 21 and *WBUR* (2020), "HBO's 'Beforeigners' Presents Sci-Fi Spin on the Refugee Crisis," March 6.
249. The adjective *glocal* is a blend of "global" and "local" and refers to something that is characterized by both local and global considerations at the same time. In the context of television, it refers to networks and companies that try to reach a global audience by positioning themselves locally in various nations and producing regional content.
250. Chalaby, Jean K. (2005), *Transnational Television Worldwide: Towards a New Media Order*. London: I.B. Tauris, p. 1.
251. Lobato, Ramon (2019), *Netflix Nations*, pp. 50-51.
252. Ibid., pp. 51-52.
253. As Lobato notes, it is important to distinguish between *global television* and *transnational television*. In Lobato's terminology, a service is only global if it "operates on a large number of international markets simultaneously," whereas the term *transnational television* is broa-

der, also covering channels and services that only offer their content in selected markets. Ibid., pp. 49-50.
254. Ibid, p. 52.
255. Hammett-Jamart, Julia et al. (2018), "Introduction: European Film and Television Co-Production," in Hammett-Jamart, Julia et al. (2018), *European Film and Television Co-Production: Policy and Practice*. London: Palgrave Macmillan, p. 11.
256. The estimated budget was 100,000,000 SEK.
257. McCabe, Janet & Catherine Grant (2019), "Bodies at the border: Transnational co-produced TV drama and its gender politics in the pilots of 'Bron/Broen' and adaptations 'The Bridge' and 'The Tunnel'," *Necsus*, May 27. necsus-ejms.org/bodies-at-the-border-transnational-co-produced-tv-drama-and-its-gender-politics-in-the-pilots-of-bron-broen-and-adaptations-the-bridge-and-the-tunnel.
258. Ibid.
259. Bolin, Alice (2018), *Dead Girls: Essays on Surviving an American Obsession*. William Morrow Paperbacks.
260. Hale, Mike (2020), "Missing 'Gomorrah'? Watch This," *The New York Times*, March 5. www.nytimes.com/2020/03/05/arts/television/review-gomorrah-zerozerozero.html.
261. Author interview, March 9, 2020.
262. *The Wire* and *Breaking Bad* are specifically mentioned in connection with *ZeroZeroZero* in the reviews that were published in *The Hollywood Reporter* and *Soundvenue*. Cf. Fienberg, Daniel (2020), "'ZeroZeroZero': TV Review," *The Hollywood Reporter*, March 6. www.hollywoodreporter.com/review/zerozerozero-review-1282768 and Freuendal, Jakob (2020), "'ZeroZeroZero': Ambitiøs narkoserie på HBO Nordic er et kludetæppe af tilfældigheder," *Soundvenue*, February 18. soundvenue.com/film/2020/02/zerozerozero-ambitioes-narko-serie-paa-hbo-nordic-er-et-kludetaeppe-af-tilfaeldigheder-397663.
263. Author interview, March 9, 2020.
264. Ibid.
265. Herzog & Company (2013), "Television Comes of Age", from the documentary series about *The Sixties*, CNN.
266. Kompare, Derek (2005), *Rerun Nation: How Repeats Invented American Television*. New York: Routledge, pp. x-xi.
267. Cf. Adorno, Theodor & Max Horkheimer (1991), *Kulturindustri*. Oslo: Cappelen.
268. There are numerous examples of reality and game shows that are being adapted and remade transnationally, e.g. *Miljoenenjacht* (TROS/Tien/RTL4, 2000-)/*Deal or No Deal* (Channel 4) and *Ramsay's Kitchen Nightmares* (Channel 4, 2004-2014)/*Kitchen Nightmares* (Fox, 2007-2014)/*Pesadilla en la cocina* (laSexta, 2012-). It would be virtually impossible to give an exhaustive list of reality and game show formats that are being adapted across different countries, however, and an in-depth exploration of this particular aspect is beyond the scope of this book.
269. Lavigne, Carlen (2014), "Introduction," in *Remake Television: Reboot, Re-use, Recycle*. Lanham: Lexington, p. 1.
270. A *telenovela* is a Latin-American form of soap opera.
271. Perrotta, Marta & Lothar Mikos (2011), "Traveling style: Aesthetic differences and similarities in national adaptations of *Yo soy Betty, la fea*," *International Journal of Cultural Studies* 15(1), p. 2.
272. Ibid, p. 3.
273. McMillin, Divya (2013), "How Ugly Can Betty Be in India?", in McCabe, Janet & Kim Akass (eds.), *TV's Betty Goes Global: From Telenovela to International Brand*. London: I.B. Tauris, p. 148.
274. Ibid., p. 146.
275. Ibid., p. 149.
276. Cf. Bordwell, David (1986): "Classical Hollywood Cinema: Narrational Principles and Procedures" and Nielsen, Jakob Isak (2013b), "The Oscars og den klassiske Hollywoodfilm", in Højer, Henrik et al. (eds.), *Guldfeber – på sporet af Oscarfilmen*. Aarhus: Turbine, p. 87.

277. This title alludes to the interesting book *Beyond the Bridge: Contemporary Danish Television Drama* (Hochscherf & Philipsen, 2017) about the global success of current Danish television, but it also, indirectly, references an old project proposal from 2016.
278. Cf. Agger, Gunhild (2012), "Thrillerens kunst: *Forbrydelsen I-III*," *16:9* 10(48), November. www.16-9.dk/2012-11/side08_feature1.htm; Hellekson, Karen (2014), *Forbrydelsen, The Killing,* Duty, and Ethics," in Lavigne, Carlen (ed.), *Remake Television: Reboot, Re-use, Recycle*. Lanham: Lexington Books, pp. 131-140; Hochscherf, Tobias & Heidi Philipsen (2017), *Beyond the Bridge: Contemporary Danish Television Drama*. London: Tauris Academic Studies; Gemzøe, Lynge Stegger (2018), *The Showrunner Effect: System, Culture and Individual Agency in American Remakes of Danish Television Series*. PhD dissertation, Institut for Kommunikation og Kultur, Aarhus Universitet.
279. Frost, Vicky (2011): "*The Killing* puts torchlight on subtitled drama," *The Guardian*, November 18. www.theguardian.com/tv-and-radio/2011/nov/18/the-killing-torchlight-subtitled-drama.
280. Cf. Agger, Gunhild (2012), "Thrillerens kunst: *Forbrydelsen I-III*."
281. Cf. Agger, Gunhild (2012), "Thrillerens kunst: *Forbrydelsen I-III*."
282. Gemzøe, Lynge Stegger (2018), *The Showrunner Effect*.
283. Jensen, Pia Majbritt et al. (2016), "When public service drama travels," *The Journal of Popular Television*, January 1.
284. Nordstrøm, Pernille (2004), *Fra Riget til Bella – bag om tv-seriens golden age*. København: DR.
285. Nielsen, Jakob Isak (2016), "The Danish Way to Do It the American Way," *Kosmorama*, May 13. www.kosmorama.org/en/kosmorama/artikler/danish-way-do-it-american-way.
286. Gemzøe, Lynge Stegger (2018), *The Showrunner Effect*, p. 71.
287. Hale, Mike (2012), "The Danes Do Murder Differently," *The New York Times*, March 28. www.nytimes.com/2012/04/01/arts/television/comparing-the-killing-to-the-show-forbrydelsen.html.
288. Nielsen, Jakob Isak (2012), "Solen må aldrig skinne, og Sofie må aldrig smile: Interview med Piv Bernth," *16:9* 10(48), November. www.16-9.dk/2012-11/side06_interview3.htm.
289. Sundet, Vilde Schanke (2017), "'Det er bare du som kan føle det du føler - emosjonell investering og engasjement i nettdramaet SKAM," *16:9*, June 25.
290. Sundet, Vilde Schanke (2020), " 'Will it Translate?': *SKAM* som remake," in Nielsen, Jakob Isak et al. (eds.), *Streaming for viderekomne*, p. 71.
291. Bazin, André (1952), "Remade in USA," *Cahiers du Cinéma* #11.
292. Lobato, Ramon (2019), *Netflix Nations*, p. 110.
293. Lotz, Amanda (2020), "Storytelling in the World of Streaming," p. 31.
294. Author interview, May 6, 2020.
295. Author interview, May 5, 2020.
296. Chalaby, Jean K. (2005), *Transnational Television Worldwide: Towards a New Media Order*. London: I.B. Tauris, p. 62.
297. Lobato, Ramon (2019), *Netflix Nations*, p. 111.
298. Ibid., p. 114.
299. Author interview, March 5, 2020.
300. Author interview, March 3, 2020.
301. Cf. Svensson, Henrik & Pontus Möller (2019), *The conherency between Fjällräven's brand identity and brand image*. Jönköping University, Jönköping International Business School, Master's Degree Project, pp. 33-34. Fjällräven is also used as a demographic or social signifier in HBO's *The Undoing* (2020).
302. Other critics have noted this combination, and in *The Atlantic*, the series was described as "ludicrous climate fiction." Cf. Gilbert, Sophie (2018), "*The Rain* Is a Taut Dystopian Thriller," *The Atlantic*, May 3. www.theatlantic.com/entertainment/archive/2018/05/the-rain-review-netflix/559439. See also Bastholm, Søren (2018), "Interview med Jannik Tai Mosholt - hovedforfatter på *The Rain*, den første danske Netflixserie," *16:9*, April 17. www.16-9.dk/2018/04/interview-med-jannik-tai-mosholt-showrunner-paa-the-rain.

303. Cf. Cappelen, John (2020), "Nedbør og sol i Danmark," *DMI*, January 31. www.dmi.dk/klima/temaforside-klimaet-frem-til-i-dag/nedboer-og-sol-i-danmark.
304. Adalian, Josef (2018), "Inside the Binge Factory."
305. Cf. Grater, Tom (2020), "Netflix Unveils Its Most-Watched Series and Films in America: 'The Platform' & 'Barbarians' Top Lists Also Featuring 'Cuties', 'Money Heist', 'Dark'," *Deadline*, December 10. deadline.com/2020/12/netflix-most-watched-international-series-films-america-the-platform-barbarians-cuties-1234653658.
306. Author interview, March 5, 2020.
307. Author interviews, October 6 and November 26, 2020.
308. Katz, Brandon (2020), "Why Netflix's 'Money Heist' Is the Most In-Demand Show in the World," *Observer*, April 9.
309. Author interview, May 18, 2020.
310. Author interview, May 18, 2020.
311. Frater, Patrick (2020), "Netflix to Launch Korean Version of 'Money Heist' Hit Spanish Series," *Variety*, November 30.
312. Nussbaum, Emily (2014), "Small Differences: He-said, she-said on 'The Affair'," *The New Yorker*. December 8. www.newyorker.com/magazine/2014/12/15/small-differences.
313. Author interview, April 28, 2020.
314. Ibid.
315. Ibid.
316. Ibid.
317. Keslassy, Elsa (2019), "'The Intouchables' Helmers to Direct French Adaptation of 'In Treatment'," *Variety*, November 15. variety.com/2019/tv/news/the-intouchables-helmers-to-direct-french-tv-adaptation-of-in-treatment-1203405971.
318. Author interview, April 28, 2020.
319. Ibid.
320. Author interview, April 28, 2020.
321. Kustanowitz, Esther D. (2019), "'Our Boys' will make you uncomfortable, which is exactly why you should watch it," *The Jewish News of Northern California*, August 29. www.jweekly.com/2019/08/29/our-boys-will-make-you-uncomfortable-which-is-exactly-why-you-should-watch-it.
322. Snider, Mike (2018), "AT&T CEO Says HBO is 'Tiffany' to Netflix's 'Walmart'," *USA Today*, December 14. eu.usatoday.com/story/money/business/2018/09/13/randall-stephenson-att-ceo-netflix-walmart-hbo-tiffany/1288253002.
323. Cf. Alexander, Julia (2019), "Can HBO Now survive HBO Max", *The Verge*, September 27.
324. Mittell, Jason (2015), *Complex TV*, pp. 2-3.
325. Author interview, May 11, 2020.
326. Quoted in Schaal, Eric (2020), "Why David Lynch Would Rather Make a TV Series Than a Feature Film These Days," *Showbiz CheatSheet*, April 20.
327. Dunleavy, Trisha (2018), *Complex Serial Drama and Multiplatform Television*, p. 11.
328. Newman, Michael Z. & Elana Levine (2011), *Legitimating Television: Media Convergence and Cultural Status*. London: Routledge, p. 5.
329. Author interview, April 28, 2020.
330. Cf. Mittell, Jason (2015), *Complex TV*, p. 32.
331. Mittell, Jason (2015), *Complex TV*, p. 216.
332. Author interview, April 28, 2020.
333. Author interview, February 23, 2015.
334. Jason Mittell defines narrative complexity in the following way: "At its most basic level, narrative complexity is a redefinition of episodic forms under the influence of serial narration – not necessarily a complete merger of episodic and serial forms but a shifting balance. Rejecting the need for plot closure within every episode that typifies conventional episodic form, narrative complexity foregrounds ongoing stories across a range of genres." Cf. Mittell, Jason (2006), "Narrative Complexity in Contemporary American Television," *The Velvet Light Trap* #58, Fall, p. 32.

335. Bordwell, David (2006), *The Way Hollywood Tells It: Stories and Style in Modern Movies*. Berkeley: University of California Press, p. 89.
336. Mittell, Jason (2015), *Complex TV*, p. 237.
337. Cf. Mittell, Jason (2015), *Complex TV*, pp. 38, 197.
338. As Jason Mittell puts it, "the consumer of complexity needs to engage fully and attentively." The distinction between *erratic viewer* and *comprehensive viewer* is taken from Mittell. Cf. Mittell, Jason (2013), "The Qualities of Complexity: Vast versus Dense Seriality in Contemporary Television," in Jacobs, Jason & Stephen Peacock (eds.), *Television Aesthetics and Style*. New York: Bloomsbury, p. 46.
339. Dunleavy, Trisha (2018), *Complex Serial Drama and Multiplatform Television*, p. 3.
340. For more on this and other plot arcs from *Mad Men*, see Nielsen, Jakob Isak (2011b), "Rundt om *Mad Men*," in Nielsen, Jakob Isak et al. (eds.), *Fjernsyn for viderekomne - de nye amerikanske tv-serier*. Aarhus: Turbine, pp. 202-223.
341. Dunleavy, Trisha (2018), *Complex Serial Drama and Multiplatform Television*, p. 4.
342. Ibid, pp. 5-7.
343. Bordwell, David (1985), *Narration in the Fiction Film*. Madison: University of Wisconsin Press, p. 49.
344. Ibid., p. 50.
345. Bronwen, Thomas (2016), *Narrative: The Basics*. London: Routledge, p. 113.
346. Author interview, February 12, 2019.
347. Mikanowski, Jacob (2014), "'True Detective': Down the Bayou (Far From Any Road)," *Los Angeles Review of Books*, March 8. lareviewofbooks.org/article/bayou-far-road.
348. Author interview, April 28, 2020.
349. Kiss, Miklós & Steven Willemsen (2017), *Impossible Puzzle Films: A Complex Approach to Contemporary Complex Cinema*. Edinburg: Edinburgh University Press, p. 11.
350. Cf. Nussbaum, Emily (2014), "Small Differences: He-said, she-said on 'The Affair'," *The New Yorker*. December 8.
351. Author interview, April 28, 2020.
352. In a conversation with the French filmmaker François Truffaut, Alfred Hitchcock admitted that the lying flashback in *Stage Fright* was a flaw, in the sense that the audiences believed what they saw and did not understand the element of unreliability. Cf. Truffaut, François (1967), *Hitchcock*. New York: Simon and Schuster, p. 139.
353. Gay, Verne (2015), "American Crime review," *Newsday*, March 3.
354. Chion, Michel (1999), *The Voice in Cinema*. Translated by Claudia Gorbman. New York: Columbia University Press, pp. 23-32.
355. Damico, Amy M. & Sara E. Quay (2016), *21st-Century TV Dramas: Exploring the New Golden Age*. Praeger, p. 29.
356. Ibid., p. 164.
357. Højer, Henrik (2018), "Et billedes anatomi: American Crime," *16:9*, June 11. www.16-9.dk/2018/06/american-crime.
358. Cf. Hopewell, John (2020), "'When the Dust Settles': Dorte W. Høgh, Ida Maria Rydén Drill Down on the New DR Series," *Variety*, January 24. variety.com/2020/tv/global/when-the-dust-settles-dorte-w-hogh-ida-maria-ryden-drill-down-new-dr-series-1203478542.
359. Author interview, May 6, 2020.
360. Ibid.
361. Mittell, Jason (2013), "The qualities of complexity: Vast versus dense seriality in contemporary television," p. 52.
362. Author interview, May 6, 2020.
363. Author interview, February 17, 2020.
364. Cf. Halskov, Andreas (2011), "Carnivàle - støvskålens magi," *16:9 books*. www.16-9.dk/fjernsynforviderekomne/carnivale.htm.
365. Author interview, February 17, 2020.
366. Ibid.
367. Ibid.

368. Ibid.
369. Ibid.
370. Mikos, Lothar (2020), "Streaming Services and the Changing Nature of Drama Series Production in Germany - The example of *Dark* and *You Are Wanted*, in Nielsen, Jakob Isak et al. (eds.), *Streaming for viderekomne: Fra* Doggystyle *til* Black Mirror *og* The Jinx. Aarhus: VIA Film & Transmedia, p. 112.
371. Translated from German: "[W]enn du lange in einen Abgrund blickst, blickt der Abgrund auch in dich hinein." Nietzsche, Friederich (2013 [1886]), *Jenseits von Gut und Böse: Vorspiel einer Philosophie der Zukunft*. JiaHu Books, p. 98, ¶146.
372. Jerslev, Anne (2001), "Vildledninger: Den overrumplende dramaturgi,"*Ekko* #9, September.
373. Thanks to Per Martin Halskov for giving me valuable insights and comments on *Dark*.
374. Herson, Kellie (2019), "The biggest mystery on TV is how every show became a puzzle box," *Culture*, March 25.
375. Cf. Petersen, Brian (2017), "Gådefuldt spild af tid", *EKKO* #76 and Nystrøm, Camilla Gyldendal (2017), "The Leftovers er fyldt med mening", *EKKO*, October 13.
376. Chaney, Jen (2015), "Damon Lindelof on 'The Leftovers' Finale, the Show's Future and his Afterlife Obsession," *The New York Times*, December 7.
377. Author interview, October 2, 2020.
378. Quoted in Baker, Djoymi (2017), "Terms of Excess: Binge-Viewing as Epic-Viewing in the Netflix Era," in Barker, Cory & Myc Wiatrowski (eds.), *The Age of Netflix: Critical Essays on Streaming Media, Digital Delivery and Instant Access*. Jefferson, NC: McFarland & Co., p. 41; Lotz, Amanda D. (2006), "Rethinking Meaning Making: Watching Serial TV on DVD, *Flow* 4.12. www.flowjournal.org/2006/09/rethinking-meaning-making-watching-serial-tv-on-dvd/#fn2.
379. Mittell, Jason (2013), "The Qualities of Complexity," p. 49.
380. Jenkins, Henry (2006), *Convergence Culture: Where Old and New Media Collide*. New York: New York University Press, pp. 2, 95.
381. Jenkins, Henry (2007), "Transmedia Storytelling 101," *Confessions of an Aca-Fan*, March 21. henryjenkins.org/blog/2007/03/transmedia_storytelling_101.html.
382. According to Ryan: "[T]his important trend in contemporary culture comes in two types. The first could be called the "snowball effect": a certain story enjoys so much popularity, or becomes culturally so prominent, that it spontaneously generates a variety of either same-medium or cross-media prequels, sequels, fan fiction and adaptations. In this case there is a central text that functions as common reference for all the other texts. Harry Potter and Lord of the Rings are good examples of the snowball effect: they started out in the medium of the novel, created by a single author, and they expanded to film and computer games by popular demand. In the other type of transmedial narration, illustrated by the commercial "franchise" of The Matrix, which comprises films, computer games and comics, a certain story is conceived from the very beginning as a project that develops over many different media platforms." Cf. Ryan, Marie-Laure (2014), "Story/Worlds/Media: Tuning the Instruments of a Media-Conscious Narratology," in Ryan, Marie-Laure & Jan-Noël Thon (eds), *Storyworlds across Media: Toward a Media-Conscious Narratology*. Lincoln: University of Nebraska Press, pp. 25-49. See also Ryan, Marie-Laure (2013), "Transmedial Storytelling and Transfictionality," *Poetics Today*, 34(3), pp. 361-388.
383. Jenkins, Henry (2009), "The Revenge of the Origami Unicorn: The Remaining Four Principles of Transmedia Storytelling," *Confessions of an Aca-Fan*, December 12. henryjenkins.org/2009/12/revenge_of_the_origami_unicorn.html.
384. Jenkins, Henry (2006), *Convergence Culture*, p. 33. See also Halskov, Andreas (2015a), *TV Peaks*, p. 172.
385. Mittell, Jason (2015), *Complex TV*, p. 289.
386. Cf. Bruns, Axel (2008), *Blogs, Wikipedia, Second Life and Beyond*. Peter Lang.
387. Pearson, Roberta & Máire Messenger Davies (2014), *Star Trek and American Television*. Berkeley: University of California Press, p. 126.
388. Hills, Matt (2005), "Cult TV, Quality, and the Role of the Episode/Programme Guide," in Ham-

mond, Michael & Lucy Mazdon (eds.), *The Contemporary Television Series*. Edinburgh: Edinburgh University Press, pp. 190-191.
389. Sue Short defines these types of series as *cult telefantasy*. Cf. Short, Sue (2011), *Cult Telefantasy Series: A Critical Analysis of The Prisoner, Twin Peaks, The X-Files, Buffy the Vampire Slayer, Lost, Heroes, Doctor Who and Star Trek*. London: McFarland & Company.
390. Henrik Højer has written an article about *transmedia storytelling* for the Danish anthology *Det nye mediefag* (2017), focusing on *The Walking Dead* and *Westworld* (cf. Højer 2017b). For more on *Cobra Kai*, nostalgia and fan engagement, see Halskov, Andreas (2019), *Remakes, sequels og serialisering*. København: Samfundslitteratur.
391. Cf. Ferguson, Latoya (2020), "'The Lord of the Rings': Everything You Need to Know About Amazon's Big Money Adaptation," *Indiewire*, July 6. www.indiewire.com/gallery/amazons-lord-of-the-rings-explained-plot-cast/the-lord-of-the-rings-the-fellowship-of-the-ring-2001-2.
392. Sconce, Jeffrey (2004), "What If? Charting Television's New Textual Boundaries," in Spiegel, Lynn & Jan Olsson (eds.), *Television after TV: Essays on a Medium in Transition* Durham, NC: Duke University Press, p. 95.
393. "We are currently working on Season 11," Angela Kang says. "We will be telling a very Western-themed mission story, and also meeting the largest community our people have come across yet. I can't say much more without spoiling it!" Cf. Author interview, May 19, 2020, and Debnath, Neela (2020), "Walking Dead season 11: Has Maggie changed amid time-jump? Star drops cryptic clue," *Express*, June 23. www.express.co.uk/showbiz/tv-radio/1299810/Walking-Dead-season-11-Maggie-Rhee-time-jump-Lauren-Cohan-AMC-series.
394. Nielsen, Jakob Isak (2013c), "Blockbuster TV," conference paper delivered at the conference *Bestseller & Blockbuster Culture: Books, Cinema and Television* at Aalborg University.
395. Author interview, May 19, 2020.
396. Cf. Altman, Rick (2012 [1984]), "A Semantic/Syntactic Approach to Film Genre," in Grant, Barry Keith (ed.), *Film Genre Reader IV*. Austin: University of Texas Press, p. 32.
397. Author interview, May 14, 2020.
398. Author interview, May 19, 2020.
399. The *Walking Dead* attraction has closed. Cf. Newman, Sydney (2020), "The Walking Dead Attraction closes at Universal Studios Hollywood," *Inside Universal*, March 4. www.insideuniversal.net/category/universal-studios-hollywood.
400. Cf. Henderson, Rik (2018), "The Walking Dead Pokemon Go-Style AR Game is out now for iOS and Android," *Pocket-lint*, July 12. www.pocket-lint.com/games/news/pokemon/143939-the-walking-dead-our-world-ar-game-is-pokemon-go-for-zombie-lovers.
401. Cf. *Steam*. store.steampowered.com/app/207610/The_Walking_Dead.
402. Cf. Chitwood, Adam (2014), "*The Walking Dead* Season 5 Premiere Shatters Ratings Records with 17.3 Million Viewers," *Collider*, October 13. collider.com/the-walking-dead-season-5-premiere-ratings.
403. Author interview, May 19, 2020.
404. Author interview, October 31, 2017.
405. Cf. Thompson, Robert J. (1996), *Television's Second Golden Age*, p. 163 and Halskov, Andreas (2015a), *TV Peaks*, p. 10.
406. Author interview, April 16, 2019.
407. Molloy, Tim (2018), "Twin Peaks' Origin Story 'Blonde, Beautiful and Dead' Optioned by Part2 Pictures (Exclusive)", *The Wrap*, d. 19. november. www.thewrap.com/twin-peaks-origin-story-blonde-beautiful-and-dead-optioned-by-part2-pictures.
408. Murray, Noel (2017), "'Twin Peaks' Season 1, Episode 1: Wrapped in Plastic," *New York Times*, April 20. www.nytimes.com/2017/04/20/watching/twin-peaks-recap-season-1-episode-1.html.
409. Lotz, Amanda D. (2007), *The Television Will Be Revolutionized*. New York, NY: New York University Press, p. 53.
410. Cf. Halskov, Andreas (2015a), *TV Peaks*, p. 11. David Lynch attended David Letterman's

Late Show on February 27, 1991. The interview can be watched here: www.youtube.com/watch?v=jH2tyK3eQ8c.
411. *Twin Peaks: Fire Walk with Me*, Japanese Promo from 1992. www.youtube.com/watch?v=MoltYM2EW7s.
412. Alexander, John (1993). *The Films of David Lynch*. London: Letts, p. 138.
413. Iversen, Ebbe (1992), "Tomme mysterier", *Berlingske Tidende*, October 9 and Canby, Vincent (1992): "One Long Last Gasp for Laura Palmer", *The New York Times*, August 29.
414. Cf. Jerslev, Anne (1993), *David Lynch i vore øjne*. København: Frydenlund, pp. 166-178 and George, Diane Hume (1995), "Lynching Women: A Feminist Reading of *Twin Peaks*," in Lavery, David (ed.), *Full of Secrets: Critical Approaches to Twin Peaks*. Detroit: Wayne State University Press, pp. 110-117.
415. Cousins, Mark (2014), *The Story of Film*. BCA/Pavilion Books, p. 396.
416. For more on *Twin Peaks: Fire Walk with Me* and its relation to the TV series, see Halskov, Andreas (2014b), "'The worst movie ever made': en revurdering af *Twin Peaks: Fire Walk with Me*," *16:9*, May 29. www.16-9.dk/2014/05/the-worst-movie-ever-made; McHugh, Maura (2017): *Twin Peaks: Fire Walk with Me*. PS Publishing; Hallam, Lindsay (2018), *Twin Peaks: Fire Walk with Me*. Devil's Advocate. Auteur.
417. For more on the Georgia Coffee commercials, see Malkinson, Agnes (2016): "'Damn Fine Coffee' Advertising: David Lynch's TV Commercial Adaptation of *Twin Peaks*," *Senses of Cinema*, #29, July. sensesofcinema.com/2016/twin-peaks/26839.
418. Jensen, Jeff (2017a), "*Twin Peaks* Recap: *The Return* Parts 3-4," *Entertainment Weekly*, May 28.
419. Cf. Jerslev, Anne (2017), "Twin Peaks peaker," *Kommunikationsforum*, May 24.
420. Author interview, April 13, 2019.
421. For more on the connections between *Twin Peaks: The Return* and avant-garde cinema, see Pedersen, Peter Ole (2018), "Dette er vandet, dette er brønden," *Passage* 33:1, pp. 77-88.
422. In Denmark, there is a Facebook group called *For alle os der hader James fra Twin Peaks* (*For Everyone Who Hates James from Twin Peaks*), and there are numerous examples of humorous GIFs and memes that ridicule James Hurley as an overly melodramatic character and/or James Marshall for having a narrow emotional range and a protruding forehead. Only a few of them are mean-spirited, but parts of the community have reacted by disallowing demeaning posts.
423. Author interview, April 13, 2019.
424. The term *forensic fandom* was originally coined by Jason Mittell. Cf. Mittell, Jason (2006): "Narrative Complexity in Contemporary American Television", *Velvet Light Trap* 58, pp. 29-40.
425. Author interview, February 12, 2019.
426. Cf. Halskov, Andreas (2017a), "No Place Like Home: Returning to *Twin Peaks*," *16:9*, May 30. www.16-9.dk/2017/05/returning-to-twin-peaks.
427. BOB's comment to Laura in *The Secret Diary of Laura Palmer*, "I DON'T NEED THINGS… I WANT THINGS", is repeated by Mr. C. (Kyle MacLachlan) in *Twin Peaks: The Return*, which has also been subject to debate on Reddit. And the strange combination of frog and flying insect in Part 8 looks like a visual reference to an animal from the fictional guide book *Welcome to Twin Peaks: An Access Guide to the Town* (1991) and to the frog-moth that David Lynch has mentioned in various contexts. He mentions this strange creature both in a featurette from the *Inland Empire* DVD where he cooks quinoa and in the book *Room to Dream* (2018). Cf. www.reddit.com/r/twinpeaks/comments/94nxg9/all_the_secret_diary_of_laura_palmer.
428. The Swiss journalist and documentarian Matteo Maccarinelli is working on a documentary about the *Twin Peaks* fan community and how it has affected the *Twin Peaks* universe. The film does not have a definite release date yet, but is expected in 2021.
429. Cf. Williams, Rebecca (2016), "'No Lynch, No Peaks!': Auteurism, Fan/Actor Campaigns and the Challenges of *Twin Peaks' Return*(s)," *Series*, 2:1, Spring, pp. 5-19.
430. Cf. Jensen, Jeff (2017b), "*Twin Peaks*: David Lynch Breaks Down the First Four Episo-

des," *Entertainment Weekly*, May 26.
431. Garner, Ross (2017),"What We Learned from Sam and Tracey: Does the New *Twin Peaks* Differ from Contemporary Quality TV," *CST*, May 27.
432. Cf. Fiske, John (1987), "Intertextuality," in *Television Culture*. London: Routledge. For more on transmedia storytelling and how these kinds of stories can evolve and mutate, see Waade, Anne Marit & Claus Toft-Nielsen (2015), "Harry Potter som transmedia storytelling - franchise, fantasy og fans," in Lauridsen, Palle Schantz & Erik Svendsen (eds.), *Medieanalyse*. København: Samfundslitteratur.
433. Silver, Stephen (2017), "Twin Peaks Revival Draws Record Showtime Signups & Soft Ratings," *Sceen Rant*, May 22. screenrant.com/twin-peaks-revival-season-3-showtime-subscribers-streaming.
434. Thompson, Kristin (2003), *Storytelling in Film and Television*. Cambridge, MA & London, England: Harvard University Press, pp. 107-108.
435. Jacobs, Jason & Steven Peacock (2013), "Introduction," in Jacobs, Jason & Steven Peacock (eds.), *Television Aesthetics and Style*. New York & London: Bloomsbury, pp. 6, 8.
436. Cardwell, Sarah & Steven Peacock (2006), "Introduction," in Cardwell, Sarah & Steven Peacock (eds.), "Good Television?", *Journal of British Cinema and Television* 3:1, p. 1.
437. Jacobs, Jason & Steven Peacock (2016), "Introduction", in *Television Aesthetics and Style*, p. 7.
438. Quoted in Flitterman-Lewis, Sandy (1992), "Psychoanalysis, Film, and Television," in Allen, Robert C. (ed.), *Channels of Discourse, Reassembled*. London: Routledge, p. 217.
439. Cf. Caldwell, John T. (1995), *Televisuality: Style, Crisis, and Authority in American Television*. New Brunswick: Rutgers University Press and Butler, Jeremy G. (2010), *Television Style*. New York: Routledge, pp. 15-16, 26, 56 and 82.
440. Ellis, John (1992 [1982]), *Visible Fictions: Cinema, Television, Video*. London & New York: Routledge, p. 128.
441. Ibid.
442. Cf. Carroll, Noël (1996), "The Specificity of Media in the Arts."
443. Cf. Pudovkin, Vsevolod (2009 [1958]), "Film Technique [On Editing]," in Braudy, Leo & Marhsall Cohen (eds.), *Film Theory & Criticism*. Oxford: Oxford University Press, pp. 7-12; Eistenstein, Sergei (2009 [1988]), "Film Form: Beyond the Shot & The Dramaturgy of Film Form," pp. 13-40; Bazin, André (2005 [1967]), *What is Cinema?*, pp. 23-40; Epstein, Jean (1993 [1924]), "On Certain Characteristics of *Photogénie*", in Abel, Richard (ed.), *French Film Theory and Criticism: A History/Anthology, 1907-1939: Vol.1: 1907-1929*. Princeton University Press, p. 314.
444. Caldwell, John T. (1995), *Televisuality: Style, Crisis and Authority in American Television*. New Brunswick, NJ: Rutgers University Press, p. 110.
445. Mills, Brett (2016), "What Does It Mean to Call Television 'Cinematic'?", Jacobs, Jason & Steven Peacock (eds.), *Television Aesthetics and Style*. New York & London: Bloomsbury, pp. 64-65.
446. Dunleavy, Trisha (2009), *Television Drama: Form, Agency, Innovation*. Basingstoke: Palgrave Macmillaa, p. 211.
447. Levine, Elana (2008), "Distinguishing Television: The Changing Meanings of Television Liveness," *Media, Culture & Society* 30:3, pp. 393-394.
448. Bordwell, David (1979), "The Art Cinema as a Mode of Film Practice," *Film Criticism* 4, No. 1, pp. 57-61.
449. Thompson, Kristin (2003), *Storytelling in Film and Television*, p. 110. Thompson specifically distinguishes between *art TV* and "prestige" television in the form of renowned literary adaptations (a long-standing tradition for BBC and various other broadcasters and public services channels). As Thomson writes, that strand of television is actually related to a major Hollywood tradition (rather than art cinema). It should be noted, however, that the term "prestige" television is usually used in a broader sense to describe TV series that are stylized and/or critically acclaimed, whereas "prestige" film is used, more specifically, as a reference to literary adaptations, gaining their "prestige" from their literary ancestors.

450. Author interview, January 29, 2018.
451. Karpovich, Angelina (2010): "Dissecting the Opening Sequence," in *Dexter – Investigating Cutting Edge Television*. London & New York: I.B. Tauris, p. 29. See also Genette, Gérard (1997), *Palimpsests: Literature in the Second Degree*. Lincoln: University of Nebraska Press.
452. Author interview, July 2, 2019.
453. Cf. Halskov, Andreas (2014c), "Indledningens kunst: Den moderne titelsekvens," *16:9*, www.16-9.dk/2014/04/indledningens-kunst-den-moderne-titelsekvens.
454. Author interview, April 10, 2020.
455. Author interview, February 24, 2020.
456. Halskov, Andreas (2014c), "Indledningens kunst."
457. Cardwell, Sarah (2007). "Is Quality Television Any Good? Generic Distinctions, Evaluations and the Troubling Matter of Critical Judgement," in McCabe, Janet & Kim Akass (eds.), *Quality TV: Contemporary American Television and Beyond*. London: I.B. Tauris, p. 28.
458. Halskov, Andreas (2014c), "Indledningens kunst."
459. Cf. Højer, Henrik & Andreas Halskov (2009), "It's Not TV… (Part 2)", *16:9* #34.
460. Author interview, January 1, 2018.
461. Author interview, April 18, 2019.
462. Cf. Lirette, Christopher (2014), "Something True about Louisiana: HBO's *True Detective* and the *Petrochemical American* Aesthetic," *Southern Spaces*. August 13.
463. Author interview, February 24, 2020.
464. Author interview, April 28, 2020.
465. Cf. Halskov, Andreas (2015b), "My Least Favorite Life," *16:9*, June 18 and Bastholm, Søren Rørdam (2014), "I mørket findes frelsen," *16:9*, August 15.
466. Author interview, March 14, 2019.
467. Cf. Johnson, Catherine (2012), *Branding Television*. London: Routledge.
468. Author interview, June 8, 2020.
469. The title sequence to *Mindhunter* (Netflix, 2017-) is also quite evocative, and Søren Rørdam Bastholm has presented an insightful authorial reading of that particular title sequence, arguing that the title sequence is meant to promote the series as a part of Fincher's oeuvre. Cf. Bastholm, Søren Rørdam (2019), "Tænk på Fincher - *Mindhunters* titelsekvens," *16:9*, August 10.
470. Landekic, Lola (2018), "Babylon Berlin", *Art of the Title*, April 24.
471. Cf. e.g. the interview with Craig Henighan (February 13, 2018) elsewhere in this book.
472. Author interview, April 10, 2020.
473. Karpovich, Angelina (2010): "Dissecting the Opening Sequence," p. 29.
474. Author interview, April 10, 2020.
475. Author interview, July 5, 2019.
476. Film historian John Fawell presents a convincing defense of "the invisible, seamless style of classical Hollywood" where he argues that the "seamlessness," the "clipped efficiency" and "the elegant continuity" of traditional mainstream films is an under-appreciated quality, compared to the "lavish technique" and "overt stylistic devices" of modern (art) films. Cf. Fawell, John (2008), *The Hidden Art of Hollywood: In Defense of the Studio Era Film*. Westport, CT & London: Praeger, p. 77.
477. Martin, Adrian (2014), *Mise en Scéne and Film Style: From Classical Hollywood to New Media Art*. New York: Palgrave Macmillan, pp. 21-42.
478. Bordwell, David et al. (1985), *The Classical Hollywood Cinema: Film Style & Mode of Production to 1960*. New York: Columbia University Press, p. 3.
479. Cf. Thurm, Eric (2017), "Farewell to *Halt and Catch Fire*, the best show that nobody watched," *The Guardian*, October 16. www.theguardian.com/tv-and-radio/2017/oct/16/farewell-to-halt-and-catch-fire-the-best-show-that-nobody-watched.
480. Cf. Giannetti, Louis (2002), *Understanding Movies*. 9th Edition. Upper Saddle River, New Jersey: Prentice Hall, pp. 218-219.
481. Author interview, May 14, 2020.
482. Author interview, February 11, 2019.

483. Gorman, Bill (2011), "'Doctor Who,' 'Top Gear,' & 'Luther' Lead BBC America To Best Ratings Quarter Ever", *TV By the Numbers*, October 14.
484. Chion, Michel (1999), *The Voice of Cinema*, p. 5.
485. Author interview, May 14, 2020.
486. Author interview, April 2, 2020.
487. Hellerman, Jason (2019), "HBO's 'Succession' Will Change How You Shoot and Edit," *No Film School*, August 23. nofilmschool.com/succession-hbo-technical-specs.
488. Author interview, February 16, 2020.
489. Cf. Schepelern, Peter (2003), "Filmen ifølge Dogme: Spilleregler, forhindringer og befrielser," in Toftgaard, Anders & Ian Halvdan Hawkesworth (eds.), *Nationale spejlinger: Tendenser i ny dansk film*. København: Museum Tusculanums Forlag, pp. 61-108.
490. Author interview, February 16, 2020.
491. Author interview, February 16, 2020.
492. Ibid.
493. Ibid.
494. Ibid.
495. Author interview, February 14, 2020.
496. Author interview, December 7, 2020.
497. Cf. the feature interview (April 6, 2020) with Sam Levinson at the end of this book.
498. Author interview, April 15, 2019.
499. The main principles behind Hollywood's so-called "seamless style" were established in the early 1900s, and many of the techniques are often attributed to pioneers like Edwin S. Porter and D.W. Griffith. For more on this, see Salt, Barry (1983), "The Early Development of Film Form," in Fell, John L. (ed.), *Film Before Griffith*. Berkeley & Los Angeles: The University of California Press, pp. 284-298.
500. Author interview, September 1, 2016.
501. Adorno, Theodor & Hanns Eisler (1947), *Composing for the Films*. London: The Athlone Press, p. 10.
502. Gorbman, Claudian (1987), *Unheard Melodies: Narrative Film Music*. Bloomington: Indiana University Press, pp. 76-79.
503. Chion, Michel (1994), *Audio-Vision: Sound on Screen*. Translated by Claudia Gorbman. New York: Columbia University Press, p. 148.
504. For more on the so-called *Dolby Era*, see Sergi, Gianluca (2004), *The Dolby Era: Film Sound in Contemporary Hollywood*. Manchester: Manchester University Press and Kerins, Mark (2011), *Beyond Dolby (Stereo): Cinema in the Digital Sound Age*. Indiana: Indiana University Press.
505. Cf. Beck, Jay (2016), *Designing Sound: Audiovisual Aesthetics in 1970s American Cinema*. Rutgers University Press.
506. Author interview, January 10, 2018.
507. Chion, Michel (1994), *Audio-Vision: Sound on Screen*, p 150.
508. Cf. Sergi, Gianluca (1998), "A cry in the dark: The role of post-classical film sound," in Neale, Steve & Murray Smith (eds.), *Contemporary Hollywood Cinema*. New York: Routledge, pp. 156-165 and Langkjær, Birger (2000), *Den lyttende tilskuer: Perception af lyd og musik i film*. København: Museum Tusculanums Forlag, pp. 132-164.
509. Adams, Sam (2016), "*The Night Of* Is More Than a Crime Thriller. It's Also a Great Prison Drama," *Slate*. August 10. slate.com/culture/2016/08/the-night-of-is-more-than-a-crime-thriller-it-s-also-a-great-prison-drama.html.
510. Author interview, February 12, 2019.
511. Cf. Reay, Pauline (2004), *Music in Film: Soundtracks and Synergy*. London: Wallflower Press.
512. Smith, Jeff (1998), *The Sounds of Commerce: Marketing Popular Film Music*. New York: Columbia University Press, pp. 205-207.
513. Author interview, September 10, 2016.
514. Altman, Rick (2001), "Cinema and Popular Song: The Last Tradition," in Wojcik, Pamela Robertson & Arthur Knights (eds.). Durham: Duke University Press, pp. 19-30.
515. Smith, Jeff (1998), *The Sounds of Commerce*, p. 2.

516. Author interview, May 6, 2017.
517. Ibid.
518. Korsgaard, Mathias Bonde (2020), "'Musical Moments' i nyere serier," in Nielsen, Jakob Isak et al. (eds.), *Streaming for viderekomne: Fra* Doggystyle *til* Black Mirror *og* The Jinx. Aarhus: VIA Film & Transmedia, pp. 196-216.
519. Author interview, December 21, 2020.
520. Author interview, April 14, 2019.
521. Pudovkin, Vsevolod (2009 [1958]), "Film Technique: On Editing," p. 12.
522. Cf. Dibdin, Emma (2006), "Is *Six Feet Under*'s final episode the best TV finale of all time?", *Digital Spy*, March 6. www.digitalspy.com/tv/ustv/a663836/is-six-feet-under-the-best-tv-finale-of-all-time/-
523. Author interview, March 2, 2020.
524. Author interview, February 12, 2019.
525. Author interview, April 14, 2019.
526. Author interview, April 15, 2019.
527. Author interview with Charlotte Sieling, December 28, 2020. See also, Split Screens TV (2018), "Split Screens 2018 presents THE AMERICANS Debriefing with Showrunners Joe Weisberg and Joel Fields" (interviewer Matt Zoller Seitz), and Højer, Henrik (2015), "Family Noir", 16:9, June 10. www.16-9.dk/2015/06/family-noir.
528. Author interview, January 5, 2021.
529. Author interview, January 9, 2016.
530. Cf. Bojalad, Alec (2017), "Stranger Things: In Defence of Nostalgia," *Den of Geek*, November 2. www.denofgeek.com/tv/stranger-things-in-defense-of-nostalgia/ and Halskov, Andreas (2018b), "Echoes of the Past: Popular Music and Nostalgia in Modern Television Drama," *16:9*, May 28. www.16-9.dk/2018/05/nostalgia.
531. Author interview, July 5, 2019.
532. Langkjær, Birger (2000), *Den lyttende tilskuer*, p. 195.
533. Author interview, January 10, 2018.
534. TV critic Anna Leszkiewicz convincingly argues that the campiness of Jane's punk 'adventure' in *Stranger Things 2* is intentional. Cf. Leszkiewicz, Anna (2017), "Eleven's 'Stranger Things 2' Punk Revamp Is Corny But That's the Point," *Vice*, November 2. www.vice.com/en_us/article/vb33m3/eleven-stranger-things-2-episode-7-lost-sister-punk.
535. Cf. Gooden, Tai (2019), "The Song Dustin & Suzie Sing in 'Stranger Things' from 'The Neverending Story' Was an Epic Choice for the Teen Coule," *Bustle*, July 4, and Codero, Rosy (2019), "The NeverEnding Story theme singer Limahl celebrates newfound interest thanks to 'Stranger Thing', *Entertainment Weekly*, July 9.
536. Author interview, August 21, 2016.
537. Author interview, May 29, 2017.
538. Author interview, April 12, 2019.
539. Cf. e.g. Dornbush, Jonathan (2015): "25 Years Later: The 5 Ways *Twin Peaks* Changed TV," *Entertainment Weekly*, April 8 and Dane, Benjamin (2020), "For 30 år siden vendte ét afsnit op og ned på tv-landskabet: Her er historien om Twin Peaks, der måske ændrede modern tv for altid," *Børsen*, May 31.
540. Quoted in Grimes, William (1991), "Television; Welcome to Twin Peaks and Valleys," *New York Times*, May 5, 1991.
541. Author interview, October 14, 2014.
542. Author interview, November 25, 2014.
543. According to both Duwayne Dunham and Sabrina Sutherland, all of the Roadhouse songs from *Twin Peaks: The Return* were recorded "live" in one day. Author interviews, April 13, 2019.
544. For more on the wall-to-wall music in the original series, see Dean Hurley's comments in Paula Mejia's article "Charting the Vast Musical Universe of *Twin Peaks*," *Vulture*, July 27, 2017.
545. Author interview, May 29, 2017.

546. For more on this, see Halskov, Andreas (2015c), "What's the Frequency, David? Noise and Interference in the Films of David Lynch," *16:9*, August 16.
547. Author interview, May 29, 2017.
548. Author interview, March 6, 2017.
549. Schrader, Paul (2018 [1972]), *Transcendental Style in Film: Ozu, Bresson, Dreyer*. University of California Press.
550. Author interview, April 12, 2019. There is no evidence to support that *Twin Peaks: The Return* in general has an extraordinary ASL (average shot length). In fact, Parts 1 and 2 of the new series have an ASL of 8 and 7.5 seconds, which is not markedly higher than a traditional mainstream film or series. Cf. Chavez, Mercedes (2019), "Twin Peaks S3 EP1 & Twin Peaks S3 EP2," *Cinemetrics*, January 19. cinemetrics.lv/movie.php?movie_ID=23613.
551. Author interview, March 14, 2017.
552. Author interviews, July 19, 2017 and April 13, 2019.
553. Ibid.
554. Author interview, February 27, 2015.
555. Author interview, July 2, 2019. Or as the synthesist Kinny Landrum puts it: "David Lynch had to edit the picture to fit the music and not vice versa. That's a pretty radical concept in terms of television." Author interview, November 15, 2014.
556. Author interview, August 24, 2016.
557. Author interview, September 1, 2016.
558. Author interview, August 24, 2016.
559. Author interview, March 16, 2020.
560. There were exceptions, though. As Dave Porter explains: *"There are only two dramatic moments where I broke that rule — and every rule is designed to be broken — one is the Salamanca cartel cousins, who by design are a very specific and unshakeable threat. The other appeared only in Breaking Bad in a few dramatic instances when Walter White donned his Heisenberg hat… and even that was just a simple motif that required very different orchestration behind it in each instance because the circumstances were always very different."* Author interview, March 16, 2020.
561. Author interview, September 1, 2016.
562. Author interview, August 24, 2016.
563. Author interview, March 16, 2020.
564. Author interview, May 6, 2017. Nick Forshager gives a similar explanation: *"I am happy you mention that title sequence. A lot of people think it's a mistake. "Why is the music cut off that way?" But it was very intentional and, as you say, it was supposed to mirror Jimmy. It's not perfect, not polished, exactly like Jimmy. We struggled to find the music for the title sequence, and it was the last piece we ever found. We actually had an extension of it where it ended, but we wanted to cut it off, and we didn't want it to be elegant."* Author interview, August 24, 2016.
565. Author interview, June 11, 2016.
566. Pudovkin, Vsevolod (2009 [1958]), "Film Technique: On Editing," pp. 11-12.
567. Author interview, August 24, 2016.
568. Author interview, May 6, 2017.
569. Author interview, August 24, 2016.
570. Cf. Jensen, Troels Peter Mourits (2019), "Serieverdenens populære flagskibe: Et blik på underholdningsværdien i *bottle episodes*," *16:9*, March 10.
571. Author interview, June 11, 2016.
572. Ibid.
573. Author interview, March 16, 2020.
574. Author interview, May 6, 2017.
575. Author interview, September 1, 2016.
576. Author interview, June 11, 2016.
577. Author interview, May 6, 2017.
578. Ibid. For more on Barack Obama's appraisal of *Better Call Saul*, see Rankin, Selja (2020), "Barack Obama on the pop culture (and more) that inspired *A Promised Land*," Entertainment

Weekly, December 15. ew.com/books/barack-obama-a-promised-land-interview.
579. Kant, Immanuel (1892 [1790]), *The Critique of Judgement*. Translated by J.H. Bernard, §46.
580. Butler, Jeremy (2010), *Television Style*. New York & London: Routledge, p. 16.
581. Astruc, Alexandre (1948): "The Birth of a New Avant-Garde: La Camera-Stylo," in Vincendeau, Ginette & Peter Graham (eds.)(2009), *The French New Wave: Critical Landmarks*. London: Palgrave.
582. Truffaut, François (1954), "A Certain Tendency of the French Cinema." soma.sbcc.edu/users/davega/FILMST_113/Filmst113_ExFilm_Movements/FrenchNewWave/A_certain_tendency_tr%23540A3.pdf.
583. Sarris, Andrew (2009 [1962]), "Notes on the Auteur Theory in 1962," in Braudy, Leo & Marshall Cohen (eds.), *Film Theory & Criticism*. Oxford: Oxford University Press, 9th edition, p. 453.
584. Cf. Hodsdon, Barrett (2017), *The Elusive Auteur: The Question of Film Authorship Throughout the Age of Cinema*. Jefferson, North Carolina: McFarland & Co., p. 3.
585. Jaramillo, Deborah L. (2013), "Rescuing Television from the 'Cinematic'," in Jacobs, Jason & Steven Peacock (eds.), *Television Aesthetics and Style*, p. 74.
586. Cf. Newcomb, Horace & Robert S. Alley (1983), *The Producer's Medium: Conversations with Creators of American TV*. New York: Oxford University Press.
587. Author interview, April 18, 2019.
588. Author interview, March 23, 2018.
589. Author interview, March 12, 2018.
590. Mittell, Jason (2015), *Complex TV*, p. 95.
591. Ibid.
592. Ibid., pp. 88-89.
593. Caughie, John (1981)(ed.), *Theories of Authorship: A Reader*. London: BFI, p. 15.
594. Author interview, February 28, 2020.
595. Blair, Iain (2018), "Showtime's *Homeland*: Producer/director Lesli Linka Glatter", *Randi Altman's postPerspective*, June 18. postperspective.com/showrunner-lesli-linka-glatter-showtimes-homeland.
596. Cf. Nietzsche, Friederich (1872), *Zur Genealogie der Moral* (*On the Geneaology of Morality*). Translated by Carol Diethe. Cambridge: Cambridge University Press.
597. Gilbert, Sandra & Susan Gubar (1979), *The Madwoman in the Attic: The Woman Writer of the Nineteenth-Century Literary Imagination*. Yale University Press.
598. Author interview, May 11, 2020.
599. Kildebæk, Morten (2020), "'I Know This Much Is True': Ny HBO-serie med dobbel Mark Ruffalo rammer hårdt og nådesløst," *Soundvenue*, May 11.
600. Tom Santopietro has argued that *The Godfather* not only reflected Italian-Americans, but changed how Italian-Americans perceived themselves. Cf. Santopietro, Tom (2012), *The Godfather Effect*. St. Martin's Press.
601. O'Malley, Sheila (2020), "I Know This Much Is True," *RogerEbert.com*, May 8. www.rogerebert.com/reviews/i-know-this-much-is-true-movie-review-2020.
602. Lattanzio, Ryan (2015), "Lynch, Fincher, 'True Detective' and the Unknowable Future of Auteur TV," *IndieWire*. August 11. www.indiewire.com/2015/08/lynch-fincher-true-detective-and-the-unknowable-future-of-auteur-tv-184757.
603. Author interviews, May 23, 2017 and February 5, 2015.
604. Author interview, May 14, 2020.
605. Cf. Travers, Ben (2017), "'Twin Peaks', New Ratings, Facing Off with 'Game of Thrones,' and What It All Means for the Future of TV," *Indiewire*, July 12. and Seitz, Matt Zoller (2017), "The Best Show on TV Is *Twin Peaks: The Return*," *Vulture*, July.
606. Mittell, Jason (2004), *Genre and Television: From Cop Shows to Cartoons in American Culture*. New York & London: Routledge, p. 11.
607. Croce, Benedetto (1929), *Aesthetic*. Trans. Douglas Ainsley. London: Macmillan, pp. 36-37.
608. Mittell, Jason (2004), *Genre and Television*, p. 30.
609. Cawelti, John G. (1976), *Adventure, Mystery and Romance*. Chicago: The University of Chica-

go Press.
610. Cawelti, John G. (2001), "The Concept of Formula in the Study of Popular Literature," in Harrington, Lee & Denise Bielby (eds.), *Popular Culture. Production and consumption*. Oxford: Blackwell Publishing, pp. 203-209.
611. Altman, Rick (1999), *Film/Genre*. London: BFI, p. 14.
612. Tudor, Andrew (1974), *Theories of Film*. Viking Press, p. 139.
613. The finale of *Transparent* has a totally separate format of 1h38 min. and it is also generically different.
614. Author interview, April 2, 2020.
615. Quoted in Hochscherf, Tobias & Heidi Philipsen (2017), *Beyond the Bridge*, Chapter 3.
616. Cf. Lauridsen, Palle Schantz (2014), *Sherlock Holmes i Danmark*. København: Rosenkilde & Bahnhof, pp. 21-26.
617. Todorov, Tzvetan (1977), *The Poetics of Prose*. Cornell University Press, p. 45.
618. Vincentelli, Elisabeth (2020), "Comfort Viewing: 3 Reasons I Love 'Columbo'," *The New York Times*, July 24. www.nytimes.com/2020/07/24/arts/television/columbo-watch.html
619. Mittell, Jason (2004), *Genre and Television*, p. 130.
620. Forster Hirsch describes the *noir* films made from 1940 to 1950 as *high noir*. Cf. Hirsch, Forster (1999), *Detours and Lost Highways: A Map of Neo-Noir*. New York: Limelight, pp. 12-15.
621. Schrader, Paul (1972), "Notes of Film Noir," *Film Comment* 8:1, Spring, pp. 8-13.
622. For more on this, see Koepnick, Lutz (2002), *The Dark Mirror: German Cinema Between Hitler and Hollywood*. Berkeley: University of California Press.
623. Cf. Bordwell, David (2017), *Reinventing Hollywood: How 1940s Filmmakers Changed Movie Storytelling*. Chicago & London: The University of Chicago Press.
624. Author interview, March 23, 2018.
625. Mittell, Jason (2004), *Genre and Television*, pp. 130-131.
626. Author interview, April 18, 2019.
627. Cf. Truelove, Thom (2016), "Amazon's *Bosch*: Echoes of Black", *Criminal Element*, March 18. www.criminalelement.com/amazon-bosch-echoes-of-black-harry-bosch-amazon-prime-michael-connelly.
628. Author interview, April 18, 2019.
629. Mittell, Jason (2004), *Genre and Television*, p. 130.
630. Author interview, April 16, 2019.
631. Cf. Schneider, Michael (2016), "Watch My Show: *Bosch* Is 'The Next Binge Experience,' Says Henrik Bastin," *TV Insider*, April 19. www.tvinsider.com/86432/watch-my-show-bosch-is-the-next-binge-experience-says-henrik-bastin.
632. Ibid. and Skinner, Jessica E. (2020), "Bosch Season 7: Release Date, Cast, Plot, And All the Latest News", *NewsreaderWeb*, July 16. www.newsreaderweb.com/bosch-season-7-release-date-cast-plot-and-all-latest-news.
633. Author interview, April 28, 2020.
634. Author interview, February 12, 2019.
635. Conklin, Micah (2014), "Fort Macomb and True Detective," *Deep South Magazine*, March 17. deepsouthmag.com/2014/03/17/fort-macomb-and-true-detective.
636. Author interview, March 14, 2019.
637. Author interview, February 12, 2019. For more on *Sharp Objects* and its use of editing, see Oxholm, Jan (2019), "*Sharp Objects*: Det dystre dukkehus", *16:9*, August 18.
638. Cf. Vincendeau, Ginette (2019), "How the French birthed film noir," *Sight and Sound*, May 7.
639. This unofficial trilogy has also been described as his *Los Angeles Trilogy*. Cf. Elsaesser, Thomas (2012), "Actions Have Consequences: Logics in the Mind-Game Films in David Lynch's Los Angeles-Trilogy. Paper presented at *The Art of the Real: An Interdisciplinary International Conference* in Berlin (Roter Salon, Volksbühne), June 28-30.
640. Author interview, December 8, 2016.
641. Andersen, Kim Jong (2019), "*Too Old to Die Young* - 13 timer i skærsilden," *P.O.V.*, June 26.
642. Author interview, November 24, 2014.
643. Nielsen, Jakob Isak (2016), "The Danish Way to Do It the American Way."

644. Cf. Ennis, Rikke & Helene Aurø (2020), "Nordic Series – What's Trending," presentation at Aarhus Series Festival, October 30.
645. Ibid.
646. Cf. Bendtsen, Johan Varning (2018), "DR laver ny sæson af drama-succes med afdøde Nedim Yasar på rollelisten," *Politiken*, December 12. politiken.dk/kultur/film_og_tv/art6913752/DR-laver-ny-s%C3%A6son-af-drama-succes-med-afd%C3%B8de-Nedim-Yasar-p%C3%A5-rollelisten.
647. Ibid.
648. Author interview, February 17, 2020.
649. Ibid.
650. Nikolajsen, Lone (2016), "Storslået landskabsporno i islandsk krimiserie," *Information*, December 16. www.information.dk/kultur/anmeldelse/2016/12/storslaaet-landskabsporno-islandsk-krimiserie.
651. Author interview, June 25, 2020.
652. Ibid.
653. Ibid.
654. Author interview, December 29, 2020.
655. Author interview, April 2, 2020.
656. Cf. Fry, Naomi (2020), "'The Undoing' Is Empty Life-Style Porn," *The New Yorker*, November 9 and Agger, Gunhild (2020), "Dream a Little Dream of Me," *Kommunikationsforum*, December 1.
657. For more on this, see Granild, Dorte Schmidt (2020), "*Crime Spree*: Om true crime-bølgen og *The Jinx*," in Nielsen, Jakob Isak et al. (eds.), *Streaming for viderekomne: Fra* Doggystyle *til* Black Mirror *og* The Jinx. Aarhus: VIA Film & Transmedia, pp. 140-160.
658. For more on the different tropes in crime fiction, see Christensen, Jørgen Riber (2018), "Troper i krimiserier," *16:9*, November 14. www.16-9.dk/2018/11/troper-i-krimiserier.
659. Cf. Lauridsen, Palle Schantz (2016), "Audience Involving Strategies," *16:9*, January 28. www.16-9.dk/2016/01/audience-involving-strategies-in-sherlock.
660. Author interview, April 6, 2020.
661. Author interview, April 6, 2020.
662. Cf. Mittell, Jason (2004), *Genre and Television*, p. 11.
663. Højer, Michael (2011), "Teen Noir - Veronica Mars og den moderne ungdomsserie," in Nielsen, Jakob Isak et al. (eds.), *Fjernsyn for viderekomne - de nye amerikanske tv-serier*. Aarhus: Turbine, p. 271.
664. Davis, Glyn & Kay Dickinson (2008), "Introduction," in *Teen TV - Genre, Consumption and Identity*. London: BFI, p. 1
665. Ross, Sharon Marie & Louisa Ellen Stein (2008), *Teen Television: Essays on programming and fandom*. Jefferson, NC: McFarland, pp. 7-9.
666. Lysne, Anders (2013), "At forstå en teenager," *16:9* #52. www.16-9.dk/2013-09/side04_feature1.htm.
667. Driscoll, Catherine (2011), *Teen Film: A Critical Introduction*. Oxford & New York: Berg, p. 3.
668. Driscoll, Catherine (2011), *Teen Film*, p. 3.
669. Martin, Adrian (1994), "Teen Movies: The Forgetting of Wisdom", in *Phantasms*. Ringwood, Vic: McPhee Gribble, pp. 66-67.
670. Author interview, December 18, 2020.
671. Driscoll, Catherine (2011), *Teen Film*, p. 2.
672. Shary, Timothy (2005), *Teen Movies: American Youth on Screen*. London & New York: Wallflower, p. 5.
673. Ibid., p. 6.
674. Altman, Rick (1999), *Film/Genre*, p. 50.
675. Shary, Timothy (2005), *Teen Movies*, pp. 6-7.
676. Cf. Thompson, Derek (2018), "A Brief History of Teenagers," *The Saturday Evening Post*, February 13. www.saturdayeveningpost.com/2018/02/brief-history-teenagers.
677. For more on the teen movies of the 1980s and John Hughes' influence on modern teen dra-

mas in film and television, see Christie, Thomas A. (2009), *John Hughes and Eighties Cinema: Teenage Hopes and American Dreams*. Crescent Moon and Gora, Susannah (2010), *"You Couldn't Ignore Me If You Tried": The Brat Pack, John Hughes, and Their Impact on a Generation*. New York: Three Rivers Press.

678. In Ep. 2:1, Brenda breaks up with Dylan due to their pregnancy scare. During the break-up scene in Dylan's car, "Losing My Religion" is playing in the background. Later, after Dylan has chosen Kelly (Jennie Garth) over Brenda, there is a scene (in Ep. 3:20) where Brenda is listening to "Losing My Religion" in her room and where she explains to Brandon how the song relates to her and Dylan. "What's with playing the song over and over?", Brandon asks her. "It's 'Losing My Religion'. It was playing in Dylan's car the first time we broke up. [...] At the time, I thought nothing could ever feel that bad," she replies. These instances, including the dialogue connected to the song, have been cut from Hulu's version of the series, presumably due to licensing issues, but they are still included in the version on TV2 Play that is available to Danish audiences.
679. Povlsen, Karen Klitgaard (1999), *Beverly Hills 90210 - Soaps, ironi og danske unge*. Aarhus: Klim.
680. Author interview, March 23, 2018.
681. Quoted in McFadden, Kay (1999), "WB Hitting the Mark with Target Audience," *Chicago Tribune*. January 13. www.chicagotribune.com/news/ct-xpm-1999-01-13-9901130071-story.html. The WB was replaced by The CW in 2006.
682. Author interview, March 23, 2018.
683. Sconce, Jeffrey (2002), "Irony, Nihilism and the New American Smart Film," *Screen* 43:4, pp. 349-369.
684. Author interview, March 23, 2018.
685. Hjarvard, Stig (2013), *The Mediatization of Culture and Society*. London: Routledge.
686. Cf. Krüger, Steffen & Gry C. Rustad (2019 [2017]), "Coping with Shame in a Media-saturated Society: Norwegian Web-series *SKAM* as Transitional Object," *Television and New Media* 20:1.
687. Author interview, April 6, 2020.
688. Modleski, Tania (2003), "The Search for Tomorrow in Today's Soap Operas," p. 298.
689. Rustad, Gry (2016), "Producing feminist teen television," paper presented at the Console-ing Passions Conference at Notre Dame University.
690. Cf. Nikolajsen, Lone (2017), "Der var gråd, og det var fantastisk, indtil antimobbekampagnen tog over," *Information*, June 3. www.information.dk/kultur/anmeldelse/2017/06/graad-fantastisk-indtil-antimobbekampagnen-tog.
691. Author interview, April 6, 2020.
692. Sundet, Vilde Schanke (2020), "'Will it translate?': *SKAM* som remake," in Nielsen, Jakob Isak et al. (eds.), *Streaming for viderekomne*, p. 74.
693. Cf. Andersen, Tore Rye (2019), *Serier*. Aarhus: Aarhus Universitetsforlag, pp. 44-45.
694. Ibid.
695. Author interview, April 6, 2020.
696. Cf. McFadden, Kay (1999), "WB Hitting the Mark With Target Audience," *Chicago Tribune*, January 13. www.chicagotribune.com/news/ct-xpm-1999-01-13-9901130071-story.html.
697. Sundet, Vilde Schanke (2020), "'Will It Translate?'," p. 72.
698. For more on *Friday Night Lights* as an 'arthouse teen drama,' see McNeil, Kenneth (2011), "*Friday Night Lights* - imellem amerikansk drøm og virkelighed," in Nielsen, Jakob Isak et al. (eds.), *Fjernsyn for viderekomne - de nye amerikanske tv-serier*. Aarhus: Turbine, pp. 286-301.
699. Ibid.
700. Author interview, March 17, 2020.
701. Author interview, February 27, 2020.
702. Cf. Baudrillard, Jean (1994 [1981]), *Simulacra and Simulation*. Translated by Sheila Faria Glaser. Michigan: The University of Michigan Press and Jensen, Jakob Linaa (2009), "Fra onlinefællesskaber til onlinenetværk: Facebook som augmentering af den sociale virkelig-

hed, *Mediekultur* #46, pp. 86-99.
703. Author interview, February 25, 2020.
704. Ibid.
705. Ibid.
706. Author interview, March 30, 2020.
707. Ibid.
708. Cf. Grusin, Richard & Jay Bolter (1999), *Remediation: Understanding New Media*. MIT Press.
709. Author interview, April 18, 2019.
710. MarBelle (2020), "How Lenny Abrahamson Transformed Sally Rooney's Best Selling Novel Into the Record-Breaking TV Event of the Year," *Directors Notes*, July 27. directorsnotes.com/2020/07/27/lenny-abrahamson-normal-people.
711. Cf. Kelly, Emma (2020), "'It's what you'd see in a porno': Normal People 'immoral' sex scenes spark major debate on Irish radio," *Metro*, May 1.
712. Author interview, May 25, 2020.
713. Ibid.
714. Puschak, Evan (2017): "The Handmaid's Tale Won Emmy Best Drama," *Nerdwriter*, August 31.
715. Author interview, February 20, 2020.
716. Ibid.
717. Cf. Lee, Benjamin (2019), "*Euphoria* review - dizzying high school drama is one of the year's best," *The Guardian*, June 14; Nicholson, Rebecca (2019), "*Euphoria* review - so explicit it makes *Skins* look positively Victorian", *The Guardian*, August 6; Madsen, Sarah Gerlach (2019), "Fucking råt for usødet: *Euphoria* taler et helt andet sprog," *Kommunikationsforum*, September 24; Hale, Mike (2019), " 'Euphoria' Review: HBO Raises the Stakes on Teenage Transgression," *The New York Times*, June 14.
718. Travers, Ben (2019), "'Euphoria' Review: Zendaya's HBO Series Is a Teens-in-Crisis Horror Show," *Indiewire*, June 4.
719. Cf. Cusumano, Katherine (2018), "Rising Model Hunter Schafer Is Fighting for the Future of Trans Individuals On and Off the Runway," *W*, March 21. www.wmagazine.com/story/hunter-schafer-model-bathroom-bill and Somoma, Serena (2019), "What Trans Teens Are Saying About Jules on 'Euphoria'," *Teen Vogue*, August 5. www.teenvogue.com/story/euphoria-jules-trans-teens.
720. Author interview, March 3, 2020.
721. Ibid.
722. Ibid.
723. Cf. Grigoriadis, Vanessa (2008), "The Tragedy of Britney Spears," *Rolling Stone*, February 21. www.rollingstone.com/music/music-news/the-tragedy-of-britney-spears-rolling-stones-2008-cover-story-254735.
724. Author interview, February 25, 2020.
725. This allusion is fairly obvious, and many critics have mentioned it. Cf. e.g. Moestrup, Steffen (2020), "Interview with Michael Højer," in *Film:syn - den om ungdomsserier*, DK4. www.dk4.dk/item/6231/filmsyn-den-om-ungdomsserier.
726. Sundet, Vilde Schanke (2020), "'Will It Translate? *SKAM* som remake," p. 76.
727. Author interview, April 6, 2020.
728. In *Bande à part* (1964), the young bohemian Franz (Sami Frey) proposes that they should take a one-minute break without words, and this is followed by absolute silence for 37 seconds. For more on this, see Halskov, Andreas (2014d), "The Sound of Silence: Stilhed på film," *16:9*, August 28. www.16-9.dk/2014/08/the-sound-of-silence-stilhed-paa-film.
729. Cf. Gilbert, Sophie (2020), "The Teen Dramas That Reject Modernity," *The Atlantic*, March 4. www.theatlantic.com/culture/archive/2020/03/netflix-new-teen-nostalgia-i-am-not-okay-with-this-sex-education-stranger-things/607366.
730. Kaveney, Roz (2006), *Teen Dreams: Reading Teen Films and Television from* Heathers *to* Veronica Mars. London: I.B. Tauris.
731. Author interview, May 25, 2020.
732. Spencer, Samuel (2020), "'Euphoria' Cast and Crew Tease 'Special COVID Episode' Before

Season 2", *Newsweek*, September 23. www.newsweek.com/euphoria-season-2-release-date-filming-special-hbo-zendaya-1533839.
733. Hale, James (2020), "Brat Brings in TikTok Star Dixie D'Amelio to Front New Series 'Attaway General'," *Tubefilter*, February 17.
734. Quoted in Adalian, Josef (2016), "How Amazon Became a Major Player in Half-Hour Television," *Vulture*, October 6. www.vulture.com/2016/10/amazon-became-a-major-player-in-half-hour-tv.html.
735. Author interview, May 5, 2020.
736. Havas, Julia & Maria Sulimma (2020 [2018]), "Through the Gaps of My Fingers: Genre, Femininity, and Cringe Aesthetics in Dramedy Television," *Television & New Media* 21:1, p. 76.
737. Moestrup, Steffen (2017), "Lena, Louie og Derek: et blik på den eksistentialistisk dramedie," in Nielsen, Jakob Isak et al. (eds.), *Helt til grin: Moderne audiovisual komik på tværs af medier*. Aarhus: VIA Film & Transmedia, pp. 145-164.
738. Landau Neil (2018), "Blurring the Lines: Redefining TV Genre and Tone in the Dramedy," *Creative Screenwriting*, June 13. creativescreenwriting.com/blurring-lines-redefining-tv-genre-tone-dramedy.
739. Havas, Julia & Maria Sulimma (2020 [2018]), "Through the Gaps of My Fingers," pp. 75-77.
740. Sabroe, Iben Albinus (2010), *Da Sex and the City ændrede verden*. København: Sabroe & Sabroe.
741. *M*A*S*H* is also mentioned by Helle Kannik Haastrup as a crucial series. Cf. Haastrup, Helle Kannik (2011), "Dramedien som genre - fra livsstilsserie til krisefortælling," in Nielsen, Jakob Isak et al. (eds.), *Fjernsyn for viderekomne - de nye amerikanske tv-serier*. Aarhus: Turbine, p. 55.
742. Landau Neil (2018), "Blurring the Lines: Redefining TV Genre and Tone in the Dramedy."
743. Page, Adrian (2005), "Post-Modern Drama," in Creeber, Glen (ed.), *The Television Genre Book*. London: BFI, pp. 45-46.
744. Quoted in Sammond, Nicholas & Chandra Mukerjo (2001), "'What Are You? ... I Wouldn't Eat': Ethnicity, Whiteness and Performing 'the Jew' in Hollywood's Golden Age," in Bernardi, Daniel (ed.), *Classic Hollywood, Classic Whiteness*. Minnesota: University of University Press, p. 24.
745. Page, Adrian (2005 [2001]), "Post-Modern Drama," in Creeber, Glen (ed.), *The Television Genre Book*. London: BFI Publishing, pp. 45-46.
746. Landau Neil (2018), "Blurring the Lines: Redefining TV Genre and Tone in the Dramedy."
747. Cf. Haastrup, Helle Kannik (2011), "Dramedien som genre," p. 56 and Berg, Leah R. Vande (1991), "Dramedy: Moonlighting as an Emergent Generic Hybrid," in Berg, Leah R. Vande & Lawrence R. Wenner (eds.), *Television Criticism: Approaches and Applications*. New York & London: Longman, pp. 95-109.
748. The term *smartcom*, which is inspired by Jeffrey Sconce, refers to a group of modern comedy series that veer away from the conventional sitcom grammar. These series are often recognized for their high degree of stylization, playfulness and intertextuality, and as such they target a "blue-chip demographic" (as Robert J. Thompson would call it). Cf. Halskov, Andreas (2017b), "Fra Lucy til Louie: smarte sitcoms til smarte seere," in Nielsen, Jakob Isak et al. (eds.), *Helt til grin: Moderne audiovisual komik på tværs af medier*. Aarhus: VIA Film & Transmedia, pp. 118-144.
749. Barra, Luca (2017), "*Master of None*, *Atlanta* and Audience Engagement in Contemporary US TV Drama," *16:9*, November 19. www.16-9.dk/2017/11/master-of-none.
750. There are also noteworthy examples of dramedies made by broadcast networks, however, e.g. *Gilmore Girls* (The WB/The CW, 2000-20007), *Desperate Housewives* (ABC, 2004-2012) and *House, M.D.* (Fox, 2004-2012).
751. Haastrup, Helle Kannik (2011), "Dramedien som genre," pp. 59-73.
752. The designation *domestic dramedy* is used by Jay Duplass when talking about *Togetherness*, as seen in the "Feature Interview" at the end of this chapter. Author interview, May 22, 2020.
753. Gheciu, Alex Nino (2018), "Why the Duplass Brothers Are Done Directing (Unless It's the

754. See the feature interview with Jay Duplass (May 22, 2020) at the end of this chapter.
755. The scene from *Wayne's World*, which *Togetherness* apparently paraphrases, is mentioned by Jeff Smith as a noteworthy example of *musical moments* and *cross-promotion* in modern films. Cf. Smith, Jeff (1998), *The Sounds of Commerce: Marketing Popular Films*. New York: Columbia University Press, p. 2.
756. Author interview, October 2, 2020.
757. Ibid.
758. Ibid.
759. Cf. Halskov, Andreas (2013), "*Girls* - Degradation and the City," *16:9 Books*. www.16-9.dk/fjernsynforviderekomne/girls.html.
760. Adelborg, Jeppe Kondrup (2019), "'Girls', 'Game of Thrones' og 'Chernobyl' satte standarden for tv-serier i 10'erne," *Politiken*, December 19. politiken.dk/kultur/film_og_tv/art7559746/Girls-Game-of-Thrones-og-Chernobyl-satte-standarden-for-tv-serier-i-10erne.
761. VanDerWerff, Emily Todd (2012), "*Looking* reaches beyond simply being "the gay *Girls*," *AV Club*, January 17. tv.avclub.com/looking-reaches-beyond-simply-being-the-gay-girls-1798179204.
762. Author interview, May 17, 2020.
763. Ibid.
764. Ibid.
765. Miller, Liz Shannon (2015), "'Looking' Canceled by HBO After 2 Seasons, Though the Story Isn't Over," *Indiewire*, March 25..
766. Author interview, May 17, 2020.
767. Author interview, May 22, 2020.
768. Cf. Højer, Henrik (2017a), "It's Not TV, It's Art TV."
769. Film historian Barry Salt also argues that long takes are associated with art cinema. As he writes, "The higher the pretentions, the longer the take." Cf. Salt, Barry (1992), *Film Style and Technology: History and Analysis* (2. Ed.). London: Starwood, p. 283.
770. Author interview, May 22, 2020.
771. The same thing could be said of *Orange Is the New Block* and *Mrs. Fletcher* (HBO, 2019), two dramedies that also depict non-binary people and that also feature transgender actors.
772. Filippo, Maria San (2016), "Transparent Family Values: Unmasking Sitcom Myths of Gender, Sex(uality), and Money," in Dalton, Mart M. & Laura R. Linder (eds.), *The Sitcom Reader*. New York: SUNY Press, p. 306.
773. Goddard, Michael & Christopher Hogg (eds.)(2018), "Trans TV Dossier 1: Platform Television, Netflix and Industrial Transformations," *Critical Studies in Television* 13(4). See also Romano, Nick (2021), "Just four creators are tied to nearly a fifth of all LGBTQ representation on TV," Entertainment Weekly, January 14.
774. Jones, Gerard (1993), *Honey, I'm Home! Sitcoms, Selling the American Dream*. Grove, PR, p. 4.
775. Cf. Halskov, Andreas (2017c), "Komedieserien er ikke længere sjov," *Soundvenue*, March 6.
776. For more on this, see Halskov, Andreas (2018c), "*BoJack Horseman* og situationskomedie," in Agger, Gunhild et al. (eds.), *TV-analyse*. Universitet. Aarhus: Systime, pp. 251-168.
777. Author interview, May 5, 2020.
778. Camus, Albert (1991), *The Myth of Sisyphus*. Translated by Justin O'Brien. Alfred A. Knopf.
779. Author interview, May 5, 2020.
780. Ibid.
781. Ibid.
782. Thorpe, Vanessa (2019), "Seriously funny: why we fell in love with dramedies," *The Guardian*, May 11. www.theguardian.com/tv-and-radio/2019/may/11/why-we-fell-in-love-with-dramedies.
783. Cf. Bloodsworth, Adam (2020), "How *I May Destroy You* Should Open the Door for More Groundbreaking TV Shows," *Huffpost*, August 19, and Barra, Luca (2017), "*Master of None*, *Atlanta*, and Audience Engagement in Contemporary US TV Comedy," and Goldberg, Lesley

(2020), "'Emily in Paris' Creator Darren Star Responds to French Critics and Gives Update on 'Younger' Spinoff," *The Hollywood Reporter*, October 22.
784. Alexander, Julia (2020b), "Streaming was part of the future – now it's the only future," *The Verge*, October 28. www.theverge.com/21536842/streaming-disney-hbo-max-peacock-cbs-all-access-warnermedia-viacom-nbcuniversal.
785. As David Lynch said at the Lucca Film Festival in 2017: "For me, the key to why *Twin Peaks* changed television is because we see it as a film, not a TV show. One film broken into 18 parts [...] A beautiful picture and beautiful sound. And I would like to tell you and ask you to tell your friends around the world, that when you see *Twin Peaks* on a television, or a computer, or even worse, a telephone, you are not hearing the full soundtrack." Cf. Dom, Pieter (2017), "David Lynch's Personal Recommendations on How to Watch *Twin Peaks* Properly," *Welcome to Twin Peaks*, June 23. welcometotwinpeaks.com/news/david-lynch-how-to-watch-twin-peaks-recommendations.
786. Author interview, February 4, 2015.
787. Author interview, October 2, 2020.
788. Cf. Ludvigsen, Jacob (2020), "Fra Netflix til TV2 Play: Vi vurderer de otte største tjenester efter streamingkrigens første år," *Soundvenue*, December 28. soundvenue.com/film/2020/12/fra-netflix-til-tv-2-play-vi-vurderer-otte-tjenester-efter-streamingkrigens-foerste-aar-435993, and Ulrich, Lise (2021), "Netflix, Disney og HBO kaster vanvittigt beløb efter din underholdning i 2021," Soundvenue, January 13. soundvenue.com/film/2021/01/netflix-disney-og-hbo-kaster-vanvittigt-beloeb-og-kaempestjerner-efter-din-underholdning-i-2021-437536.
789. Hans, Simran (2019), "Does it matter if a television show tops the best-film lists?", *The Guardian*, December 12. www.theguardian.com/commentisfree/2019/dec/12/best-film-twin-peaks-cinema-tv.